International Business
Challenges and Choices

Second edition

Alan Sitkin and Nick Bowen

OXFORD
UNIVERSITY PRESS

OXFORD
UNIVERSITY PRESS

Great Clarendon Street, Oxford, OX2 6DP,
United Kingdom

Oxford University Press is a department of the University of Oxford.
It furthers the University's objective of excellence in research, scholarship,
and education by publishing worldwide. Oxford is a registered trade mark of
Oxford University Press in the UK and in certain other countries

British Library Cataloguing in Publication Data
Data available

ISBN 978–0–19–964696–8

Printed in Italy by
L.E.G.O. S.p.A.—Lavis TN

International Business

Preface

The world has experienced some major upheavals in the three years since the publication of this textbook's successful first edition, and this new edition reflects these changing circumstances.

Although the origins of many current trends could perhaps be sensed a few years ago, several have assumed a magnitude that few would have predicted. For instance, by the year 2010 some of the world's larger developing countries had already embarked upon a process of economic, political, and social emergence. The speed at which this has happened has been astonishing and is starting to upset many assumptions about the ongoing domination of the older industrialized countries. As a result, political discussions about the competition between these two categories of country have become less relevant: leading developing countries like China are no longer waiting to negotiate greater power on the world stage but are simply assuming a bigger role. This justifies the decision made in this second edition to devote an entire chapter to the changing geography of international business, which is no longer interesting merely for reasons relating to the location of global manufacturing, but increasingly due to the rising purchasing power of millions of new consumers emerging from a state of poverty. This too is changing the focus of international business in 2013 and beyond.

Similarly, the ecological crisis that some observers had started to recognize a few years (and even decades) ago has worsened, in part because economic growth in countries lacking modern energy-efficient equipment has worsened the twin problems of resource depletion and pollution. Whereas environmental management could still be presented in our 2010 edition as a sub-section of corporate responsibility, it now merits its own chapter to detail the new operational and strategic approaches being followed by the increasing number of multinational managers concerned about this trend that is both a potentially catastrophic problem and an exciting new opportunity.

Lastly, our first edition was written in the aftermath of the subprime crisis which spread out from the United States in 2008 to cause a global credit crunch. The main questions in international business at the time was whether this general setback would cause protectionist sentiments, and how long it would take trade and investment volumes to return to their pre-crisis levels. Given the state of the global economy in 2013, following a new financial upheaval caused by the European sovereign debt crisis, the whole tone of this discussion has become more ominous. The difficulties in which the world economy finds itself at the start of the second decade of the twenty-first century means that many countries would accept any solution to their problems, and no longer worry so much whether help is supposed to come from domestic or international business, or whether globalization is advantageous. To some extent, desperation has de-politicized the international business debate, with observers expressing anger at the banking sector but asking fewer ideological questions about the benefits of open borders. This too is reflected in our second edition.

New to this edition:

- revised structure to reflect students' knowledge as they progress through an International Business module;
- streamlined coverage of finance to enable greater focus on future trends in emerging markets and sustainability;
- addition of longer end-of-part cases to promote a holistic understanding of international business;

- more in-depth focus of the core international business theories carefully integrated with online coverage of more advanced theories; and
- increased number of in-text examples to help students envisage how companies and countries put theory into practice.

Acknowledgements

I would like to express my deepest gratitude to all friends and family members acknowledged in the book's first edition, not to forget a number of others from locations worldwide (ranging from Abergavenny/Clodock to l'Hexagone, CRESC, and the West Coast) whom there was no room to mention last time.

Also, since change is the only thing that never changes, I'd like to acknowledge colleagues new and old at the European Business School. More locally, there is the privilege I have had since 2010 of serving London Borough of Enfield as a member of the majority group. Thanks also to friends from Southgate CLP as well as Bowes constituents. Debate sharpens the mind.

Lastly, there are three acknowledgements that I would like to repeat. To my sf Lea and Dani—you make me incredibly happy (not to mention proud). And to my Verena, echt die beste Frau der Welt—may the next 30 years be as great as the past 30.

AS

For this edition, I would like to thank all those who contributed to the first, including many colleagues, students, and alumni at the European Business School London and Regent's College. I would also like to thank colleagues at the Chartered Institute of Linguists for adding to my understanding of international cultures.

My thanks also go to friends around the world and, of course, particularly to members of my family: again, my wife, Joan, as always for all her support and love; my three sons and daughters-in-law; my mother, Beryl, still as optimistic as ever at 92; my sister, Jane, with whom I have shared so much over the last six decades; and my two special grand-daughters, Eleanor and Amelia.

NB

The authors would also like to thank the following reviewers:

Sjoerd Beugelsdijk, University of Groningen
Alfredo D'Angelo, Glasgow University
Amit Das, Qatar University
Robert Inklaar, University of Groningen
Keith Medhurst, INHolland
Lutao Ning, Queen Mary, University of London
Stefania Paladini, Coventry University Business School
Shameen Prashantham, Nottingham University Business School China
Paul Ryan, NUI Galway

QR Code images are used throughout this book. QR Code is a registered trademark of DENSO WAVE INCORPORATED. If your mobile device does not have a QR Code reader, try this website for advice: www.mobile-barcodes.com/qr-code-software.

Outline contents

Detailed contents

List of case studies and practitioner insights

Walk-through of the textbook features

Chapter-opening features

Learning objectives

Learning objectives

After reading this chapter, you will be able to:
- identify the principles guiding MNEs' historic efforts to shape the international environment
- identify SMEs' main international strengths and weaknesses
- discuss foreign direct investment (FDI) drivers
- describe how FDI affects host economies
- characterize international lobbying

Each chapter contains a bulleted list of its main concepts and ideas. These serve as helpful indicators of what you can expect to learn in the chapter.

Opening case study

Case study 5.1

MNEs and international operations: IBM's Indian summer

Since 1991, market liberalization has been a core policy for all Indian governments. The result is that many MNEs have reappraised this huge continent-sized country, a land of contrasts where terrible poverty coexists with an education system turning out millions of world-class mathematicians and engineers. With many multinationals expanding their presence in India, the country has become a global hub for a variety of activities, ranging from bank administration to pharmaceutical research and information technology (IT). IBM (http://www.ibm.com/) is part of this wave.

A case study at the beginning of each chapter provides you with an introduction to the subject and helps to set the scene.

In-text features

Practitioner insights

Practitioner insight

Robert Dennis, Advisory Board Member, Zafesoft.

Zafesoft, a small hi-tech company operating in the field of digital information security, faces particular challenges in the international marketing of its security solutions. As a niche vertical player, it needs to make decisions on how it generates leads and how it delivers solutions to customers in different sectors with different needs and of different sizes. Zafesoft has to be smart in its approach in order to be competitive with its larger rivals.

Zafesoft is a software start-up company focused on the security and control of digital information. It targets government agencies, companies that deal with electronic health information, financial information, other proprietary and commercially valuable information, where the loss or compromise of this information can result in a breach of national security, loss of privacy and/or

Practitioners provide short summaries of their experiences in the world of business and explain how the theories and concepts discussed within the chapter are used in practice.

Case studies

Case study 12.3

Facebook: The present and future of international network marketing

The great marketing phenomenon of the early part of the twenty-first century was the development of advertising and sales through social networking. The main social networks included Facebook, Twitter, MySpace, Bebo, LinkedIn, and Flickr. The market leader was Facebook, which made a rapid fortune for its young founder, Mark Zuckerberg. Born in 1984, he was estimated to be worth $15 billion at the age of 23 in 2007 and in 2012, in an minority stake (1.6 per cent) in the company, thus buying the exclusive rights to sell advertising on Facebook. The value of this small stake was estimated to be $1.6 billion in 2012.

Facebook and the other social networks are inevitable developments from the user-generated content feature of the Internet. Whereas earlier developments within the

The book is packed full of examples to help link business theory and concepts to the real business world.

Online Resource Centre references

Specific links to extension material hosted on the Online Resource Centre (ORC) allow you to expand your knowledge and understanding.

s to enhance product development and satisfy
ns about both the functional and experiential
n material 12.1 on consumer behaviour).   > Go online

mentation are at the heart of success or failure
te within international marketing is whether
ruly global goods, thus requiring little or no

Challenges and choices

This feature highlights the challenges and choices that business practitioners face in each particular subject area.

Challenges and choices

→ A key challenge for international marketing over the next few years is the extent to which the use of the Internet and social networking sites becomes the industry norm, and the impact this will have on other methods of marketing.

→ This involves difficult decisions about the information management systems to be purchased, maintained, and extended; the staffing levels required in this new marketing world; and the likely development of affordable, single-platform home-entertainment systems

that combine the current features of TV, DVD, comput telephone, gaming, and the purchase of goods and services. A key choice for the industry is the extension online marketing to children. As long ago as 2008, ther were about 100 youth-focused virtual worlds, some aimed at children as young as 5 years old; by 2012 this had grown to nearly 500. For the industry, the key challenge is to provide 'legitimate reassurance to pare that the sites their children use adhere to strict codes a standards' (Richard Deverell, Controller of BBC Childre cited in Carter 2008).

Key terms and glossary

Key terms are highlighted where they first appear. They are also defined in the glossary.

→ Polycentric
Company adapts its marketing and sales strategy as closely as possible to the target country—that is, the market that it is entering is so particular

(ethnocentric) or corporate accommo
(polycentric).

    Some of the world's largest retailer
and some of the classic cases are set o
do well in a number of markets, incl
problems for Walmart included an ina
ment (Japan), too much emphasis on
the same store format (Brazil) (Gand

End-of-chapter features

Chapter summary

Chapters conclude with a brief summary of the key concepts and points discussed.

Chapter summary

The chapter started by identifying a group of emerging economies (the BRICs and Next 11 countries) whose positive outlook means that they are destined to become a key focus of international business. The countries' development dynamics often started with political reform encouraging inwards investment by MNEs, albeit in an operating environment quite different from the Global North. LDCs' improved manufacturing capabilities caused national household income levels to rise, leading in turn to the arrival of a newly solvent middle class characterized by its own particular consumption patterns. The final section discussed how this population has become a target for MNEs but also a launchpad for local companies, which can leverage their experience to develop a new international profile. Given the growing capabilities of companies originating from the Global South, in time they can be expected to compete with their older established rivals. In turn, this is likely to impact upon international

Closing case study and questions

At the end of each chapter is a case study accompanied by questions which enable you to test your knowledge.

Case study 16.3
Powering the renewal of international business

Given current technology, wind power is closer than solar power to achieving grid parity, or the level of performance that makes it competitive with traditional fuel sources. This should mean better short-term growth prospects for wind as countries try to stabilize energy supplies and fulfil their climate change-related

(the Sahara in Africa, the Gobi in Asia, the Arabian Peninsula, or the Mojave/Sonora in California/Mexico) that are almost uninhabitable. At that point, exploiting solar power requires enormous investments in long-te distribution networks that consume much of the prima energy captured in the first place. The loss of power ca

Discussion questions

These stimulating questions are designed to help you to engage with and reflect upon the chapter.

Discussion questions

1 What other development models exist asides from the manufacturing-for-export path followed by most of today's emerging economies?

2 Which countries might be added or subtracted from economist Jim O'Neill's list of Next 11 emerging markets?

3 How quickly might MNEs be expected to adapt their product ranges to meet the specific demands of emerging market consumers?

4 Is 'frugal innovation' destined to become a major gl marketing trend in the future?

5 What implications does Asia's rise as a centre of international business have for the political paradigm that shapes the international business framework?

Further research

Suggestions for further reading are contained at the end of each chapter.

Further research

Gipouloux, F. (2011). *The Asian Mediterranean.* Cheltenham: Edward Elgar Publishing

Uses a cross-disciplinary approach to analyse the new 'East Asian economic corridor' intertwining all of the economies between Vladivostok and Singapore.

Radjou, N., Prabhu, J., and Ahuja, S. (2012). *Jugaad Innovation: Think Frugal, Be Flexible, Generate Breakthrough Growth.* San Francisco: Jossey-Bass

Makes the argument that the West would benefit by looking to the East and copying its frugal and flexible innovation processes.

Walk-through of the Online Resource Centre

www.oxfordtextbooks.co.uk/orc/sitkin_bowen2e/

The Online Resource Centre (ORC) comprises resources for both lecturers and students.

For students

Free and open-access material available to students:

Extension material

A vast amount of material with specific references to the textbook enables you to expand your knowledge.

Self-test questions

These provide a quick and easy way to test your understanding, with instant feedback.

Key references

Includes a list of key texts and websites where you can learn more about a particular topic.

Critical skills activity

Scenarios or activities are provided to encourage you to think critically about an aspect of business, enabling you to understand alternative viewpoints and arguments.

Revision tips

Each chapter is accompanied by revision tips, which help sum up the key points.

Glossary

A fully searchable glossary helps you to quickly locate key terms.

Multimedia library

Access a wealth of carefully selected material including company video material, YouTube videos, and TED talks, all organized by chapter.

Interactive world map

Contains statistical country data, including imports and exports expenditure, population growth rate, CO_2 emissions, and inflation rates.

For lecturers

Free for all registered adopters of the textbook:

PowerPoint lecture slides

A suite of customizable PowerPoint slides has been provided to use in your lecture presentations.

Internal drivers of IB activity

- Expanding sales
  - Leverage existing competencies
  - Activities that are international by their very nature (commodities)
  - Achieve critical mass

Additional case studies

An additional case study accompanies every chapter and can be used to provide students with a further example of how theory is applied in practice.

2.4. Additional case study: The UNHDI and the economics of happiness

A true Renaissance man, the Indian philosopher Amartya Sen was awarded a Nobel Prize for Economics in 1998 for his political work convincing governments worldwide that the aim of economic policy should be qualitative outcomes supporting the well-being of the whole of a population, rather than abstract numerical indicators like GDP neglecting the importance of wealth distribution and of many non-monetary outcomes to people's daily lives. In his words, 'Economic growth can make a very large contribution to improving people's lives, but single-

Running a seminar

The authors have provided suggestions for structuring a seminar and integrating the textbook and its resources in your teaching.

1.a. Running seminars

- For a one-hour seminar:
- Ask students to answer 'in-text' seminar discussion questions based on chapter reading. Calculate 20 minutes
- Discussion of chapter case studies. Get individual student(s) to recap two case studies of lecturer's choosing, then ask case study questions to the whole of the class. Calculate 15-20 minutes

Project tasks

Suggestions for various projects on which students can embark are provided for use in tutorial work.

1.d. Project Task

The whole class should brainstorm the general themes that students predict will be covered during each lesson/workshop, explaining why they consider them to be relevant to an international business module. At the end of this process, the lecturer should confirm the contents covered in each session. At that point, students should be asked to suggest five or six possible presentation topics for each week. Once these have been logged, students, either individually or on a group basis (depending on class size), will be asked to volunteer for the particular topic that will be the focus of their PowerPoint presentation.

Seminar discussion questions

These can be used to help spark debate amongst students during seminars.

1.b. Seminar discussion questions

  i.   In-text questions

1. Is globalization inevitable?
2. Is nationality an important factor in the way people do business?
3. To what extent is international business beneficial to wealthy and/or poor countries?
4. How would international business be affected if national regulations were stricter?

Case study questions and indicative answers

Questions and answers are provided for each case study from the textbook for use in class or to set as homework.

Case Study 1 International business in the wake of a crisis – Looking for the bright side of life

1. Which social, political and economic events have had the strongest influence on international business confidence levels in recent years?

Generally there is a distinction between events seen as one off occurrences and others that form part of a deeper, long-term trend. The former category might include natural disasters like earthquakes, even if the implications that companies draw from them can also have major consequences (i.e. leading, for instance, to a reorganization of their international supply chains). The same can be said about the

Oral presentation

Ideas for individual and group oral presentations are provided.

Oral presentation

This should be a 10-minute presentation to whole class, followed by a 5 minute Q+A session. The presentation should be made using PowerPoint; otherwise student should prepare, photocopy and distribute the structure of the talk beforehand. Normally, the marking will be largely based on the student's substantive performance (breadth, depth, independent thinking, research, exemplification) although some consideration might be given to format (cohesion, spontaneity).

Possible oral presentation topics for lessons for which Chapter 2 serves as background reading:

Test bank

A ready-made electronic testing resource which is fully customizable and contains feedback for students will help you to save time creating assessments.

What is corporate responsibility?

- a. The idea that a company should ensure that all its actions are both legal and ethical
- b. The idea that a company should ensure that all its actions are legal
- c. The idea that a company should ensure that all its actions are ethical
- d. The idea that a company should ensure that all its actions are geared to social and philanthropic ideals

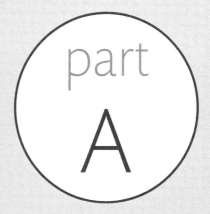

part
A

Introduction

1 Introduction to international business

Learning objectives

After reading this chapter, you will be able to:

✦ compare the concepts of international as opposed to global business

✦ determine the value for international managers of developing a flexible mindset

✦ understand the main terminology used in international business studies

✦ perceive the link between politics, economics, and international business

✦ analyse the internal and external drivers of international business

Case study 1.1

International business in the wake of a crisis—looking for the bright side of life

Like many management disciplines, international business is divided between company-internal topics, such as corporate philosophies or cultures, and things happening outside companies but shaping the general environment in which they operate. It may be impossible to survey every external factor affecting companies' cross-border dealings but the main ones can be identified and their effects analysed. This is what consultancy Grant Thornton does in its International Business Report, whose winter 2012 issue offered findings from interviews with more than 13,000 practitioners in 40 economies.

2011 was tumultuous, featuring among other events the European sovereign debt crisis, the Japanese tsunami and the Arab Spring. Add to this sustainability problems like the rising global population or political problems like the US Congress's budgetary problems and it is no surprise that global business confidence fell very low, particularly in the older industrialized countries. The Grant Thornton scale started 2011 at a mere 34 per cent level of confidence that profit growth prospects were improving. By the third quarter of 2011, confidence had shrunk to 3 per cent, reflecting a growing sense of hopelessness. General sentiments like this are extremely important in a social science like business, which is often driven by personal psychology. In the absence of confidence, many initiatives will never happen, particularly in foreign environments that are considered riskier because they are comparatively unknown.

The factors determining confidence in 2012 were expected to be a continuation of longstanding trends, led by a shift of economic activity to the newer industrialized countries. Significant variations in gross domestic product (GDP) growth rates in different parts of the world have been mirrored in the fact that businesses operating in emerging economies like Vietnam, India, and Mexico are expressing an optimistic view of the future, with 90, 79, and 68 per cent of all companies, respectively, forecasting profit growth in 2012. This should be compared with figures in troubled older industrialized countries like Spain, Japan, and Greece, where confidence figures were 15, −8, and −11 per cent respectively.

The study also identified other constraints impeding countries' growth prospects. Companies in the more mature markets, especially the European Union, were concerned that high debt levels would prevent them from making the kinds of investment they need to consolidate their future, particularly involving research and development. Emerging economy players did not have the same worries but faced another constraint, namely poor transportation and ICT infrastructure. Of course, companies that are sufficiently 'agile and adaptable to change' might also view these problems as opportunities. In international business, many clouds have a silver lining.

International business benefits when managers have confidence in their ability to predict the situation abroad

Case study questions

1. Which social, political, and economic events have had the strongest influence on international business confidence levels in recent years?
2. Looking ahead, what scenarios are most likely to affect confidence in the future?

Introduction

+ Gross domestic
product (GDP)
National income,
defined by national
consumption plus/
minus investment
activity plus/minus
government spending
plus/minus balance of
trade.

The simplest definition for international business is 'cross-border economic activity'. This has existed in various forms ever since human communities first began to interact with one another. When prehistoric tribes started trading beads or useful minerals like flint, they were engaging in early forms of international business (Watson 2005). Of course, trade has become somewhat more complicated since then. Nowadays, international business refers to the exchange not only of physical goods but also of services, capital, technology, and human resources. The first point to make about international business is that it covers a very broad spectrum of activities.

Just as important is to recognize what makes international business distinct from other areas of study, and where it overlaps with them. Many aspects of domestic business are also reproduced in international business, but they are treated differently because of the emphasis on cross-border aspects. Similarly, international business covers most if not all of the same topics as international management but goes much further. Where international management focuses mainly on decisions made by individuals operating within a corporate environment, international business also encompasses the broader political, economic, social, technological, philosophical, and environmental contexts within which firms operate. It is a very broad discipline with connections to many if not most of the issues that affect people's daily lives. Top international business students and practitioners are capable of carrying out analysis on many different levels and tend not to build artificial borders between business, economics, politics (White 2001), and society. Indeed, the ability and desire to embrace diversity is what gives this discipline its distinct philosophy and enduring attraction.

Section I: The international context

+ Globalization
Process whereby
the world becomes
increasingly
interconnected at an
economic, political,
and social level.

A useful starting point is the distinction between the concept of international business and the neighbouring notion of globalization with which it is often confused (Hirst and Thompson 1999). 'International' stresses differences; 'global' tries to highlight oneness. The emphasis on 'international' in this book is based on the expectation that strategies and behaviour that apply in one situation may not be appropriate in another, suggesting that there is no 'one best way' of doing business. This may seem obvious to people whose culture of origin emphasizes the need to seek multiple solutions to any one problem, but it can be a difficult adjustment for people from a culture where the emphasis is on discovering a single optimal solution to a problem.

A prime example of this focus on single solutions was in the early 1990s when certain academics claimed that the industrial methods that Toyota was implementing were so clearly superior to any other possibilities that they constituted a 'one-best-way' for the whole of the world (Womack et al. 1991). This caused a storm in university circles, with many academics opposing the idea that a universal solution to a business problem even exists. It is best to say from the outset that this book adheres to the second school of thought. Certainly, this is a more constructive approach from an educational perspective, since learners are better prepared for the diversity of the international business experience if they start with the expectation that things tend to be different in different places. Otherwise, it would be hard to spot the difference between international business and normal management studies.

Terminology and useful concepts

Every discipline has its own vocabulary, and it is useful to introduce certain key terms early on. This will be followed by a brief look at some of the many different approaches that companies take to international business. Lastly, a few statistics will be analysed to give readers a sense of some of the latest developments in this field.

International business features a number of specific challenges that business practitioners and academics ignore at their peril. It can be a very difficult adjustment for companies or individuals leaving a familiar home country to work in a host country where the environment and people are foreign to them. There is no doubt that the psychic distance between the world's different societies has shrunk over time, meaning that for many people, the 'foreignness' of operating in a country other than their own seems less challenging than it used to be (**go online to ORC Extension material 1.1**). It is also clear that globalization has been a key factor in this shift (MacGillivray 2006).

At the same time, it would be unrealistic and even dangerous to assume that societies worldwide have converged to the extent that there is no longer any need to study their economic, political, and cultural differences. The recognition that the world remains a complex and diverse place is best expressed by distinguishing between the basic terms of 'global' as opposed to 'international'. The word 'global' is associated with the idea of a single world and therefore stresses similarities between different communities. The word 'international', on the other hand, starts with an emphasis on the lack of similarity. This book will argue that this is a more useful approach, since it acknowledges the many obstacles that arise when people from different nations and cultures come together. Similarly, it is clear that most people have an identity that reflects, at least in part, the specificities of their culture of origin and/or the paradigm they use to make sense of the world. In our opinion, there is nothing inevitable about globalization or, indeed, any other socio-economic or cultural trend.

The book also prepares practitioners to develop the insiderization strategies that they need to overcome the barriers that people so often face when operating abroad (Ohmae 1999). In an ideal world, no such barriers would exist. Unfortunately, humankind does not live in such a world, if only because of 'home bias' and the feelings of 'animosity' that some populations have towards others (Amine 2008). This is not to deny growing similarities between many societies at certain levels, or that some sectors of activity operate along global rather than national lines (see Chapter 10). Indeed, there is little doubt that greater global interconnectedness has had a very deep effect on business and individuals, and some sociologists have identified what should be greeted as a positive trend towards greater cosmopolitanism and tolerance among the world's many citizens (Giddens 2002). By the same token, others express doubt about how long this new religion of 'globalism' will last, preferring to highlight the enduring and even resurgent nature of national awareness (Saul 2006). As shown in the wake of the 2008 credit crunch and 2011 European sovereign debt crisis, when times are hard, many people's first concern is to protect their domestic interest.

Companies doing international business

Now that we have outlined how the term 'international' will be used here, the next task is to define what kind of 'business' will be covered. It could be argued that 'international business' is already occurring whenever an individual engages in a cross-border transaction. Indeed, private individuals working by themselves have always had an important role to play in the world economy, whether investors purchasing currencies or shares in foreign companies (see Chapter 13), or local agents acting as representatives and providing firms with information on countries with which they are unfamiliar (see Chapter 9). Unsurprisingly, however, most international business is done by companies, ranging from huge firms to small and medium-sized enterprises (SMEs) to micro-firms that may or may not be 'born global' from the very outset. It is impossible to generalize why firms might want to seek their fortune abroad. In very general terms, many operators' motivation for going abroad used to be to acquire resources, whereas nowadays it tends to be to develop knowledge and markets (Aharoni and Ramamurti 2008). Paradigms vary strongly from one generation to the next, however. As Chapter 3 demonstrates, history is another discipline that has much to offer the international business student.

+ Home/host countries
People and companies originate from a 'home country'. When they operate abroad, they are working in a 'host country'.

+ Psychic distance
People's sense of the degree to which a foreign business culture differs from their own, adding to the sense of 'foreignness'.

> Go online

+ Paradigm
Worldview or vision of how things are and/or should be organized.

+ Insiderization
Where a person or company has become so integrated into a particular host society that locals forget its foreign origins.

+ Small and medium-sized enterprises (SMEs)
- 'Enterprises which employ fewer than 250 persons and which have an annual turnover not exceeding 50 million euros, and/or an annual balance sheet total not exceeding 43 million euros' (Extract of Article 2 of the Annex of Recommendation 2003/361/EC; European Commission 2003).

Despite its smaller size, German piano-maker Steinway dominates its sector globally

Source: Steinway & Sons

+ **Multinational enterprises (MNEs)**
Companies whose regular activities cause them to engage with and/or operate in more than one country at a time.

+ **Global firm**
Company designed to serve a single world market instead of different national markets.

+ **Configuration**
How a company locates its different corporate functions like research, production, marketing, and finance.

+ **Subsidiaries**
(Foreign) Unit belonging to a company's head office.

+ **Foreign direct investment (FDI)**
Where companies fund a permanent or semi-permanent unit overseas. The OECD defines FDI as a situation where a foreign owner has an equity stake of at least 10 per cent in a company's ordinary shares and aims to establish a 'lasting interest' in the host country.

The general terminology that this book uses to refer to companies that have regular dealings outside their home country is multinational enterprises (MNEs). Other international business books will often use other terms, such as multinational corporation (MNC), transnational corporation (TNC), and global firm. The problem with these other expressions is that each refers to a specific kind of company and is therefore not general enough. For instance, talking about MNCs neglects the fact that not all actors playing a role in international business are corporations or even privately owned enterprises. Similarly, terms such as TNCs and global firms do not sufficiently communicate the connections that continue to tie most companies with international interests to their country of origin. MNE is a more neutral term to describe the broad category of firms that, according to some statistics, account for more than a quarter of global GDP (UNCTAD 2011) and an even higher percentage of global trade. Thus, for the rest of this book, MNEs (a term including those SMEs that do business overseas) will be the basic unit of analysis.

A firm that owns facilities in a single country but regularly does business outside its borders may qualify as an MNE, but a far more typical and informative example is one whose international configuration is comprised of a head office and foreign subsidiaries. It has been estimated that MNE subsidiaries are responsible for more than 10 per cent of global economic activity and up to a third of world exports (UNCTAD 2011). The scale of their activities can vary widely between countries like France or the UK, where foreign subsidiaries account for up to 30 per cent of national sales, and others like Japan, where they play almost no role at all in key economic functions like manufacturing. In general, however, there is a trend towards MNEs expanding their international presence through subsidiaries. Alongside trade, companies' foreign direct investment (FDI) is the second main pillar of international business and a key focus in this field (see Figure 1.1).

Figure 1.1
Companies can choose different configurations when engaging in international business.

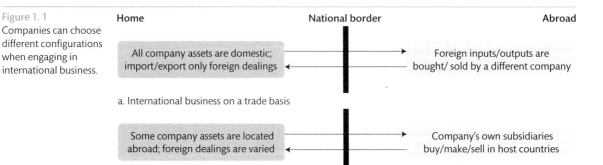

a. International business on a trade basis

b. International business on a foreign direct investment basis

The tendency over recent decades has been for MNEs to try to integrate their different operational units' activities into a coherent unit. This is the concrete application of certain leading international business theories (see Chapter 2) postulating that particular locations should specialize in those specific activities in which they have a competitive advantage. There is also a connection here to the growing body of academic research measuring how a company's degree of internationalization affects its performance. One consequence is that an increasing proportion of international business involves MNE subsidiaries trading with one another or with subcontractors (Economist 2011). This is one reason why it is so important to understand the different ways in which MNE head offices organize their relational networks (see Chapter 10).

+ Economies of scale
When a company increases output using the same equipment, its per-unit production costs fall.

+ Value chain
Succession of acts that successfully add value to an item as it is transformed from a raw material or input stage to a finished product or service.

Case study 1.2

MNEs' many strategic options

Since 2005, *Fortune Magazine*, the US business magazine, has published an annual list of the world's largest multinational enterprises, ranked by the revenues they produce globally (http://money.cnn.com/magazines/fortune/global500/). This data is of some interest to international business students; particularly year-to-year comparisons revealing, for instance, which sectors dominate the top of the list (with energy companies having largely displaced banks in recent years). It is also worth noting the decreasing number of global top 500 MNEs with headquarters located in the older industrialized countries (133 in the USA in 2011 vs. 176 in 2005) matched by the rising number of top MNEs over this period of time with their head office in China (61 vs. 16). Above and beyond discussions of location, however, understanding MNEs means having a sense of the main strategic choices they face. To some extent, 'where' they do things simply reflects 'how' they do them.

Despite the inherent advantage for most companies of reaching a critical mass that will enable them to achieve economies of scale (thus lower unit production costs) different sectors of activity are usually guided by different business paradigms. For instance, culturally more sensitive sectors such as food often emphasize national differentiation, with leading MNEs operating in this field, including Nestlé, Unilever, or General Mills, tending to prefer localized operations. On the other hand, hi-tech pioneers like Microsoft or Intel generally emphasize global operations that are easier to streamline

(see Chapter 10's discussion on MNEs' 'push' or 'pull' orientations). It is important to remember that international business is not a science but involves trying to understand managers' highly informed yet ultimately subjective appreciation of what constitutes the appropriate response to their circumstances.

In terms of MNE locations, contemporary analysts tend to be less interested in where a company runs its own operation and focus instead on the global value chains that they have developed through their dealings with suppliers and customers worldwide (Gereffi and Fernandez-Stark 2011). This new understanding of MNEs reflects the fact that many modern products are too complex to be manufactured by a single company working alone. Instead, as Chapter 5 will discuss, there is a growing trend towards a lead MNE working with an initial tier of counterparts, whose own suppliers or customers then become the lead MNE's second tier of counterparts. In the end, studying MNEs without identifying the relationships they build with other companies provides an incomplete picture of their strategic possibilities.

Case study questions

1. What factors explain why certain sectors are more or less represented at the top of the Fortune 500 rankings in certain years?
2. In which sectors of activity are MNEs particularly dependent on external counterparts, and why?

Like many if not most products, jeans are the result of a multitude of international supply chains coming together

Source: iStock

Accumulation of value in value chains

+ **Upstream**
Early value chain activities undertaken when processing or transforming a product or service.

+ **Downstream**
Late value chain activities undertaken when selling or distributing a product or service.

The most useful way of picturing MNEs' work organization is to imagine the production and sale of a good or service as a series of acts adding to the item's value as it is transformed from a raw material into a semi-processed stage, before ending up as a finished good or service (see Figure 1.2). This series of acts is called the value chain. It is split into production-related upstream activities (see Chapter 11) and marketing-related downstream activities (see Chapter 12). A key feature of international business today is that many firms do not perform by themselves all of the activities comprising the value chain in which they are involved. Instead, they might ask external partners to take responsibility for certain phases. As such, it is more accurate to represent international value chains as the sum of several intermediary value chains. A good example is provided by jeans, which should be analysed

Figure 1.2
Visualizing the transformation of a good or service. Each level adds value and also has its own intermediary supply chains.

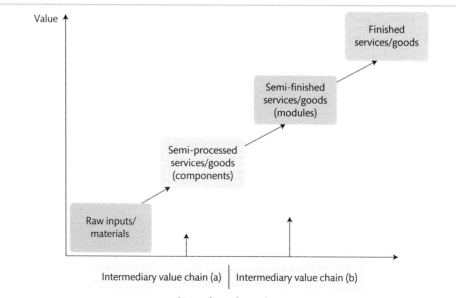

not just as a finished product but as the sum of many lower level generic products. One of these is the zip, which is the culmination of several intermediary businesses, starting with the extraction of minerals, the processing of basic metals, and their subsequent transformation into zips. It is important to understand that the end product of one company's international value chain (for example, zip-makers) is just an intermediate phase in the value chain of another company (the jeans-maker).

This portrayal of international business as a series of cross-border value chains raises questions about the rate at which value accumulates as a service or good is being transformed into its final form. For presentational purposes, Figure 1.2 shows value accumulating at a linear rate. This is generally unrealistic, since, depending on the sector in question, value tends to accumulate more or less quickly when the good or service passes through the upstream or downstream side of the value chain. For instance, in the coffee business, a tiny percentage of what consumers pay for a cup at many coffee shops goes to upstream bean-growers. To some extent, this reflects poor coffee bean growers' lack of bargaining power when dealing with powerful MNEs that dominate the value chain at the point where value accumulates more rapidly—in this case, further downstream, closer to consumers. Inversely, in a sellers' market (like oil) marked by less competition among producers, value tends to accumulate in the hands of upstream producers. Figure 1.3 offers a more realistic picture of (international) value chain curves.

Clearly it is more efficient to operate at that part of the value chain where value accumulates most rapidly (i.e. where the value-added curve is steepest). This is just as true for national economies as for companies. Those countries whose firms specialize in high value-added production clearly have an advantage over those that specialize in low value-added goods, or, as economists would put it, they enjoy better terms of trade. For example, if US firms are global champions in computers and Sri Lankan companies lead the world in the tea business, the USA is clearly at an advantage, since the market where it dominates creates greater value than the market where Sri Lanka dominates. National governments are very aware of this factor and will often take measures to improve their country's competitive position. Such efforts are part of the political environment within which MNEs operate, as are the measures enacted by global bodies (see Chapter 4) to control the actions that states might wish to take in the marketplace. Certain regions' tendency to concentrate on higher or (less advantageously) lower value-added activities is another major topic in international business, especially where this affects the international flow of wealth. Without underestimating the ongoing strength of the MNEs from the older industrialized world—often referred to as the Triad or the OECD countries—as discussed in Chapter 15, a growing number of companies from newly industrialized emerging economies (also known

+ Generic
Reference to goods that are not meant for a specific use but serve a variety of applications.

+ Terms of trade
Relationship between the value added inherent to the goods/services that a country imports or exports.

+ Triad/OECD countries
World's older industrialized nations. Triad refers to the three regions of Western Europe, North America and Japan/Oceania. The Organization for Economic Cooperation and Development (OECD) is a Paris-based association whose membership is comprised of the world's advanced economies.

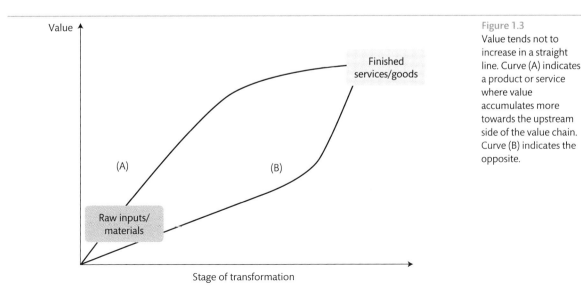

Figure 1.3
Value tends not to increase in a straight line. Curve (A) indicates a product or service where value accumulates more towards the upstream side of the value chain. Curve (B) indicates the opposite.

+ Less developed
countries (LDCs)
Countries whose
industrial base and
general level of human
welfare does not
enable most citizens to
achieve a decent living
standard. This is
an umbrella term
covering a vast range
of economic, social,
and demographic
situations, ranging
from 'emerging' or
'newly industrialized'
countries that are on
a clear industrialization
path to 'heavily
indebted poor
countries' (HIPC)
with very poor
growth prospects.

> Go online

+ Offshore
Transactions or actors
over which national
regulators have no
authority.

as less developed countries (LDCs) have become leading players on today's international business scene. The challenge for them is whether the activities in which they specialize create greater or lesser value added.

Some observers point to the industrial emergence of many LDCs as showing that power is shared more widely nowadays. Others might emphasize the fact that most of the world's largest MNEs still come from OECD countries. Indeed, the Triad continues to host many if not most of the world's hi-tech production activities, meaning that the distribution of global economic power remains very uneven to this day (Mann 2004). MNEs' role in aggravating or reducing income inequalities, on a national but also a global scale, constitutes another major topic of debate in international business (**go online to ORC Extension material 1.2**).

When devising their value chain strategies, companies need to be aware of all relevant political and legislative frameworks, because they must obey the laws of the different countries where they will be operating. The problem today is that many operate on an offshore basis outside the control of any single government. Further confusion is caused by the fact that many of the policies shaping the international business framework (like the level of import taxes or export subsidies) vary greatly in time and place. In international business, political considerations are a key aspect of corporate strategizing (Scholte 2005). It is important for theory in this field to juggle the subjective nature of human attitudes with the hard facts on the ground.

Key statistics

International business is very much a living subject, rooted in the relationship between actions and outcomes. For this reason, it is crucial that practitioners and students develop the ability to analyse the basic concepts of this discipline in terms of what happens in the real world. Viewing international business in context necessitates linking theory to front-page news.

International trade data

Recent crises have been harmful to world trade and raised a number of issues that are key to the study of international business. The first question relates to the relative strength of cross-border as opposed to purely domestic activities during times of economic difficulty. As indicated in Figure 1.4, over the years there has been a definite trend towards international business expanding at a faster rate than business as a whole. Yet following the 2008 credit crunch, both trade and FDI fell much more quickly than global GDP did. This was exemplified most poignantly by the 46 per cent collapse between January 2008 and January 2009 in exports from Japan, one of the world's most competitive trading nations. For the global economy as a whole, total trade fell by about 12 per cent over this period. At one level, the disproportionate slump in international business was unsurprising, since national governments tend during a recession to provide 'stabilizing' financial resources (i.e. paying welfare benefits or running budget deficits) that are mainly spent on more domestic activities such as services. At the same time, it is very significant that many if not most economies react to crises by becoming more inwardly focused, at least temporarily. In a sense, the 'de-globalization' fears associated with the crisis of the late 2000s reveal the potential limitations of international business.

It remains that longer term statistics have shown a very strong trend towards cross-border activities increasing as a percentage of total business. In the decade preceding the 2008 credit crunch, for instance, world trade had expanded by an annual average of nearly 5.5 per cent, or about 2 per cent faster than the global economy as a whole. The result of this trend is that international business had already become a dominant aspect of many people's lives by the mid-2000s. Just one generation ago, trade accounted for a mere 10 per cent of the US GDP; around 25 to 30 per cent of GDP in medium-sized industrial exporting

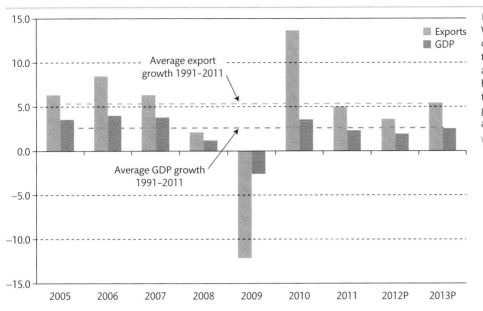

Figure 1.4
With the exception of 2009 (following the crisis in 2008), average export growth has been much faster than average economic growth for more than a decade.

WTO 2012

nations such as Germany, France, and Japan; and around 50 per cent of GDP in a few smaller, open economies like the Netherlands. By 2008, almost all of these countries' openness to trade, measured as the sum of their imports and exports divided by national GDP, had at least doubled (see Figure 3.2). Even more dramatically, by the late 2000s the sum total of imports and exports in countries like China, Russia, and India, which for political reasons had engaged in very little trade before the 1990s, had jumped to somewhere between 45 and 65 per cent of national GDP. Of course, it could be argued that simply adding imports and exports overstates an economy's degree of openness. Admittedly, this is an inadequate way of accounting for certain situations, like the temporary import of components assembled in final goods that will be resold in export markets. Moreover, in the wake of the 2008 credit crunch, some observers were predicting that, within a few short years, global trade would fall from a peak of around two-thirds of global GDP to a more sustainable figure of 40–50 per cent (Munchau 2009). This would remain very high, however. Even after the recent turbulences, there is little doubt that international business will continue for the foreseeable future to account for a large proportion of all economic activity.

Within this general trend, however, regional performances vary widely, as indicated in Figure 1.5. This reflects differences in economic performance or orientations and has clear implications for the politics of international business.

This data set is interesting for both historical and current reasons. Compared with global trade's breakdown in 1990, exports from North America and Western Europe have fallen as a percentage of the world total, matched by rising exports from Africa, the ex-Soviet Union, the Middle East, and above all Asia. For the first three regions, the change is largely explained by higher commodity prices. For Asia, it reflects the region's growing role as a global manufacturing centre. It is also worth exploring the topic of how world trade breaks down between the primary sector (raw materials and agricultural products), the secondary sector (manufactured goods), and the tertiary sector (services) (**go online to ORC Extension material 1.3**). Changes in the relative pricing of goods can be an important factor in determining the current and future prospects of one sector of activity as opposed to another. All of these trends are largely driven by MNEs' behaviour—before shaping, in turn, the contexts to which MNEs are forced to adapt.

Figure 1.6 reveals the enormous gap between merchandise imports and exports in some of the world's leading economies—starting with the largest, the USA. When analysing national economic performance, it is always worth examining whether a country is in surplus or deficit, if only to anticipate the likely impact upon economic indicators such as

> Go online

+ Relative pricing
Price of a given category of goods or services expressed in relation to the price of a different category.

FIGURE 1.5
World merchandise
trade, by region and
selected country,
in US$ billion and
percentages; exports
accounted for FOB
(free on board) imports
on CIF (cost insurance
freight) basis.

WTO 2012

	FOB value exports 2011	Percentage global exports 2011, in % (% in 1990)	CIF value imports 2011	Percentage global imports 2011, in %
World	17,779		18,000	
North America	2283	12.8 (16.6)	3090	17.2
USA	1481	8.3	2265	12.6
South and Central America	749	4.2	727	4.0
Mercosur*	354	2.0	334	2.0
Europe	6601	37.1 (49.6)	6854	38.1
EU 27	6029	33.9	6241	34.7
Germany	1474	8.3	1254	7.0
Netherlands	660	3.7	597	3.3
France	597	3.4	715	4.0
UK	473	2.7	636	3.5
Russia	522	2.9	323	1.8
Africa	597	3.4 (3.1)	555	3.1
Middle East	1228	6.9 (4.1)	665	3.7
Asia	5534	31.1 (21.8)	5568	3.1
China	1890	10.6	1743	9.7
Japan	823	4.6	854	4.7
India	297	1.7	451	2.5
Asian NICs†	1290	7.3	1302	7.2
ASEAN‡	1244	7.0	1151	6.4

(*) Argentina, Brazil, Paraguay, Uruguay
(†) Hong Kong, Republic of Korea, Singapore, Chinese Taipei
(‡) Brunei, Cambodia, Indonesia, Laos, Malaysia, Myanmar, Philippines, Singapore, Thailand, Vietnam

unemployment or inflation. For example, despite the size of its economy, the USA is only the world's second leading exporter, far behind China. Germany comes a close third—a remarkable performance by Europe's leading trading power, given its much smaller population. The USA did claw back some of its 2011 merchandise trade deficit with a $187 billion surplus on the trade in services—a sector that accounts for upwards of 30 per cent of total trade volumes in Europe and around 15 per cent elsewhere. However, with the country's already large trade deficit aggravated by large FDI outflows, all in all the USA ran a significant current account deficit in 2011, as it had in fact done for quite a few years previously. Questions must be raised about the viability of a system whose leading economy runs such large deficits. The global financial architecture (see Chapter 4) is another major debate in international business today.

Lastly, it is also worth commenting upon the growing percentage of world trade accounted for by newly industrialized countries, led by China and other emerging Asian powers. Some observers analyse this as a sign that globalization offers poorer nations greater opportunities, especially considering that, as recently as 1990, LDCs accounted for only around 25 per cent of total volumes. This view is encapsulated in the body of theory

+ Current account
Country's 'balance of trade' (exports minus imports) plus or minus its financial flows from abroad (interest or dividend payments, cash transfers).

	Trade balance (FOB exports – CIF imports)
World	−221
North America	−807
USA	−784
South and Central America	+22
Mercosur*	+20
Europe	−253
EU 27	−212
Germany	+220
Netherlands	+63
France	−118
UK	−163
Russia	+199
Africa	+42
Middle East	+563
Asia	−34
China	+147
Japan	−31
India	−154
Asian NICs†	−12
ASEAN‡	−93

Figure 1.6
Trade balances for selected countries and regions.
WTO 2012

(*) Argentina, Brazil, Paraguay, Uruguay
(†) Hong Kong, Republic of Korea, Singapore, Chinese Taipei
(‡) Brunei, Cambodia, Indonesia, Laos, Malaysia, Myanmar, Philippines, Singapore, Thailand, Vietnam

supporting the idea that, one way or another, all countries stand to gain from international trade (see Chapter 2). Whether this is true or not, the shifting geography of international business (see Chapter 15) is another key feature of the modern era. With its enormous impact on MNEs' structures and the global distribution of capital, this is a trend that affects managers' decisions at many different levels.

Introduction to foreign direct investment

As indicated above, trade is just one of international business's two main pillars. The second, foreign direct investment, has gained in importance over recent decades, characterized by a growth rate that has often surpassed the increase in trade itself. Being able to analyse the rise of FDI is also key to understanding this discipline as a whole.

FDI can involve any part of a value chain, from the upstream extraction of raw materials to the downstream retailing of services or finished goods. Recent FDI data should be handled with care given statistical categorization problems but also because the long-term uptrend has been very inconsistent, featuring strong rises followed by interruptions such as the events of 2001 (the 9/11 attacks on New York's World Trade Center and bursting of the 'dot.com' stock market bubble) and the 2008 credit crunch. One of the main explanations

Figure 1.7
FDI inflows and
outflows for selected
nations, from Q4 2010
through Q3 2011, in
US$ billion.

(FDI in figures
http://www.oecd.org/
dataoecd/60/43/
48462282.pdf OECD
2012)

Total global inflows, Q4 2010 through Q3 2011	1362.8	
Breakdown	FDI inflows	FDI outflows
OECD countries	790.1	1276.3
USA	226.5	391.5
EU	385.9	565.5
France	28.9	89.7
Germany	29.6	57.6
UK	70.8	109.1
Brazil	76.4	–5.2
Russia	54.2	64
India	31.0	17.5
China	217.8	57.3

+ Protectionist
General attitude that a
national government
should adopt policies
restricting foreign
interests' ability to
access its domestic
market.

> Go online

+ Outsourcing
Where a company
delegates to another
company certain tasks
(like the production
of components) that
it might otherwise
undertake itself.

for the collapse in FDI following this crisis was a 77 per cent fall in international mergers and acquisitions (see Chapter 9), one of the main drivers of FDI (UNCTAD 2009). At times of trouble, MNEs may be reluctant to invest abroad, especially if funding dries up. Managers might also become more pessimistic about foreign markets' growth prospects.

A similar reaction can also be witnessed in the kinds of attitudes that policy-makers often display during times of economic hardship. Thus, some observers have predicted that the 2008 and 2011–2012 crises could lead to the resurrection of old protectionist attitudes and trigger a process of 'de-globalization' **(go online to ORC Extension material 1.4)**, reversing the major trend of the past half-century. In general, this pessimism was met with widespread declarations of support for open borders (e.g. statements made at the April 2009 G20 meeting in London), with many economists and politicians asserting that it is precisely during an economic slowdown that governments must avoid the kinds of discriminatory nationalistic measures that impede the cross-border flow of goods, services, and capital. Having said that, in times of crisis there is a natural tendency, especially in certain political cultures, to prioritize domestic investment and restrict capital outflows. One example of this was the decision by France's old Sarkozy administration in 2009 to require automaker Renault, in exchange for government aid, to close a plant in Slovenia and bring the work back home. MNEs will also have their own ways of reacting to weak economic conditions, often speeding up their ongoing cost-cutting drive. Under certain circumstances, however, this can have the effect of a further acceleration in international outsourcing, a trend that for several decades now has been a key factor in the explosion of cross-border trade volumes. These interrelationships explain why, at a certain level, it can be inaccurate to analyse FDI in isolation from companies' other international trade decisions.

All in all, the global stock of foreign direct investment has risen substantially since the turn of the twenty-first century. Unlike the international trade of goods and services, however, with FDI there has been relatively little variation in recent years in terms of the breakdown between the developed and the developing worlds' share of total volumes, with the OECD countries still accounting for nearly two-thirds of global totals. This may even out in the future given sharp rises in FDI flow to (and increasingly from) the developing world. Moreover, it is also worth exploring the relative variation in LDCs' share of global trade as opposed to FDI because of what this reveals about managers' varying levels of comfort in different business environments and the impact on MNEs' internationalization decisions (see Chapter 9). In international business, there are many different levels where political 'macro' analyses of national interest link to more 'micro' discussions of corporate (and even personal) strategy.

Practitioner insight

John Browne has had a very successful career in the international energy sector, including as Chief Executive of British Petroleum (later BP) between 1995 and 2007, and more recently as Managing Director of Riverstone Holdings LLC. As Baron Browne of Madingley, he has been a member of the House of Lords since 2001. He is also President of the Royal Academy of Engineering.

'The three main drivers of economic globalization have been: communications technology and infrastructure; the reduction in global tariffs and establishment of free trade areas (lowering the cost of international business); and the emergence of new trading partners for the developed world, like the BRICs. Some drivers are both a cause and an effect of globalization.

International and domestic business have an interesting relationship. When the whole world is in crisis, globalized international industries often suffer the most. This is because most global industries are, for various industry-specific reasons, very vulnerable to downturns. Examples include: oil, where turnover falls sharply in global recessions; luxury consumer goods, where customers cut back heavily during a downturn; and finance, because of lending constraints during recessions. Domestic industries, on the other hand, tend to be more resilient because they provide essential goods for which demand is less sensitive to income. Examples include agriculture, healthcare, transport, and the public sector, which often increases spending at times of crisis to stimulate the economy.

In general, however, I predict that international business will continue to expand faster than its domestic counterpart. Every firm above a certain size wants to spread overheads across a larger market to reduce costs per unit sold. I also think the growth of foreign direct investment will remain strong. Even when national or regional shocks occur, the diversity of international business should protect it.

Regarding corporate decisions to internationalize, I see three main drivers. The first is comparative growth rates. If you face a shrinking market at home and booming markets abroad, the signal to internationalize is strong. Second is the wider environment abroad: infrastructure, education, stability, and taxation. There is no point accelerating international expansion if you can't hire appropriately skilled staff or are likely to lose everything in a war. The third factor is confidence in your company's internal capability to succeed in a foreign market. You need to have the right skills, relationships, and structures to cope with the many challenges that each move presents. You must become an apparently domestic player in each market.

Lastly, there is the management of MNEs, typically vast organizations with tens of thousands of employees operating in very different environments. You need a structure that leverages local information close to the ground, ensuring that people from every background, including local people, are equally valued. In general, you need to balance power between the centre and subsidiaries, which should be given the maximum possible freedom to operate within defined boundaries. As a rule-of-thumb, decisions should be taken at the lowest level possible. Country-specific decisions should be taken within the country.'

Section II: The international business framework

Chapter 9 discusses a range of motivations explaining why and where companies operate abroad. Some MNEs internationalize systematically, taking advantage of the relationships they have built up to exploit any and all opportunities (Ellis 2011). Others might only

Figure 1.8
Summary of the main
strategic drivers of
international business
today.

Internal drivers

– Expand sales

– Leverage existing competencies

– Use extra capacities

– Spread risks

– Avoid saturation

– Internalize competencies

– Acquire resources

– Access more efficient inputs

External drivers

– Technology

– Liberalized regulatory framework

– Free trade friendly institutions

– Global competitive paradigm

– Deregulated finance

venture abroad on specific, ad hoc occasions. The following section (see Figure 1.8) offers an overview of some of the main factors driving companies' international business projects.

Strategic drivers

Some of the motives driving international business are 'micro' in nature and primarily related to firms' profit-seeking initiatives and strategic intent. Others involve companies' reactions to external 'macro' trends such as political, governmental, macro-economic, and socio-cultural factors over which they have little control (Yip 1989). Of course, 'micro' and 'macro' motivations are often interrelated. One example of this linkage can be found in the corporate philosophy of internalization. This is the idea that when markets function poorly (for example, where market participants do not receive a fair reward for their efforts) companies may wish to run their international value chain operations themselves, because they need to maintain in-house any knowledge that they may possess (Buckley and Casson 1976). In this view, firms will not need external partners to lead their internationalization drive as long as they have high-quality managers capable of assuming responsibilities abroad, and as long as the host countries are not too different from the ones to which the company and its managers are accustomed. This is a case where international business springs from the interface between a company's internal attributes (managers' qualities) and the characteristics (foreignness and/or market mechanisms) of the host country where it is hoping to move. Another example of the interconnection between micro vs. macro-drivers of international business is when an MNE calculates that the costs of going abroad are lower than its potential gains from operating in a regulatory, labour, or tax system where it is well placed to pressure the host country government into offering it certain facilities (Ietto-Gillies 2003). This is because a company's cross-border success depends not only on how suitable its behaviour is to the market(s) where it is operating (Porter 1986) but also on how effectively it deals with non-business actors such as politicians or regulators. In short, separating micro and macro-drivers of international business may be a useful categorization (see Figure 1.8) but it is necessarily an artificial one.

+ **Internalization**
When a company decides to run a particular function itself (using its own employees) instead of delegating it to an external party.

Internal drivers of international business

Companies often operate outside their borders because they are in a sector shaped by international rather than domestic factors. At the same time, it is rare to find companies launched as multinationals from the very outset. The vast majority of MNEs throughout history, with the exception of 'born-globals' (see Chapter 9), have started in their home market and moved abroad later: expanding downstream to increase sales; upstream to acquire resources; or in both directions to diversify risk. Each of these actions is based on a different logic that the company will have developed for its own internal reasons.

Expand sales

Once a firm has built a system allowing it to produce and market a product or service efficiently, it will usually want to leverage this competency by selling the finished good, with or without modification, into a new market. Thus, on the downstream side, the expansion of sales is the main driver of international business. There are countless examples of this rationale being put to use. For instance, Dutch vegetable farmers have developed the green-house technology to grow tomatoes and peppers even during cold North European winters. Because consumer demand for these products from neighbouring countries such as Germany and the UK remains strong all year long, doing business across borders is a natural step for Dutch agribusiness companies like The Greenery, which sources fresh produce and sells it to foreign retailers.

A related example is the trade between Japan, a dynamic but mineral-poor industrial giant whose factories require enormous amounts of raw materials, and Australia, which has an abundance of minerals as well as an industrial sector capable of refining ore (like bauxite) into usable production inputs (like aluminium). For Australian mining or refining companies, exporting to Japan is a logical extension of what started out as a domestic activity. A third example from the service sector is the way that huge pension funds like Jupiter or Allianz RCM leverage their expensive management infrastructure (often located in London) to sell their products to customers worldwide. Expanding sales worldwide is a quick way of paying for the enormous costs that they incurred building their trading rooms in the first place. Lastly, cross-border sales can also be a natural move for companies that are small or medium-sized but operating in sectors that are by their very nature international in

Dutch food manufacturers use their facilities to serve domestic and foreign markets alike

Source: The Greenery

scope. One example here would be the engineering consulting business, which in Europe and neighbouring regions like the Middle East is 96 per cent dominated by companies with fewer than 20 employees (http://www.ecceengineers.eu). In all these instances, international business is as relevant to a company's mission as the work that it does in its home market. This is especially true when the company is looking to move into a foreign country that is similar in political, economic, and/or cultural terms, not to mention close geographically. Without minimizing the real differences that exist between the USA and Canada, when McDonald's first began expanding across America, setting up outlets across its northern border must have seemed a relatively easy step. The skills developed selling in one country can sometimes be transplanted seamlessly to another.

There are also strategic reasons why companies organize their commercial functions to embrace international sales as a matter of course. As mentioned above, a basic principle of modern production is that selling large volumes is beneficial because it creates economies of scale. In a similar vein, the greater the experience that a company has acquired in producing something, the better it becomes at this activity. This is because it appropriates skills that will allow it to achieve productivity gains. As a result, many companies size their production operations to obtain critical mass. To justify these investments and avoid surplus capacities, they often need to sell more than they would if they were simply serving domestic customers. This is especially true if the firm comes from a small country. For example, discount airliner Ryanair would have been at a disadvantage using its Dublin home as its only hub. With so many more passengers travelling through the UK, it made sense for this Irish company to run its main operations out of London Stansted Airport, which is, after all, a foreign location. Another way of looking at the issue of the size of a company's international operations is in financial terms. In the mid-2000s, the cost of building a new automotive plant was roughly $1 billion. To have any hope of recovering such a large upfront investment, a car company would have to make sure that its new plant produced enough cars to justify the expense. This is not possible if the plant is located either in a small country (Luxembourg does not have a car plant serving its domestic market alone, for instance) or in one where demand is already saturated due to competition. In both cases, the production scale must be international or else the investment becomes impracticable.

+ Critical mass
Minimum threshold beyond which positive, size-related benefits arise.

Risk diversification

Another strategic driver of international business is the desire to spread risk by working in more than one country at a time. Evidence shows that this kind of 'multinationality' not only increases flexibility, thereby increasing profit-making opportunities, but also reduces risk by preventing over-dependence on a single location or market (Andersen 2011). One way of looking at this is from an upstream, production perspective. If a firm had all its industrial assets in northern Turkey and another earthquake were to hit the region, its chances of continuing manufacturing operations would be worse than if it also had plants in zones not affected by the earthquake. That is why so many firms have disaster plans allowing them to continue functioning in case a catastrophe affects one of their main locations. The same logic can be applied on the downstream, sales side. A company that sells into one market alone runs the risk that its outlet might collapse for whatever reason (natural disaster, bad policy, war) without any other customers to compensate for lost sales. Any firm whose entire business revolved around exports to Syria at the time of the 2012 civil war, for instance, would have experienced major problems. The adversity that a company experiences in one location has less of an impact when it has interests in many others.

Spreading risk through international operations can be done in different ways. The 'product life cycle' (PLC) is the idea that, from an international marketing perspective, a product or service that is on an upward trend in some countries may be in decline elsewhere (see Chapter 12). Clearly, it is advantageous for firms to sell goods in markets where demand is on the rise, since they will be able to command higher prices. One example from the 1970s and 1980s is the way that jeans were so much more expensive in Western Europe, where they were new and fashionable, than in California, where they had long been a commodity product. The PLC variation enabled San Francisco firm Levi Strauss to supplement revenues in its home market with exports to Europe. International business can be used to diversify other risks as well. For instance, foreign sales can be used to offset the risk of accumulating liabilities in the currency concerned (see Chapter 13). Despite the challenges of operating in a foreign environment, diversification means that international business can actually be a way for a company to reduce risk.

Acquire inputs

The final internal driver of international business is the acquisition of resources (materials and labour but also capital and technology) used during a firm's production process. Sometimes this involves inputs that are unavailable at home. For example, non-oil-producing countries such as Japan, Germany, and France must look abroad to source this commodity. At other times, the cost of an input might be so much lower overseas that a company would be at a competitive disadvantage if, unlike its rivals, it did not source the factor where it can be acquired most cheaply. As discussed in Chapter 9, this can be done via FDI or trade. UK vacuum cleaner manufacturer Dyson provides one example of a firm engaging in FDI to reduce input costs. Portrayed as a symbol of the rebirth of British manufacturing in the 1990s, Dyson had decided by 2002 that it needed to lower its cost base. Accordingly, it moved almost all its production activities to Malaysia, where workers' wages were less than those paid to British production staff. However, the company continued to run higher end tasks out of the UK, with its founder and CEO sponsoring annual awards from 2009 onwards to encourage young British design engineers.

Trade can also be used to reduce return costs. The budding solar energy business is a good case in point. Builders worldwide seeking to enter this fast-growing sector must source solar panels at a competitive price. However, few countries can make these components as cheaply as Germany, where companies like Solarworld or Q-Cells that were relatively small SMEs until recently have now achieved critical mass, allowing them to compete successfully in the global markets. Thus, it is in the interest of energy system installers worldwide to import from Germany if they want to acquire resources cheaply. In short, international business is often driven by firms focusing more on the advantages inherent to a given production location and less on whether this site is in their country of origin or not.

External factors

Business decisions are always shaped by trends and events that escape a company's direct control. This can be particularly significant in an international situation, as most multinationals are less able to influence multiple global events affecting their fortunes, as opposed to trends unfolding within a single country where they might have greater influence.

Dyson famously moved its manufacturing facilities to Malaysia, while maintaining most of its engineering activities in the UK

Source: Dyson

Technology

It is not always easy to determine which drivers a company can control, and which it cannot. One case in point is technology, a key factor in today's global economy. This is an umbrella term that refers to companies' internal innovation efforts (see Chapter 11's section on knowledge management) but also to the technological advances that a particular society achieves. Thus, technology affects the international business environment at many different levels. On the upstream side, for instance, improved telecommunications enable companies to stretch their value chains to distant locations offering competitive advantages. One example is when hospitals in the West use remote diagnostics facilities to get advice from doctors located, for instance, in India. Out of a service that was once as localized as medical treatment is, modern technology has created an opportunity for an international work organization. The same applies to downstream activities, for instance, where company–customer relationships extend worldwide due to technological advances like the Internet. When consumers worldwide purchase their books through Amazon instead of at their local bookstore, they are cementing technology's role as a key organizing principle in international business. Indeed, given the positive impact that technology-related transportation improvements have traditionally had on trade, it can be argued that technology is one of the main causes of today's shrinking world. It is rare that a community chooses to remain completely isolated once the means exist for it to interact with other communities. Google's rapid rise in China, despite the obstacles raised by the Beijing government, is a good example of this. Before China had any exposure to Western consumption goods (or ideas), its population was less focused on them. People's outlooks and desires often change when they see how foreigners live. Cross-border comparison has always been a significant driver of international business.

Regulatory framework

However, just because a technology exists that enables something to happen does not mean that it will necessarily occur. For international business to take place, it must be enabled by a general regulatory framework. National governments' main responsibility is to ensure the well-being of their population in the face of danger from abroad. The main threat is clearly war, but foreign competition can also be damaging to local interests, for instance, by crowding home country companies out of their domestic marketplace. The state must therefore determine to what extent it wants to use regulation as protection against this international business threat. Chapter 3 looks at the issue of state intervention in greater depth. For the moment, it is worth stating that the general paradigm in many countries since the early 1980s has been to accept and indeed promote cross-border flows by allowing foreign actors to enter domestic marketplaces. The effect of this deregulation (also known as 'liberalization') trend has been to reduce barriers to entry, making it easier for companies to operate on an international scale.

+ Barriers to entry
Regulatory, competitive, financial, and other obstacles that make it difficult for a firm to enter a particular market.

A liberalization philosophy has affected the trade and FDI regulations of most if not all of the world's nation-states, but, as Chapter 4 details, it has also led to the creation of a global framework that is conducive to international business. One aspect is the rise of regional trading arrangements like the EU. These are groups of neighbouring countries that have signed agreements enabling easier access to one another's markets. Their degree of integration can vary, but in general such arrangements promote free trade among members. The same philosophy has also led to the creation of trade-friendly international institutions like the WTO, whose laws create a framework in which countries are positively discouraged from adopting isolationist policies. The idea is to create a world where cross-border transactions are no longer considered unusual.

Global competition

In terms of corporate strategy, a whole new vision has arisen regarding what it means to compete. Before the arrival of a world of free trade, companies would position themselves in terms of local and national rivals, competing for a share of their domestic markets. Today, with increasingly penetrable national borders, economic competitors can come from any-where, taking advantage of any experiences that they have accumulated at home or abroad. This means that some companies that have worked very hard over the years to improve productivity or quality, and that would be very competitive in a purely domestic framework, might suddenly lose market share because of the arrival of hyper-competitive foreign companies. For example, where Bordeaux wineries used to compete successfully with domestic rivals from France's Burgundy region, they must now face challenges from New World winemakers from Australia, Chile, and South Africa. With rivals achieving economies of scale because they already operate globally, Bordeaux winemakers can no longer afford to think in domestic terms alone. Furthermore, the profits that global groups make in one market can be used to fund their activities in another, which is why it is sometimes just as important to go abroad specifically to limit rivals' profitability as it is to turn a profit oneself. This explains the outcry when companies like US aircraft-maker Boeing and its European rival Airbus suspect one another of receiving different kinds of preferential treatment at home, enabling them to subsidize lower prices to foreign customers and thereby gaining global market share to their rivals' detriment. The new competition involves fighting not just in rivals' home markets but also in markets all across the world, which is why business has become so much tougher in many sectors today.

The main consequence of the new competitive paradigm is that producers are no longer able to rely on the comfortable positions they used to hold in their domestic markets. Consumers' greater awareness of possible foreign alternatives to domestic products, and their ability to access rival products at competitive prices, has given buyers greater power. For example, in the mid to late twentieth century, when German consumers could buy their television sets only from local companies AEG Telefunken and Grundig (or Dutch rival Philips), these proud old firms were in a position to sell their high-quality products at a good profit. Once the market began to be flooded with equally good but cheaper Japanese alternatives, the two German companies were forced to compete at a level to which they were unaccustomed. Today both survive only as brand names listed in other firms' product portfolios. Given the partial convergence of consumer behaviour and demand patterns worldwide (see Chapter 12), companies have come to realize that, regardless of how directly or indirectly they operate outside their national borders, international business will affect them at one level or the other. As Chapter 10 discusses, MNEs running worldwide operations increasingly look to integrate their units' management, in a bid for greater coherency (Held et al. 1999). Everyone's playing field has expanded.

International finance

Corporate finance has also been affected by the trend towards a more globalized world. To source the capital needed to run vast multinational empires, MNEs often have to rely on different funding sources, many of which operate offshore and thus free from domestic controls. The deregulation of the finance industry since the 1980s, part of an overall 'liberalization' paradigm, has led to an explosion in cross-border capital flows. Much of this money is free floating, that is, not directly associated with the production of goods and services. This partial separation of finance from real business activity—one of the causes of the 2008 global credit crunch—has added to pressures weighing on MNE managers today. On the one hand, financial asset prices are becoming increasingly volatile and difficult to predict, adding to the uncertainty of international business. On the other, whereas many MNEs used to be owned by 'passive shareholders' mainly interested in the safety of their investments, in the new 'shareholder value' paradigm international managers are under pressure to maximize short-term financial returns by running tighter operations and taking greater risks. In a similar vein, the deregulation of the world's financial markets means that problems first affecting just one country have become more contagious and are therefore more likely to affect other economies (see Chapter 4). A more globalized world has advantages but also creates particular challenges.

+ Shareholder value
Idea that the purpose of a company is to maximize returns to shareholders.

Challenges and choices

→ The demanding and constantly evolving nature of modern international business is the final point to be made in this introductory chapter. Some textbooks adopt what seems at times to be a checklist approach to international business, giving readers the impression that they will necessarily succeed in their foreign endeavours if they simply tick certain action boxes. This is misleading, in the opinion of the authors of this book and based on their personal experience and research. If readers are led to believe that international business is a mere subcategory of domestic business, they will not develop the diverse worldview characterizing the vast majority of successful international practitioners. Thinking internationally is something new for many people.

→ It is true that international business is capable of creating the greatest opportunities for profit maximization, as proven by the fact that most if not all the wealthiest companies (and people) in the world operate on a cross-border basis. At the same time, operating internationally requires an ability to cope with challenges that do not arise at the domestic level. Politically, despite the trend towards more internationalist thinking, resistance to foreign competition for markets, resources, and jobs remains very widespread. Economically, many foreign operations (like technological transfers or global funding) are associated with distinct sets of problems. Socially, there is widespread condemnation of the unequal distribution of globalization's costs and benefits. Environmentally, there is the extra usage of resources and generation of waste caused by the organization of trade

over long distances. Last but not least, psychologically there is the obstacle of xenophobia. Despite the authors' personal rejection of discriminatory attitudes, the academic value of this textbook would be undermined if xenophobia's impact on international business relationships were underplayed. Now, some might argue that globalization stems from (and/or causes) lesser xenophobia. Conversely, others would argue that increased contact with foreigners sparks, at least in certain communities, greater dislike of the outside world (Huntingdon 2002; Barber 2003). If an international business book overestimates the cross-border obstacles that managers face, then at worst it is guilty of advocating excessive caution. If, on the other hand, it underestimates these obstacles, then it is guilty of leaving readers totally unprepared for the situations that they will face in the future. The consequences of the latter error would be much more severe than the former.

→ For this reason, the chapters in this book will include special sections highlighting different challenges inherent to international business, as well as choices that managers might make to overcome them. Each of these choices— how to allocate resources, target markets and customers, and relate to foreign individuals or governments— should be grounded in managers' ability to provide an appropriate response to a specific set of circumstances. This book's fundamental philosophy is that it is more important to help readers learn how to make choices than to dictate to them what choices they should be making.

Chapter summary

+ Xenophobia
Fear of things that are foreign.

This brief introduction set the scene by identifying the differences between global and international approaches, and asking whether it is more effective to seek a 'one best way' approach that can be applied in all circumstances or to develop an ability to respond flexibly to different environments. In both cases, an argument was made in support of the second alternative. This is justified in part by the chapter's statistical analysis of the recent rise in world trade and FDI. Depending on their personal and national interests, people will react in different ways to the presence of foreign companies. Successful international managers will therefore be those whose thinking incorporates a range of views. Business is, after all, a social science.

The second section studied in greater depth the drivers of modern international business, categorizing them as macro-factors external to a firm's internal workings and micro-factors reflecting the policies it chooses to adopt. A distinction was made between factors that might be applicable irrespective of circumstances and others that are directly linked to modern globalization. The chapter's final section stated the importance for future practitioners of respecting the challenges associated with international business.

Case study 1.3

The sun rises in the East

International business has been conducted in many different ways in many places over many centuries. The one constant in this field is change, meaning that practitioners and students must always remain attentive to new trends. This is particularly true at present, with the astonishing rise of countries that used to be much more peripheral to the international trade system, starting with China.

As job markets get tighter in many of the world's older industrialized countries, more and more business school graduates from Western universities find themselves tempted by opportunities found in Asia. The phenomenon is not new but what has changed is the speed and extent of Asia's emergence. This has changed the trickle of international business hopefuls relocating to the East into a flood.

In Singapore and Hong Kong, for instance, the community of French business expatriates more than doubled between 2006 and 2011 to number more than 9000 and 10,000 practitioners, respectively (Wassener 2012). The same phenomenon has also been observed in Thailand and India. This is particularly noteworthy given that these are parts of the world where French entrepreneurs and managers have always accounted for a much smaller proportion of the foreign business community than their American and British counterparts. The sudden interest can be explained by the fact that China's emergence process is now at a stage where there is a growing population of middle class households with enough spending power to purchase the kind of luxury items in which many French companies have traditionally specialized. Indeed, as Chapter 15 discusses, whereas export used to be the prime driver behind Chinese development, today this role is played by domestic consumption in both the private and public sectors, a category of economic activity that accounted for more than half of Chinese GDP in 2011, for the first time in a decade (Economist 2012). The 'what' and the 'where' of international business are often closely interconnected.

As Chinese households' disposable income rises, so has their demand for items from a number of sectors

dominated by longer established foreign multinationals. One example is bottled water. China's rapid industrialization has been accompanied by many environmental problems (see Chapter 16) and it has been estimated that only a small proportion of the country's overall water resources are clean (Jing 2011). Thus, there is a very good health reason for local consumers to pay for bottled water, especially now that they can afford it. The market has enjoyed an annual growth rate of 20 per cent over the past decade and its high-priced, premium sector is predicted to grow by a further 80 per cent over the next few years, reaching annual sales of around $1.5 billion. Of course, what remains to be seen is whether the famous international brands (led by French household names such as Perrier and Evian) will be the ones that benefit most from this trend, or if local companies, such as Tibet 5100 Water Resources Holding Ltd (first listed on the Hong Kong stock exchange in June 2011) will gain market share. Domestic water is much less expensive than the foreign variety. What remains uncertain, however, is whether Chinese consumers will trust its quality.

This uncertainty reflects widespread problems in China with the quality of manufactured goods. One example is the market for tyres. Up to 43 per cent of all Chinese highway accidents and casualties in 2010 were blamed on the poor quality of tyres, most of which had been manufactured in local factories (Nan 2011). Following a long series of negative headlines, six large and medium-sized Chinese tyre-makers went out of business. A market survey published the same year found that 64 per cent of all car owners in the Shanghai area preferred European, US, or Japanese tyres to ones made in China. Well-established international rivals like Continental AG from Germany or Michelin from France took note of the situation and moved quickly to intensify their market presence in China. Opportunism has always been a key part of international business strategies.

It is not at all evident, however, that in the future foreign producers will dominate as many market sectors in China as is currently the case. Chinese companies have proved themselves very capable of learning quickly,

As Chinese consumers' purchasing power increases, their preferences will dictate a number of global markets

Source: Corbis

and their growing exposure to the quality levels that are taken for granted in many overseas markets will have a major impact on their domestic activities as well. When

this occurs, there is every chance that they might regain some domestic market share back from the foreign MNEs. Deciding if and when this will happen is crucial to the career plans of anyone interested in moving East. Having a coherent vision of the future is an essential skill for any international business practitioner.

Case study questions

1. What are the arguments in favour of an international business graduate seeking employment in different parts of the world?
2. How certain is it that China will continue to emerge at its current pace?
3. To what extent will local or foreign companies take advantage of Chinese households' rising purchasing power?

Discussion questions

1. Is globalization inevitable?
2. Is nationality an important factor in the way people do business?
3. To what extent is international business beneficial to wealthy and/or poor countries?
4. How would international business work if national regulatory environments were stricter?
5. To what extent is international business based on objective science vs. human psychology?

Online resource centre

Go online to test your understanding by trying multiple-choice questions, and assignment and examination questions.

Further research

Axford, B. and Huggins, R. (2011). *Cultures and/of Globalization*. Newcastle upon Tyne: Cambridge Scholars Publishing

Quelch, J. and Jocz, K. (2012). *All Business is Local: Why Place Matters More than Ever in a Global, Virtual World*. London: Penguin

In some academic circles, there has been a consensus in recent years that the phenomenon of globalization is inevitable and will lead to ever-greater convergence between different countries' economic, political, and social characteristics. Partially in reaction to this assumption, there is a growing body of literature arguing instead that national differences will remain in place for the foreseeable future. Axford and Huggins' book looks at increasing interconnectedness in the cultural arena; Quelch and Jocz's book highlights divergences.

References

Aharoni, Y. and Ramamurti, R. (2008). 'The internationalization of multinationals', *Research in Global Strategic Management*, 14 (June), pp. 177–201

Amine, L. (2008). 'Country-of-origin, animosity and consumer response: Marketing implications of anti-Americanism and Francophobia', *International Business Review*, 17/4 (August), pp. 402–422

Andersen, T. J. (2011). 'The risk implications of multinational enterprise', *International Journal of Organizational Analysis*, 19/1, pp. 49–70

Barber, B. (2003). *Jihad vs. McWorld: Terrorism's Challenge to Democracy*. London: Corgi Books

Buckley, P. and Casson, M. (1976). *The Future of the Multinational Enterprise*. New York: Holmes and Meier Publishers

Economist (2011). 'Exports to Mars', 20 November 2011, available at http://www.economist.com/, accessed 12 February 2011

Economist (2012). 'Two twists in the dragon's tail', *The Economist*, 21 January, p. 74

Ellis, P. (2011). 'Social ties and international entrepreneurship: Opportunities and constraints affecting firm internationalization', *Journal of International Business Studies*, 42, pp. 99–127

European Commission (2003). 'The new SME definition', available at http://ec.europa.eu, accessed 2 June 2012

Gereffi, G. and Fernandez-Stark, K. (2011). 'Global value chain analysis: A primer', 31 May 2011, available at http://www.cggc.duke.edu, accessed 18 May 2012

Giddens, A. (2002). *Runaway World: How Globalization is Shaping our Lives*. New York: Routledge

Grant Thornton (2012). 'The global economy in 2012: A rocky road to recovery', available at http://www.internationalbusinessreport.com/, accessed 13 February 2012

Held, D., McGrew, A., Goldblatt, D., and Perraton, J. (1999). *Global Transformations: Politics, Economics and Culture*. Stanford, CA: Stanford University Press

Hirst, P. and Thompson, G. (1999). *Globalization in Question*, 2nd edn. Cambridge: Polity Press

Huntingdon, S. (2002). *The Clash of Civilizations: And the Remaking of World Order*. London: Simon & Schuster

Ietto-Gillies, G. (2003). 'The nation-state and the theory of the transnational corporation', available at http://www.econ.cam.ac.uk, accessed 2 June 2012

Jing, M. (2011). 'China gushes over high-end bottled water', *China Daily–European Weekly*, 7–13 October, p. 20

MacGillivray, A. (2006). *A Brief History of Globalization: The Untold Story of our Incredible Shrinking Planet*. London: Robinson

Mann, M. (2004). 'Has globalization ended the rise and rise of the nation-state?', in D. Held and A. McGrew (eds.). *The Global Transformations Reader: An Introduction to the Globalization Debate*. Cambridge: Polity

Munchau, W. (2009). ICES European Business School London conference, discussion with the author, 17 February

Nan, Z. (2011). 'Driving force', *China Daily–European Weekly*, 7–13 October, p. 12

OECD (2012). 'FDI in figures', January 2012, available at http://www.oecd.org, accessed 3 May 2012

Ohmae, K. (1999). *The Borderless World: Power and Strategy in the Interlinked Economy*, revised edn. New York: Collins

Porter, M. (1986). *Competition in Global Industries*. Boston, MA: Harvard Business School Press

Saul, J. (2006). *The Collapse of Globalism and the Reinvention of the World*. London: Atlantic Books

Scholte, J. A. (2005). *Globalization: A Critical Introduction*. Basingstoke: Palgrave MacMillan

UNCTAD (2009). 'Global FDI flows halved in 1st quarter of 2009, UNCTAD data show; prospects remain low for rest of year', 24 June 2009, available at http://www.unctad.org/, accessed 2 June 2012

UNCTAD (2011). 'World Investment Report', available at http://www.unctad.org/, accessed 12 February 2012

Wassener, B. (2012). 'Asia's nouveau riche lure the French', *The Observer–New York Times insert*, 11 March, p. 6

Watson, P. (2005). *Ideas: A History of Thought and Invention, from Fire to Freud*. New York: HarperCollins

White, H. (2001). *Markets from Networks: Socioeconomic Models of Production*. Princeton: Princeton University Press

Womack, J., Jones, D. T., and Roos, D. (1991). *The Machine that Changed the World: The Story of Lean Production*. New York: Harper Perennial

WTO (World Trade Organization) (2012). 'World Trade 2011, Prospects for 2011', available at http://www.wto.org/, accessed 17 April 2012

Yip, G. (1989). 'Global strategy . . . in a world of nations?', *MIT Sloan Management Review*, 31/1, pp. 29–41

2 Theories of international business

Learning objectives

After reading this chapter, you will be able to:

✦ understand the development of international theories in their historical context

✦ determine why certain countries specialize in certain industries

✦ discuss free trade theory in cost/benefit terms

✦ analyse historical transition of theory from country to company focus

✦ trace historical shifts in political paradigms and their diffusion worldwide

Case study 2.1

Theories and trade policy: South Korea's commercial soul

The general image of South Korea today is that of a thriving manufacturing economy, home to many successful products including Hyundai cars, Samsung mobile phones, and LG refrigerators. South Korea is a member of the Organization for Economic Cooperation and Development (OECD), a body representing the world's advanced economies; its school leavers regularly rank among the world's top performers; and the country is making steady progress up the international GDP per capita charts. Yet, just a century ago, Korea was a nation of poor farmers whose limited relations with the outside world had earned it the name 'The Hermit Kingdom'. The policies that South Korea has implemented during its industrial ascension offer many lessons about the real world application of trade theories.

One starting point for studying Korea's development might be the country's occupation by Japan during the first half of the twentieth century, given that Korea's first real steps towards industrialization were enforced by its former colonizer. After Japan's defeat in the Second World War, two competing powers, China and America, stepped into the vacuum, triggering a civil war that split the Korean peninsula in half. After an armistice was signed in 1953, North Korea ended up with a communist regime and closed its borders to international trade. South Korea, on the other hand, joined the capitalist world's relatively open trade regime.

Throughout the 1950s, the South Korean government fell in line with the many other newly independent less developed countries (LDCs) that were trying to industrialize rapidly to improve their terms of trade. The preferred policy at the time was import substitution where the state would provide support to help domestic industries manufacture those goods that South Korea used to import, and protect these sectors from international competition. The idea behind this policy was that South Korea's new industries needed time to develop the financial strength and knowledge they required to compete successfully with more established foreign rivals.

One of the side effects of excluding efficient foreign producers from the South Korean market was high inflation. The government of General Park Chung Hee decided to change gears in the 1960s by adopting a strategic trade policy. Now, instead of trying to improve South Korea's trade balance by minimizing imports, the new priority was to increase exports by strengthening high value-added industries in sectors such as machine tools or electronics through low interest rate loans and direct state subsidies. Accompanied by a devaluation of the national currency (the won), the new policy triggered a period of export-driven growth. Alongside this, it also required substantial investment in target industries such as shipbuilding, steel, and chemicals. Because it lacked sufficient domestic capital, South Korea had to increase its borrowings from abroad. The deficits it accumulated in this way eventually caused a financial crisis—a major factor in the Park regime's demise in 1979.

Partially in reaction to this crisis but also mirroring the ideological shifts occurring in the rest of the world, South Korea again changed course in the 1980s, opting for a policy of 'trade liberalization'. Key elements of the new approach included relaxing earlier import restrictions and eliminating many export subsidies. South Korean industry was increasingly expected to compete with foreign rivals without receiving any state funding. Henceforth, governmental interventions would be mainly limited to two kinds of indirect action: a big investment in workforce education; and government coordination of private economic decisions.

South Korea has expanded rapidly over the past 20 years, to the extent that this once-poor developing country is now a modern industrial economy. Nevertheless, its reliance on Western product markets—and its vulnerability to international financial storms such as the 1997 Asian currency crisis—means that it is increasingly dependent on events decided outside its borders. Autonomy, once a key goal for policy-makers, is much less of a factor today.

The three trade policies that South Korea has pursued since the 1950s (import substitution, strategic export promotion, and trade liberalization) all had their own rationales, strengths, and weaknesses. Each served a purpose in getting South Korea to where it is today. The conclusion is that no trade policy is appropriate in all circumstances and at all times. The same might be said about the theories underlying these policies (Lee 1996; Soo Cha 2010).

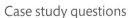

Korea, an industrial powerhouse today, was a mainly agricultural nation until a few decades ago

Source: Photodisc

Case study questions

1. To what extent has Korea's political history dictated its economic policies?
2. Why did South Korea move from an import substitution policy to a strategic trade policy?

+ Import substitution
Trade policy of
supporting the
domestic production
of goods that would
otherwise be imported.

+ Strategic trade
policy
Trade policy of
strengthening local
firms' export
competitiveness in
specific sectors.

Introduction

'The ideas of economists and political philosophers, both when they are right and when they are wrong, are more powerful than is commonly understood. Indeed, the world is ruled by little else. Practical men, who believe themselves to be quite exempt from intellectual influences, are usually the slaves of some defunct economist . . .'

(Keynes 1936)

To understand the policy environment in which international business takes place, it is crucial that managers gain awareness of the trade and investment theories underlying policy-makers' decisions. In turn, theories can be fully appreciated only if they are considered in the historical context in which they were first developed. Learning how past theorists reacted to the circumstances they faced can also provide lessons for today. Some of the main theoretical economic debates recur over the centuries, with strong ideas reborn in forms that may differ from their initial expression but translate the same vision (Klug 2009). The long-term effect of theorists' attempts to make sense of the world is to create schools of thought that shape people's beliefs, and thus their behaviour. 'If enough people believe a theory, even a false one, it becomes self-fulfilling and therefore true' (Caulkin 2005). In international business, as in all social sciences, reality and perception influence one another.

Section I: Economic theories

For centuries, international business economists and practitioners have developed different theories to explain why nations produce what they do. An associated question is whether policies can be implemented to improve a country's trade performance. The first section of this chapter will explore the most famous of these theories in chronological order. The economic environment at the time that each of these theories was developed should be kept in mind, given the links between people's material circumstances and the world views they develop. Putting opinions into the context where they are being developed is a crucial skill for international managers.

Pre-Second World War theories

Thinkers have long grappled with trade as a topic, with some of the oldest arguments in this debate still resonating today. Many of Ancient Greece's earliest philosophers, for instance, expressed a negative reaction to foreign merchants (Irwin 1996). This sentiment came to be known as xenophobia (from the Greek for 'fear', *phobia*, and 'foreign', *xenos*) and to varying degrees it is something that international managers continue to encounter today, along with home bias, its more moderate form.

+ Home bias
Preference for
domestic counterparts
rather than foreign
ones.

In the European Middle Ages, trade's image as a fundamentally immoral activity slowly began to change under the influence of thinkers like Thomas Aquinas. By the sixteenth century, legal experts like Spain's Francisco de Vitoria were writing that it was 'natural' for nations to trade with foreigners as long as this did not damage domestic interests. The new vision paved the way for a doctrine that became known as 'the right of nations' to trade. Once this was legitimized, it was a short step to mercantilism, the first fully fledged trade theory.

Mercantilism

This school of thought dominated from about 1550 until 1776. Its main driver was that the purpose of a national trade policy should be to ensure higher exports than imports. This was based on the notion that national wealth materializes not in the economic activities that a country hosts but in its accumulation of currency (mainly gold at the time), with trade being the prime vehicle for sourcing currency. This doctrine views trade as a zero sum proposition where some parties win, meaning that others necessarily lose. For this reason, all nations have the right to compete, using almost any means, to improve their trade balance. Generally, this would involve subsidies, 'industrial regulations, state-created monopolies, import and export restrictions [and] price controls' (Lal 2006: 305–19).

To many thinkers this was and remains a logical proposition, in large part because it seems normal behaviour for a society, organized into a nation-state, to try to accumulate surpluses. Yet mercantilism has received much criticism. As we will see below, the founders of what came to be known as 'classical economics' accused it of incentivizing governments to distort market conditions to protect the interests of inefficient domestic producers, who instead of taking the steps required to become competitive might simply exert undue influence on local politicians to get them to adopt a policy serving the interests of a particular constituency as opposed to the whole of society. Consumers would be doubly harmed: by the higher price paid for goods; and because aid to local industry is a drain on national resources. As for those companies that did not receive state aid, their reaction might be to avoid paying the extra costs of this policy by resorting to tax evasion and capital flight. This would undermine the state's tax base and reduce government revenues—the very problem that mercantilism was supposed to resolve.

Some leading mercantilist thinkers, such as Thomas Mun (1571–1641), were aware of the 'defensive' problems associated with taxing imports and proposed more 'proactive' solutions where governments focus instead on helping national industry to produce better quality exports. This positive version of mercantilism is more accepting of the need for international competitiveness but its success depends on the government's ability to pick winners. It also opposes some modern analysts' belief that a country's trade balance does not matter any more, since the more important objective is to ensure domestic firms' profitability. Conversely, other voices protest that a policy of facilitating MNE profits does an economy no good if it means that companies shift work from domestic employees to cheaper foreign workers. In short, arguments over mercantilism (in its new, 'neo' form) remain highly topical. It is an honest philosophy in the sense that it recognizes the reality of national interest. It can also be a wasteful one if it undermines efficiency.

Classical economics

The father of 'classical' economics is the Scotsman Adam Smith (1723–1790), whose seminal work *The Wealth of Nations* (1776) laid the foundations for many of the economic and trade principles that still dominate today (see Figure 2.1). A keen observer of the changes that Britain was experiencing as a result of the first Industrial Revolution, Smith believed that governments should stay out of the marketplace, which should be run by an 'invisible hand of God' and individuals' pursuit of self-interest (which he called 'utility'). In this conception, economics have their own laws, irrespective of vested interests. What matters is market performance, not which social partners plead their case most loudly or who has inherited the most wealth.

Such was the power of Smith's 'classical-liberal' principle that it continues to dominate economic debate today. Smith's supporters continue to find evidence of strong links between lighter regulations on companies, meaning less state interference in the business sphere, and the kind of entrepreneurial dynamism that they view as key to economic renewal (Levie and Autio 2011). Other thinkers, however, would tend to highlight the strength of successful trading nations such as China and even Germany, both of which maintain, each in their own manner, strong regulatory frameworks. It is important that international business students master both sides of this debate since it is likely that they will encounter it in many professional situations.

Classical economics are driven by the idea that when markets are left to their own devices they will tend towards an optimal allocation of resources, called 'equilibrium'. One of

+ Trade balance
Relationship between the value of a country's exports and imports. When exports exceed imports, the country has a trade surplus. When imports exceed exports, the country has a trade deficit.

+ Capital flight
When investors or savers take large sums of money out of a country because of concerns about local risks or disagreements with policy.

Figure 2.1
Adam Smith's classical economics.

+ **Trickle-down economics**
Idea that policy should reward the economically successful because their gains ultimately benefit the rest of society. Often used to justify low tax regimes.

Smith's ideas	Modern application	Modern manifestation
Maximizing individual outcomes optimizes overall welfare	Trickle-down economics	WTO rulings discouraging subsidies to weak producers, import tariffs, etc.
The market can organize itself most efficiently without state interference	Market liberalization	Privatization programmes, deregulation
Efficiency comes from specializing in certain operations	(International) Division of labour	Countries should focus on different parts of product value chains and trade with one another

the main ways that an economy achieves this is by allowing uncompetitive industries to die naturally to free up resources supporting growth sectors (a process the economist Joseph Schumpeter called 'creative destruction'). In trade economics, this means that countries should only support industries that have a competitive advantage in the international markets. Conversely, they should be willing to abandon all others, even at the price of temporary, 'frictional unemployment' when workers losing their jobs in the less competitive sectors transition into new, more productive activities.

At an extreme, this thinking translates into the view that open borders are beneficial because pressure from foreign industry forces national producers to become efficient. One example of this kind of willing self-discipline was the newly unified German government's refusal during the 1990s to support the Trabant automotive company, which had a dominant position in the former East Germany's protected market but crumbled when exposed to Western competition. In 2011 joblessness in Germany's eastern provinces still stood at 12.7 per cent vs. 6.8 per cent for the country as a whole—a situation that continues to cause social problems. Yet it is quite clear that Germany stands a better chance of competing in international markets with BMW, Mercedes, and Volkswagen cars than it could have done trying to sell Trabants. Moreover, using state funds to prop up inefficient firms like this old East German car-maker would have become a drain on national resources. Another

After German unification, a decision was made not to continue producing the Trabant cars that used to be manufactured in the communist East

Source: iStock

example from the same decade was Mexico's signing of the North American Free Trade Agreement (see Chapter 4), a treaty forcing Mexican farmers to compete with more mechanized (but also highly subsidized) American rivals. Many Mexicans struggled to adapt to this market liberalization, resulting in mass rural emigration and social disruption (Sitkin and Bowen 2010).

Critics of classical economists often accuse them of over-confidence in market mechanisms. For example, in an increasingly globalized world, there is always a risk that international competition will kill off entire sectors of domestic activity. The improvement in the country's overall economic efficiency is of little consolation to the many citizens who will then lose their jobs (Held and McGrew 2007). As the British economist John Maynard Keynes once wrote, the problem with classical economists' focus on long-term equilibrium is that 'in the long-term, we are all dead'. Classical economists emphasize that market mechanisms have their own laws. Other thinkers might tend to focus more on political realities.

Absolute advantage

One robust aspect of Smith's theory is the idea that it is most efficient for different parties to an economic process to specialize in different tasks and become experts in them. The end result is an overall work organization often referred to as the 'division of labour'. When two countries both have absolute advantage in different products (say the British in textiles and the Portuguese in wine), it is in the interest of each to import the other's speciality product instead of making it at home. This is an idealized vision of trade as enabling one country to benefit from another's strengths. The emphasis here is on a country's overall productive capacities, not the amount of currency it earns from any one deal (Zhang 2010). To that extent, there is greater sophistication here than was the case with mercantilism.

+ **Absolute advantage** Where one country, providing the same input of a good as another, achieves greater output and can therefore be said to produce it more cheaply.

Smith's argument is evidenced every time a country uses cheap imported components in its domestic production process instead of manufacturing the same items locally but at a higher cost. It is remarkable, for instance, how little resistance the WTO (see Chapter 4) faced in 1997 when it made the decision to promote global free trade in computer goods. Instead of complaining about imports, almost all governments listened to local manufacturers who were more than happy to get cheap access to intermediary goods such as microprocessors because they could put them to good use in their production processes. The foreign origin of the component was irrelevant. What mattered was the beneficial effect on the local value chain. Conversely, Brazilian government moves in 2011 to put extra import taxes on stainless steel imports from China were not to the liking of all domestic manufacturers. The added cost of a 'generic' input such as steel (see Chapter 11) has a knock-on effect all the way down the value chain. Manufacturers who are no longer able to access the foreign component at its cheaper international price will either have to accept lower margins or else pass the added cost on to consumers, making them less competitive.

Yet despite these examples, Smith's absolute advantage theory remains insufficient and imperfect. It may speak to the micro-level realities of corporate transactions but it ignores certain macro-level problems on a broader national scale. In the real world, economic advantage is distributed unevenly, with some countries enjoying greater factor endowments (such as land, capital, or natural resources) than others. Some consider this a question of size, since larger countries often benefit from greater access to labour (China), natural resources (Russia and Australia) or a big home market (the USA). Others, however, may possess no particular advantages at all. This then raises the question of why they would even want to open their borders to trade. Moreover, analysing countries in terms of the 'natural advantages' they inherit from their geographic or demographic situation is a static approach since it neglects their ability to develop new advantages (especially technology). Japan, for example, has few natural advantages yet is an economic powerhouse, in part thanks to advanced coordination between the state and the private sector (see Chapter 3). Smith did not consider this scenario.

+ **Factor endowments** The human, financial, and physical capital that an economic entity (often a country) can use in its production process.

Another weakness in Smith's theory is that countries lacking any absolute advantage whatsoever (i.e. countries that suffer from poor 'terms of trade', a possibility that Smith also did not imagine) will be too poor to buy the goods that their more competitive counterparts produce. International trade can function only if sellers find solvent customers. Western Europe, for example, was able to purchase American goods after the Second World War only because the USA came up with Marshall Plan funding that re-injected cash into European economies. The same argument is often used today to justify aid to LDCs. To organize a successful market, it is not enough to have efficient producers, as Smith thought; there must also be customers with enough money to spend.

The aftermath of the 2008 financial crisis revealed another way in which Smith's trade theory is conditioned by solvency. Substantial trade surpluses had been built up before the crisis by a number of countries whose industries, in line with Smith's reasoning, were oriented towards the kinds of activities in which each had an advantage (technology for Germany, cheap labour for China, and services for India). As global demand dried up in the wake of the crisis, however, output plummeted in these economies, largely because their buyers' sudden unwillingness (or inability) to spend left them without sufficient outlets. As noted by a senior Taiwanese official, a 2 or 3 per cent fall in global consumption can cause a 40 per cent fall in some countries' exports, a contraction that can be especially dramatic in small internationalized countries where trade accounts for a disproportionate percentage of total GDP (Bradsher 2009). By spring 2009, regional bodies such as the Association of Southeast Asian Nations (see Chapter 4) were meeting to discuss ways of replacing some of the business being conducted outside the region with business conducted within it, in much the same way that China was counting on domestic infrastructure projects to reduce its dependency on overseas buyers. By 2012, Germany had rearranged its export focus with many leading companies, such as BMW, selling more to China than to the USA. Smith's theory does not satisfactorily address this question of why some countries are more dynamic economically than others.

None of this is meant to deny the wealth of statistical evidence that exists to support Smith's basic premise that free trade in the form of lower imports contributes positively to productivity gains (Luong 2011) and that, in turn, this leads to national growth, not just in the older industrialized countries but also in the developing world (Cieślik and Tarsalewska 2011). Yet from the outset, it was clear that his theories were simple and required greater elaboration. This would be achieved by what has become the seminal concept in modern (neo-)classical trade theory.

Comparative advantage

David Ricardo's *Principles of Political Economy and Taxation* (1817) presented the idea of comparative advantage, which remains the basis of most trade models today. Ricardo's idea addressed the basic shortcoming of Smith's theory when applied to trade, namely, how to interest countries that lack any absolute advantage whatsoever in opening up their borders. The great novelty of Ricardo's work was its vision that under certain conditions international trade could become a 'win–win' proposition and benefit all countries, even less competitive ones. In this view, it can still be in a country's interest to open its borders to international trade even if it does not have an absolute advantage in any particular field. This is because the people employed in the country's less productive fields of activity can simply receive lower wages to reflect their lower level of efficiency. This was a first step towards resolving certain problems associated with Smith's absolute advantage construct.

Like Smith, Ricardo used a wine versus textiles example to demonstrate his thinking. Unlike Smith, however, his starting point was the idea that Portugal produces both items more cheaply than England does. Ricardo then set out to prove that England might still have a reason to open its borders despite lacking an absolute advantage in either market.

+ Solvent
Having sufficient funds to pay for goods or services.

+ Comparative advantage
Where one country makes all goods more efficiently than another but agrees not to make (hence to import) those goods whose production makes the least efficient use of its resources.

	Wine cost	Textiles cost	Domestic price structure (autarky)	At international price of 1 unit of wine = 0.75 units of textiles
In Portugal	5	10	1 wine = 0.5 textiles (5/10)	Receives an extra 0.25 units of textiles when exporting 1 unit of wine
In England	15	15	1 wine = 1 textiles (15/15)	Receives an extra 1.33 units of wine (1/0.75) when exporting 1 unit of textiles

Figure 2.2
The basic Ricardian model. Both parties benefit.

Ricardo's starting point was to calculate the price structure if both countries were to work in autarky, with consumers only trading locally produced goods. The domestic prices in this case might be one unit of wine and one unit of textiles each costing 15 points in England. As per the conditions of the demonstration, however, both items would be cheaper in Portugal—especially wine, for which one unit would cost 5 points, with one unit of textiles costing 10 points.

+ Autarky
Where an entity operates self-sufficiently and in isolation.

It is at this point that Ricardo had his crucial insight. With Portuguese wine trading domestically at half the price of local textiles, it stood to reason that if the country could receive more than one half unit of textile for each unit of wine that it sells, there would be an advantage for it to export wine but import textiles, leaving the production of the latter good to England as a trading partner. The question then becomes what international price meets this condition. In the present example (see Figure 2.2) this happens when one unit of wine trades at the equivalent of 0.75 units of textiles.

The same demonstration can be made from the English perspective. Here, because domestic wine and textiles sell at the same price (15 units), it would only be worth engaging in international trade if this allowed consumers to buy one unit of wine for less than one unit of textiles. This condition would also be satisfied at the aforementioned international price, one where England would only need to produce 0.75 units of textiles to receive one unit of wine. It would therefore save 33 per cent (1 unit of wine divided by 0.75 units of wine) by purchasing Portuguese wine—and it could pay for this import by selling to Portugal the good in which it has a comparative advantage, in this case, textiles. Thus, despite England not having Smith's absolute advantage in any product, it would still be in England's and Portugal's interests to open their borders to one another, and both countries would have the means to buy the other's output. International trade can exist as long as the international price properly reflects the difference in the two countries' levels of efficiency (which Ricardo attributed to technology).

A simplified explanation for Ricardo's insight comes from an anecdote that some have attributed to US economist Paul Samuelson. The premise here is that one person, say Sally, is the best solicitor but also the best typist at her firm. Despite being the most productive person at both jobs, it makes more sense to use Sally for legal work and hire someone else as secretary. The opportunity cost of not using a comparatively worse typist to do the administrative work is less than if a comparatively worse solicitor were hired to do the legal work.

+ Opportunity cost
Cost of doing something in a certain way, thus not receiving the benefits of doing it another way.

Ricardo's theory was also imperfect and has been criticized; for instance, because it ignores factors such as capital mobility and technological transfers. These are important because they affect the international distribution of comparative advantages. Yet it is a strong theory and one that is corroborated in countless international trade situations today. One example is the agricultural trade between France and Russia. France produces both cereals and farm equipment more efficiently (thus cheaply) than Russia. Under Smith's theorem, this would mean that Russia must import both items from France. Yet in actual fact it imports tractors but exports grains, since its productivity disadvantage in the former is greater than in the latter. This real-life outcome is perfectly predictable under Ricardo's theorem.

Infant industries

The English philosopher John Stuart Mill (1806–1873) saw three main advantages to free trade. The first two followed on from Smith's and Ricardo's theories about the advantage of specialization and the need for countries to focus on whatever activities increase global productivity. Mill's third construct, the 'intellectual and moral gains' that a country makes from its contacts with foreigners, was new and remains topical, with analysts continuing today to debate to what extent free markets strengthen democracy. One of the ideas associated with this construct is that open borders help to prevent wars, because countries that trade with one another are less likely to fight. This ultimately became one of the drivers behind the foundation of the WTO (see Chapter 4).

+ **Infant industry**
Sector of activity that has only recently developed in a particular country and whose prospects for survival are uncertain because it lacks the capital and experience to compete with existing (foreign) producers.

Mill's most significant contribution to international trade theory was the infant industry argument that he developed at the same time as a German economist, Friedrich List, and following previous work done by an early American politician, Alexander Hamilton. In Mill's opinion, government intervention is justified when a country nurtures a new industry in a sector where it might have a natural advantage. Since this industry is new, it is at risk from foreign producers who have a temporary competitive advantage simply because they are already up and running. 'The superiority of one country over another in a branch of production often arises only from having begun sooner. There may be no inherent advantage on one part, or disadvantage on the other, but only a present superiority of acquired skill and experience' (Mill 1848). This idea is relevant to modern concerns about the ability of countries, particularly LDCs, to enter sectors where MNEs are already firmly entrenched. Examples include India's interest in developing its own semiconductor manufacturing capabilities, despite the global overcapacities that already exist in this sector.

Trade as exploitation

Underlying Smith's classical liberal theory was the optimistic view that an efficient market economy benefits society as a whole. Ricardo's opposition to England's early nineteenth-century Corn Laws led him, on the other hand, to observe that some social classes (industrialists, workers) were more dynamic than others (landowners). This implied that economic benefits can be distributed unevenly and unfairly. German philosopher Karl Marx (1818–1883) built on this insight, stating that the starting point for all economic analysis should be acknowledgement that capitalism is rooted in the exploitation of one social group by another. His accusations of unfairness still resonate today, for instance when LDCs accuse wealthy nations of using open-border globalization as a smoke screen for continued domination—or 're-colonization', as Malaysia's ex-President Mahathir called it (Fuller 1999). It is a mistake to study capitalism without considering the views of its leading critics. This is especially true in the wake of the 2008 and 2011 crises.

One Marxian theory with direct relevance to international business today is the 'law of diminishing returns', which holds that firms operating in a closed capitalist economy will, for a number of reasons, suffer from falling profit rates. In this view, firms have no choice but to internationalize if they want to survive. The theorem is subject to some criticism, having been at least partially disproved by Joseph Schumpeter's 1912 demonstration of how growth within a national economy can be sustained through 'technological progress'—a key factor in modern explanations of MNE location (see discussion on 'New Trade Theory' later in this chapter). It remains that many business analysts are unintentionally arguing a Marxian position when they assert that internationalization is a necessary condition for firms' survival.

Case study 2.2

Theory and economic dependency: Bolivia Cochabamba

After many years as a Spanish colony, Bolivia became independent in 1825 but immediately ran into difficulties due to insufficient agricultural output, scarce investment capital, and heavy national debt (Lobina 2000). The economy improved somewhat in the 1830s after tariffs had been implemented to protect Bolivia's infant textile industry. However, it remained very poor for most of the nineteenth century.

The turn of the twentieth century saw a brief period of expansion following temporary rises in the global price of tin, one of Bolivia's few natural resources. When this market collapsed in the 1920s, Bolivia again started running up large debts, mainly owed to the USA. There was a growing sense during the 1940s that reform was needed, in part because of the widening gulf between Bolivia's rich and poor. Local conservative and socialist parties had very different ideas about how to solve these problems, however, and the country fell victim to decades of political unrest and economic mismanagement. During this time, the USA provided much needed aid but also increased its control over the economy. This sparked great resentment, with new Bolivian regimes sporadically deciding to renationalize American assets. It also led to an intellectual revolution across Latin America, encapsulated in the 'dependency theories' formulated by the Argentine theorist, Raul Prebisch.

When Bolivia turned to the World Bank in the 1990s for loans to fund a water system near its third largest city, Cochabamba, it was told to structure the project as a private initiative run by a consortium comprised mainly of US and Italian firms (Klaus 2005). Bolivia's financially strapped government agreed but the ensuing privatization (and abandonment of public subsidies)

Privatizing staples like water, and letting them be run by private foreign interests, can be a recipe for social unrest

Source: iStock

caused a sharp rise in water rates that the citizens of Cochabamba, a poor city, could not afford. Tensions ran high because the high rates were not only meant to reimburse the project's construction costs but also pay for foreign shareholders' dividends. Violent riots erupted and the Cochabamba water system was ultimately renationalized and a socialist president elected in 2006. The incident led to widespread criticism of global free markets and became one element in South America's 'pink revolutions', with most countries voting in left-wing governments throughout the first decade of the twenty-first century to help protect national interests in the face of rampant globalization.

Case study questions

1. How did Bolivia's economic troubles affect its politics?
2. What other methods might have been used to finance the Cochabamba project?

Factor proportions (Heckscher–Ohlin)

Returning to certain principles of classical economics that Ricardo had developed, Swedish economists Eli Heckscher (1879–1952) and Bertil Ohlin (1899–1979) devised a model stating that, when two countries trade, each will export the good that makes the most intensive use of the particular factor input (labour, capital, or material resources) that it has in abundance. This is because each can source the abundant factor cheaply, thereby raising its (export) competitiveness in the sectors where this factor is key. Conversely, a country

Figure 2.3
Application of the
Heckscher–Ohlin
model, which focuses
on differences in
countries' factor
endowments.

Country	Abundant factor input	Exports
France	Capital	Industrial carpets
Turkey	Labour	Handmade rugs

> Go online

should import the good that makes the most intensive use of the factor input that is most scarce locally. This is a strong construct and one that is consistent with a great deal of other trade theories developed in the mid-twentieth century (**see ORC Extension material 2.1**).

Figure 2.3 illustrates the Heckscher–Ohlin (H–O) model. In France, for example, capital is abundant, and the country specializes in the export of factory-made carpets. In Turkey, on the other hand, labour is abundant, so wages are low, making it economically more viable to produce and export handmade rugs. At its simplest level, this elegant model is the core of neo-classical trade theory.

H–O's power to explain real data is severely limited, however (Feenstra 2004). The most famous criticism of H–O was formulated in 1953 as Leontief's Paradox, which asked why the USA, the world's most capital-intensive country at the time, imported capital-intensive goods and exported labour-intensive goods—the exact opposite of what H–O would have predicted. Although Leontief's findings have lost weight over time, doubts still remain as to H–O's applicability in its original form. H–O seems to fully perform only when cross-border differences in productivity and technology are introduced. Otherwise, it tends to ignore the reality of international factor mobility (Zhang 2010).

+ Factor mobility
Propensity of factor
inputs (capital,
resources, labour, etc.)
to move in time
and/or place.

It is one thing assuming that countries will differ in terms of their abilities; it is another explaining why this is so. Ricardo and other classical economists (see Figure 2.4) suggested that national factor inputs remain constant, because to a large extent this was the world they inhabited. Since the mid-twentieth century, however, market liberalization and improved telecommunications have intensified the international mobility of certain factor inputs, such as technology and capital. To reflect the new reality, theory has had to broaden its scope beyond trading nations' characteristics to include the behaviour of the corporate actors who had become responsible over time for driving factor mobility.

Post-Second World War theories

The leading business theories since the mid-twentieth century, summarized in Figure 2.6, focus on company behaviour more than national economies. Alongside this, more recent

Figure 2.4
Most pre-Second
World War theories
focused on national
circumstances.

	Key economist(s)	Main points
Mercantilism	Thomas Mun	Trade creates winners and losers Policy aim should be trade surplus
Classical economics, absolute advantage	Adam Smith	Markets find their own equilibrium Specialization means efficiency (International) division of labour
Comparative advantage	David Ricardo	Trade is a win–win proposal as long as opportunity costs are minimized
Infant industries	John Stuart Mill	The only domestic producers deserving help are young firms in key sectors
Trade as exploitation	Karl Marx	Trade is a form of domination
Factor proportions	Eli Heckscher/ Bertil Ohlin	Countries export goods using their abundant factor most intensively

'welfare economics', which work at the intersection of economic, political, and business thinking, tend to pass judgement on the overall distribution of the benefits of globalization (**see ORC Extension material 2.2**). The search for an all-encompassing theory of international business is ongoing.

> Go online

Product life cycle

In a seminal article published in 1966, Raymond Vernon linked international manufacturing location decisions to what he called the 'product life cycle' (PLC). Note that the name chosen by Vernon for his theory was the same as one used in a marketing concept developed by the Boston Consulting Group (http://www.bcg.com). Vernon's concept (see Figure 2.5) covers four phases.

1. *Introduction.* A good is manufactured in the technologically advanced country where it is invented (often the USA in Vernon's original model). At this early stage, what matters is the MNE headquarters' ability to control the risks involved in the new product launch. Price competition is not an issue yet, especially if the product is innovative. Demand may spread rapidly in the home country and other industrialized markets can only access it through imports.

2. *Growth.* As demand spreads through the rest of the developed world and foreign rivals set up plants in their home markets, it becomes worthwhile for the original MNE to do the same, especially since it can leverage the manufacturing experience it gained back home. This international production reduces the need for exports and the market starts to organize itself on a country-by-country basis.

3. *Maturity.* The technology begins to age and the market gets saturated in the industrialized world. Prices fall and cost becomes key. This leads to manufacturing facilities being built in low-cost LDCs.

4. *Decline.* Cost pressures become so severe that all plants shut down in the industrialized world. The remaining sites are located in LDCs, with output being re-exported back to the original markets.

A prime example of PLC at work is the historical changes in the location of Xerox photocopier manufacturing plants. Output began in the USA in the 1940s and 1950s, before moving to Europe within a decade, and finally, as the technology matured, to India in the 1970s and 1980s. The automotive industry offers a similarly useful example, with Ford and GM undertaking their first FDI in Europe in the 1920s before subsequently opening plants in the developing world and closing more sites in its original markets.

Vernon's theory does not apply in all circumstances. Products with a short life span (like microprocessors) may not last long enough to experience the entire PLC. Also, products like luxury goods, whose perceived value can be altered through marketing campaigns, may not age in the way that the model predicts. However, it is useful to note that products can find themselves at different stages of their life cycle at different times in different countries. This is a key factor in international marketing (see Chapter 12).

Phase	Introduction	Growth	Maturity	Decline
Market dynamics	High-priced new good	Demand spreads	Competition intensifies	Demand declines
Key factors of success	R&D, confidentiality	Market coverage	Rejuvenation via marketing	Low prices
Production location	OECD home country	All OECD countries	OECD & LDC countries	LDC countries only

Figure 2.5
Vernon's product life cycle construct.

New Trade Theory

The starting point for the New Trade Theory was John Dunning's 1977 proposal of an Eclectic Paradigm, partially derived from earlier analysis by Stephen Hymer regarding the advantages for a firm of controlling its internal capabilities (Dunning and Pitelis 2007). The idea here is that because markets often function imperfectly, MNEs are likely to face higher costs in a foreign market than domestic firms will. Thus, FDI is attractive only if internationalization offers specific incentives.

Dunning's insights are often referred to as the OLI theory:

- *Ownership advantages*. The foreign MNE must have a special product or production process that it can use against rivals operating in their home market. This explains why technologically advanced companies guard secrets so jealously.

- *Location advantages*. Moving production abroad must offer some advantage, like the possibility of achieving economies of scale.

- *Internalization advantages*. It must be useful for MNEs to exploit any ownership advantage by themselves, instead of licensing or selling it to someone else. The company must control a larger portion of its total value chain.

Following on from Dunning, Markusen (2002) observed that most trade and FDI occurs between neighbouring countries with similar levels of industrial development. This finding, which contradicts classical economists' predictions that trade should occur between countries that differ, is called the 'gravity model' (Krugman 1997). Markusen researched this discovery and found that FDI often involves 'horizontal integration' or companies producing similar goods at home and abroad, rather than 'vertical integration' where the internationalization involves making different goods at different stages of the value chain (see Chapter 5). His conclusion was that the key factor in MNE internationalization is knowledge, a finding substantiated by the disproportionate concentration of MNEs in hi-tech and research-oriented sectors, such as computing or pharmaceuticals, where intangible, firm-specific assets are key factors of success.

In Dunning and Markusen's vision, international business has two main drivers. The first is learning effects, or the idea that, because knowledge is easier and cheaper to transfer than other forms of capital, it can be fragmented relatively efficiently between an MNE's research and development (R&D) team, working out of corporate headquarters, and its manufacturing teams, working in different subsidiaries. The second driver is first-mover advantage, or the idea that the first firm to enter a new market and leverage its existing experience is in a good position to shut out future rivals.

Unlike Heckscher-Ohlin's emphasis on countries' particular endowments, the New Trade Theory's main explanation for international success is a company's knowledge, and its ability to apply this worldwide. This introduces the notion that the location of a particular activity may be a simple accident of history and have nothing to do with a country's absolute or comparative advantage. After all, there is nothing that predestines Seattle or Toulouse (respectively centres for Boeing and Airbus operations) to dominate global aircraft manu-facturing. The New Trade Theory highlights the consequences of international managers' very human decisions. It is this ability to incorporate human factors that makes this the most interesting of all post-Second World War theories (**see ORC Extension material 2.3**).

+ **Learning effects**
Added production efficiency and lower costs that companies gain from accumulating experience in a particular activity.

+ **First-mover advantage**
Benefit of being the first party to move into a market segment in a certain location.

> Go online

Competitive advantage

Michael Porter's famous 1990 text, *The Competitive Advantage of Nations*, focused less on FDI than on the connection between countries' relative factors (endowments in capital, natural resources, and labour), on one hand, and MNEs' historical development, on the other. Porter's 'Diamond' construct identifies four sources of competitive advantage for companies, some involving actions that companies might choose to implement and others reflecting the external conditions they face in any one country.

Theory	Key economist(s)	Main points
Product life cycle	Raymond Vernon/BCG	Production location depends on phase in product's life
New Trade Theory: Eclectic Paradigm	John Dunning	FDI undertaken to maintain advantages
New Trade Theory: knowledge capital	James Markusen	FDI driven by knowledge; first-mover advantage
Competitive advantage	Michael Porter	Diamond model; national circumstances affect MNEs

Figure 2.6
Post-Second World War international business theories have focused on FDI as well as trade.

- *Factor conditions*. Porter considers this to be the main driver of competitive advantage. The distinction made here is between basic factors of production (natural resources, climate) and advanced, productivity-enhancing factors associated with the long-term investments that a country has made in technology and education. Companies operating in this latter context have a better chance to benefit from knowledge spillovers (see Chapter 11).

+ Knowledge spillover
When companies gain knowledge through proximity to external sources such as universities, research centres, or other companies.

- *Demand conditions*. The variables here are the size of a company's domestic market and the sophistication of buyers. MNEs that have flourished in large home markets characterized by demanding consumers are better equipped to succeed abroad. This is because they have already been 'battle hardened' before leaving home.

- *Firm strategy, structure, and rivalry*. A firm's managerial orientation (focus on finance, engineering, and so on) is crucial to its success.

- *Related and supporting industry*. Firms benefit from the proximity of 'clusters' of efficient upstream suppliers that offer inexpensive components and up-to-date technology. Some consider this to be Porter's main contribution to modern theory, as this insight opens the door to considerations of firms working as part of a network instead of in isolation—a model that has become increasingly widespread over the years in many international value chains.

Porter's insights are often exemplified by the existence of 'industrial districts', with one famous case being the cluster of small and medium-sized companies located near Sassuolo in Italy's Modena province and specializing in the production of ceramic roof tiles. This is a high-performance local economy where information is shared vertically up and down the value chain, and where companies export goods only once they have had a long apprenticeship in their local marketplace. It is an organization that fits Porter's predictions.

+ Cluster
Where firms in a similar line of business operate in close physical proximity to one another and build close ties. This can reflect historical factors or strategic intent.

Despite specifying the conditions in which companies can become an international success, Porter's theory does not explain why failures continue to occur even when these conditions are fulfilled. Clearly other factors are at work as well—one strong possibility being the 'organizational learning' discussed in Chapter 10.

The company-oriented theories outlined above do not account for all of the attempts made in recent decades to understand why certain activities are run out of particular countries, and how MNEs fit into this process. Chapter 9 gives a greater airing to these more hybrid models.

Section II: Political economy frameworks

One common thread throughout this chapter is the idea that thinkers are children of their era, so that the theories they develop can be understood only within a given historical context, characterized by its particular political, economic, social, and technological factors (Hibou 2004). Indeed, it would be worth analysing why it is that mercantilism dominated the early ages of exploration; why liberalism (and socialism) arose during the first Industrial Revolution; and how the rise of modern globalization has coincided with the pure corporate focus of the New Trade Theory. It remains an open question whether economic philosophy determines political action or vice versa.

The spectrum of political principles

It is one thing calculating the kinds of economic decisions that policy-makers might consider useful in different contexts. It is another to determine their power to act. At the most basic level, trade theories cannot be addressed without an understanding of the relative power of public and private sectors. Opinions as to which of these spheres should dominate the other have tended to alternate over history. It is useful to understand why.

Neo-liberalism

+ Neo-liberalism
Belief in minimal interference from government in the economy.

The political expression of classical economists' general outlook has gone under many names but is often referred to currently as neo-liberalism, or the idea that governments should 'allow people to do as they like' (the French translation of this expression, *laissez-faire*, is also used frequently). 'Free market' neo-liberalism states that government should run few if any areas of economic activity. It is grounded in a strong belief in personal initiative, market efficiency, and the sanctity of private property.

The first point to make clear is that some policy-makers implement neo-liberal policies in domestic markets but not international ones, or vice versa. Examples abound of this kind of mixed approach. Despite claiming to promote free market principles, the US government laid itself open to criticism in 2011 after awarding a $35 billion Air Force refuelling contract to domestic company Boeing instead of accepting an arguably more competitive bid from EADS, a European defence consortium (Cassata and Baldor 2011). That same year, Canada's very neo-liberal regime contradicted its supposed principles to invoke an Act preventing the Australian mining giant BHP Billiton from taking over a provincial fertilizer maker because this was not a 'net benefit' to the country. Ideological attitudes as to what constitutes an ideal economic philosophy can be easily overshadowed by a country's sense of its immediate political interests.

General support for a paradigm such as neo-liberalism also depends on attitudes towards the leading countries advocating this philosophy. For example, as the global superpower ('hegemon') not only in economic and political terms but also academically and culturally, in recent decades the USA has influenced many other nations' political views. This implies that if the general desire worldwide to copy US policy were to fade, support for its preferred neo-liberal policies would probably decline as well (Jacques 2008). It is likely that the future popularity of the American model will depend on its ability to survive crises such as those experienced in 2008 and 2011, and on the relative attraction of different models, like the one embodied by China with its tradition of greater government interference in economic affairs (see Chapter 15).

Lastly, consensus opinion will also depend on how well the global economy is doing in general. There is some tendency for governments to take a step back during boom years, confident in the market's ability to enhance general welfare, but for people to expect the state to intervene when times are bad. A prime example was the many different stimulus packages implemented in the wake of the credit crunch by governments that otherwise define themselves as neo-liberal. The Obama administration's 2009 bail-out of the US automotive industry, notably helping once bankrupt General Motors to return to profitability by 2011, is a textbook case of this kind of cyclical involvement. As Chapter 3 will demonstrate, having less of a state is not the same thing as having no state.

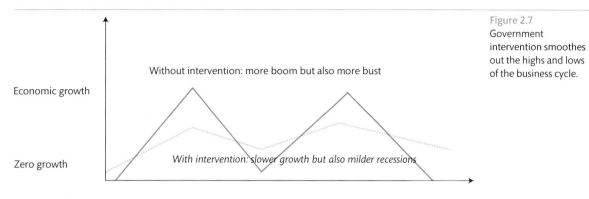

Figure 2.7
Government
intervention smoothes
out the highs and lows
of the business cycle.

Interventionism

This philosophy encompasses a range of ideas. At one extreme, it includes communism and the belief in state ownership of all means of production. There are very few communists any more, and modern interventionism is dominated by 'social-democratic' thinking of the kind advocated by Keynes (and implemented by US President Franklin Delano Roosevelt) during the 1930s battle against the Great Depression. Keynesians believe that capitalism is prone to alternating periods of expansion and recession, and that even if policy-makers cannot always be certain about the effects of their plans, it is more prudent for them to prepare stabilizing measures (involving fiscal or monetary instruments but also industrial policy) to correct recurring breakdowns in market conditions (Parsons 2010). Such planned interventions smooth out business cycles and support the vulnerable in society (see Figure 2.7). This safety net prevents the kind of tensions that have historically caused extremist revolutions. It has, for instance, been argued that it is precisely because Roosevelt adopted Keynesian policies that the USA did not experience even more social unrest during the Great Depression of the 1930s (Yergin and Stanislaw 2002).

Like neo-liberals, interventionists sometimes pursue international policies that are at odds with their domestic approach. Keynes himself was a strong supporter of free trade and one of the architects of the Bretton Woods international agreements (see Chapter 4). Contradictory political philosophies can combine in different ways at different times. Many nations pursue mixed economic policies that borrow to varying degrees from both schools.

Critics of interventionism say that it can be 'dysfunctional [and] bad economics' because it distorts market behaviour and causes a poor allocation of resources (Lal 2006). This might affect international business in several ways. For instance, when a national government intervenes to protect domestic producers from foreign rivals by taxing imports (see Chapter 3), domestic industries will have less of an incentive to modernize. Restricting consumers' access to cheap foreign goods also raises the costs thereof. State support for uncompetitive local producers can become an endless drain on public funds, when the local producers have no hope of ever being able to survive on their own. This may be acceptable if the beneficiaries are strategically important (for example, Europe's Common Agricultural Policy was originally designed to subsidize farmers to ensure that the region produced enough food), but it is wasteful when the same product can be produced much more efficiently abroad.

Neo-liberalism and interventionism each have their strengths and weaknesses. They also constitute, in their most radical forms, the two extremes of the policy frameworks that international managers are likely to encounter in their careers. Most societies operate somewhere in the middle of this spectrum. So do most managers.

Shifts in the dominant political economic paradigm

One skill that most leading international businesspeople share is extreme intellectual flexibility. In part, this is because their encounters with foreign counterparts will regularly bring them into contact with philosophies that are both different and constantly evolving.

+ **Interventionism**
Belief that the state
has a role to play in
ensuring that market
mechanisms are both
efficient and lead
to a fair and viable
distribution of income.

+ **Business cycle**
Period during which
the economy alternates
between boom and
bust.

+ **Free trade**
Belief that goods and
services should be
negotiated in private
domestic and foreign
markets without
government
interference.

Throughout history, countries have run border patrols to protect domestic interests

© European Union, 2011

Changes over time

From the late nineteenth to the early twentieth century, many politicians in the world's leading power at the time, the UK, believed in minimal government intervention. This attitude applied not only to international trade but also to domestic business cycles, viewed by classical economists at the time as natural phenomena best left untouched.

Such passivity came under widespread criticism when the 1929 Wall Street Crash was followed by the Great Depression. The crisis led to widespread calls for a new policy framework, one where the state would manage the business cycle more proactively. The result was the rise of interventionism, largely based on the views of Keynes, who believed that government's first priority is to address short-term human needs that the market does not satisfy.

By the mid-twentieth century, Keynesianism had become the dominant paradigm in much of the capitalist world. The consensus was that states should control many domestic sectors, develop welfare systems, undertake economic planning, and manage entire industries, including aviation, steel, and communications. State involvement often exceeded Keynes original advice, but criticisms were muffled as long as economies boomed—as many did following the Second World War.

Once again, it was an economic crisis that changed policy ideals (see Figure 2.8). The global economy slumped in the 1970s, suffering from high oil prices, budget deficits, inflation, unemployment, and saturated markets. There was widespread disenchantment with Keynesianism and renewed support for classical economics, renamed neo-liberalism. This led in 1979 and 1980 to the elections of UK Prime Minister Margaret Thatcher and

+ Welfare systems
Provisions made alongside the productive economy to support vulnerable members of society. Usually government-sponsored.

Figure 2.8
Crisis-related paradigm changes during the twentieth century in the world's dominant economies (UK then USA).

Laissez-faire	Crisis=shift	Interventionism	Crisis=shift	Laissez-faire
1st wave of globalization	Depression World War II	Keynesianism Post-war boom	Oil shocks Inflation	Neo-liberalism 2nd wave of globalization
ca. 1880s–1929	1929–1945	1945–1973	1973–1979	1979–ongoing

- Private sector becomes the main engine of economic growth; subsidies must be slashed and state-owned enterprises privatized

- Budget deficits, taxes, and public spending have to be minimized

- Price stability becomes a priority; interest rates are set by the market

- Deregulation becomes a priority; property rights become paramount

- Financial markets are deregulated and pension schemes privatized

- Exchange rates become competitive and completely convertible

- Trade becomes liberalized: no barriers to entry; export orientation

- Foreign direct investment and ownership must be accepted and domestic monopolies discouraged

Figure 2.9
Washington Consensus principles that became the hallmark of modern neo-liberal economic management (adapted from Williamson 2002).

US President Ronald Reagan, supporters of the economist Milton Friedman, who thought that a state's main priority was to ensure stable prices and not promote welfare directly, a philosophy that came to be known as 'monetarism'. Laissez-faire ideology was back in fashion.

After communism crumbled in Eastern Europe in 1989, influential thinkers floated the idea that nation-states had arrived at the 'end of history', with the superiority of free market capitalism being proven once and for all (Fukuyama 1993). Associated with this vision was a package of policies that all states were advised to implement, called the 'Washington Consensus' (see Figure 2.9) or, more humorously, the 'Golden Straitjacket' (Friedman 2000). The basic concept was that states exist for three reasons only: to help markets function by producing necessary goods that markets cannot provide by themselves; to remedy market failure (**see ORC Extension material 2.4**); and to help the most vulnerable in society (Wolf 2004). The expectation was that, except in extreme cases, politics are secondary to business.

The question is how long neo-liberalism will dominate. History teaches that paradigms only last as long as enough people support them. If neo-liberalism becomes incapable of resolving the twin crises of 2008 and 2011–2012, there is every chance that support will decline. Indeed, by early 2009, governments everywhere were intervening massively in the economy, with countless voices asking for the re-empowerment of the state, even in the neo-liberal UK, where a re-nationalization of banks was demanded even by many normally anti-interventionist observers (Wolf 2009). Attitudes towards state power have always depended on circumstances at a given point in time.

+ Market failure
Where markets perform inefficiently by not allocating resources optimally.

> Go online

Changes in place

Policy frameworks are further complicated by the fact that different paradigms can coexist at any moment in time. This can make analysis very confusing. For instance, one explanation for East Asia's excellent trade performance since the mid-1990s is its market orientation. Yet governments in this part of the world have retained significant power. The East Asian form of neo-liberalism comes in many different forms, ranging from China's special market zones to Singapore's hi-tech government-aided research centres (Ong 2006). There is no such thing as a single model of free market capitalism.

The international diffusion of a particular paradigm also depends on broader political factors. For most of the twentieth century, two ideological blocs (communism and capitalism) vied for world dominance. The fall of communism removed a major obstacle to global integration. Paradigms tend to spread more easily in the absence of geopolitical tensions.

One consequence of the end of the Cold War was that many LDCs that used to be strongly opposed to the neo-liberal model began embracing it to varying degrees. After gaining independence in the mid-twentieth century, many former colonies had opted for interventionist policies that they felt better reflected their newfound sovereignty. By the end of the century, however, several of these governments were being criticized as 'predatory' and corrupt bureaucracies (Lal 2006). Tellingly, a neo-liberal approach began to take root in places that used to be hotbeds of interventionism, like once socialist Tanzania in Africa, or the Indian state of Kerala, which had famously prioritized state-run education and health programmes over business-oriented growth policies. With increasing numbers of LDC elites being educated in Western business schools, many began to favour the kind of market-friendly policies to which they had been exposed there.

This is not to say that the neo-liberal agenda has gained unanimous approval across the developing world. In some places, the philosophy has only been imposed through violence—one example being Chile, where Salvador Allende's democratically elected socialist government was overthrown on 11 September 1973 by a US-supported military dictatorship that soon became a laboratory for Milton Friedman's free market ideas (Perkins 2004). Ongoing Latin American resentment following this episode is one reason why the

Practitioner insight

Dr Judy Willetts has much experience of international business, strategy, and entrepreneurship research, with a particular focus on SMEs in Africa. This body of work underpins Judy's former collaborations on World Bank and UNCTAD projects. She is currently a lecturer in international business at Regents College (London).

'Despite the strength of Smith and Ricardo's theories, I also have some sympathy for protectionism, largely because the "invisible hand of God" does not really exist in the real world. There are always political interests behind every national policy and this cannot help but have an effect on markets. Secondly, the world is full of inequalities in terms of access to resources and the ability to use whatever resources a population can find. This too affects markets but is not represented in Smith's thinking.

On the other hand, I also see a problem with too much protectionism, namely that it can lead to a great deal of inefficiency. Many developing countries have had infant industry laws in place over the past 40 or 50 years, yet the industries concerned continue to be inefficient and underdeveloped. It's complicated, because when we look back at the history of today's developed economies, they used protectionism during their own development phases. So there is also an issue of fairness in allowing countries to adopt the same policies. For instance, the USA and many European countries continue to protect their farming industries without allowing African countries to do the same. We could say that the Africans shouldn't hide behind protectionism but it's still not a level playing field when their competitors maintain that advantage. There is a lot of this kind of hypocrisy in international business today.

If there were no such thing as political interference, we could say that Ricardo's theories, even more than Smith's, are quite strong. But since this will never be true in the real world, we're stuck with imperfect economic theory. Which leaves us with discussions about politics. I believe that countries are increasingly showing a willingness to negotiate compromises with one another beyond their national political interests, which leaves me hopeful that they can make up for some of the imperfections in theory. This hope is based on political leaders, particularly (but not only) in Africa, learning to negotiate better quality contracts that benefit the whole of their nation, not just a few powerful interest groups. I even think that as South-South international business flows expand, things will get even better. Africa should be able to transcend the absolute advantage trade position in which it has been stuck for a long time and industrialize based on its comparative advantages. This would be a beneficial change.'

region ended up rejecting the initiative of the Free Trade Area of the Americas that George W. Bush's US administration tried to implement in the early 2000s. Similarly, the world's largest LDCs joined forces later in the decade to reject the WTO's efforts during the 'Doha Round' to force open their service sectors (see Chapter 4). Still, despite this resistance to certain aspects of liberalization, the main feature of economic policy in most of the world's leading emerging nations over the past two decades has been the adoption of an increasingly market-friendly stance.

The same phenomenon has been witnessed in Europe, despite the region's traditional support for state power. A prime example of this attitude was the famous 1966 dictum by France's ex-President Charles de Gaulle that *La politique de la France ne se fait pas à la corbeille* ('The stock market does not dictate French policy'). There would be nothing surprising about this statement except for the fact that de Gaulle was a democratic conservative who defined himself in opposition to communism. In the European tradition, opposition to laissez-faire economics has deep roots. Yet European attachment to state-oriented solutions also faded somewhat in the 1990s and 2000s, with some analysts blaming the region's generous welfare systems for its economies' comparative under-performance ('Euro-sclerosis'). Evidence of newfound interest in market mechanisms has been particularly strong in Eastern European transition countries rejecting their communist past. In Western Europe (as in the USA), however, there is greater ideological confusion at present, with some sections of the population blaming an inflated state apparatus for the 2011–2012 European sovereign debt crisis, and others blaming the private sector for decades of paying insufficient tax. As President Barack Obama said in the run-up to the 2012 US presidential election, the question now is whether the policies of Ronald Reagan and Margaret Thatcher remain appropriate in the brave new world of the early twenty-first century (Pace 2012). It is doubtful that readers of this book will have a definitive answer any time soon.

Challenges and choices

→ During the course of their careers, international managers are likely to be introduced to all sorts of different political cultures, many associated with protectionist attitudes that can become major obstacles to cross-border activity. The challenge is learning how to overcome these barriers. Clearly, it is less problematic working in countries with a strong tradition of open borders. The challenge then becomes determining how much success firms can expect to have in countries where other policy frameworks prevail. At a certain point, managers need to decide whether to invest substantial resources in such difficult environments, or whether the level of foreignness is too hard to manage.

Chapter summary

Since the dawn of civilization, people have tried to develop theories to explain trade and, more recently, FDI. The chapter began with a brief review of the crucial and ongoing philosophical debate about the justification for protectionism vs. free trade. It then went on to divide the main trade theories into pre-Second World War theories focusing on national policies (and including ideas such as absolute or comparative advantage) vs. modern company-focused theories highlighting constructs such as product life cycle, FDI, and knowledge management. The second section looked at the two main political economic frameworks that constitute the spectrum of attitudes concerning state interference in the economy. The demonstration was made that these approaches have tended to evolve in time and place.

Case study 2.3

Theory and regime change: Russia from Gorbachev to Putin

The Union of Soviet Socialist Republics (USSR), of which Russia was the founder state, ran a communist regime from 1917 until 1990. One of the most noteworthy features of this system was its command economy, with bureaucrats making most decisions about investment, pricing, incomes, and trade. Communism's worthy goal of social equality paled alongside its other faults, which in the field of economics included its inefficient industrialization processes and consumer rationing. In the end, Mikhail Gorbachev oversaw the dissolution of the Soviet regime, which officially ended on 25 December 1991.

The new President, Boris Yeltsin, and his main economic adviser, Yegor Gaidar, were strongly influenced by the radical neo-liberal attitudes of the 1990s. Their policy was to apply a 'shock therapy' of market-oriented reforms, including the phase-out of price controls and subsidies, privatization of national industries, and acceptance of foreign entities such as the International Monetary Fund (IMF). The IMF provided much needed loans but also exerted strong influence over Yeltsin's budgetary and monetary policies. The mid-1990s were a period of extreme inflation and fiscal deficits, with the new regime seemingly incapable of raising enough tax revenues to meet its budgetary needs. Soaring interest rates made it difficult for Russian industry to fund its ambitious modernization investments. National GDP fell by an estimated 50 per cent as the economy restructured. The Russian currency suffered from volatility, culminating in a 1998 financial crisis when the rouble's value was halved and many financial institutions went bankrupt, destroying the savings of millions of households. Such was the lack of confidence in Russia's future that the country recorded an estimated annual net capital outflow of $20 billion during the 1990s (Bank of Russia 2008).

By 2007 about $35 billion of private capital was flowing into Russia on an annual basis, a phenomenal turnaround. Russia's unique endowment in natural resources such as gas, coal, and minerals meant that it was well placed to benefit from the sharp rise in world commodity prices that began in the late 1990s. Whereas in 1998 Russia's balance of payments was more or less zero, by 2006 it had a surplus of $92.5 billion. The

annualized interbank lending rate, which had reached 140 per cent in September 1998, was down to 3.3 per cent in 2007. Russia had experienced uninterrupted strong GDP growth since 1999, with annual rises averaging around 6 per cent over this period. Indeed, surpluses accumulated to such an extent that when the country started experiencing outflows over 2010–2012, this was no longer presented as a crisis but instead as a sign that Russia had enriched to the extent that its entrepreneurs could afford to start acquiring foreign assets without destabilizing their mother country.

Some observers analyse the improvement in Russia's economic fortunes as the by-product of its conversion to a market economy. There is no doubt that the new regime eliminated many distortions found in the old one, but it would be wrong to assume that Russia has embraced free trade wholeheartedly. The country only joined the WTO in 2012 and continues to levy

Demand for Russian energy products has skyrocketed with the country's emergence

Source: iStock

high tariffs on imports. As unpopular as this policy is among Russian importers and consumers, it indicates ongoing mercantilist attitudes in many parts of government.

Russia's strength during the 2000s was partially explained by the world's thirst for its natural resources, allowing Russia to put strong pressure on trading partners without fearing a loss of business. Another factor contributing to Russia's strength was its centralized political culture. Many Kremlin leaders felt unhappy with the dictates that foreign creditors had imposed during the Yeltsin years. On 31 December 1999, Vladimir Putin came to power and not only proceeded to restore the central state's internal authority but also began wielding Russian power in the international arena. One instrument implemented towards this end was greater state control over national energy giants such as Gazprom and Lukoil. Foreign MNEs like BP and Shell were made to understand that Russia

intended to reign supreme over its domestic economy, with both MNEs being convinced to sell their stakes in local projects (Parker 2011). Many analysts came to consider the leading Russian energy companies as quasi-nationalized firms run by an inner circle of Kremlin leaders. Clearly, although Russia has adopted many capitalist attributes, it has chosen a direction quite distinct from the one imagined by the free market thinkers who flocked to Moscow at the end of the communist era.

Case study questions

1. To what extent did Russia benefit from, or was damaged by, the neo-liberal policies it applied in the 1990s?
2. How justifiable is Russia's pursuit of its perceived national interest?
3. How sustainable are Russia's current mercantilist policies?

Discussion questions

1. Adam Smith's theory views the international division of labour favourably. How does this approach fit the needs of the modern world?

2. Citing current examples, how well does Ricardo's comparative advantage theory explain countries' varying fortunes?

3. Are there any limitations to the idea that countries should be allowed to protect infant industries?

4. Give examples of industries where Vernon's product life cycle theory does or does not apply.

5. Paul Krugman disagrees with the idea that 'the people who lose from free trade tend to be small, well-organized groups and the winners are more widely spread'. He thinks that it may be the other way around. Comment.

Online resource centre

Go online to test your understanding by trying multiple-choice questions, and assignment and examination questions.

Further research

Kemp, M. (2011). *International Trade Theory: A Critical Review*. Abingdon, Oxon: Routledge

This book raises questions about a number of theories that are widely accepted today, ranging from comparative advantage to faith in the universal benefit of free trade.

Hufbauer, G. and Suominen, K. (2012). *The Economics of Free Trade*. Cheltenham, UK: Edward Elgar Publishing

Authoritative compilation of reflections on free trade by many of the world's leading economists, including Gary Becker, Jagdish Bhagwati, John Maynard Keynes, Paul Krugman, Dani Rodrik, and Jeffrey Sachs.

References

Bank of Russia (2008). 'Monetary Statistics', available at http://www.cbr.ru, accessed 15 October 2008

Bradsher, K. (2009). 'East Asia rethinking reliance on exports', *International Herald Tribune*, 5 March, p. 9

Cassata, D. and Baldor, L. (2011). 'Boeing gets $35 billion Air Force tanker order', 24 February 2011, available at http://www.msnbc.com, accessed 3 April 2012

Caulkin, S. (2005). 'That's the theory, and it matters', available at http://observer.guardian.co.uk, accessed 3 June 2012

Cieślik, A. and Tarsalewska, M. (2011). 'External openness and economic growth in developing countries', *Review of Development Economics*, 15/4, pp. 729–744

Dunning, J. and Pitelis, C. (2007). 'Stephen Hymer's contribution to international business scholarship: An assessment and extension', *Journal of International Business*, available at http://www.palgrave-journals.com, accessed 29 June 2008

Feenstra, R. (2004). *Advanced International Trade: Theory and Evidence*. Woodstock: Princeton University Press

Friedman, T. (2000). *The Lexus and the Olive Tree*. New York: Anchor Books

Fukuyama, F. (1993). *The End of History and the Last Man*. New York: Harper Perennial

Fuller, T. (1999). 'Mahathir discerns threat from "ethnic European" colonizers: A fiery warning in Malaysia', 19 June, available at http://iht.com, accessed 14 October 2008

Held, D. and McGrew, A. (eds.) (2007). *Globalization Theory: Approaches and Controversies*. Cambridge: Polity Press

Hibou, B. (2004). *Privatising the State*. London: Hurst and Company

Irwin, D. (1996). *Against the Tide: An Intellectual History of Free Trade*. Chichester: Princeton University Press

Jacques, M. (2008). 'Northern Rock's rescue is part of a geopolitical sea change', *The Guardian*, 18 February, p. 29

Keynes, J. M. (1936). *The General Theory of Employment, Interest and Money*. London: Macmillan

Klaus, E. (2005). 'Bolivia National History', available at http://www.aeroflight.co.uk, accessed 15 October 2008

Klug, A. (2009). *Theories of International Trade*. Abingdon, Oxon: Routledge

Krugman, P. (1997). *Pop Internationalism*. Boston: MIT Press

Lal, D. (2006). 'The contemporary relevance of Heckscher's mercantilism', in R. Findlay, R. Henriksson, H. Lindgren, and M. R. Lundahl (eds.). *Eli Heckscher, International Trade, and Economic History*. Cambridge, MA: MIT Press

Lee, J. (1996). 'Economic growth and human development in the Republic of Korea 1945–1992', available at http://hdr.undp.org, accessed 15 October 2008

Leontief, W. (1953). 'Domestic production and foreign trade: The American capital position re-examined', *Proceedings of the American Philosophical Society*, 97/4, pp. 332–349

Levie, J. and Autio, E. (2011). 'Regulatory burden, rule of law, and entry of strategic entrepreneurs: An international panel study', *Journal of Management Studies*, 48/6, pp. 1392–1419

Lobina, E. (2000). 'Cochabamba—Water War', University of Greenwich, available at http://www.psiru.org, accessed 15 October 2008

Luong, T. (2011). 'The impact of input and output tariffs on firms' productivity: Theory and evidence', *Review of International Economics*, 19/5, pp. 821–835

Markusen, J. (2002). *Multinational Firms and the Theory of International Trade*. London: MIT Press

Mill, J. S. (1848). *Principles of Political Economy*. London: Prometheus Books

Ong, A. (2006). *Neoliberalism as Exception: Mutations in Citizenship and Sovereignty*. Durham, NC: Duke University Press

Pace, J. (2012). 'Obama accuses Republicans of "madness" in Maine', 31 March 2012, available at http://www.guardian.co.uk, accessed 3 April 2012

Parker, L. (2011). 'Trouble comes calling for BP again', 31 August 2011, available at blogs.wsj.com, accessed 3 April 2012

Parsons, W. (2010). *Keynes and the Quest for a Moral Science*. Cheltenham, UK: Elgar Publishing

Perkins, J. (2004). *Confessions of an Economic Hit Man*. San Francisco: Berrett Koehler Publishers

Porter, M. (1990). *The Competitive Advantage of Nations*. London: Palgrave Macmillan

Ricardo, D. (1817). *Principles of Political Economy and Taxation*. Oxford World's Classics. Oxford: Oxford University Press

Schumpeter, J. (1912). *Economic Doctrine and Method*. New York: Oxford University Press (1954, translated from the German 1912)

Sitkin, A. and Bowen, N. (2010). *International Business: Challenges and Choices*. Oxford: Oxford University Press

Smith, A. (1776). *The Wealth of Nations*. Oxford: Oxford University Press

Soo Cha, M. (2010). 'The economic history of Korea', available at http://eh.net/encyclopedia/, accessed 8 June 2012

Vernon, R. (1966). 'International investment and international trade in the product cycle', *Quarterly Journal of Economics*, 80/2, pp. 190–207

Williamson, J. (2002). 'What Washington means by policy reform', available at http://www.iie.com, accessed 17 July 2008

Wolf, M. (2004). *Why Globalization Works*. London: Yale University Press

Wolf, M. (2009). 'To nationalise or not is the question', *Financial Times*, 4 March, p. 15

Yergin, D. and Stanislaw, J. (2002). *The Commanding Heights: The Battle for the World Economy*. New York: Touchstone

Zhang, W-B. (2010). *International Trade Theory: Capital, Knowledge, Economic Structure, Money, and Prices over Time*. Heidelberg: Springer

Part case study

The global automotive markets: Detroit falls behind before catching up again

The first foreign producers to gain a significant share of the US automotive market were the Japanese in the 1970s, led by Toyota, Honda, and Nissan (or Datsun, as it was known). Offering fuel-efficient models that were better adapted to the high oil prices of the time, the Japanese helped to build a new market niche in a country where low fuel prices had always been taken for granted. The American car-makers, led by the 'Big 3' (General Motors, Ford, and Chrysler), reacted to this competition in their home market by lobbying Washington to put restrictions on Japanese imports. This seemed a cheaper option than redesigning their product ranges away from the big gas-guzzlers that American consumers had traditionally favoured (Freyssenet 2009).

The sharp fall in oil prices from 1986 onwards seemed to justify the Big 3's decision not to worry too much about fuel efficiency, at which point they decided to invest massively in the light truck segment, promoting household purchases of minivans, 4×4s, pick-ups, and sport utility vehicles. These vehicles were anything but fuel-efficient and, despite enormous technological progress between the 1980s and the 2000s, fuel consumption averages actually rose in the USA during this period. At the same time, strong sales in the light truck segment, which by 2008 accounted for around half of all new vehicle purchases in the USA vs. one-fifth in the 1980s, helped to temporarily restore the Big 3's profitability (Sitkin and Bowen 2010). This strategic decision came with a heavy cost, however, since it lulled US auto executives into believing that they still did not have to incorporate long-term global trends into their planning.

The energy crisis of 2006–2007 shook up the global economic environment, with oil prices hitting new records, stimulating US consumers' interest in fuel-efficient cars. This was a great opportunity for Toyota, whose entire strategy was focused on saving energy, partially reflecting Japan's relative lack of natural resources. The Japanese car-maker had used the period since the 1980s to develop a hybrid model (the Prius) that consumed less fuel and emitted less carbon dioxide (a key contributor to global warming). This positioning gave Toyota a tremendous edge when oil prices spiked in the mid-2000s and revealed serious flaws in the Big 3's strategic outlook.

The financial crisis of 2008, which caused a collapse in new car model sales worldwide, added to the pressure on the American car-makers. Not only were the Big 3 car-makers unable to count on export markets to offset falling domestic demand, but the recession meant that it had become harder for them, even at home, to sell the big, expensive vehicles in which they specialized. This positioning was especially unfortunate given the likelihood that much future growth in the global automotive markets will occur in emerging economies, where most households can only afford modest-sized vehicles, like the small cars being developed by companies such as Romania's Dacia or India's Tata.

With hindsight, the decision by America's Big 3 car-makers during the 1980s and 1990s to focus on domestic market conditions and consumer preferences was very damaging to their chances of long-term survival in what became an increasingly globalized business. By summer 2009 General Motors (GM) had declared bankruptcy and Italian car-maker Fiat had taken over Chrysler. At that point, the US government was looking at the loss of an estimated 1 million jobs, many concentrated in the Midwest states (including Michigan and Ohio) where some of the Big 3's domestic suppliers were located. Newly elected President Barack Obama had to decide whether to provide government support or watch the US automotive industry continue its decline.

It could be argued that it is important for governments not to interfere in the marketplace, especially where this has the effect of distorting international competition by protecting inefficient domestic producers. A number of leading economists advised the President to 'fight the protectionist virus' (Bhagwati 2009), in part because any measures supporting American industry might be taken as a signal by countries across the world to do the same with their own producers, thereby restricting US exporters' access to foreign markets. Furthermore, an argument was made that bailing out Detroit auto executives would only allow them to continue their failed policies and essentially mean throwing good money after bad. In this view, it was acceptable to 'let Detroit go bankrupt' (Romney 2008).

President Obama chose to provide the Big 3 with financial resources, allowing them to restructure their finances but even more importantly their product lines, specifically by developing new fuel-efficient models matching the standards set by rivals in markets across the world. The turnaround was remarkable. Within three years, GM had regained its lost status as the world's largest car-maker and was generating the highest profits in its century-old history (UPI 2012). In total, from early 2009 through year-end 2011, the whole of the US auto industry added 200,000 jobs. Most significantly, GM was able to reimburse the bailout funds that had allowed it to survive.

International business economists will be analysing these events for years to come. A more sceptical view would be that GM's recovery can also be explained by advantageous conditions that it negotiated in terms of paying workers' pension liabilities or supplier contracts. Others have highlighted numerous examples where government bailouts did not prevent non-competitive industries from ultimately going bankrupt and simply added to the overall economic cost. Yet there is no question that the recent events in Detroit indicate the possibility of at least some role for governments in the conduct of international business. They also support the idea that in many sectors of activity, global trends tend to have a greater impact than domestic ones.

Case study questions

1. Why did the US auto industry fall behind its Japanese rival?
2. What were the arguments for and against President Obama's administration bailing out the US auto industry?
3. What is the outlook for the US auto industry?

References

Bhagwati, J. (2009). 'Obama must fight the protectionist virus', *Financial Times*, 4 February, available at http://www.ft.com, accessed 3 April 2012

Freyssenet, M. (2009). *The Second Automobile Revolution: Trajectories of World Carmakers in the 21st Century*. New York: Palgrave Macmillan

Romney, M. (2008). 'Let Detroit go bankrupt', 18 November, available at http://www.nytimes.com, accessed 3 April 2012

Sitkin, A. and Bowen, N. (2010). *International Business: Challenges and Choices*. Oxford: Oxford University Press

UPI (2012). 'Obama calls out critics of Detroit bailout', 28 February, available at http://www.upi.com, accessed 3 April 2012

Key players

3 International business and national politics

Learning objectives

After reading this chapter, you will be able to:

✦ assess the rationale for government intervention in international business

✦ ascertain to what extent globalization affects the power of the state

✦ measure the political constraints weighing on international business

✦ identify the different tools that states use to control trade and FDI

Case study 3.1

Globalization and deregulation: Food retailing in India

With a need to feed more than 1.1 billion consumers—many of whom are desperately poor—India is a country that takes food distribution very seriously. Not only is ensuring the availability of affordable staples a social and political imperative, but given the large number of small grocers who make their living selling food, the sector's organization is also economically crucial. The problems arise when these two considerations conflict.

India's population centres are traditionally organized around a vast network of family-owned shops. These stores are often too small to bulk-purchase large volumes at a cheap price, much less invest in the kinds of modern logistics capabilities that make huge global players like Walmart, Carrefour, Tesco, Metro, or Shiseido so effective. The consequence of India's shop network being so fragmented is that the country suffers from poor retail infrastructure (Bharee 2011), exemplified by a severe shortage of the refrigerated lorries needed to transport perishables to market before they rot. The problem is particularly acute given India's growing population and because consumers' rising standard of living increases their expectation of improvements in this area. The question for the government has been how to achieve this.

Although the country as a whole famously changed course in 1991 to open up many previously closed sectors of activity to international business, the Indian government had protected the food retailing sector for the simple reason that it feared that competition from efficient foreign companies with global experience in this activity would put millions of domestic grocers out of business. In line with the new philosophy, however, some change was welcomed, resulting in a situation that might be described as partial globalization: food retail MNEs would henceforth be allowed to invest in India, but they had to do this via a domestic partner and could not take a majority stake in a local company.

Modernizing India's traditional distribution networks will be a major challenge

Source: Photodisc

Several companies pursued this option, most notably Walmart, which teamed up with rising Indian giant Bharti to develop a wholesale cash and carry business, the kind of integrated supply chain that had been lacking in the country until now. Progress towards greater efficiency was slow, however, and as global commodity prices began to rise, India suffered high food inflation. Conscious of the social problems this might cause, the government decided to accept a full globalization of the sector and amended legislation in late 2011 to let MNEs become majority owners of Indian retailers. This move will not have been to the liking of certain constituencies but the decision was taken that it is in the greater national interest.

Case study questions

1. Why did the Indian government protect local retailers' interest for so long to consumers' detriment?
2. Will foreign MNEs necessarily be interested in investing in India now that the government has changed the law?

Introduction

Companies operate in frameworks defined by the laws, regulations, and institutions that governments create. What can be confusing is the way that different countries pursue different objectives, and the consequences for international business. For some governments, the policy priority is to protect domestic producers from foreign competitors, improve national terms of trade, and raise revenues by taxing imports. This general attitude is referred to as an interventionist or 'neo-mercantilist' approach. Other countries take more of a free market, 'neo-liberal' approach, based on the idea that the state should exert as little influence as possible, preferring to trust in the efficiency of market mechanisms. This is the basic theoretical debate that Chapter 2 started to explore. It is useful to analyse it more fully in the light of the forces of globalization that have dominated international business since the early 1980s.

Before doing this, however, it is also important to state that these two approaches are two extremes in a spectrum of possible national policies. There is no question, for instance, that the past 30 years have witnessed a widespread 'neo-liberal' trend towards less government interference in international business. Yet even governments that have actively adopted this approach continue to intervene at times—after all, one of the main functions of any government is to safeguard a population's relationship with the outside world. It is almost impossible to conceive of a political regime so opposed to the idea of intervention that it refuses to wield any power at all.

Section I: State power in an era of globalization

The argument over the ideal role of the state is crucial to understanding both the national frameworks within which international business exists, and the global governance structures (see Chapter 4) that have been created to help shape this environment. The 'global economic order is not founded on state power and rules alone, but also on sets of policy ideas and beliefs' (Woods 2004: 467). Few topics are as hotly argued in business as state power—and few historical phenomena have ever created so much uncertainty in this area as globalization.

Analysis is not made easier by the fact that debate in this area can often be highly emotive, particularly as people disagree about the distribution of the costs and benefits of contemporary trends. Yet such arguments also have a very real role to play, if only because of the way they advocate one paradigm as opposed to another, shaping policy-making in turn. In international business as in many social sciences, it can be just as important to understand how people view things as it is to understand the things themselves.

Factors undermining state power

The aspects of modern globalization that have tended to cause the 'retreat of the state' (Strange 1997) and undermine state power include:

- the way in which technology has brought about a greater decentralization of informational powers that states used to monopolize
- the fact that MNEs are much more mobile than national governments
- the rise of alternative forms of governance
- the power invested in the global financial markets.

It is worth remembering, however, that the influence exerted by each of these aspects of globalization can vary considerably (**see ORC Extension materials 3.1**). This will depend

> Go online

on many different factors, not least of which is the paradigm dominating a given society at a particular moment in time.

Technology

Advances in telecommunications mean that an increasing percentage of the world's population today can 'act on the world stage directly—unmediated by a state' (Friedman 2000: 14). Among other effects, the free transfer of information via the Internet empowers consumers to compare prices and, if advantageous, shop across borders. This weakens the position of national producers, who are no longer free to impose prices as they see fit in a given market. In turn, this contributes to the retreat of the state, since it is easier for governments to affect the behaviour of companies that are deeply rooted in the local economy than to control consumers capable of spending their money abroad.

In addition and with the exception of countries where research programmes are dominated by public sector bodies (see Chapter 11), today it is mainly private sector companies, often large MNEs, that develop new technologies, hence the processes determining many aspects of people's economic behaviour. Where an MNE's technological capabilities exceed a government's ability to monitor its activities, it may become tempting for the company to hide transactions from public scrutiny. In turn, this creates a further incentive for managers to separate their interests from those of the nation hosting their activities. One example of this behaviour was the 2008 subprime crisis, when US financial institutions disseminated financial assets that regulators worldwide were unable to analyse accurately. A second example is the ease with which MNEs can transfer funds anywhere in the world without government tax collectors always having a clear picture of the transactions (see Chapter 13). The asymmetry between governments and MNEs' technological prowess is one factor changing the balance of power between these two actors.

MNEs' advantages

One of the main attributes of modern globalization is the rise of private sector multinational enterprises that are increasingly in a position to dominate national governments. There are two key reasons why MNEs' bargaining position has improved: many have grown to a size where they dwarf the government bodies with whom they are negotiating; and, above all, MNEs are generally mobile and free to move operations between worldwide locations, whereas national governments are necessarily bound to a specific territory.

Size

As explained in Chapter 2, the trend towards greater globalization has been established for several decades now. As such, many companies have had the time to take full advantage of the possibilities for expansion that are associated with this trend. They have developed global networks whose size, measured in revenue terms, surpasses the gross domestic product (GDP) of some very large countries. By itself, the MNE with the largest global sales in 2011 (Walmart) already generated revenues matching the GDP of the world's 23rd largest economy, Norway. As illustrated in Figure 3.1, a number of MNEs outweigh all but the world's very largest economies. This contrast in economic power is particularly striking when one compares company staff numbers with national population sizes.

One possible effect of this growing imbalance is that it often occurs that sovereign states are in a far weaker bargaining position than MNEs (see Chapter 5). This is particularly true when developing country governments desperate for inwards investment negotiate the conditions surrounding an MNE's market entry. The trend towards giant MNEs has also created a situation where certain areas of activity, such as infrastructure projects or technological research, can no longer be managed in many countries without business involvement. This is another factor shifting the historical borders between companies and governments' spheres of influence (Scherer and Palazzo 2011).

Figure 3.1
Corporate revenues equalling GDP of much larger countries. Comparison of sample of MNEs ranked approximately by 2011 revenues and featuring global staff numbers (taken from annual reports) vs. countries ranked by GDP (CIA 2012).

MNEs ranked by 2011 global revenues (with number of global staff members)	Countries ranked by 2011 GDP (with population size)
Global top 5: Walmart $444 billion (2.1 million staff)	Ranked nr. 30: Malaysia $444 billion (28.7 million inhabitants)
Global top 10: Toyota $235 billion (315,000 staff)	Ranked nr. 52: Israel $235 billion (7.7 million inhabitants)
Global top 20: General Electric $142 billion (301,000 staff)	Ranked nr. 61: Belarus $142 billion (9.5 million inhabitants)
Global top 80: Proctor & Gamble $83 billion (45,000 staff)	Ranked nr. 77: Myanmar $83 billion (48 million inhabitants)
Global top 100: Deutsche Post $71 billion (423,348 staff)	Ranked nr. 83: Kenya $71 billion (41 million inhabitants)

Mobility

Politicians worldwide are acutely aware that getting MNEs to trade and invest in their country helps to create jobs and enhance economic prosperity. Thus, except in those instances where the host country features some particularly attractive characteristics (i.e. natural resources or a dynamic consumer market), MNEs' desirability gives them a strong bargaining chip in their negotiations with host country governments. The advantage is compounded by the fact that, in many situations, MNEs are free to take their business elsewhere if the host government does not accommodate their interests. This possibility, called regime shopping or arbitrage, happens if social, environmental, tax, or other regulations dissuade MNEs from investing or trading in a particular country (see the discussion on lobbying in Chapter 5). In turn, the threat of regime shopping creates a kind of inter-state competition, putting pressure on countries to make fewer demands on companies. The ensuing race to the bottom weakens state power, since governments find they cannot apply certain preferred policies and still hope to attract MNEs.

In 2010, for instance, Ireland was suffering a huge budget deficit and could conceivably have increased its comparatively very low corporation tax rate of 12.5 per cent to raise revenue. Indeed, the country came under pressure from its European partners to do exactly this. Irish politicians resisted, however (McDonald et al. 2010), largely because of their concern that this might further weaken the economy by persuading MNEs with operations in Ireland to move elsewhere, for instance to Bulgaria, Cyprus, Serbia, or Hungary, all countries with a corporation tax rate of only 10 per cent at the time. The end result was that it became harder for Ireland to fund the kinds of social spending that would otherwise be desirable given the country's rising unemployment levels.

Of course, government attempts to attract companies through low tax rates can also be portrayed in a more positive light as simple 'regime competition'. There is nothing controversial, for instance, about investment or marketing agencies advertising a country's charms. Such competition becomes problematic only when it breaches international agreements, like if EU member states try to attract FDI away from fellow members by not observing stringent European labour laws. One example is when countries offer mobile MNEs tax holidays, grants, and/or infrastructure investments. The common point in all these situations is that MNEs' mobility gives them a bargaining power that they can use to good effect against immobile national governments.

+ **Regime shopping/ arbitrage**
Decision to locate an MNE's activities based on the relative laxness of a host country's requirements (taxes, regulations, etc.).

+ **Race to the bottom**
Where competition among disadvantaged producers forces them to accept lower remuneration for their services.

Global governance

Many areas of international business cannot be negotiated within a national framework alone. Examples include regional trading policies, environmental action, or currency regimes. Consequently, bodies operating at a higher level than the individual state must be formed to deal with such issues. At the same time, such bodies—generically referred to as 'global governance'—undermine the power of nation-states since they are no longer the only actors operating on the world stage. 'Enmeshed within horizontal and vertical networks of multiple supra-state, sub-state and non-state actors' (El-Ojeili and Hayden 2006: 97), national governments find there are fewer policy areas where they wield uncontested sovereignty.

For reasons that Chapter 4 explores in further detail, most countries have joined regional associations and/or intergovernmental organizations (IGOs) where they agree to be bound by the rules that these bodies impose on their member states. One of the main IGOs shaping international business is the World Trade Organization (WTO), whose purpose is to promote a free trade regime. One of the principles guiding the WTO is non-discrimination, or the idea that a country's trade policies should not benefit national producers to the detriment of fellow WTO members. This takes away sovereign states' old mercantilist prerogative of being able to favour domestic interests. By joining the WTO, national governments accept that they will no longer have a monopoly over economic policy decisions. In essence, this means swapping the dominant role in a smaller framework (the nation-state) for a smaller role within a larger structure (the WTO). It is tempting for a state to try to have the best of both worlds, maintaining absolute sovereignty at home while having a greater say on the global stage. This is more feasible for larger countries, which find it easier to dominate IGO proceedings. At the same time, one of the original aims in the development of IGOs was to ensure that every country has a voice.

Finance

The gigantic sums traded in today's deregulated financial markets match and often exceed the funds available to national governments, whose ability to raise money is constrained by international tax competition and by the fact that the countries with the greatest capital

+ **International tax competition**
Where countries try to attract offshore funds by offering investors lower tax rates than they can find in competitor nations.

WTO conferences are often accompanied by protests aimed at the protection of national interests

© WTO | Photo: Studio Casagrande (Jay Louvion/Kryvosheiev Nikita)

needs are often those with the lowest savings rates. Because of this imbalance between public and private wealth, states are often forced to tailor their policies to appeal to global investors who tend to prefer governments accepting the 'Golden Straitjacket' (Friedman 2000: 86–7) of reduced state spending, whether or not this suits domestic circumstances or preferences.

Practitioner insight

Andy Love is a British Member of Parliament, first elected to represent the North London constituency of Edmonton in 1997. Since 2005 he has sat on the Treasury Select Committee, which examines the spending, administration, and policies of the UK Treasury along with associated bodies such as Revenue & Customs and the Bank of England.

'The UK has traditionally been an open economy and an instigator of free trade. The associated process of globalization has sometimes been good for us—but not always. Moreover, it can be hard determining where our best interests lie.

For instance, there is a strong argument in the current downturn that we should use public sector investment to revive demand. Yet doing this by ourselves would aggravate the trade deficit, particularly in sectors like construction, where many value-added goods (i.e. boilers) are imported. Another risk with bucking global trends is that financial centres like Wall Street might lose confidence and withdraw capital. In short, the openness that makes us successful at attracting capital also restricts our margin to manoeuvre during a crisis.

Globalization is also a double-edged sword for emerging economies. China and India have benefited from entering the world economy but to get here they had to erect barriers, giving them space to develop their infrastructure. Such protectionism is problematic in a down-cycle, as people saw during the 1930s when competitive tariffs and currency devaluations worsened the Depression. Governments must be careful that policies improving things nationally do not worsen them internationally.

One example is governments' problem with the international capital markets. I believe that globalization must go hand in glove with financial regulation. The absence of such mechanisms patently contributed to the 2007 crisis. The West used to be relaxed about capital flows when they affected Latin America or Russia but now we are suffering. This is not only due to deregulation, however. There is also the problem of imbalances between massive national surpluses and deficits. China must lodge its funds somewhere but such huge inflows of capital can distort pricing in the financial markets.

We need structural change but also regulatory progress. The IMF may be best placed to help since it now has a mandate to suggest things to blocs of countries and not just single governments. The problem is that it cannot impose sanctions. National governments are reluctant to hand sovereignty over to the IMF or EU. This is often due to resentment at their past interference. Yet many problems can only be resolved through collective acceptance of risks. Currently, for instance, big banks suffering problems abroad seek bailouts from home country taxpayers. This is unsustainable. Unfortunately the G20 ignores the problem.

Many governments argue that they should not control banks directly. I agree but this means that governments limit themselves to a 'bully pulpit' discourse where they are powerless to do anything more than lecture other countries and I doubt this is enough. Some agreements, like the Basel III capital adequacy measures, are actually designed to be implemented within a national framework but this can be very complicated. I see too many paradoxes.'

The problem for governments prioritizing domestic needs is that their policies may not be to offshore investors' liking. For instance, if a government tries to accelerate national growth through lower interest rates, investors might decide to withdraw funds and invest them in another currency offering higher interest. In the worst-case scenario, as detailed in Chapter 13, this can cause capital flight and a currency crisis. The lesson is clear: where governments depend on overseas funding (as has increasingly been the case over the past 25 years of financial globalization), politicians cannot govern without taking stock of foreign investors' judgements.

+ Financial globalization
Deregulation of global capital markets leading to an acceleration in cross-border capital transfers.

Factors bolstering state power

Even if some aspects of globalization have undermined governments' ability to make policy autonomously, it would be wrong to conclude that states no longer matter at all. Quite the contrary: there are many signs that nation-states continue to have a crucial role to play in economic decision-making in general, and in international business in particular. In part, this is because government remains the actor with the most direct control over a population in a given territory (**see ORC Extension material 3.2**). This was dramatically exemplified in the wake of the 2008 and 2011 crises by the way in which massive interventions by governments worldwide prevented the collapse of the global financial system. Of course, these actions were jointly planned and coordinated, meaning that even if there is little question that states still matter, there is also no doubt that they exercise power differently nowadays. Thus, the more accurate analysis might be to identify a new kind of sovereignty, one where 'nation-states are simply one class of powers and political agencies in a complex system of power from world to local levels' (Hirst and Thompson 1999: 16, 276). Chapter 4 will explore this vision of mixed governance in greater detail.

> Go online

The following arguments illustrate the ongoing strength of national political power despite the trend towards greater globalization.

The domestic setting remains crucial to many business activities

Notwithstanding the expansion of international business, 'all economic and financial activity, from production, R&D [research and development] to trading and consumption, occurs in geographical not virtual space' (Held and McGrew 2002: 42), one that is basically subject to the authority of a national government. Local officials continue to establish and collect corporation and personal tax rates and taxes, determine macro-economic policy targets, operate welfare and education programmes, invest in infrastructure, and determine immigration regulations (El-Ojeili and Hayden 2006)—this final point offering clear proof that the world is not entirely 'borderless', as some globalization enthusiasts would have it (Ohmae 2005). They also retain the power to penalize MNEs operating on their home space, as exemplified by the fine of upwards of £5 billion that the Indian authorities have tried to levy on Vodafone, which was accused of using an 'artificial tax avoidance scheme' to avoid paying what the company really owes (Garside 2011). Moreover, despite talk about companies being global, statistics show that home regions tend to account for most MNE activity (see Chapter 9). It is useful to recall the many different barriers to entry that companies face whenever they transact outside their original homeland: foreign accounting rules and legal systems; unfamiliar supply chains; the absence of any brand history; not to mention cultural and linguistic differences. At home, on the other hand, companies benefit from the experience they have accumulated in managing their physical assets; tried and trusted supplier networks; a superior knowledge of human resources; and, above all, brand loyalty. It should never be forgotten that, despite all its attractions, international business remains a big challenge for many companies.

One way to demonstrate this is by analysing the data contained in Figure 3.2, which shows the world's 16 largest exporting economies' degree of openness, defined as their

Figure 3.2

Total 2011 trade in goods and services, in US$ billion and as percentage of GDP (CIA 2012)

* *Source*: http://www.singstat.gov.sg/pubn/reference/sif2012.pdf

Countries ranked by degree of openness	Total exports (trade/services)	Total imports (trade/services)	GDP, current prices	Total trade/GDP (per cent)
Hong Kong	507	483	242	409.1
Singapore	540*	455*	267	372.7
Netherlands	577	514	858	127.2
Belgium	332	332	529	125.6
Taiwan	325	299	505	123.5
South Korea	557	524	1164	91.2
Germany	1408	1198	3629	71.8
China	1898	1743	6989	52.1
Canada	451	460	1759	51.8
Italy	522	556	2246	48.0
UK	495	655	2481	46.4
Russia	499	310	1791	45.2
France	578	685	2803	45.1
India	298	451	1843	40.6
Japan	801	795	5459	29.2
USA	1511	2314	15,060	25.4

total exports and imports of goods and services, expressed as a percentage of GDP. This is an imperfect calculation that does not reflect certain factors, especially the fact that some sectors (i.e. pharmaceutical products) are inherently more international than others (i.e. healthcare administration) that are necessarily organized on a more local basis.

Figure 3.2 is a snapshot taken in the year 2011 and therefore does not mention the long-term upwards trend in many countries' degree of openness, with numbers for most older industrialized countries having at least doubled over the past 25 years (see Chapter 1).

Analysing countries' degree of openness is very instructive. In many of the world's leading exporting countries, between 40 and 50 per cent of GDP involves products or services that have no overseas aspect whatsoever at any point in their production process or supply chain. Indeed, in two of them (Japan and the US), around 70 per cent of total GDP is entirely untouched by international business. This is significant because these are two of the world's three largest economies—indicating that a relatively strong reverse relationship exists between country size and degree of openness. In fact, the only countries in the sample where total trade volumes are equal to 100 per cent or more of GDP are the smaller countries (translating a situation where large volumes of goods and services are being imported and subsequently re-exported). Otherwise, the larger the economy, the higher the percentage of purely domestic business. As for China, its emergence over the past 20 years (see Chapter 15) has been largely based on foreign trade alone, but this is likely to represent a smaller part of the national economy in the future, when greater emphasis will be placed on domestic activity. The same can be said about India and, to a lesser extent, Russia. Clearly, announcements of the death of domestic business are premature.

At a more individual level, the existence of 'cosmopolitan' citizens of the world should not take attention away from the fact that most people continue to live near where they were born, consume domestically manufactured goods, invest savings locally (Legrain 2003), and pay taxes to their national government. Indeed, for many economists, the best proof of states' continued power is the general rise in most countries' tax revenues over the past few decades. It is easier to measure this phenomenon in the older industrialized world than in the in less-developed countries (LDCs), which can lack reliable statistics (often due to black market activity) and where inefficient tax collection systems mean that state power tends to be administered via direct control or regulation rather than by taxation. Figure 3.3 measures the tax burden in selected OECD member states, defined as the percentage of national GDP collected in the form of corporate or personal taxes and levies. If states have truly lost their power over their national economies, the ratio would have fallen.

+ Black market
Economic activities occurring outside an official framework.

In reality, with few exceptions, tax burdens rose more or less worldwide from 1975 through 2000—the period that was supposed to have been defined by the free market, 'neo-liberal' prescription of low taxation. Since 2000 tax rates have generally fallen, but rather than analysing this as a loss of state power, it could merely translate the modernization of state interventions, with more functions being subcontracted to private intermediaries, largely in reaction to criticisms of government bureaucracy (Hibou 2004). Moreover, states continue to set the tone for these activities even if they no longer run them directly. Indirect governance does not mean less governance.

Economic patriotism

One key aspect in many countries' social history has been the 'reluctance of people to be ruled by politicians and bureaucrats from the other side of the world, over whom they have no democratic or other control' (Friedman 2000: 205). The fact that there are so many examples

	1975	1985	1995	2000	2005	2010
Belgium	39.5	44.3	43.5	44.7	44.6	43.8
Denmark	38.4	46.1	48.8	49.4	50.8	48.2
France	35.5	42.8	42.9	44.4	44.1	42.9
Germany	34.3	36.1	37.2	37.5	35.0	36.3
Greece	19.4	25.5	28.9	34.0	31.9	30.9
Ireland	28.7	34.6	32.5	31.2	30.3	28.0
Italy	25.4	33.6	40.1	42.2	40.8	43.0
Japan	20.7	27.1	26.8	27.0	27.4	n.a.
Korea	14.9	16.1	20.0	22.6	24.0	25.1
Mexico	..	15.5	15.2	16.9	18.1	18.7
Netherlands	40.7	42.4	41.5	39.6	38.4	n.a.
Spain	18.4	27.6	32.1	34.2	35.7	31.7
Sweden	41.3	47.4	47.5	51.4	48.9	45.8
Switzerland	24.4	25.8	27.7	30.0	29.2	29.8
Turkey	11.9	11.5	16.8	24.2	24.3	26.0
UK	34.9	37.0	34.0	36.3	35.7	35.0
USA	25.6	25.6	27.8	29.5	27.1	24.8

Figure 3.3
Total tax revenues as a percentage of GDP.
(OECD 2011: reprinted with the kind permission of the OECD)

French activist José Bové, a European parliamentarian, has supported a number of localism or environmental causes over the course of his career

Source: José Bové's EU office

of this attitude—at a time when globalized thinking is assumed to be so dominant—indicates how premature it is to talk about geography no longer being important (Bauman 1998). Borders still count in today's world.

'Home bias' (see Chapter 1) has taken different forms over the years. Current references to this attitude tend to be encapsulated in the idea of economic patriotism, which plays out at several levels. In marketing, this involves consumers being encouraged to prefer goods manufactured domestically. This is exemplified by the food localization campaigns being waged, for instance, by José Bové in France, so-called 'localvores' in the US state of Vermont, or Italy's Via Campesina movement (Ayres and Bosia 2011). There are also discriminatory rules promoting the national ownership of national assets to the detriment of foreign shareholders (see Figure 3.4). Resembling the trade philosophy adopted by many states before the rise of Adam Smith's classical economics, this policy array is sometimes referred to as 'neo-mercantilism'.

Advocates of economic patriotism may stress that foreign shareholders lacking personal ties to a country are likely to be less sensitive to local populations' needs (jobs, the reinvestment of profits) or domestic politicians' social influence (Matelly and Nies 2006). In December 2010, for instance, Ugandan economists were expressing concern about their

+ Economic patriotism
Idea that a society might show preference for domestic firms by purchasing their products and/or preventing foreign ownership.

Figure 3.4
Recent examples of economic patriotism.

Year	Example
2007	Spanish government prevents E.ON a German energy firm, from acquiring Endesa, a local energy provider—even though Germany is a fellow EU member state.
2008–2012	Russian government places unusual pressure on BP's joint venture with local oil firm TNK, visibly to reassert national control over a strategic sector (Wachman 2008).
2009–2010	China enacts 'indigenous innovation' policies reserving government contracts to those MNEs that have produced technology in the country. The purpose of this new form of protectionism is to accelerate China's transition to higher value added production.
2011	After Italian milk producer Parmalat and watchmaker Bulgari are acquired by French companies Lactalis and LVMH, respectively, Italy draws up anti-foreign takeover legislation and creates a fund to 'defend' so-called strategic national assets.

government wilfully selling foreigners a number of key domestic assets, including the National Insurance Corporation to Nigerians, the Uganda Commercial Bank to South Africans, and the National Housing Corporation to Libyans (Kizito 2010). Like all theories, internationalism has its limitations. Even the most hardened internationalists would accept that governments have a duty to protect some national interests. US authorities generally argue against protectionism but fund American space, military, and energy research projects in which US companies alone can participate. Japanese governments support open international markets as a general policy but fight to achieve food autonomy by protecting local rice farmers. A nation-state can accept certain aspects of global deregulation without abandoning all of its powers to protect people at home. Conversely, governments may say they favour a policy of economic patriotism, but when it is in their national interest to compromise with foreigners, they will do so.

The argument against economic patriotism is that it constitutes a danger to a world that has benefited greatly from free trade. Some commentators view economic patriotism as a new form of mercantilism—the old trade theory that Adam Smith and his classical successors worked so hard to discredit (see Chapter 2). In the UK, for instance, there is general acceptance that foreign shareholders own many if not most national industries. The term commonly used for this process is 'Wimbledonization', in reference to the tennis tournament that the British host but (almost) never win. This rejection of narrow patriotic reasoning is exemplified by the lack of strong opposition in the country to American MNE Hewlett Packard's August 2011 takeover of UK software specialist, Autonomy, at a time when there was widespread discussion about the best way to re-balance the British economy towards exactly the kind of higher value-added operation that was being sold to the Americans. The reason for this relaxed attitude may be the domestic consensus that it is not very important whether British industry is kept in national hands. The UK is the world's second leading buyer of foreign firms and benefits from a high 'cross-border net score', meaning the number of acquisitions that British interests make abroad vs. the number of UK firms taken over by non-British shareholders (Kollewe 2011). The end result is that takeovers by foreigners are rarely framed in 'patriotism' terms in the UK. In international business, patriotism is a multi-layered and variable concept.

Case study 3.2

States and economic patriotism: Who owns Britain?

One consequence of the free market revolution of the 1980s has been the displacement of manufacturing to lower cost developing countries. This trend has undermined factory work in the older industrialized countries even as it benefits consumers by helping to keep prices low. Many supporters of the change argue that workers in the Global North should transition into the service sector and let the Global South specialize in simple manufacturing activities. Of course, this is only possible if there are enough service jobs available to absorb the ex-factory workers. As the world economy soured in 2011–2012, the prospects for this adjustment seemed poor. In turn, most politicians in the EU and the

USA started to advocate economic 're-balancing' based on the revitalization of domestic manufacturing. The challenge, however, was how to achieve this goal in a meaningful way.

In the UK, many of the industrial goods being manufactured in domestic factories involve assembling components that have been manufactured abroad and imported into the country. Examples range from almost any British-made car to the kinds of high-quality diggers sold by English construction company JCB, for which 36 per cent of the parts are now made domestically vs. 96 per cent in 1979 (Chakrabortty 2011). International supply chains may allow companies to cut costs and pass the benefits on to local customers. Moreover, many components are not even produced in the UK any more. This explains the national government's interest in trying out new industrialization approaches.

JCB is a British company but a large percentage of its components come from outside the country

Source: JCB

State authorities can support local industry through procurement policies reserving preferential treatment for domestic producers. One example is when national railway companies order trains. In France or Germany, it would be unheard of for foreign firms to win a large order from the national operator, instead of domestic manufacturers such as Alstom and Siemens, respectively (Economist 2011). Hence the general surprise in spring 2011 when the British government ordered 1200 train carriages from Siemens instead of Bombardier, which would have used facilities at Derby in England to fill the order, thereby preserving British jobs (Wright 2011). The British government knew that its decision would damage the UK's last functional train factory but argued that it had no choice because EU and WTO guidelines prevent national preference, and because Siemens was simply cheaper. At that point, the question becomes whether the benefits of running a national manufacturing activity outweigh the costs of supporting this sector.

Case study questions

1. Why is Britain struggling to re-balance its economy towards more manufacturing?
2. Was the UK government right to prefer Siemens to Bombardier?

States as tools of international competition

There are at least three levels at which governments intervene proactively to bolster national competitiveness: by developing capabilities in sectors considered essential to international competition; by orienting international agreements in the national interest; and by engaging in so-called 'state capitalism'.

Developmental capitalism

Despite the frequent argument that it is not a government's role to pick winners, this often happens. Alongside classical economic criticisms of public money being wasted on 'lame duck' companies incapable of surviving without state aid (see Chapter 2), there are just as many cases where timely government interventions, coming in a variety of forms, have secured the future for an industry that subsequently competed successfully in international markets. Such actions can involve helping a company through temporary difficulties, exemplified by General Motors becoming profitable in 2011, as well as a global leader in electric vehicles just two years after the Obama administration had bailed it out (see the Part case study at the end of Part A). More strategically, states will work in conjunction with domestic companies to develop sectors of activity where the country hopes to have an international competitive advantage. This approach, known as 'developmental capitalism', is particularly rife in political cultures that have traditionally favoured a strong state, many of which are in Asia. One example is the rise of the Chinese automotive industry (Chin 2010), whose modernization has been driven by government pressure on MNEs to transfer investment capital and advanced technologies into the country. Even in less interventionist cultures

Temporary government support gave General Motors an opportunity to restructure

Source: General Motors

such as the USA, there are many examples of this kind of developmental activity. For instance, in one remarkable study of the American cotton industry (Rivoli 2006), farmers' success stemmed not only from their entrepreneurial spirit and competency but also from more than a century of government support, whether this involved manipulating the labour market to provide cotton growers with cheap, captive workers, or state-funded R&D facilities disseminating cutting-edge knowledge. The lesson here is that an active and/or powerful state is not necessarily incompatible with a country's pursuit of market success. The example of Japan Incorporated, where many if not most of the country's industries have come together under government coordination to create an export powerhouse, attests to the role that states can play in enhancing national competitiveness (**see ORC Extension material 3.3**).

A more recent example of how states help to develop national capabilities is the new global market for environmentally friendly energy-efficiency products (see Chapter 16). Debates about whether the new industry should be shaped by private entrepreneurship or state intervention seem sterile given the way both of these drivers have been interacting with one another. Figure 3.5 provides examples of various actions that governments take to encourage local companies to enter this sector.

> Go online

Name	Discussion
Elimination of tariffs on green goods/services	Facilitate cross-border trade in green technologies and other energy-saving devices by minimizing protectionism
Standards (including carbon trading schemes)	Governments set quantitative targets (CO_2 emissions, fuel efficiency, etc.) and levy sanctions if they are missed
State sponsored R&D	Due to the expense and long payback period associated with green innovations, governments can provide financial, infrastructure, and/or scientific assistance
Green taxes	Motivate consumers to opt for greener products (cars) and/or behaviour (fuel taxes, airport taxes)
Green subsidies (including tax credits)	Payments enabling operators to offer green products/services even if they are uneconomic at current price levels. Often monitored by international body (WTO, EU) to prevent national producers from gaining an unfair advantage
Direct state investment	Government-owned and managed enterprises specializing in the creation/operation of a green activity

Figure 3.5
State actions developing a global environmental industry (Sitkin 2011).

International negotiations

Despite the growing power of regional and global bodies of governance, most political decisions are still made at the national level. Indeed, some observers argue that the shift from traditional bilateral forums (where one state deals directly with another) to multilateral negotiations actually increases states' bargaining power (Kelly and Grant 2005). One example of this would be the way that a small country like Luxembourg can use its EU membership to have a louder voice on the international stage than would otherwise be the case. Conversely, there is also the argument that big countries like the USA might be tempted to use these very same organizations as a 'Trojan horse' serving American interests (Mathews 2005).

One example of the way that international forums offer states an opportunity to increase their power is the ongoing negotiations between the world's older industrialized countries and the developing world. The USA, EU, and Japan, for instance, have long tried to get the WTO to adopt an agenda entitled Trade Related Aspects of Intellectual Property Rights (TRIPS). With the majority of global patents still being registered in these countries, the idea is that it will become easier to protect their innovators' intellectual property rights if multilateral instead of bilateral agreements are reached. Critics have described this as an attempt to preserve Western pharmaceutical MNEs' advance against Indian and Brazilian rivals capable of producing cheaper generic substitutes (Papaioannou 2006). The dilemma is best exemplified by the negotiations surrounding appropriate pricing for anti-AIDS retroviral drugs whose retail price needed to be high to remunerate MNEs for innovating in this area but was too expensive for poor populations requiring treatment.

+ Intellectual property rights
Exclusive enjoyment of the benefits derived from intangible assets like trademarks, patents, and copyrights.

Developing countries also use international forums to advance their interests. One example was the 2011 Durban climate change conference, where India and China negotiated less binding CO_2 obligations for themselves, arguing that their relative poverty—and recent industrialization—meant they should face lesser burdens than the advanced nations (see Chapter 16). To the extent that India and China used this forum to achieve national policy goals, global governance enhanced state power.

State-capitalism

The most direct way in which states exercise power over international business is by running economic bodies that operate on the world stage. The two main actors in this category are state-owned enterprises (SOEs) and sovereign wealth funds (SWFs), which are government-run pools of national currency reserves used to acquire assets worldwide.

The main difference between having MNEs owned by public rather than private sector shareholders is that the two groups tend not to pursue the same goals. Normally, private shareholders focus more on short-term financial returns (see the Chapter 5 discussion on 'financialization') whereas state sector shareholders focus on outcomes like providing jobs at a time of high unemployment or using international expansion to acquire technology or natural resources. A prime example of this latter situation is Chinese government-owned SOEs engaging in mining and oil drilling activities in Africa, where they compete with private sector MNEs.

Similar concerns have been expressed about SWFs (see Figure 3.6), which mainly originate from countries with large oil surpluses (often from the Arabian Gulf) and/or where the state has traditionally played a major economic role (like China). There is nothing new about such funds, but their recent expansion is noteworthy. In 2011, for instance, the Abu Dhabi investment company became the largest 'cornerstone' shareholder in the giant commodities company, Glencore, when its shares were floated on the international stock markets, taking a stake worth at least $850 million. GIC, Singapore's sovereign wealth fund, took a further $400 million stake in Glencore at the time. In part, these moves were motivated by the SWFs' desire to speculate on a company whose shares they hoped would rise in future. But they also reflected the desire of the states standing behind them to access Glencore's physical resources. When governments have such enormous sums at their disposal, it is hard to argue that the state is in retreat.

Sovereign wealth fund	Estimated May 2012 holdings	Founded	Origin of funds
Abu Dhabi Investment Authority	$627	1976	Oil
Government Pension Fund–Global (Norway)	$611	1990	Oil
SAFE Investment Company (China)	$567.9	1997	Non-commodity
SAMA Foreign Holdings (Saudi Arabia)	$532.8	n/a	Oil
China Investment Corporation	$439.6	2007	Non-commodity
Kuwait Investment Authority	$296	1953	Oil
Hong Kong Monetary Authority Investment Portfolio	$293.3	1993	Non-commodity
Government of Singapore Investment Corporation	$247.5	1981	Non-commodity
Temasek Holdings (Singapore)	$157.2	1974	Non-commodity
National Welfare Fund (Russia)	$149.7	2008	Oil
National Social Security Fund (China)	$134.5	2000	Non-commodity
Qatar Investment Authority	$100	2005	Oil

Figure 3.6
World's largest sovereign wealth funds.
www.swfinstitute.org/

Section II: States as actors in international business

State intervention in trade matters often means supporting local producers' interests to the detriment of foreign producers (and even local consumers). Chapter 2 showed that protecting local industry can be politically advantageous but economically sub-optimal: because domestic producers have less of an incentive to modernize and become more competitive; but also because the countries in question tend to have weaker corporate governance mechanisms (Talamo 2011). Conversely, organizing 'efficient', internationally open markets where participants are free to succeed but also fail, can be politically damaging but economically advantageous, if only because such regimes generally attract more FDI. These tensions are reflected in the political economic tools that governments routinely wield.

+ Corporate governance
Laws and processes regulating corporate management, including composition of the Board of Directors, protection of minority interests, executive control, and accounting practices.

Motives for intervention

Some state interventions are internally oriented and aimed at ensuring a country's well-being. Others are intended to improve its external positioning.

Interventions for internal purposes

Jobs

A country's unemployment rate can skyrocket if foreign producers take a big share of the domestic market. In recent years, this issue has had increasing political resonance in the world's older industrialized countries. It explains, for instance, why one key clause in US President Barack Obama's 2012 budget involved modifying the US tax system to penalize American companies that ship jobs abroad, while offering tax credits to firms employing workers at home. Such interventions are particularly politic when they involve sectors considered crucial to the national identity, such as rice in Japan or wine in France.

+ Industrialization policies

Concerted efforts by states to increase the role of value-added manufacturing in their national economy or support industrial sectors they consider strategic.

> Go online

Development

Because of the structures that they have inherited from the past, some economies specialize in the production of low value-added goods. This is sub-optimal from a wealth creation perspective. Moreover, having open borders can penalize countries in this position, since their tendency to import higher value-added goods than they export (see Chapter 1 discussion on 'terms of trade') will lead to an accumulation of deficits. To change things, governments can implement targeted industrialization policies to build up national capabilities in particular sectors. When financed using domestic resources alone, many such interventions will have to be funded via higher taxes—a key lever in the exercise of state power.

Safety/security

One area where governments can intervene to protect citizens' welfare is public health, as exemplified by measures taken by the US Food and Drug Administration to open an office in China in 2008 following a series of medicine and food safety scares in that country (**see ORC Extension material 3.4**). Otherwise, governments will often fulfil their basic national security duties by keeping a close eye on the trade of arms or hi-tech computer systems. For example, the United States Department of Commerce's Bureau of Industry and Security (http://www.bis.doc.gov) restricts trade in items that potentially hostile countries (or individuals) might use for military purposes. Such controls often involve implementing export licensing systems.

Interventions for external purposes

Reciprocity

Governments are not in the business of handing out favours without expecting something in return. This means that they will usually expect a foreign market to be as open to national producers as the domestic market is to the foreign interest. Things can degenerate where people sense a lack of reciprocity. In extreme cases, this can lead to trade wars, as exemplified by the dispute between the EU and the USA over genetically modified (GM) food. The background to this case was when an American multinational, Monsanto, developed a seed technology that resulted in higher crop yields. This was poorly received in Europe, largely because many EU citizens prefer natural food processes. In addition, the technology forced European farmers to order new seeds from Monsanto every year. In American eyes, EU resistance to GM imports was a pretext for refusing American companies access to European markets. The end result was a complaint filed by the USA in 2003 against the EU to the WTO, which ultimately took issue with both sides' arguments.

Influence

Trade can be used to influence an external partner's behaviour either defensively or proactively. During the 2000s, one example of the former approach came when several partners (including the EU) signed preferential trade agreements with Afghanistan offering farmers incentives to grow crops other than opiate poppy seeds. The aim here was to reduce international drugs trafficking. A more proactive approach might be exemplified by the French Socialist Party's 2012 manifesto demand that EU member states be allowed to levy tariffs on imports from other countries lacking certain labour and environmental standards. The goal here was to create a level playing field preventing Europe's trading partners from benefiting competitively from the fact that they did not have to finance the same costly welfare systems as Europeans do.

Sanctions

Governments usually restrict trade with governments, investment funds, or MNEs from countries with whom they entertain a hostile relationship. Examples include many Arab countries' boycott of Israeli goods due to political tensions in the Middle East, the US government's blockade of Cuba, or EU and US threats against Iran because of its nuclear enrichment programme.

Tools of intervention

Some of the tools that states use to influence international business (such as import quotas and anti-dumping provisions) target trade specifically. Others, like ownership restrictions, apply to FDI. Lastly, some intervention tools, such as subsidies and macro-economic policies, are more general in nature and affect the economy as a whole.

Trade tools

The main distinction for government intervention in trade is whether the foreign partner must pay a sum of money and/or be subject to administrative controls.

Tariffs

Tariffs (or 'customs duties' that companies pay to the government on foreign goods) are usually assessed as a percentage of a shipment's value—that is, on a so-called *ad valorem* basis. However, they can also be 'specific' and represent a lump sum for a given physical quantity of goods. Governments often try to improve their country's terms of trade by levying higher tariffs on processed goods (i.e. whose transformation has advanced further along the value chain). This also has the effect of not penalizing domestic industries that import more basic goods. For instance, tariffs on finished goods like shoes are usually higher than on raw materials like leather.

+ Tariffs
Taxes that governments levy on goods (usually imports) when they cross national borders.

By artificially raising the price of foreign goods, import tariffs affect consumer preferences. Historically, they have also been the main tool that governments use to intervene in the trade arena. In March 2011, for instance, Ukraine imposed additional excise taxes on distilled spirit imports from its neighbour and fellow WTO member, Moldova. When a complaint was made to the WTO Dispute Settlement Body (see Chapter 4), countries ranging from China to Colombia and the USA added their names to the case to increase the pressure on Ukraine.

Non-tariff barriers

Higher oil prices in 1973 raised national energy import costs worldwide and sparked a wave of protectionist sentiment. Obliged by their General Agreement on Trade and Tariffs (GATT) commitments to keep import tariffs low (see Chapter 4), many countries started looking for other intervention tools. The end result was the development of a series of non-tariff barriers (NTBs), led by quantitative restrictions (QRs), standards, and anti-dumping provisions.

- *QRs.* There are two main variants of quantitative restrictions: voluntary export restraints (VERs) and import quotas. VERs refer to one country's agreement to limit the volume and/or value of its exports to another country, usually to avoid the kind of hostile response that can arise when a domestic market is dominated by foreigners. This tool was famously used by the USA during the 1970s to persuade Japan to reduce exports. Japanese companies' growing share of the American car market had destroyed jobs in the USA and caused much resentment. Japan's VER policy was one way to prevent Washington from taking more drastic measures. A similar case from 2007 was when China voluntarily cut steel exports to the USA to reduce tensions with its main trading partner.

Quotas specify the maximum quantity of a good that a country is prepared to import (or occasionally export). Volumes are usually agreed in licensing arrangements that, under WTO regulations, must be transparent and non-discriminatory. Note that under the rules that used to apply before the WTO was founded in 1995, LDCs were permitted to apply QRs or other non-tariff measures if they needed to protect infant industries (Hoekman and Kostecki 2001). Whether developing countries should be afforded special treatment remains a key topic in debates about state intervention in trade.

By restricting the supply of foreign goods, both VERs and import quotas increase the price that consumers pay. Higher prices mean extra revenue for the foreign producer selling the goods. On the other hand, when import tariffs are applied, it is the domestic government that collects the surcharge, in the form of taxes collected as the goods enter the country. In this sense, tariffs are a more effective way of protecting national interests than quotas.

Standards. Where consumer health is at stake, governments often require scientific evidence that a product is safe. Problems arise when one country accuses another of misusing controls to disguise its protectionist intent. One example is the debate over whether countries with tough environmental legislation should be allowed to restrict imports of goods produced using a lower standard. In 1998, for instance, the WTO rejected a US ban on the import of shrimp caught in nets that harm sea turtles. Attitudes have changed since then, however, and it is increasingly acceptable to the WTO for countries to prohibit products manufactured in a less environmentally friendly manner. A basic question for many states is whether economic issues should be prioritized over other concerns (see Chapter 8).

Governments sometimes apply technical standards that have no health implications but reflect national interests. One example is a German law (*Reinheitsgebot*) that was used to prevent foreign breweries from calling their exports to Germany 'beer' until the EU ruled in 2004 that this comprised disguised protectionism. Along similar lines, the International Organization for Standardization (ISO) tries to harmonize national quality regimes by providing guidelines that companies worldwide can use to audit internal performance (see Chapter 11). It is sometimes hard to detect whether import standards are a protectionist tool or an honest attempt to ensure quality and/or protect public health.

+ **Dumping**
Where exporters sell goods at a loss or below the normal price to gain market share and put rivals out of business.

Anti-dumping provisions. Businesses can try to gain market share by dumping goods at artificially low prices. The problem is determining whether imports are cheap because foreign producers have manipulated prices or simply manufactured more competitively. Governments that accuse foreign producers of dumping will often levy a fine—one example from 2011 being penalties that the EU levied on coated fine paper imported from China, accused of selling at below-market rates. The frequency with which countries accuse one another of dumping raises suspicions that many such fines hide protectionist intent.

Lastly, note that some NTBs are administrative in nature. These include product labelling or place-of-origin requirements, as well as assorted bureaucratic controls.

FDI tools

An increasing number of intervention tools specifically target MNEs' overseas subsidiaries. This trend reflects FDI's growing role in global economic activity.

Performance requirements

Governments impose conditions on MNE subsidiaries for various reasons. Sometimes the purpose is to monitor how state aid is being used. On other occasions, it is to control foreign subsidiaries' behaviour locally, often to ensure that their actions improve the host country's balance of trade. The main performance requirements are:

- *Local contents ratios.* This means that a minimum percentage of the value of the goods being sold has to involve components sourced from local manufacturers. For instance, to benefit from preferential tariffs, at least 40 per cent of the value of goods (re-)exported from the Association of Southeast Asian Nations (ASEAN) zone must be manufactured in a member state.

- *Dividend repatriation restrictions.* These are limits that are sometimes placed on the quantity of money that an MNE can take out of a country in the form of dividends. Similarly, there is often an assumption that MNE subsidiaries will reinvest some of their profits. The failure to do so can create angry reactions, as Spanish oil producer Repsol YPF learnt when the Argentine government threatened to revoke its drilling licences because of dissatisfaction with the company's local investment policies (Webber and Johnson 2012).

- *Technology transfers.* Here the goal is to ensure that MNEs bring knowledge into the host country and/or undertake a modicum of research locally.

- *Employment measures.* These are initiatives aimed at accelerating local recruitment, improving domestic pay scales, or enhancing worker training.

Many neo-liberal opponents of government intervention particularly dislike performance requirements, which they accuse of being a vehicle for politicizing FDI decisions that they think should be made by market participants alone. During the 1990s, one notable effort to disband performance requirements involved a controversial proposal by the OECD called the Multilateral Agreement on Investment (MAI), which would have harmonized the global deregulation of FDI and allowed MNEs to sue any state whose interventionism cost them money. Many non-governmental organizations (NGOs) viewed MAI as an attack on national sovereignty, and the proposal was ultimately shelved in 2000. Subsequently, the WTO developed a similar proposal called Trade Related Investment Measures (TRIMs), although this also encountered serious opposition (see Chapter 4). Performance requirements are strongly supported by those who argue that, without such protections, FDI-related gains would benefit MNEs more than host countries. Because FDI penetrates host economies more deeply than trade does, it also causes greater suspicion.

Ownership restrictions

As Chapter 9 will discuss, national governments often have good reason to try to ensure that domestic interests have an equity stake in MNEs' local units, with studies showing that strong local ownership helps to ensure that FDI-related productivity gains spread more widely through the host economy (Marcin 2008). Ownership restrictions can range from limiting foreign stakes in local ventures to the nationalization of MNE subsidiaries. Similarly, in many countries the FDI environment is shaped by competition regulators whose role is to ensure that foreign interests do not abuse a dominant position. An interesting source of information in this area is the OECD's 'FDI Regulatory Restriction Index' (http://www.oecd.org/), whose 2012 study found, for instance, that China was the sample's most restrictive country and Luxembourg the least. Policies of this sort are usually justified by alleging the desire to protect domestic competition. Often enough, however, the real goal is to protect domestic competitors.

General intervention tools

This category, referring to actions affecting the economic environment within a particular host country, is comprised of domestic initiatives that have international repercussions.

Subsidies

The most common variety of trade-related subsidies involves direct payments to domestic exporters and/or producers operating in sectors exposed to foreign competition. One example from year-end 2011 was when the US Congress decided to stop paying subsidies to domestic farmers to help them compete against cheap ethanol imports from Brazil. A second category of subsidies is comprised of loans or insurance offered to exporters at preferential rates.

Subsidies enabling uncompetitive companies to stay alive are deemed to be market-distorting. They are a cause of much conflict in international business—as exemplified in 2012 by the angry reaction by many solar panel manufacturers worldwide to the subsidies that Chinese authorities were paying to local manufacturers with interests in this sector.

Figure 3.7
Summary of some
of the ways that
governments intervene
in trade and FDI.

Government tool	Examples
Tariffs	*Ad valorem* or specific duties
Non-tariff barriers	Quantitative restrictions, standards
Anti-dumping	Retaliatory measures
Performance requirements	Local contents, dividend repatriation
Ownership restrictions	Joint ventures, (re-)nationalizations
Subsidies	Cash payments, preferential terms
Macro-economic policy	Fiscal, monetary, and currency actions

This ultimately led to China eliminating some of these support mechanisms. Had it not done this, foreign governments might have started levying fines on Chinese solar panel exporters to reduce their advantage. Penalties of this kind, called 'countervailing duties', are meant to restore a semblance of fairness to markets. The complication is that in some situations—for instance, where infant industries are involved—it can be argued that subsidies are actually needed to re-establish a level playing field.

Macro-economic policy

A country's trading position is also affected by its general economic policies. Thus, tax systems can be used to shift domestic demand towards home-made products (for instance, by raising VAT on goods that the country traditionally imports). Governments can establish 'free trade zones' (see Chapter 11) allowing domestic firms to import components destined for re-exportation on a tax-free basis. Interest rates can be raised or lowered, respectively, to reduce demand when the country has a trade deficit and needs to consume less, or increase demand when it has a trade surplus and can afford to consume more. Countries can keep currency rates artificially low to facilitate exports, or set them artificially high to reduce the price of imports. Many national economic decisions are taken with an eye on the international business outcomes that will also result from them.

Governments can also set up a variety of targeted competitiveness schemes. Examples include state-sponsored workforce training programmes aimed at developing national capabilities in a particularly promising export sector; payroll tax relief to help export-oriented companies; preferential treatment for domestic companies bidding on public procurement contracts; and export assistance packages specifically targeting local small and medium-sized enterprises (SMEs). Few countries in the world will enact policy without giving at least some consideration to its international effects.

Challenges and choices

→ It can be very difficult for MNE executives to calculate how much leeway they have when negotiating with a host country. The answer largely depends on the extent to which the company needs the country or vice versa. If managers perceive the country as being crucial to their internationalization plans, they will tend to show greater flexibility. Conversely, where a particular location is important to them, they might drive a harder bargain to get better market entry conditions. This latter approach is often constrained by ethical considerations. It is bad for a company's reputation to be seen as bullying a host government, especially where a developing country is involved.

Chapter summary

The chapter's first section was concerned with the question of whether states have lost their power to control their economic environment. After reviewing arguments that some aspects of modern globalization—such as global governance, technology, and deregulated finance —have weakened national governments, the counter-argument was presented, suggesting that they still retain significant power. This was based on the continued importance of domestic business, the rise of economic patriotism, and states' important roles as tools of international competition.

After detailing some of the main internal and external reasons why states continue to intervene in international business, the second section then reviewed the different instruments that they use. The main distinction at this level was between trade-related tools, which tend to be divided into tariffs and non-tariff barriers; FDI tools, largely relating to ownership restrictions; and general tools, often coming in the shape of macro-economic policy.

Case study 3.3

States and their protective role: *Vive la différence*

France's protectionist reputation is not entirely justified, given the open border policies that this key EU member state implements. In addition, many of the companies operating in France are foreign-owned—not to mention that power of foreign investors to influence prices on the Paris stock exchange.

Yet the reputation does exist and not entirely without reason. For centuries, French national leaders have pursued what is commonly referred to as a *colbertiste* policy of strong state intervention in both domestic and international business. In recent decades, this has been expressed through opposition by both conservative and progressive parties to what the French commonly refer to as 'Anglo-Saxon' capitalism, or the free-trade, neo-liberal approach that advocates letting market forces alone to dictate economic processes. One example is the global market for culture products (film, music, etc.). French

authorities started to become concerned a few decades ago that the growing global domination of English-language products might undermine France's long and proud heritage as a cultural force. The consensus in favour of protecting domestic artists ultimately led in the early 1990s to Culture Minister Jack Lang successfully negotiating a 'cultural exception' (*exception culturelle*) waiver exempting French cinema, music, and TV production from the kinds of restrictions that the WTO normally places on state aid. Instead, France follows a different set of rules (see Figure 3.8) ensuring that some of the receipts from any cultural activity taking place on national territory, i.e. when people go to watch Hollywood blockbusters, are recycled in the form of subsidies for French artists, whose outlets are further protected by a quota system forcing broadcasters to offer minimum thresholds of national output. The end result is that unlike many other similarly sized

Domain	*Exception culturelle* policies
Radio	At least 40 per cent of all songs played must be French in origin
TV	At least 45 per cent of all programmes broadcast must be French in origin
Cinema	Revenues from tax levied on cinema tickets are used to fund domestic productions
Language	Public posters must contain French translations

Figure 3.8
Cultural protectionism in France.

(or even larger) countries, France's cultural production continues, in quantitative terms at least, to punch above its weight.

Recent French business history also abounds with examples of protectionism. There is the country's decades-long unwillingness to permit any significant reform of the EU's Common Agricultural Policy, which subsidizes French farmers but places a huge burden on the EU budget. Then in 2000, at a time when the banking sector was experiencing a wave of cross-border takeovers as companies tried to maximize their global presence, the French state preferred to broker a merger between two domestic banks (BNP and Paribas) to ensure continued national control. This was followed in 2003 by the French government's formal categorization of 14 sectors as 'strategic', meaning that foreign shareholders would no longer be allowed to take a controlling share of companies operating in certain areas. This measure was not unprecedented, with other countries having adopted similar policies in relation to clearly strategic industries like energy—although even in this sector, it was remarkable that France used its new powers to prevent

Italian energy company ENEL from taking over French consortium Suez only a few years after Electricité de France had acquired the Italian utility Montedison. What was striking about the new 'strategic list' was that it also included Danone, a food processing company that the French government protected from being taken over by PepsiCo, the American soft drinks maker. Decisions of this kind reflect the general support in France for *intelligence économique*, best translated as industrial espionage. Figures such as conservative Member of Parliament Bernard Carayon have built an entire media career around the idea that economics is a war that companies wage on governments' behalf. In this view, it becomes legitimate to adopt any means necessary to advance national economic interests, even if this involves bending international trade rules.

The crises of 2008 and 2011–2012 did nothing to change the French approach, quite the contrary. Having learnt that it is dangerous to restrict trade during times of reduced economic activity (a policy that had worsened the Great Depression of the 1930s), most heads of state pledged this time around to avoid the temptation of protectionism. Yet once again, French leaders on both sides of the political spectrum showed an entirely different sensitivity. In 2009, for instance, conservative president Nicolas Sarkozy announced that he would only provide additional loans to French automaker Renault if the company promised to close a plant it was operating in Slovenia to move production back home. Two years later, the French Socialist Party declared that if its candidate, François Hollande, were to win the 2012 presidential election (which he ultimately did), it would require that labour, environmental, and other standards be built into world trade rules, failing which it would try to increase import tariffs on non-European partners lacking such standards (Taylor 2011). Whether this is analysed as a new form of mercantilism or simply as common sense in re-establishing a level playing field, there can be no doubt that in terms of the relationship between globalization and state power, France continues to march to the beat of its own drum.

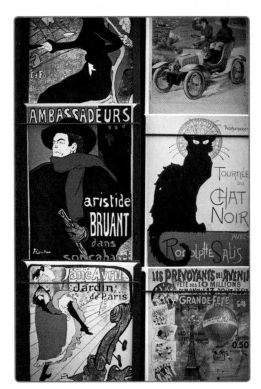

France has a tradition of state intervention in most sectors of activity, including cultural production

Source: Photodisc

Case study questions

1. To what extent can a country like France be called protectionist when it practises open border policies in so many different areas?
2. What is the basis for many French politicians' rejection of pure free trade?
3. Should France be criticized for its economic patriotism?

Discussion questions

1. Is the rising power of international business a good or bad thing for democracy?

2. Advocating the union of all human interests, musician John Lennon once asked people to 'imagine there's no countries'. Is this an attractive or realistic prospect?

3. To what extent should, and can, a political economic system that succeeds in one country become a model for another?

4. Buckman (2004) has alleged that globalization is similar to communism in so far as it concentrates power in fewer hands. Is this a reasonable assertion?

5. Which sectors of business activity might national governments find easier or less easy to control? Why?

Online resource centre

Go online to test your understanding by trying multiple-choice questions, and assignment and examination questions.

Further research

Engelen, E., Ertürk, I., Froud, J., Johal, S., Leaver, A., Moran, M., Nilsson, A., and Williams, K. (2011). *After the Great Complacence: Financial Crisis and the Politics of Reform*. Oxford: Oxford University Press

This challenging analysis of particular features of the contemporary capitalist economy in Britain, the USA, and Western Europe raises questions about the relationship between the financial system and politics, what kind of control elected governments have over the financial markets, and the role that elite and non-elite citizens play in operating and regulating these markets.

Bremmer, I. (2010). *The End of the Free Market: Who Wins the War Between States and Corporations*? New York: Viking

The rise of state-owned firms in China, Russia, the Arab states of the Persian Gulf, Iran, Venezuela, and elsewhere exemplifies how state capitalism challenges the global economy's current neo-liberal form.

References

Ayres, J. and Bosia, M. (2011). 'Beyond global summitry: Food sovereignty as localized resistance to globalization', *Globalizations*, 8/1 (February)

Bauman, Z. (1998). *Globalization: The Human Consequences*. New York: Columbia University Press

Bharee, M. (2011). 'India unlocks doors for global retailers', 25 November, available at http://online.wsj.com, accessed 11 June 2012

Buckman, G. (2004). *Globalization: Tame it or Scrap it*. London: Zed Books

Chakrabortty, A. (2011). 'What JCB's yellow digger tells us about our manufacturing malaise', *The Guardian*, G2, 8 February, p. 5

Chin, G. (2010). *China's Automotive Modernization: The Party-State and Multinational Corporations*. London: Palgrave Macmillan

CIA (2012). 'The World Factbook', available at http://www.cia.gov/, accessed 11 June 2012

Economist (2011). 'Less paper, more iron', 7 July, available at http://www.economist.com, accessed 9 October 2011

El-Ojeili, C. and Hayden, P. (2006). *Critical Theories of Globalization*. Basingstoke: Palgrave Macmillan

Friedman, T. (2000). *The Lexus and the Olive Tree*. New York: Anchor Books

Garside, J. (2011). 'Vodafone may have thrown away £12bn in Indian venture', *The Guardian*, 21 November, p. 26

Held, D. and McGrew, A. (2002). *Globalization/Anti-Globalization*. Cambridge: Polity Press

Hibou, B. (2004). *Privatising the State*. London: Hurst and Company

Hirst, P. and Thompson, G. (1999). *Globalization in Question*. Cambridge: Polity Press

Hoekman, B. and Kostecki, M. (2001). *The Political Economy of the World Trading System*, 2nd edn. New York: Oxford University Press

Kelly, D. and Grant, W. (2005). 'Introduction: Trade politics in context', in Kelly and Grant (eds.). *The Politics of International Trade in the Twenty-First Century: Actors, Issues and Regional Dynamics*. Basingstoke: Palgrave Macmillan

Kizito, J. (2010). 'Opinion: No economic patriotism today', 10 December, available at http://dispatch.ug/no-economic-patriotism-today/905/, accessed 27 December 2011

Kollewe, J. (2011). 'UK is second-largest buyer of foreign firms', *The Guardian*, 13 October, p. 34

Legrain, P. (2003). *Open World: The Truth about Globalization*. London: Abacus

Marcin, K. (2008). 'How does FDI inflow affect productivity of domestic firms? The role of horizontal and vertical spillovers, absorptive capacity and competition', *Journal of International Trade and Economic Development*, 17/1 (March)

Matelly, S. and Nies, S. (eds.) (2006). 'La Nationalité des enterprises en Europe', *La Revue internationale et stratégique*. Paris: Dalloz

Mathews, R. (2005). 'Free trade and an emerging revolutionary planet', 8 October, available at http://www.vivelecanada.ca, accessed 14 December 2007

McDonald, H., Elliott, L., and Treanor, J. (2010). 'Ireland takes hardline stance on corporation tax as bailout talks begin', 18 November, available at http://www.guardian.co.uk, accessed 11 April 2012

OECD—Organization for Economic Cooperation and Development (2011). 'Revenue statistics', available at http://www.oecd.org/, accessed 25 December 2011

Ohmae, K. (2005). *The Next Global Stage: The Challenges and Opportunities in Our Borderless World*. Upper Saddle River, NJ: Wharton School Publishing

Papaioannou, T. (2006). 'Towards a critique of the moral foundations of intellectual property rights', *Journal of Global Ethics*, 2/1 (June)

Rivoli, P. (2006). *The Travels of a Shirt in the Global Economy*. Hoboken, NJ: John Wiley and Son

Scherer, A. and Palazzo, G. (2011). 'The new political role of business in a globalized world: A review of a new perspective on CSR and its implications for the firm, governance, and democracy', *Journal of Management Studies*, 48/4, pp. 899–931 (June)

Sitkin, A. (2011). *Principles of Ecology and Management: International Challenges for Future Practitioners*. Oxford: Goodfellow Publications

Strange, S. (1997). *The Retreat of the State: The Diffusion of Power in the World Economy*. Cambridge: Cambridge University Press

Talamo, G. (2011). 'Corporate governance and capital flows', *International Journal of Business in Society*, 11/3, pp. 228–243

Taylor, P. (2011). 'France flirts with Euro-protectionism', 18 April, available at http://uk.reuters.com, accessed 21 December 2011

Wachman, R. (2008). 'Kremlin leaves BP shaken, but it won't stir', *Observer*, 6 June, Business and Media section, p. 7

Webber, J. and Johnson, M. (2012). 'Argentina hits out at Repsol YPF', *Financial Times*, 27 February, p. 23

Woods, N. (2004). 'Order, globalization and inequality', in D. Held and A. McGrew (eds.). *The Global Transformations Reader: An Introduction to the Globalization Debate*. Cambridge: Polity Press

Wright, R. (2011). 'Bombardier loses out to Siemens on train order', *Financial Times*, 16 June, available at http://www.ft.com, accessed 2 October 2011

4 Global frameworks

Learning objectives

After reading this chapter, you will be able to:

✦ distinguish between different kinds of regional associations

✦ critique the Bretton Woods organizations' methods and performance

✦ analyse the relevance of single purpose intergovernmental organizations

✦ judge the efficiency of the international finance system's current architecture

Case study 4.1

Defining the capacities of a regional association: A good plumber is hard to find

In its biggest enlargement move ever, the EU accepted ten new members in 2004, mostly from the Continent's ex-communist East. The path followed by these countries since the Second World War had failed to afford them the standard of living that their Western neighbours enjoyed. Their hope was that joining the EU would help them to catch up. What was less certain was how this integration would affect the older EU states.

The prospect of tens of thousands of young East European immigrants sparked an emotional debate in the West. The French prime minister expressed concern that the EU's proposed Bolkestein Directive, which would have let foreigners operate under their home countries' less stringent labour laws, might put host country workers and contractors at a disadvantage. In France, commentators stoked fears that hordes of 'Polish plumbers' would take up to one million French jobs and undermine the country's long-standing social model, characterized by its generous but expensive welfare system. A media panic erupted, leading in May 2005 to French rejection of a constitutional referendum aimed at modernizing EU operating procedures. The vote was a defeat for European integration and Bolkestein was quietly sidelined.

Organizational enlargement is a difficult process requiring major efforts to satisfy existing members' concerns. In summer 2005, the Polish government sponsored humorous advertisements showing a handsome plumber inviting people to visit Poland. The point was to remind French society that it too might benefit from the new EU members. The situation gradually calmed down, especially once it became clear that mass migration to France was not going to take place. Between May and November 2006, French authorities received a mere 10,165 residency requests from Eastern bloc workers (RTL 2006). This was much lower than expected and reflected developments keeping Polish workers at home, like the country's growing role as an outsourcing destination for many multinational banks' administrative operations (Wilkinson 2007). Ultimately, by mid-2008 the French population was sufficiently reassured for the government to lift any restrictions on the immigration of Polish workers. Nor was this measure followed by an accelerated emigration of Poles to France, with Germany and the UK remaining their preferred destinations. The end result was that unlike the UK, where accusations of Poles taking 'British jobs' received a wide airing from politicians, Eastern Europeans were barely mentioned in the run-up to France's 2012 presidential election. At one level, this reflected the French population's greater acceptance of the EU. At another, it translated people's relief that EU enlargement had had less of an effect than they originally feared.

Advertising Poland to the French: a good plumber is hard to find!
Source: ONT Pologne

Case study questions

1. Why did so many French fear the arrival of a Polish workforce in France?
2. What are the prospects over the next few years for the regional migration of professional workers within the EU?

Introduction

Over the years, it has become increasingly apparent that the only way of addressing many of the problems facing MNEs is by developing an international regime capable of defining the cross-border framework within which international business takes place. The impossibility of resolving certain issues at a domestic level explains why national governments are increasingly transferring some of their sovereign prerogatives to international bodies. The usual way of categorizing these bodies is by differentiating between regional associations (RAs) that neighbouring countries create to coordinate interests in their part of the world; intergovernmental organizations (IGOs) empowered by member countries to assume governance functions in specific policy areas; and international systems (led by the global financial markets) requiring global coordination. This chapter reviews these three categories in turn.

The new cross-border framework has been very successful in many respects, contributing to the explosion in trade volumes in recent decades. In particular, IGOs such as the World Trade Organization (WTO) have become major players on the international business stage, serving as forums for debate and policy coordination, and offering an efficient vehicle for counterbalancing MNEs' growing power (see Chapter 3). The same can be said about RAs, which often serve a coordinating function, enabling neighbouring governments to create a mutually agreed framework for international business.

However, there have also been many problems with this architecture of power, often because once IGOs are established, they do not always operate in line with their original mission or member states' current interests. A prime example is the debate surrounding the usefulness of the world's leading multi-purpose IGO, the United Nations (**see ORC Extension material 4.1**). In addition, there are entire areas of cross-border policy that remain insufficiently controlled , first and foremost the environment (see Chapter 16) and the global financial system. Thus, even as some observers criticize IGOs' rising powers, others argue that they are not yet powerful enough.

> Go online

Section I: Regional associations

+ **Regional association (RA)**
Cooperation between neighbouring countries in building an institutional platform where issues of mutual interest can be discussed and decided.

The general term 'regional association' (RA) can refer to anything from loose arrangements where neighbouring countries have agreed to simply debate specific issues, to highly integrated bodies like the EU, which has been transferred the power to manage entire areas of policy-making. RA member states are necessarily geographically close to one another. This is one key characteristic distinguishing them from other IGOs.

Forerunners of RAs have existed for centuries. Many earlier versions involved a central imperial power imposing its will on a zone's weaker periphery (for example, Turkey's Ottoman Empire dominating the states it administered or the French dominion in Northern Africa). Friendlier arrangements, like the late nineteenth-century *Zollverein* (Customs Union) between independent German states, were few and far between. It is only recently that the world has witnessed voluntary RAs involving neighbours and trading partners promoting similar values and purposes.

One of the main factors driving modern RAs is the sense that economies that organize their division of labour along regional rather than national lines tend to suffer less protectionism on the part of neighbouring trading partners. They also enjoy higher inwards investment (Davis 2011) and, as long as trade diversion effects are not too strong, generally higher productivity, largely because companies are forced to hone their skills in a larger, hence more competitive, environment. Learning effects are also particularly strong with MNEs increasingly innovating along regional lines today (see Chapter 11) largely because this helps

+ **Trade diversion**
When imports come from less efficient producers located within an RA instead of from more efficient outside producers.

Advantages of RA membership	Disadvantages of RA membership
Raises efficiency: work allocated in a way that reflects members' particular advantages	Possibility of 'trade diversion'
Corporate innovation increasingly developed on a regional basis	Some MNEs become overly dependent on regional linkages and neglect global prospects
Products sold across bigger markets	Increased competition for jobs
Greater currency stability	Loss of national sovereignty
Poorer members' living standards might converge with wealthier neighbours	Division of labour benefits some members but may be disadvantageous to others
Peaceful relations	Domination of larger member states

Figure 4.1
Advantages and disadvantages of joining a regional association.

them to develop technology on a larger scale (Cantwell and Iammarino 2011). The regional level is also more manageable than the global and, as Chapter 5 discusses, there is strong evidence that most MNEs have a stronger presence in their home region than globally. Yet by definition, RAs also offer lesser economies of scale than global business. One explanation, for instance, for Mexico and Central American companies' lesser performance compared with their Chinese and Indian rivals is that the former group is too closely tied to the fortunes of the USA alone, whereas China and India have developed relationships worldwide (Sturgeon and Biesebroeck 2011; Frederick and Gereffi 2011).

In political terms, regions constitute an intermediary level of governance between global and national policy-making. The proliferation of RAs is due partly to the changing definition of national sovereignty in today's increasingly globalized world (see Chapter 3). With MNEs increasingly integrating their global supply chains, and given how easy it has become for investors to shift funds everywhere, national borders are penetrated more easily than ever. Since decisions taken abroad affect many domestic outcomes, governments are finding that they must carry out more and more of their traditional functions on a wider regional scale. The extent to which they transfer sovereignty will depend on numerous factors, primarily the degree to which their local RA integrates member states into a single entity (see Figure 4.2), something that can vary in both time and place. It should also be noted that, in some parts of the world, a country can belong to more than one RA at a time.

Least integrated
↓

Preferential trading area: where countries decide to eliminate some barriers to trade with one another; implemented via trade pacts (e.g. EU–ACP agreements)

Free trade area: where countries decide to eliminate most barriers to trade with one another; there is no common external tariff, however (e.g. NAFTA)

Customs union: free trade area where members have also adopted a common tariff on goods from outside the region (e.g. ASEAN)

Common market: customs unions where members have also implemented a free movement of capital and labour (e.g. Mercosur)

Single market: common market whose members have also pooled many of their government functions, including tax policies; member states might pursue a joint monetary policy (e.g. European Union)

Currency union: single market whose members also share a single currency and therefore coordinate monetary policy (e.g. Eurozone)

↓
Most integrated

Figure 4.2
Regional associations range from loose pacts to fully integrated unions. The loosest tend to focus on trade matters alone, with the most integrated encompassing all kinds of policy areas.

RAs in Europe

The European Union (EU): http://europa.eu/index_en.htm

The world's most politically and economically integrated RA was founded in the 1950s. At the time, the EU's six founder members—France, Germany, Belgium, Holland, Luxembourg, Italy—had been trying to rebuild their economies after the Second World War while counterbalancing US and Soviet Russian power. The ambition to avoid future wars explains Europe's desire for an RA that is as tightly knit as possible. The EU's philosophy has always been that peace requires regional loyalties above and beyond national patriotism. Its remit is, therefore, much wider than a purely economic RA, and many of its bodies are endowed with supranational powers. This activism often leads to accusations that the EU's Brussels headquarters has become a giant, unaccountable bureaucracy. Yet it is precisely because so many citizens support European construction that the EU has been able to expand its competencies.

The EU has gone through many phases. One of the most crucial was its transformation from the EC common market to the more integrated EU single market. This happened in 1992 with the signing of the Maastricht Treaty, which paved the way for the 2002 introduction of a single currency throughout most of the region (called the Eurozone). Since its enlargement on 1 January 2007 to 27 member states, the EU has been home to nearly 500 million consumers. A huge organization with a wide range of bodies and total budget of around €100 billion, the EU is the biggest and most advanced RA in the world (see Figure 4.3). This also makes it difficult to please all members all of the time—one key example being the terrible problems that it was facing in 2012 when large budget deficits in Eurozone countries such as Greece and Italy combined with a loss of market confidence, created a financial crisis that, by common agreement, would only be overcome by closer coordination of member states' different fiscal policies. However, the idea of accelerating the political union, albeit logical, is not unanimously welcomed throughout the EU. Member states may want the benefits of belonging to a large regional association but are usually less enthusiastic about sharing the costs.

Lastly, the EU represents member states' interests at many global forums. This can involve negotiations with other OECD nations, like the dispute with the USA over the subsidies that the two powers have been paying to aeroplane manufacturers Airbus and Boeing,

The EU is the world's most advanced regional association

© European Union, 2011

Figure 4.3
Current and
prospective EU
member states (http://
europa.eu/abc/maps/).

European Commission

respectively. Other negotiations are with emerging powers such as China, occasionally rebuked by Brussels for trying to gain European market share by 'dumping' products at below-market prices (see Chapter 3). In addition, the EU often features at multilateral forums like the WTO, presenting a powerful, united front on behalf of its member states. The EU also regularly engages directly with MNEs operating on its territory, exemplified for instance by the total €161 million in antitrust fines levied, among others, against Whirlpool and Panasonic (respectively an American and a Japanese MNE) for allegedly fixing prices of refrigerator compressors (White 2011). Representing the combined interests of its member states, the EU is in a better position to bargain with MNEs than each individual government would be.

European Free Trade Association (EFTA): http://www.efta.int/

This loose association was comprised, as of November 2012, of Iceland, Liechtenstein, Norway, and Switzerland—European countries that have not sought to join the EU but need a body to organize their relations with it. Since June 1992, the EU and EFTA combined have been referred to as the European Economic Area.

RAs in Asia

Association of Southeast Asian Nations (ASEAN): http://www.aseansec.org/

The original aim of the newly decolonized less-developed countries (LDCs) that make up ASEAN was to encourage national development while preventing member states from interfering in each other's sovereign affairs. The mission changed radically over the years,

Practitioner insight

For more than 150 years, British bank Standard Chartered has been a global leader in trade finance. As part of this specialization, the company has developed a strong reputation for its mastery of international economics, with a firm focus on emerging markets. Within Standard Chartered's research group, LSE economics graduate Christine Shields runs the Country Risk Research section, a position that requires her to travel extensively to compile data and present reports.

'For many years preceding the 2011–2012 European sovereign debt crisis, we devoted substantial resources to Asia, Africa, and the Middle East, producing a "supercycle" report that analysed long-term development prospects for a world where economic power was shifting from the West to the East. But as Europe's problems worsened, I thought it important to explore the potential economic risks and the political implications for the European Union.

By mid-2011 we were witnessing the exhaustion of the slow recovery in European growth and trade that had followed the 2008–2009 recession. Purchasing managers' indices and economic confidence surveys pointed to a new downturn in the manufacturing and service sectors, especially in the continent's more peripheral economies, which were becoming less able to raise bank finance domestically and were increasingly dependent on European Central Bank (ECB) funding. This low growth problem aggravated the sovereign debt crisis that had been building up for a number of years. Our concern was that the combination of the two could not help but create political tensions, putting strain on the solidarity that is at the heart of the EU project.

There was the strong possibility of what we called "Euro-area scepticism" or "bailout fatigue". The fear here was that the Northern European countries with capital surpluses (led by Germany) could quickly lose sympathy for their Mediterranean partners, who had been pursuing much less rigorous policies. The risk would then have been that the creditor nations might decide not to fully fund the various bailout funds that had been created to help the debtor nations meet their payment schedules and avoid a chain reaction of bank failures that in turn would push the EU into deep recession or even depression.

We were also concerned about the possibility of "austerity fatigue" on Europe's periphery, with Greece, Italy etc. resisting the massive spending cuts that were the only way to stabilize their books. In this case, ECB support would have been insufficient, since the imbalances that had caused the deficits in the first place would have continued. In the absence of such austerity programmes, Germany's reluctance to let the ECB become the "lender of the last resort" and make good on all debts issued by Eurozone member states seemed logical in its anti-inflation mindset. The EU may be well integrated by comparison with other regional associations but it is far from unified like a single country. Indeed, there is a strong argument that it either has to achieve full fiscal union, with the political implications that would have, or the Euro will ultimately break up. In any event, the 2011–2012 crisis shows that the EU's current intermediate status cannot be sustained much longer.'

with ASEAN's 'Vision 2020' agenda targeting full-blown economic integration. One milestone in this transformation was the 1992 launch of the ASEAN Free Trade Area, whose purpose (according to the RA's website) is to enhance 'the region's competitive advantage as a single production unit'. Since 2010, most trade within the core group of ASEAN-6 countries (Brunei, Indonesia, Malaysia, Philippines, Singapore, and Thailand) has been subject to zero tariffs, with many non-tariff barriers (NTBs) having been eliminated entirely. Unsurprisingly, this has deepened the integration of member states' economies. Moreover, there is every chance that this process will accelerate in the years to come. In February 2009,

ASEAN leaders met to discuss their concerns over the particularly sharp fall in member states' industrial output as a result of the credit crunch. This was one consequence of the region's over-reliance on exports to non-ASEAN markets (the West but also China and Japan), all of which had been deeply affected by the crisis. The decision was made to place greater priority on trade within the RA, which up to that point had accounted for only one-quarter of members' exports. What had become apparent was the limits of the decades-long policy followed by Asia's newly industrialized countries (the so-called 'Tiger economies') of depending on external demand. Clearly, the time had come for a fuller development of their internal markets (see Chapter 15).

ASEAN+3

ASEAN summits regularly include extra meetings between the original six members and the region's three other economic powerhouses, China, Japan, and South Korea. The ASEAN+3 forum was created in response to the perceived need for a larger body representing regional interests following the 1997 currency crisis, which some Asian governments blamed on Western speculators. This is a regional grouping of nations that share certain cultural and philosophical affinities. It also reflects the rise in intra-Asian commerce, which now accounts for more than 50 per cent of all trade in this region. The purpose of ASEAN+3 is to give greater resonance to Asian ideas and interests. The region may lag behind Europe in terms of political integration, but it is one of the main drivers of the world economy and therefore understandably seeking a louder voice on the world stage.

Asian Pacific Economic Cooperation (APEC): http://www.apec.org/

This is a minimalist forum for voluntary economic cooperation. It is comprised of all major Pacific Rim economies (including the USA, Russia, and Australia), and characterized by informal arrangements rather than strict regulations. In the past, trade liberalization in the Asia–Pacific region was mainly done on a voluntary, unilateral basis, with countries often deciding individually whether to offer one another lower tariffs. APEC members do not have a common tariff on imports from outside the region, and each can negotiate deals with non-members as it sees fit. It is true that APEC's 1996 Bogor declaration had stated that the grouping's more industrialized members would try to cut internal tariffs to 5 per cent by the year 2010 (with LDC members doing the same by 2020) but progress has been unsatisfactory. In reality, APEC is little more than a forum to 'promote dialogue amongst the world's most dynamic economies' (Higgott 1998).

RAs in the Americas

North American Free Trade Agreement (NAFTA): http://www.nafta-sec-alena.org/

Founded on 1 January 1994, partly in reaction to the European integration process, NAFTA links Canada, Mexico, and the USA in a pact aimed at eliminating intra-regional tariffs on many types of products, especially consumer durables, textiles, and agricultural produce. Other goals include the relaxation of FDI restrictions (see Chapter 3, 'Performance requirements'); protection of intellectual property such as patents and trademarks; and creation of trade dispute mechanisms. What NAFTA does not seek are single tariffs on imports from outside the region. Nor does it allow the free movement of labour. Above all, it is not trying to become a single market, much less a replacement for national government.

NAFTA has succeeded in so far as intra-regional trade and FDI have risen, but it has also had a few less fortunate outcomes. By opening Mexico's food markets up to highly subsidized (and industrialized) American agribusiness interests, NAFTA has made life very

difficult for small Mexican farmers. This has had several consequences, including a rise in the number of displaced Mexican agricultural workers seeking employment in the USA. Secondly, many North American industries' supply chains now stretch south of the border to include low-cost Mexican *maquiladora* plants that import American components to assemble them on goods re-exported to the USA. This 'offshoring' and outsourcing movement has lowered production costs for many American companies and provided work for people in northern Mexico. At the same time, it has had a negative effect on many local labour markets in the USA and raised concerns that Mexico might become a 'pollution haven' for dirtier US industries (Ederington 2007). This explains why, when President Bill Clinton negotiated the original NAFTA agreement in the 1990s, he also drafted labour and environmental standards to deal with certain negative outcomes that almost inevitably arise when production is displaced from a wealthy nation to a poorer one. Whereas the consensus used to be that RAs will only succeed if member states have converged towards a similar level of socio-economic development, NAFTA presents an interesting case of an RA that associates advanced economies (the USA and Canada) with an LDC (Mexico). In this way, it reproduces within a regional framework the kind of cross-border relationships that have come to typify modern globalization. At a certain level, this is comparable to the hierarchy that now exists within the EU after it incorporated poorer Eastern European transition countries. Unlike the EU, however, NAFTA is not expected to have a major impact on people's lives. Indeed, tensions tend to heighten when this occurs.

Mercosur: http://www.mercosur.int/

In 1991, Brazil, Argentina, Uruguay, and Paraguay signed a treaty promoting free trade in goods and free circulation of persons. This was an attempt to counterbalance repeated US efforts to open Latin American markets, most recently via the so-called Free Trade of the Americas initiative. Mercosur has at best made slow progress towards economic integration, although there has been an acceleration over the course of the 2000s with the development of closer trade relations to the Andean Community (Bolivia, Colombia, Ecuador, and Peru), and with the 2004 launch of a South American Community of Nations (UNADOL), whose long-term ambition is to grow along EU lines.

Caribbean Community (CARICOM): http://www.caricom.org/

Replacing an old free trade agreement, CARICOM has the explicit goal of developing into a single market characterized by harmonized economic legislation and policy. This RA also seeks to fulfil wider, non-economic missions, including actions on sustainability, HIV/AIDS, and security. Given most member states' status as LDCs, CARICOM mainly exists to formulate a 'single development vision'.

RAs in Africa and elsewhere

African Economic Community (AEC): http://www.au.int/

This is an umbrella organization for the different regional economic communities to which African countries belong, sometimes with overlapping memberships. Driven by principles of unity, decolonization, and development, the AEC aims to advance towards full integration, although frequent conflicts have impeded progress. The most successful grouping at present is probably the Economic Community of West African States (ECOWAS), a common market characterized by harmonized economic policies, single external tariffs, and a joint currency, the Central African franc.

African, Caribbean, and Pacific states (ACP): http://www.acp.int/

This is a loose confederation of developing countries that have signed joint pacts with the EU (most recently, the 2010 revised Cotonou Agreement) to create preferential, low-tariff access to European markets for many agricultural and mining products. The ACP also tries to use development aid to foster price stability in the primary goods sectors that are so important to many of its members.

+ **Global governance**
Regulatory and supervisory functions fulfilled by authorities whose responsibilities exceed national borders.

> Go online

Section II: Single-purpose IGOs

There are hundreds of specialist IGOs today, each focusing on the global governance of a particular issue that cannot be dealt with sufficiently within a national framework (**see ORC Extension material 4.2**). In the field of international business, however, the most important IGOs are the three that came out of the 1944 Bretton Woods conference that set the architecture for today's post-Second World War international trade and finance regime (see Figure 4.4).

+ **Regime**
General system organizing interactions between different groups. Often refers to a system of regulations and the institutions that formulate and enforce them.

Bretton Woods institutions

Much research has been undertaken into the motivations underlying the birth of the WTO, the International Monetary Fund (IMF), and the World Bank. Analysts usually speak of participants' desire to avoid future tensions by creating coordinating IGOs where cross-border concerns could be discussed and decided in a transparent and friendly manner. This followed many countries' beggar-thy-neighbour response to the Great Depression of the 1930s, a protectionist stance that worsened the crisis by placing obstacles in the path of international business. It can therefore be argued that Bretton Woods applied and institutionalized a free trade, neo-liberal approach. Moreover, many voices have been raised over the years criticizing this orientation (Kelly and Grant 2005), accusing the three IGOs of consolidating the power of the older industrialized countries in general and the USA in particular (Drezner 2007). However, instead of commenting on the validity of these and

+ **'Beggar thy neighbour' policies**
Where one country manipulates its competitive position (i.e. via currency devaluations) to its trading partners' detriment.

Figure 4.4
Overview of the
Bretton Woods
organizations.

		World Trade Organization http://www.wto.org/	International Monetary Fund http://www.imf.org/external/index.htm	World Bank http://www.worldbank.org/
	Headquarters	Geneva	Washington DC	Washington DC
	Director (mid-2012)	Director-General Pascal Lamy (France)	Managing Director Christine Lagarde (France)	President Jim Yonk Kim (USA)
	Executive decisions by:	Consensus: one country, one vote (in reality, agenda set during 'Green Room' negotiations)	Executive Board: MD & 24 Directors representing countries or groups of countries. Votes weighted to reflect block 'quotas' (role in world economy)	Boards of Executive Directors: President plus 25 Members
	Staff numbers	640	2470	>10,000
	Key data 2011/2012	Operating budget: Swiss francs 196 million	Loans committed: ca. $285 billion	FY11 group new commitments: $57.4 billion

> Go online

other critiques of multilaterism encapsulated in the Bretton Woods organizations (**see ORC Extension material 4.3**), the following analysis will merely highlight their aims and actions.

The World Trade Organization (WTO)

The Bretton Woods conference had originally envisaged the creation of a strong International Trade Organization (ITO) with formal links to the IMF, the World Bank, and the International Labour Organization (ILO). When the US Congress decided in 1948 not to approve the ITO, what remained in the trade arena was the less ambitious GATT treaty. Unlike the ITO, the GATT had no links to other IGOs; did not seek to promote full employment (as the ILO did); and had an ineffective dispute settlement mechanism. It did, however, provide a loose framework for step-by-step reductions in quantitative tariffs on the cross-border flow of goods. Trade ministers from signatory nations would engage in targeted discussions called 'rounds' (see Figure 4.5). Any problems arising between sessions would be dealt with in ad hoc committees, meaning that the GATT did not have much of a

Figure 4.5
The main rounds of GATT and, since 1995, WTO meetings (BBC 2009).

Year(s)	Name of round	Main features
1948	Geneva	45,000 tariff concessions affecting $10 billion (around 20 per cent) of world trade; kick-started liberalization
1949	Annecy	5000 tariff concessions
1951	Torquay	8700 concessions, cutting 1948 tariff levels by 25 per cent
1955–1956	Geneva	$2.5bn in tariff reductions
1960–1962	Dillon	Concessions worth $4.9bn of world trade; negotiations about birth of European Economic Community
1964–1967	Kennedy	$2.5bn in tariff reductions; anti-dumping agreement
1973–1979	Tokyo	$300bn in tariff reductions; focus on non-tariff barriers
1986–1994	Uruguay	Agricultural subsidies cut, full access for LDC textiles, intellectual property rights extended; birth of WTO
2001–	Doha	Development agenda; deadlocked due to conflicts between advanced countries/LDCs

- There should be no discrimination in the world trade system

- A gradual, negotiated move towards open borders is intrinsically beneficial

- Trade decisions should be transparent and not arbitrary

- Competition is desirable as long as it is fair

- Trade should be used to encourage development and economic reform

Figure 4.6
The WTO's
fundamental beliefs.

permanent oversight function (Wilkinson 2006). On the other hand, this regime balanced the need for an open world economy with the sovereignty concerns that many countries had at the time—GATT had no 'supranational' mandate to interfere in domestic decision-making (Kelly and Grant 2005).

GATT weathered several storms, in particular the protectionist policies (like the wave of non-tariff barriers; see Chapter 3) that accompanied the global recession of the 1970s. By the 1980s, supporters of free trade were suggesting that a stronger body was needed. GATT's relatively modest remit meant that it did not cover several key international sectors, such as agriculture and textiles—areas of prime importance for many LDCs. Additionally, it had made so much progress in lowering tariffs that little more could be done. For some, this meant that it was time to move market deregulation on to a wider agenda that would include the trade in services, FDI, and intellectual property.

The Uruguay round of GATT negotiations concluded with the Marrakesh Agreement, which gave birth to the WTO on 1 January 1995. On its own website, the WTO defines itself as a negotiating forum; the embodiment of a set of rules; and a venue for settling disputes. Its functions are to administer WTO trade agreements; host trade negotiations; handle trade disputes; monitor national trade policies; offer technical assistance and training for developing countries; and cooperate with other international organizations. This is an extremely broad mandate. The WTO is the cornerstone of today's global trading regime (**see ORC Extension material 4.4**).

> Go online

In political terms, the WTO fights for free trade, which it equates with economic progress (see Figure 4.6). It is in no way a neutral body giving equal support to members' free trade and protectionist policies. Quite the contrary: it explicitly encourages the former and opposes the latter—a divide that causes deep-seated contradictions in its decision-making processes. On the one hand, the WTO requires consensus among members. On the other, it officially opposes any policies that run counter to its own 'neo-liberal' inclinations. This means that the WTO often enters into conflict with its own members. Hence its requirement that members accept its authority to judge any trading disputes that may arise. Acting simultaneously as lawmaker, judge, and police, the WTO has greater scope than most other IGOs.

At a technical level, five principles guide the WTO's actions:

1. *Most-favoured nation (MFN)*. If a WTO member grants favourable treatment (like lower tariffs) to goods made in one member state, it must offer the same preferences to all members. There are exceptions to this rule. First, regional free trade blocs (like the EU Single Market) can favour internal flows over extra-regional trade, even if the latter involves a fellow WTO member. Secondly, under certain circumstances, a country can offer LDC producers special access to its market. Lastly, some discrimination is allowed if the goods in question have suffered from unfair market practices (like 'dumping'). On the whole, however, the MFN arrangement facilitates exports by WTO members. It is usually the main reason why countries want to join this IGO.

2. *National treatment*. The WTO also specifies that members should strive to give similar treatment to all goods, regardless of whether they are produced locally or by a fellow member state. This acceptance of imports is the main price that a country pays to join the WTO and serves as a counterbalance to MFN. Together, the two principles are

what cement 'reciprocity' as a key WTO value, the idea being that any pain caused by WTO membership will be offset by gains. Note that some (mainly industrialized) countries have tried to get national treatment to apply also to services and copyrights/patents, the two 'new issues' that became part of the WTO agenda in the mid-1990s when interest rose in a General Agreement on Trade in Services (GATS) and Trade Related Aspects of Intellectual Property Rights (TRIPS).

3. *Fairness*. A common misunderstanding is that the WTO advocates free trade in all circumstances. In reality, there are situations (balance-of-payments crises, temporary surges in imports, unfair competition) in which it does tolerate countries adopting 'safeguard' protections. Conversely, the WTO will object when countries adapt barriers to trade that it considers 'unfair' or market-distorting.

4. *Special and Differentiated Treatment for LDCs*. Various WTO clauses recognize developing countries' special needs. As shown by philosopher Robert Nozick's 'time slices of history' theory (Singer 2004), establishing a single set of rules for everyone neglects the effects that a country's past has on its present capabilities. In this view, it is unfair to LDCs to force them to play by the same rules as the OECD countries, since the former cannot afford 'safety nets' (for example, welfare systems). When citizens of wealthy countries lose their job because of foreign competition, they can expect help until they find new employment—unlike LDC citizens. In a similar vein, very poor countries cannot even afford the capital equipment and technologies that they need to take advantage of the improved market access that is the main reason for joining the WTO. One of the ways in which Special and Differentiated Treatment materializes for LDCs is in the diffusion of a General System of Preferences (GSP) exempting them from MFN reciprocity requirements. The system's implementation has been patchy, however, with the world's advanced economies often setting up a GSP only in high value-added sectors where LDCs are hardly present, as opposed to the more commoditized sectors (such as steel, shoes, or textiles) where LDCs' price advantage makes them more competitive. It is true that a greater distinction is needed between the treatment of LDCs that are 'emerging' and those that are not. Understandably, OECD countries are 'reluctant to extend to China the special treatment they may grant to Cameroon' (Dadush and Nielson 2007). In general, the least straightforward (and most contentious) aspects of WTO governance are development-related.

5. *Dispute resolution*. WTO members who believe that they have suffered from unfair trade practices can make use of structured complaints processes. The hope is that they will turn to this facility instead of retaliating unilaterally against trading partners whom they believe have treated them badly. Parties are encouraged to come to out-of-court settlements, with only about one-third of all cases completing the Dispute Settlement panel process. For those cases (see Figure 4.7) that are judged, however, the panel's ruling is binding, unless a consensus agreement exists to reject it. Countries are expected to comply with Dispute Settlement rulings by ceasing the practice in question—although some continue and simply compensate the injured party for any damages suffered. For instance, for most of the 2000s the EU in general (and France in particular) preferred to pay a yearly fine of around $150 million rather than abandon its ban on US beef with excessive levels of growth hormones.

At a certain level, the WTO is a very useful tool. Its consensual decision-making process (one nation, one vote) should ensure that all participants, from the largest to the smallest, get a fair hearing. Its transparency commitments should promote good governance practices, shielding member states from powerful lobbies—only governments are authorized to negotiate at the WTO, and they are expected to argue for the interests of the nation as a whole. Lastly, its multilateral nature should mean less bullying by the world's more powerful states—one example being the way that the USA, out of fear of WTO condemnation, has more or less stopped resorting to the 'Special 301' unilateral trade retaliations that the country's 1974 Trade Act once allowed (Iida 2005).

Issue	Complainant
Measures Relating to the (Renewable Energy) Feed-in Tariff Program	EU (vs. Canada)
Taxes on Distilled Spirits	Moldova (vs. Ukraine)
Countervailing and Anti-dumping Measures on Certain Products	China (vs. USA)
Measures Affecting the Importation and Internal Sale of Goods (Environmental Change)	Ukraine (vs. Moldova)
Measures Affecting the Automobile and Automobile-Parts Industries	USA (vs. China)
Measures Prohibiting the Importation and Marketing of Seal Products	Norway/Canada (vs. European Communities)

Figure 4.7
Sample 2010–2012 disputes brought before the WTO Dispute Settlement Body (www.wto.org).

At the same time, the WTO remains the most contested of the major IGOs. Its ministerial conferences are usually accompanied by enormous protests. A few of the demonstrators may be indiscriminate critics of modern capitalism but, as ex-US President Bill Clinton pointed out in 1999 at the first major anti-WTO riots in Seattle, other critics have well-founded arguments. Like all governance bodies, the WTO is destined to evolve. Some argue in favour of empowering it to deal with non-trade-related matters. Others would simply change its agenda-setting process. Others still call for its dissolution. Given the current deadlock in the Doha Development Round, the future of this key IGO is very unclear.

Case study 4.2
The WTO's Doha deadlock

One motive underlying the WTO's foundation in 1995 was to expand the liberalization process beyond the cross-border trade in goods alone. International business not only involves physical products but also services, capital, and intellectual property. Supporters of free trade were looking to add these aspects to the policy areas that are subject to global governance. The problem is that each penetrates national economies to a different extent, and therefore provokes a different level of resistance.

One tool that the WTO and other intergovernmental organizations use to implement an agenda is the 'round' system. This starts with the identification of a policy goal (i.e. lower trade barriers). Officials working behind the scenes then negotiate a broad framework of agreement.

Finally, the document is publicly debated and hopefully ratified by political leaders, usually trade ministers. Many older industrialized countries tried this approach in 2001 when the WTO organized ministerial-level meetings at Doha, Qatar. Their goal was to introduce several policy frameworks: GATS; TRIMs; and TRIPs. The proposals were not entirely new, however, having been rejected at an earlier meeting in Singapore by the WTO's poorer member states. When the WTO raised them again and neither side changed position, the liberalization process ground to a halt.

The main criticism of the WTO was that it had turned into a tool for wealthy members alone. This argument was based on the WTO allowing Japan, the USA, and Europe to protect domestic agriculture while pushing a Doha agenda that advanced their interests alone. For instance, many developing countries that had opened their product markets to international trade continued to protect their banking sectors. GATS would have made this impossible and opened the way for Western MNEs to acquire local banks. TRIMs would have prevented government procurement projects from offering national companies preferential treatment, even though this is an important driver in many poor countries' development processes. Lastly, TRIPS seemed specifically designed to stop Indian and Brazilian pharmaceutical companies from taking market share away from Western MNEs. An intergovernmental organization that fights for some members but not others is destined to fail (Wilkinson 2006). The WTO organized other meetings

to try to repair Doha (Cancun 2003, Hong Kong 2005, and Potsdam 2007) but by 2011 commentators were pointing out that given fundamental differences in developed and developing countries' policies regarding import tariffs on manufactured goods, a decade of negotiations seem to 'have sharpened divisions, not smoothed them' (Economist 2011). The experience has been a lesson in the limitations of global governance.

Case study questions

1. Is the WTO right to be pushing the GATS, TRIMs, and TRIPS agenda?
2. Can the Doha Development Round be salvaged and, if so, how?

The International Monetary Fund (IMF) and the World Bank

The IMF is an international financial institution (IFI) specializing in crisis lending. Set up after the Second World War to revive the international financial system, it provides temporary funding, often at concessionary, below-market interest rates, to countries suffering from balance-of-payments problems. Its sister organization, the World Bank, whose original mission was to support European reconstruction, provides long-term funding, mainly to developing countries seeking to build up their infrastructure. Thus, the World Bank's actions are more strategic in nature, whereas the IMF has a much higher profile during times of crisis.

For the first few years of their existence, the two organizations fulfilled their missions in a flexible manner, adapting their aid packages and technical advice to suit borrowers' various needs. This changed in the 1980s when the IMF and World Bank adopted a 'one size fits all', approach requiring all prospective borrowers, regardless of their situation, to adopt the same 'structural adjustment'. As per Washington Consensus principles (see Chapter 3), this involved governments having to slash spending, including on social programmes, while opening their domestic financial markets up to international investors (Drezner 2007). The reason given for putting so many conditions on loans was the assumption that governments forced to seek external funding were necessarily guilty of mismanagement and needed to change their economic approach. The problem was that in many cases, the policies suggested by the IMF and the World Bank would have disastrous effects on recipient countries' poorer populations. This laid the IMF and World Bank open to angry accusations that their real aim was to ensure the 'hegemony of capitalism on a global scale' (Cammack 2003: 170); that they were anti-democratic (Woods 2004); and that, by imposing capital market liberalization on poor countries lacking sufficiently mature financial institutions, they were contributing to 'global instability [and] political chaos' (Stiglitz 2004). By the early twenty-first century, the IMF and World Bank had become figures of hate for many reformers.

In response, they started to modify their approaches. The first change was witnessed in 1999, when several lending packages were renamed 'Poverty Reduction and Growth Facilities'. This coincided with a new attitude towards borrowers, who, instead of being forced to adopt policies primarily aimed at solving short-term problems such as capital flows or trade deficits, were now being asked to focus on more structural problems, such as financial sector modernization (Gomel 2002). The World Bank also began experimenting in the early 2000s with what it called a more 'holistic' approach to financial intervention, adapting loan conditions to ensure a better fit with borrowers' specific needs. More emphasis was placed on the two bodies' advisory roles, focused on achieving improvements in debtor nations' monetary policies and banking systems. IMF and World Bank forecasts are key inputs in many countries' economic planning process. Even the fiercest of their critics now accept that they are priceless sources of information.

Subsequently, however, a new set of problems began to arise. Resentful at past interference and sitting on growing piles of cash following years of rapid export growth, the larger emerging countries began reimbursing all of their outstanding loans from the IMF and World Bank, which by 2007 had very few customers beyond a circle of highly indebted poor countries (HIPCs) largely incapable of repaying their debt. Even for these HIPC borrowers, funding from these two sources often paled in comparison with direct government aid (Weisman 2007) or loans from sovereign wealth funds (see Chapter 3). This was a time when questions were being raised about the IMF and World Bank's continued relevance. Oddly enough, the 2008 credit crunch served to restore their power, with a wide range of countries (not just HIPCs) being forced to turn to them (especially the IMF) for crisis funding. What remains to be seen is the shape that they will assume in the future to ensure their continued usefulness. In terms of technical advice, there is widespread agreement that the Bretton Woods IFIs possess a great deal of data and intellectual firepower that can serve in the formulation of national economic policy. In terms of funding, however, their importance will depend on the sums they can mobilize.

Member states are supposed to fund the IMF and the World Bank proportionately to their relative importance in the global economy. Voting rights are distributed along the same lines. The global hegemony of the USA at the time of the IMF birth was reflected in its very high initial share quota, but as of November 2012 the USA was down to 16.75 per cent of all voting rights. Yet this still exceeded the combined vote of Western Europe's three leading economies (Germany, France, and the UK, totalling 14.39), not to mention Japan (6.23) and China (3.81).

The USA's ongoing domination of the Bretton Woods organizations' governance appears an anomaly in an era when the country suffers from huge long-term capital deficits. This explains the common expectation that the IMF and World Bank's governance structures are destined for further reform in the future. An initial step consisted of the World Bank appointing a Chinese citizen (Professor Justin Yifu Lin) as chief economist for the first time ever in 2007. The idea is that a senior officer from a non-Western background would bring a new way of analysing economics and ensure policy-making that is more representative of the different economic philosophies found worldwide. The fact remains, however, that the IMF and the World Bank both continue to be run out of Washington DC and traditionally appoint, respectively, a Western European and a US citizen as their managing directors. This is out of tune with the changing geography of international business, since cash-rich emerging economies increasingly provide the financial resources that IGOs need to fulfil their missions and can, quite naturally, be expected to require greater say in the way such organizations are run. Seen in this light, reforming the Bretton Woods IFIs is not just desirable; it is crucial to their long-term survival.

Other specialist organizations

One way to categorize single-purpose IGOs is to distinguish between groups that represent specific sectors' interests and others that promote general policy frameworks. The former category is comprised of producer organizations fighting on behalf of specific sectors. The latter is comprised of ad hoc government associations, think tanks, lobbyists (see Chapter 5), NGOs (see Chapter 8), and international financial institutions.

Producer IGOs

These organizations exist to represent the interests of particular sectors engaged in international trade negotiations. Some struggle for legitimacy, accused by policy-makers of

Despite variations in local drilling conditions, oil prices tend to be determined globally based on OPEC policies

Source: Photodisc

+ **Cartel**
Group of producers that collaborate with one another on supply quantity and pricing decisions instead of competing.

+ **Oligopoly**
Market dominated by few sellers, who might therefore have a disproportionate power to collude outside the market framework and fix prices in a non-competitive manner.

+ **Debt relief**
Idea that poorest borrowers should not be asked to reimburse debt: because the original borrowings had been misused or embezzled; or because the borrower is too poor to pay.

behaving like cartels. Yet as Chapter 1 has shown, countries locked into the production of low value-added goods suffer if they cannot improve their terms of trade. One way to do this is by negotiating higher prices for the good(s) in which they specialize, either by reducing supply or by engaging in oligopolistic practices. This explains many African nations' long-standing support for the International Cocoa Association (ICA), which tries to keep cocoa-bean prices at a level that will provide farmers with sufficient income. The most successful example of this approach is the Organization for Petroleum Exporting Countries (OPEC), a key player in the global energy sector. OPEC's remarkable power derives largely from consumer nations' inability to reduce their dependency on this particular resource (Rose 2004). Producer IGOs representing so-called strategic sectors will always wield more power than ones specializing in less crucial activities.

Policy IGOs

G8/G20

Alongside the UN and the RAs, the main multi-purpose international organization is the G8, which is not so much an organization as an ad hoc body that exists to call regular meetings between the leaders of the world's most influential countries. In recent years, topics have ranged from debt relief and poverty in Africa to terrorism, climate change, energy, and food. In recent years, recurring financial crises have concentrated attention. For instance, in April 2009 an expanded forum called the G20 convened in London to discuss possible responses to the 'credit crunch' that was in the process of freezing the world's banking system. The general consensus at the time was that national responses to the global crisis (fiscal stimulus packages, re-regulation of the global banking system, repression of tax havens) could be effective only if designed and coordinated at the highest level. Three years later in May 2012, a G20 summit in Chicago discussed a coordinated response to Europe's sovereign debt crisis. The global economy is generally too integrated today for leaders in one part of the world to ignore the consequences of problems arising elsewhere.

Organization for Economic Cooperation and Development (OECD)

The OECD (http://www.oecd.org) was created in 1961 to represent the world's advanced economies and support free markets. Working out of its Paris headquarters, this IO uses its

Along with the Bretton Woods organizations, the G8 has come under increased public scrutiny in recent years

Source: iStock

enormous data resources to monitor all kinds of economic developments and produce analyses that it hopes will be taken up by policy-makers everywhere (and not just member states). As highlighted throughout this book, ideas are an important part of the international business framework. Thus, despite its lack of formal competencies, OECD does have some authority in so far as it influences people in power.

Financial IGOs

Sector-specific organizations include the international financial institutions (IFIs) that countries establish on a joint basis to conduct a certain number of banking activities. The IMF and the World Bank can be categorized in this way, as can regional development banks such as the European Bank for Reconstruction and Development (EBRD), the Inter-American Development Bank (IADB), and the Asian Development Bank (ADB). In recent decades, these entities have often been used to funnel aid or loans to emerging or transition economies—one example being the €32 million package that the EBRD, the European Investment Bank, and other IFIs, working on a combined basis, put together in March 2009 for East European banks caught up in the credit crunch. Also worthy of note is the Bank for International Settlements (http://www.bis.org), which specializes in providing national central banks with information and coordinating their transactions. IFIs have key roles to play in the wider debate about the need for a more coordinated international financial system (Ikhide 2004). Their existence highlights many policy-makers' sense that much as the WTO provides mechanisms structuring the cross-border trade in goods, international capital flows also require governance. Yet there is no single body in the financial arena with powers equivalent to those exercised by the WTO. Instead, global governance in this field largely reflects the mechanisms that market participants have set up to structure their own activities.

Section III: Architecture of the international financial system

Financial globalization has become as much of a central focus in international business as trade and investment. Yet observers have been expressing doubts about the efficiency of the world's financial architecture for several decades. Some analysts have focused on financial speculators' growing power over national governments, criticizing the unequal battle between mobile capital investors ('absentee landlords') and immobile, 'space-constrained' local communities (Bauman 1998: 68). Others express concern about the way in which financial interests now determine entire areas of activity—like health and housing—that were once driven by political considerations alone (Monbiot 2001). Still others attribute rising income inequality to the growing disparity between the wages paid to people employed in the financial sector as opposed to the remuneration levels witnessed throughout the rest of the economy (Anderson 2008).

However, some observers support the empowerment of financial speculators specifically because they advocate a 'global vision, in contrast to the often insular views of national government leaders worried about electability' (Mazlish and Morss 2005:172). Indeed, many university graduates still seek employment in a sector that is often considered exciting, innovative, and cutting-edge.

Of course, due to the aforementioned absence of a global body empowered to supervise the financial markets, discussions of their organization will necessarily be piecemeal, particularly given the many different categories of financial assets traded across borders. The best way to approach the topic is probably by following the organization found in many of the world's larger banks, which often distinguish between the foreign currency (FX) and capital markets, broken down into stocks and bonds (and other debt instruments).

Foreign exchange regimes and markets

The world has witnessed a number of different currency regimes. For a long time, countries would prioritize keeping their national currency stable against an external standard, usually gold. Most organized regimes since the Second World War have revolved around the US dollar—although there are growing signs that it now has competition from the Chinese yuan and conceivably an IMF 'basket currency' called Special Drawing Rights.

There are basically three rival regimes governing national currencies today. Where they differ is the extent to which market participants or state authorities set prices (Caramazza and Aziz 1998). In *fixed* regimes, a country's central bank pegs its national currency to a benchmark—often the US dollar or baskets of currencies—and ensures that this rate is maintained. Examples include the Kuwaiti or Bahraini dinars, and to some extent the Chinese yuan, which is allowed to move only under strict government supervision. With a *managed float*, a country's central bank sets a target trading range and intervenes in the market, as needs be, to keep its currency within the range. Prime examples include the Russian rouble and Malaysian ringgit. Lastly, the price for *free floating* currencies (most of the world's 'major' currencies, including euros, yen, and dollars) is determined solely by supply and demand from private interests. Each of these systems is associated with different levels of *convertibility*, which is the degree to which the authorities in a country allow transactions in their national currency to be traded without prior administrative authorization.

In line with the general paradigm that has dominated policy-making since the 1980s (see Chapter 2), the trend has been towards free-floating currency systems. Some studies view this as a positive trend, having found, for instance, that economic shocks are less likely to damage countries with flexible exchange rate systems than those whose currencies are fixed (Edwards and Levy Yeyati 2005). Other countries maintain a preference for fixed FX regimes, often because this corresponds to their view of how states and private interests should interact. Between these extremes, managed float systems have lost much of their attraction (Fischer 2001). This is because since the late 1980s, private sector resources have been so much larger than the funds available to central banks that it is almost impossible for the latter to control a national currency once it has been made convertible and can be freely traded by investors. Indeed, in the absence of global coordination, nowadays central banks find it almost impossible to impose their will on the FX markets (Ghosh 2008). This means that governments have one less policy weapon at their disposal in times of crisis.

Theoretically, foreign exchange markets are supposed to fulfil two main functions: price currencies at their fair value so that people have valid information about an economy's real situation and can make appropriate decisions; and provide liquidity to support international business. The problem is that neither fixed nor floating currency regimes fulfil these missions perfectly. Fixed regimes can be criticized, for instance, because of the tendency of central banks and/or politicians to price currencies wrongly by allowing non-currency-related considerations to affect their judgement. If national authorities want their economy to export its way out of a slump, for example, they will be tempted to price its currency at an artificially low rate. This might temporarily make its goods more attractive on the international markets, but it will also stoke inflationary pressures and mask the need for productivity efforts. Indeed, over the years many countries have been accused of these kinds of 'beggar-thy-neighbour' devaluations, most recently the USA, with its 'benign-neglect' policy of tolerating and even encouraging a weaker dollar in the mid-2000s. Conversely, if a government's priority is to cut inflation by reducing import costs—as Argentina did in the 1990s, largely under IMF pressure—the authorities might overvalue their currency. One problem then is that consumers' temporarily inflated purchasing power will tempt them to go on a shopping spree for foreign goods. These and other mistakes have sustained deregulation advocates in their conviction that politicians should stay out of the foreign exchange markets.

Yet markets driven by speculative interests alone are just as likely to price currencies wrongly. Traders are often motivated by short-term psychological factors like 'irrational exuberance' (over-excitement) and 'herd mentality' (or the tendency of crowds of investors to imitate one another). Such behaviours, which skew currency pricing mechanisms, are aggravated by the disproportionate power wielded by just a few leading financial institutions, with the world's six leading currency traders in 2011 (in order, Deutsche Bank, Barclays, Union Bank of Switzerland, Citigroup, JPMorgan, and HSBC) having a combined market share of nearly 60 per cent (Euromoney 2011). Centralization to this extent means that the trading decisions of a few very large players will have a disproportionate effect on market behaviour. As a result, currencies often spend long periods of time trading at prices that do not reflect the true economic situation of the countries they represent. The inevitable corrections are painful, especially when the country involved lacks the resources to protect itself from the volatility resulting from this adjustment process. This can be particularly upsetting when the country has been advised by an IGO like the IMF to abandon whatever currency controls it may have had in place (Bhagwati 2007; Daneshku 2007). It bears repeating that currency volatility is usually a bad thing for businesspeople engaged in real economic activities, because it obscures their vision of the true value of the goods and services involved in a cross-border transaction.

However, uncontrolled foreign exchange markets also have their supporters, some of whom consider that the repeated currency crises of the 1990s actually had a healthy effect, forcing the countries involved to reform their financial systems and paving the way for renewed growth in the 2000s (Rowe 2007). The argument has also been made that occasional turmoil in the FX markets is a price worth paying for the advantages derived from greater access to foreign currency (Obstfeld 2005). Like most international business topics, the architecture of the currency market provokes passionate debate. As crucial as currency trading is to most MNEs, analysts frequently estimate that only 2–3 per cent of all transactions in this market relate directly to real trade or FDI. In other words, the FX markets are predominantly run by financial interests but not in the interest of non-financial MNEs. Whether that was the original intention behind their design is very doubtful.

+ Currency/capital controls
Where a government places administrative restrictions on people's ability to buy/sell or lend/borrow assets denominated in the national currency.

Figure 4.8
Recent examples of global capital market crises.

Year	Description
1995	Mexican banking sector requires bailout after excessive lending spree
1997	Contagion effect leads to capital flight out of economies across Southeast Asia
1998	Russia defaults on 'GKO' government bonds, causing major outflows and bank shutdown. Results in bankruptcy of US hedge fund Long Term Capital Management
2001	Global market crash as 'dot.com' bubble bursts. Further panic after 9/11 bombings
1999–2003	Argentina balance of payment crisis causes government default on debt repayments
2007–2008	US subprime mortgage crisis, with global effects. See Case study 4.3
2011–2012	European sovereign debt crisis, with global effects. See Case study 4.3

International capital markets

For most of the 2000s, a key international business debate has been whether open capital markets are the best way of providing the liquidity that enables productive activity, or whether the deregulation trend of the past 25 years has created a 'casino capitalism' that benefits speculators to the detriment of everyone else (Sinn 2010) and ultimately results in crises that destroy value (see Figure 4.8).

Deregulation advocates assert that the best way of disciplining managers is to subject them to the scrutiny of the international capital markets, the idea being that investors will withdraw their money from any company (or country) that does not show financial good sense and, conversely, support anyone who is on the right path. This is not only important in big MNEs to ensure that managers' short-term personal incentives do not conflict with companies' long-term strategic objectives, but also in small family-owned firms that might otherwise hesitate to take tough but necessary productivity-enhancing decisions. Pressure from the financial markets also induces companies originating from countries lacking a tradition of financial discipline to pay closer attention to budgetary constraints. In this view, having demanding shareholders is good for companies precisely because it requires so much from them.

The contrasting vision holds that finance markets exist to support real business activity, not the other way around. What managers representing non-financial MNEs need to conduct international business is confidence in their ability to predict the present and future value of their international operations or assets. However, having this kind of clear picture is almost impossible when financial market deregulation means that huge volumes of 'hot capital' flow across borders in seconds, affecting prices in totally unforeseeable ways. Such volatility is compounded by the difference between the instantaneous time framework within which financial speculators work, and the much longer period of time that it takes for 'stickier' prices to change in the markets for real goods and services. The net effect of the ensuing confusion is less global investment than would otherwise be the case.

This enables the argument that open capital markets are actually less conducive to international business than older, more bureaucratic regimes where host countries retain control over foreign capital movements. As unexciting as administrative models might sound, it is worth recalling that several of today's leading investment destinations, starting with China, have kept capital (and currency) controls specifically because their governments want to supervise hot flows and necessarily have to do this at a national level due to the absence of any body empowered to fulfil this function on a global scale. This does not prevent China from receiving huge amounts of inwards investment, with entrepreneurs calculating that the advantages associated with establishing a long-term commercial or industrial presence here exceed the disadvantage of not being able to withdraw their funds as quickly as they might like in case of an emergency. Yet one of the main theoretical justifications given for deregulating the international capital markets is precisely that investors supposedly must be confident that they will be able to withdraw their funds quickly and freely before consenting to invest in the first place. Of course, such conditions may still apply where riskier countries are concerned—but this would intimate that the attractiveness of a host economy determines investment decisions, not the openness of the capital regime. The implication is that markets could be re-regulated yet continue to perform. The question is which global body would have the overview and power to implement re-regulation.

There is little doubt that open financial markets have facilitated the international recycling of surplus funds held by cash-rich countries and investors. Since the late 1990s, this has increasingly meant moving capital held by Asian and Middle Eastern interests to MNEs or indebted countries across the world—a function that many governments find useful. At the same time, it is partially because the markets were so open in the first place that these imbalances were able to accumulate. Thus, the first question in judging the adequacy of the financial system's design is whether capital flows simply reflect the realities characterizing the global economy, or instead, cause the erratic boom-bust cycles from which many countries suffer today (Pintus 2011).

Challenges and choices

→ One of the main business justifications for a regional association is that it enables firms from member states to work in a bigger marketplace, thereby enhancing their ability to withstand more robust global competition. The problem is that many leading MNEs are more regional than global in terms of their outlook. The challenge for managers is to avoid the temptation of developing strategies that will prepare their company only for regional rivals, ignoring the benchmarks set by companies strategizing on a more global plane. The feasibility of this choice depends on whether the world is going to start to converge in terms of consumers' purchasing power and the international distribution of wealth.

Chapter summary

Much of the framework within which international business takes place is determined by governance bodies operating outside national governments' control. The chapter has explored the three main categories for such bodies, starting with RAs that try to replicate, internationally, some of the functions that nation-states fulfil on a domestic basis. This was followed by a section on single-purpose IGOs, led first and foremost by the three Bretton Woods IGOs that have been so important in determining today's international business framework—particularly the WTO, whose political approach has a great many supporters but also critics worldwide. The final section discussed the global financial system that creates the framework for MNEs' foreign exchange and funding operations, which Chapter 13 treats from a more corporate perspective.

Case study 4.3

Global regulations for global crises

The history of modern finance is sprinkled with periods of market upheaval (such as the implosion of the European Monetary System in 1992 or the 1997 Asian currency crisis) but as long as the effects were more or less contained, many observers were willing to accept uncertainty as the cost of ensuring greater global access to capital. However, the severity of the two most recent crises in 2008 and 2011–2012 undermined this complacency (Engelen et al. 2011), causing widespread concern about the extent to which the international capital markets remain fit for purpose—or whether they have become dysfunctional. An increasing number of observers, even ones broadly in favour of free market globalization (Bhagwati 2007), have arrived at the latter conclusion. The case for an at least partial re-regulation of global finance has become mainstream.

To understand the new consensus, it is worth reviewing the causes of the two recent crises. The 2008 subprime crisis was rooted in the availability of cheap credit in the USA during the early 2000; a time when American lenders awarded huge mortgages to property developers and households without controlling their ability to repay. Unsurprisingly, defaults began accumulating, forcing several major US financial institutions to borrow increasing amounts of capital to restore their balance sheets. This led in turn to rumours about their financial health; panic spread; and institutions sitting on surplus funds became much less willing to lend them. The ensuing 'credit crunch' affected other banks whose relative lack of depositor funds meant that they relied excessively on interbank funding. By mid-2008, a full-blown crisis had erupted, culminating in the disappearance of powerful investment banks such as Lehman Brothers and Bear Stearns.

On the face of things, the problem was purely American in origin. Yet it ended up having a global impact, demonstrating the coupling between different national capital markets—or, as the expression goes, how everyone catches a cold when Washington sneezes. There were two main reasons for this knock-on effect. First, the squeeze in the USA reduced the global supply of capital. Foreign victims of the credit crunch included Britain's Virgin Money (ex-Northern Rock Bank), which

ultimately required government support to survive, and Belgium's Fortis bank, which was taken over by France's BNP-Paribas. Secondly, with US lenders having often repackaged their outstanding mortgage loans and sold them on to non-American banks and funds—and with cross-border bank credit to non-banks having risen more than twice as fast as domestic lending during the boom years of the early 2000s (Economist 2012)—investors worldwide recorded losses as the value of these assets plummeted. This caused further concern about the viability of the world's financial system and raised questions about the lack of a central authority capable of supervising the external effects of actions that financial institutions take in their internal markets. Ultimately, the decision was made at an April 2009 G20 meeting in London to empower Basel's Bank for International Settlements (BIS) to convince banks to increase their equity capital (in absolute terms and as a ratio of their outstanding loans), in the hope that this would stabilize the global financial system. Although the implementation of these ratios would be supervised by national authorities, the fact that they were specified by an international financial institution indicated the growing sense that the solution to the crisis would only be found in global re-regulation.

The 2011–2012 financial crisis, on the other hand, started in Europe. Several Eurozone governments, most notably Portugal, Ireland, Italy, Greece, and Spain, struggled to reimburse debt accumulated after years of low tax revenues and high public spending (aggravated by the huge sums spent bailing out banks following the 2008 crisis). The spectre of government default was particularly frightening given that 'sovereign' Eurozone debt had previously been classified as a virtually risk-free asset category, with many European banks having invested heavily in reputedly safe government bonds. These institutions stood to lose substantial sums if their holdings were written off, leading to serious concerns about their long-term survival. Like the 2008 crisis, the first consequence was the growing unwillingness by banks with surplus funds to lend to normal counterparts, a renewed credit crunch that aggravated the economic recession by reducing the amount of capital available to non-financial companies. The subsequent recession meant lower fiscal revenues for Eurozone governments, creating a vicious cycle of rising debt slowing down economic activity and leading to further debt. Instead of enabling business, once again the financial markets were becoming an obstacle to growth.

With encouragement from Washington, Beijing, and Tokyo, the EU member states met on numerous occasions over 2011 and 2012 to seek a solution. The agreement they reached reflected the global nature of the crisis, largely attributed to the fact that the fiscal policies being pursued in some Eurozone countries were much less disciplined than in others (like Germany). The idea was advanced that the euro could only survive if the management of member states' domestic budgets converged, thus if a global body (like the EU) assumed a greater role in coordinating national actions. This was similar to some of the conclusions reached following the 2008 subprime crisis. It confirmed the growing sense that the best response to global problems is to adopt global solutions.

Financial crises in 2008 and in 2011–2012 both had significant knock-on effects in the real economy

Source: Corbis

Case study questions

1. What are the different ways in which problems in one country's financial markets might affect the rest of the global financial system?
2. How effective have global institutions (such as the BIS or the EU) been in addressing, respectively, the 2008 and 2011–2012 financial crises?
3. What architecture can the global financial system be expected to assume in the future?

+ Default
Where a debtor does not fulfil a contractual obligation to repay a debt.

+ Coupling
Where countries' economic fortunes are linked due to the inseparability of their economic and financial interests.

Discussion questions

1. Why might international organizations' focus change over the course of their lifetime?

2. Has regionalization led to a convergence in national economic policies?

3. Why should a national government hand power over to an IGO such as the WTO?

4. What possibilities exist for supervising the global currency and capital markets in the future?

Online resource centre

Go online to test your understanding by trying multiple-choice questions, and assignment and examination questions.

Further research

Eccleston, R. (2012). *The Dynamics of Global Economic Governance*. Cheltenham: Edward Elgar Publishing Ltd

Recurring crises have revealed a lack of global coordination in terms of fiscal policy-making. This reflects the incoherency of countries trying to stabilize their shared financial markets while each implements a different tax regime. The book focuses on how greater transparency in international tax dealings might improve the situation.

Ku, C. (2012). *International Law, International Relations and Global Governance*. Abingdon: Routledge

This general text covers a wide spectrum of international parties and explores the many different ways in which they regulate the world's governing capacity.

References

Anderson, G. (2008). *Cityboy: Beer and Loathing in the Square Mile*. London: Headline

Bauman, Z. (1998). *Globalization: The Human Consequences*. Cambridge: Polity Press

BBC—British Broadcasting Corporation (2009). 'Timeline: World Trade Organization', 7 January, available at http://news.bbc.co.uk, accessed 1 July 2009

Bhagwati, J. (2007). *In Defense of Globalization*. New York: Oxford University Press

Cammack, P. (2003). 'The governance of global capitalism: A new materialist perspective', in R. Wilkinson (ed.) *The Global Governance Reader*. London: Routledge

Cantwell, J. and Iammarino, S. (2011). *Multinational Corporations and European Regional Systems of Innovation*. London: Routledge

Caramazza, F. and Aziz, J. (1998). 'Fixed or flexible: Getting the exchange rate right in the 1990s', available at http://www.imf.org/, accessed 3 December 2008

Dadush, U. and Nielson, J. (2007). 'Governing global trade', *IMF: Finance & Development*, December

Daneshku, S. (2007). 'IMF accused of poor exchange rate guidance', *Financial Times*, 18 May, available at http://www.ft.com/, accessed 15 June 2007

Davis, D. (2011). 'Regional trade agreements and foreign direct investment', *Politics & Policy*, 39/3, pp. 401–419 (June)

Drezner, D. (2007). 'The new world order', available at http://www.realclearpolitics.com, accessed 2 May 2007

Economist (2011). 'Dead man talking', *The Economist*, 28 April, available at http://www.economist.com/, accessed 11 June 2012

Economist (2012). 'The retreat from everywhere', *The Economist*, 14 April, p. 27

Ederington, J. (2007). 'NAFTA and the pollution haven hypothesis', *Policy Studies Journal*, 35/2 (May)

Edwards, S. and Levy Yeyati, E. (2005). 'Flexible exchange rates as shock absorbers', *European Economic Review*, 49/8 (November)

Engelen, E., Ertürk, I., Froud, J., Johal, S., Leaver, A., Moran, M., Nilsson, A., and Williams, K. (2011). *After the Great Complacence: Financial Crisis and the Politics of Reform*. Oxford: Oxford University Press

Euromoney (2011). 'Euromoney's 2011 FX survey results', 4 May, available at http://www.euromoney.com, accessed 18 January 2012

Fischer, S. (2001). 'Exchange rate regimes: Is the bipolar view correct?', *IMF Finance and Development*, 38/2 (June)

Frederick, S. and Gereffi, G. (2011). 'Upgrading and restructuring in the global apparel value chain: Why China and Asia are outperforming Mexico and Central America', *International Journal of Technological Learning, Innovation and Development*, 4/1–2, pp. 67–95 (August)

Ghosh, A. (2008). 'Turning currencies around', *IMF Finance and Development*, 45/2 (June)

Gomel, G. (2002). 'Crisis prevention and the role of IMF conditionality', in M. Fratianni et al. (eds.). *Governing Global Finance: New Challenges, G7 and IMF Contributions*. Aldershot: Ashgate

Higgott, R. (1998). 'The international political economy of regionalism', in W. D. Coleman and G. R. D. Underhill (eds.). *Regional and Global Economic Integration*. London: Routledge

Iida, K. (2005). 'Is WTO dispute settlement effective?' in D. Kelly and W. Grant (eds.). *The Politics of International Trade in the Twenty-First Century: Actors, Issues and Regional Dynamics*. Basingstoke: Palgrave Macmillan

Ikhide, S. (2004). 'Reforming the international financial system for effective aid delivery', *World Economy*, 27/2 (February)

Kelly, D. and Grant, W. (2005). *The Politics of International Trade in the Twenty-First Century: Actors, Issues and Regional Dynamics*. Basingstoke: Palgrave Macmillan

Mazlish, B. and Morss, E. (2005). 'A global elite?', in Chandler, A. and Mazlish, B. (eds.). *Leviathans: Multinational Corporations and the New Global History*. Cambridge: Cambridge University Press

Monbiot, G. (2001). *Captive State: The Corporate Takeover of Britain*. London: Pan Books

Obstfeld, M. (2005). 'Reflections upon re-reading "The Capital Myth"', available at http://elsa.berkeley.edu/, accessed 11 June 2008

Pintus, P. (2011). 'International capital flows, debt overhang and volatility', *International Journal of Economic Theory*, 7/4, pp. 301–315 (1 December)

Rose, E. (2004). 'OPEC's dominance of the global oil market: The rise of the world's dependency on oil', *Middle East Journal*, 58/3 (July)

Rowe, J. (2007). 'Countries take stock of financial soundness exercise', *IMF Survey*, 36/10 (June)

RTL (2006). 'L'invasion du plombier polonais n'a pas eu lieu', 20 November, available at http://www.rtl.fr, accessed 24 October 2008

Singer, P. (2004). *One World: The Ethics of Globalization*. London: Yale University Press

Sinn, H.W. (2010). *How the Financial Crisis Came About and What Needs to be Done Now*. Oxford: Oxford University Press

Stiglitz, J. (2004). 'The promise of global institutions', in D. Held and A. McGrew (eds.). *The Global Transformations Reader: An Introduction to the Globalization Debate*. Cambridge: Polity Press

Sturgeon, T. and Biesebroeck, J. (2011). 'Global value chains in the automotive industry: An enhanced role for developing countries?', *International Journal of Technological Learning, Innovation and Development*, 4/1–2, pp. 181–205 (August)

Weisman, S. (2007). 'Old guard of banking struggles to adjust to global economy', *Observer*, 3 June, *New York Times* insert, p. 5

White, A. (2011). 'Whirlpool, Panasonic among four fined $216 million over compressor cartel', 7 December, available at http://www.bloomberg.com/, accessed 1 January 2012

Wilkinson, R. (2006). *The WTO: Crisis and the Governance of Global Trade*. Abingdon: Routledge

Wilkinson, T. L. (2007). 'Eastern Europe challenges India as hub for bank-office work', *Wall Street Journal – Europe*, 19 November

Woods, N. (2004). 'Order, globalization and inequality', in D. Held and A. McGrew (eds.). *The Global Transformations Reader: An Introduction to the Globalization Debate*. Cambridge: Polity Press

5 Multinational enterprises and foreign direct investment

Learning objectives

After reading this chapter, you will be able to:

✦ identify the principles guiding MNEs' historic efforts to shape the international environment

✦ identify SMEs' main international strengths and weaknesses

✦ discuss foreign direct investment (FDI) drivers

✦ describe how FDI affects host economies

✦ characterize international lobbying

Case study 5.1

MNEs and international operations: IBM's Indian summer

Since 1991, market liberalization has been a core policy for all Indian governments. The result is that many MNEs have reappraised this huge continent-sized country, a land of contrasts where terrible poverty coexists with an education system turning out millions of world-class mathematicians and engineers. With many multinationals expanding their presence in India, the country has become a global hub for a variety of activities, ranging from bank administration to pharmaceutical research and information technology (IT). IBM (http://www.ibm.com/) is part of this wave.

By 2011, IBM had become India's second largest private sector employer, with more than a million staff members, up from 53,000 in 2006 (*Times of India* 2010). The company operates the full range of computing and business service activities, ranging from low-cost call centres and business process outsourcing to high value-added research and development, software production, and cloud computing.

One of the main reasons behind IBM's decision to expand in India is that competition from emerging local software companies like Infosys had put it under pressure to cut costs. With highly competent Indian programmers earning far less than their US counterparts, one obvious response for IBM was to invade Infosys's home market. From an Indian perspective, FDI of this kind is a double-edged sword. It brings funding and management knowledge while offering much needed jobs. Yet it also drains some of India's human capital away from domestic companies and distorts national wage structures by widening the gap between workers who benefit from globalization and those who do not. Issues relating to the fair distribution of the benefits of globalization played strongly in the country's 2012 parliamentary elections. In India, as elsewhere, foreign firms often meet with mixed reactions.

The US no longer dominates the global programming market to the extent that it once did

Source: iStock

As IBM's ex-CEO Sam Palmisano said at the 2006 INSEAD Global Leaders Series: 'Work flows to the places where it will be done best.' In its early years, IBM was mainly a domestic US company but by the 1990s it was already running distinct supply chains all across the world. Now, in the early 2010s, it is IBM's executive functions that have internationalized, as exemplified by the group's chief procurement officer recently moving from Shenzen (China) to Budapest (Hungary) to gain proximity to new suppliers in Eastern Europe and Africa. IBM maintains headquarters in New York and many executives are American, but it is unclear to what extent it remains an American company.

Case study questions:

1. What are India's attractions for MNEs seeking to offshore their operations?
2. IBM has had operations in India for a while but recently decided to increase its investment. Why?

Introduction

Alongside nation-states and intergovernmental organizations, the main actors shaping international business are multinational enterprises (MNEs) themselves. Mobile and free to allocate resources as they see fit, MNEs create markets and determine standards of living. They have left few societies untouched. At the same time, many populations resent this domination. However powerful multinationals may be, they are also under pressure to accommodate local interests.

Section I: Business across borders

Companies with international activities come in many shapes and sizes, ranging from small domestic firms with one-off foreign interests to huge firms transacting constantly outside their national borders. The composition of MNEs' foreign activities at any given time depends on many factors, including political and economic circumstances, technology, management paradigms, and company size. It is interesting to study how the importance of each of these factors has varied historically (**see ORC Extension material 5.1**). One example of a historical shift, further detailed in Chapter 15, is the way that many of today's leading MNEs come from emerging economies or upper middle income countries like Spain, South Korea, or Taiwan (Guillen and Garcia-Canal 2010), whereas almost all of their nineteenth and twentieth century predecessors originated in the world's more technologically advanced countries. The key factors of success have also changed: instead of necessarily competing in technological or marketing terms, today many MNEs find strength in their ability to collaborate and manage corporate networks. The one constant in international business is that the rules are never constant.

> Go online

Multinational enterprises

MNE behaviour is partially a reaction to external circumstances (see Figure 5.1). Some drivers (funding, political environment, logistics, and communications) were briefly introduced in Chapter 1, but it is useful to keep track of their different manifestations over time. As stressed throughout this book, corporate behaviour is only significant if put into a particular context.

MNE behaviour also reflects internal factors like structure, decision-making processes, and managers' personal value systems, all of which materialize within the particular organizational configuration that each company has chosen. Hence the need to review different managerial paradigms that have dominated international business historically, a topic whose theoretical and practical aspects will be further discussed in Chapter 10.

		Pre-twentieth century drivers of globalization	Drivers of globalization in the modern era
Figure 5.1 MNE drivers have remained constant over the years—only their forms have changed.	Funding	Companies with publicly traded shares	Globalized financial markets
	Policy framework	Mercantilism, then free trade	Deregulation
	Logistics	Ships, rail	Trucking, planes
	Communications	Telegraph, telephone	Internet

External drivers of multinational activity

One key driver of multinational activity is *funding*. Logically, distant markets are riskier and harder to service, thus more expensive, than domestic ones. In the past, states were the prime source of funding for international business. As the merchant classes accumulated wealth, however, they gradually assumed this role. An early example is the creation of the British East India Company, recognized as one of the world's first MNEs, following the development of stock markets and limited liability companies in the seventeenth century. Today it would be impossible to analyse MNE expansion without reference to the international financial markets where they access the capital they need (see Chapter 13).

The *political environment* is another key factor affecting MNEs, which, because of their foreign status, have always been subject to scrutiny from national authorities. Poor relations with host governments can cause problems for companies, leading in extreme cases to expropriation—one 2011 example being the way that ownership of online payment company Alipay was transferred to Chinese interests without any prior notification being given to Yahoo, despite its 43 per cent stake in the company (Economist 2011). Diplomatic tensions can also affect MNEs' dealings in certain states, as exemplified by the way that the USA has repeatedly pressured European MNEs like oil companies Total, Statoil, and ENI to reduce their Iranian operations (RTRS 2011). MNEs may also be affected by zealous regulations, one case being when the French competition authority levied a $312 million fine on US consumer goods MNE Proctor and Gamble, accused of coordinating product promotions and offerings (Monk 2011). Yet another political factor is the degree of economic patriotism (see Chapter 3), as exemplified by the 'Buy American' rhetoric that marked the 2012 US presidential campaign. Lastly, host populations may suspect an MNE of undermining national interests, causing in turn a negative political reaction. The extent of the hostility will depend on different factors, including the host country's historic relations with the company's country of origin (Makino and Tsang 2011). Clearly, international business does not exist in a political vacuum.

The third constant is *logistics*. Early exploration was often driven by improved naval technology. Similarly, the invention of the steam engine stimulated the Industrial Revolution of the eighteenth century. The first great era of globalization that materialized in the late nineteenth century featured major projects like the Suez and Panama canals and the Trans-Siberian railway. This infrastructure work facilitated the movement of goods , but also managers, who diffused corporate knowledge in turn, further driving MNE expansion (Jones

+ Expropriation
Where private property is seized by a government, often without compensation.

High performance logistics allow MNEs to plan their operations on a global scale

Source: Digital vision

2005; Wilkins 2005). Today, truck and aeroplane fleets help companies ship components, finished products, and human resources worldwide. In the absence of rapid transportation, global supply chains linking remote sites would be impossible. Without cargo planes, for instance, European retailers would be unable to import Kenyan roses or New Zealand apples during the Northern winter. Globalization in its current form requires affordable logistics.

Lastly, MNE operations have always mobilized rapid and reliable *communications*. It was only after the telegraph and telephone spread a century ago that MNEs could integrate operations worldwide (Wilkins 2005). The Internet fulfils a similar function today, helping companies not only to improve market intelligence but also coordinate foreign subsidiaries to form effective value chains. The intra-firm transfer of knowledge that Internet technology enables is as important to MNEs as trading goods.

The kinds of knowledge that MNEs typically share not only involve products and processes but also management systems. Historically, different principles have dominated thinking about the best way to structure cross-border operations. Paradigms vary in time in the same way as economic or political conditions do.

Evolving multinational paradigms

MNEs tend to develop subsidiaries according to two principles. Much early FDI involved horizontal integration, where companies would open overseas units doing roughly the same things abroad as at home, in countries characterized by roughly the same level of industrial development. These similarities made it easier for companies to internationalize. Examples include German engineering group Siemens' launch of UK operations in 1852, or the plant that Scottish thread maker Clark's built in New Jersey in 1865.

Early MNEs had less information about foreign environments than companies today. They also faced greater barriers to entry and suffered from slower communications and transportation. All these factors hindered inter-subsidiary relationships and meant that most units had to be managed separately. In reality, given how erratic cross-border deliveries were at the time, it would have been risky for one plant's production to rely on components shipped from distant sister units. Where foreign subsidiaries traded, it usually involved finished products.

MNE paradigms during the first 'golden era of globalization'

From the late eighteenth century until the 1929 Wall Street Crash, the spread of free-trade politics and improved transportation and communications deepened many companies' cross-border connections and generated what is known as the first 'golden era of globalization' (Jones 2005). Multinationals in this period generally developed cross-border networks by pursuing one of the following models (see Figure 5.2):

- An 'American' model: MNEs developed competencies at home and either exported goods or undertook FDI specifically to overcome trade barriers (for example, Ford and General Motors' entry into Europe in the 1920s).

- A 'British' model: MNEs established subsidiaries depending on local competencies and embedded these units into a wider global network (for example, the Jardine trading company in Hong Kong).

+ Integration
Where different units' activities are coordinated to the extent that their missions are defined in light of one another.

+ Intra-firm
Activities occurring within the confines of one and the same firm.

+ Horizontal integration
Where a firm establishes a presence in a new market by running activities similar to the ones operating in its home market.

+ Sister units
Separate corporate entities sharing the same parent company.

Figure 5.2
MNE models during the first era of globalization (1880–1929). The arrows indicate the direction of cross-border knowledge flows (Jones 2005).

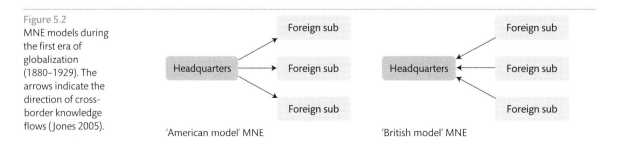

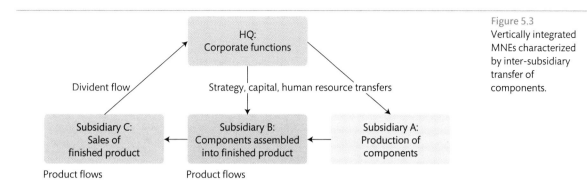

Figure 5.3
Vertically integrated
MNEs characterized
by inter-subsidiary
transfer of
components.

Both models contained the seeds of the HQ–subsidiary configuration typifying modern MNEs (see Chapter 9). By accepting that different sites can specialize in different activities that reflect their strengths, the British model came closer to applying Adam Smith's international division of labour principles (see Chapter 2). Associated with this vision was the question of whether sites necessarily had to have the same parent company. Companies that ended up owning all units working upstream and downstream from themselves are described as vertically integrated (see Figure 5.3). This remains a common mode of MNE organization. Indeed, by some accounts, intra-firm trade of unfinished goods represents up to 60 per cent of all international trade. Vertical and horizontal integration are topics lying at the very heart of FDI and internationalization studies.

As Chapter 2 discussed, the first era of globalization ended in the 1930s and 1940s following the Great Depression, the Second World War, and the Decolonization Era. The net effect of these upheavals was that national governments were generally more interested at the time in protecting their domestic economies and less focused on the benefits of open borders. This led to a sharp contraction in international trade and FDI, with many firms deciding to manage their foreign subsidiaries as standalone, multi-domestic units. This was a partial return to the horizontal logic that had dominated before the first golden era of globalization.

After the 1944 Bretton Woods conference (see Chapter 4), a series of global negotiations launched within the framework of the General Agreement on Trade and Tariffs breathed new life into international business. By the 1960s, barriers to trade and FDI were falling again, and a 'big is beautiful' paradigm took root in many boardrooms. This convinced many managers that, where possible, companies should maximize economies of scale by integrating operations into their international value chain. The renaissance of vertical integration was particularly widespread among American MNEs trying to apply overseas the same mass production logic that they had long pursued in their huge home market. It also dominated Europe, which was rising from the ashes of the Second World War, and whose Western half was moving to create a common market. Many European MNEs, ranging from financial institutions like Deutsche Bank to industrial firms like Philips or food companies like Danone, integrated their regional value chains in an attempt to achieve the critical mass that would help them serve the EU's increasingly unified market. A similar example in Asia was the adoption of this model a few years later by Sri Lankan textiles firm Hirdaramani, which started out by manufacturing both fabrics and shirts at its home factory before offshoring operations to a specialist fabrics plant in Cambodia, where a particular skill exists for this kind of activity. With the world shrinking every day, the new paradigm demanded that companies be large enough to service regional and even global markets.

MNE paradigms during today's second 'golden era of globalization'

The 1970s were a watershed in MNE history because of the rise of Japanese firms, whose 'Toyotaist' model was soon considered more adapted to a world of differentiated global consumers than the old 'Fordist' model, geared towards the mass production of a limited range of goods (see Chapter 11). With firms that were much more energy-efficient than their US

+ Vertical integration
Where a firm controls, and/or moves towards controlling, both the *upstream* and the *downstream* sides of its value chain.

+ Multi-domestic
Management approach emphasizing autonomy of differentiated national markets as opposed to the coordination of unified global or regional markets.

+ Offshoring
Where a firm moves an activity that it once ran domestically into a subsidiary that it owns abroad, usually to cut costs.

Figure 5.4
An MNE can either cover the entire international value chain with its own subsidiaries or contract overseas operations to outside parties.

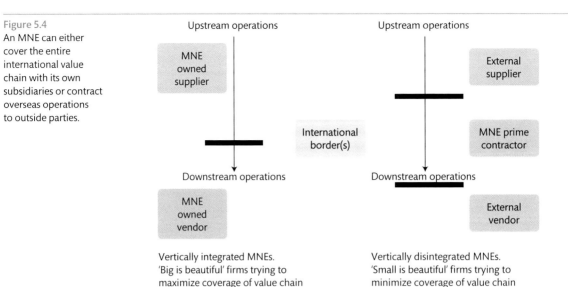

Vertically integrated MNEs.
'Big is beautiful' firms trying to maximize coverage of value chain

Vertically disintegrated MNEs.
'Small is beautiful' firms trying to minimize coverage of value chain

rivals (Glyn 2006) and had positioned themselves cleverly in fast-growing sectors like consumer electronics (Sony and Matsushita) and computing (Fujitsu and Toshiba), Japan became the world's industrial powerhouse. Just as importantly, its management systems became the benchmark for MNEs everywhere.

One of the main characteristics of the Japanese model is that MNEs no longer necessarily had to own the foreign units comprising their value chains (see Figure 5.4) but could opt for 'vertical disintegration'. In this approach, a central prime contractor assumes little direct responsibility for operations and instead organizes a network of trusted external partners to whom work is outsourced. Many household names, like Toyota or Panasonic, have successfully applied this 'small is beautiful' paradigm, which dominates MNE thinking today. Despite signs that Japanese multinationals no longer set the pace internationally as they did in the 1990s (Black and Morrison 2010), the country remains a laboratory for cutting-edge international business practices.

The first lesson from this new Japanese paradigm is that prime contractors coordinating a network of companies covering the whole value chain will view international business differently from vertically integrated firms that run all operations by themselves. Costs are a primary concern for vertically integrated MNEs, whereas the main factor for MNE networks is partners' interdependency (hence coordination). This is conditioned by several factors, including partners' relative sizes; who possesses the more valuable technology; and the balance of political power (with companies from poorer developing countries often finding themselves in a weaker bargaining position than their network partners). Corporate culture is another key factor, since some firms are more disposed towards entertaining friendly relations with potential partners whereas others are more inclined to compete. MNE network relationships (see Figure 5.5) are one of the areas where companies' micro-level strategies intersect most visibly with the macro-level international business environment.

Although this brief review of multinational history has uncovered many common themes over the years, the reality is that MNEs as a whole tend to pursue a range of different behaviours at any one moment in time. This diversity can be categorized by companies' region of origin. Indeed, most global authorities, including the Organization for Economic Cooperation and Development (OECD) and the United Nations, classify MNEs along regional lines. This is logical, given the many studies showing that most MNEs conduct the lion's share of their business in their home region (Rugman 2005). Working in an MNE may require a cosmopolitan outlook, but the fact is that many managers are connected to their culture of origin. This does not mean that everyone working in a particular region behaves similarly, or that companies in one part of the world do not imitate counterparts elsewhere.

+ Prime contractor
Company at the heart of a corporate network and whose orders trigger partners' production plans.

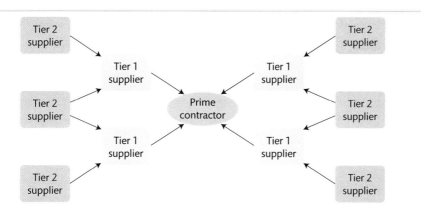

Figure 5.5
Prime contractors
at the heart of MNE
networks coordinating
relationships between
supplier tiers.

There is simply a strong argument supporting the notion that between the global and national perspectives, the region offers a useful level of analysis.

MNEs' regional characteristics

One way to compare MNEs from different regions is in terms of their research efforts. For instance, North American MNEs have recently benefited in many sectors from fast productivity growth driven by advances in IT. The continuous development of new products and processes is rooted in US companies' strong connections to universities (see Chapter 11 discussion on knowledge spillovers). On the other hand, the financialization ethos that dominates in the USA (Froud et al. 2006) means that American MNEs are also under greater pressure than their foreign counterparts to maximize short-term returns (**see ORC Extension materials 5.2**). This tends to create riskier corporate behaviour, something often manifested in companies' investment policies and financial or product innovation strategies. Lastly, the North American corporate environment is also noteworthy because of the role FDI plays here. The USA is the world's leading recipient of FDI, although it is hard to say whether this reflects its financial imbalances or attractiveness as a destination— probably both.

   One of the most significant trends characterizing European companies in the years since the fall of communism and arrival of a single EU market is the drive towards greater sectorial consolidation. Many companies that used to dominate their national markets have been forced to adopt a transcontinental strategy, one consequence of which has been an increase in the number of cross-border mergers and acquisitions. Also noteworthy is the region's strong FDI growth in recent years, largely driven by West European companies investing in Eastern transition economies. At the same time, many European MNEs remain vulnerable because of their comparatively lower R&D spending. One outcome is that despite clear improvements in recent years, the productivity of European labour (measured in GDP per worker) lags far behind US levels. The EU's 2000 Lisbon strategy aimed to address some of these weaknesses through the promotion of a more 'knowledge-based' economy, but much work remains to be done.

   Lastly, Asian MNEs can be divided into two categories. First, there are longer established companies from Japan and Korea, often with particular strengths in consumer durables and capital goods. Secondly, there are younger MNEs from two emerging giants: China, now the world's leading manufacturing centre; and India, which specializes more in services but also has certain industrial strengths (see Chapter 15, which also highlights new MNEs from other emerging regions). Factors such as economic patriotism, the global financial crisis, and ecological constraints may slow Asia's rise, and it is noteworthy that a disproportionate percentage of Western dealings in this part of the world continue to involve trade rather than FDI. Nevertheless, since the 1990s, Asia has been the world's most dynamic region, and it is a safe bet that Asian MNEs will continue to out-perform rivals from other regions as

+ **Financialization**
View that a firm's mission is to maximize financial returns and shareholder value.

> Go online

+ **Consolidation**
Where producers within a sector join forces via takeovers or mergers in an attempt to reduce over-capacities.

+ **Mergers and acquisitions**
Mergers are when two companies agree to combine their operations into a new company and both have more or less equal powers. Acquisitions indicate that one company has become the main shareholder of another.

their home markets catch up to Western standards of living. To some extent, this is driven by Asian firms' above-average R&D spending, and by the enormous numbers of young engineers being trained in this region. Such developments bode well for MNEs' future in the East.

Regions also vary in terms of average company size. One global constant is that SMEs account for most companies involved in international business. This justifies specific analysis.

Small and medium-sized enterprises (SMEs)

It is impossible to determine how trade and FDI break down exactly among the many different types of companies engaging in such activities. Even within the SME category, there are significant variations between companies with sporadic international dealings, others that transact abroad regularly, and tiny, start-up 'micro-multinationals' that use the Internet to 'go global' from the very outset (Copeland 2006). Irrespective of these variations, the lack of attention that SMEs receive in much international business analysis is a mistake: in many countries, they account for a significant proportion of all trade and FDI.

A prime example is Germany, where *Mittelstand* ('medium-level') companies are responsible for around 70 per cent of national exports. The country is home to upwards of 250 SMEs that can be classified as world-class champions in their respective markets. *Mittelstand* firms often operate profitably in niches that are too narrow to be exploited profitably using larger MNEs' heavier (hence more expensive) industrial assets. Examples include finished products (i.e. Neumann microphones or Bechstein pianos) and intermediary goods (i.e. Zeiss glass lenses or Solar-Fabrik photovoltaic cells) that larger companies subsequently use for their own production needs. Successful *Mittelstand* firms are characterized by narrow product portfolios (they rarely engage in diversification strategies); ongoing efforts to innovate gradually in their specialist areas; and the ambition to dominate their respective markets. A common trait for companies in this category is the refusal to outsource sales or production. Despite their small size, German SMEs strive unusually to maximize control over their international value chains. Otherwise, another key feature of these 'hidden champions' is their close relationship with the local community, translating into strong support for young recruits' vocational training and a culture emphasizing long-term market share over short-term profits or wages (Economist 2012b). Above all, they are very commercially oriented, constantly communicating with customers in their different target national markets to stay informed of changing preferences.

SMEs' flexibility contrasts with many larger companies, where size often creates a 'diseconomy of scale' materializing in heavy bureaucracies and procedures. Many large MNEs struggle to develop the responsiveness they need to keep up in fast-moving international environments. Thus, instead of being rivals, small and large MNEs often complement one another, with each tending to thrive in a different setting. Even so, SMEs' internationalization processes often follow a very different path from large MNEs. One example is the importance of key individuals' 'social capital' in SMEs, which therefore tend to internationalize at a slower, more incremental pace (Lindstrand et al. 2011). Similarly, family-run firms' generally smaller size means that they cannot be as proactive about foreign opportunities and must try instead to take advantage of intermediary network arrangements such as international trade exhibitions (Kontinen and Ojala 2011). In sum, SMEs' weakness, which is that they are too small to shape their international environment, often constitutes their strength, since it forces them to be more flexible than a larger MNE might be.

SMEs generally play a relatively greater role in locations (like Southern Europe or certain LDCs) where a lack of equity funding makes it harder for companies to access the financial resources they need to expand. Indeed, smaller companies are catalysts for economic progress in many parts of the world. This is particularly true in countries blessed with large numbers of tiny but dynamic micro-multinationals. These are a new category of SMEs offering many if not most of the knowledge-related service activities that drive much international

SME handicaps	Comments	
Bureaucracy	Same amount of paperwork as larger firms (i.e. customs forms) but spread over smaller volumes	Figure 5.6 Main external barriers to SME internationalization.
Product and service range	SMEs' narrower portfolios make it harder to attack diverse international markets	
Language/cultural barriers	SMEs have less human capital to cope with differences	
Commercialization	SMEs can rarely afford foreign retail outlets yet struggle to control external vendors	
Branding	SMEs cannot invest as much as large firms in overcoming consumers' home bias	
Supply chain pressures	Payment delays, price wars—larger firms' deeper pockets allow them to squeeze SMEs	
Scale	SMEs do not have the same size advantages as larger firms (bulk purchases/scale output)	
Government support	Larger firms are more effective than SMEs at lobbying for export assistance	
Intellectual property	SMEs have fewer resources to monitor possible infractions	

business today (basic and applied technologies, IT, consulting, or legal advice). Individually, SMEs may not have as much power as their larger counterparts, but their combined impact is substantial.

Nevertheless, it is clear that size is ultimately a severe handicap for smaller firms. This is a topic of great concern for many business economists, to the extent that the UN has organized several conferences devoted specifically to SMEs' internationalization difficulties (UNECE 2001). As demonstrated by Figures 5.6 and 5.7, such problems are often divided into two categories: external barriers and internal handicaps.

SMEs and politicians are aware of these various problems and constantly try to remedy them. At a political level and in recognition of SMEs' contribution to employment (with some EU estimates finding that smaller companies account for up to 70 per cent of all European jobs), governments often try to help this category of companies by offering export promotion facilities, financial aid, and/or data on international markets. Some countries have restructured their corporation tax systems so that SMEs pay lower marginal rates than big companies. At a more strategic level, many help SMEs to modernize their telecommunications systems, the idea being that this will improve their intelligence about foreign consumers or potential partners. Lastly, a number of specialist federations exist worldwide to represent the wide range of SME interests.

SME handicaps	Comment	
Lack of entrepreneurial, managerial, and/or marketing skills	Many top graduates go to big name firms	Figure 5.7 Main internal handicaps for SME internationalization.
Difficulties in accessing financial resources	Banks often penalize SME borrowers	
Lesser quality management capabilities	SMEs might not have enough spare staff to pursue a quality agenda	
Trade documentation (i.e. packaging, labelling requirements)	SMEs might not be able to afford trade specialists to deal with complexities	
Insufficient investment in technological assets and know-how	SMEs' size means that they struggle to fund crucial non-productive functions like R&D	

Having reviewed the different ways in which MNE and SME behaviour is shaped by political, economic, and technological variables, it is useful to study the reverse effect and see how MNEs affect the host countries where they operate. It is this focus on the two-way interaction between companies and their environments that makes international business such a special discipline.

Case study 5.2
Small companies in international business: Green and Black's

In 1991, Josephine Fairley and her husband, Craig Sams, founders of a pioneering organic food company named Whole Earth, set out to develop the world's first organic chocolate bar. Working out of small premises on London's Portobello Road, they began by launching a new label that would be called Green and Black's (http://www.greenandblacks.com) and would be defined by its ethical supply chain. By 1994, they were ready to market 'Maya Gold', a product made from Central American cocoa beans whose growers received a premium payment of 10 per cent. By offering suppliers a 'living wage', Green and Black's soon became the first UK brand to receive 'fair trade' certification (see Chapter 8). Thus, the SME had an international dimension from the outset, although more on the purchasing than on the sales side.

Sainsbury's, a large British retailer, began selling the label in the 1990s but market coverage was patchy and Fairley and Sams could not afford to develop a larger

distribution network (Jeffries 2005). External funding had to be found, so in 1999 the couple sold an 80 per cent stake to an investor group led by the former head of the New Covent Garden Soup Company. The move worked, in part because the new partners were also experienced in high-quality foods. Soon Green and Black's was carried by all UK supermarkets and achieved double digit annual growth rates.

Despite this success, size remained a handicap, limiting both how much Green and Black's could pay Central American suppliers (a crucial part of its brand image) and the company's market coverage in Britain. Supermarkets account for 80 per cent of the UK food market but only 60 per cent of sweets sales. Most confectionery products are impulse purchases made at newsagents and other small retail outlets. Green and Black's needed capital to attack more channels and, just as importantly, explore overseas opportunities. The lengthy supply lines that are part of an international network can be prohibitively expensive for an SME but, if Green and Black's did not go abroad, better-funded rivals would invade its niche. Hence Fairley and Sams' decision to accept a takeover bid from British food manufacturer Cadbury's (BBC 2005), itself acquired by the giant US MNE Kraft in 2010. Green and Black's declared that this change was desirable because it helped the company, still run by the same people implementing the same ethical practices, to expand more quickly. The question is whether fans of a charming little SME will retain the same loyalty to a small division in a huge MNE.

Case study questions

1. What sorts of constraints did Green and Black's face as a result of its size?
2. Why did the company necessarily have to go international?

SMEs tend to develop their international presence in niche markets
Reproduced with the kind permission of Green and Black's

Section II: MNE interactions with host countries

Whereas trade mainly impacts upon the point when goods cross national borders, the impact of FDI and lobbying is felt at the very heart of a host country's economy. Hence the idea that these factors deserve a special mention in the study of companies' international behaviour and interaction with host countries.

+ Lobbying
Attempts to influence policy-makers, often elected officials.

Foreign direct investment

As aforementioned, international business analysts commonly distinguish between horizontal FDI, where a company operates in the foreign country at a similar stage of its international value chain, and vertical FDI, where the cross-border move involves operating at a different stage than it does at home. Horizontal FDI is usually considered 'market-seeking', since it is generally motivated by the desire to expand sales—although, for some upstream companies, horizontal FDI can involve the acquisition of resources and/or domination of competitors (one 2011 example being French pharmaceutical giant Sanofi-Aventi's $19 billion takeover of US biotechnology rival Genzyme). Vertical FDI, on the other hand, is considered more 'efficiency-seeking', since its purpose is to help a company control its value chain more effectively. There are two ways of doing this. In the case of 'backwards' integration, the MNE expands its operations upstream (towards the supply side). 'Forward' vertical integration, on the other hand, means that the company is making a downstream FDI, usually to increase sales. An example of a company that has integrated in both directions is the Indian alloy manufacturer Rohit Ferro Tech, whose website refers to efforts both to backwards-integrate by acquiring coal mines in Indonesia to provide raw materials for its value chain, and to forward-integrate by setting up a stainless steel manufacturing facility processing the company's basic alloy products.

The United Nations Conference on Trade and Development (UNCTAD) has calculated that the value added generated by 'transnational corporations' (UNCTAD's expression for MNEs) amounts to nearly one-quarter of the world's combined GDP. Moreover, a further 10 per cent of GDP and a whopping one-third of total global exports are accounted for by MNE affiliates, defined as foreign holdings where the parent company only has a minority shareholding (as opposed to subsidiaries, where it has a majority stake). Given these enormous volumes, it is clear that FDI constitutes a central topic in international business today.

Assessing FDI from a country perspective

The macro-economic value of FDI can be assessed in terms of the benefits but also the disadvantages for home and host country alike.

Inwards investment benefits the home country

One frequently heard argument over the past 30 years is that a country benefits when its MNEs transfer abroad low-wage activities, simple business processes, or unsophisticated manufacturing operations. This supposedly frees up the home country to concentrate on higher value-added activities like R&D and finance, reducing the negative employment effects of the simpler jobs being offshored (Cuyvers and Soeng 2011). This was the reasoning applied, for instance, by Italian–French hi-tech company STMicroelectronics when it off-shored the production of basic components like silicon wafers to Singapore and concentrated its home European units on more advanced activities such as smartcards and micro-controllers. By focusing its home country units on strategic, higher value-added activities, STMicroelectronics was improving its macro-economic performance and arguably increasing employment opportunities.

Moving production
abroad can have
devastating
consequences in
an MNE's country
of origin

Source: iStock

Inwards investment damages the home country

The home country's main criticism of FDI is its negative effects on employment. Many OECD economies have suffered from widespread de-industrialization (that is, a shrinking industrial base) because of competition from foreign manufacturers working out of low-cost countries. The social consequences can be particularly devastating due to the fact that, in many countries, factory jobs are concentrated in just a few regions. For instance, mass plant closures have destroyed a number of communities in France (Lorraine region), Germany (Ruhr region), and the USA (Ohio/Western Pennsylvania), in part because it is so difficult for unemployed workers and their families to migrate to new employment centres.

Aggravating this problem is the growing displacement of service sector activities such as banking or research away from OECD countries, a trend shown to have a particularly negative impact on public attitudes towards globalization (Coe 2008). There is also the issue of rising disparities between those who benefit from globalization, including shareholders or workers with secure jobs, and those who lose their jobs or whose wages are being squeezed (Glyn 2006). One analyst has calculated that, despite rising average earnings in the USA, from the mid-1990s onwards median earnings stagnated. The analysis suggests that globalization tends to benefit a few people enormously but most not at all (Altman 2007). Home country governments also lose out on tax revenues when MNEs use FDI to move operations (and declare profits) overseas.

Inwards investment benefits the host country

Host country firms can benefit from MNEs' intangible competencies, comprised not only of technological know-how but also managerial competencies (Wei and Liu 2006). The knock-on effect for local firms and workers' skill levels can be very positive, especially when foreign units manufacture intermediary goods and services that domestic firms put to good use in their own production processes, often leading to the birth of innovative new SMEs (Leitao and Baptista 2011). Examples include how the arrival of Western retailers like Tesco, Carrefour, and Walmart has helped to modernize retailing in several emerging economies. In addition, foreign MNEs are often more productive than domestic firms, because their larger size allows them to perform more R&D, handle a wider variety of products, and employ more skilled labour (Barba Navaretti and Venables 2004; Bhagwati 2004). Studies have also shown that inwards FDI can have a positive effect on a country's outwards FDI (Gu and Lu 2011), exports (Bhatt 2011), and productivity—although the last factor will depend on whether the FDI is technology-based (Vlachos 2011) or if it is vertical in nature and transfers technology to domestic firms, unlike horizontal FDI that takes business away from locals (Le and Pomfret 2011). Lastly, FDI can improve human resource management in the host country, one example being the way that companies in formerly communist Eastern Europe imitate more sophisticated employment relationships practised by Western newcomers like French hotel group Accor or German automaker Volkswagen (Contrepois et al. 2010).

Inwards investment damages the host country

FDI critics often accuse MNEs of causing social tensions by increasing regional wage differentials (Damijan and Kostevc 2011). Others go so far as to say that MNEs plunder resources and exploit workers (Palast 2003), a line of reasoning partially contradicted by evidence that MNEs engage in significantly higher FDI in LDCs characterized by stronger labour rights (Busse et al. 2011). Another frequently heard criticism is that MNEs tend to transfer little useful technology and often use their units to import expensive components that will worsen the host country's trade balance. There is also concern in some quarters that big MNEs might squeeze small local firms out of their home markets. Lastly, there is the criticism that highly mobile MNEs find it easier to pressure national governments into offering tax breaks not available to national firms (Barba Navaretti and Venables 2004). This is the view that many if not most international investment agreements are imbalanced because they give MNEs rights but force obligations on host countries (Muchlinski 2011). For some critics, FDI embodies all that is bad about globalization.

Figure 5.8 provides a cost/benefit assessment of FDI's impact on host countries. The picture is ultimately mixed. Like most international business topics, FDI is neither intrinsically good nor bad.

Economic aspect	How does FDI affect the host country?
Capital flows	Inflows; outflows. Were the funds imported or raised locally? How much does the MNE take out in dividends? What policies has the government had to implement to attract FDI? How easily can foreign investors withdraw funds?
Development	Infrastructure; industrialization; terms of trade. Does the FDI involve high or low value-added activities? Does the FDI encourage local entrepreneurship? Had the FDI never occurred, could local goods or imports have served the country's needs? What social damage is caused by changing the country's old structures?
Competition	Short-term disruptions; long-term productivity effects. Has the FDI broken up existing monopolies and created more local competition? Or is it crowding out local producers? Are MNEs competing or acting as a cartel?
Flow of goods	Imports; exports. Does the FDI rely on imports of components or finished products rather than locally sourced inputs? What are the knock-on effects for local firms? Is the MNE exporting its output or selling it locally?
Labour	Job volatility; comparative pay scales; standards. Is the FDI creating new jobs or taking staff away from local employers? Does the FDI involve part-time workers or local contractors? Are workers/unions put under pressure? Is extra training offered?
Knowledge spillovers	Technology transfers; new management practices. Has the FDI raised local productivity? Have learning clusters developed? Is the host country capable of absorbing new knowledge or hosting hi-tech activities?
Sustainability	Pollution policies; competition for (and use of) resources. What pollution mitigation/abatement policies come with the FDI? Does it use best practices and clean technology?

Figure 5.8
Judging MNEs' impact on host economies (adapted from Barba Navaretti and Venables 2004).

Assessing FDI from a corporate perspective

The decision to do business in another country via FDI as opposed to another, less capital-intensive entry mode—such as trade, outsourcing, or licensing (see Chapter 9)—is one of the most important decisions that an MNE must make. Because of the extra costs and knowledge that FDI requires, companies embark upon this course only if they expect substantial gains.

Proactive reasons for engaging in FDI

Vertical integration. Where companies open specialist production units overseas to maximize each location's particular advantages, they put themselves in a position to increase their economies of scale and develop expertise. As long as intra-firm flows can be coordinated, the result will be a more rational production organization. This kind of 'internalization' (see Dunning's 'Eclectic Paradigm' theory in Chapter 2) helps companies to protect and enhance their competitive knowledge, since they retain responsibility for all operations and can therefore control and even monopolize the learning associated with this. One example is Apple's direct stake in many of the businesses (chips, software) whose output goes into its iPod products. This is an efficient way to ensure the coherency of any technological progress achieved in its value chain.

Proximity to resources. One leading factor in most international production is manual labour. This is often the key driver behind FDI, with companies seeking to take advantage of the wage differentials that exist across the planet. On other occasions, the resource sought through FDI is a physical commodity like oil or minerals. This rationale will become increasingly important as global demand for finite commodities creates supply shortages (see Chapter 16). Lastly, it is not only primary resources that companies seek through FDI but also access to knowledge, a crucial factor in many hi-tech sectors. One example of this was the decision taken by French computer company Honeywell-Bull to set up a representative office in California's Silicon Valley, thereby increasing its exposure to trendsetters in the world of computing. The main question at this level is whether the MNE will try to access local knowledge by working in partnership with domestic firms; with companies from their own country of origin; or with companies from elsewhere. Studies based on a sample of firms in Vietnam indicate that this collaboration decision (see Chapter 9) largely depends on investors' perception of the strength of host country institutions (Tan and Meyer 2011). FDI seems less challenging in countries where local institutional counterparts have a trustworthy reputation.

Proximity to customers. Companies often try to locate manufacturing facilities near or in emerging economies such as China or India for the obvious reason that this increases their chances of gaining a foothold in a dynamic market offering good growth prospects. This is particularly important if the host country government requires its national market to be served via FDI rather than imports, often because of the positive impact that inward investment is expected to have on local employment. A second proximity strategy involves replicating the internationalization moves of a customer with whom a company has a longstanding supply relationship. One example is the factory that Japanese automotive manufacturer Chuo Spring, built in Thailand following the decision by its main customer, Toyota, to undertake FDI in this country.

International economies of scale. The critical mass that firms achieve through FDI can occur on the upstream production side but also on the downstream sales side. This can be useful when domestic manufacturing capacities exceed home country demand. For instance, large British banks including HSBC have opened branches across continental Europe to sell financial products originating in the UK. By increasing the number of outlets selling products developed in its London trading room, they reduce their per-unit manufacturing costs.

Government incentives. Lastly, FDI can also involve opportunistic behaviour by MNEs taking advantage of government measures to encourage inwards investment. Chapter 3 detailed some of these incentives, which include competitively low corporation tax rates, industrial grants, and specific infrastructure outlays maximizing the productivity of new facilities.

Defensive reasons for engaging in FDI

Government interference. Because of the frequent perception that investment (through the capital, knowledge, and jobs that it provides) is more advantageous to a host country than imports are, governments sometimes establish barriers to trade specifically because they want to induce MNEs to enter their markets via FDI rather than through trade. Such policies, which during the 1970s motivated FDI decisions by Japanese car-makers in the USA or Volkswagen in Brazil, have become somewhat less prevalent in recent years. This is because the WTO criticizes them as a hidden form of protectionism, but also because of growing awareness by many host countries that a policy of economic openness can be a strong magnet for inwards FDI, especially when they combine with other industrial and economic development factors including market size, rich human resources, and good infrastructure (Zheng 2011).

Lack of domestic capacities. The importance of economies of scale in many price-sensitive sectors of activity can put companies originating from smaller countries at a disadvantage. This obstacle was one of several reasons underlying the series of acquisitions that Swedish 'white goods' appliances maker Electrolux made in 2011 in emerging economies ranging from Egypt to Chile and Argentina. Above and beyond the need to reduce logistics costs, Electrolux's plants in Sweden were not large enough to serve the demand volumes potentially emanating from these new locations.

Foreignness. A foreign brand will sometimes be penalized by consumers simply because they are more familiar with domestic alternatives. One way for MNEs to overcome this obstacle is by engaging in FDI, thereby showing greater commitment to the host country. Foreign firms can show their devotion to a local population through employment policies. Local marketing is another tool that companies can use to great effect. For instance, Tottenham Hotspur, one of London's leading football clubs, used to be sponsored by Holsten, a brewery from Hamburg seeking to raise its profile in the already crowded UK beer market.

Need to diversify exposures. As discussed in Chapter 1, there are two strategic risks that MNEs can address via FDI. One relates to foreign exchange, or the danger of accumulating costs in countries prone to currency rises and/or revenues in countries prone to currency devaluations. The second involves marketing, since products can grow old and unprofitable in one country while remaining young and attractive in another. Indeed, much FDI by food sector companies such as Nestlé or General Foods is specifically aimed at juggling global variations in product life cycles. Otherwise, FDI also allows companies to diversify their general macro-economic exposure. At any given moment in time, different countries will find themselves at varying stages of the economic cycle, with some experiencing a period of growth even as others enter recession. An MNE with operations in just one country risks losing out on a boom occurring elsewhere. Lastly, global FDI also increases a company's chance of benefiting from an LDC's emergence from poverty (see Chapter 15).

Undermining competitors. Some MNEs engage in FDI without any great hope of making much money from this action. Instead, their goal is to create greater competition in a rival's market of origin, undercutting its profits there to prevent it from engaging in price wars elsewhere. This is one explanation for the decision taken by US food manufacturer General Mills to take a stake in French yoghurt maker Yoplait in 2011. By controlling this brand, with its good expansion prospects in several emerging markets, the American MNE was preventing its giant French rival Danone from doing the same.

Recent FDI trends

As highlighted in UNCTAD's 2012 World Investment Report, 2011 global FDI flows of $1.5 trillion were still 23 per cent below the record level achieved the year before the 2008 subprime crisis broke out. The document went on to predict that the all-time record of $1.9 trillion would be reached in 2014, but this forecast was endangered by the European sovereign debt crisis, a second financial upheaval that could have a long-term dampening effect on investor confidence. The key observation here is that FDI appears to decline even more than total economic output does during times of trouble (a tendency also observed when the dot.com bubble burst in 2001). One implication is that crises diminish international managers' appetite for risk, including for the risks inherent to capital investments abroad.

There has also been a change in the dominant type of FDI practised during the crisis period compared with what could be witnessed previously. As detailed in Chapter 9, one way of categorizing FDI is by distinguishing between cross-border mergers and acquisitions (M&A) involving the takeover of existing foreign assets, and investment in new, so-called 'greenfield' facilities. The 2008 credit crunch and 2011–2012 European sovereign debt crisis both witnessed a sharp drop in M&A volumes, partially due to banks' growing unwillingness to fund such activities in an era when capital was short. There is always a question over whether M&A activity is driven more by strategic thinking or by opportunistic behaviour, instigated by the availability of funding.

Conversely, FDI involving the construction of brand new facilities seems to have suffered somewhat less in recent years, first and foremost because of the growing consensus that to remain competitive, companies need to expand their presence in emerging economies that have been altogether less affected by the recession than the older industrialized countries. The lesson here is that recession in one part of the world no longer necessarily signals that the same conditions will apply everywhere. More significantly, the fortunes of developing countries are no longer entirely dependent on the health of their more developed counterparts. For the first time ever, nearly half of global FDI flows in 2010 were directed at developing and transition (former communist) countries—with an increasing percentage of these sums originating from other LDCs (**see ORC Extension materials 5.3**). Developing countries used to receive less FDI due to their lesser intellectual property rights (Lung 2007) and the relative lack of democratic institutions (Jensen 2008) and good governance (Adhikary 2011). These obstacles no longer seem to carry as much weight in managers' minds.

> Go online

Lastly, in terms of the sectors where global FDI is occurring, currently around three-fifths involve services (including trade and finance), one-quarter manufacturing, and the rest primary goods. The expectation is that FDI in primary goods will rise in the future as energy and commodity prices continue their long-term uptrend (see Chapter 16). This prediction is based on fundamental demand conditions, partially driven by the rapid industrialization of the developing world, above all China. For instance, by some measures, Petrochina became the world's largest oil company in November 2007, following a series of investments that this state-owned MNE undertook in African countries including Sudan, Angola, and Nigeria. The expected growth in primary sector FDI will tend to benefit resource-rich countries like Russia and Brazil (and increasingly Mongolia), as well as those MNEs that have already secured their global supplies of raw materials. Conversely, downstream processors like Baoshan Iron and Steel, China's leading steel-maker, might struggle to secure the iron ore that they currently import from international mining companies such as Australia's BHP. To remedy this vulnerability, and much in the same way as European industrialists acquired foreign mines and oilfields a century ago to fuel the first era of globalization, there is a possibility that a large number of industrial MNEs will use FDI in the future to integrate backwards. One effect of this strategy, in a world afflicted by resource depletion, would be to intensify their interactions with host country governments concerning the management of their countries' natural resources.

Practitioner insight

After graduating from Bath University with an MSc in Development Studies, Achilleas Georgiou started his career working in international development before going on to advise multinational enterprises on their communications strategies with both internal and external partners. This latter responsibility involved his participating in the formulation of market entry and exit strategies, mainly across the European continent, where he has worked with both public and private sector counterparts.

'The first question when companies take the strategic position to enter or exit a market is where this decision is made. Usually it is corporate headquarters, meaning that in the host country itself, you need a partner familiar with the local legal and parliamentary context and capable of offering advice on how to achieve your objectives. At home you might have the capabilities to do this with in-house people but, unless your foreign affiliates already have public affairs and communications expertise abroad, there will always be a need to bring in outside help.

Many countries have local intermediaries happy to engage on incoming multinationals' behalf with politicians, regional or central government, business bodies, or unions. The question then becomes how (and especially when) this engagement should occur. Companies might take the view that they will enter a foreign market by buying land, assets, or a company without talking to the powers that be. They might have the same attitude when it comes down to closing an existing plant, saying they'll only talk with the staff members concerned. But this is wrong, if only because unionized workforces will nearly always mobilize under such conditions. So you need to get ahead of the game, think what your counterparts are thinking, engage with local politicians to help smooth the process.

I'll give you a well-known counter-example—the problems that Marks & Spencer experienced in France, when they shut down outlets in 2001. The French government backed union moves to stop the closures and Minister for Labour Elisabeth Guigou called for a Europe-wide trade union protest (Webster 2001). M&S's actions serve as a good lesson for other multinationals that followed in its tracks on how to manage relations in countries like France, and also on how to protect their global brand when exiting a country.

At the same time, it is very interesting that many politicians criticizing an MNE sometimes only do this to show a populist face. In reality, you can often get them on board by remembering the two things they normally want: inwards investment and jobs. You might not even have the choice, seeing how more and more host governments have taken to enacting legislation that requires multinationals to join forces with host country partners, either as joint ventures or through supply chain alliances.

Similarly, we are also seeing host governments requiring some form of corporate social responsibility and asking multinationals to train and up-skill local people. I generally have the impression that states want to be stronger in achieving things for their nationals.'

Lobbying

Negotiations between MNEs and host countries are extremely complicated bargaining situations (Agmon 2003). A good example is the concept of 'obsolescing bargaining', which states that an MNE can put greater pressure on a host country government before it invests in the country than afterwards. The amount of pressure that can be applied depends on how important the MNE is to the country, or vice versa. Logically, a company will have to be more conciliatory when entering a dynamic growth market such as India or China.

Conversely, where the host country is desperate for the capital, knowledge, and jobs that the FDI is offering to bring, the MNE will be in a stronger bargaining position (Grosse 2005). This is especially true if the host government is aware that the company has a large multinational network enabling it to shift production elsewhere quickly and for relatively little cost (Ietto-Gillies 2004). Much depends on whether the MNE plans to use the FDI to produce goods that will be re-exported, thus earning foreign currency for the host country, or to sell goods and services into the local market, thereby displacing national firms.

On other occasions, the factors influencing MNE–host country relationships are more subjective in nature. These can include the host government's general attitude towards foreign interests. In all likelihood, governments run by politicians who are partisans of free trade will be more welcoming to FDI than ones whose sole priority is to protect domestic constituents' interests. Trust in a foreign MNE will also depend on its track record. A feeling of mistrust can arise if there is the perception that an MNE has a pattern of trying to take advantage of countries' weaknesses. One reason why so many LDCs still require MNEs to sign 'joint venture' mixed ownership alliances with local partners (see Chapter 9) is suspicion of the motives and methods of what some critics have come to denounce as the 'corporacracy' of large firms (Palast 2003). Even globalization-friendly economists often have some sympathy with LDCs' aversion to MNEs' lobbying activities. Jagdish Bhagwati (2004), for instance, noted the inappropriateness of some US companies' successful lobbying to get Washington to force Mexico into accepting an intellectual property regime that was specifically tailored towards American interests before agreeing to sign the NAFTA treaty. Another controversial instance related to the way in which the US government allowed itself to be lobbied in 1999 by American firms that wanted to prevent Thailand from placing any restrictions on foreign cigarette sales, the argument being that public health measures of this sort were 'GATT-inconsistent'. This kind of aggressive lobbying, which sometimes involves MNEs getting their home country government to put added pressure on the host country in question, unsurprisingly generates feelings of hostility that, in turn, get in the way of harmonious international business relationships. The short-term advantages that an MNE is able to negotiate may be offset over the long run by the negative brand image that the local population will attribute to it—or to other companies from the same country of origin.

Nonetheless, there is no doubt that interactions between many MNEs and national governments are friendlier than they were before the 1990s, when the world was torn between communism, and capitalism, and subject to greater ideological polarization than is the case today. One explanation for this generally broader acceptance of foreign companies' influence is the greater global awareness developed in many modern universities, as well as the 'insiderization' effects of several decades of globalization (which has had the consequence of making many MNEs seem less foreign than they used to). Feelings of economic patriotism may continue to undermine foreign ownership in some countries, but obstacles of this kind can generally be overcome if the MNE is perceived as adding real value to the local economy and is not accused of causing cultural, social, or environmental harm. As discussed in Chapter 8, widespread recognition of the benefits of a positive reputation has changed the nature of international lobbying. Nowadays, MNEs tend to resort to advocacy approaches involving the organization of well-publicized open forums where they try to win the battle for hearts and minds. The focus is no longer on heavy-handed threats behind closed doors but on convincing friendly foreign audiences of the advantages of establishing a partnership relationship—although often on the MNE's terms.

Lobbying is already widespread in many OECD countries. It came under repeated criticism, for example during the 2012 US presidential campaign, for providing companies with an unfair advantage to the detriment of other interest groups. This explains the adoption of different codes (like the European Commission's 2001 Green Paper on Governance) aimed at restricting lobbyists' conduct. At the same time, some observers take the opposite view that advocacy lobbying is nothing more than managers' democratic right to influence

+ Advocacy
Speaking out on behalf of a certain constituency in order to influence policy-makers to adopt a friendly stance.

political decisions in areas of interest to MNEs, which include topics like foreign trade, agriculture, technical standards, and intellectual property rights (Coen and Grant 2005). Lobbying cannot be deemed to be intrinsically unfair as long as everyone has a similar opportunity to employ lobbyists (Hoekman and Kostecki 2001). There is no doubt that, in much of the world, joining an advocacy group (**see ORC Extension materials 5.4**) has become a standard way for MNEs to gain the attention of home and host country governments alike.

> Go online

It is also worth noting international variations in lobbying approaches. The US legislative process, for instance, is marked by so-called 'pork barrel' politics where members of Congress actively seek funds for projects benefiting the constituencies they represent. In a certain sense, this means that power is less centralized in this country than it is in Europe, where almost all EU-wide decisions are made in Brussels (Guégen 2007). At the same time, EU member states hold much more power than US federal states do. The USA and the EU also have different systems in terms of how they fund political parties and campaigns. These considerations all affect the ways in which international lobbyists might try to influence local politicians.

Lastly, there is a striking difference between lobbying in the Western hemisphere and in Asia, where companies might apply what the Chinese call a *guanxi* approach to construct personal relationships and a sense of social obligation with politicians (see Chapter 6). Government–business relations in this region are deeply rooted in local cultures, meaning that professional lobbying in the US or European styles will be less effective here. Yet Western MNEs also need good relationships with local authorities in Asia, especially in countries like China, where bureaucratic decisions like licensing are not always made in a way that is particularly transparent to foreigners. This explains why so many MNEs retain the services of individuals capable of developing good political connections. In this as in many other areas of international business, 'insiderization' is a key factor of success.

Challenges and choices

→ Size is a major challenge for many firms considering international operations, especially during their formative early years. If a company remains small, it will struggle to achieve the critical mass required for certain aspects of international business. This means that it may be condemned to act as a niche player and remains vulnerable to the risk that larger rivals might one day force their way into its sector of activity. Conversely, for various strategic, financial, and human resource reasons, rapid growth can be very risky for young companies. Size for size's sake is rarely a reliable internationalization strategy.

Chapter summary

This final chapter in the trilogy examining the main actors in international business focuses on MNEs, the constraints they face, and the impact of their actions on the home and especially host countries where they operate. Multinationals' room to manoeuvre across borders is limited by several factors, including the funds available to them, the political support they enjoy, and the logistics and communications obstacles that they face. Size is another key variable affecting companies' performance in the international markets. All these factors vary in time and place, as do MNEs' responses, first and foremost being their FDI actions and the relationships they entertain with the host country governments that they lobby.

Case study 5.3

MNE internationalization: It's SAB Miller time

The giant South African beer multinational SAB Miller is today recognized as a world leader in its sector, but few of the millions of customers consuming its 200 brands will be aware of the many different strategic moves that created this global empire.

SAB (http://www.sabmiller.com) was founded in 1895 and quickly achieved success selling its Castle Lager brand to thirsty gold miners. Once South Africa's relationships with the rest of the British Empire normalized following the Boer War, SAB took advantage of its preferential access to the London Stock Exchange to source funds enabling its expansion into Rhodesia (now Zimbabwe), a friendly neighbour that did not put obstacles in the way of imports coming from a fellow Commonwealth member. The company also worked together with a domestic rival to develop the production of hops in South African farming, a vertical integration ensuring its ability to source the key raw material for its beer products. For the first half of the twentieth century, SAB was happy to consolidate its regional presence, but after moving its headquarters to Johannesburg in 1950, management decided to accelerate the company's growth rate. The first step involved the acquisition of local rivals. This helped SAB to achieve economies of scale and escape competition in its home market.

From the 1960s onwards, however, further expansion for SAB, like for all South African firms, was restricted by international boycotts following global condemnation of the apartheid regime's racial policies. To overcome this obstacle, the company started working together with non-South African brands such as Amstel (Amsterdam) and Carling (Cleveland, Ohio) while diversifying into non-beer-related activities. The apartheid regime fell in 1990 and the ensuing cessation of sanctions paved the way for SAB's renewed internationalization. With the world's communist bloc also opening up that same year, SAB developed an opportunistic horizontal integration strategy, purchasing a series of breweries in Eastern European, Asian, and Central American countries with new regimes hungry to attract inwards investment. These moves also reflected SAB's level of comfort with operations located in the developing world, a specialty that its main international rivals, originating in the world's more advanced economies, did not possess.

By the turn of the century, this unique growth strategy gave SAB the size enabling it to finally compete directly with some of its older rivals. This ultimately led in 2002 to the acquisition of Miller, the USA's second largest brewer in volume. The following year, the new combined entity, now called SAB Miller, began to move into Western Europe, acquiring a majority stake in leading Italian brand Peroni. Whereas most of today's better known MNEs started in the developed world and only recently expanded into emerging economies, SAB Miller stands out for having followed the opposite trajectory. Its success demonstrates that the path to international success is never written in stone but reflects the particular circumstances in which a company finds itself at different points in time.

Once SAB Miller had achieved sufficient geographical diversification to avoid being over-exposed to any one region, it returned to its previous pattern of focusing on growth markets, starting with its home region of Africa, which attracted nearly one-third of the group's total investments in the early 2010s (Economist 2012a). This often involved joint ventures with partners like the French company Castel, to consolidate market share (SAB Miller has a 60 per cent market share in Africa for commercial beer) but also because the company's rapid expansion stretched its finances. There had been a growing consensus within this industry that consolidation was necessary to protect profit margins withered by global competition and SAB Miller's management paradigm was fairly typical of its peers. Thus, the late 2000s saw more and more horizontal actions where the company would either launch its own brands in new markets or acquire existing brands abroad, most notably Australia's famous Foster's beer in 2011. Along the way, it has also become one of the world's largest bottlers of Coca-Cola products while also launching innovative new cassava or sorghum-based beers—a diversification that offers synergies with the competencies it has developed through its core business.

With fewer of the brand creations that marked the company's early years, SAB Miller's recent focus has been on other areas, starting with sustainable development (environmental, social, and health-related) and corporate governance. The new priorities are entirely in line with modern concerns about corporate ethics above and beyond its products. They have not prevented SAB Miller from achieving exemplary financial results: 2011 pre-tax profits of $3.63 billion (up 24 per cent year-on-year) for group revenues of $28.3 billion (up 7 per cent) and net debt down 16 per cent to $7.09 billion. Yet they have laid the company open to increased scrutiny in areas unrelated to its core beer business, starting with recent

accusations that it has avoided 'millions of pounds of tax in India and African countries by routing profits through a web of tax-haven subsidiaries' (Lawrence 2011). Depriving poor countries of tax revenues is not good for the image of an MNE that has historically specialized in gaining dominant positions in LDCs. The dilemma for the company is its need to generate maximum cash flow to fund its global expansion.

All in all, it would be difficult to analyse SAB Miller's multinational trajectory without bringing many different factors into the equation. The company states that its focus has always been 'excelling locally'. By definition, this requires a track record of strategic flexibility.

MNEs like SAB Miller apply abroad many of the lessons they learn in their home market

Case study questions

1. Why did SAB Miller prefer vertical integration at certain moments in history, and horizontal integration at others?
2. Describe SAB Miller's different negotiations over time with host governments.
3. What motives explain the company's historic acquisitions?

Discussion questions

1. List the different ways in which FDI has a positive or detrimental effect on host countries.

2. Now that Ford has manufactured and sold cars in Europe for nearly a century, how important is it that the company originally came from the USA?

3. Is SMEs' share of international business destined to rise or fall? Why?

4. Which sectors are likely to dominate FDI flows in the future?

5. Is MNE lobbying an example of democracy at work or a case of institutionalized corruption?

Online resource centre

Go online to test your understanding by trying multiple-choice questions, and assignment and examination questions.

Further research

Buckley, P. and Casson, M. (2010). *The Multinational Enterprise Revisited: The Essential Buckley and Casson*. Basingstoke: Palgrave Macmillan

This book identifies certain crucial problems in understanding multinational enterprises: the nature of such companies; the determinants of the international division of labour; the rationale for joint ventures; and the role of trust in international business transactions.

Jones, G. and Friedman, W. (2011). *The Rise of the Modern Firm*. Northampton, MA: Edward Elgar Publishing Ltd

This book traces the historical rise of modern firms, depicted as agents shaping economic growth in national and international settings. Focus is placed on the role of laws and contracts in determining corporate influence, and also on entrepreneurs and executives' personal actions.

References

Adhikary, B. (2011). 'Foreign direct investment, governance, and economic growth: A panel analysis of Asian economies', *Asia Pacific World*, 2/1, pp. 72–94

Agmon, T. (2003). 'Who gets what: The MNE, the national state and the distributional effects of globalization', *Journal of International Business Studies*, 34/5 (September)

Altman, D. (2007). 'Managing globalization: Has it hurt US workers?', 17 April, available at http://www.iht.com, accessed 31 October 2008

Barba Navaretti, G., and Venables, A. (2004). *Multinational Firms in the World Economy*. Princeton: Princeton University Press

BBC (2005). 'Cadbury gobbles up organic rival', 13 May, available at http://news.bbc.co.uk, accessed 31 October 2008

Bhagwati, J. (2004). *In Defense of Globalization*. New York: Oxford University Press

Bhatt, P. (2011). 'A causal relationship between exports, foreign direct investment and income for Malaysia', *Journal for Global Business Advancement*, 4/2, pp. 155–166 (July)

Black, S. and Morrison, A. (2010). *Sunset in the Land of the Rising Sun: Why Japanese Multinational Corporations Will Struggle in the Global Future*. Basingstoke: Palgrave Macmillan

Busse, M., Nunnenkamp, P., and Spatareanu, M. (2011). 'Foreign direct investment and labour rights: A panel analysis of bilateral FDI flows', *Applied Economics Letters*, 18/2, pp. 149–152 (February)

Coe, D. (2008). 'Jobs on another shore', *IMF: Finance and Development*, March

Coen, D. and Grant, W. (2005). 'Business and government in international policymaking: The transatlantic business dialogue as an emerging style?', in D. Kelly and W. Grant (eds.). *The Politics of International Trade in the Twenty-First Century: Actors, Issues and Regional Dynamics*. Basingstoke: Palgrave Macmillan

Contrepois, S., Delteil, V., Dieuaide, P., and Jefferys, S. (eds.) (2010). *Globalizing Employment Relations: Multinational Firms and Central and Eastern Europe Transitions*. London: Palgrave Macmillan

Copeland, M. (2006). 'How startups go global', 29 June, available at http://money.cnn.com, accessed 7 July 2008

Cuyvers, L. and Soeng, R. (2011). 'The effects of Belgian outward direct investment in European high-wage and low-wage countries on employment in Belgium', *International Journal of Manpower*, 32/3, pp. 300–312

Damijan, J. and Kostevc, C. (2011). 'Trade liberalisation and economic geography in CEE countries: The role of FDI in the adjustment pattern of regional wages', *Post-Communist Economies*, 23/2, pp. 163–189

Economist (2011). 'What was ours is now mine', 13 May, available at http://www.economist.com, accessed 19 January 2012

Economist (2012a). 'Beer in Africa: From lumps to lager', *The Economist*, 24 March, p. 75

Economist (2012b). 'What Germany offers the world', *The Economist*, 14 April, p. 27

Froud, J., Johal, S., Leaver, A., and Williams, K. (2006). *Financialization and Strategy: Narrative and Numbers*. London: Routledge

Glyn, A. (2006). *Capitalism Unleashed: Finance, Globalization and Welfare*. Oxford: Oxford University Press

Grosse, R. (ed.) (2005). *International Business and Government Relations in the 21st Century*. Cambridge: Cambridge University Press

Gu, Q. and Lu, J. (2011). 'Effects of inward investment on outward investment: The venture capital industry worldwide 1985–2007', *Journal of International Business Studies*, 42/2, pp. 263–284 (February)

Guégen, D. (2007). *European Lobbying*, 2nd edn. Brussels: European Politics

Guillen, M. and Garcia-Canal, E. (2010). *The New Multinationals: Spanish Firms in a Global Context*. Cambridge: Cambridge University Press

Hoekman, B. and Kostecki, M. (2001). *The Political Economy of the World Trading System*, 2nd edn. New York: Oxford University Press

Ietto-Gillies, G. (2004). 'The nation-state and the theory of the transnational corporation', available at http://www.econ.cam.ac.uk, accessed 31 October 2008

Jeffries, S. (2005). 'I should cocoa', 16 May, available at http://www.guardian.co.uk, accessed 31 October 2008

Jensen, N. (2008). *Nation-States and the Multinational Corporation: A Political Economy of Foreign Direct Investment*. Princeton, NJ: Princeton University Press

Jones, G. (2005). *Multinationals and Global Capitalism: From the Nineteenth to the Twenty-First Century*. Oxford: Oxford University Press

Kontinen, T. and Ojala, A. (2011). 'Network ties in the international opportunity recognition of family SMEs', *International Business Review*, 20/4, pp. 440–453 (August)

Lawrence, F. (2011). 'Brewer accused of depriving poor countries of millions in revenue', *The Guardian*, 29 November, p. 21

Le, H. and Pomfret, R. (2011). 'Technology spillovers from foreign direct investment in Vietnam: Horizontal or vertical spillovers?', *Journal of the Asia Pacific Economy*, 16/2, pp. 183–201

Leitao, J. and Baptista, R. (2011). 'Inward FDI and ICT: Are they a joint technological driver of entrepreneurship?', *International Journal of Technology Transfer and Commercialisation*, 10/3–4, pp. 268–288

Lindstrand, A., Melén, S., and Nordman, E. (2011). 'Turning social capital into business: A study of the internationalization of biotech SMEs', *International Business Review*, 20/2, pp. 194–212 (April)

Lung, Y. (2007). 'Une mondialisation à un rythme effrené', *Sud-Ouest*, 30 March

Makino, S. and Tsang, E. (2011). 'Historical ties and foreign direct investment: An exploratory study', *Journal of International Business Studies*, 42/4, pp. 545–557 (May)

Monk, D. (2011). 'Proctor & Gamble hit with $312M price-fixing fine in Europe', 8 December, available at http://www.bizjournals.com, accessed 19 January 2012

Muchlinski, P. (2011). 'Regulating multinationals: Foreign investment, development, and the balance of corporate and home country rights and responsibilities in a globalizing world', *The Evolving International Investment Regime*, pp. 30–60 (April)

Palast, G. (2003). *The Best Democracy Money Can Buy: The Truth about Corporate Cons, Globalization and High-Finance Fraudsters*. New York: Plume

RTRS (2011). 'European oil companies resist US pressure to withdraw from Teheran', 1 October, available at http://ww.arabtimesonline.com/, accessed 19 January 2012

Rugman, A. (2005). *The Regional Multinationals: MNEs and 'Global' Strategic Management*. Cambridge: Cambridge University Press

Tan, D. and Meyer, K. (2011). 'Country-of-origin and industry FDI agglomeration of foreign investors in an emerging economy', *Journal of International Business Studies*, 42/4, pp. 504–520 (May)

Times of India (2010). 'IBM is India's second largest private sector employer', 18 August, available at http://www.indiatimes.com/, accessed 18 January 2012

UNCTAD (2011). *World Investment Report 2011: Non-Equity Modes of International Production and Development*, available at http://www.unctad-docs.org/files/UNCTAD-WIR2011-Full-en.pdf, accessed 10 August 2012

UNECE (2001). *Entrepreneurship and SME Development*, available at http://www.unece.org, accessed 1 November 2007

Vlachos, V. (2011). 'International business spillovers in South Eastern Europe: Members of the stability pact', *International Journal of Economic Policy in Emerging Economies*, 4/2, pp. 197–210 (April)

Webster, P. (2001). 'France calls for protests at M&S closures', 6 April, available at http://www.guardian.co.uk, accessed 25 March 2012

Wei, Y. and Liu, X. (2006). 'Productivity spillovers from R&D, exports and FDI in China's manufacturing sector', *Journal of International Business Studies*, 7/5 (September)

Wilkins, M. (2005). 'Multinational enterprise to 1930: Discontinuities and continuities', in A. Chandler and B. Mazlish (eds.). *Leviathans: Multinational Corporations and the New Global History*. Cambridge: Cambridge University Press

Zheng, P. (2011). 'The determinants of disparities in inward FDI flows to the three macro-regions of China', *Post-Communist Economies*, 23/2, pp. 257–270 (June)

Part case study

A tale of two regions: Global governance strategies in Europe and Asia

Much has been written on the rising number of intermediary-level institutions operating between the global level of decision-making, where bodies like the UN or the WTO function, and the local level, where national governments rule supreme. This intermediary space of governance features very different kinds of players, ranging from non-governmental organizations to international financial institutions and regional associations (see Chapter 4). In addition, there is no real consensus on the powers awarded to the bodies acting within this category, or the extent to which they have the right to be involved in decision-making on other levels. Hence the growing number of countries today with political movements that loudly proclaim their reluctance to see any real power transferred to a regional association. On the other hand, there is also an understanding that the increasingly cross-border nature of finance demands an 'adequate institutional infrastructure' (Obstfeld 2012). Here the question is no longer whether power should be shifted to the regional level, but how much and in what form.

An example of this debate can be witnessed in the European and Asian approaches to two major international business dilemmas facing these regions, respectively trade and finance. The EU experienced severe economic hardship in late 2011 and early 2012 when a number of longstanding problems came together, led by the sovereign debt crisis epitomized by Greece's inability to reimburse its debts. The consequence of the crisis was lower demand for products resulting in massive job losses across the continent. As often happens at times of crisis, politicians representing their struggling constituencies focused on protecting narrow national interests, especially in countries whose open border policies have led to trade deficits and the perception that jobs are being shipped abroad. History has shown that there is greater consensus in favour of free trade during a strong economy than in a recession. For instance, with an election coming up in May 2012, it was no surprise when incumbent French President Nicolas Sarkozy used a campaign speech to advocate government intervention in the allocation of public contracts to ensure that the business is given to local companies instead of foreign competitors (Economist 2012a). More noteworthy is the fact that this stance was supported by Karel de Gucht,

a Belgian serving as EU Trade Commissioner (Barker et al. 2012), a role traditionally fulfilled by strong advocates of free trade.

The market for public procurement contracts amounts in many countries to as much as 15–20 per cent of GDP. To open up these particular kinds of markets, around 40 countries worldwide have signed a 'government-procurement agreement' (GPA) framework. The problem is that China is not one of these signatories. Moreover, in volume terms, twice as many EU contracts are open to foreign bidders than in the USA and 13 times more than in Japan. Sensitive to this imbalance, Mr De Gucht claimed that it would be 'naïve' not to level the playing field by ensuring that European producers receive the same market access abroad as foreign interests enjoy in Europe. Frenchman Michel Barnier, the EU's Single Market Commissioner, further supported the approach with the suggestion that foreign bidders might be shut out of any state contracts exceeding €5 million (and featuring at least 50 per cent foreign product content) if local municipalities, national governments, or the EU itself determined that the bids came from countries that discriminated against European producers. In the eyes of the proposal's authors, this tougher attitude should result in greater 'reciprocity'.

Not all EU members were happy with the new focus, however, with Germany in particular expressing a great deal of concern. The possibility that the new legislation might be used by one European member state against another, undermining the whole mission of the EU, was a real fear. The new preference for European producers could also result in increasing public procurement costs and therefore waste taxpayers' money. Lastly, this kind of aggressive attitude might increase the likelihood of further trade wars between EU member states and their partners. Of course, given Germany's strong export performance, it is in this country's interest to maintain the status quo in the international trade system, unlike fellow EU members who tend to do less well in competitive global markets. One lesson here is that neighbouring countries might join forces in a regional association yet maintain completely opposed policy objectives in certain areas.

This European furore can be contrasted with the more serene arrangements found in Asia in spring 2012, when

China, Japan, and South Korea came together with ASEAN members (see Chapter 4) to devise a framework defending the region against the kind of financial instability from which it suffered in the late 1990s (Economist 2012b). The common purpose of the countries involved was to find a mechanism for mutual aid in case of a liquidity crisis. This was not the first attempt at such an understanding. In 2000, for instance, the Chiang Mai Initiative (CMI) culminated in bilateral agreements between national central banks, with signatories promising to provide one another with liquidities if needed. This was followed by years of economic dialogue, culminating in the 2010 CMI agreement where the earlier promises were turned into something binding. Only a relatively small amount of money was involved, however—$240 billion, a sum well below what would be needed to stave off a capital outflow crisis. This suggests that the relative tranquillity with which a regional consensus has been reached in Asia can be partially explained by the modest sums involved. What then becomes questionable is how friendly intra-regional relations would become if bold plans to develop a heavily resourced 'Asian Monetary Fund' were ever to take shape. It is easy to get along with one's neighbours when this does not cost very much. It is quite a bit more difficult when the stakes get higher.

Case study questions

1. To what extent should the EU dictate public procurement policies to its member states?
2. What are the advantages and disadvantages of the particular policy that Mr de Gucht and Mr Barnier have suggested?
3. What is the likelihood that the Asian countries in the CMI will ever agree to pool larger sums?

References

Barker, A., Chaffin, J., and Pignal, S. (2012). 'Germany warns on keeping EU market open', *Financial Times*, 21 March, available at http://www.ft.com, accessed 9 April 2012

Economist (2012a). 'Charlemagne: Unfree trade', *The Economist*, 24 March, p. 46

Economist (2012b). 'Banyan: A rather flimsy firewall', *The Economist*, 7 April, p. 46

Obstfeld, M. (2012). 'Financial flows, financial crises and global imbalances', *Journal of International Money and Finance*, 31, 469–480

part

C

Cultural perspectives

6 National cultures

Learning objectives

By the end of this chapter, you should be able to:

✦ appreciate and understand definitions and uses of the concept of national cultures

✦ recognize and understand the different models of culture, particularly as applied to international business

✦ evaluate the implications of national cultures for business and employment relationships

✦ recognize the relationship between cultural attitudes and business behaviour

✦ assess the abilities required by managers to navigate their way through a world of different cultures

Case study 6.1

Food courts and the globalization of national tastes

Hawaiian pizza with pineapple? Lasagne with the flavours of Mexican tortilla or chicken tikka masala? Lattes not café au lait in French patisseries? Le Big Mac and a Royale with cheese? Black pudding mousse au chocolat? Sherry with ice? Brazilian sushi?

The development towards a world culture has introduced global food to consumers, but there are many issues with the globalization of food and drink. These include whether people are eating the genuine or original form of the food or drink, and how far companies can afford to alter the 'pure' form of the food or drink before it can really no longer be sold as belonging to that culture. Above all, if the item that consumers eat or drink is not authentic, will they have an incorrect impression of the country of its supposed origin?

The food court acts as a telling microcosm of the globalization and homogenization of food. Originating in the shopping malls of the USA, food courts are now widespread throughout the world. The food court offers many different types of food and drink provided by specialist outlets—noodles from Asia, pizza from Italy, burgers from America, sushi from Japan, curry from India, doughnuts and pretzels. Commercial logic has resulted in single sites providing an international range of food.

A regular feature in food courts and in other internationalized eating and shopping locations is pizza. Originally an Italian dish, pizza has spread throughout the world as an international food, available for home consumption and for eating out in restaurants. Much of the development of pizza as a world food has come from the creations of Italian immigrants to the USA and, indeed, from Greek immigrants and their version—the Greek pizza. Among the international industry leaders are Pizza Hut and Dominos.

One of the most unusual pizza offerings comes from a US-based company called California Pizza Kitchen (CPK), founded in 1985 and since 2011 owned by a private equity firm (Golden Gate Capital). The company has about 14,000 employees worldwide and had revenues of $642 million at the end of 2010. CPK has over 260 outlets in 32 states in the USA and in 11 other countries— including the United Arab Emirates, the Philippines, Mexico, Japan, and China, including Hong Kong (California Pizza Kitchen 2012; Yahoo Finance 2012). CPK's menu now includes many other items, but the pizzas offered cover such non-Italian varieties as mango tandoori chicken pizza, Jamaican jerk chicken pizza, Habanero Carnitas (with pulled pork), chipotle chicken (with roasted corn and black bean sauce), and Thai chicken pizza. Is this the ultimate departure from an original national food into an internationalized commodity designed to appeal to a universal set of customers?

The combination of the pizza outlet and the range of other drink and food provided in a food court is a striking expression of the globalization of eating and drinking. Food courts are simultaneously evidence of the international market for restaurants and showcases for national tastes in food and drink. They are a fascinating illustration of both the clash of national cultures and the possibilities of a new world culture.

Domino's is among the market leaders in the pizza industry

+ World culture
Growing concept of a universal culture that rises above national cultures and emphasizes global events and world organizations.

+ Culture
Broad term that covers many patterns of human activity that exemplify the ways of life of a certain population.

+ Internationalize
Decision to enter foreign markets; involves upstream and/or downstream activities.

Introduction: What is culture?

Most successful international business relies on factors such as clear strategy, cost control, pricing, product quality, meeting customer needs, and an understanding of national cultures. Each MNE operates within internal and external contexts, and one of the most significant aspects of the external environment is national culture. The simplest international form of the impact of national culture is when the MNE comes from one country, is 100 per cent staffed by people from that country, and operates in only one foreign country. Although this might have been true of international activities many decades ago, it is now far more common that any MNE is staffed by nationals of many different countries, that it operates throughout the world, and that its 'original' country of origin may be hidden behind the international image that it projects to its worldwide customers.

An accepted view of culture is that it is like an onion with several different layers that can be peeled back to reveal deep meanings and core values, as noted in Figure 6.1. The outside layers feature explicit manifestations of the culture—products, artefacts, food, language, shrines, markets, houses, monuments, art, and so on. The intermediate layers contain the norms and values of the individual culture; these include the mutual and agreed sense of what is meant by 'right' and 'wrong', whether these are expressed as formal laws and/or as informal social control, and what is understood to be 'good' or 'bad'. For two of the key experts in this field, the difference between norms and values is that norms 'give us a feeling of "this is how I normally should behave"' whereas values 'give us a feeling of "this is how I aspire or desire to behave"' (Trompenaars and Hampden-Turner 1997). People engaged in international business must not only have empathy with other cultures, they also need to know how to behave and how to devise strategies for conducting business successfully within the constraints of the organization for which they work.

Section I: Interpretations of culture

+ Hierarchy of needs
Maslow's concept sets out a pyramid of layers of human need, from basic needs such as food, water, and shelter to the realization of personal potential and self-fulfilment.

As noted above, one of the interpretations of culture, as indicated in Figure 6.1, is that it consists of different layers, with the centre containing the fundamental aspects of human culture and human existence. At the most basic, these are survival in the face of natural elements, security from hunger and want, and provision of people's basic and physical needs, such as shelter. At the higher end of the spectrum, human beings have aspirations towards greater self-fulfilment. The many variations in human values, needs, and wants have also been explored by other writers (e.g. Kluckhohn and Strodtbeck 1961). All these layers of culture can also be expressed in Maslow's hierarchy of needs—an attempted

Figure 6.1
Layers of culture (adapted from Trompenaars and Hampden-Turner 1997).

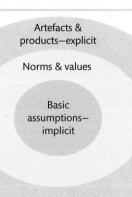

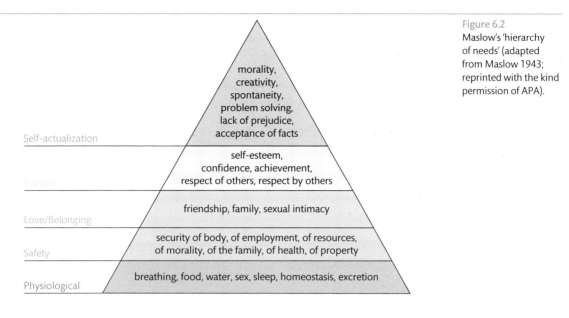

Figure 6.2
Maslow's 'hierarchy of needs' (adapted from Maslow 1943; reprinted with the kind permission of APA).

gradation of human needs from the most ordinary (at the bottom of the pyramid) to the most extraordinary (at the top of the pyramid).

In the 1940s and 1950s, Abraham Maslow set out an approach for understanding the full range of human needs. He originally stressed that each person is motivated by needs, starting from the most basic, which are innate, having evolved over tens of thousands of years. Maslow's 'hierarchy of needs' is designed to help explain how these needs motivate all humans. It states that people must satisfy each need in turn, starting with the first, which deals with survival itself. Only when the lower-order needs of physical and emotional well-being are satisfied are people concerned with the higher-order needs of influence and personal development. Conversely, if the factors that guarantee the satisfaction of lower-order needs are removed, people are no longer concerned about the maintenance of the higher-order needs.

Over time the model of the 'hierarchy of needs' has developed from an original set of five needs, as illustrated in Figure 6.2, to seven needs, with the addition of cognitive (knowledge and meaning) and aesthetic (appreciation and search for beauty, balance, and form). For people engaged in business, whether domestic or international, there can be real applications of Maslow's concepts and the models of the hierarchy.

The highest concept of self-actualization relates directly to the present-day challenges and opportunities for employers and organizations; that is, the need to provide real meaning, purpose, and true personal development for employees. This supports the view that people in employment need to have a true life–work balance; their key needs relate to their whole life, not just the time and effort that is devoted to work. For some companies, typically in Scandinavian business cultures, strenuous efforts are made to ensure that staff efficiency comes from a combination of working hard while taking regular work breaks and holidays. Similarly, but in a different national and business context, a company such as Mont Blanc, now part of the Richemont Group (luxury pens, watches, jewellery, and other products) insists that staff take a certain number of holiday weeks and cultural breaks, such as visits to the theatre and concerts (personal communication 2012).

Maslow noted the fact that employees at all levels of the company have a basic human need and right to strive for self-actualization, just as much as corporate directors and owners do. Increasingly, the successful organizations and employers in many cultures will be those that genuinely care about, understand, encourage, and enable their people's personal growth towards self-actualization. This means that MNEs, and other firms engaged in international business, realize that they need to go beyond traditional work-related training

+ Autocratic management
Management style that is domineering and dictatorial, sometimes with the exercise of unrestricted authority.

+ Corporate culture
Common values shared by employees at all levels of a business. This can sometimes form an implicit or explicit control mechanism within the company.

and development, and abandon the concepts and behaviour of old-style autocratic management. Modern business employers have learnt that ongoing and sustainable success is built on a serious commitment to helping people identify, pursue, and reach their own unique potential. The assumption is that when people are encouraged to grow, they automatically become more effective and valuable as employees. Most personal growth is seen as producing new skills, attributes, behaviour, and wisdom that are directly or indirectly transferable to any sort of job or employment role. In the most effective national and corporate cultures, the best modern employers recognize the importance of personal growth and offer development support to their members of staff so that each person seeks to grow and become more fulfilled (see Chapter 7).

Religions and languages

As noted above, the outer layers of the culture 'onion' contain elements such as art, literature, religions, and languages. The latter two are significant constituents and main determinants of national cultures, thus forming the backdrop to countries, and indeed to other entities, such as communities or regions. As can be seen from Figures 6.3–6.6, the variety of religious adherence and faith, and of languages, contributes massively to the kaleidoscope that contains all the coloured pieces constituting the culture of a nation or a society.

Figure 6.3 demonstrates that the main global religions of the world are clearly Christianity and Islam but, as is evident from many of the social and political disputes in the world, some of the main divisions are within these broad religious categories. The separation in terms of belief, faith, and values between Shiite and Sunni Islam or between Catholic and Protestant Christianity are often greater than between the two main religions. Each of these world religions is really a classification of multiple distinct movements, sects, divisions, and denominations. None of these world religions is a single, unified, monolithic organization, but the diversity within these groupings varies. Hinduism, for example, is sometimes described as a collection of very different traditions, bound by a geographical and national identity—that is, within the Indian subcontinent. At the other extreme, and in contrast to complex religious groupings such as Christianity and Hinduism, there is the Babi and Baha'i tradition, which is probably the most unified of the classical world religions. The

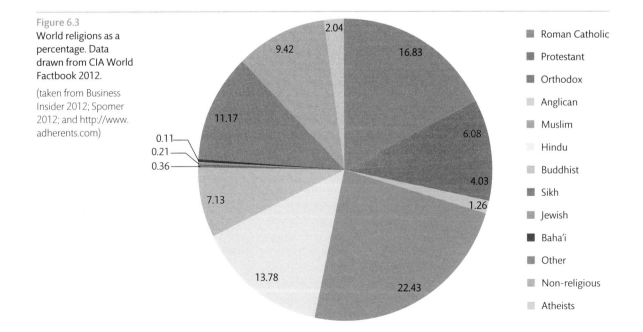

Figure 6.3
World religions as a percentage. Data drawn from CIA World Factbook 2012.

(taken from Business Insider 2012; Spomer 2012; and http://www.adherents.com)

Roman Catholic
Protestant
Orthodox
Anglican
Muslim
Hindu
Buddhist
Sikh
Jewish
Baha'i
Other
Non-religious
Atheists

Branch	Number of adherents
Christianity	
Catholic	968,000,000
Protestant	395,867,000
Other Christians	275,583,000
Orthodox	217,948,000
Anglicans	70,530,000
Islam	
Sunni	940,000,000
Shiite	120,000,000
Ahmadiyya	10,000,000
Druze	450,000

Figure 6.4

Major groups within Christianity and Islam by number.

(taken from http://www.adherents.com)

Baha'i faith, based in Haifa, Israel, is almost entirely contained within one highly organized and very hierarchical denomination.

Most adherents of a single religion usually share at least some commonalities, such as a common historical heritage and some shared doctrines or practices. But these common factors are often limited by the many exceptions. A listing of doctrinally and organizationally meaningful divisions or denominational branches for all religions would be much more complex. Figure 6.4 summarizes the main divisions of the world's two largest religions, Christianity and Islam.

From these figures, it can be seen that the largest single groupings are Catholics and Sunnis at 968 million and 940 million respectively. Within these two massive sections of the world's population, there is sometimes little direct contact. The most significant considerations for understanding of national cultures come not from these raw figures and listings but from a more detailed analysis of the role of religions within geopolitical regions. The impact of religion has often affected the conduct of international business, whether in the days of Venetian maritime trade, the difficulties of commerce along the central Asian silk road (or route), or the triangular trade involving the transportation of African slaves to North America in the eighteenth and nineteenth centuries.

At the heart of the complex conflict within the Middle East, there is the separation between Christianity and Islam that has affected the region, both politically and economically, since the rise of Islam over 1200 years ago. The battle for Jerusalem, which is a holy site for both religions, as well as for Judaism, has exemplified the bitter nature of the religious (and other) differences that have arisen. A further cultural complication within the Middle East is the division of the region into the Sunni and Shiite branches of Islam. However, even when two of the major countries in the region are dominated by Shiites—Iran (89 per cent) and Iraq (65 per cent)—it does not prevent them from engaging in conflict, including the long war of 1980–1988, which cost well over a million lives (Global Security 2012). The differences of language (Farsi in Iran and Arabic in Iraq) and the differences of politics, economics, and society overrode the similarities of religion.

Another major determinant of national cultures is the language (or languages) spoken in each nation-state and in different parts of the world (see Figure 6.5). As with religion, it is sometimes the divisions created by languages that have most impact on the world and on the interplay between national cultures. The understanding and mastery of another language is often a great advantage for managers in their conduct of international business.

Figure 6.5
Major language
groups in the world
(numbers of people).

(Adapted from Lewis
(2009). *Ethnologue:
Languages of the
World*, 16th edn.
SIL International,
Ethnologue.com—used
with permission)

Language	Family	Number of 'speakers' in millions (2000–2009 estimates)
Mandarin	Sino-Tibetan, Chinese	1151
Hindustani	Indo-European, Indo-Iranian, Indo-Aryan	490
Spanish	Indo-European, Italic, Romance	500
English	Indo-European, Germanic, West	1000
Arabic	Afro-Asiatic, Semitic	255
Portuguese	Indo-European, Italic, Romance	240
Bengali	Indo-European, Indo-Iranian, Indo-Aryan	215
Russian	Indo-European, Slavic, East	277
Japanese	Japanese–Ryukyuan	132
German	Indo-European, Germanic, West	166

The period from the seventeenth to the nineteenth centuries witnessed the spread of European languages around the world as part of the expansion of various empires, especially those of Spain, Portugal, the Netherlands, France, and the UK. This accounts for the continued spread of European languages (see Figure 6.5). In particular, the nineteenth and twentieth centuries saw the increasing dominance of English as the language of business and culture, as Anglicization and then Americanization spread throughout the world. Accordingly, English is usually ranked as the most commonly learnt and spoken second language, with possibly nearly two billion speakers using it as either first or second language (Crystal 1997, 2003).

Within the large families of language (see Figure 6.5), it is evident that the proximity of some languages, both geographically and linguistically, can sometimes lead to conflict. Within the medium-sized country of Spain (total population of about 47 million in 2012), there is harmony of religion (94 per cent Roman Catholic) but divisions arising from several different languages: Castilian Spanish (74 per cent), Catalan (17 per cent), Galician (7 per cent), and Basque (2 per cent) (CIA 2012). The linguistic and cultural divisions have led to political and armed campaigns opposed to control by Madrid from the Basques and Euskadi Ta Askatasuna (ETA—Basque for 'Homeland and Freedom'), to the creation of more autonomous regions (such as Catalonia), and to regular cultural rivalries such as football club allegiances (including Real Madrid vs. Barcelona).

Religion and language can be sources of both friction and stability for a national culture, or for a region within the world. The tendency towards friction and conflict arises from the apparently small differences that communities can magnify. As shown above, conflicts within the Christian or the Islamic worlds can stem from differences of belief such as those between Catholics and Protestants, or Sunnis and Shiites. The best international managers and their companies need to design and implement strategies for overcoming these differences.

Unity of language, culture, and religion can lead to greater political and economic harmony and the development of successful international commerce. The linkages between some of the predominantly Christian and English-speaking countries of the Commonwealth, such as Canada, Australia, New Zealand, and the UK, have led to major migrations of people and considerably eased cross-border transactions between those who share language and culture. In the same way, the influence of Spanish, Portuguese, and Italian companies in Latin America is partially a product of cultural and linguistic similarity, as well as historical and commercial ties.

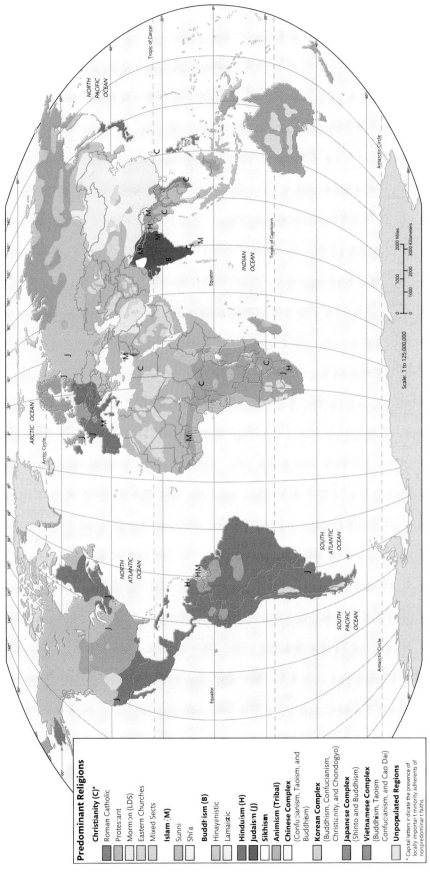

Figure 6.6

World map depicting predominant religions.

Adapted from CIA World Factbook 2012

Practitioner insight

Denitza Roussinova, former Managing Director, Portfolio Manager Eastern Europe Middle East Africa Fund, Black River Asset Management (speaking in a personal capacity).

'I was born in Bulgaria and after graduating from the European Business School London (EBS London) in 1994, I started working for Cargill, one of the largest multinational companies. Cargill is an international provider of food, agricultural, and risk management products and services operating in 67 countries and is privately owned.

I spent 6 years at Black River Asset Management, which is an alternative asset management company operating in global financial markets. It was created in 2003 as an independently managed subsidiary of Cargill Incorporated. Black River operated out of 14 offices in 12 countries. I was responsible for local markets trading in Central Europe, the Middle East, and Africa. The mandate covered a broad range of products: currencies, local currency debt, derivatives, and equities. I focused mainly on Hungary, Poland, Czech Republic, Slovakia, and Bulgaria in Europe, as well as South Africa, Israel, Egypt, and Nigeria.

Speaking different languages (Bulgarian, English, Russian, Italian, and Spanish) has been extremely important for me. It gave me the opportunity to come and study in London; to go to Italy and Spain in my year of study abroad while at EBS London; and to start my professional life in the UK. In the sphere of finance, English has undoubtedly been the most essential language. This is partially due to the fact that there are specific terms in finance that people know mainly in English. I am surrounded by people who are fluent in two or three languages, which now has become more of a norm than an exception.

In my interaction with colleagues and counterparts, I have not experienced specific differences coming from religious beliefs. Certain markets can be closed for longer periods because of religious holidays, but ultimately people everywhere are looking for an attractive return on their investment, regardless of their religion.

Most people in my profession, regardless of nationality or cultural background, seek higher returns and are willing to tolerate a higher level of risk. However, if we look at individual retail investors, you can see differences in their investment behaviour. For example, in my opinion, Polish people stand out as more entrepreneurial and they manage their financial investments pretty actively. This is different from Bulgaria, where most middle-aged and old people keep their savings in property or deposits. This is perhaps a legacy of the communist time when shortages prompted people to be very economical and save everything. People in the Czech Republic also come across as more prudent and conservative.

My job has given me many opportunities for professional and personal development, which was encouraged and supported by my employer. Throughout my job, my areas of responsibility evolved and broadened and I have certainly not experienced a "glass ceiling". Financial markets recognize and reward good performance and, from this point of view, if you do a good job there are no career limitations. I think the main challenge for women in business is to achieve the appropriate balance of work and family.'

Demography
Statistical study of all populations and the specific features of such populations related to their size, structure, and distribution.

World demography

Another fundamental factor in the development of national cultures—and their changes over time—is demography. The field of demography includes age (and age distribution), gender (and gender distribution), life expectancy, literacy and education levels, opportunities of employment, and socio-economic level (including income and wealth per person). Implications of the possible developments in age demography are dramatic, such as the key drivers of the move towards an ageing world population being the combination of rising life expectancy and low or falling fertility. As Magnus (2008) indicated, there are four main characteristics of the ageing population. The first is that the proportion of people over 60 worldwide is 'going to more than double to 22 per cent by 2050'; the second is that the under-15 age group is 'going to shrink or stagnate'; the third is that 'the number of people of working age will also decline'—by 16 per cent in the EU and by nearly 40 per cent in Japan; finally 'the welfare and prospects of older, economically inactive people will become increasingly dependent on a falling, or slowly growing, population of working age' (Magnus 2008: 14–15).

As noted above, demography covers the key elements of the structure of each country. Even among a selection of major countries there can be some large variations. Figure 6.7 supplies details for 2007–2008, showing, for example, the high life expectancy in Japan and France (over 80 years) compared not only with South Africa (49 years) but also with India (69 years) and Russia (66 years). Similarly, the male–female ratio ranges from Russia, where it is 0.8 male to 1.2 female, to China and India, where it is the reverse (1.04 and 1.03 male to 0.96 and 0.97 respectively). The largest discrepancy in Figure 6.7 is, of course, per capita income (GDP per head at purchasing power parity): the world average is $10,000, the lowest is India with $2,700, and the highest is the USA with $45,800.

The demographics of nations throughout the world have major impacts on the kinds of products and services that MNEs will decide to provide in each country. Products for elderly people will clearly have a larger market, both in real terms and in proportion to the population, in Japan than in South Africa. Attempts to reach a literate public will be different in India from what they are in European countries.

Caution must be exercised about some of the statistics cited in Figure 6.7 and in any comparable listing of figures drawn from a variety of national and international sources. Literacy figures, for example, are surprisingly similar, with seven countries, ranging from Russia to the USA, all claiming that 99 per cent of the population are 'literate'. They are also suspiciously high for certain countries, and it is clear that the national determination of what is meant by the ability to 'read and write' has differed considerably.

	Pop.	GDP	Life	Literacy	Gender
World	7.0 bn	11,800	68	84	1.01
China	1.3 bn	8400	75	92	1.06
India	1.2 bn	3700	67	61	1.08
USA	314 m	48,100	78	99	0.97
Indonesia	248 m	4700	72	90	1.00
Brazil	206 m	11,600	71	99	0.90
Russia	138 m	16,700	66	99	0.85
Japan	127 m	34,300	84	99	0.94
Germany	81 m	37,900	80	99	0.97
France	66 m	35,000	81	99	0.96
UK	63 m	35,900	80	99	0.99
South Africa	49 m	11,000	49	86	0.99

Figure 6.7
Selected demographic statistics; figures generally rounded up.
(adapted from CIA 2012)

Pop. = Population in millions (m) or billions (bn)
GDP = GDP per capita in $ at purchasing power parity
Life = life expectancy at birth (in years, total population)
Literacy = percentage of those over 15 who can read and write
Gender = sex ratio of males (total population)

As noted above, at the heart of the successful conduct of international business is a full understanding of the key determinants of the market, especially its demographic structure. The size of the market as a whole—as specified by factors such as population, age group, and income level—is vital information for any business, and successful international companies research demographic basics very carefully.

Section II: Models of national culture and the conduct of international business

Models of national culture

When national, or regional and local, cultures are considered, the concern is with the extent to which these cultures differ and how this might affect the conduct of international business. For managers and others engaged in the practicalities of business, one of the key questions is: 'What sort of accommodation do "we" have to make to "you"?' For the purposes of understanding culture and national cultures within international business, the emphasis is on certain limited aspects of this exceptionally broad topic.

The focus in this book, therefore, is on Hall's notions of high and low context, on the categories established by Hofstede and Trompenaars, and on the experiences of businesspeople in the ways in which they have confronted these varieties of culture. As the Chinese philosopher Confucius has been quoted as saying: 'All people are the same. It's only their habits that are so different.' Businesspeople can optimize their activities and those of their companies only when they understand the vital differences in national habits.

High-context and low-context cultures

+ Cultural context (high and low) Definition of the situational framework by which it is possible to distinguish the degree to which a special code is needed to understand the signals and communications of a culture.

A key insight into understanding national cultures is Edward Hall's (1976) identification of countries that have 'high-context' or 'low-context' cultures. The broad distinction that was made by Hall is that low-context cultures require explicit communication through language and specific signals. This means that low-context cultures value verbal abilities, logic, and reasoning. By contrast, high-context cultures are identified by the fact that physical context and the nature of the people are key means by which communication is made. Hall set out a view that high-context cultures make greater distinction between insiders and outsiders than do low-context cultures. He also commented that people raised in high-context systems expect more of others than do the participants in low-context systems. When talking about something that she has on her mind, a high-context individual will expect other people to know what is bothering her, so that she does not have to be specific.

As can be seen in Figure 6.8, there are countries where important information and messages—for example, about whether a deal can be done—are going to be communicated very clearly and directly (low context). The opposite way of communicating (high context)

Figure 6.8
Level of context, identified by culture.

(adapted from Jandt 2009)

High	Low
China	Switzerland
Japan	Germany
Korea	USA and Canada
Latin America (most countries)	Nordic/Scandinavian countries
Arab countries (most)	

is done more subtly and indirectly; much of the business will be done because the people know each other or get on well. In both cases, it is assumed that the basic features of the deal (product, quantity, quality, costs, and timescale) make it feasible. The high-context social and business culture is reflected very clearly among the Chinese, expressed by the concept of *guanxi*. This is a concept that promotes personal relationships and mutual trust. It also stresses family and personal relationships and the hierarchy of age and experience over youth and inexperience. *Guanxi* emphasizes the importance of reciprocal ties and personal relationships for the successful conduct of business. It can also be seen as a system that appears difficult to understand and impenetrable for outsiders (that is, non-Chinese).

What does high- and low-context actually mean for the conduct of business in specific situations? Take the hypothetical case of a Saudi Arabian businessperson trying to work with a company in North America; assume, too, that the Saudi is male. The Saudi will assume that there should be social courtesies before any discussions take place; that a considerable amount of time will be required to conduct the business; that any exchange of information with his counterparts does not imply any agreement to the deal; that he will need to refer major decisions and certainly the final decision back to his superiors in Saudi Arabia; and that the final deal will have to be agreed and signed in a relatively formal ceremony, probably accompanied by some lavish hospitality. The difference in context and formality may lead to all sorts of misunderstandings: feeling downgraded because there has been no ceremony (the Saudi); feeling insulted (the Saudi) by the forceful, direct approach (of the North American); thinking (the North American) that discussions are proceeding too slowly; feeling misled because the information given (by the North American) has not been fully passed on to his own superiors (by the Saudi); possibly feeling uncomfortable if he (the Saudi) has to deal with a woman (the North American) who is at a higher level; feeling 'tricked' (the North American) by the politeness (of the Saudi) when no agreement is reached; and, by contrast, feeling 'tricked' (the Saudi) by the degree to which his counterpart (the North American) had assumed that everything was going very well. In so many instances, business arrangements have been harmed by cultural misunderstandings and the inability to communicate on the same level or with the same objectives.

This gap between the 'high-context' Saudi and the 'low-context' North American may not be so wide if they know each other from other social or business connections; for example, if they went to the same university or have previously done business with each other. In such circumstances, there would be a level of contact and personal relationship that would overcome the gap in the contexts.

Dimensions of culture: Hampden-Turner, Trompenaars, Hofstede, and others

Among the other main aspects of national culture that are relevant to international business, there are a number of factors identified by Fons Trompenaars and his collaborators. The principal finding from Trompenaars and Hampden-Turner is that 'foreign cultures are not arbitrarily or randomly different from one another. They are instead mirror images of one another's values . . .' (Hampden-Turner and Trompenaars 2000). This finding derives from 'eighteen years of cross-cultural research' and is reflected in the posing of opposites such as 'universalism–particularism', 'individualism–communitarianism', and 'specificity–diffuseness' (**see ORC Extension material 6.1**). In addition, their research uncovered three other opposites or dilemmas: 'achieved status–ascribed status', 'inner direction–outer direction', and 'sequential time–synchronous time' (Hampden-Turner and Trompenaars 2000).

These six factors have been identified through extensive longitudinal studies, originally conducted by the Centre for International Business Studies, established by Trompenaars. These studies were based on a series of questionnaires designed to discover the values of managers around the world. As far as business is concerned, the general meanings of these pairs of opposed dimensions are explained briefly below, with some business cultures cited as examples:

+ *Guanxi*
Chinese concept in which personal relations and the establishment of mutual trust and obligations are seen as essential for the conduct of business.

> Go online

- *Universalism–particularism.* People in a universalist culture respect rules and often value them more highly than relationships. Universalist people (Americans and northern Europeans) are less likely to do business with others simply because of a personal contact. For particularists (Asians and people from the Middle East), it seems very strange not to base their business dealings around the people they know and trust.

- *Individualism–communitarianism.* The most important values for individualists are competition, self-reliance, self-interest, personal growth, and fulfilment. These give them a view of business where individuals need to compete and struggle. By contrast, the business principles within a communitarian society (Chinese, Japanese, Arab cultures) are cooperation, social concern, altruism, public service, and societal legacy. These encourage connections between business, education, finance, labour, and government, so that the society as a whole benefits from shared knowledge.

- *Specificity–diffuseness.* Cultures that tend towards specificity in business value analysis, action research, measurement of results, and feedback on performance. By contrast, diffuse business cultures emphasize work as a process, complex interactions, and the sharing of commitment to quality.

- *Achieved status–ascribed status.* The culture that values achieved status puts emphasis on what people have actually done in business—their track record (Northern Europeans, North Americans). The other side of this dimension values people's potential and connections—*who* people are, rather than *what* they are (Southern Europeans, Latin Americans).

- *Inner direction–outer direction.* This dimension focuses on the origin of people's convictions and beliefs. The inner-direction culture looks at people's inner convictions and conscience, while the outer-direction cultures stress that the most important influences and examples come from outside the self.

- *Sequential time–synchronous time.* The time dimension is quite a stark contrast between those people who think that time is a race along a set course (sequential) and those who see it as a matter of precise coordination (synchronous). Those people in the synchronous category are likely to be able to multi-task better than others. (Men are thought to be sequential and women synchronous.)

It is surely no coincidence that, like Trompenaars, one of the other main experts in the area of cross-cultural research, Geert Hofstede, is Dutch. Perhaps the special position of the Dutch within Europe explains the prominence of Trompenaars and Hofstede in this field. They come from a relatively small country with an open culture, a trading and imperial heritage, a gift for other languages, a multi-ethnic society, and a capacity to survive while surrounded by more powerful neighbours. Like Trompenaars, Hofstede has undertaken a lifetime of research on national cultures in business, much of it based on original studies of employees in IBM.

Stephan Dahl, a commentator on intercultural research, has indicated the similarities between the main factors identified by Trompenaars and Hofstede. He has suggested that over half of the different factors are closely related and claimed that some of Trompenaars and Hampden-Turner's 'value orientations can be regarded as nearly identical to Hofstede's dimensions' (Dahl 2006). (**See ORC Extension material 6.2 for more about cross-cultural studies**)

> Go online

There are six key dimensions identified by Hofstede, the first four of which have always been part of this cultural analysis; time orientation and indulgence–restraint are later additions.

Power distance

The concept of power distance is an attempt to measure 'the extent to which the less powerful members of institutions and organizations within a country expect and accept that power is distributed unequally' (Hofstede et al. 2010). This represents a view of inequality, of more vs. less, that is shared and supported by the followers as much as by the leaders.

The variations of power distance in its simplest form are demonstrated by the national societies with the highest measures (Malaysia, Slovakia, Guatemala, and Panama) and the lowest ones (Austria, Israel, Denmark, and New Zealand) (Hofstede et al. 2010). The implication for the conduct of international business is that people from the lowest power-distance countries, such as Scandinavians and Israelis, tend to be more informal and relaxed in their attitude to approaching their counterparts, carrying out negotiations, and making deals.

Individualism–collectivism

Individualism is a measure of the extent to which individuals are integrated into groups within society or business. On the individualist side, there are 'societies in which the ties between individuals are loose: everyone is expected to look after himself or herself and his or her immediate family' (Hofstede et al. 2010). By contrast, on the collectivist side, there are 'societies in which people from birth onward are integrated into strong, cohesive in-groups which, throughout people's lifetimes, continue to protect them in exchange for unquestioning loyalty' (Hofstede et al. 2010). The idea of 'collectivism' in this sense has no political meaning because it refers to the group, rather than to the state.

In the general measures that Hofstede has developed for these factors, the most contrasting cultures in terms of individualism and collectivism are the USA, Australia, the UK, Canada, Hungary, and the Netherlands as the most individualist, and, on the collectivist side, a group of Latin American countries (Guatemala, Ecuador, Panama, Venezuela, and Colombia), and Pakistan and Indonesia (Hofstede et al. 2010). The international business implication is that more individualist people, such as the North Americans and the British, are inclined to work independently, to take decisions on their own, and to lead a team or group 'from the front'. They are less likely to seek consensus or wait for their team to come up with solutions.

Masculinity–femininity

The third of Hofstede's measures is perhaps the one that is most puzzlingly named, masculinity–femininity. The measure refers to the distribution of roles between the genders, which can be regarded as another fundamental issue for any society.

One of the main sources of evidence within Hofstede's research has been the two phases of studies based on employees at IBM, the large IT company. These studies revealed that women's values differed less among societies than did men's values, which tended to contain a dimension that was very assertive and competitive, and very different from women's values. The assertive pole was called 'masculine' and the modest, caring pole 'feminine'. A feminine society is one where 'emotional gender roles overlap', so that both men and women are perceived to be 'modest, tender, and concerned with the quality of life' (Hofstede et al. 2010). In masculine societies, 'gender roles are clearly distinct: men are supposed to be assertive, tough and focussed on material success'. These countries thus show a gap between men's and women's values (Hofstede et al. 2010).

On this measure, the national cultures at the extremes are the most 'masculine': Slovakia, Japan, Hungary, Austria, Venezuela, Switzerland (German part), and Italy; the most 'feminine' are the Scandinavian/Nordic countries (Sweden, Norway, Denmark, Finland), the Netherlands, Slovenia, Costa Rica, and Chile (Hofstede et al. 2010). The consequence for the conduct of international business is that the Scandinavians and the Dutch tend to be less impressed with outward status symbols and are inclined to work cooperatively with both their fellow-workers and their opposite numbers in other companies.

Uncertainty avoidance (risk aversion)

The fourth of Hofstede's factors is called either uncertainty avoidance or risk aversion. In general, it deals with a society's tolerance for uncertainty and ambiguity, and indicates 'the extent to which the members of a culture feel threatened by ambiguous or unknown situations' (Hofstede et al. 2010). Cultures that tend towards 'uncertainty avoidance' try to minimize the possibility of such situations by strict laws and rules, by safety and security measures, and, on the philosophical and religious level, by a belief in absolute truth. Hofstede also draws the conclusion that people in uncertainty-avoiding countries are generally more emotional, and motivated by inner nervous energy. By contrast, his research suggests that the opposite cultures—those that accept uncertainty—are more likely to be tolerant of different opinions. It is claimed that these cultures try to have as few rules as possible. People within them are more phlegmatic and contemplative, and are less likely to express emotions.

The national cultures at the extreme ends of this measure are Greece, Portugal, Guatemala, Uruguay, Belgium (Flemish part), Malta, and Russia (most risk averse), contrasting with Singapore, Jamaica, Denmark, Sweden, and Hong Kong (least risk averse) (Hofstede et al. 2010). As with the conclusions from the other measures cited above, the business and management implications of uncertainty avoidance/risk aversion is that the nationals of such countries as Singapore and Hong Kong are most likely to take business risks, and that these countries are the ones that have created a risk-welcoming business environment.

Long-term orientation (time)

The fifth factor in the Hofstede scheme—and one that is common to most other views of national cultural differences—relates to time. This fifth dimension was originally found in a study among students from 23 countries around the world, the Chinese Value Survey. This was then expanded by Hofstede into a further survey covering a total of 39 societies. Values associated with long-term orientation are thrift and perseverance, whereas values associated with short-term orientation are respecting tradition, fulfilling social obligations, and protecting one's 'face'. Both the positively and negatively rated values of this dimension are found in the teachings of Confucius, but 'the dimension also applies to countries without a Confucian heritage'. There are other interesting measures related to time that are especially important for international business, such as a concern for the start, duration, and finish (let alone the purpose) of meetings, attitudes towards punctuality, and emphasis on deadlines.

As far as this factor is concerned, the countries with the greatest long-term orientations are almost all Asian (China, Hong Kong, Taiwan, Japan, Vietnam, South Korea) and Brazil; at the other end of the spectrum, the short-term cultures are Pakistan, Czech Republic, Nigeria, Spain, Philippines, Canada, Zimbabwe, the UK, and the USA (Hofstede et al. 2010).

Indulgence–restraint

The final factor was introduced as a result of analysis by Michael Minkov of the World Values Survey data for 93 countries (Minkov 2009). This sixth factor is a measure of the extent to which a society allows relatively free gratification of basic and natural human drives related to enjoying life and having fun—indulgence—or the reverse, where gratification of needs is suppressed and regulated by strict social norms (Hofstede et al. 2010). In essence, it appears to be a measure of elements of personal happiness, satisfaction, and well-being, and the degree of control that people have over their own lives.

On his website and in his many books, Hofstede and his collaborators have provided interesting three-dimensional maps of the combinations of these characteristics in the national cultures of over 100 countries. They have also managed to ensure the updating of this information, as, for example, Russia has emerged from the Soviet Union or South Africa has moved on from the apartheid era of white domination. Some early tables and figures provided by Hofstede (and by Trompenaars and others) have proved to be very fixed in time and place. As the societies have changed, so have their orientations and, consequently, what the indicators have been measuring.

Rank	PDI	I-C	M-F	Uncertainty	Time	Indulgence
Brazil	4	10	9	4	9	4
Canada	9	3	8	7	10	2
China	2	11	3	11	2	10
France	5	5	10	3	5	5
Germany	10	6	4	6	3	7
India	3	7	7	9	8	9
Italy	7	4	2	5	6	8
Japan	6	8	1	2	1	6
Russia	1	9	11	1	4	11
UK	11	2	5	10	7	1
USA	8	1	6	8	11	3

Figure 6.9
Summary of selected countries, ranked against each other for each category (ranking of 1 for PDI = most distance; I–C = most individual; M–F = most masculine; Uncertainty = most keen to avoid uncertainty; Time = most long-term orientation; Indulgence = highest indulgence in society).

(Derived from Hofstede, Hofstede and Minkov 2010; © Geert Hofstede B.V. quoted with permission.)

For the immediate purposes of this book and as a rough guide to understanding the relative measures for 11 major countries, Figure 6.9 measures their rankings in relation to each other for the six Hofstede dimensions. It can be seen from the rankings in Figure 6.9 that even among these 11 countries there are significant differences of approach to business, so that the conduct of commerce and trade is complex. Looking at the relationship between two of the Asian giants, China and Japan, the greatest gulf is the factor of uncertainty avoidance (a ranking difference of 9). Not only does this suggest that the business environment in China is more attuned to and welcoming of taking risks, whether in investments or trading, but it also provides evidence to confirm the stereotype that Chinese businesspeople are more adventurous than their Japanese counterparts. Doing business in Japan takes place within a more cautious environment in which long-term planning plays a large part, decisions are made more slowly, and the prevailing attitude is a conservatism rejecting outside influences that the Japanese perceive as designed to change the system.

There is an equally large difference between Russia and Germany (a ranking difference of 9) on the factor of power distance. This confirms the experience of those who have carried out business in or between these two countries. For Russians, there is still a view that the gulf between the top and bottom of the business world, let alone in society as a whole, is wide. This confirms the new oligarchs' view of themselves as superior creatures and that their new-found wealth requires them to be aloof in their business dealings.

As with the demographic figures cited above, these ranking differences are very broad and mask the complexities of the mapping that the detailed Hofstede system can uncover. The implications and conclusions drawn from these indicators should be regarded with some degree of scepticism.

+ Stereotype
Simplified and/or standardized conception or image with specific meaning, often held in common by people about another group.

Stereotyping and 'world culture'

There are inherent difficulties in ascribing certain characteristics to specific cultures as though such cultures are homogeneous. It is usually only an average characteristic that is being described. This is the false currency of stereotypes.

A possible advantage of stereotypes and stereotyping is being able to make some general comments about peoples, rather than having to keep stating that general types do not exist. The view that all Germans or all Indonesians, or even all Bavarians and all Javanese, think, behave, or act in a certain way is clearly erroneous but, used carefully, there can be a valid

The Olympic Games, held in London in 2012, is an example of a world culture

© iStockphoto.com/ Andrea Zanchi

+ Infographics
Graphic visual representations of information, data, or knowledge.

+ Social network
A social structure consisting of a set of individuals and/or organizations and the dyadic (or bilateral) links between them.

+ Viral marketing
Strategy that encourages individuals to pass on marketing messages to others, creating a multiplier effect spreading the message's exposure and influence.

possibility of stating that, in general, when doing business with Germans, Bavarians, Indonesians, or Javanese, certain things may be true and distinctive.

A modern view, sometimes hotly debated, suggests that it is possible to abandon the use of stereotypes and to rise above the focus on national cultures; this view is associated with the development of the concept of a world culture. Some writers have argued that world culture is 'a global, distinct, complex, and dynamic phenomenon' (Lechner and Boli 2005). Some of the examples of a world culture include the Olympic movement and the Olympic Games, the worldwide rituals and experiences of the United Nations organization (and its many agencies), and the various worldwide activities of non-governmental organizations and social movements. The central argument behind the idea of world culture is that 'it concerns the routine realities of everyday life. Most directly involved are people of the relatively affluent countries and social classes but increasingly we find world culture influencing the lives of even the most remote places and poorest people' (Lechner and Boli 2005).

Case study 6.2

Visuals and graphics: Do you see what I see?

A common form of communication in international business is through visual displays and graphic representations; this has become particularly the case through the development of the fields of business intelligence and business analytics (Evans 2011). The importance of infographics and data visualization has had a particularly significant impact within social networks, viral marketing, and the exchange of information via smartphone and computer applications.

This use of visualization is done on the assumption that businesses are thereby avoiding the difficulties of communication through language. Recent research has indicated, however, that 'communicating with diagrams can be problematic' (Eppler and Gee 2008).

The general view among international managers is that graphic formats (pie charts, bar charts, matrices, decision trees, Venn diagrams, flow charts) are

intuitively understood by employees who have different levels of qualification and experience. Similarly, it is expected that this understanding is extended across cultural, national, and linguistic boundaries. In the modern world, too, the presentation of facts and figures is increasingly fast, instant, and changing. It is sufficient to look at the scrolling of such data in onscreen displays (OSDs) across split screens, the use of graphical user interfaces (GUIs), and straplines by financial media producers such as Bloomberg, Thomson Reuters, CNBC, and CNN to acknowledge the danger of the assumption that all people might interpret this information in the same way. MNEs regularly use 'standardized graphic formats' in corporate newsletters, annual reports, video screen displays, team meetings, wikis and blogs, strategy workshops, and PowerPoint presentations. MNE managers assume that they know what the most crucial information to be cascaded down to staff is, and the best format for its graphic representations.

There has been some specific analysis of cultural differences in the interpretation of data, figures, and graphic representations. Eppler and Gee's study (2008) examined the perception of business graphics by over 100 Chinese and British business students in Beijing and Cambridge. They asked the students (58 men and 43 women) to categorize a number of typical business visualizations. Accepting that their findings are tentative and limited, Eppler and Gee note a number of significant differences in the interpretation of figures. These are:

1. 'Diagram understanding is neither intuitive nor cross-cultural.'

2. There may be 'considerable differences among male and female groupings'.

Infographics are an increasingly popular way of sharing information
Source: iStock

3. Asians are generally less keen to strictly 'group or classify elements based on their attributes compared to people from the West'.

4. Asians are more likely to 'emphasize the context in which something is used'.

These points confirm some of the assumptions made about Eastern and Western differences and the need for intercultural sensitivity. The lesson for European and Asian MNEs working together is 'that Europeans should be especially careful when using visual means of communication in China, as Chinese employees may not be highly familiar with these formats or interpret them differently (i.e. as with regard to quantitative vs. qualitative charts)' (Eppler and Gee 2008).

The evidence is clear: not only do people not necessarily hear the same thing; they do not always see the same thing. The cultural differences of the world are very deep, and this is a key lesson for international businesspeople to learn and understand.

The impacts of culture on international business

As businesspeople navigate their way through the complexities of culture, they acknowledge that these cultures will have varying effects on international business. This section deals, therefore, with these different aspects.

Culture and the regulatory framework

Around the world, the variance in national cultures forms (or reflects) different attitudes towards rights of ownership and property. In more highly regulated and legalistic cultures (such as the Northern European or Northern American cultures), the legal rights and obligations of landowners, tenants, lease holders, and so on are clearly defined. Any disputes over the title of lands are governed by the legal and court system and, in the vast majority of cases, the judgments and rulings of the court authorities are accepted by participants in the case. This is not always so in the less legalistic cultures where the 'rule of law' is regarded less highly.

Firms engaged in international business need to know the status of the land that they occupy—whether it is an office, a factory or processing plant, agricultural land, or land for hotel and leisure facilities. Not only can companies not afford doubts about their right to carry out business on a particular piece of land, they must have certainty over other legal issues as well, such as laws relating to ecology and environment, health and safety, insurance, and security. For MNEs, the legal culture of nation-states is also revealed in the rules and customs surrounding competition law—an essential element for the successful conduct of international business (**see ORC extension material 6.3**).

> Go online

Companies must also be aware of the prevailing philosophy underlying the regulatory framework. The national culture sometimes plays a key role in determining the nature of the economic system operated by the state. There are three key systems that can be operated by different countries: laissez-faire, interventionism, and command economy and central planning. The political philosophies that underlie these different systems are explored more fully in Chapters 2 and 3. As far as the cultural implications are concerned, those countries with the greatest degree of laissez-faire, such as Singapore and the USA, tend to permit business to operate with as little involvement of the government as possible. At the other end of the spectrum, there used to be countries, such as the old communist bloc, where the governments dictated the central elements of the economy and the business environment.

There are other forms of national culture that can affect business operations. These include a system often called 'cronyism' in which the majority of business decisions are made on the basis of economic and political calculation that directly favours friends or 'cronies' of those in power. There is also the possibility of a business system that can be classified as 'theocracy' (Ferrero and Wintrobe 2009). In this system, the culture is based on some form of religious rule, and the regulation of business stems from the fundamental beliefs and tenets of that religion. Modern examples of theocratic states are those where Islam is the dominant religion and where banking and other forms of business are governed by Muslim principles, such as the Islamic Republic of Iran. Rather different from a theocratic state are countries such as Saudi Arabia and many of the Gulf states, such as Dubai and Bahrain, which combine modern capitalism in its laissez-faire manifestation with strong social and economic policies derived from Islam.

Culture and the employment relationship

The relationships between employees and the MNEs that employ them can be characterized by different forms of behaviour and attitude that may be reflective of national cultures. In some cases, these relationships can be viewed through the models of Hofstede or Trompenaars. These observations of culture and the employment relationship are gathered under the headings of identification with the job, attitudes towards technology, education and training, culture's effect on demand and consumption, and business leadership and national culture.

Identification with the job

One of the main aspects of employees' identification with the job is their approach towards working collectively or individually. This aspect can be connected to the second of Hofstede's dimensions (individualism–collectivism) and is very observable in the approach that different cultures have towards teamwork or individual efforts. A great deal of research has been undertaken on the role of teams within teamwork (Ryan 2012; Lee and Tseng 2012), both at high and low levels of work. There is evidence that the experience of what is a team and teamwork can vary sufficiently widely across cultures that, in some cases, the actions of individuals contribute very little to the overall effort of the team. An interesting example of this relates to the French view of teamwork in which French employees are sometimes reluctant to share the knowledge and the skills that they have with other members of the team. As Luan Greenwood, International Communications Manager at Ondeo, noted in a BBC TV programme: 'in France you can say there is a team and a team set-up, but each member of that team will work separately' (BBC Languages 2008).

A further example of the individualist end of this working spectrum is revealed in the American approach towards what they would call 'rugged individualism'. This implies that people stand or fall on their own efforts. Each employee has to take responsibility for his or her own actions, and there can be no possibility of hiding behind others' efforts. This view of employment is strongly reflected in those societies that, as pointed out by Hofstede, are at the individualist end of the individualism–collectivism spectrum: USA, Australia, Hungary, Netherlands, UK, Canada, and Italy.

In addition to the view of the individual or the team in international business, there are also different attitudes towards hierarchy (reflected by Hofstede's concept of power distance), labour mobility in general, flexibility of working, and the work ethic itself. Within these aspects of employment relations, there is a fundamental difference between those societies and national cultures in which work is seen as an expression of self and those in which it is viewed as an obligation imposed on the individual. For the latter societies, there is a tendency to take work more lightly; to be happy with a job that is completed though not perhaps to the highest quality; to resist moving from one job to another, let alone from one part of the country (or the world) to another; and to hide behind the function of the job and the hierarchy of the company that has imposed it.

Attitudes towards technology

As far as culture and attitudes towards technology are concerned, there is often a direct connection to the behaviours and attitudes attributed to the national cultures commented upon above. The key aspects of international attitudes towards technology in business are: (1) Luddism; (2) views of education and training, embracing the attitude towards learning and change, and the willingness to share and spread knowledge; and (3) the view of whether industrial and scientific research should be applied or theoretical.

The complexity of cultural attitudes towards technology is affected by economic issues facing different countries and groups of people, and by individual and specific national and personal responses to changes in the external environment. It is impossible to say that certain cultures are intrinsically in favour of or hostile to technology. For example, in the Gulf states (United Arab Emirates, Qatar, Bahrain, and so on), the wealth of the top sectors of society has inspired people to embrace many aspects of the new technologies. There is an abundance of advanced communications (mobile phones, MP3 players, satellite navigation systems, and so on) and an extraordinary development of modern architecture and construction, such as the Burj Khalifa in Dubai—the world's tallest building, officially opened in January 2010. Side by side with this impressive encouragement of high technology, the society remains rooted in its conservative and traditional socio-cultural ways and its adherence to old-fashioned courtesies.

+ **Luddism**
Term used to characterize any resistance to change and innovation in technology. It is derived from the actions of the Luddites, who campaigned against the introduction of textile machinery in the early nineteenth century.

Education and training

Different cultures' views on the value of education and training can also impact on business. The cultural attitudes towards education, training, and research are conditioned by a country's relative wealth, but there can also be a strong aspirational element where importance is placed on education by the family, or the society as a whole, and is disproportionate to the per capita GDP of the country.

The Burj Khalifa in
Dubai—the tallest
artificial structure
on earth

© iStockphoto

In relation to population and investment in education, Figure 6.10 shows the immense focus of the USA on the need for public investment in the sector. Within the UNESCO figures, also noteworthy is the relatively high attainment of regions such as South and West Asia, and Latin America and the Caribbean, where the investment in education is 6.9 per cent and 7.6 per cent of the world total, respectively. Although well behind the industrialized and developed countries of North America and Western Europe (55.1 per cent) and the region of East Asia and the Pacific (17.9 per cent), these are the parts of the world where most attention is paid to education (UIS 2007).

Figure 6.10
Global distribution of
public expenditure on
education for selected
countries, 2004.

(Adapted from UIS
2007)

Country	Percentage of world total (international PPP (percentage purchasing power))
Brazil	2.7
Italy	3.1
France	4.2
UK	4.1
Germany	4.4
India	5.2
Japan	5.5
China	5.9
USA	28.0

Culture's effect on demand and consumption

From another perspective, socio-economic conditions can affect people's relationship to spending and buying. In line with the ideas of Maslow's hierarchy (see above), some historical periods of economic development of economies and certain socio-economic classes have led to the phenomenon of conspicuous consumption.

The theories of conspicuous consumption suggest that certain classes of people (or sectors of society) like to consume goods and services almost as a function of their status and ability to show that their level of consumption is higher than other people's. The main proponent of this theory was Thorstein Veblen, who wrote in the late nineteenth century about the growth of a leisure class that engaged in extravagant consumption of expensive goods and services in order to demonstrate status and wealth (Bullock et al. 2000). There are many contemporary examples of this kind of consumption—the Russian (and other former Soviet Union) elites since the fall of communism and the wealthy Gulf state elites—that demonstrate very clearly that it is not particular to any national culture. It is also reflected in the purchase of football clubs (both Chelsea FC by Roman Abramovich and Manchester City FC by Sheikh Mansour bin Zayed Al-Nahyan's Abu Dhabi United Group within the English Premier League), in the use of large yachts and personal aeroplanes, in the development of extensive art collections, and through the ownership of many very expensive houses around the world (Kane 2008).

Associated with the melding of cultures and consumption is the notion that the wealth of certain elites allows them to consider instant rather than delayed gratification; they can have what they want immediately rather than having to wait for it. At certain socio-economic levels below the elites, this kind of behaviour can also be enjoyed. As people move up through the classes, it is often possible for them to buy goods and services at a more expensive level or more rapidly than was possible before. Examples of this form of consumption can be found in many advanced industrialized societies in the expansion of exclusive shopping outlets, the growth of luxury advertising, and a mass desire to own sophisticated products and services.

A further consideration within the bounds of demand and consumption is the different perceptions of value that exist. The tension between aesthetic beauty and functionality, so often dependent on one's socio-economic level and national culture, means that consumers can indulge in more aesthetic and less functional purchases. This can be seen in everyday life, as purchasing decisions are made whether to buy a device for boiling water (a pot or a kettle priced purely for its function) or an extravagant and expensive piece of equipment that does the same thing but costs a great deal more.

+ Conspicuous consumption
Extravagant purchase and use of expensive goods and services, usually by a leisured class, in order to demonstrate status and wealth.

Designer outfits for pampered pets illustrate consumers' indulgence in luxury items

© iStock

Business leadership and national culture

A further aspect of the expression of national culture can be seen in the function of the chief executive officer (CEO) of leading companies in the world of international business. There have been some recent extensive studies of the relationship between organizations, leaders, and cultures, especially in the work of Mansour Javidan, Robert House, and others: the GLOBE study of many societies across the world (House et al. 2007; Javidan et al. 2010). The more specific aspects of corporate culture are explored in Chapter 7, but the following example is useful for understanding the differences in national cultures.

Within three of the key countries in the EU, there are some significant areas of agreement among the views of 200 CEOs surveyed on the best and worst things they perceived about leading companies. As Figure 6.11 indicates, there is very strong agreement about the lack of personal time. Similarly, about seven other factors are close enough to indicate that North European chief executives agree on their major items of concern. However, it is also most striking that there is a fundamental difference in the category that suggests that the French and German CEOs are much more affected by conflict within their management team than British ones.

The more qualitative aspects of the MORI–DDI survey used for Figure 6.11 revealed various other key differences between the national characteristics of the 200 chief executives. The research labelled 'French captains of industry as "autocrats", Germans as "democrats" and British as "meritocrats"' (Maitland 2006). While this may seem a sweeping generalization and typical stereotyping, the survey revealed that 'fewer than three in ten French bosses are happy to be challenged about the decisions they make, compared with half of Germans and more than nine out of ten business leaders in the UK' (Maitland 2006).

The managing director of DDI noted that executives of international companies need to be able to adapt to the corporate and national culture in which they work, without forsaking their individualism. He stressed: 'The danger for any leader is only being able to operate within one of these styles. If you take an autocratic style into a culture that expects a more democratic or meritocratic style, the chances are that you will trip up' (Maitland 2006).

+ Meritocracy
Form of social organization in which the leaders have achieved their status by their own efforts—on merit.

Success in international business comes, therefore, from an ability to adapt as need be to different national cultures and to know the limits of action and operation for the MNE in its conduct of international deals. This applies at the personal level for directors and managers, as well as for the company as a whole.

Figure 6.11
Ranking the worst things about being a leader.
(Adapted from Maitland 2006, DDI 2006)

	UK	France	Germany
Keeping pace with legislation	1	8	4=
Lack of personal time	2	1	1
Having to make tough decisions affecting people's future	3	7	2
Addressing corporate governance issues	4	6	11=
Concerns about having the right talent/best people	5	3	4=
Knowing that failure at this level is big failure	6	4=	3
The loneliness of knowing the buck stops with me	7	4=	7
Dealing with the press	8	10=	10
Conflict/warring egos within the management team	9	2	4=
Keeping ahead of the competition	10	9	9
Dealing with financial stakeholders, such as analysts	11=	10=	8
Public view of company directors/directors' pay	11=	10=	11=

Challenges and choices

→ Understanding cultures is very important for managers in international companies wanting to do business successfully. Whether managers need to be able to comprehend and manipulate such complex systems as Chinese *guanxi* or simply accept the impact of cultural differences on commercial deals, there is no doubt that cross-cultural awareness and perspectives are essential. The challenge for each manager is to know the best ways of making the right choices in selecting overseas business partners, in committing his/her own company to the best investment, and in enjoying productive business relationships around the world.

→ In the late twentieth and early twenty-first centuries, the trend towards a globalized world suggested that cultures were becoming increasingly homogenized and that a world culture might become a reality. The cultural, financial, and economic challenges of the early 2000s have subsequently revealed that cultural differences remain strong at a national level. The business that needs to be conducted over the next few decades will still require businesspeople to develop and maintain awareness and sensitivity to the particular nature of the foreign companies and organizations with which they have to deal.

Chapter summary

The points to be drawn from this chapter are the importance of an awareness and understanding of the complexity of national cultures, and the models that have been devised as a means of assisting managers to comprehend this complexity and carry out international business successfully.

The first section outlined the global variations in factors such as demography, culture, religion, and language. Not only is there a massive diversity among the 200 national cultures that exist, but their subsets—that is, local and regional cultures—add immeasurably to the difficulties of drawing sensible and solid conclusions on which to base business activity and MNE policies, decisions, and actions. In addition to all of this, there is the growth of some aspects of a 'world culture' and the global manifestations of other cultural attitudes and activities.

The many aspects of culture that are relevant to conducting business successfully include understanding languages, fostering awareness of other people's cultures, developing sensitivity to counterparts, and recognizing what is appropriate in different business settings and cultures. This means that the culture of a nation or a society could be viewed as a kaleidoscope containing the colours of language, literature, art, customs, religion, attitudes, and patterns of behaviour.

The second section of the chapter explored the impact of national cultures on factors such as the employment relationships within MNEs, attitudes towards technology, education and training, culture's effect on demand and consumption, and business leadership.

Case study 6.3

Taking medicine

The pharmaceutical industry, featuring some of the world's major MNEs, including Johnson & Johnson, Pfizer, Bayer, GlaxoSmithKline, Sanofi Aventis, AstraZeneca, Roche, and Novartis, is ranked as one of the key industries in the world. As an example, one of the leading companies in the field, Johnson & Johnson, had total worldwide sales of $65 billion, net income of $9.7 billion, and 117,000 employees in 2011 (Johnson & Johnson 2011). Many of the features of the pharmaceutical business are exactly what would be expected of such a massive industry: international production, a complex supply chain, extensive research and development (R&D), multiple locations, and complicated structure and control systems. However, one of the surprising aspects of the industry is how 'national' it can be, and perhaps has to be, when it comes to the delivery of medicine to the patient. It seems that people in different countries like to take their medicine in different ways, such that the major MNEs have to manufacture and sell their end product in many different forms.

From the patients' perspective, there is only one imperative: when they are ill, they want only to be cured. But how best to administer the medicine? In general, it seems that the 'Latins' within Europe, such as the French, Italians, and Spanish, generally like to take their medicine by means of suppository, the Germans by injection/vaccine, the British and the Americans by tablet, and the rest of the world in powder or liquid form. This is a reflection of personal preferences on a large scale and thus an aspect of national culture. As John Barrable, leader of a pharmaceutical marketing survey in the 1990s, noted: 'What's fascinating is that what we've learnt seems to reflect what one thinks of as national characteristics . . . Different nations seem preoccupied with different parts of the body.' In relation to medicine-taking in the UK, he commented that 'there is a positive advantage . . . to making something taste nasty because [British] people then think it must be doing them good' (Gill 1991).

However, it is also a major cost item for the pharmaceutical companies. They need to establish the special compound for a particular treatment and then produce it, if possible, in a range of delivery modes, depending on where it is to be sold. In some cases, this is relatively simple, but in others it takes time and effort to convert one successful delivery mode into another. The extent of the technical work usually requires the deployment of a multidisciplinary team, with chemists for synthesis and structure determination, biochemists and pharmacologists for testing and biological investigation including toxicology studies, and clinicians for evaluation of drug efficacy. To be effective in the pharmaceutical industry, the team requires people with experience in synthetic organic chemistry, with the ability to carry out structural characterization by spectroscopic techniques, and with familiarity in chromatography. All these skills are required for the testing and trialling of different compounds and for bringing the products to market.

When a new formulation is developed by a pharmaceutical company, it is initially produced in tablet (pill) form,

especially when the primary method of administering the drug is by the patient at home. Capsules have also become a popular method of delivery, although in certain markets, such as Islamic countries and Jewish communities, it is not possible to sell capsules as they are made with gelatin, derived from pigs and thus unacceptable to religions that prohibit the eating of pork. Liquid preparations, in the form of syrups or powders to be dissolved in water, are generally acceptable throughout the world. There has recently been a tendency to move away from syrups, which were heavily based on sugar, to lighter liquids or other forms of treatment.

It is thought that one of the simpler modes of delivery for the future may turn out to be the patch, since it may be culture neutral. The patch has proved to be very successful in getting people in many different cultures to reduce or stop smoking—the use of nicotine patches—and there are various companies, including smaller ones such as Novosis (acquired by Schweizerhall in 2008, and now renamed Acino), working on the application of patches and other forms of pharmaceutical treatment. The work of Novosis ('A success story that gets under your skin') is primarily in taking drugs that are already patent protected and devising new dosage formats; the company is particularly involved in transdermal therapeutic treatments—that is, patches that deliver the drug through the skin. It is anticipated that such transdermal treatments, as well as being more effective for the patient, may be more applicable to all cultures and thus a universal way of delivering treatments.

People around the world have differing access to health and medicine. In some countries, people have virtually no access to basic health care, whereas in others people can be treated in the most modern and sophisticated ways. Regardless of these disparities, there appear to be some basic and possibly innate differences in the ways in which people like to administer medication. National cultures have an impact all the way down to the methods by which people prefer to take their medicines.

Case study questions

1. What is the impact on international pharmaceutical companies of having to make products sold in different markets?
2. What methods of medicine taking are most common in different parts of the world? Why may new methods, like patches, become more acceptable?
3. Assess the importance of multidisciplinary teams in the design and delivery of pharmaceutical products.

Discussion questions

1. How far are the key determinants of national culture likely to vary from one country to another?

2. What is the relevance of Hofstede's work on companies' ability to do business in different countries?

3. How much do different religions affect commercial and business relationships?

4. Does a world culture exist? If so, what are its advantages and disadvantages?

5. What benefits would a universal language have for international business?

Online resource centre

Go online to test your understanding by trying multiple-choice questions, and assignment and examination questions.

Further research

Hofstede's and Trompenaars' extensive and complex body of work has been the subject of considerable commentary, criticism, and discussion. Some key participants in this discussion include Jean-Louis Barsoux (INSEAD, Fontainebleau, France), Stephan Dahl (Middlesex University, UK), J. Patrick Gray (University of Wisconsin-Milwaukee, USA), Mansour Javidan (Thunderbird School of Global Management), Brendan McSweeney (University of Essex, UK), and Susan Schneider (HEC University of Geneva and INSEAD). The cross-cultural research undertaken by these academics and others has emphasized the complexities of understanding different cultures and the difficulties of applying this in a meaningful way to the conduct of international business.

It is worth consulting any of the texts by the authors cited above, as well as the following journals:

Journal of International and Cross-Cultural Studies
Cross-Cultural Research
Communal/Plural: Journal of Transnational and Cross-Cultural Studies
World Cultures eJournal

References

BBC Languages (2008). 'Working with the French', available at http://www.bbc.co.uk/languages, accessed August 2008

Bullock, A., Stallybrass, O., and Trombley, S. (2000). *The New Fontana Dictionary of Modern Thought*, 3rd edn. London: Fontana Press

Business Insider (2012). 'Huge Map of the World's Religions', *Business Insider*, 16 April

California Pizza Kitchen (2012). http://www.cpk.com, accessed April 2012

CIA (2012). 'The World Factbook', available at http://www.cia.gov, accessed May 2012

Crystal, D. (1997). *English as a Global Language*. Cambridge: Cambridge University Press

Crystal, D. (2003). *The Cambridge Encyclopedia of the English Language*, 2nd edn. Cambridge: Cambridge University Press

Dahl, S. (2006). 'Trompenaars and Hampden-Turner', available at http://stephan.dahl.at, accessed 31 August 2008

DDI (2006). *Leaders on Leadership*, MORI–DDI survey. Development Dimensions International

Eppler, M. J. and Gee, J. (2008). 'Communicating with diagrams: How intuitive and cross-cultural are business graphics?' *Euro Asia Journal of Management*, 18/1 (June)

Evans, S. (2011). 'Top 10 trends in business intelligence: To visualise or not, that is the question', *Computer Business Review*, 13 December

Ferrero, M. and Wintrobe, R. (eds.) (2009). *The Political Economy of Theocracy*. Basingstoke: Palgrave Macmillan

Gill, L. (1991). 'Uncommon market: What is medicine for one European can often be poison for another', *The Times*, 10 October

Global Security (2012). 'Iran–Iraq War, 1980–1988', available at http://www.globalsecurity.org, accessed 12 May 2012

Hall, E. T. (1976). *Beyond Culture*. New York: Anchor

Hampden-Turner, C. and Trompenaars, F. (2000). *Building Cross-Cultural Competence: How to Create Wealth from Conflicting Values*. Chichester: Wiley

Hofstede, G., Hofstede, G. J., and Minkov, M. (2010). *Cultures and Organizations: Software of the Mind*, 3rd edn. London: McGraw-Hill

House, R. J., Hanges, P. J., Javidan, M., Dorfman, P. W., and Gupta, V. (2007). *Culture, Leadership and Organizations: The GLOBE Study of 62 Societies*. Thousand Oaks, CA: Sage

Jandt, F. E. (2009). *An Introduction to Intercultural Communication: Identities in a Global Community*, 6th edn. London: Sage

Javidan, M., Teagarden, M., and Bowen, D. (2010). 'Managing yourself: Making it overseas', *Harvard Business Review Magazine*, April

Johnson & Johnson (2011) *Johnson & Johnson Annual Report 2011*, available at htp://www.investor.jnj.com/2011annualreport, accessed 29 June 2012

Kane, F. (2008). 'The Gulf's new bling kings', *Observer*, 7 September

Kluckhohn, F. R. and Strodtbeck, F. L. (1961). *Variations in Value Orientation*. Evanston, IL: Row Peterson

Lechner, F. J. and Boli, J. (2005). *World Culture: Origins and Consequences*. Oxford: Blackwell

Lee, H-Y. and Tseng, H-H. (2012). 'A Team Ant Colony Optimization (TACO) model for planning work assignments', *Advanced Science Letters*, 9/1, April

Lewis, M. P. (2009). *Ethnologue: Languages of the World*, 16th edn. Dallas, Texas: SIL International (online version: http://www.ethnologue.com)

Magnus, G. (2008). 'Financial crisis and ageing', *World Today*, 64/12

Maitland, A. (2006). 'Le patron, der chef and the boss', *Financial Times*, 9 January

Maslow, A. H. (1943). 'A theory of human motivation', *Psychological Review*, 50: pp. 370–96, available at http://psychclassics.yorku.ca, accessed 6 September 2008

Minkov, M. (2009). 'Predictors of difference in subjective well-being across 97 nations', *Cross-Cultural Research*, 43/2, May

Ryan, S. (2012). 'When is a team a team?' *Employee Relations*, 34/3

Spomer, M. (2012). 'Facts on File: World Religions Online,' *The Charleston Adviser*, 13/4, pp. 39–42

Trompenaars, F. and Hampden-Turner, C. (1997). *Riding the Waves of Culture: Understanding Cultural Diversity in Business*, 2nd edn. London: Nicholas Brealey

UIS (2007). 'Global education spending concentrated in a handful of countries', *UIS Factsheet*, 03 (October). Montreal, Canada: UNESCO Institute of Statistics

Yahoo Finance (2012). Company information for CPK, available at http://biz.yahoo.com/ic/47/47669.html, accessed April 2012

Other sources of information

Barron, A. (2011). 'The impact of national business cultures on large firm lobbying in the European Union: Evidence from a large-scale survey of government affairs managers', *Journal of European Integration*, 33/4, July

Dahl, S. (2004). 'Intercultural research: The current state of knowledge', *Middlesex University Discussion Paper*, No. 26 (January)

Gould, S. J. and Grein, A. F. (2009). 'Think glocally, act glocally', *Journal of International Business Studies*, 40

Hagen, S. (2005). *Language and Culture in British Business*. London: CILT

Harris, S. and Carr, C. (2008). 'National cultural values and the purposes of businesses', *International Business Review*, 17/3 (February)

Helmreich, R. L. and Merritt, A. C. (2001). *Culture at Work in Aviation and Medicine: National, Organizational and Professional Influences*, 2nd edn. Aldershot: Ashgate

Hofstede, G. (1980). *Culture's Consequences: International Differences in Work-Related Values*. London: Sage

Hofstede, G. (2001). *Culture's Consequences: Comparing Values, Behaviors, Institutions and Organizations across Nations*. London: Sage

Leung, K., Bhagat, R., Buchan, N. R., Erez, M., and Gibson, C. B. (2011). 'Beyond national culture and culture-centrism: A reply to Gould and Grein (2009)', *Journal of International Business Studies*, 42/1, January

McSweeney, B. (2002). 'Hofstede's model of national cultural differences and their consequences: A triumph of faith—a failure of analysis', *Human Relations*, 55, pp. 89–118

Maddison, A. (2007). *Contours of the World Economy, 1–2030 AD: Essays in Macro-Economic History*. Oxford: Oxford University Press

Muethel, M., Hoegl, M., and Praveen Parboteeah, K. (2011). 'National business ideology and employees' prosocial values', *Journal of International Business Studies*, 42/2, February

Pan, Y., Rowney, J.A., and Peterson, M.F. (2012). 'The structure of Chinese cultural traditions: An empirical study of business employees in China', *Management and Organization Review*, 8/1, March

Novosis (2009). http://www.novosis.de, accessed 26 June 2012; and via http://www.acino-pharma.com

Schneider, S. C. and Barsoux, J.-L. (2003). *Managing Across Cultures*, 2nd edn. Harlow: FT Prentice Hall

Trompenaars, F. (1993). *Riding the Waves of Culture: Understanding Cultural Diversity in Business*. London: Nicholas Brealey

UIS (2004). UNESCO Institute of Statistics, 'A decade of investment in research and development (R&D)', *UIS Bulletin on Science and Technology Statistics*, 1 (April)

Webster, C. and White, A. (2010). 'Exploring the national and organizational culture mix in service firms', *Journal of the Academy of Marketing Science*, 38/6, December

7 International corporate cultures

Learning objectives

After reading this chapter, you should be able to:

+ evaluate the significance of MNEs' values and ethos
+ assess the importance of corporate culture models in analysing MNEs
+ analyse the key factors in variations in corporate culture
+ evaluate rationales and methods of corporate change
+ appreciate the international manager's role in the process of change

Case study 7.1

Olayan: Corporate culture in a privately owned group

The Olayan Group was founded in Saudi Arabia in 1947 as a trucking and supply company (the General Contracting Company) working on the Trans-Arabian Pipeline. It has grown into one of the world's largest privately owned companies, with an increasingly global reach and offices in Athens, London, New York, and Vienna, as well as in Saudi Arabia. The Group is a multinational enterprise with about 50 wholly owned companies, joint ventures, and affiliated businesses and about 10,000 employees; it has a sizeable stake in Credit Suisse. In the Middle East, Olayan has numerous operating companies and substantial equity holdings, with partners and principals such as Kimberly-Clark, Toshiba, Colgate-Palmolive, Burger King, Coca-Cola, Nestlé, and Cardinal Health. The Group's CEO is now Lubna Olayan, ranked by Forbes in 2011 as the 63rd most powerful woman in the world (Broomhall 2011).

Like many privately owned international groups, Olayan is able to take decisions quickly, change direction, be closer to the customer, and make new investments in ways that publicly owned companies that have Stock Exchange listings sometimes find more difficult. The advantages to being privately owned include being able to take a longer term view of the business because the company is not tied to concerns about its share price, the interests of stockholders, and the sometimes hostile views of market analysts. This flexibility has not, however, prevented the Group from restructuring itself so that its divisions reflect its multinational development. It has done this while retaining an element of family focus and contact with its regional origins.

In 2012 the company celebrated its 65th anniversary and concluded its maiden issue of an Islamic bond (or *sukuk*) with a value of $173.3 million; this was a privately placed transaction that was 2½ times over-subscribed (Arabian Business 2012).

One reflection of the Olayan Group's ability to combine the operations of an MNE with its Middle Eastern and family orientation has been the range of its philanthropic activities, from its contribution to the establishment of

The Riyadh headquarters of the Olayan Group's Middle East operations
Reproduced courtesy of the Olayan Group

renal-care training centres in Saudi Arabia to pioneering recruitment policies in non-traditional job opportunities for women. The new generation of Olayan directors and managers have continued to emphasize that 'good deeds mean good business' and that companies such as Olayan need to 'become good corporate citizens with a keen awareness of social responsibility' (Olayan 2012).

The contribution of the Olayan Group and its charismatic founder, Suliman S. Olayan, to international business throughout the Middle East has been recognized in many ways, but none more profound than the decision in 2003 of the American University of Beirut to name its Business School the Suliman S. Olayan School of Business. The University's trustees hailed Mr Olayan (who died in 2002) as 'one of the world's most astute and highly trusted private investors . . . a valuable bridge between cultures and economies . . . a man with vision and unimpeachable integrity, and . . . an eminent role model for younger generations'. Olayan's growth illustrates the ability of companies to grow organically, take on different roles, and adopt a new corporate culture that is suitable to its stage of development. It demonstrates that it is possible for a small company to grow into an MNE, with a range of international activities and achievements that permit it to be measured alongside other MNEs, both public and private, from around the world.

Introduction

This chapter focuses on the corporate cultures of firms that operate internationally, primarily MNEs. As was seen in the previous chapter (Chapter 6) on national cultures, such companies operate in an environment where they have to face and adapt to external cultures. To be successful, they must get the business basics right—reducing costs, devising the right product, setting the right price, managing people, operating efficiently, and so on—and adapt to the national cultures where they are carrying out their activities. Some firms are more successful at international business than others, and this can be because of another key factor: their internal culture.

Beyond these aspects of corporate culture, there is also the driving ethos of the organization—its reason for being or *raison d'être*—that marks it out as unique in its field. This ethos is often displayed in the company's statement about itself: a set of values, a slogan, or a motto. This chapter, therefore, discusses a range of analytical models that enable managers to understand their own corporate culture and the key factors that need to be considered when assessing the possibilities of planning and implementing strategies for corporate change. In addition, managers need to identify, understand, and analyse the corporate culture of their competitors and partners. The chapter also reviews the external and internal contexts that have an impact on corporate cultures, looking at the values and ethos of different types of companies and the importance of understanding these within different national economic structures.

Section I: Understanding corporate culture and change

Many analytical models have been proposed by academics and practitioners to understand corporate culture. These models range from those that are deliberately limited in scope, with a simple set of categories, to others that construct an analysis of many dimensions. Many of the models are equally applicable to domestic companies as to MNEs.

The international business scene is constantly changing, and some of the models put forward are designed to assist managers in assessing the degree to which change will be accepted or rejected within an organization. An understanding of strategies for business change is essential for managers as they progress through their corporate careers.

Models for understanding corporate culture

To understand both domestic and international corporate cultures, it is essential to use a variety of models. A straightforward guide to organizational culture is that of the British management writer Charles Handy (1993), who classified it by the power of individuals' roles and functions, and identified four archetypes: those of Power, Role, Task, and Person. Handy also attached the names of Greek gods to the four different cultures (see Figure 7.1).

Figure 7.1 The four cultures (Handy 1993).	Power	Zeus	(spider's web)
	Role	Apollo	(temple)
	Task	Athena	(matrix/net)
	Person	Dionysius	(amoeba)

The Power culture (Zeus) emphasizes the concentration of power in the hands of one individual, the boss. The lines of control are exercised by the priority of personal contacts over procedures; the most powerful person dominates the decision-making process. This organizational culture is typical of companies where ownership is private or held by a single family, led by a charismatic leader or the founder. Examples of this sort of international company and corporate style include Facebook, still dominated by Mark Zuckerberg (see Chapter 12 Case study 12.3), the Virgin Group, led by Sir Richard Branson, the Olayan Group, led by Lubna Olayan (see Case study 7.1 above), and the Alibaba Group, led by Yun Ma (Jack Ma) (see Case study 7.2). International investment banks and brokerage firms are also often organized on the lines of a dominant Power culture. Proximity to the boss is vitally important and key decisions are made quickly. The company's administration is small, and costs are kept low.

Order and efficiency are valued most highly within the Role culture (Apollo). Decision-making takes place at the top, and power is derived from the hierarchical structure of the company. Responsibilities and powers are clearly defined in the job descriptions for each employee. Examples of this are large MNEs such as Shell, IBM, Nestlé, and General Motors, as well as former 'public-sector' corporations such as the French utilities and energy company EDF and the British Broadcasting Corporation (BBC). The size and structure of the international company can mean that such organizations are slow in responding to changes, often relying on their existing routines and trying to ignore changed circumstances. Some life insurance companies that offer wider financial services, such as Fortis, had this form of organization. The company was slow to react to external change in the events of the 2008 credit crunch and the 2011–2012 European sovereign debt crisis to the extent that it was absorbed by other companies or broken up into smaller constituent parts. Fortis slumped from being the 20th largest business in the world by revenue to the point where its banking operations were split up and sold—some to BNP Paribas, and others to ABN AMRO (Fassin and Gosselin 2011). The insurance remnants of Fortis changed name to Ageas in April 2010, while the ownership of the once strong Fortis brand was acquired by BNP Paribas.

Handy's third model of corporate culture is the Task culture (Athena). Power comes from the expertise required to complete a task or project, with decision-making occurring through meritocracy. Key emphases in this model are coordination, organization into groups and teams, and tasks based on specific projects. It fosters a high level of adaptation and innovation by emphasizing talent, youth, and team problem-solving. In many international pharmaceutical companies, advertising agencies, management and technical consultancies, and technologically innovative companies such as Microsoft and Apple, this Task culture tends to be dominant. Task cultures require highly paid experts who are driven to analyse organizational problems in depth. Because of the high costs incurred, such companies often construct more formal routines and move towards the more hierarchical culture of the Role model.

The fourth organizational format is the Person culture (Dionysius), which is highly individualistic. Accordingly, this model is often adopted by universities and professional service firms, such as partnerships of architects, doctors, or lawyers. Employees see themselves as independent professionals who are keen to exercise independent and individual judgement in finding solutions and making decisions. The phrase often used about trying to manage academic members of staff in universities—'it's like trying to herd cats'—summarizes the independent nature of employees in this model. The Person culture can lead to strong ideological conflict among its professionals, because they see themselves as having hired out their services or skills to the organization.

The four models set out by Handy enable managers to be aware of the different cultures within a variety of businesses. While it is rare for these models to be seen in their pure form in practice, it is possible to locate any company as being closer to one model rather than another. This is essential when managers are viewing their own organizations and any that they have to work with.

Organizations and culture change

The idea of corporate culture is a contentious area and there is little agreement on its nature, structure, and influence. In the main, however, there are both external and internal influences. Each organization has its own culture, consisting of its set of beliefs, values, learnt ways of managing (Lynch 2012), systems and structures, approach to strategy, and ability to change. The organizational culture is the 'filter and shaper' through which all levels within the business—workers, managers, leaders, CEOs—understand, develop, and implement strategies and any changes or adaptations to the direction of the company (Lynch 2012).

The principal external influences on corporate culture include factors such as demographics (age profile, socio-economic groups, gender roles), language and communication, religion and beliefs, and governments' policies on social developments. These factors are very complex within a single country; in international business, the complexities are multiplied many times. For example, as shown in Chapter 6, countries vary widely in terms of their social attitudes towards religion and the relative equality of men and women. For international companies, the impact of these external influences may be on their approaches to the shape and structure of their own workforce, the kinds of products that suit the market, the advertising and media that can be used, and the effect on the relationship between the company and the community.

A key model, devised by Trompenaars (1993), Trompenaars and Hampden-Turner (1997), and Hampden-Turner and Trompenaars (2000) for the organization of international corporations, is called the four diversity cultures (see Figure 7.2). This assumes the major dimensions of person vs. task and of centralization (which is also assumed to be hierarchical) vs. decentralization (which is assumed to be more egalitarian). Both dimensions are very common measures and can often be easily determined.

The four diversity cultures derived from this model were named by Trompenaars as shown in Figure 7.2. The key features of the four different types—Incubator, Guided Missile, Family, and Eiffel Tower—are outlined below. Some of the implications for managing international businesses involve employee relations, attitude to authority, ways of thinking and learning, attitudes to people, and managing change.

As far as relationships between employees are concerned, the Eiffel Tower model suggests that the employee has a specific role in a mechanical system of required interactions, whereas the Incubator model features more diffused and spontaneous relationships that grow out of shared creative processes. Thus, the Eiffel Tower model can be applied to the workings of a large hierarchical and formal MNE such as Shell or IBM; the Incubator model

Figure 7.2
Four diversity cultures models, derived from Trompenaars (1993), Trompenaars and Hampden-Turner (1997), and Hampden-Turner and Trompenaars (2000) (Nicholas Brealey Publishing/NB Ltd).

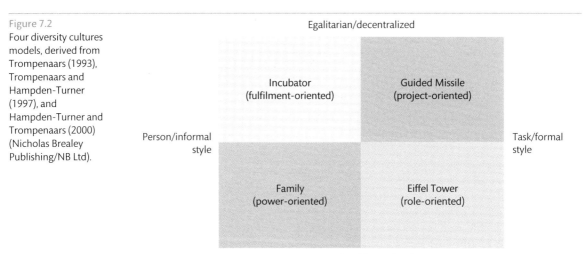

Ways of thinking & learning	Family:	Eiffel Tower:
	Intuitive, holistic, lateral, and error-correcting	Logical, analytical, vertical, and rationally efficient
Attitudes to people	As family members	Human resources
Ways of thinking & learning	Guided Missile:	Incubator:
	Problem-centred, professional, practical, cross-disciplinary	Process oriented, creative, ad-hoc, inspirational
Attitudes to people	Specialists and experts	Co-creators

Figure 7.3
Ways of thinking and learning, and attitudes to people (adapted from Trompenaars and Hampden-Turner 1997; Hampden-Turner and Trompenaars 2000).

describes more accurately the close relations that exist in a small, creative business such as an IT consultancy or an advertising agency.

For the dimension of attitude to authority, the Family model ascribes status to parent figures who are close to each other and are all powerful within the company, whether international or domestic; this is true, for example, of the family-run businesses like the Olayan Group (see Case study 7.1) and the Hirdaramani Group (see Chapter 8). By contrast, the achievement of status in the Guided Missile model is earned by project group members who work together and contribute to the targeted goal.

With respect to thinking and learning, and attitudes to people, the models operate as set out in Figure 7.3.

As far as the final factor is concerned, which is often crucial to the development of international corporations, the different models in relation to managing change indicate that, in the Family model, the 'Father' changes course, whereas in the Eiffel Tower model, the organization has to change rules and procedures. In the Guided Missile model, the company has to shift aim as the target moves, whereas in the Incubator model, the imperative is to improvise and attune. When applied to specific MNEs, the ability of the 'family-oriented' businesses to take the lead in change management from the 'boss' is contrasted with the more hierarchical, publicly quoted, profits-driven companies such as Unilever (Case study 10.1), where the organization has to undertake major changes in its rules, procedures, and operations.

A further model that is useful for analysing and understanding MNEs' corporate culture is the 'cultural web', which identifies six interrelated elements, as originally devised by Gerry Johnson (1987, 1992) and used in *Exploring Corporate Strategy* by Johnson et al. (2010). These help to make up the 'paradigm'—the pattern or model—of the work environment. Analysing the factors in each element helps to reveal the bigger picture of the company's culture: what is working, what is not working, and what needs to be changed. In addition to monitoring change, Johnson's view of strategic management suggested that executives had to be able to signal changes in corporate culture. Planning change is required to alter the everyday routines that affect the behaviour of those who work in the MNE.

The six elements in Johnson's cultural web are outlined below.

Stories

Stories refer to the past events and people that are talked about inside and outside the company. The focus here is on what matters in the organization and what the company chooses to emphasize. The stories told and the examples used are good indicators of what the MNE values and what is perceived as appropriate behaviour. The emphasis is also on what constitutes success or failure.

This is often revealed in the statements made in the history or the background of a company, such as the attention paid to the character and life story of Suliman S. Olayan, the founder of the Olayan Group (see Case study 7.1).

Symbols

Symbols are the visual representations of the company, including logos, the standard of the offices and other facilities, and formal or informal dress codes. Symbols can also include whether there are separate restaurants for different levels of employees, and how managers and workers are rewarded through fringe benefits, including travel, health insurance, and gym membership.

Throughout this book, there are a number of images and other pictorial representations of the MNEs that have contributed to it. They can be viewed as the first symbols of how the company wants to visualize itself (Walsh et al. 2010). Some companies spend a vast amount of money on changing logos and corporate colours in order to signal shifts in corporate intentions and strategy, such as the oil company Esso/EXXON in the early 1970s (Giddens 1973; Exxon Digital History 2012); others change their logo on a regular basis, such as Rede Globo (or Globo), the Brazilian media group, which made alterations in 1976, 1986, and 2008–2009. Still others, such as FedEx (operating as Federal Express between 1973 and 2000), have used variations of the logo, depending on the operating unit of the company.

Power structures

This refers to the location of real power in the company. It may involve one or two key senior executives, a group of executives (the inner circle, as mentioned by Handy's Power culture above), or even a department. The most significant aspect is identifying those people who have the greatest amount of influence on decisions, operations, and strategic direction.

As with the organizational structures below, the existence of key decision-makers may not be obvious from the external representation of the structure. For example, stereo-typically, but also with some basis in reality, decision-making in some MNEs (and other companies) may still be significantly determined on the golf course.

Organizational structure

This includes both the structure defined by the organization chart, and the unwritten lines of power and influence that indicate whose contributions are most valued, as suggested through rituals and routines.

The organizational structures adopted by MNEs and other companies are explored in depth in Chapter 10. For some managers, it is important to understand that, particularly in some 'high-context cultures' (see Chapter 6), the key decisions will be made in ways that are not always evident from the highly intricate chart of how the company works internationally. The experience of 'westerners' working in many BRIC (Brazil, Russia, India, and China) or CIVET (Colombia, Indonesia, Vietnam, Egypt, Turkey, and South Africa) countries is that the formal hierarchy of the business organizations does not reveal how and where the decisions are made. The informal linkages within business are usually more significant than the formal ones.

Control systems

The ways that the organization is controlled include financial systems, quality systems, and the measurement and distribution of rewards.

An important element within the control system can be decisions made on the type of pay rewards. In MNEs in some countries, it is automatic that employees can take a reasonable proportion of their pay in overtime; for others, such as Nordic or Scandinavian workers, there is both a social inhibition on working beyond the set hours and a belief that, if work is carried out efficiently, it can be accomplished within the working day. A 2011 study examined some interesting facets of pay for about 900 businesspeople in the three Baltic states, confirming some of the key aspects of northern Europeans' attitudes towards work and pay (Carraher 2011).

Rituals and routines

These include the daily actions of people that signal acceptable behaviour. The emphasis in this element is on the normal ways of doing things. In some cases, the guide to these acceptable procedures is not written down but still regulates what is expected to happen in given situations, and what is valued by management, including such things as long service, quality standards, innovation, and sales achievements. These elements can really only be learnt 'on the job'—when people are working in a company, they realize what they have to do under the special circumstances they find there. Such rituals and routines also vary between offices and factories within the same MNE but located in different countries (Deal and Kennedy 2000).

All these models help to explain how companies operate internationally. What is even more crucial for MNEs are the intersecting forms of national culture and corporate culture that impact on each other and on how the MNE is viewed. Companies with a particular national base have developed differently from others with a different national origin. For example, although it was rare for successful MNEs to have joint national origins, the achievements of Unilever and Shell proved that Anglo-Dutch companies could work well. For many decades, these two MNEs maintained joint management boards with decisions being made in both Netherlands and the UK. For some companies, their national origins have been retained regardless of how large and global they have become. It is difficult to think of MNEs such as Levi's, Disney, Coca-Cola, Kellogg's, and Ford as being anything other than American, or of BA (airline), BP (petroleum and energy), BG (gas and energy), or BT (telecommunications) being anything other than British in origin. As a result of the merger in 2006, the steel company ArcelorMittal has combined Asian and European operations but retained the very strong operational and directorial control of the Mittal family, with Lakshmi Mittal as Chairman and CEO; his son, Aditya Mittal as CFO (Chief Financial Officer); and his daughter, Vanisha Mittal Bhatia, as a member of the Board of Directors (ArcelorMittal 2012). This highlights the confusing tension between Asian and European management styles, and between the corporate culture of a family firm and a publicly quoted company.

The ArcelorMittal Orbit at the London Olympics

Source: Corbis

> Go online

Another topic in international corporate culture is the rise of multicultural teams. Such teams demonstrate the complexity of how different cultures fit together (**see ORC Extension material 7.1**). A key factor is the conjunction of each team member's personal and national background within the company's own organizational culture. To what extent is it possible for the corporate culture to overcome each individual's personal or national culture? How strongly does each person retain his or her national characteristics?

Section II: Corporate values and ethos

Visions, missions, and values

All MNEs (and most other organizations in the world, whether business related or not) have adopted some form of words that are intended to encapsulate their *raison d'être* (their reason for being). These words usually form the organization's vision, set of values, or mission statement (Mission Statements 2012). The mission statement is designed to provide a focus for the attention, activities, and purposes of the organization, its employees, and all other stakeholders. Although these wordings may appear rather simple and open to criticism, they often express clearly and directly what the company stands for and why it is successful. The vision or mission statement is usually supported by a slogan or motto (sometimes called a strapline) that will be used on a website, marketing emails, and throughout trade and promotional literature.

+ Mission statement
Defines in a few words or sentences the reason for existence of any entity or organization. It embodies its philosophies, goals, ambitions, and values.

One of the world's largest facility and project management corporations, Johnson Controls, has 162,000 employees in more than 1300 locations in over 150 countries, with global sales in 2011 of $40.8 billion (Johnson Controls 2012). Based in Milwaukee, USA, the company is engaged in the sectors of automotive experience, building efficiency, and power solutions. It has a straightforward vision: 'Creating a more comfortable, safe and sustainable world', supported by five values: integrity, customer satisfaction, employee engagement, innovation, and sustainability (Johnson Controls 2012). Johnson Controls' international presence is emphasized by being world leader in integrated facility management for Fortune 500 companies, managing 1.8 billion square feet of commercial real estate worldwide. However, the simple message of its vision is apparently maintained throughout the MNE.

The Olayan Group (see Case study 7.1) has a complex set of statements indicating its *raison d'être*: four paragraphs setting out its mission statement (Olayan 2012); four core values focusing on customers, business partners, people, and shareholders; seven operating principles, including integrity, excellence, and accountability; and its vision, consisting of five areas (opportunity, alliances, impact, strength, and vision). By contrast, the Hirdaramani Group has a single statement for its 'motto': 'Your Company, Your Future' (Hirdaramani 2012), but also has several sentences for its mission and a sentence for each of the six elements of its vision: design, customer first, enable, sustainability, productivity, and commitment. This is a considerable change from the vision of 2009: 'To offer quality customer service through innovation, leadership and excellence and to be responsive to change in a competitive world' and the mission: 'To instil professionalism by embracing a positive spirit of enterprise within the group, with the aim of gaining a global market share' (Hirdaramani 2009).

Nestlé expresses its Corporate Business Principles in a long statement, noting that these ten principles will be adapted and changed over time as the world changes, but its motto/slogan is still short and sweet: 'Good Food, Good Life' (Nestlé 2012). In recent years Nestlé has attached to its ten principles a range of links to its more detailed descriptions and operational corporate policies. Similarly, Nokia (see Chapter 13) has a simple strapline of 'Connecting People' and a more formal and complex statement that 'our goal is to build great mobile products that enable billions of people worldwide to enjoy more of what life has to offer. Our challenge is to achieve this in an increasingly dynamic and competitive environment. Ideas. Energy. Excitement. Opportunities. In today's mobile world, it feels like anything is possible—and that's what inspires us to get out of bed every day' (Nokia 2012).

As can be seen from the small selection above, the international nature of these statements usually consists of stressing the movement of the company into the international arena, either as a player seeking 'a global market share' or as a 'world leader'. They can provide a solid clue as to the international achievements and aspirations of MNEs and they are sometimes a reflection of whether the company's main motivation to internationalize is 'push' or 'pull' (see Chapter 10). Companies such as Olayan and Hirdaramani have started on a small scale from a national base (respectively Saudi Arabia and Sri Lanka) before expanding onto the global scene in a mix of push and pull: the push from the development and saturation of their domestic activities; and the pull of the opportunities afforded by the international market.

Global corporate ethos

Each company has its own way of doing things. As people move from one job to another and from one company to another, they are able to notice visible and also less tangible things that define the working environment and the working practices of each. Visible characteristics include the structure as defined by the MNE's organization chart, the nature of the factory or office building, the corporate logo, the layout of the rooms and offices, and the type of clothing that staff wear. The less tangible factors include the values and mission, the reporting and control systems, and the global corporate ethos.

+ global corporate ethos
Essential set of characteristics that define the ways in which the MNE is organized and has its staff operate and behave.

There are three broad types of global corporate ethos, each related to a particular form of identification that a firm has sought, or by which it is known internationally. These types are values, brand, and sector.

A good example of a values ethos is the BBC, which prides itself on being 'objective'. Its large team of reporters across the world and its extensive range of radio, television, and Internet broadcast outlets are its attempt to guarantee comprehensive and objective news coverage, as well as providing a full service of programming in other areas. Behind the original straightforward principles of 'Inform, Educate, Entertain', the BBC has developed mission and vision statements, and a set of six values. These corporate statements are based on the Royal Charter and Agreement, and have resulted from a strategic review in 2009–2010 (BBC 2012).

Examples of the brand ethos are those companies that are identifiable on a worldwide basis by their names and their brands. These include MNEs such as Nike, Google, Toyota, McDonald's, Microsoft, Sony, Apple, Coca-Cola, Santander, and NTT Group.

The sector ethos MNEs are those that, regardless of brand and/or values, see themselves most significantly as identifiable by the sector of business in which they operate. Major firms in the capital markets—banks, investment houses, private equity firms—may identify themselves primarily by their function: that they are in business to make money. Such companies include Deutsche Bank (see 'Practitioner insight' in this chapter), Morgan Stanley, Nomura, HSBC, and Goldman Sachs. Despite the dramatic events of the world's financial crises of 2008–2012, the companies that survived have an even stronger identification with the sector as the defining factor in their corporate ethos.

It is rare, of course, for MNEs to associate themselves with only one type of identity. Not only do they normally have a more complex view of themselves but they are also very competitive within each industrial sector as to who has the right to regard themselves as the pioneer or the innovator, or as the leading brand.

International business negotiations

An important feature of corporate culture—and national culture (see Chapter 6)—is that companies need to be able to negotiate successfully with each other, with national governments, and with international institutions. The distinctive culture of each firm impacts on the stance that it may take in such negotiations. Increasingly, employees of many companies are operating internationally and it is estimated that about 50 per cent of an international manager's time may be spent on negotiations (Pynchon 2011; Potgieter 2010; Hendon et al. 1996). These managers need to be trained in sensitivity towards the differing national cultures in which they operate and in understanding how culture can affect the negotiating position of their own business and other organization(s) in the deal.

As with domestic negotiations, managers must look at the balance between their competitive and collaborative approaches, the framework for the negotiation, including strategy, tactics, and implementation, the phases of preparation, interaction, and post-negotiation, and key issues such as communication, price, timing, and legal agreements. The success of international business negotiations can bring the massive financial and cost-cutting benefits associated with cross-national mergers and acquisitions, but just as often do not work.

There are two major cases of short-lived mergers where the correct fit was not negotiated and the apparently 'good marriage' was dissolved within a few years: AOL with Time Warner (2000–2009) and Daimler-Benz with Chrysler (1998–2007). The $360 billion AOL–Time Warner merger fell foul of a failure to meld the two organizations so as to maximize benefits from the digital media revolution; what should have been a perfect merger between two American giants within the media industry turned out to be a nightmare (Quittner 2009). For the Daimler–Chrysler merger (Martelin 2008), there was a long-term failure to build the right vehicles and serious misunderstandings that arose in the original negotiations between the German and American corporations. The charismatic leadership of Jürgen Schremp, the German boss, managed to persuade the management and shareholders of Daimler–Benz that the merger with Chrysler was the right move in trying to create a global corporation. From the American perspective, the merger was immediately contentious, with many investors contesting in the law courts whether the transaction was the 'merger of equals' or a straightforward German acquisition. From the beginning, the growing pains of a marriage of opposites were evident: the formality and hierarchy of the German conglomerate did not match well with a Chrysler method of operation that was informal, with cross-functional teams and free-flowing discussions (Vlasic and Stertz 2000). There were also financial and legal issues involved in the inability to get the two sides to fit together, but at the heart of the failure was a mismatch in corporate culture that had echoes within the perceived and/or real national differences (Martelin 2008; Casestudyinc.com 2010).

External contexts for international corporate culture

The corporate culture of a firm is derived from internal and external factors. External factors are drawn from the widest aspects of society such as national culture, art and literature, language, and spiritual and religious beliefs, as discussed in Chapter 6. The impact of the MNE's country of origin is sometimes more long-lasting and prevalent than might be imagined. However international certain companies become, they also remain rooted in their original culture. Despite the adoption of abbreviations and acronyms by many companies (see BP, BA, BT, and BG as noted above), it is clear in these examples that the 'B' stands for British and that these large MNEs remain essentially British in their corporate cultures.

For MNEs and other companies operating across the globe, their corporate culture becomes even more complex. There is the human dimension of having many people from different cultures interacting around the world; the architectural complexity of MNEs' structures of geographical divisions and functional departments; and the strategic challenge of maintaining control over a massive organization and ensuring that it retains its single purpose and direction. The culture of a successful MNE is multifaceted and exceptionally complicated.

A key development for workers and managers is the change that has come about in some countries and that is forecast for others: the arrival of the post-industrial society. Heralded by a number of social commentators as early as the 1960s and 1970s, the key features of the

+ **Post-industrial society**
Defines the development of a late capitalist society with such features as the growth of free markets, greater mass consumption, and, ultimately, more leisure time.

post-industrial society were identified, particularly by the late Daniel Bell (who lived from 1919 to 2011), as being related not only to economic and social structures but also to norms and values. Bell's seminal work, *The Coming of Post-Industrial Society* (1974), highlighted a shift from manufacturing to services; the centrality of industries based on new scientific developments; an emphasis on rationality and efficiency; the rise of new technical elites; and the advent of new principles of social stratification. Bell's concern about the post-industrial society was that its new values might cause a disconnection between socio-economic structures and culture, such as the domination of free market regimes, the growth of economic inequality, the outsourcing of domestic jobs, and a surge in mass consumption (**see ORC Extension material 7.2**).

The positive aspects of the post-industrial society are intended to be greater leisure, a better work–life balance, and the greater availability of consumer products and services for more and more consumers. Whereas some of this has been achieved in certain countries—especially the developed, Western, industrialized societies (the OECD countries) and the oil-rich countries of the Middle East—the post-industrial or leisure society has sometimes come at the social cost of a loss of job security, higher structural unemployment, and the fragility of economic interdependence. All these developments have an impact on the external business environment in which international companies operate in the twenty-first century and on their corporate cultures. In the post-industrial society, companies make choices about work–life balance for their employees, structural and hierarchical arrangements within the company, and the extent to which the offering of products and services may change. In their articles and their book on work–life balance (Gambles et al. 2006), the authors cite instances of the dilemmas from the 'global front line' faced by real people, working in countries such as South Africa and India, as well as Norway and Japan.

A step beyond the post-industrial or leisure society has been the beginnings of the emergence of a virtual society and economy (**see ORC Extension material 7.3**). One of the key features of online advertising and purchasing has been the massive growth of the medium itself and many associated developments: social networking, blogging, podcasting, texting, and tweeting. Beyond the virtual economy, there has been the idea of using gaming and virtual worlds in order to model the real economy in a way that, it is hoped, will provide simulated predictors of future development (see Further research).

> Go online

+ Work–life balance
Life choices that many people make in order to balance the demands of work with other important areas of their lives, such as family, friends, and hobbies.

> Go online

Cultural differences

A prime consideration for all managers is not only their personal attitudes and responses to cultural differences but how they influence their company's attitudes towards the countries they work in and from which they originate. The impetus for the company to do business internationally is a 'push' or a 'pull' factor. For some companies, their prime reaction to carrying out international business is to prioritize the home country (where they originate) over their host country; this is known as an 'ethnocentric' policy. Other companies adopt a policy in which the company responds more directly to local considerations—that is, those of the host country; this is generally known as polycentric or indeed geocentric, where the policy is to act regardless of national origins (see Chapter 12).

At a personal level, managers of MNEs need not only be aware of cultural and linguistic differences but must be able to act and respond appropriately in a range of different national and cultural situations. In some cases, particularly in 'high-context' cultures (see Chapter 6), many of the cultural signals are subliminal, consisting of forms of social behaviour, expressions of language used, and body language, including gestures (**see ORC Extension material 7.4**). Whereas participation in drinking after work and karaoke evenings is commonly expected in Japan, it would be unexpected and unacceptable in most countries of the Middle East. For many Europeans and Americans, it would not be unusual behaviour but would be seen as an additional part of the need to do business, rather than an essential component.

+ Geocentric
Company adopts the most suitable marketing strategy, taking into account the values of the company and those of the target market.

> Go online

Gestures and body
language vary
significantly between
cultures

Source: Ariel Skelley

For those 'westerners' doing business in the Middle East and in many parts of Asia, it is essential to understand the need to build long-lasting relationships. It is not acceptable in such cultures to fly in, do the business, and fly out; it is necessary to get to know business counterparts and build the deal from the viewpoint of successful personal relationships.

Practitioner insight

Shona Milne, Managing Director, EMEA Finance, Deutsche Bank AG, London

'My role as a regional CFO in Finance is overseeing the financial aspects of Deutsche Bank in my region (Europe, Middle East, and Africa—EMEA) and protecting the interest of Deutsche Bank's shareholders to ensure their returns are maximized over time. This includes all aspects of internal and external financial and regulatory reporting, and maintaining appropriate internal control systems. In addition, my role is to partner with internal stakeholders to monitor performance, manage costs, and deliver their strategic agenda.

Deutsche Bank is a leading global investment bank with more than 100,000 employees in 72 countries and our mission statement is: "To compete to be the leading global provider of financial solutions, creating lasting value for its clients, shareholders, people and the communities in which it operates." Our mission gives our business a clear purpose and direction, and is rooted in our brand so that it captures and projects a clear idea of who we are.

Deutsche Bank is clear about what its purpose is: we are here to perform—in business and beyond. My experience is that we do this with a measured approach that gives us the confidence to enable our own employees to look beyond the obvious, gaining advantage for people with whom we work. Strong brands evoke strong emotions. Today everyone looks for personality in business, for the same reasons they look for it in people. It helps us decide whom we trust, whom we admire, and whom we would like to work with.

Deutsche Bank actively works on facilitating work–life balance through a number of initiatives including the family network, one of the diversity networks existing in Deutsche Bank globally. Deutsche Bank's commitment to working mothers in the UK was recognized in 2011 when the Bank won the Best for Mothers Award at the annual Working Families Awards 2011. The award was given to the Bank in recognition of its programme of maternity coaching.

Working for an organization existing in 72 countries, it has been my experience that I have had to adapt to many different cultures. Cultural awareness courses are offered for our staff involved in global roles. Ensuring the right fit of local culture with a global organization is key to the Bank's success; I and other staff members have become accustomed to dealing with and adapting to different cultures. My current EMEA job is a perfect example of this, requiring regular travel and interaction with people from many countries.

Over the last 20 years, the globalization of the business has led to a strong global management structure for each business line. In addition, there is a regional structure to ensure appropriate regional governance in EMEA, Asia Pacific, and the Americas with regional management and local country level management. It is my responsibility to manage this global–regional balance.'

Internal contexts for MNEs

The many factors related to external culture for companies are virtually matched by the internal ones. The different layers of a company in terms of, for example, hierarchy, structure, control systems, responsibilities, and tasks are sufficient to create very individual cultures for each firm. When the variations of personality, attitude towards work, team or individualist orientation, and national and ethnic background are added, the complexity of internal dimensions creates a further set of considerations. To attempt to uncover and explain the internal cultures of MNEs, the following sections explore departmental issues, interpersonal relationships, and social aspects of corporate culture.

Departmental cultures

Within business there are different departmental or divisional cultures that are obvious to anybody who visits offices, factories, or production facilities around the world. Without wishing to uphold stereotypes, it is possible to distinguish a number of cultures that can exist within the same firm or, where a company is predominantly focused on a particular activity, that can permeate the whole operation. These different cultures can be represented by the way in which people dress and behave.

There is a tendency for the focus in the research departments to be on their scientific and professional nature, thus represented by white coats. The demeanour of the staff in such an operation tends towards engagement with serious enquiry, intellectual debate, and attention to testing and results. This tends to be less the case with the high-technology companies, especially those in the computer and IT industry. Here the research side of the company is often composed of mavericks with a casual sense of dress but a hard-driving outlook to getting the work done. This has been exemplified at CEO level by the hard-working but casual demeanour and dress of such leaders as the late Steve Jobs (Apple, NeXT, and Pixar) and Bill Gates (Microsoft).

Within the manufacturing and production sections of the firm, the focus is on work on the assembly line, hard manual labour, or the manipulation of technical equipment, such as fork-lift trucks. Such members of staff are characterized by their working uniforms and are still traditionally known as 'blue collar' workers. Any visitor to an international logistics, transport, or delivery firm, such as DHL, TNT, Fedex, and UPS, will witness their massive operations, which, though highly technical, are still based on labour-intensive and mechanized activity.

For those people within departments such as marketing, including advertising and public relations, there is often a more relaxed dress style. This may be reflected in the permission for members of staff to dress down more than they would in other areas of the business, perhaps even to the point of unusual hair styles or of earrings or other piercings for men.

Steve Jobs often wore casual dress

Source: Corbis

This apparently more casual corporate culture, including the adoption of less formal dress, has been shown in very market-oriented MNEs by leaders such as Sir Richard Branson (Virgin) and Charles Dunstone (Carphone Warehouse). The most formal corporate culture has tended to be within finance departments or among staff who are predominantly concerned with accounting and finance functions. In terms of dress, this is exemplified by the wearing of formal suits, including pinstripes, and white shirts—hence the common terminology of 'white collars'. This most formal culture is exemplified among CEOs by the style and dress of leaders, such as almost all bankers and many others from so-called blue chip companies. Women managers in these companies are also inclined to wear the same uniform of dark suits and white shirts.

Interpersonal relationships at work

Among MNEs there is a range of differences that derive from both national and corporate cultures. At one extreme, there is Japan: the life of the Japanese employee can be arduous and hard-working, with a dedication to the office and the business that is thought in other cultures to be far too serious. Typically, Japanese salarymen will often work very long hours, including late evenings and weekends (Hays 2009–2010 and Dasgupta 2012) and are expected to fulfil 'even the most unreasonable demands of their bosses' (Hays 2009–2010).

The socializing side of business is regarded as an essential part of working life, with bouts of excessive drinking and wild karaoke (Economist 2007). The flip side of this extensive commitment of the managerial class to this kind of business life is that they are (or were) guaranteed jobs for life and the 'cradle to grave' security of the company. This commitment on both sides of the corporation began to diminish in the 1980s and 1990s, and the trend away from the permanent worker in Japan continued into the early part of the twenty-first century. The permanent workforce, among which were the salarymen, declined from over 80 per cent to only just over 60 per cent and there was significant restructuring of executive levels within Japanese companies (Economist 2010 and Matsuura et al. 2011). Thus, as the economic conditions changed in Japan in the 1990s, the matching values of staff loyalty to the company and the company's guarantee of lifetime employment were no longer as viable.

There are further indicators of the differences that can be shown in the working relationships within MNEs. An interesting—and physical—manifestation of this comes from the ways in which North Americans and Japanese organize their office and other working spaces, as shown in Figure 7.4. The individualist nature of the American layout is dramatically

+ **salaryman**
White-collar worker (based on a Japanese model) who works in the large bureaucracy of a business (or government office). The salaryman has long working hours, low prestige in the corporate hierarchy, and an absence of significant sources of income other than salary; the term is almost always used only for male employees.

American organization of working

Large spaces, with large desks and distance between desks/offices.
Workers have separate cubicles, separate offices.
Sit with backs to others—work requires privacy, concentration.
Each employee has a set of their own papers, information, PC etc. in their office.
To communicate with someone, use phone, or get up and walk to their desk.
Work spaces are personalized (photos, art etc.).
Windows mean status

Japanese organization of working

Compact use of space, with small desks, closely spaced.
Desks of a work unit are put together to form one large table.
Everyone faces other people.
Not much room for papers, etc. Must be very neat; use collective supplies.
Supervisor sits at the head, the most junior sits at the foot.
You work on projects with those who sit nearest you.
Communication is continuous because you talk to or overhear everyone else's business.
Workspaces are for work only; only a few personal touches are allowed, if any.
Window means exile from active working group.

Figure 7.4
American and Japanese organization of working (adapted from JB Intercultural Consulting 2012).

different from the more collectivist set-up of the Japanese office. The emphasis in the latter is on teamwork rather than on individual endeavour.

Social aspects of corporate culture

Many people spend a substantial amount of their life at work, rather than at home. Even the modern developments of computer access from home, wireless-free facilities, hot-desking, video conferencing, and teleworking have not significantly reduced the amount of time that most workers and managers have to spend in the office or the factory. The quantity of international business conducted by video conferencing, sometimes as much as 3–4 hour conferences or a series of such conferences spread over a couple of days (JCI 2012; GSK 2011–2012), has not prevented managers from having to be physically in the office most of their working life. Given the continuing centrality of working time, it is not surprising that a key factor of corporate life is the bringing together of business and social lives within MNE activities.

A great development in modern business life is team-building through corporate events. Such activities are designed to help companies develop their business and ensure that managers and workers from the same company understand the strengths of the people they work with on a day-to-day basis (Ferdinand and Kitchin 2012). Organizers of corporate events offer a range of physical and mental challenges that are designed to tackle some of the issues in the workplace such as time management, delegation, and communication. Beyond the team-building activities, there are MNE events such as conference organizing, motivational days, themed evening events, corporate entertainment, and corporate hospitality (Shone and Parry 2010; Bowdin 2011).

In the USA, a significant feature of business life is the celebration within companies of certain American holidays, especially the 4th of July. In many US companies, there is a company picnic on Independence Day, with a series of sports and games played (usually touch football and softball) and a barbecue. The purpose of the company's 4th of July picnic is both social and corporate. On the social side, it is an opportunity for managers and workers to meet with their families and friends; on the corporate side, it provides an opportunity to encourage teamwork and bonding between members of staff.

By contrast, for French companies, there is considerable focus on permitting a separation between private life (*la vie privée*) and company life. It is assumed that these two aspects of a worker's life are separate and should be kept so. There is some reluctance, therefore, to engage in team-building through corporate events or to arrange for business and private life to coexist.

Case study 7.2

Alibaba

The company that is 'the world's largest business-to-business marketplace for global trade' is owned and run by Yun Ma (known as Jack Ma), is based in Hong Kong, and is called Alibaba. While this may seem improbable to many in the Western world of business, Alibaba is very clearly part of the corporate future, not just in China and Asia but across the world. The Alibaba Group is worth over $20 billion and one of its subsidiaries, Taobao, is the largest online marketplace in China with over 800 million product listings and 370 million registered users (http://news.alibaba.com). In recent years, a main issue for Alibaba has been their connection to Yahoo! Inc., the California-based Internet giant. In 2005, Yahoo! gave control of its website in China to Alibaba, as well as taking a 40 per cent stake in Alibaba for $1 billion. This arrangement worked well over the first couple of years, but in 2009 Yahoo! indicated its intention to extricate itself from this deal. By May 2012, it was agreed that Alibaba would pay $7.1 billion in cash and stock to buy back about half of the Yahoo! stake.

The Yahoo! buyback is part of a new competitive business environment for Alibaba: the rise of a Chinese Internet sector that has many 'fast-growing domestic Web companies that are rivalling their Western counterparts in size and increasingly forging their own business models' (Chao 2012). Alibaba's share of the market has declined as other websites, such as 360buy.com (Beijing Jingdong Century Trading Co.), have increased in popularity and usage within China. Jack Ma's response to this increasing domestic competition was to begin a corporate restructuring that took Alibaba from a company dominated from the top to one that created more back-end infrastructure services to merchants and divided it into smaller units that can make decisions more quickly via each unit's own executive team. The main units are Tmall (online retail for MNEs and larger companies), Taobao Marketplace (a free platform for smaller merchants that generates revenue from advertising), and ETao (an online shopping search engine). As the president of Tmall (Daniel Zhang) noted: 'The whole company has been going through a period of rapid growth . . . We needed fast decision-making. We needed to be more focused' (quoted in Chao 2012).

In the mythical story of Ali Baba, he is, of course, the honest man who knows the secret of where the treasure has been hidden by the 40 thieves and his greedy brother. So, rather like the Ali Baba of the legend, Jack Ma is the 'good guy' who has managed to navigate his way through difficult business waters and come out the other side with a more effective and dynamic company, and still on the side of the corporate angels.

Strategic change in MNEs

Making a strategic change and the means for its execution and implementation is one of the fundamental activities that an MNE can undertake. Although MNEs are continuously changing, often at a gradual pace, the strategic change that really matters is the one that can be identified as the proactive management of change, so as to achieve clearly identified strategic objectives (Lynch 2012). This often includes a high degree of risk and uncertainty, both for the organization as a whole and for many of the employees. Among the many different views of what causes change and how it should be implemented, as examined from an academic and philosophical viewpoint (see Smith and Graetz 2011), it is useful to focus on the following three reasons for strategic change in MNEs, as classically proposed by Kanter et al. (1992).

- *Response to changes in the business environment*. An MNE's strengths and weaknesses need to be constantly evaluated in relation to the external world.

- *Life-cycle differences.* Changes in one division or department of an MNE require a change of emphasis or funding. For example, the development of the interface between mobile telephony and the Internet has brought about internal changes to companies such as Sony and Apple. The issues of change in these areas include the relative size, shape, and power of one division compared with others, and the need for reallocation and coordination of resources.

- *Power changes within an MNE.* Various individuals and teams within an organization struggle for control and power on a regular basis but, when a strategic change is being proposed, implemented, or concluded, the struggle for influence and benefits is intensified.

An interesting study of a now infamous American company, Enron—now the subject not only of business case studies but a book (*Enron: The Smartest Guys in the Room*, written by Bethany McLean and Peter Elkind in 2003), a documentary film (with the same name as the book and based on it, produced in 2005), and a play (ENRON, written in 2009 by Lucy Prebble)—is very clear about the interplay between the company's perception of the external environment and its internal corporate changes (Dillard et al. 2011). The collapse of Enron in 2000–2001 is regarded as the greatest audit failure at the time, amounting to a bankruptcy of about $20 billion and the consequent break-up of Arthur Andersen, then one of the world's five largest accountancy and audit partnership firms. The company culture of Enron changed from one grounded in a regulatory ethos to one committed to unregulated free markets and the consequent exploitation of the opportunities within an unfettered capitalist system. This change led it to make a series of fatal errors in its internal organization and operations (McLean and Elkind 2003).

Once the change managers within an MNE understand the motives for strategic change, they need to be able to shape and control the process. This requires a clear plan, a determination to stick to the plan, and an intelligent management of the people involved as both winners and losers in the process of change. This is a difficult task within a domestic company operating within a single national culture; it is even more complex in a large multinational enterprise with a range of subsidiaries, competing regional bases, and the involvement of external influences, including national governments and official international bodies. At BP, for instance, between 1995 and 2007, John Browne led a strategic change that transformed the company from a key UK-based energy player, with some American connections, to the world's third largest global energy company. This was done partially through the setting of strong strategic goals and determined adherence to them, as well as through some bold acquisitions: Amoco (1998), ARCO (2000), and Burmah Castrol (2000), and a Russian joint venture, TNK-BP (2003). As of the end of 2012, the last of these acquisitions—the TNK-BP joint venture—is in the final stages of being ended (Dean and Marson 2012; Werdigier 2012).

As with any major strategic corporate change, there is inevitably some resistance. In order to overcome this, the MNE's management team needs to create the major conditions for change (recognizing the need, setting standards, monitoring performance), to identify and support those individuals and groups who will help them to lead the change, and also to promote those individuals and groups on the basis of their commitment and contribution to the new strategic direction. Only in this way can MNEs bring about changes to their corporate culture.

The most dramatic changes to corporate culture will come from the massive expansion by the new developments within the Internet, gaming, and social networking as applied to corporate ventures. The unpredictable outcome of these developments does not mean that they should be ignored, and there are indications that throughout the world the younger generations are on the brink of changing many ways of viewing and understanding economies, business structures, and corporate cultures. Probably only economic historians will in the future be able to assess the relative impacts of key changes since the 1980s: the move in many economies in the 1980s–90s from large, state-run corporations to privately owned and operated ones; the massive state intervention in the highly capitalistic financial and banking sector in 2008–2009; the continuation into 2012–2013 of the European sovereign debt crisis; and the charges against Barclays Bank (and other banks) of the alleged manipulation of the setting of interest rates (Watts 2012). All these changes brought about—or will bring about—deeply significant changes to the corporate structures and cultures of major companies.

Challenges and choices

→ Internationally operating managers face the challenges of assessing not only their own companies in terms of corporate structure but also their overseas partners and competitors. Regarding competing companies, managers need to have analytical models that assist them in working out the threats that such competitors may pose. Their rivals' corporate culture is a key factor that can aid them in working out the appropriate strategy for successfully challenging them.

→ Companies' choice of local partner can be vital to their success. Their knowledge and understanding of which other companies might be best suited to a joint venture, or other partnership, depends on many factors. A vital factor is whether the values, missions, and corporate cultures of the partners are going to be a good fit. As the business world moves into the relatively unknown and unpredictable exploitation of the Internet, gaming, and social networking, the challenges and choices can only be expected to be even more dramatic.

Chapter summary

The first section of this chapter set out the key determinants and models for understanding corporate culture and assessing how change takes place within the world of international companies. It is difficult to encapsulate the complex interplay of internal and external influences into a simple model. However, the different examples of MNE image and activity illustrate the factors that may have a bearing on the culture and the way it may be changed.

The attempts to change structures, direction, or strategy are usually conducted within the framework of the prevailing culture of the company; such changes are often relatively minor and incremental. From time to time, however, the managers of change—usually a new CEO supported by outside consultants—think that a radical alteration is required. Such was the case with British Airways (see Case study 7.3) and with many other public-sector privatizations, whether in Britain, Bulgaria, or Brazil.

The second section of the chapter outlined the factors underlying existing international corporate cultures. This helps the drivers of change to know where they will find points of resistance and where they will be able to enlist allies for the new direction of the organization. It is not an exaggeration to say that changing an MNE's corporate culture is a task that is similar to turning a large cargo ship around. It takes a great deal of effort, patience, communication, and time but also means that the captain or CEO must not deviate from the changed strategy.

The culture of multinational corporations is the context in which their structures, systems, and operations take place. To understand these is the first step towards being able to manage MNEs and direct them along routes that lead to greater success, market share, and profitability.

Case study 7.3

BA: Successfully changing an international corporate culture

Part of the business landscape throughout most of the twentieth century was the existence of national airlines, the so-called 'flag carriers'. In the UK, for example, it was clearly BOAC (British Overseas Airways Corporation) and BEA (British European Airlines) that were the flag carriers, representing Britain in all parts of Europe and the wider world. For Germany, it was Lufthansa; for the Netherlands, KLM; for Italy, Alitalia; and for Belgium, Sabena. In these national airlines, the government was directly or indirectly in control through share holdings, other forms of ownership, or being a 'public corporation'. The ethos and values of these companies were solidly public: they were designed to be a public service rather than competitive and profit-seeking.

In newly decolonized countries in the late twentieth century, an essential symbol of independence was a national airline. This period saw the rise of airlines such as Air India, Iran Air, Syrian Arab Airlines, Royal Air Maroc, Air Burundi, and EgyptAir. In general, the national airlines were advertised and designated as the favoured carrier for all nationals, and the principal airline for all businesspeople travelling abroad. For all government members and officials, it was virtually forbidden for them to fly on any airline other than a flag carrier.

State-owned national carriers were reputed to be generally inefficient and badly managed, with a lack of any kind of service ethos. This seemed to be true not only of the new flag carriers but also of the larger, older airlines from European countries (Hensher 2008).

In the 1980s and the 1990s, the wave of privatization and airline deregulation meant that the dominance of the national carriers diminished. For some such as Sabena and Swissair, this meant rapid or slow death to the point where, by the early part of the twenty-first century, they had disappeared. For others, they remained much as they were and continued to receive large government subsidies. Others gained immensely as privately run, better managed, efficient, and profit-seeking airlines. A great example of this was the transformation of the British state-run airlines that became BA (British Airways). As a private company, operating principally out of London's Heathrow airport, it carries the colours of the national flag and, from time to time, behaves like a national carrier, but it has undergone a massive cultural change from public to private. In 2011, BA became the dominant part of a newly created company—International Airlines Group (IAG)—in which it had merged with Iberia, the Spanish national carrier. IAG then acquired BMI (British Midland International) from Lufthansa in 2012 and, with its operational headquarters in London and its corporate headquarters in Madrid, IAG is now the 7th largest airline company in the world.

The change in BA's corporate culture has occurred over the three decades since its privatization in 1982. On a regular basis and under successive CEOs and chairmen, the company underwent cost-cutting through reductions in staffing levels, reorganization of its flight operations, the creation of profit centres, and the development of a streamlined IT system (Shibata 1994; Orlov 2008). New subdivisions were created, and each manager was tasked with certain profit objectives. Within this new structure, there was greater delegation of authority and a focus on management by objectives. In the first decade of the twenty-first century, the development of an information management division and the creation of the Single IT Solution (SITS) system enabled BA to save about £100 million per year (Orlov 2008).

At various times since the 1980s it has been acknowledged that BA has transformed itself from a loss-making state-owned carrier to one of the world's most profitable airlines. More recently, BA appears to have survived the rapidly changing nature of aviation, airport ownership, and airline restructuring: it has managed to enter—and then exit—the world of budget airlines (with its short-lived venture with GO), to retain its hold on flight slots at major airports, including its base at Heathrow, to undergo further cost-cutting under successive CEOs, and to retain its position as one of the world's major carriers. Even with the changes that have come with BA's merger with Iberia, and the consequent difficulties of dealing with the problems of the Spanish economy in 2011–2012 (Wild 2012), in contrast with many of its competitors, whether private or state owned, BA has undergone many adjustments to its corporate culture, and has emerged successfully as one of the world's major airlines.

Case study questions

1. What changes to corporate culture stemmed from the decision to privatize BA (or other national carriers)?
2. Why did newly independent countries want their own national airlines?
3. What other cultural changes may be faced by BA within IAG in the next 5–10 years?

Discussion questions

1. How do MNEs try to guarantee adherence to their vision, values, and mission? How does this vary in different parts of the business and in different regions of the world where companies operate?

2. What efforts do MNEs make in order to establish a corporate culture that allows for 'work–life' balance?

3. What conclusions can be drawn about corporate culture from the ways in which MNEs organize their working space?

4. Is corporate change within international business more complex now than it was in the 1990s?

5. In 2012–2013, has the world (or some countries and regions of the world) achieved a post-industrial or a leisure society?

Online resource centre

Go online to test your understanding by trying multiple-choice questions, and assignment and examination questions.

Further research

Castronova, E. (2005). *Synthetic Worlds: The Business and Culture of Online Games*. Chicago: University of Chicago Press

Castronova, E. (2007). *Exodus to the Virtual World*. Basingstoke: Palgrave Macmillan

Glasser, A.J. (2010). 'How MMOs decriminalize real money trading,' *The Monetary Future*, 29 January, available at http://www.gamepro.com/article/news/213786/analysis-how-mmos-decriminalize-real-money-trading/, accessed 31 May 2012

Guomundsson, E. (2008). 'An economist on the virtual economy', *Business Week*, available at http://www.businessweek.com (accessed 24 May 2012)

Taylor, T. L. (2009). *Play between Worlds: Exploring Online Game Culture*. Cambridge, MA: MIT Press

Taylor, T. L. (2012). *Raising the Stakes: E-Sports and the Professionalization of E-Gaming*. Cambridge, MA: MIT Press

Woolgar, S. (ed.) (2002). *Virtual Society? Technology, Cyberbole, Reality*. Oxford: Oxford University Press

The role of corporate culture and change in a post-industrial or leisure society is likely to be affected in the next few years by the radical developments taking place on the Internet. In particular, the blurring of the line between the virtual and real worlds has come from the growth in people's Internet use. People now rely on the Internet not only for information but for the purchasing of services and goods.

Various people, such as T. L. Taylor, Steve Woolgar, Edward Castronova, and Eyjolfur Guomundsson, are among the leading commentators on gaming, virtual societies, and virtual economies, and their impact on the development of international business. One of the key features of online gaming and virtual (or synthetic) worlds is that the growth rates are exponential; the number of new games doubles every 12 to 18 months. Demand growth has persisted over the last few years, although it had seemed almost certain that there would be too much supply, too many new games, and too rapid a growth in capacity.

References

Arabian Business (2012). 'Saudi's Olayan issues $173m sukuk', available at http://www.arabianbusiness.com, accessed 29 June 2012

ArcelorMittal (2012). http://www.arcelormittal.com/corp, accessed 29 May 2012

BBC (2012). http://www.bbc.co.uk/aboutthebbc, accessed 30 May 2012

Bell, D. (1974). *The Coming of Post-Industrial Society*. New York: Harper Colophon Books

Bowdin, G., Allen, J., O'Toole, W., Harris, R., and McDonnell, I. (2011). *Events Management*. Oxford: Butterworth-Heinemann/Elsevier

Broomhall, E. (2011). 'Queen Rania, Lubna Olayan named in global power list,' *Arabian Business*, 25 August, available at http://www.arabianbusiness.com, accessed 29 June 2012

Carraher, S. (2011). 'Turnover prediction using attitudes towards benefits, pay, and pay satisfaction among employees and entrepreneurs in Estonia, Latvia and Lithuania', *Baltic Journal of Management*, 6/1

Casestudyinc.com (2010). 'Daimler, Chrysler and the Failed Merger', available at http://www.casestudyinc.com, accessed 31 May 2012

Chao, L. (2012). 'Alibaba regains control: With Yahoo deal in hand, Chinese firm must tackle obstacles to growth', *Wall Street Journal*, 22 May

Dasgupta, R. (2012–forthcoming). *Re-reading the Salaryman in Japan: Crafting masculinities*. Abingdon: Routledge

Deal, T.E. and Kennedy, A.A. (2000). *Corporate Cultures: The Rites and Rituals of Corporate Life*. New York: Perseus Books

Dean, C. & Marson, J. (2012). 'Rosneft Seeks Loans for TNK-BP Deal', *Wall Street Journal*, 7 November

Dillard, J., Rogers, R. and Yuthas, K. (2011). 'Organizational change: in search of the golden mean', *Journal of Accounting and Organizational Change*, 7/1, March

Economist (2007). 'Sozzled salarymen', *The Economist*, 15 February

Economist (2010). 'Spartan salarymen: Japanese executive pay', *The Economist*, 30 June

Exxon Digital History (2012). 'Exxon: History of the name and logo', available at http://exxondigitalhistory.blogspot.co.uk/2012/04, accessed 29 May 2012

Fassin, Y. and Gosselin, D. (2011). 'The collapse of a European bank in the financial crisis', *Working Paper 2011/726*, Universiteit Gent, Faculteit Economie en Bedrijfskunde, June

Ferdinand, N. and Kitchin, P. (2012) *Events Management: An International Approach*. London: Sage

Gambles, R., Lewis, S., and Rapoport, R. (2006). *The Myth of Work-Life Balance: The Challenge of Our Time for Men, Women and Societies*. John Wiley

Giddens, S. H. (1973). 'Historical origins of the adoption of the EXXON name and trademark', *The Business History Review*, 47/3, autumn

GSK (2011–12). GlaxoSmithKline (GSK) employees, confidential information Macmillan.

Hampden-Turner, C. and Trompenaars, F. (2000). *Building Cross-Cultural Competence: How to Create Wealth from Conflicting Values*. Chichester: John Wiley

Handy, C. (1993). *Understanding Organizations*. London: Penguin

Hays, J. (2009–10). 'Japanese salarymen,' available at http://factsanddetails.com/Japan (written 2009 and updated 2010), accessed 29 May 2012

Hendon, D. W., Hendon, R. A., and Herbig, P. (1996). *Cross-Cultural Business Negotiations*. London: Quorum

Hensher, P. (2008). 'Alitalia flies into the sunset, and not before time', *Independent*, 16 September

Hirdaramani (2009) http://www.hirdaramani.com, accessed May 2009

Hirdaramani (2012) http://www.hirdaramani.com, accessed May 2012

JB Intercultural Consulting (2012). http://www.culture-at-work/jworklife.com.html, accessed 31 May 2012

JCI (2012). Johnson Controls International (JCI) employees, confidential information

Johnson Controls (2012). http://www.johnsoncontrols.com, accessed 29 May 2012

Johnson, G. (1987). *Strategic Change and the Management Process*. Oxford: Blackwell

Johnson, G. (1992). 'Managing strategic change: Strategy, culture and action', *Long Range Planning*, 25

Johnson, G., Scholes, K., and Whittington, R. (2010). *Exploring Corporate Strategy*, 8th edn. Harlow: Pearson Education

Kanter, R. M., Stein, B., and Jick, T. (1992). *The Challenge of Organizational Change*. New York: Free Press

Lynch, R. (2012). *Strategic Management*, 6th edn. Harlow: FT Pearson

Martelin, N. (2008). *Daimler-Chrysler Merger Case: Rationale of a Failure*. GRIN Verlag, available at http://www.grin.com, accessed 31 May 2012

Matsuura, T., Sato, H., and Wakasugi, R. (2011). 'Temporary workers, permanent workers, and international trade: Evidence from Japanese firm-level data', *Research Institute of Economy, Trade and Industry*, IAA, March

McLean, B. and Elkind, P. (2003). *Enron: The Smartest Guys in the Room*. New York: Portfolio Trade

Mission Statements (2012). http://www.missionstatements.com, accessed 29 May. 2012

Nestlé (2012). http://www.nestle.com, accessed 29 May 2012

Nokia (2012). http://www.nokia.com, accessed 30 May 2012

Olayan (2012). http://www.olayangroup.com, accessed 29 May 2012

Orlov, L. (2008). 'British Airways: A case study in "Lean IT"', *CIO Update*, available at www.cioupdate.com/insights/article.php/3767846, accessed May 2012

Potgieter, J. (2010). 'The top 5 components of preparing for a negotiation', Jan Potgieter's Negotiation Skills Blog, available at http://biznegotiation.typepad.com/jan-potgieter-blog, accessed 30 June 2012

Pynchon, V. (2011). 'Slate's negotiation academy and first offers', *Forbes*, 18 October, available at http://www.forbes.com, accessed 30 June 2012

Quittner, J. (2009). 'Why AOL-Time Warner wasn't doomed to failure', *Time*, 28 May

Shibata, K. (1994). 'Privatisation of British Airways: Its management and politics, 1982–1987', *EUI Working Paper EPU No. 93/9*. Florence: European University Institute

Shone, A. and Parry, B. (2010). *Successful Event Management: A Practical Handbook*, 3rd edn. Stamford, CT: Cengage Business Press

Smith, A.C.T. and Graetz, F.M. (2011). *Philosophies of Organizational Change*. Cheltenham, UK: Edward Elgar

Trompenaars, F. (1993). *Riding the Waves of Culture: Understanding Cultural Diversity in Business*. London: Nicholas Brealey

Trompenaars, F. and Hampden-Turner, C. (1997). *Riding the Waves of Culture: Understanding Cultural Diversity in Business*, 2nd edn. London: Nicholas Brealey

Vlasic, B. and Stertz, B. (2000). *Taken for a Ride: How Daimler-Benz Drove Off with Chrysler*. Chichester: John Wiley

Walsh, M.F., Winterich, K.P., and Mittal, V. (2010). 'Do logo redesigns help or hurt your brand? The role of brand commitment', *Journal of Product and Brand Management*, 19/2

Watts, R. (2012). 'Bankers fear reviews into interest-rate fixing scandal will be "witch-hunt"', *Daily Telegraph*, 30 June

Werdigier, J. (2012). 'BP to seek sale of Russian venture TNK-BP', *New York Times*, 1 June

Wild, L. (2012). 'Pain in Spain for IAG', *Investors Chronicle*, 14 May

Other sources of information

Alibaba Group (2012). 'Company overview', available at http://www.alibaba.com, accessed 30 June 2012

Coonan, C. and Foley, S. (2011). 'Meet Jack Ma, the man who might just buy Yahoo', *The Independent*, 4 October

Economist (2008). 'Sayonara, Salaryman', *The Economist*, 3 January

Flannery, R. (2012). 'China Internet billionaire Jack Ma's wealth steady under Yahoo deal', *Forbes*, 21 May

Guirdham, M. (2005). *Communicating across Cultures at Work*, 2nd edn. Basingstoke: Palgrave

Hofstede, G. (1984). *Cultures Consequences: International Differences in Work-Related Values*. London: Sage

Hofstede, G. and Hofstede, G. J. (2005). *Cultures and Organizations: Software of the Mind*, 2nd edn. London: McGraw-Hill

Peters, T. and Waterman, R. H. (1995). *In Search of Excellence*. London: HarperCollins

Schneider, S. C. and Barsoux, J.-L. (2003). *Managing across Cultures*, 2nd edn. Harlow: FT Prentice Hall

Soble, J. (2010). 'Japan finalises bill on temporary workers', *Financial Times*, 19 March

Trompenaars, F. and Asser, M. N. (2010). *The Global M&A Tango: Cross-cultural Dimensions of Mergers and Acquisitions*. Infinite Ideas Ltd.

8 Multinational corporate social responsibility

Learning objectives

After reading this chapter, you will be able to:

✦ put multinational business ethics into its historic context

✦ apply ethics in (international) business frameworks

✦ discuss leading corporate social responsibility (CSR) issues

✦ analyse problems inherent to the codification and enforcement of multinational CSR

✦ monitor the role of non-governmental organizations (NGOs)

Case study 8.1

Multinational CSR: Pepsi faces the development challenge

Multinational enterprises (MNEs) are often scrutinized for the impact they have on host countries, particularly in the developing world. The picture is generally mixed, with praise for the capital, jobs, and technology that MNEs provide sometimes tempered by criticisms that, notwithstanding the above-average wage packages they often pay (Wessel 2011), many offer lower salaries than they need to remain competitive. Clearly, MNEs' reputation and market share stand to benefit if they can devise a win-win CSR business model that maximizes local welfare without affecting profits unduly.

One example is a CSR initiative that US drinks giant Pepsi has launched in Mexico. In a major strategic decision, the MNE started sourcing crops directly from local farmers and agricultural cooperatives, instead of buying from intermediaries, whose cut of the total profits accumulating in the value chain meant less money for the farmers themselves. Pepsi's idea was that by offering farmers extra income and providing credit guarantees (Strom 2011), it could help them to purchase new equipment and fertilizers. In turn, this would enhance their overall productivity and ensure more sustainable development. From Pepsi's perspective, the new scheme saved money on transportation costs (since crop inputs were now being sourced near its production facilities); improved quality control; and above all, offered insight into the lifestyles of potential future customers. This latter aspect was particularly useful since by paying farmers more, Pepsi was helping to raise levels of nutrition and education locally. The ensuing growth dynamic would hopefully raise standards of living and, from the company's perspective, ensure future customers' solvency.

Enthusiasm about the programme led to Pepsi signing a five-year partnership agreement with the Inter-American Development Bank to implement similar approaches in 26 countries across Latin America and the Caribbean (IADB 2011). Of course, some of the proposed activities, like the work being done to help local communities access safe water, also had a reputational effect and helped Pepsi avoid the kinds of criticisms that other MNEs faced following allegations of water mismanagement. In either case, whether the goal was to stave off negative publicity or something more positive, Pepsi could be confident that it had a good chance of ultimately recovering the costs of its Mexican CSR agenda.

Case study questions

1. To what extent is Pepsi's CSR initiative in Mexico driven by self-interest?
2. Does this matter, and why?

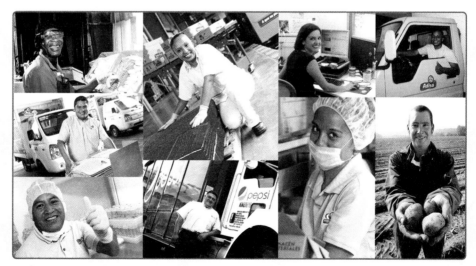

CSR is a key aspect of Pepsi's Mexican operations

Source: PepsiCo

Introduction

Multinational corporate social responsibility (CSR) involves companies acting ethically in the international business arena. The difference from domestic CSR is the difficulty that analysts face in determining what constitutes good behaviour—understood here in the traditional 'moral' sense used by philosophers (**see ORC Extension materials 8.1**)—in countries with very different value systems.

The confusion over multinational CSR can reign at several different levels. One debate is whether the benefits derived from an MNE's presence in a foreign country (such as jobs and capital) offset the damage that it may cause either through its practices (for instance, in cases of child labour) or because of the outcomes that it produces (like pollution). Another debate asks if it is companies or state authorities who should take responsibility for shaping CSR programmes and to what extent campaigns for so-called ethical supply chains actually help workers (Economist 2012a). In the wake of the 2008 and 2011 financial crises, the ethics debate has been extended even further to raise questions about the wider morality of companies engaging in actions that may lead to an uneven distribution of risks and rewards within society. Multinational CSR is an area of international business that must be analysed at both the micro and the macro levels.

> Go online

+ Ethics
Study of moral values. For the purposes of this book, behaviour is considered ethical when it is characterized by an intention not to cause harm.

Section I: Foundations of multinational corporate social responsibility

Moral philosophy, which is the cornerstone of modern business ethics, is an ancient field of study. One starting point for analysing its application in a purely business context is to look at the factors guiding individual managers' conduct. In a sense, people are 'moral navigators' balancing their values against those of the firm for which they work (Morgan 1998). As Figure 8.1 demonstrates, a dilemma arises if the two value systems clash. This can happen if an employer's code of conduct is too vague, or if executives provide contradictory signals. International managers also have the challenge of trying to differentiate between an MNE's 'core' and 'peripheral' values and decide which to apply in response to a particular host country's ethical expectations (Tan and Wang 2011).

People often join a firm specifically because they identify with its stated values. At some point, however, many if not most employees can be made to feel pressures that will affect their decision-making, whether consciously or otherwise. This means that individual ethics cannot be understood without considering the values of the company for which a person works (see Chapter 7), as well as the interface between these values and the 'national business ideology' in a given country at a given moment in time (Miriam et al. 2011).

Figure 8.1
The 'ethical fit' can vary between the personal, company, and societal values.

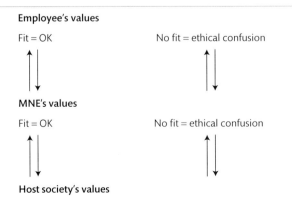

The variability of multinational business ethics in time and space

Ethical behaviour must always be analysed in context. Slave traders, 'robber barons', and 'imperial corporations' are universally condemned today, but in many societies they were once highly praised figures (Schwartz 1999). Practices like child labour that are highly criticized in Europe today were widespread before nineteenth-century reformers such as the UK's Charles Dickens or France's Émile Zola first denounced them. A country that is desperate to accept industrialization might accept higher levels of corruption or pollution than at a later stage when it is more affluent. Many of the people who blamed investment bankers for the 2008 subprime financial crisis had previously glorified them as wealth creators. Indeed, many actions are considered unethical only once their uglier sides have been revealed.

A watershed moment for business ethics came in the early twentieth century, when the birth of large, multi-divisional firms (see Chapter 10) led to a split between owners' and managers' roles. The significance of this shift lies in the opposition between managers' allegedly greater sense of responsibility to the wider community and owners' greater focus on profits (Vogel 2006). By the 1960s, influential thinkers like J. K. Galbraith stated that, above and beyond any direct business aims, a manager's mission in a company was to promote the overall welfare of a society. Some leading executives of the time, like Chase Manhattan Bank's David Rockefeller, understood this to mean that companies should engage in philanthropy.

+ Philanthropy
Long-term charitable donations to worthy causes.

Although clearly constituting a form of ethical behaviour, this approach was not particularly effective at addressing larger social problems. A leading explanation is that charity giving is not systematic enough to have a sustained effect. A more recent revelation that nearly 90 per cent of all companies engaging in philanthropy are actually looking for something in return (Bonini and Chênevert 2008) also limits the effectiveness of charitable actions.

The philanthropic model remains dominant in certain parts of the world, including Asia and Africa (Hopkins 2007). In the USA and a few other economies, however, the general paradigm has moved on, largely because of the growing alignment of managers' and shareholders' interests since the 1980s, resulting from profit-sharing bonus schemes that motivate managers to prioritize short-term profits to the exclusion of broader societal considerations. This approach is not uncontroversial, however, and has been largely rejected in countries like Germany, whose iconic *Mittelstand* firms tend to neglect aims like maximized short-term profits to focus instead on 'where we want to be when we hand over to the next generation' (Economist 2012b). In turn, this helped the country to avoid the worst of the 2008 subprime crisis, often attributed to self-serving (but ultimately anti-social) behaviour by US and UK mortgage bankers (Inman and Kingsley 2011).

An understanding of how and why ethics varies worldwide is an important topic in international business, with philosophers such as Thomas Donaldson (**see ORC Extension material 8.2**) having made considerable efforts to develop this concept. One body of research has focused on the national level, concentrating on factors like a country's socio-economic development or cultural values. Another highlights corporate-level factors, like the size of a firm and its degree of internationalization (Laudal 2011), or whether it operates alone or within a network (Weltzien and Shankar 2011). In a sense, the best proof that multinational ethics are relative and not absolute is the fact that very different actions and motivations can all be associated with ethical behaviour.

> Go online

Is CSR an appropriate response to problems in multinational business ethics?

CSR is widely but not unanimously popular today. There is an ongoing argument between supporters, who think that CSR provides a remedy to the market's failure to address international business's negative side effects; critics, who feel that MNEs should focus on profitability alone; and cynics, who doubt the authenticity of most CSR efforts.

Figure 8.2
Externalities can have a positive or negative impact on someone who is not party to a deal.

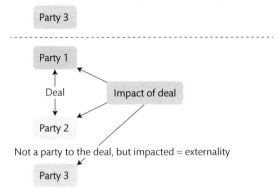

For corporate social responsibility

+ Externalities
When the effect of an economic action falls upon parties not directly involved in it. This effect can be positive or negative.

In theoretical terms, the argument in favour of CSR is the need to offset market failure, one example of which is the concept of externalities (see Figure 8.2), which occur when a transaction has a positive or negative effect on a party that did not sign up to it. Examples include Chinese property developers signing agreements with local authorities to pave over agricultural land that farmers need for their livelihood, or when non-drivers' health is affected by air pollution from automobiles. As formulated by Nobel laureate Joseph Stiglitz (2006: 190–5), there is a 'misalignment of economic incentives when corporations do not bear the downside costs [of their actions]: social welfare is not maximized if corporations single-mindedly maximize profits'. Thus, the economic argument for CSR is that it might help to remedy the unfair distribution of the costs and benefits of doing (international) business.

The moral case for CSR is that companies profiting from an activity should also be expected to take responsibility when things go wrong. An infamous example was when 3000 citizens in the Indian town of Bhopal died in 1986 because of leaks at Union Carbide's local chemicals plant. The company ultimately had to pay reparations eating into its earnings because it would have been unthinkable to expect anyone else to assume this charge. Another example from the year 2006 was the death of ten Ivory Coast citizens, and the poisoning of a further 9000, following the careless discharge of chemical waste from a ship chartered by the Dutch firm, Trafigura (Russell 2006). Because the company had benefited from the business, there was a strong argument that it also had the social responsibility to ensure that the local population suffered no ill effects as a result. In the absence of CSR, MNEs might hope to get a free ride and expect governments to compensate victims on their behalf. There might also be the consideration that the profits from the unethical behaviour exceed any potential fines.

+ Free ride
Where a party derives benefits from an economic activity without contributing to its costs.

+ Stakeholder
Anyone affected by an organization's actions. Often understood to include employees, local governments, suppliers, consumers, and host communities.

This moral argument can be strengthened by the practical consideration that CSR may no longer be a luxury but actually a necessity in certain circumstances. Given the shift of power to MNEs in recent decades (see Chapter 3), most governments simply do not have the means or the will (Frost 2004) to attend to all of the social, environmental, and other problems that stakeholders face in a society. The only question that then remains is whether companies are in a position to assume responsibility (Fyrnas 2010). MNEs such as Starbucks, Rio Tinto, BP, and Vodafone have all invested sizable sums across the world in community education, a sector that in many countries has traditionally been the responsibility of the state. Living in a 24/7 news world has increased general awareness of good and bad corporate behaviour. In this view, CSR and profit-making are not mutually exclusive.

In sum, there is growing recognition that a strong business case exists for CSR. A triple bottom line focus will help a company in terms of reputation, access to ethical investor funds, recruitment, staff motivation, risk management, and relationships with stakeholders, especially consumers (Hopkins 2007). Above all, if customers do not trust a company, they risk taking their business elsewhere. Realizing this, many if not most management schools now provide sustainability training to tomorrow's executives. In the early twenty-first century, CSR has gone mainstream.

+ Triple bottom line
Idea that firms should report not only financial but also social and environmental outcomes.

Against corporate social responsibility

In the late 1980s, one of the authors of this book suggested launching a corporate recycling scheme, only to be criticized for 'wasting time' by his manager who argued that an employee's only concern should be making money. Based on this example alone, it is fair to say that CSR has not always been a popular topic in certain circles.

Nobel laureate Milton Friedman (2002) has expressed the opinion that corporate payments made in the name of CSR are an imposition forcing shareholders to accept lower dividends, workers to accept lower wages, and/or customers to pay higher prices. In Friedman's view, as long as a firm acts legally, it is 'subversive' to ask it to divert its attention from profit maximization. Another criticism of CSR is that it unfairly portrays firms as free riders instead of giving them credit for the taxes and wages they pay (Marcoux 2000). This discourages equity investment and risk-taking, brings 'interest-group politics into the boardroom', and imposes excessive accountability on managers—especially ones operating in legal systems that hold them personally liable for their company's conduct. Similarly, some go as far as to equate CSR with 'embezzlement', rejecting managers' right to decide on shareholders' behalf to which charity their money should be given (Whyte 2012).

+ Accountability
Idea that actors must take responsibility for their actions.

At a different level, former Czech President Vaclav Klaus (2007) criticized the 'opportunity costs of . . . wasteful environmentalist policies . . . adopted to the detriment of other policies, thus neglecting many other important needs of millions of people all over the world'. This suggests that CSR actually gets in the way of greater priorities for developing countries. In some locations (e.g. Pakistan's Sialkot region, whose soccer ball manufacturers have been criticized by the International Labour Organization (http://www.ilo.org/) for employing child labour), some have even questioned whether the current insistence on CSR standards constitutes a new 'imperialism' that the West uses to impose its values on the developing world (Khan and Lund-Thomsen 2011).

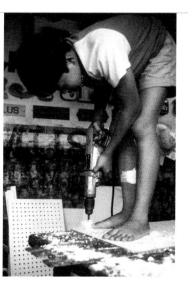

Some of the world's poorer communities may see child labour as an indispensable source of income but the practice is widely condemned

© International Labour Organization

Lastly, it is worth noting that some people criticize CSR not because it harms corporations but precisely because it helps them. Some argue that CSR constitutes a 'sham . . . bamboozling an increasingly sceptical public' (Hopkins 2007: 122–8). This suggests that many companies use CSR as a marketing tool to hide their other misdeeds—the 'greenwashing' accusation that Chapter 16 reviews in greater depth.

Case study 8.2

CSR and international supply chains: The real cost of cheap food

In a colder Northern European country like the UK, being able to buy all kinds of vegetables during the cold winter season is a luxury that consumers take for granted. Giant British supermarkets like Tesco, Sainsbury's, and Asda have all set up efficient cross-border supply chains enabling them to source fresh produce all year long at a reasonable price.

British customers spend around €2 billion a year purchasing fruit and vegetables from Spain, much of it from the agricultural region around the southern city of Almeria (Lawrence 2011a). However, farmers in Spain, like elsewhere, have been terribly squeezed in recent years by rising fertilizer and fuel costs, and because supermarkets have put suppliers under tremendous pressure to keep their costs down. Lacking the power to change this situation, farmers have tried to make savings in the one area they still control—labour costs. This has had a terrible impact on agricultural workers.

Working conditions in some industrial greenhouses have been compared to a form of modern slavery
Source: Corbis

Investigative journalists cooperating with Anti-Slavery International (http://www.antislavery.org), one of the world's oldest charities, discovered that immigrant Africans brought to Spain to harvest local produce are regularly being employed under conditions that might technically be defined as slavery. The migrants are paid less than half Spain's national minimum wage and forced to live in unhygienic shacks lacking any modern conveniences. The work itself is incredibly strenuous, involving long shifts in greenhouses where temperatures routinely exceed 40°C. Many of the workers lack immigration papers, in which case they run a risk of being reported to the police if they complain about conditions. Most are segregated in unhealthy shanty towns and aggressively dissuaded by the police or local residents from mixing with the indigenous Spanish or tourist populations. In some instances, their circumstances are so dire that the Red Cross

has been called in to hand out food (Lawrence 2011a).

There is no doubt that many of these workers come from developing countries where conditions are just as harsh. The ethical dilemma is whether this justifies their mistreatment in Europe, which has reached a stage of development where such practices are no longer tolerated. Redressing the injustice would have inevitably led to higher prices for winter vegetables in Britain. The question then becomes whether consumers' consciences have a greater influence than their wallets.

Case study questions

1. What moral issues surround the employment of African agricultural workers in Spain?
2. Do consumer boycotts work, and why?

Corporate social responsibility in specifically international contexts

The section above showed that the divide between shareholder and stakeholder perspectives permeates all business ethics. This can become particularly poignant in cross-border situations, however. One such situation is when an MNE tries to pressure an LDC into lowering taxes and/or regulatory standards, threatening to take its much needed investment elsewhere. This kind of regime shopping (see Chapter 3) puts pressure on host governments to abandon one crucial need (for example, a clean environment or workers' health and safety) in the hope of satisfying another (jobs from the new investor). Forcing countries into these kinds of trade-off is ethically dubious. MNEs could respond, with some truthfulness, that global competition obliges them to run tight operations. This is yet another instance where CSR can improve a company's image. One example was Anglo American's contribution to the fight against AIDS in Africa, in a conscious effort to overcome local mistrust of Western mining companies (Cronin 2006). Similarly, Chiquita has engaged in a number of very positive CSR initiatives (including sustainable farming and measures against sexual harassment) in some of the Central American countries that it used to treat like 'banana republics' (Economist 2012a). In this vision, multinational CSR becomes a vehicle for regaining lost trust. The debate then becomes how long it takes the host population to forget past misdeeds.

One factor determining a host country's attitude towards an MNE is general acceptance of the profit motive. In Germany, for instance, longstanding support for worker rights and traditional resistance to 'Anglo-Saxon capitalism' meant that there was a great uproar in the 1990s when Walmart tried to make employees work overtime. This put the American retailer under great pressure to find ways of proving its good faith. Resentment can also be fuelled if the host country is ethnically or politically divided, and if the MNE is seen as siding with one community vs. another. During the 1990s, for instance, Shell's relationship with the population inhabiting the region where the company's Nigerian oil platforms were located, the Ogonis, was very much at odds with its connections to the country's distant central government, to whom it paid duties and taxes (**see Chapter 8 ORC Case study**). If a legal system accepts unethical behaviour, then acting legally does not necessarily mean acting ethically.

> Go online

This is an important distinction, since it undermines the argument of CSR opponents like Milton Friedman that the only thing companies need to do to be considered ethical is to respect the law. The reality is much more complicated (see Figure 8.3). Laws reflect the balance of power in a society at a particular moment in time. A much more meaningful measurement of international CSR is 'ethical compliance', or the idea that MNEs might be held to certain minimum standards wherever they operate, regardless of local legislation.

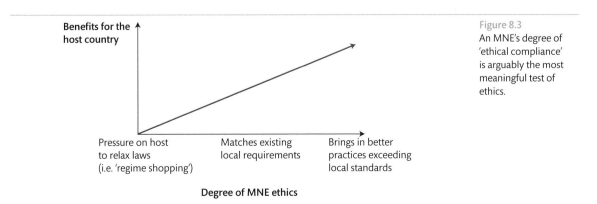

Figure 8.3
An MNE's degree of 'ethical compliance' is arguably the most meaningful test of ethics.

HIRDARAMANI GROUP

Practitioner insight

The Hirdaramani Group (http://www.hirdaramani.com) is a family-run group whose main historic business is apparel manufacturing. The company originates in Sri Lanka but also runs major operations in Bangladesh and Vietnam. Rakhil Hirdaramani is a Director of Hirdaramani International Exports, primarily overseeing several key accounts, including Marks & Spencer, Levi Strauss, Adidas, and Debenhams.

'Generally, it is our customers who dictate the ethical terms of business. For our part, we're one of the founder members in Sri Lanka of the Ethical Trading Initiative, meaning that we're committed to fair working practices, fair wages, and limited overtime. We adhere to these ethical standards even though they put us at a competitive disadvantage vs. less compliant competition. As a family, we do not believe it fair to overwork our staff. In the long run, it burns them out and you end up losing efficiency. We also want to be staff members' employer of choice. Understanding that they all have lives of their own, we want to offer them the same work–life balance as employees receive all over the world.

Sustainability
Approach where activities are organized in a way that will ensure their long-term economic, social, and ecological viability.

As for ecological sustainability, our cost-cutting measures have actually made us greener. This has involved using as much natural daylight as possible instead of artificial lighting, and recycling and reusing waste materials with an aim of zero product to landfill. Reducing waste reduces cost and we've become such firm believers that we're building in 2012 South Asia's first carbon neutral apparel manufacturing facility. Located on a greenfield site, it primarily uses locally sourced materials, lowering the carbon footprint. We've also got a zero carbon evaporative cooling system instead of traditional air conditioning, a natural paddy field to feed workers organic food, an effluent treatment plant recycling water that can be used for gardening and drinking, and a closed loop farming project composting food waste and offering it for free as fertilizer to farmers whose crops we then buy again.

In terms of our main ethical priority, workers are our most important asset and it is essential that people be allowed fair working conditions. Moreover, with about 90 per cent of our 20,000 strong workforce being women, our responsibility is to make sure that they are well looked after. Most of the ladies working for us are the primary breadwinners in their families, which have limited earning potential. We're aware of the responsibilities they face in their villages, and the abuse from which they sometimes suffer. So we do things like give them a bank card to which they alone have access. We also provide classes on personal hygiene, health and safety, and setting aside funds for retirement and also offer training to increase their skills.

Lastly, our Hirdaramani Memorial Trust contributes every year to good causes, one example being the tsunami relief, where we actually rebuilt a school from scratch. But again, we primarily focus on our workers, because we feel that our first responsibility is to them.'

Section II: Multinational corporate social responsibility in practice

In recent years, there has been a tendency to widen the scope of CSR to include all ethical issues affecting MNEs (see Figure 8.4). Some tend to be more prevalent globally than others, however. The section below reviews the main CSR issues that most MNEs face today.

Leading CSR issues

Human rights

One serious dilemma for MNEs is whether they should do business in countries that violate basic principles of freedom and humanity. This question often arises when extractive

Main CSR issues for multinationals

Human rights

Labour relations/Supply chain management

Corruption

Environment/Sustainability (also see Chapter 16)

Other CSR issues (see ORC Extension materials 8.3)

Cultural imperialism

Socially responsible investing

Corporate governance

Corporate philanthropy and community service

Product and process safety

Figure 8.4
CSR questions arise in many different areas of international business.

> Go online

industries need to access assets in countries run by non-democratic regimes. Examples include accusations that energy giant Shell paid violent gangs in Nigeria large sums to protect its pipelines (Smith 2011); companies buying 'blood diamonds' from war-torn Sierra Leone; or the mines that the large mining company Anglo-American runs in Zimbabwe. Similarly, there are numerous cases of MNEs moving manufacturing activities to countries that limit union rights and where labour leaders suffer acts of violence. A number of sources, including the activist non-governmental organization (NGO) called War on Want, have tried to associate Coca-Cola with anti-union violence across the world (War on Want 2006). Thus, a lawsuit was lodged in a US court in 2001 accusing the MNE of complicity in the murders of Colombian union members employed by FEMSA, the franchise bottler with whom Coca-Cola works in this country (Borger 2001). Coca-Cola was also criticized after police in Turkey allegedly beat local trade unionists. The company has responded that it is deeply concerned for workers' safety everywhere and takes protective measures to ensure their well-being. What is clear, in any event, is that being even remotely associated with these kinds of human rights violations is damaging to any MNE's reputation.

+ Non-governmental organizations (NGOs)
Associations created by members of the general public to address specific problems or promote an overall ethos or policy.

Other examples highlight similar dilemmas. Apple came under criticism in 2012 because of poor working conditions and unethical practices at a large Chinese manufacturer, Foxconn, which is responsible for much of the MNE's assembly work (Economist 2012a). Yet despite efforts by the company's executives to improve the situation—in part by calling in the services of a leading NGO called the Fair Labor Association (http://www.fairlabor.org)—progress is expected to be slow due to a lack of transparency, with inspectors not necessarily being able to monitor what is happening at every single level within the supply chain.

If MNEs feel that a particular regime tolerates unethical practice, they might refuse to work with it. Yet this could further harm the local population by starving the economy of much needed capital, jobs, and technology. According to Kline (2005), MNEs' responsibilities in countries where human rights are being flouted depend on their intentions, awareness of the situation, and proximity to the misdeeds. By itself, business cannot be expected to solve all of the world's problems. However, MNEs should at the very least avoid making things worse for victims of human rights abuses. They can do this by considering which populations within a particular host country are most likely to benefit from their activities—and which will not.

Labour relations and supply chain management

Labour relations includes the 'hiring and firing' of employees, wage policies, overtime, health and safety, treatment of female workers, child labour, union relations, and fair trade. This category rivals the environment as the main focus of multinational CSR today.

+ Fair trade
Business defined by the equitable distribution of profits up and down the value chain to ensure that upstream producers receive a decent 'living wage'.

As discussed throughout this book, one of the main drivers behind modern globalization is the movement of companies' upstream production activities to low-cost countries, either by outsourcing to local suppliers or via foreign direct investment (FDI). These actions all have major political and strategic implications. They also raise a number of ethical challenges.

Many people worldwide have benefited from the internationalization of supply chains. In MNEs' home countries, consumers tend to benefit from lower prices and shareholders from higher profits; in the host countries, workers get jobs and governments collect tax revenues. Indeed, in countries like South Korea and Singapore, the entire development trajectory was sparked by MNEs' outsourcing contracts or FDI initiatives. Yet the internationalization of production has also hurt many people in the MNEs' home countries and it is here that an ethical dilemma arises. When MNEs move jobs to low-wage countries, the home country workers who are made redundant can easily suffer from a 'spectre of uselessness' if they do not find new employment quickly enough (Sennett 2006). Conversely, host countries (often LDCs) are often forced to compete with one another to attract the new business. This creates a 'race to the bottom', with jobs only being created in countries whose poor citizens, lacking any union representation, are willing to accept wages that are hard to survive on.

One example is Cambodia, where workers' standard of living has stopped rising due to renewed competition from China after the Multi Fibre Agreement on textile quotas was lifted in January 2005 (Bradshaw 2005). Today, Cambodian workers must choose between wage cuts or job losses. Another example is South Africa, where, according to Human Rights Watch (http://www.hrw.org/), Western Cape province workers producing 'the country's renowned wines and fruit are being denied adequate housing, proper safety equipment, and basic labour rights, [living in] conditions that include on-site housing that is unfit for living, exposure to pesticides without proper safety equipment, lack of access to toilets or drinking water while working.' A final example involved the nature of certain mining activities run by commodities giant Glencore in Congo, accused in 2012 by BBC's Panorama programme of allegedly dumping raw acid into local waterways and using child labour (Sweeney 2012).

Of course, a whole host of MNEs pay their LDC workers above-average wages and/or pressure local subcontractors to improve labour standards. This clearly constitutes ethical behaviour, yet it can also cause problems, as witnessed by the dilemma of child labour. On one hand, education is crucial to children's long-term prospects. On the other, the press is full of images of very young children—in India and Pakistan, for instance—spending long days sewing cheap clothes for major Western brand names instead of going to school. By 2012, most leading MNEs like Gap and Primark had implemented social audit systems to detect and punish subcontractors that rely on child labour. Yet local companies can be very adept at misleading MNE inspectors. The practice therefore remains widespread and continues to be documented worldwide, from South Asian sweatshops to Egyptian cotton fields and El Salvadorean sugar plantations.

The reality is that innumerable families across the world need whatever income their children can provide. This explains why LDCs themselves have often been the strongest opponents of attempts to outlaw child labour. The ethical dilemma for MNEs is that boycotting suppliers in a particular country because of disgust with their practices can lead to greater unemployment, making things worse for the very populations that they are supposed help (Kline 2005). Indeed, most activists today encourage MNEs to work with suppliers to improve conditions, rather than abandoning a particular supply chain.

Corruption

Corruption has long been an area of concern in international business, to the extent that anti-corruption has come to be seen as a risk management industry like any other (Hansen 2011). Above and beyond examples of MNEs having to contend with corruption in a particular host country, they can also be just as guilty of this behaviour. In Nigeria, for instance, studies have found evidence of MNEs serving as 'engines of corrupt practices' and designing 'schemes to circumvent laws and regulations' in the country (Otusanya 2011).

It is important to avoid the common misconception that multinational corruption is a one-way street.

Moreover, it can be difficult allocating responsibility for an act of corruption. In a case famously denounced by Indian novelist Arundhati Roy, the now disbanded US energy company Enron paid a small sum to an official in Maharashtra state, who then awarded it a power plant construction contract despite receiving lower bids from rival Deutsche Babcock. The end result was that local residents had to pay much higher utilities bills than they should have done (Hamilton 2002). Large-scale corruption like this skews market transactions to the benefit of the few and the detriment of the many. Sometimes the problem is knowing how to differentiate between fully fledged bribery and the giving of gifts, which can be innocent enough.

Accusations of corruption can also be very inconsistent. No one calls for a boycott of the EU or the USA, yet extensive political lobbying in Brussels and Washington (see Chapter 5) is by some measures tantamount to corruption. A very topical debate also surrounds the morality of countries like the UK, Switzerland, Luxembourg, or Hong Kong, generally perceived as being among the least corrupt in the world (see Figure 8.5), yet who behave as 'secretive tax havens [encouraging] global financial crime and malpractice' (Lawrence 2011b). At a certain level, corruption discussions can easily spill over into debates about political ideology.

Lastly, there is the cultural aspect of perceived corruption. Depending on a country's heritage, practices considered corrupt in some environments may be acceptable in others. For instance, the Arab habit of *bakshish* can be analysed as a bribe or, alternatively, as something as harmless as a tip or a finder's fee. Classifying an act as corrupt is less straightforward than it first seems. An added complication is that firms or individuals who act ethically most of the time may be capable of acting unethically on the odd occasion. This inconsistency makes it very hard to audit corruption, either internally by MNEs' compliance departments, or externally by national authorities. It also explains why a number of major global initiatives have been launched (notably by the UN or the OECD) to deal with this problem.

Environment and sustainability

With few exceptions (such as when BP changed its advertising strapline in 1998 to 'Beyond Petroleum' so as to highlight its interest in renewable energies), until recently green issues

Rank	Country	Score	Rank	Country	Score	Rank	Country	Score
1	New Zealand	9.5	13	Japan	8.0	75	China	3.6
2	Denmark	9.4	16	UK	7.8	95	India	3.1
2	Finland	9.4	24	US	7.1	100	Indonesia	3.0
4	Sweden	9.3	25	France	7.0	112	Egypt	2.9
5	Singapore	9.2	41	Poland	5.5	120	Iran	2.7
6	Norway	9.0	43	South Korea	5.4	134	Pakistan	2.5
7	Netherlands	8.9	57	Saudi Arabia	4.4	143	Nigeria	2.4
8	Australia	8.8	61	Turkey	4.2	143	Russia	2.4
8	Switzerland	8.8	64	South Africa	4.1	175	Iraq	1.8
10	Canada	8.7	69	Italy	3.9	180	Myanmar	1.5
11	Hong Kong	8.4	73	Brazil	3.8	182	Somalia	1.0
13	Germany	8.0						

Figure 8.5

Selected countries and perceived level of public sector corruption.

Reprinted from the 2011 Corruption Perceptions Index. © 2011. Transparency International: the global coalition against corruption. Used with kind permission. For more information, visit http://www. transparency.org.

were less central to multinationals' CSR image than labour standards or human rights. Chapter 16 takes an in-depth look at the environment's impact on the future of international business focusing among other topics on the allocation of responsibility for ecological behaviour. Things are easy enough when a problem in this respect affects just one country, since the national government will be in charge of policing behaviour. Unfortunately, environmental damage often knows no borders, and the absence of an all-powerful international authority makes it easier to commit 'enviro-crimes'. The UN has tried to lead in this area, but its lack of policing powers means that it can do no more than develop idealistic codes that are hard to enforce. A further complication is that whereas some countries view sustainability as an absolute imperative, others do not, with many LDCs considering it unfair that their social development must be curtailed simply because the older industrialized countries have already exhausted the world's ecological possibilities (Giamporcaro 2011). Many consumers are also unwilling or unable to pay for the true environmental costs of the products they buy. Identifying an ethical issue in international business is usually much easier than agreeing on how to deal with it.

International codes

There have been many attempts over the years to codify ethical behaviour on an international scale. The two main categories are comprised of the work done by the UN in this area and voluntary codes drafted at the company or branch level.

United Nations conventions

> Go online

The UN is the closest thing to a global government. However, it falls short, in terms of being effective, because it lacks policing abilities and because its decisions require consensus agreement from members with often divergent interests. This means that UN declarations tend to be weak compromises or mere statements of intent. Yet the principles they establish— particularly the 1948 Declaration of Human Rights and the 2000 Global Compact (**see ORC Extension material 8.4**)—have laid the foundations for many of the principles underlying multinational CSR (see Figure 8.6).

CSR topics typically covered by the UN (like environment, corruption, human rights, and development) usually concern both corporations and non-corporate interests. Other CSR topics (such as corporate governance) that are specific to business alone tend to be addressed by bodies like the OECD, whose governance ambitions are less extensive than the UN.

Voluntary codes

+ Code of conduct
List of rules detailing accepted behaviour within an organization.

Companies generally like to publicize the fact that they have drafted a code of conduct, or signed up to an existing one, since this improves their reputation and defuses possible criticisms. However, depending on their circumstances, MNEs tend to manifest variable levels of interest in codes. Studies have shown that companies operating in countries where a 'relativistic' culture dominates (i.e. where people do not believe in absolute moral values) are less likely to try to regulate ethical behaviour than in so-called idealistic cultures (Donelson and O'Boyle 2011). Similarly, a website called Corporate.Register.com has uncovered considerable differences worldwide in companies' environmental, social, and ethical reporting activities. Logically, the formalization of CSR will be as variable as the definition of ethics.

+ Ethical reporting group
Associations of companies and other organizations promising to respect certain ethical standards.

After the UN Global Compact, the world's two largest ethical reporting groups are the Global Reporting Initiative (GRI) and the SA8000. The GRI's website calls it a large, 'multi-stakeholder network' of experts promoting triple bottom line disclosure within

1948 Declaration of Human Rights	Adopted in the wake of the Second World War, this document specifies minimum freedoms that governments must afford citizens.
1972 Stockholm Conference on the Human Environment	The purpose of this event was to determine a 'common outlook and for common principles to inspire and guide the peoples of the world in the preservation and enhancement of the human environment'. This paved the way for a great deal of research informing subsequent conferences.
1992 Rio de Janeiro Conference on Environment and Development	Famous 'Earth Summit' where the UN brought world leaders together to 'rethink economic development and find ways to halt the destruction of irreplaceable natural resources and pollution of the planet'.
1997 Kyoto Framework Convention on Climate Change	'Overall framework for intergovernmental efforts to tackle the challenge posed by climate change.' Undermined when several major polluters, notably the USA and Australia, refused to ratify. Follow-up conferences (including Bali 2007 and Durban 2011) were more successful but remained vague.
2000 Global Compact	World's largest voluntary corporate citizenship and sustainability initiative network, with over 8000 participants, including over 6000 businesses in 135 countries. Aims to 'mainstream [the] ten principles in business activities across the world' and 'catalyse actions in support of UN goals'. Has been criticized for letting MNEs pick and choose the principles they want to support and legitimizing their image while ignoring more 'structural' factors (Utting 2002). Doubts have also been expressed about its enforceability.
2001 Johannesburg World Summit on Sustainable Development	Disappointing progress since the 1992 Rio summit led to the organization of a second conference in 2001. One main topic was whether the codes of conduct that international firms adopt to promote ethical behaviour should be mandatory (Type I) or voluntary and self-enforced (Type II).
2005 Warsaw Convention against Corruption	Agreement expanding upon the 1997 OECD Convention on Combating Bribery of Foreign Public Officials by including private sector dealings. Yet the only authorities with power to punish are national governments applying domestic legislation (e.g. US Foreign Corrupt Practices Act).
2010 Convention on Biological Diversity	Recognized the threat raised by the accelerated extinction of species resulting from human activities.

Figure 8.6
Main United Nations conferences affecting multinational CSR.

The UN's strength lies more in setting ethical guidelines than in policing them

Source: UN Photo/ Eskinder Debebe

a 'Sustainability Reporting Framework'. The purpose is to give the public a full and transparent vision of the actions of its more than 3000 member organizations (companies but also state agencies and NGOs). The SA8000 is a 'Social Accountability Standard' as well as verification system aimed at 'assuring humane workplaces'. As of 30 June 2011, 3083 facilities had been SA8000 certified worldwide, representing a total of 1,840,846 workers in 65 industries in 65 countries.

Other codes of conduct are constructed at a branch level. In some sectors (like agri-business), this reflects companies' tendency to conceive of their ethical and other responsibilities not in terms of what each party does separately, but as a reflection of the behaviour of the value chain as a whole. The joint determination of an ethical code is a way of countering the confusion that arises when partner companies have different understandings of CSR (Hartmann 2011). Examples of these branch-level agreements include the International Council of Toy Industries and the International Code of Conduct on the Distribution and Use of Pesticides. Branch codes often focus on labour practices, product safety, and environmental standards (see Figure 8.7). They tend to be used by consumers and other stakeholders as evidence of a company's devotion to CSR policies. The same applies to environmental and social ratings agencies like Environmental Resources Management (ERM) in the USA/UK or BMJ Ratings in France, which fulfil, in their respective fields, a function similar to the one performed by financial ratings agencies like Standard & Poor's or Moody's (see Chapter 16). Lastly, it is worth noting the important role that codes play in the fast growing category of fair trade products, which currently generate global sales of $5.8 billion, a figure that is expected to double by 2015 (Neuman 2011) unless people's willingness to pay an ethical premium diminishes in the wake of the 2011–2012 recession.

+ Ethical premium
Surcharge that consumers are prepared to pay for a good certified as being associated with ethical business practices.

The existence of a growing population of consumers willing to pay more for certifiably ethical goods might give companies an incentive to exaggerate their CSR qualifications. This is particularly tempting in international business, where dispersed global operations may prevent stakeholders in some parts of the world from perceiving misdeeds committed by group branches operating in remote or distant regions. The extent to which an MNE should be held accountable for the behaviour of the international suppliers in its value chain is also questionable. Take the famous example of Nike, which, along with other clothing giants like Adidas, came under enormous pressure in the 1990s when it was accused of looking the other way while its South East Asian suppliers abused the human rights of their sweatshop workers. After first protesting its lack of responsibility for these other firms' bad

Figure 8.7 Environmental certification categories and bodies. (www.ecolabelling.org 2010.)	Category	Number of labelling bodies	Leaders
	Buildings	64	LEED Green Building Rating System (USA)
	Carbon	15	Carbon Trust Standard (UK)
	Electronics	40	Energy Star (Canada/US), EPEAT (USA)
	Energy	31	Energy Label (EU)
	Food	90	Demeter (global)
	Forest products	36	Rainforest Alliance (USA)
	Retail goods	74	Blue Angel (Germany)
	Textiles	40	EcoLogo (Canada)
	Tourism	28	Blue Flag (Denmark)
	Misc. (marine, farms, factories)	79	Marine Stewardship Council (UK) Green Seal (USA) Soil Association (UK) Nordic Ecolabel 'Swan' (Scandinavia)

practices, Nike changed its approach and openly embraced an ethical auditing regime (Böhm and Batta 2008). Proud of its new image, the MNE then advertised how well workers in its supply chain were being treated.

There is no doubt that Nike did take concrete measures to improve suppliers' working conditions. It signed an Apparel Industry Partnership code, set up a Labour Practices Department, and implemented a tight and transparent supplier audit system. It also received favourable reviews from the World Business Council for Sustainable Development (www.wbcsd.org), an association of around 200 companies working to develop the link between business and sustainable development. Yet Nike remains exposed to the possibility of suppliers' lack of ethics, largely because of the difficulty it has in monitoring their behaviour (Economist 2012a). This means that, fairly or unfairly, some mistrust remains to this day. It is very hard for MNEs to regain an ethical reputation once this has been damaged.

Enforcing CSR

It is one thing to specify the ethical standards that MNEs should adopt. It is another to ensure that they actually comply. Some standards materialize in so-called 'hard' regulations that carry legal weight and will be policed by the authorities; other, 'soft' forms involve influencing market behaviour (Dunning and Lundan 2011). Enforcing multinational CSR usually means balancing both approaches. However, this can be difficult to achieve in the absence of universal standards (Adeyeye 2011), especially in LDCs lacking strong governance institutions (Brown and Woods 2007).

Because ethical behaviour is easier to identify within a national framework where everyone answers to a single authority (the government), enforcement is also more straightforward at this level. International organizations like the EU or WTO may be able to sanction multinational wrongdoers in a few limited areas (see Chapter 4), but they generally lack the power to enforce global codes relating to basic ethical dilemmas like relative poverty and inequality (Eckert 2008). Indeed, there is a strong argument that it is in the world's interests to unify its 'fragmented legal systems [since] making firms pay for the damage they inflict [gives them] greater incentive to act more responsibly and ensure their employees do' (Stiglitz 2006: 205–7). One step in this direction would be to let companies be sanctioned in one country for actions taken elsewhere, an example being the lawsuit that was launched against Unocal in the US state of California condemning its alleged conduct in distant Myanmar. For the foreseeable future, however, with the exception of global NGO campaigns aimed at raising consumers' global ethical awareness, CSR enforcement mainly occurs within national borders. This means that it can take very different forms worldwide.

CSR in the USA

According to one school of thought (Matten and Moon 2004), due to the comparative vagueness of American liability legislation, firms in the USA may feel greater pressure to prove that they are behaving ethically even when they are obeying the law. Before the Sarbanes-Oxley corporate governance law was enacted in 2002, US executives were often able to avoid personal responsibility for their actions at work by 'hiding behind the corporate veil' of limited liability (Stiglitz 2006). One example of overt CSR efforts by US companies to reassure the public is McDonald's publication of ingredient quality standards going well beyond Food and Drug Administration minimum requirements. In an environment where accountability is less formalized, overt CSR reassures the public and becomes a competitive tool. US firms Ben and Jerry's and American Apparel have turned this to their advantage, bolstering customer loyalty by highlighting their progressive values and commitment to sustainability. CSR has provided a new market niche for a wide range of American companies.

CSR in Europe

In Europe, on the other hand, there is a 'long tradition of business/government cooperation' (Vogel 2006: 10), reflected in strong philosophical traditions like the German notion that *Eigentum verpflichtet* (loosely translated as 'ownership implies duties' and not just rights). More recently, there has also been the appearance of triple bottom line legislation such as France's *Nouvelles Régulations Economiques* requiring most companies to publish environmental and social accounts alongside their financial statements. Some analysts are of the mind that Europe 'outshines' the USA in CSR matters (Maitland 2002). Others see this differently, based on the recognition that US companies are leading signatories of global ethical reporting initiatives. It is risky generalizing about whether one business culture is more ethical than another.

CSR in Asia and the developing world

Japan's CSR profile resembles Europe's to the extent that it is a more collective culture where self-interest is less of a priority than social harmony, an Asian cultural value enshrined in the writings of the philosopher Confucius. This is not to say that the country has never experienced ethical scandals. On 18 February 2011, for instance, the environmental NGO Greenpeace published an article on its website denouncing corruption in the Japanese whaling industry. Many countries in Asia share similar values to Japan without CSR necessarily being as prevalent as it is in Japan. This is further proof that a society's attitudes towards ethics in business can be conditioned by factors other than culture alone.

More generally, there seems to be a fundamental difference in the way that CSR is viewed in the developed and developing worlds (Barkemeyer 2011). Studies about the relationship between business, government, and society in China have attributed the recurrence of scandals in this country to the relative absence of independent watchdogs and advocacy groups, as well as the comparative powerlessness of the Chinese media, which makes it harder to expose unethical behaviour in the country (Wu and Davidson 2011). To compensate, there tends to be the expectation that provincial and other local authorities will step in and police irresponsible companies. This is not always effective, however, often because political interests impact on the relationship between Chinese companies and government bodies (Lam 2011).

On a more structural level, income inequality and poor working conditions in China have led to serious industrial unrest in recent years, and MNEs operating here are increasingly obliged to give consideration to how they might entertain responsible relationships with their workforce. Thus, Walmart was forced by the Chinese government to accept the unionization of its Chinese staff members (Barboza 2006). Note that the union in question was state-run, exemplifying the fact that stakeholder relations in developing countries generally differ from those found in the industrialized world.

This is not to say that all LDCs experience CSR in a similar manner. India, the world's largest democracy, is characterized by the coexistence of a vibrant civil society. It also features MNEs that have started to act on the global stage and must therefore bolster their CSR image in much the same way that Western MNEs have had to do. The key driver here and in certain other developing regions (like the Middle East) is a long tradition of philanthropy —although, as discussed above, charity is not the same thing as CSR. Indeed, Hopkins (2007) criticizes philanthropy in places like Africa because of the risk that firms might use it 'as a respectable means of buying off stakeholders to accept operating practices' that might not be considered ethical under other circumstances. Even worse, in countries like Brazil, studies have determined that CSR might actually be 'value-destroying', given the significant negative correlation between this approach and corporate value (Crisóstomo et al. 2011).

CSR can still seem like a luxury in some areas of the world. Historically, the main priority for most developing countries has been to create jobs and spark growth by attracting inward FDI. Corruption can be very widespread, often because living standards are so low that potential recipients of bribes cannot afford to turn their backs on any sources of extra income. Many LDCs do not have sufficiently strong civil institutions to exert moral pressure on companies. CSR reporting systems can be poor quality; there may be no real obligation for companies to implement whatever national regulations exist in this domain; and even if the local population is aware of CSR, it may lack the means to force companies to report their environmental and social behaviour (Utama 2011). In the absence of strong governments, what other parties might influence the situation?

Non-governmental organizations and international charities

It is difficult to come up with a single definition for the NGO sector, a key component of what is sometimes globally referred to as 'civil society'. The first recognized NGO, founded in the USA in 1839, was the Anti-Slavery Society. At one point, non-profit organizations, ranging from family groups to small advocacy networks, were the main actors offering the kind of anti-politics of the powerless (Kaldor 2003) that typifies the sector. In every nation of the world, there are countless local charities run by volunteers seeking to right a perceived wrong. Nowadays, however, civil society actors are just as likely to be huge, professionally run organizations focused on all kinds of global issues, ranging from the environment to war, poverty, and women's rights (see Figure 8.8). Indeed, it is hard to conceive of a major international social, political, economic, cultural, or ecological issue that has not received the attention of an NGO. Their legitimacy and ability to lead cross-border campaigns is rooted in the growing acceptance of the concept of global citizenship (Bieri and Boli 2011).

No one knows exactly how many NGOs exist today, but the number is assumed to run into tens of thousands. At a time when the Internet has both broadened awareness of global problems and empowered people to express themselves on all varieties of topics, it is no surprise that like-minded individuals end up joining advocacy groups focused on globalization-related problems. Declining participation in many national elections attests to widespread disillusionment with local politicians' ability to shape events. For many citizens, NGOs offer a substitute platform for action.

NGOs come in all sizes and shapes. Since the 1980s and 1990s there has been a proliferation of loosely organized grassroots networks that the economist Joseph Stiglitz has called the 'discontents of globalization'. These are many of the people seen protesting publicly at major global governance events like WTO trade conferences or G8 annual meetings. They can be contrasted with the big professional NGOs like Greenpeace or Oxfam, many of whom regularly participate nowadays in all kinds of global policy forums. This is because MNEs have become increasingly willing to listen to civil society actors. Indeed, some transnational NGO alliances have become so adept at manipulating the global media to broadcast their views that it would be impossible for MNEs (or national governments) to ignore them. The importance attached to these organizations' opinions is quite normal—complaints about international business have always been an integral part of international business.

Names	Focus
Greenpeace; Friends of the Earth	Environment
Oxfam; War on Want; Wateraid	Poverty
Amnesty International; Human Rights Watch	Human rights
Focus on Global South; Trade Justice Movement	Trade
Child Rights Information Network; Save the Children	Child labour
Wateraid; World Wildlife Fund	Conservation

Figure 8.8
Leading NGOs dealing with globalization-related issues.

It is relatively easy to generalize about the kinds of things that globalization-critical NGOs believe in. Many oppose radical free market neo-liberalism, which they accuse of glorifying greed, weakening national governments, creating financial instability, aggravating income disparities, lowering many individuals' standard of living, damaging human health, endangering the environment, and destroying cultural diversity (Wolf 2005). What is harder to ascertain is any consensus about a replacement system. At one level, a distinction might be made between 'alter-globalizers' organizing large-scale protests and 'anti-globalizers' mobilizing around more specific issues (Ayres and Bosia 2011). The former category includes 'egalitarians' who recognize globalization's capacity to create wealth but are disappointed by the gap growing between haves and have-nots (Steger 2002; Cohen 2006), plus 'reformists' who denounce excessive deregulation and seek a more rules-based and/or fairer trading system (Buckman 2004). Anti-globalizers, on the other hand, reject globalized capitalism, demand that power be returned to the local economic level, and denounce what they see as free market neo-liberalism's 'malign intent' (Bhagwati 2004). Their attitudes range from antipathy towards all MNEs to the rejection of materialism, blind anti-Americanism, and even outright xenophobia. It should be recognized in any event that international business debates are often framed in highly emotive terms, by NGOs but also by their critics. As stated in Chapter 1, it is easy to argue that the discipline has deeper roots in human psychology than in hard science.

A rapidly expanding feature of the international ethics landscape is NGOs' use of high-profile communications (media, conferences, demonstrations, and Internet magazines such as *Ethical Corporation* or *Corpwatch*) to influence how the general public views MNEs. This often involves denouncing some MNEs' refusal to accept responsibility for the direct costs of their activities (or for the more indirect costs, such as resource depletion and subcontractors' unethical labour practices). Examples from the year 2011 include a mass campaign led by the Occupy movement, which marched in cities worldwide denouncing rising income inequality (famously expressed as the '1 per cent versus the 99 per cent'), along with more domestically oriented groups like UK Uncut, which organized a series of sit-ins alleging the underpayment of taxes by some of Britain's leading companies. NGOs' public exposure of corporate behaviour is intended to attract the attention of both politicians and legislators, in the hope that they will intervene, and consumers, in the hope that they will boycott products or services marketed by a company accused of being unethical.

It remains to be seen how effective NGO protests (or consumer boycotts) are as vehicles for enforcing CSR. Despite greater collaboration between MNEs and NGOs, companies sometimes suffer from 'CSR fatigue', perhaps because they resent some NGOs' constantly doubting their motives (Leisinger 2007). In many situations, the bottom line benefits of unethical behaviour may be higher than the costs of complying with legal and/or CSR standards—especially when the misdeeds in question occur in some remote location and are invisible to most consumers elsewhere. Empirical studies have found, for instance, that some companies only select a level of CSR compliance based on their perception of the extent to which customers are likely to punish them in the case of non-compliance (Christmann and Taylor 2006). In certain MNE boardrooms, CSR is a pure business decision.

On the other hand, MNEs who fear that a lack of CSR will put them at odds with public opinion might also decide that it is in their interest to be proactive about taking the moral high ground. For instance, there had been no particular pressure on European food conglomerate Unilever News Corporation to accelerate its sustainability programme when new CEO Paul Polman announced a raft of measures in January 2012, translating his vision that this should become the MNE's main core value. That same month saw American rival Proctor & Gamble announce a Facebook campaign supporting its global Children's Safe Drinking Water campaign; Apple released its list of suppliers for the first time ever (to facilitate scrutiny of their labour practices); and IKEA made a €300,000 donation to a Haitian children's literacy project (https://twitter.com/#!/bwcsrnews). The question is the extent to which such volunteer CSR actions are a reflection of managers' sincere goodwill (because they do not 'leave their values at home when they arrive at work') or else their fear of becoming a target of 'supermarket activism' (Hertz 2001: 179, 113). In all likelihood, it is a combination of the two. Indeed, as MNEs build up their 'community affairs' or 'sustainability' departments and staff them with former public-sector workers whose personal ethos is not necessarily profit-oriented, there is every chance that ethical attitudes will become increasingly widespread in the business world (Murray 2006). At the same time, it is just as likely that headlines will continue to denounce unethical corporate behaviour somewhere in the world. Few MNEs are 100 per cent ethical or unethical and most are capable of doing both good and bad (Strike et al. 2006). In this, as in other areas of international business, the only rule is that there are no rules.

Challenges and choices

→ Corporate social responsibility can sometimes require significant investment, at least when the programme in question is in its early stages. The challenge for managers is determining whether they are spending enough in the right areas to satisfy their ethical ambitions without wasting money. Since this cannot be answered objectively, the choice that they generally have to make is whether to err by spending too much or too little on CSR. It is also debatable whether companies should allow a CSR ethos to filter into every aspect of their value chain, or restrict it to certain well-defined functions. The answer often depends on the dominant corporate culture.

Chapter summary

Despite a few remaining pockets of opposition to CSR, expectations of ethics in business have become so widespread that CSR is likely to be one cornerstone of international business for years to come. Indeed, companies that ignore repeated criticism in this area risk their long-term survival (Singer 2004). The problem, as discussed in the chapter's first section, is defining what constitutes ethical behaviour in cross-border situations characterized by divergent value systems and national interests. The main international CSR issues (human rights, labour standards, corruption, and the environment) are viewed differently across the world.

The chapter's second section discussed international efforts to codify business ethics, many of which built on the foundation of UN conference declarations. Since the UN lacks the power to ensure compliance with its codes, and given variations in national CSR traditions, enforcement remains patchy. Currently, the NGO sector is one of the main constraints on MNE behaviour. The question then becomes which processes motivate MNEs to behave responsibly in which areas.

Case study 8.3

Global governance and NGOs: David takes on the Goliaths

Reformist NGOs have long accused the agents of globalization (MNEs, speculators) of aggravating income inequalities. Some analysts believed that the wave of currency attacks that hit South East Asia in 1997 had beneficial effects, since they revealed to local governments the unsustainable nature of their currency management policies. However, for other observers, ranging from anti-business protestors to globalization-friendly economists like Jagdish Bhagwati, the sight of rich Western financiers breaking LDC central banks was a sign that all is not right in the global currency regime.

The goal for these critics then became raising public awareness of the devastation that speculative currency attacks can cause by creating instability in a country's financial system. In the 1970s, Nobel laureate James

Tobin had floated the idea that a 1 per cent tax on currency transactions could stop the traders who destabilize national currency markets for purely speculative reasons. Reform-minded campaigners, shocked by the 1997 crisis, revived this proposal and lobbied governments to implement it.

NGOs exist in part so that reformers have a vehicle to express their views. Worldwide there are many idealistic NGO professionals who devote their lives to spotting injustices and seeking remedies. One such individual, a veteran of earlier campaigns against apartheid South Africa and landmines, is Londoner David Hillman. Like many others, David was dismayed by what happened in Thailand and Indonesia in 1997 and reacted favourably when anti-poverty NGO, War on Want, asked if he would spearhead its Tobin Tax campaign. This required coordination with like-minded campaigns in the UK and abroad. In international business, as in many other areas, governments can only be convinced of the need to change policy if this has widespread support. David Hillman set about making the case.

The first step was to marshal all Tobin Tax forces into a single network speaking with a single, coherent voice. Many proposed reforms exist in different versions and it is crucial that NGOs speak clearly when engaging with decision-makers. Hillman's next step was a multi-pronged communications effort, revolving around public conferences in the UK and abroad, the production of short explanatory films, their distribution to key opinion-makers, and media exposure in the written and online press. This entire stage began with an educational phase, during which time David would teach key players about the details of this relatively technical proposition. Then, after about 18 months and once key figureheads had been brought on board, greater focus was put on targeting decision-makers. In the UK, this went as high as the Chancellor of the Exchequer.

By the mid-2000s, several heads of state and/or governments (in France and Brazil, for example) were showing interest in what was now known as the currency transaction tax (CTT). To keep the pressure on, David organized debates, once pitting Jim O'Neill, a well-known economist from Goldman Sachs, against a CTT advocate. The purpose was to convince the public of the proposal's seriousness by showing that it could withstand criticism. David also made a decision to move the CTT effort out of the War on Want NGO and lodge it in a smaller new entity called Stamp Out Poverty. This was to ensure continued focus on the campaign, which might

The Robin Hood Tax Campaign has over 115 supporter organizations and 262,000 Facebook friends. It is part of a movement of campaigns in more than 25 countries
© Andrew Aitchison

otherwise have been swamped by War on Want's broader development agenda. In 2007, a new video called *Can Pay, Should Pay* was released (http://www.stampoutpoverty.org/?lid=10652), featuring a number of activist politicians, NGO leaders, and academics. NGOs like Stamp Out Poverty are constantly competing for media attention; the problem of a dysfunctional currency trading regime is only one issue among the many that politicians are asked to address.

The financial crises of 2008 and 2011–2012 gave further impetus to David Hillman's project by popularizing global doubts about the suitability of the global financial system in its current form (see Chapter 4). In 2009, working together with Richard Curtis and the UK's longstanding Comic Relief charity team, David helped launch the Robin Hood Tax campaign with a short film featuring Bill Nighy as The Banker (http://www.youtube.com/watch?v=qYtNwmXKIvM). By 2012, European politicians such as German Chancellor Angela Merkel and French President François Hollande were openly calling for the implementation of what was now called the Financial Transaction Tax (FTT). Even if success depends on overcoming continued resistance by bodies like the British government, which fears that the FTT will disproportionately affect the City of London, David's cause has finally become prominent on the international agenda. For a campaigning NGO, that is the ultimate accolade.

Case study questions

1. To what extent can groups of concerned citizens achieve change in the world?
2. What, if anything, legitimizes NGO efforts to influence policy-makers?
3. How can NGOs avoid 'charity fatigue' on the part of politicians or donors?

Discussion questions

1. What kind of positive and/or negative connection exists between the corporate profit motive and the greater social good?

2. Is Kline right to fear that MNEs might use the pretext that definitions of morality vary from one country to another to avoid responsibility for ethical behaviour?

3. To what extent are smaller MNEs likely to be more ethically sensitive than larger ones?

4. What should MNEs do if ethical behaviour puts them at a competitive disadvantage?

Online resource centre

Go online to test your understanding by trying multiple-choice questions, and assignment and examination questions.

Further research

International Journal of Business Governance and Ethics (IJBGE)

(http://www.inderscience.com/browse/index.php?journalCODE=ijbge)

IJBGE's purpose is to critically explore business and managerial strategies, actions, responsibilities, and accountabilities, publishing high quality papers from a range of disciplines.

Ethical corporation website (http://www.ethicalcorp.com/)

A UK entity '100% focused on global ethical business and how large companies are responding to the sustainable business agenda'.

References

Adeyeye, A. (2011). 'Universal standards in CSR: Are we prepared?', *Corporate Governance: International Journal of Business in Society*, 11/1, pp. 107–119

Ayres, J. and Bosia, M. (2011). 'Beyond global summitry: Food sovereignty as localized resistance to globalization', *Globalizations*, 8/1, pp. 47–63 (February)

Barboza, D. (2006). 'China drafts law to boost unions and end abuse', *The New York Times*, 13 October, available at http://www.nytimes.com, accessed 15 April 2012

Barkemeyer, R. (2011). 'Corporate perceptions of sustainability challenges in developed and developing countries: Constituting a CSR divide?', *Social Responsibility Journal*, 7/2, pp. 257–281

Bhagwati, J. (2004). *In Defense of Globalization*. New York: Oxford University Press

Bieri, F. and Boli, J. (2011). 'Trading diamonds responsibly: Institutional explanations for corporate social responsibility', *Sociological Forum*, 26/3, pp. 501–526 (September)

Böhm, S. and Batta, A. (2008). 'Just doing it. The imaginary, the symbolic and the real in Nike's commodity fetish', University of Essex working paper, No. WP 08/11, available at http://www.essex.ac.uk, accessed 14 June 2012

Bonini, S. and Chênevert, S. (2008). 'The state of corporate philanthropy: A McKinsey Global Survey', February, available at http://www.mckinseyquarterly.com, accessed 24 June 2008

Borger, J. (2001). 'Coca-Cola sued over bottling plant "terror campaign"', *The Guardian*, 21 July, available at http://www.guardian.co.uk, accessed 14 June 2012

Bradshaw, S. (2005). 'Free Trade, After a Fashion', *Panorama* series, 7 March, available at http://news.bbc.co.uk, accessed 8 October 2008

Brown, D. and Woods, N. (eds.) (2007) *Making Global Self-Regulation Effective in Developing Countries*. Oxford: Oxford University Press

Buckman, G. (2004). *Globalization: Tame It or Scrap It? Mapping the Alternatives of the Anti-Globalization Movement*. London and New York: Zed Books

Christmann, P. and Taylor, G. (2006). 'Firm self-regulation through international certifiable standards: Determinants of symbolic versus substantive implementation', *Journal of International Business Studies*, 37/6 (November)

Cohen, D. (2006). *Globalization and its Enemies*. Cambridge, Mass.: MIT Press

Crisóstomo, V., Freire, F., and Vasconcellos, F. (2011). 'Corporate social responsibility, firm value and financial performance in Brazil', *Social Responsibility Journal*, 7/2, pp. 295–309

Cronin, J. (2006). 'Let business lift Africa out of poverty', *BBC online*, 4 July, available at http://news.bbc.co.uk, accessed 8 October 2008

Donelson, R. and O'Boyle, E. (2011). 'Rules, standards, and ethics: Relativism predicts cross-national differences in the codification of moral standards', *International Business Review*, 20/3, pp. 353–361 (June)

Dunning, J. and Lundan, S. (2011). 'The changing political economy of foreign investment: Finding a balance between hard and soft forms of regulation', *The Evolving International Investment Regime*, pp. 125–153 (April)

Eckert, A. (2008). 'Obligations beyond national borders: International institutions and distributive justice', *Journal of Global Ethics*, 4/1 (April)

Economist (2012a). 'When the jobs inspector calls', *The Economist*, 31 March, p. 69

Economist (2012b). 'What Germany offers the world', *The Economist*, 14 April, p. 28

Friedman, M. (2002). *Capitalism and Freedom*, 40th edn. Chicago: University of Chicago Press

Frost, R. (2004). 'Corporate social responsibility and globalization: A reassessment', *IABC's Online Newsletter for Communication Management*, 2/2, available at http:// www.iabc.com, accessed 20 July 2009

Fyrnas, J. (2010). *Beyond Corporate Social Responsibility: Oil Multinationals and Social Challenges*. Cambridge: Cambridge University Press

Giamporcaro, S. (2011). 'Sustainable and responsible investment in emerging markets: Integrating environmental risks in the South African investment industry', *Journal of Sustainable Finance & Investment*, 1/2, pp. 121–137 (April)

Hamilton, J. (2002). 'How Arundhati Roy took back the power in India', available at http://www.commondreams.org, accessed 8 October 2008

Hansen, H. (2011). 'Managing corruption risks', *Review of International Political Economy*, 18/2, pp. 251–275 (May)

Hartmann, M. (2011). 'Corporate social responsibility in the food sector', *European Review of Agricultural Economics*, 38/3, pp. 297–324

Hertz, N. (2001). *The Silent Takeover*. London: Heinemann

Hopkins, M. (2007). *Corporate Social Responsibility and International Development: Is Business the Solution?* London: Earthscan

IADB (2011). 'PepsiCo and Inter-American Development Bank sign agreement to spur development in Latin America and Caribbean', 22 February, available at http://www.iadb.org, accessed 9 October 2011

Inman, P. and Kingsley, P. (2011). 'Inside job: How bankers caused the financial crisis', *The Guardian*, 17 February, available at http://www.guardian.co.uk, accessed 15 April 2012

Kaldor, M. (2003). 'The idea of global civil society', *International Affairs (Royal Institute of International Affairs 1944–)*, 79/3 (May), pp. 583–593

Khan, F. and Lund-Thomsen, P. (2011). 'CSR as imperialism: Towards a phenomenological approach to CSR in the developing world', *Journal of Change Management*, 11/1, pp. 73–90 (March)

Klaus, V. (2007). 'Czech President warns against global warming intolerance', available at ww.hrad.cz, accessed 8 October 2008

Kline, J. (2005). *Ethics for International Business*. New York: Routledge

Lam, M. (2011). 'Successful strategies for sustainability in China and the global market economy', *International Journal of Sustainable Strategic Management*, 3/1, pp. 73–90 (June)

Laudal, T. (2011). 'Drivers and barriers of CSR and the size and internationalization of firms', *Social Responsibility Journal*, 7/2, pp. 234–256

Lawrence, F. (2011a). 'How "modern day slavery" on the Costa del Sol puts the salad in your shopping', *The Guardian*, 8 February, pp. 12–13

Lawrence, F. (2011b). 'Campaigners name secretive tax havens', *The Guardian*, 4 October, p. 12

Leisinger, K. (2007). 'Capitalism with a human face: The UN Global Compact', *Journal of Corporate Citizenship*, 28 (winter)

Maitland, A. (2002). 'Europe outshines US in corporate social responsibility', *Financial Times*, 13 February

Marcoux, A. (2000). 'Business ethics gone wrong', *Cato Policy Report*, 20/3, May–June, available at http://www.cato.org, accessed 8 October 2008

Matten, D. and Moon, J. (2004). *Implicit and Explicit CR: A Conceptual Framework for Understanding CSR in Europe*, available at http:// www.nottingham.ac.uk, accessed 8 October 2008

Miriam, M., Hoegl, M., and Parboteeah, K. (2011). 'National business ideology and employees' prosocial values', *Journal of International Business Studies*, 42, pp. 183–201

Morgan, E. (1998). *Navigating Cross-Cultural Ethics: What Global Managers Do Right to Keep from Going Wrong*. Woburn, MA: Butterworth Heinemann

Murray, S. (2006). 'Corporate social responsibility: A much more competitive market as public/private lines blur', *Financial Times*, 16 November, available at http://www.ft.com, accessed 26 June 2008

Neuman, W. (2011). 'An issue of farmers, fine coffee and Fair Trade', *The Observer: New York Times* insert, 11 December, p. 5

Otusanya, O. (2011). 'The role of multinational companies in corrupt practices: The case of Nigeria', *International Journal of Critical Accounting*, 3/2-3, pp. 171–203 (April)

Russell, J. (2006). 'Ivory Coast toxic waste—dumped on', *Ethical Corporation*, 12 October, available at http://www.ethicalcorp.com, accessed 8 October 2008

Schwartz, P. (1999). *When Good Companies do Bad Things: Responsibility and Risk in the Age of Gobalization*. New York: John Wiley & Son

Sennett, R. (2006). *The Culture of the New Capitalism*. London: Yale University Press

Singer, P. (2004). *One World: The Ethics of Globalization*. New Haven: Yale University Press

Smith, D. (2011). 'Shell accused of fuelling violence in Nigeria by paying rival militant gangs', *The Guardian*, 3 October, p. 16

Steger, M. (2002). *Globalism: The New Market Ideology*. Lanham (US), Plymouth (UK): Rowman & Littlefield

Stiglitz, J. (2006). *Making Globalization Work: The Next Steps to Global Justice*. London: Allen Lane

Strike, V. M., Gao, J., and Bansal, P. (2006). 'Being good while being bad: Social responsibility and the international diversification of US firms', *Journal of International Business Studies*, 37/6 (November)

Strom, S. (2011). 'In Mexico, a business deal with social benefits', *The Observer: New York Times* insert, 21 February, p. 5

Sweeney, J. (2012). 'Mining giant in child labour and acid dumping claims', 15 April, *The Observer*, p. 16

Tan, J. and Wang, L. (2011). 'MNC strategic responses to ethical pressure: An institutional logic perspective', *Journal of Business Ethics*, 98/3, pp. 373–390 (February)

Utama, S. (2011). 'An evaluation of support infrastructures for corporate responsibility reporting in Indonesia', *Asian Business & Management*, 10/3, pp. 405–424 (August)

Utting, P. (2002). 'The global compact and civil society: Averting a collision course', *Development in Practice*, 5 November, 12/5

Vogel, D. (2006) *The Market for Virtue*. Washington: Brookings

War on Want (2006). 'Coca Cola: The Alternative Report', March, available at http://www.waronwant.org, accessed 9 October 2008

Weltzien, H. and Shankar, D. (2011). 'How can SMEs in a cluster respond to global demands for corporate responsibility?', *Journal of Business Ethics*, 101/2, pp. 175–195 (June)

Wessel, D. (2011). 'Big US firms shift hiring abroad', 19 April, available at http://online.wsj.com, accessed 14 April 2012

Whyte, J. (2012). 'Ideological companies are not the way to go', *City AM*, 21 March, p. 29

Wolf, M. (2005). *Why Globalization Works*. New Haven: Yale Nota Bene

Wu, J. and Davidson, D. (2011). 'The business-government-society relationship: A comparison between China and the US', *The Journal of Management Development*, 30/1, pp. 112–125

Part case study

When cultures collided: The case of Olympus and Michael Woodford

Was it because the company was too Japanese for the boss? Was it because the new CEO was too British? Was it because the national cultures could not mesh? Was it because the corporate cultures clashed? Was it because of their different practices and views about corporate governance and corporate responsibility? Was it because Japanese business culture does not tolerate 'whistle-blowers', especially if they are not Japanese?

The strange case of the serious falling-out between a major Japanese hi-tech MNE (Olympus) and its newly appointed British CEO (Michael Woodford) occupied a great deal of space and time in the financial, business, and legal media in 2011–2012.

Olympus Corporation is a Japanese-based company that manufactures precision machinery and instruments, such as optics, reprography products, lenses, cameras, endoscopes, and scanners. Since its foundation in 1919, Olympus has grown to be a worldwide MNE with nearly 40,000 employees and revenues of about $10.9 billion.

Michael Woodford was appointed as CEO of Olympus in April 2011 after working for the company for 30 years. He had joined Olympus's UK agent Keymed and at the age of 29 appointed head of Olympus operations in the UK. Woodford held senior positions in the USA and took over the EMEA (Europe, Middle East, and Africa) region, overseeing its restructuring.

The appointment of a non-Japanese person as the boss of a Japanese MNE was unusual but not unprecedented: Sony had appointed Sir Howard Stringer (a British-born American) to senior positions, including CEO, chairman, and president between 2005 and 2012; and Nissan's alliance with Renault had been led since 1999 by Carlos Ghosn, a Brazilian-born Frenchman. Indeed, the chairman of Olympus, Tsuyoshi Kikukawa, had originally greeted Woodford's appointment with praise for his ability to work across cultures: 'I've been particularly impressed by the way in which he has shown great sensitivity and understanding of the different cultures across our global organisation' (cited in Goodway 2011).

Soon after his promotion to CEO, Woodford uncovered a $1.5 billion fraud within Olympus and raised his concerns with the board of directors. Part of the fraud was a $687 million advisory fee paid as part of the Olympus acquisition of Gyrus, a company involved in the production of hi-tech medical equipment. In an unprecedented case of

'whistle-blowing', Woodford also queried three other deals where it had become evident that the company had used advisory fee payments and other funds to cover losses going back to the 1990s. The ensuing differences between Woodford and the Japanese board led to a number of legal cases, concern about corporate governance and responsibility, widespread poor publicity, and a massive collapse in the company's share price.

'Whistle-blowing'—the discovery and publicizing of poor business behaviour—is a very contentious aspect of corporate governance. It is often officially encouraged but can result in serious consequences for any employee who dares to actually denounce misconduct. Japan does have a 'whistle-blowers' law' but its effectiveness is questionable. One example is the strict provision that a whistleblower can contact mass media only when it is reasonably clear that contacting a compliance section will lead to destruction of evidence (*Japan Times* 2011).

By the end of October 2011, the company resolved that Woodford should be sacked. Its announcement noted that Woodford 'has largely diverted from the rest of the management team in regard to the management direction and method, and it is now causing problems for decision making by the management team' (Olympus Global 2011). In the context of the 2010 Corporate Strategic Plan, the company judged that it would be difficult to achieve its objectives with 'the management team led by Woodford'. He was therefore dismissed.

Almost a year after Woodford's much-heralded appointment, the board of Olympus announced their conclusions on the way forward. Hiroyuki Sasa (Representative Director/President Olympus Corporation) and the new management team declared that they would implement a 'new management structure to fundamentally overhaul and improve our system of governance'. Sasa also noted that he wished to 'express our deepest apologies to Olympus shareholders, customers, business partners and all other stakeholders for the difficulties caused to them' (Olympus Global 2012).

The outcome for Olympus appears to be that the company has emerged virtually unscathed from this year-long operations and governance crisis. Critics suggest that this 'reflects a familiar Japanese formula of accommodating banks, compliant shareholders and toothless regulators' (Inagaki and Wakabayashi 2012). Despite everything, the Japanese reaction has been to carry on with 'business as usual'. Indeed, the previous chairman of Olympus, Tsuyoshi Kikukawa, tried to put the matter to bed by criticizing Woodford's inability to 'overcome the cultural barrier of Japan and Japanese companies' (cited in Goodway 2011). It is worth remembering that just one year previously, Kikukawa had been one of the many to welcome Woodford's appointment, specifically praising his cultural awareness.

The full details of this story may not be fully known for many years but it certainly has instructive lessons for international corporate governance and CSR, the running of Japanese companies by non-Japanese bosses, and differences in the proper behaviour to be observed within corporate cultures. This is one case where national and corporate cultures have truly collided.

Case study questions

1. Is there a particularly Japanese way of running MNEs?
2. What are the benefits and drawbacks for MNEs of having 'whistle-blowing' policies?
3. What is the relationship in international business between national and corporate cultures?

References

Goodway, N. (2011). 'Lost in translation: Japanese sack British boss after culture clash,' *Evening Standard*, 14 October

Inagaki, K. and Wakabayashi, D. (2012). 'At Olympus, the more things change . . . ,' *Wall Street Journal*, 18 April

Japan Times (2011). Editorial: 'Protection law fails whistleblowers,' 27 September

Olympus Global (2011). 'Olympus Corporation Resolved Dismissal of President Michael C. Woodford,' 14 October http://www.olympus-global.com; accessed 31 May 2012

Olympus Global (2012). 'Announcement, April 2012,' http://www.olympus-global.com; accessed 31 May 2012

Other sources of information

Armitage, J. (2012). 'A very honourable defeat: Ex-Olympus boss walks away', *Independent*, 7 January

Clark, N. (2011a). 'Olympus fires British boss after just two weeks', *Independent*, 15 October

Clark, N. (2011b). 'The hi-tech giant, the ousted boss, and the $680m mystery', *Independent*, 21 October

Clark, N. (2011c). 'Olympus chairman quits amid takeover scandal', *Independent*, 27 October

Clark, N. (2011d). 'Fears for Olympus increase as it faces delisting', *Independent*, 11 November

Rowley, E. (2012). 'Whistleblower reaches deal with Olympus', *Daily Telegraph*, 30 May

part

D

International strategy

9 Modes of internationalization

Learning objectives

After reading this chapter, you should be able to:

+ identify the factors motivating managers to commit resources abroad
+ evaluate the trade vs. FDI decision in terms of its impact on the boundaries of the firm
+ discuss the relative merits of greenfield vs. brownfield investments
+ assess the utility of international joint ventures and cross-border mergers and acquisitions
+ compare the costs and benefits of collaborating with foreign partners

Case study 9.1

MNEs and internationalization: Bimbo bombs along

The Mexican company Group Bimbo has become the world's largest baked packaged-goods maker, with global sales of $10 billion in 2010. Outside its home country, which accounts for around half of total sales, Bimbo brands have a significant share of markets as widely dispersed as China, the USA, and South America. It is an unusual achievement for an MNE originating in a developing country.

Bimbo's historical expansion has been more or less evenly split between organic growth and the acquisition of high profile brands in target markets. In October 2011, for example, it purchased Sara Lee's North American bakery business, and Portuguese and Spanish operations. In a 2011 interview (McKinsey 2011), CEO Daniel Servitje spoke of how Bimbo had learnt in the USA, its first big foreign market, that it could, and actually needed to, target segments beyond the Spanish-speaking communities with which it was most comfortable. This ambition required faster expansion than the company could achieve organically, explaining a series of acquisitions it has undertaken over the past 15–20 years.

Bimbo's growth strategy in Brazil has also been geared towards acquiring existing companies instead of building up house brands, even if many of the companies involved have been relatively modest in size. In part, this reflects the fragmentation of a consumer market split between modern hypermarkets and small grocery stores. The result is that Bimbo tends to react opportunistically in Brazil instead of pursuing a single growth strategy throughout this country or, indeed, the rest of South America.

Lastly, Bimbo's experience in China has been closer to what it first did in its home market in Mexico, when it had to try to develop bread as a whole new product category in a culture where the staple starch is cornmeal tortillas. This common environment has facilitated the company's learning process in China, as has the fact that it originates from another emerging economy and is therefore more accustomed to the uncertainties characterizing business in the developing world. Being comfortable with the developing world means that Bimbo CEO Servitje is less worried about the problems associated with growing Bimbo's small Chinese operations than the complications he will face integrating his MNE's American acquisition,

Mexican bakery firm Bimbo has organized market entry in different ways in different countries
Source: Bimbo

Sara Lee. Bimbo's main historical success at home in Mexico involved nurturing localized segments over the long run. It hopes to internationalize by following the same model.

Case study questions

1. To what extent is Bimbo operating in markets that resemble or differ from its home country?
2. What factors determine whether Bimbo internationalizes via organic growth or acquisition?

Figure 9.1
The ladder of
internationalization
choices.

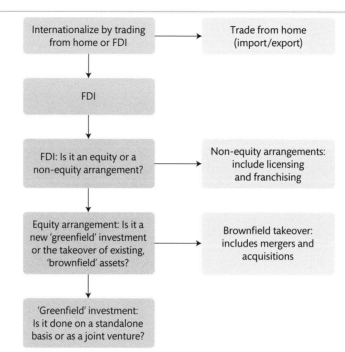

Introduction

Except for a few 'born-global' firms (Ripollés et al. 2011a), like the dot.com start-ups that arose around the year 2000, most of the world's leading MNEs were born in a home market where they grew up before venturing abroad. The actual decision to internationalize, and the way this is done, is often referred to as a 'mode of entry' choice. Figure 9.1 displays this decision, using the terminology that this chapter will teach. The figure represents a decision-making ladder showing different levels of corporate commitment to internationalization. The initial decision facing a manager who wants to internationalize is whether to trade from home or engage in FDI. Where an MNE opts for FDI, the question then becomes whether the company should commit equity capital or not. If so, the company must decide if the market entry should involve building a brand new site or if it should take over another company's current operations. Additionally, at every stage of this process it will want to consider whether it should act by itself or in cooperation with a partner.

+ Commitment to
internationalization
Depth of a company's
engagement of human,
physical, and financial
resources abroad.
Ranges from simple
import/export to
running large, wholly
owned foreign
subsidiaries.

Once the mode of entry is decided, managers must then decide how to structure relations between the different units that have been put in place. Chapter 10 deals with these organizational aspects of companies' internationalization drives. Altogether, the two chapters strengthen the argument made throughout this book that international business is not a science but the outcome of a series of decisions that are at least partially subjective in nature.

Section I: Leaving home: Theories, mindsets, and strategies

The main focus in many international business studies is why and how companies decide to go abroad. Chapter 4 discussed several theories that put such decisions into contexts defined by different national economic policies. The theories underlying this chapter, on the other hand, focus on actual market entry decisions.

The 'Uppsala' school

The main approach used in this chapter is called 'stages of internationalization' and derives from the Uppsala model that views 'the internationalization process [as being] characterized by the management of complexities and uncertainties and that requires learning and commitment building' (Vahne et al. 2011), with companies only engaging resources abroad once they become more comfortable with the environments they discover. The expectation is that MNEs usually internationalize first via simple import and export arrangements that gradually become more complex over time (Ruzzier et al. 2006). This is due to the connection between managers' perception of the degree and type of uncertainty associated with a particular market entry mode, and their overall commitment to internationalization (Li and Rugman 2007). Subsequently, once managers do feel ready to commit capital resources abroad, this will often first involve entering a neighbouring country or culture before going further afield later. The Uppsala school argues that the key factor in most companies' overseas trajectory is the confidence that managers have in their internal capabilities and accumulated expertise (Tuppura et al. 2008). It is rare for international managers to have a complete understanding of the foreign environments to which they are thinking of moving. This is illustrated in recent studies showing that Chinese private enterprises' early stage entry in Africa is more a reflection of the existence of local overseas Chinese networks raising entrepreneurs' level of comfort than of any understanding they might have of local circumstances (Song 2011). Subjective decision-making in the face of imperfect knowledge has always been an integral part of international business.

Other internationalization schools

International business literature offers a number of other theories (**see ORC Extension material 9.1**) emphasizing different aspects of companies' internationalization paths. This includes long established constructs like 'transaction cost economics', which implies, where MNEs are concerned, that internationalization decisions are largely motivated by the desire to cut costs; 'network theory', which apprehends international business decisions in terms of MNEs situating themselves within the web of companies comprising their value chain; and Professor Alan Rugman's 'FSA/CSA matrix', which highlights MNEs' search, respectively, for firm- and country-specific advantages. There are also more recent models such as the 'New Venture Theory' or the 'LLL framework', which focus on fine-tuning current understanding of internationalization processes by accounting for factors such as companies' different organizational cultures, stages of development, or sectors of activity. Lastly, some economists have highlighted factors such as home market saturation and diversification as a prime driver behind internationalization, exemplified by California bank Wells Fargo's stated priority of buying European bank assets to offset a disproportionate focus on its home market (Braithwaite 2012).

> Go online

Given the wealth of different schools of thought, the only theoretical generalization that can be made is that companies go abroad for a wide variety of reasons, which can broadly be divided between internal strategic motives vs. responses and external circumstances (Hutson et al. 2011). This diversity explains why internationalization has attracted so much attention over the years. Going abroad is one of the most crucial decisions that international managers will ever have to make.

Degrees of internationalization

Doing business outside one's home country will always be challenging, with some studies struggling to find evidence that firms with a greater cross-border presence necessarily perform better than companies that work within their national boundaries (Contractor et al. 2003). Transferring resources (mainly capital, knowledge, personnel, and materials) overseas is an expensive and difficult process for many companies and can create a wide range of new problems (Nadolska and Barkema 2007). Some of these problems are industrial in nature, like the difficulties that German car-maker BMW faced in the 1990s after buying Rover, a UK company accustomed to lower quality manufacturing standards. Others involve financial aspects, like the debt that France's Vivendi incurred to fund its 2000 acquisition of US entertainment company Universal. Still others are intellectual property-related, as exemplified by the dispute between French food company Danone and its Chinese partner Wahaha, which it accused of setting up parallel operations rivalling the joint venture that the two companies had established together. Lastly, some problems are more strategic in nature, like when Pizza Hut sought a first-mover advantage by entering Brazil in the 1990s before this volatile emerging economy had stabilized, and suffered high pioneering costs as a result. Internationalization is never an easy step.

Despite these risks, international sales can be a saving grace for companies with little room to grow at home. There are many sectors of activities (automobiles, beverages, etc.) that are more or less saturated in the world's older industrialized nations, whose MNEs must therefore seek new opportunities in emerging economies in order to expand. Others, like the accommodations business, are suffering from a great deal of volatility in once stable regions like Europe, explaining why a giant in this sector, InterContinental Hotels, is repositioning itself to centre new growth in emerging Asian and Middle Eastern markets (Thompson and Jones 2012). Seen in this light, expanding overseas is often a necessity, not a luxury. The main obstacle to internationalization then becomes managers' psychological predisposition to enter foreign markets, sometimes referred to as the opposition between companies characterized by a 'domestic mindset' (Nadkarni and Perez 2007) vs. others whose corporate culture emphasizes 'international entrepreneurship' (Ripollés et al. 2011b). Derived from the Uppsala model with its learning focus, the more confidence a company has in its ability to succeed abroad, the greater the amount of financial and other capital it will be prepared to invest. The less confidence it has, the more it will prefer interacting with foreign interests, when necessary, through less committed methods: trading (importing/exporting) from its home base; or, at most, opening a tiny representative office abroad. This spectrum of possible actions means that the main internationalization modes can be ranked (see Figure 9.2) in order of the physical, capital, and human resources that each requires.

Managerial mindsets

Managers' tendency to adopt a 'domestic' or 'international entrepreneurial' mindset varies in time and place, and also depends on whether the proposed market entry involves an operational 'exploitation' of relatively familiar capabilities or a riskier 'exploration' of something unknown (Barkema and Drogendijk 2007). One way to analyse this sense of difficulty is by using Porter's 'Diamond' model (see Chapter 2), which states that firms that

+ Joint venture
Business unit specifically created by different companies to achieve a particular mission. Usually involves pooling resources like equity capital, knowledge, processes, and/or personnel.

+ Pioneering costs
Costs associated with the mistakes that companies make when entering an unfamiliar market.

Figure 9.2	Market entry mode	Description	Scale of commitment
Different modes of market entry require the internationalization of different amounts of financial capital, human capital, and knowledge.	Import/export from home	Firm remains domestic but buys from foreign supplier/sells to foreign buyer	Low
	Licensing/franchising	Firm gives permission to an agent to manufacture/retail abroad on its behalf	
	Joint venture (form of FDI)	Firm makes equity investment abroad together with partner	
	Wholly owned subsidiary (FDI)	Firm makes standalone equity investment abroad	High

have overcome tough challenges at home feel better prepared to deal with difficulties abroad. Recent examples include Russian telecommunications operator Vimpelcom's 2010 acquisition of two companies in neighbouring Ukraine, a successful decision in light of the new subsidiaries' strong contribution to 2011 group operating profits. The move signified the MNE's growing confidence in its ability to succeed in a business environment influenced by a recent communist past, a context for which Vimpelcom was prepared given Russian's own political history. Similarly, there is also a tendency for MNEs to expand more quickly in places where the business culture is similar to the one they grew up in. US multinational Starbucks, for instance, has penetrated the English market with apparent ease in comparison with the problems that it has suffered in India, where the MNE's inability to find acceptable partners limited its market entry until it finally signed a memorandum of understanding with Tata, the giant Indian conglomerate, in January 2012.

A further factor affecting managers' internationalization attitudes is how well they process the failures of past foreign ventures (Desislava and van Witteloostuijn 2007). For example, the problems that British retailer Marks & Spencer faced in the USA and France in the mid-1990s did not prevent it from renewing its ambitions in these countries some 15 years later. Some companies are disheartened if their first internationalization efforts fail but others keep trying.

SMEs and internationalization

Lastly, company size is also a major factor in internationalization. Small and medium-sized enterprises (SMEs) face many obstacles when entering foreign markets, first and foremost being their comparative lack of resources (see Chapter 5). SMEs are often family-owned, a factor that can on occasion correlate negatively with internationalization (Fernandez and Nieto 2006). One of the reasons is that a firm lacking corporate shareholders will have problems accessing the substantial funding that foreign operations often require. Even when family-run SMEs do go abroad, observers have noted a tendency for many to go particularly slowly, especially where the internationalization move involves bridging significant 'psychic distance', or managers' sense of how great a difference there is between home and host country business cultures (Kontinen and Ojala 2010). Excluded from costlier opportunities (large company takeovers or big marketing campaigns), family-run SMEs are often restricted to smaller actions in well-defined niches. This often forces them to join a network with other firms to achieve critical mass. For example, small vineyards in south-west France have tried to optimize their international marketing operations by banding together in an association called the *Conseil Interprofessionnel du Vin de Bordeaux* (CIVB). Family-run firms may also lack the managerial competencies to attack foreign markets, although it is worth noting that this shortcoming has given birth to an entire consultancy activity for SMEs trying to enter challenging international business environments. US computer-maker Intel, for instance, has set up an alliance with partners from the Chinese city of Guangdong, establishing a payment platform facilitating SMEs' local transactions (Hooi 2011). Similarly, there is the 'Launchpad' service that the Chinese British Business Council provides to help UK businesses to hire individuals capable of representing them in China. This has become a necessity given many Chinese companies' refusal to deal with anyone other than 'the big boys' (Moody 2001).

In long-term strategic terms, SMEs can react to their size handicap in one of two ways. Some become extremely cautious and opt for a less financially committed and faster form of internationalization, such as exporting (Cassman and Golovko 2011) or licensing/franchising (Hutchinson et al. 2006). Conversely, others decide to respond even more radically and opt for 'accelerated internationalization', an approach where they change their entire focus specifically to take advantage of foreign opportunities (Chetty and Campbell-Hunt 2003). Observers have noted that these sudden shifts in strategy are often sparked by the fact that managers in the internationalizing company have developed a particular relationship with members of their ethnic community residing in the target host country (Prashantham 2011).

+ Licensing
Contract where a licensor grants permission to a licensee to use one of its assets, usually intellectual property. In return, the licensor will receive royalties.

+ Franchising
Contract where a franchiser grants permission to a franchisee to run a business bearing its name, often using supplies that it provides. In return, the franchiser will receive income, often based on the franchise's performance.

This is very different from the gradual approach envisaged under the Nordic (Uppsala) 'stages' theory. The choice between these two options depends on the strategic attitudes of the SMEs' owner-managers, whose personalities have a much greater impact within smaller structures than they would in larger MNEs (Lloyd-Reason and Mughan 2002). At this level, like so many others, the link between psychology and strategy is crucial to understanding international business.

Trade vs. FDI: Drawing the boundaries of the firm

International business theory has traditionally suggested that export is the better market entry choice if a company faces major cultural or institutional barriers (and if economies of scale are a key factor of success), whereas FDI is more suitable when the target market is very distant from the MNE's home country (Lankhuizen et al. 2011). This proposition has been somewhat weakened in recent years by the way in which ICT facilitates long-distance customer servicing and intra-firm communications (Philippe and Leo 2011). The simpler and safer explanation is therefore that managers' internationalization decisions are rooted in their corporate culture. Thus, companies characterized by a minimal commitment to internationalization might prefer, irrespective of the strategic argument, to take delivery of foreign purchases, or transfer ownership of foreign sales, at their 'factory gate', if only because they want to avoid logistics complications or similar problems. In this sense, trade is easier than FDI since it does not require the company to go beyond its current capabilities.

The attraction for easier solutions explains why some large MNEs that could afford to develop wholly owned foreign affiliates have decided otherwise. As explained in Chapter 5, since the 1980s more and more companies have opted for a 'small is beautiful' mindset, preferring to outsource certain operations to other companies who might be able to do them better and/or more cheaply. Designing the boundaries of the firm is one of the main actions that international managers must take (see Figure 9.3) and the trade vs. FDI choice is a crucial part of this decision, which has financial aspects as well as psychological and strategic ones. If the FDI costs the firm more than the profit margins that will have to be paid to external suppliers or vendors once they become part of the value chain, then using import/export as a prime mode of internationalization makes sense. If FDI costs less, then it is worth considering.

Firms that take direct responsibility for few of their value chain operations are said to have narrowly drawn boundaries **(see ORC Extension material 9.2)**. Such firms necessarily rely on having good relations with partners operating in their value chains. This dependency is a source of potential problems. Contracts with other firms may be incomplete and not cover

+ Boundaries of the firm
Range of value chain operations that a company does by itself without turning to outside partners.

> Go online

Figure 9.3
Value added in a shared international value chain.

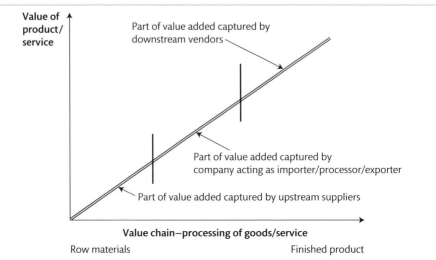

	Advantages	Disadvantages	
Trade only (import/export)	• Easier to manage, requires less knowledge • Engages less capital, thus lower risk • Keeps balance sheet smaller and more flexible, thus more responsive to changing economic situations	• Firm develops less overseas experience • The value added generated during the good's transformation will have to be shared with other companies • Depends on partners; risk of opportunistic behaviour	Figure 9.4 Trade is often a simpler option than FDI but also creates strategic vulnerabilities.
FDI	• Control/confidentiality • Higher profit potential/visibility • Increases knowledge of/comfort with foreign market	• Harder to manage • Harder to finance • Greater risk of failure	

certain scenarios, performance can be disappointing (bad quality, unreliable deliveries, late payments), and sharing crucial know-how is always a problem (Gilpin 2001). There is also the risk that an opportunistic supplier or vendor will expand its own operations down or up the value chain and become a direct competitor. These and many other problems explain why, despite the added difficulties and expense, MNEs often prefer FDI as a prime mode of internationalization (see Figure 9.4).

Even after opting for internationalization via FDI, firms still have many aspects to consider. The first is whether the FDI is more property-related or knowledge-based, with studies offering evidence that the latter has a more lasting influence on international growth than the former (Tseng et al. 2007). In 2011, for instance, Australian building materials supplier Boral bought out the interests of its French partner, cement-maker Lafarge SA, in their Asian plasterboard manufacturing joint venture. This was a useful FDI that had had some consequences for Boral's production organization, but its strategic scope was clearly far narrower, for instance, than Hewlett-Packard's purchase that same year of British software provider, Autonomy Corporation, whose online data search capabilities might help to spearhead the US computing giant's transformation from hardware manufacturing to IT services. FDI that is based on a firm developing a new line of business may be riskier than one seeking a straightforward expansion of existing commercial territory (Doukas and Lang 2003), but the potential rewards are also higher.

The most fundamental distinction in FDI analysis is whether a particular action is vertical or horizontal in nature. The cost factors associated with these two modes, first defined in Chapter 5, are worth exploring in greater detail (Barba Navaretti and Venables 2004).

Vertical vs. horizontal internationalization

As explained previously, the main reason for MNEs to engage in vertical FDI up and down their global value chains is to reduce dealings, hence potential problems, with outside partners. At an extreme, vertical FDI can lead to specialist 'focused factories' being built in different countries, each engaged in one specific aspect of the total production processes (see Chapter 11). The strength of this kind of manufacturing organization is that all units can benefit from the particular competitive advantages inherent to their location. In Asia, for example, it is noteworthy how low-skill work like textile weaving has generally moved to countries like Bangladesh, where labour is abundant, whereas more technological work like microprocessor development is centralized in scientifically more advanced countries like Singapore, where capital is abundant. This trend fits in with the Heckscher–Ohlin factor proportions theory discussed in Chapter 2.

Vertically integrated MNEs like ABB will centralize the production of certain sub-assemblies in particular plants before transferring them to sister units elsewhere

Source: ABB

Vertical internationalization

The consequence of having factories focused on a single activity (see Chapter 11) is that each plant in the value chain will then produce and/or export a larger quantity of the particular good for which it is responsible. This increases plant-level economies of scale and learning. Swiss–Swedish MNE ABB, for instance, uses its Ludvika site to make many of the electrical modules (like current transformers or voltage transformers) that it sells to customers and/ or fits into more complex products that ABB manufactures elsewhere. Many companies' internationalization efforts involve FDI creating a specialist in-house unit that will then trade with sister units worldwide up and down the value chain. The separation between MNEs' trade and FDI activities can be artificial. The two are often complementary.

The downside for MNEs with this sort of configuration is that it increases the need to ship goods (and services) between different sites, adding to 'trade costs' such as packaging, freight, and tariffs. More time can also be lost in transit. Some MNEs address this problem by running production operations on only a very few sites, often located near their final product assembly plants. Examples include the *maquiladora* components factories that several US industrials have set up in north Mexico near the American border, or automotive parts plants that German car-makers have built in neighbouring East European countries like Hungary. At a certain point, however, managers may decide that vertical internationalization's firm-wide trade costs outweigh its benefits. They might then opt for 'vertical disintegration', or the outsourcing solution that Chapter 11 describes in greater detail.

Horizontal internationalization

Chapter 5 introduced the concept of horizontal FDI, where firms reproduce abroad the same activities as the ones they run at home. This kind of internationalization is often driven by knowledge transfers and reflects MNEs' particularly strong presence in technologically advanced sectors, characterized by complex production processes. Where there is value in 'bundling' different manufacturing stages together, an approach that countless Japanese hi-tech companies have put to good use over the years, it can make more sense for manufacturers to maximize their global production activity on a single manufacturing site, especially since this helps to maintain the confidentiality that is so important in hi-tech. Some companies

	Vertical FDI	Horizontal FDI
Purpose	Internalize global value chain	Leverage existing competencies abroad
Facilities	Focused factories	Multi-function facilities
Economies of scale	Plant-level	Firm-level
Trade	Often intra-firm	Often in host country
Weakness	High trade costs	Duplication of overheads

Figure 9.5
The two main FDI strategies.

might even feel that the best way to protect trade secrets is simply to export finished products from their original plant(s) and avoid FDI altogether. However, if international sales expand too quickly, a single site can quickly run into capacity constraints. Horizontal internationalization is the logical response to this.

Of course, horizontal FDI also costs more, since it involves duplicating certain activities on several sites. This can become particularly expensive when each new site is designed to service one specific market instead of servicing customers or sister units worldwide. Moreover, output from the new plants that an MNE has built according to a horizontal logic tends to reduce the need for exports from existing units, affecting their economies of scale. It remains that these are losses felt at the individual plant level. On a broader plane, it is possible to develop firm-level economies of scale through horizontal FDI, since many assets will not have to be replicated everywhere. This includes some tangible assets but especially intangible ones like scientific know-how, patents, or brand reputation. In large MNEs with worldwide sales, shared resources of this kind go a long way towards paying the extra cost of horizontal FDI as opposed to other modes of internationalization. Figure 9.5 summarizes the advantages and disadvantages of these two modes of market entry.

In sum, most large MNEs have a variety of reasons for, and ways of, venturing abroad. The course that they choose will depend on many different factors, including whether the expansion is for upstream or downstream purposes, the depth of managers' willingness to commit to internationalization, and the kinds of resources being transferred. Like all international business decisions, there is no optimal solution—just the response that managers consider most appropriate to a given set of circumstances.

Section II: Entering foreign markets

The speed with which MNEs go abroad can vary greatly. Many companies (especially SMEs) might first enter a market via an 'intermediate step' like a small, representative office. The purpose is to increase organizational learning about a destination before risking greater resources there. Representative offices are places where company executives travelling to a country can stop off to get their bearings when first visiting. This was a common practice, for instance, for Western banks entering China in the 1990s.

Where companies opt for full-blown FDI, an initial decision is whether to build new greenfield facilities (alone or with a partner) or take over existing assets via a brownfield strategy. This choice is often referred to as the 'build or buy' dilemma.

Greenfield vs. brownfield investments

There are several reasons why an MNE might opt for a greenfield or a brownfield investment as its mode of market entry. At a strategic level, greenfield investments are preferred when the purpose of the expansion is to exploit technologies, whereas brownfield investments are

+ Greenfield investment
Where a firm enters a new market by building new facilities.

+ Brownfield investment
Where a firm enters a new market by buying existing facilities.

preferred when the purpose is to acquire downstream capabilities and service the local market (Anand and Delios 2002). This largely reflects the fact that, with a greenfield mode, it is easier to preserve the confidential nature of a company's technological knowledge, since this can be transferred internally from the MNE's existing sites to its new locations. For example, Intel's chosen method for growing its operations in Costa Rica has been to construct greenfield 'campuses' hosting research and other functions on sites located 12 miles outside the nation's capital. Novartis did something similar when it developed its Changshu Pharmaceutical Development Centre alongside the Yangtze River, using this new platform to develop, manufacture, and ship products targeting diseases that have a high incidence in China. On the other hand, where commercial knowledge is the key factor of success, a brownfield entry will usually be deemed more appropriate. One example is the decision made in 2011 by British educational specialist Pearson to enter China by acquiring successful local English language test company Global Education and Technology Group, paying $294 million instead of growing organically and building its own facilities. Among other reasons, it was felt that the target company's longstanding relationships with school networks would have taken too long to replace.

In practical terms, MNEs facing this 'build or buy' dilemma have different variables to consider. One advantage of the greenfield approach is that it saves a firm from having to spend time and effort on identifying and acquiring an appropriate target—assuming that one even exists. One example was when German retailer Metro realized that, to develop a functional supply chain in India, it needed to build its own facilities (refrigerated transportation is a key capability for modern supermarkets). The relative lack of local agents capable of this function forced Metro to start from scratch (Bellman and Rohwedder 2007).

A greenfield entry also means avoiding goodwill costs associated with the purchase of an existing asset. At times when stock market valuations are high, this can be very expensive.

The advantages of brownfield entry, on the other hand, include the fact that the approach avoids the start-up problems inherent in any new venture. One example of this is the decision by French banking giant BNP Paribas Walmart to enter the Ukrainian market by taking a large stake in UkrSibbank (totalling 84.99 per cent by 2011) instead of establishing its own subsidiary as rival Deutsche Bank had done. BNP managers had previous experience entering other Eastern European countries and possibly decided to accelerate market entry through this brownfield approach. Otherwise, a second advantage is the possibility of benefiting from the target company's brand image. This explains why target firms are often allowed to keep their old name. One example is Vivo Energy's acquisition of giant energy company Shell's retail operations in Africa, with the decision being made that while the new corporate entity will still bear the name Vivo, when the deal is completed, the 1300 stations that it runs across the continent will continue to sell products under the old Shell brand name. Brownfield expansion also means that a company is taking over an existing producer instead of adding to the sector's total production capacities and increasing the global supply, the effect of which would be to drive down market prices, something that is not in a producer's interest. In addition, increasing environmental constraints argue against the unlimited construction of new assets on previously undeveloped green fields. After all, with the notable exception of primary sectors such as agriculture or mining, many areas of economic activity already suffer from excessive productive capacities.

Lastly, it is worth mentioning that the preference for a greenfield or brownfield entry will also depend on how foreign a particular market feels to the manager making the decision. People sense different levels of (dis)comfort when entering a particular market. Research has revealed some MNEs' tendency to prefer brownfield investments when expanding into countries that are culturally very different from their home market. This is especially true if the firm lacks significant previous international experience or plans to allow the new affiliate to develop its own marketing strategy and therefore needs to acquire good customer relationship skills (Slangen and Hennart 2008). Once again, there is an apparent link between managers' willingness to commit resources abroad and their confidence in their ability to cope with foreign environments and cultures.

+ Goodwill
Difference between the price at which a company can be purchased and the break-up value of its assets.

A key FDI decision
is whether to invest
in a greenfield or
brownfield site

Equity arrangements

Greenfield investments are often motivated by managers' conviction that they can acquire a first-mover advantage in a foreign market. Chapter 10 offers a fuller explanation of this proactive, 'push' orientation. For the moment, it suffices to note that, in the absence of local knowledge, companies are usually assuming greater risk when starting a foreign operation from zero because they know less about the host market than home country professionals do. Radically new visions developed by distant corporate executives may not be very appropriate to local conditions. In many cases, it is simply safer to try to fit into a country's existing economic fabric. This is one of the reasons why brownfield investments are the prime vehicle for modern equity-based internationalization arrangements.

International mergers and acquisitions

One of the leading categories of equity-based market entry is international mergers and acquisitions (M&A). This form of brownfield entry is usually driven either by downstream motives like the search for new markets, or upstream motives such as the search for resources or the strategic assessment that a sector is suffering from over-capacity and needs to consolidate. M&A tends to occur in waves, often because managers in a given line of business have come to similar conclusions about which strategies are most appropriate at a particular moment in time. Different waves of international M&A can have different causes, but the net effect is often to consolidate a sector in the hands of a few enormous MNEs and create monopoly positions. This is what makes M&A such a controversial topic for many critics of globalization. In turn, it often receives attention from national competition agencies, one of the main areas where state authorities continue to intervene in international business (see Chapter 3).

Examples of 'merger-mania' include the telecommunications sector, which witnessed a wave of cross-border M&A operations in 2005, or the international banking sector, which went through a similar experience in 2008. This latter transition occurred largely in response to the global financial market crisis that year, raising questions as to how many international M&A deals are motivated by long-term strategy considerations as opposed to

Figure 9.6
Value of cross-border
M&As by region/
economy of seller,
in US$ billion
(UNCTAD 2012;
reproduced with the
kind permission of the
Department of Public
Information, United
Nations)

	1995	2000	2002	2007	2009	2011
World	112.5	905.2	248.4	1022.7	249.7	525.8
Developed economies	105.1	852.3	204.1	891.9	203.5	409.0
Percentage of total	93.4	94.2	82.2	87.2	81.5	78.1

MNEs simply seeking to take advantage of one-off opportunities, often in the wake of a sudden and favourable change in stock market valuations. Most noteworthy of all is the historic rise and fall in different sectors' relative share of total international business volumes at different points in time, the best example being the explosion in raw material and commodity-related international M&A activity since the turn of the century, which shot up from around 10–15 per cent of total global volumes in 2000 to nearly a third of all deals a decade later.

Figure 9.6 provides data on cross-border M&A since 1995. The first notable aspect is its cyclical nature. Activity levels tend to skyrocket during boom years but collapse completely during difficult periods, like after the 9/11 attacks on New York or the 2008 financial crisis. For instance, after embarking on a slew of acquisitions in the early 2000s (Thomas and Sakoui 2012), British telecommunications giant Vodafone had reversed its strategy by the year 2012, generating cash by selling existing subsidiaries but hesitating before using its healthy treasury position to acquire new assets (often because of fears about regulatory constraints). A second noteworthy trend in cross-border M&A is the older industrialized countries' declining share of total deal volumes. Whereas stock exchanges in the developing world used to lack the maturity to enable market-based M&A operations, this has changed in recent years, as has emerging economies' relative share of the global economy (see Chapter 15).

The 2011 European sovereign debt crisis also had a serious dampening effect on international M&A activity, with the slight recovery witnessed since the 2008 credit crunch grinding to a halt as funding possibilities (whether stock market or banking system based) froze up again. The downturn was particularly evident for MNEs with headquarters in Europe, whose share of cross-border acquisitions plunged in volume terms to 31 per cent of the global total, the lowest since 1990 (Sivertsen 2012). Conversely, the size of American and especially Asian acquisitions in Europe rose significantly, another indication of shifting geography of power in international business (see Chapter 15). The appetite for cross-border acquisitions cannot be analysed separately from the outlook for the global economy as a whole.

All in all, international M&A can be studied at many levels. The main macro-economic issue is whether a particular country is a net provider or receiver of M&A-related capital flows. Cross-border M&A operations are more widespread in the absence of capital market controls (see Chapter 4) and when a host country government tolerates foreign ownership of national companies. On the other hand, M&A will not flourish in countries where there is resistance to foreign ownership or suspicion that international oligopolies are trying to undermine competition or limit consumer choice. High stock market valuations can also be an obstacle to M&A.

At a micro-level, cross-border M&A offers two main advantages as a mode of expansion. As demonstrated by Figure 9.7, by bringing together companies with complementary capabilities, it enables significant synergies. It can also be a relatively quick way to build an international presence.

Once a cross-border M&A has been concluded, managers will still have a great deal of work to do to ensure the new entity's success. This area of international business is explored in Chapter 10's discussion of MNEs' 'change-management' strategies, but it is worth noting that screening and choosing partners who will be trustworthy and offer a good strategic fit constitutes a major challenge for all international collaborative arrangements. Of course,

Type of international acquisition	Recent examples
Upstream (backward integration): Acquisition of inputs	Ongoing purchase of mines in Africa and elsewhere by Chinese processor Minmetal Resource Ltd
Downstream (forward integration): Acquisition of market share	Indian telecoms giant Bharti's 2010 purchase of Zain's African mobile phone infrastructure to access new customers
Complementarities: Geographic (former companies had strengths in different parts of the world)	2012 Swedish telecom MNE Ericsson buys operations/business support system firm Telcordia for its US customers
Complementarities: Product (former companies had strengths in different product ranges)	US medical devices maker Johnson & Johnson buys Swiss Synthes for its portfolio of orthopaedic tools
Efficiency savings: Synergies	Italian utility Enel's purchase of Spanish counterpart Endesa. Aim: save €1 billion a year by 2012 on administration, R&D, operations, and procurement

Figure 9.7
Different kinds of business strategy in recent international M&A.

there are also many success stories in this area. One was the 2009 merger between British Airways and Iberia from Spain. The new combined entity was able to benefit from the partners' ability to rationalize existing computer systems and branch networks, and from their complementary presence in different growth markets, respectively Asia and Latin America. By 2012, the combined entity, now called International Airlines Group, was able to announce strong growth in traffic even as rival operators were announcing disappointing results. Another success story is the way that Renault has been able to learn frugal, labour-intensive low-cost manufacturing methods from its Indian joint-venture partner Mahindra and Mahindra and put these techniques to good use at Dacia, the company it had acquired in Romania. Finding a suitable foreign partner is a real concern for MNE executives. Similarly, there is hope that Mattel's 2011 takeover of Hit, the company that produces Thomas the Tank Engine and other children's favourites, will be successful because of the good relationship that already exists between the US giant and the British target. Where no friendly partner exists, however, companies may be forced to resort to risky organic growth or even turn down overseas opportunities from which their competitors might then be able to profit.

Practitioner insight

Takahiro Izuta is Chief Financial Officer at Sumitomo Corporation Europe Group and Corporate Officer, Sumitomo Corporation. Much of his career in the group has focused on market entry and FDI issues.

'Historically, Sumitomo's international operations started with trading activities where we imported raw materials and other inputs and exported production. Often, this initial arrangement was followed by our establishing overseas offices supporting these trading activities. Indeed, much of what we do is in response to changing customer relationships. For instance, where we might once have simply purchased raw mineral resources on customers' behalf, over time many could manage by themselves. In response, we would then invest directly in mines and secure long-term purchases, providing advanced solutions to customer needs.

This approach is reflected in sales activities. We generally market goods on customers' behalf—after all, if they could export themselves, they would. Sometimes we enter a market through simple sales to local agents but decide over time to establish a local distribution company and sell goods directly. It depends on factors such as local distribution capabilities and product portfolio issues. The *raison d'être* of a trading company is to provide solutions to its customers around the world, but this means different things at different times and in different places.

Generally the key questions, once we decide to enter via FDI, are the size and nature of the risk; the growth potential and strategic importance; the balance between Sumitomo and local personnel; country risk; and Sumitomo's role in any joint venture. In countries where we already have experience and are confident of investing by ourselves, acting alone is the norm. Conversely, in regions where we historically have limited experience or the investment climate is poor and we are unsure about FDI protections, we proceed cautiously. We hesitate to grow a business if we are not confident of government support.

We have worked, however, to address such issues. In Bolivia, for instance, we have overcome negative attitudes towards foreign mine owners by being a model corporate citizen. Above all, we mitigate certain risks by collaborating with trusted local business partners who share our principles and can also bring additional expertise or benefits, especially since legislation in some countries does not allow 100 per cent foreign ownership of trading entities. In these cases we devise a joint venture with local companies or seek other structures.

At that point, we weigh the advantages of an acquisition (immediate market access, established organization) against the disadvantage of having to transform the operation to meet our needs. In some instances we might have no choice. There might be not be any operations inviting us to join them or the number of concessions may be limited. Alternatively, we might find an operation requiring reorganization. The problem is that if we change an organization, this might cause customers or good managers to abandon it. Lastly, for a Japanese company such as ourselves, there are always cultural differences. The key here is to manage overseas operations fully respecting people's differences while ensuring agreement on our business principles.'

International joint ventures

Most MNEs that want to enter a foreign market via an equity arrangement but are unwilling (or not permitted by the host country's government) to do so on a standalone or M&A basis will end up opting for a 'strategic alliance' with another company. In general, the term refers to limited one-off cooperation arrangements in specific functions such as transportation or research. The alliance in question can be given a specific mission, as exemplified by the agreement between French tyre manufacturing giant Michelin and California renewable chemicals and fuels company Amyris to develop natural isoprene. Alternatively, it can be the foundation of a broader relationship, such as the ongoing technical partnership between Japanese technology giant Fujitsu and German software designer SAP. In its broadest sense (**see ORC Extension material 9.3**), a strategic alliance can include any kind of international collaboration. For clarity's sake, however, it is best to apply the term in its more limited sense and specify different classes within this category.

An international joint venture (IJV) exists when a strategic alliance involves an equity arrangement where the MNE and its partner each take a percentage stake in a new company, often built on a greenfield basis. Some IJVs feature 50–50 joint ownership, but in others one of the partners will have at least a 51 per cent share to ensure overall control.

IJVs are interesting as a market entry mode, largely because of the nature of partners' relationships. By putting up equity capital, an MNE entering a joint venture is making

> Go online

strong commitment to internationalization even as it seeks outside help. At the same time, this partnership aspect creates certain complications, particularly if the cultural fit between the foreign and local partner is suboptimal (Lu 2010). MNEs considering an IJV will often wonder whether it is worth the almost inevitable aggravation.

Some IJVs occur because the host country (often an LDC) requires incoming multinationals to enter partnerships with local firms. Such requirements are often motivated by the desire to engineer a more extensive transfer of technology, taking advantage of the R&D-intensive nature of many IJVs, particularly export-oriented ones (Zhang et al. 2007). At other times, host governments impose an IJV arrangement on incoming MNEs because they fear being dominated by interests over which they have no control. This defensive stance is particularly frequent in so-called 'strategic' areas of activity: always defence; but often banking, which most countries tend to classify as a cornerstone of national sovereignty, especially after the 2008 global financial crisis revealed the impact this one sector of activity can have on the rest of an economy.

Banking sector IJVs are particularly prevalent in countries with a strong tradition of government intervention, like China, the leading example of a country with a policy of requiring IJVs. There is no doubt that joint-venture stipulations in Chinese FDI legislation have liberalized in recent years, especially since China joined the WTO in 2001. The country's first attempts to harmonize its banking norms with global standards, including with regards to the conditions governing MNEs' market entry date from 1994. Yet many restrictions remain in place, depending on the exact kind of banking activity in question, branch location, and whether the bank is listed on a Chinese stock market. An additional consideration is whether the IJV started out as a new, 'wholly foreign-owned enterprise' or began with the takeover of an existing entity. In the latter case, foreigners' maximum shareholdings are capped at 49, 33, and 20 per cent, respectively, depending on whether the venture is a commercial bank, investment bank, or stockbroker. This patchwork of regulations may be confusing but there is one constant: in most cases, banking MNEs seeking to enter China should expect to work with a local partner. This is a country where IJV tends to be mandatory, not voluntary.

Many firms do not mind this requirement. Indeed, IJVs are an attractive solution for MNEs afraid of having to manage the market entry process without help from the outside. Liberalization has not been a one-way street in China, and national interests regularly pressure local authorities into placing tighter controls on foreign affiliates. Thus, having a local partner who knows how to handle government officials can be of great use to non-Chinese MNEs. Similarly, tax bills can vary markedly in China, depending on how bureaucrats decide to classify a particular venture. There is often a great deal of flexibility in the way such decisions are made. Here too it pays to have a good local lobbyist (see Chapter 5). In complicated foreign environments, it may be impossible for MNEs to succeed on their own.

Local government contacts are only one of several reasons that multinationals often opt for IJV. With this kind of market entry, MNEs have to put up far less equity capital than they would if operating alone. Furthermore, like international M&As, IJVs can help companies to achieve synergies, reduce competitive pressures, and implement vertical internationalization strategies—or, often even more profitably, horizontal ones (Slovin et al. 2007).

In terms of choosing local partners, MNEs tend to seek parties capable of fulfilling specific functions in the host country. This can involve personnel recruitment, supply chain operations, and/or customer relations. In turn, the incoming MNE is usually expected to offer technological expertise based on its processes and/or products, provide access to international funding sources, and, where possible, bring a recognizable brand name. The exact breakdown of partners' roles within the new venture, as well as its legal status (usually a partnership or limited liability company), depends on how each side's bargaining position evolves over time (Abdul-Aziz and Wong 2011) and whether the purpose of the IJV is to sell into the host country or use it as a manufacturing base for exports elsewhere.

The great weakness of the IJV structure is the potential for arguments between partners. In 2011, for instance, global consultant KPMG appointed as its Head of Joint Ventures

Dr Marc van Grondelle who stated on the company website that, ' In my experience, more than 80 per cent of joint ventures fail to deliver the value for which they were created'. In addition to how hard it can be to find an able and willing partner in the first place, tensions can subsequently arise for a number of reasons, including one side's sense that the other is not performing in operational terms; changes in either partner's strategic goals; and problems of culture, communications, and above all trust, defined as 'positive expectations of predictability, reliability, and competence' (Macduffie 2011). A company that loses faith in its partner will often try to limit the scope of the cooperation. An example from the early twenty-first century was when Mitsubishi engineers refused to discuss a new design with their Volvo partners simply because the latter wanted to introduce changes at the last minute. Their idea had been a good one but, because the working method was jarring to the Japanese culture, tempers flared (Manzoni and Barsoux 2006). Once trust has been lost, it is hard to restore. Managers are human, after all; irrationality is as much a part of international business as rationality.

Many IJVs are born out of a desire to split the costs associated with a new activity but, if the partners are rivals outside the joint venture, both will be concerned that the other does not benefit disproportionately. Two relevant examples taken from the automotive industry in the year 2011 include the announcement by rivals BMW and Toyota of a joint R&D programme looking into a new generation of lithium-ion batteries; and a joint venture in China between Guangzhou Automobile Group Component Company and a subsidiary of its giant Canadian rival, Magna International, aimed at allying the former's knowledge of local supply chains with the latter MNE's technical experience. It is not unfair to predict that these partnerships might face their own peculiar tensions and it should be stressed again that IJVs have a higher failure rate than other modes of internationalization. This is one explanation for the rise of international business literature devoted to market entry failures, often encapsulated in MNEs' exit and re-entry decisions (**see ORC Extension material 9.4**).

Because of these problems, there are many situations where MNEs will consider joint ventures too challenging, and standalone FDI too risky and expensive. In this case, they will start to consider other, less-committed modes of internationalization.

> Go online

Case study 9.2

For Chinese joint ventures, the sun sets in the West

China's development since the mid-1980s is possibly one of the most dramatic growth trajectories ever witnessed in international business history. Yet it can be difficult for MNEs to figure out how to take advantage of this trend. Sourcing supplies from Chinese exporters is the easiest step but has certain weaknesses, such as MNEs' lack of control over product specifications. Engaging with China on a trade basis also makes it hard for the MNE to sell into the country as its consumer markets develop. Hence the decision by growing numbers of MNEs to invest directly in China.

MNEs must consider how to choose IJV partners in a country where intellectual property theft and poor operational performance is rife. When China first

opened up in the 1980s, MNEs often partnered with agents who had a close relationship with the communist government. This did not always work, however, since the two sides often did not view the business world in the same way. Otherwise, in sectors like banking, foreign organizations must take a Chinese partner. HSBC's presence in China has been constrained, for instance, by its small 20 per cent stake in BoCom, one of the country's largest banks (Sender 2012). To raise its presence from 110 branches currently to 800, HSBC's CEO may try to increase this holding substantially.

Nowadays companies tend to choose partners with complementary interests, as US solar panel maker

Ascent did in 2011 when it licensed its photovoltaic module manufacturing technology to TFG Radiant group, a Chinese metal roofing and construction firm. This course of action can be complicated, however, by many Chinese companies' ambition to become global players in their own right. One potential response is to adopt a very narrow definition of the cooperation agreement to avoid any confusion in the future about whatever innovations the joint venture develops.

To avoid intellectual property conflicts, some analysts (Bosshart et al. 2010) advise companies to avoid bringing their newest technology to China, hide detailed design specifications, and make the local partner pay upfront for accessing intellectual property. Ascent chose the last of these routes with its Chinese partner but went one step further by organizing a cross-shareholding arrangement

in which TFG also took a hefty equity stake in Ascent. The idea was to create an incentive scheme where it would be in both companies' interest to ensure that both benefit from their long-term cooperation. By 2012, TFG had boosted its stake in Ascent to 41 per cent, effectively integrating backwards up the value chain. The lesson is that international joint ventures need to be analysed not only in terms of their current operations but also in light of their overall strategic impact.

Case study questions

1. How will FDI strategies evolve in China over the next ten years?
2. Was Ascent naive in its partnership with TFG or is the outcome of their relationship a desirable one?

Non-equity arrangements

Companies that are hesitant about investing equity capital in a foreign venture can choose instead to share intangible assets (knowledge, brand name) with a local partner in exchange for the payment of fees and/or royalties. These kinds of non-equity arrangements, called licensing or franchising contracts, are a common long-term market entry strategy. Other strategic alliances, such as turnkey projects or management contracts, tend to be devised on a more ad hoc basis.

> Turnkey projects
> Large projects where a group of companies, called a consortium, bids to win the right to build an asset (plant, infrastructure).

International licensing

There are two ways for firms to enforce private property rights. First, where they own a particular process or item, they can try to sue anyone copying their intellectual property without permission to get them to cease such behaviour and, if possible, pay compensation. Secondly, they can proactively authorize another party to borrow their intellectual property rights, specifically because this will allow them to enter a foreign market more quickly and for a lower investment (thus a lesser risk) than if they were acting on their own. The legal term for this kind of authorization is licensing, materializing in a contract between one party granting rights (the 'licensor') and another party (the 'licensee') receiving them, usually in exchange for the payment of licensing fees and/or royalties.

Licensing contracts typically contain many specific clauses, starting with a precise definition of the product or process covered in the agreement and including the geographic territory where it applies, the duration, the licensor's remuneration, and any contract termination/renewal terms. International licensing agreements apply in many different areas but are often manufacturing-related. According to the International Licensing Industry Merchandisers' Association (http://www.licensing.org), the four leading areas of licensing are: character and entertainment (replication of figures from movies, television, and so on); corporate trademarks and brands (for example, Coca-Cola licenses bottlers worldwide to produce and market its products); fashion licensing (involving the world's biggest names, such as Nike, Louis Vuitton, or Gap); and sports licensing (for example, replications worldwide of Tottenham Hotspur or David Beckham football shirts). In addition to these headline-grabbing examples, licensing also drives many other international business trans-actions. A frequent example is when a pharmaceutical MNE makes a discovery and licenses a rival in another country to market it there, partially because the cost of developing the new product means that the innovator no longer has sufficient funds to finance its distribution abroad (see Chapter 11). It is impossible to get an accurate calculation of the total volume of international licensing agreements at a given point in time. For some companies, however, this is clearly an enormous source of income. Thus, the world leader in this category, Disney Corporation, estimated its 2011 global licensed merchandise sales at $37.5 billion. By offer-ing a quick and relatively low-risk way of entering new markets, licensing overcomes some of the main obstacles to internationalization.

International franchising

Franchising's rationale and contractual aspects are similar to licensing, but the focus is more on downstream commercial actions. A 'franchisor' signs a contract ('master licence') with its local agent ('franchisee'), granting the latter the right to operate under the former's trade name and distribute its goods or services in a particular territory. To enable the franchisee to perform this function, the franchisor will typically provide all necessary support, includ-ing supplies, training, and advertising. The remuneration it receives in return is based on royalties, usually calculated as a percentage of the franchise's gross sales.

Many famous MNEs, often in the retail and fast-food sectors (Starbucks, McDonald's, Burger King), have internationalized using this mode because it is quick and easy. Indeed, franchising is used in many sectors of activity worldwide. The advantage for the MNE is that it does not need to invest equity capital in overseas commercial outlets and can take advantage of local partners' experience in operating outlets and attracting customers. The advantage for local agents is that they can benefit from the brand name and know-how of a company with a tried-and-tested business model.

Running licensing/franchising partnerships

In an ideal scenario, an MNE will sign a collaborative agreement with a local partner and things will run smoothly. Of course, like all foreign ventures, non-equity arrangements have their downsides. The royalties that the MNE receives may offer significant returns (especially since it has been able to enter the market without putting up any equity capital) but are necessarily far lower than the unshared potential profit of a wholly owned sub-sidiary. Secondly, like all collaborations, licensing/franchising is associated with a number of networking risks. These include confidentiality (industrial espionage), exclusivity (whether the partner might open up a rival operation one day), and performance (whether the materials that the partner uses or the business practices that it implements will harm the MNE's reputation).

The question then becomes how to control one's foreign partners. The contracts linking MNEs and their local agents must reflect legal conditions in the host country and be enforce-able. This is easier to achieve if the MNE has a local presence staffed by individuals with knowledge of the local environment. In the UK, for instance, McDonald's has staff members charged with monitoring local franchises' performance. This optimizes contract perform-ance but also represents an additional cost for the company.

Above all, the question is how the MNE is going to find a partner it trusts, one that has useful and compatible business competencies but can be counted upon not to turn into a rival in the future. At a certain point, companies may decide that no such partners exist—in which case consideration will be given to the possibility of the company itself taking respon-sibility for market entry, for example, via greenfield FDI. The net effect would be that the company would revert to doing in-house ('internalizing') the operations that it had hoped to allocate to external partners under a collaborative arrangement. This is an example of how an MNE's market entry possibilities shape its ultimate configuration.

Ibis, the international hotel company, uses franchising to grow in China

Source: Ibis Chengdu Yongfeng. Photographer: Fabrice Rambert

Ad hoc non-equity arrangements

When a public infrastructure project (like the Bangkok public transportation system or the Channel Tunnel) is so huge that no one company has the financial or technical resources to complete it alone, the contractor or order-giver will often organize a 'call for tender' from groups of companies organized into a consortium, inviting them to bid for the contract. Such a consortium will usually have a prime contractor who coordinates the tasks allocated to each participant. Partners in the consortium are contractually allied, in the sense that they work on the same overall project. At the same time, their ties are generally too temporary to justify an investment of equity capital. Once the project is completed, the consortium will be expected to hand over the keys of a fully functional system to the order-giver and then disband. This explains why such arrangements are known as turnkey projects.

By definition, gigantic ventures of this kind are few and far between. There is, however, every chance that as increasing amounts of capital accumulate in the hands of developing countries that, by definition, require significant infrastructure investment, turnkey projects will become a more common mode of market entry. They are already widespread in certain growth sectors, such as water systems and public transportation.

A final category of non-equity arrangements involves 'management contracts', where companies receive payment in exchange for sending competent staff members to foreign organizations on temporary work assignments. This mode of entry is relatively widespread in certain specialist sectors like health care, one example being the way that Johns Hopkins Medicine International, a subsidiary of a major university in the US state of Maryland, enhances its income by running a large hospital in Abu Dhabi. Similarly, another US-based organization (University of Pittsburgh Medical Center) has announced plans to run at least 25 cancer clinics worldwide by the year 2018, leveraging international contracts signed by its partner General Electric to build relationships with local decision-makers (Glader and Whalen 2008). Details for all such agreements (fees, ownership structure) will vary depending on local circumstances. As an entry mode, management contracts are sufficiently light and flexible to accommodate the diversity required for particular kinds of service activities.

Challenges and choices

→ MNEs are challenged by market entry more than by any other international business choice. One problem is that many key decisions must be taken without managers having sufficient understanding of the market being targeted. This could be resolved with help from a local company but that raises a new issue of whether the potential partner is trustworthy or not. Some MNEs view all competitors as rivals, whereas others focus more on doing whatever it takes to get the business done. In the absence of a crystal ball telling international managers which markets are promising, or which partners are trustworthy, their decisions will necessarily remain at least partially subjective.

Chapter summary

The chapter started by detailing why some MNEs choose to enter foreign markets via trade and others through FDI. This decision relates to how much of the global value chain a company wants to occupy by itself and how much it is willing to share with partners. Responses vary depending on different factors, including company size. The chapter continued with an analysis of international managers' varying levels of comfort with investing abroad. The section concluded with a comparison of vertical and horizontal forms of FDI.

The second section reviewed MNEs' different modalities for entering foreign markets. For companies with sufficient resources to make substantial equity investments, one of the first decisions is whether to build a new greenfield site or acquire brownfield operations, for example, through international M&A. A related question for larger MNEs is whether to develop a wholly owned subsidiary or ally with a foreign partner, for example, within an international joint venture. The chapter ended with a study of non-equity-based collaborative arrangements such as international licensing and franchising. The point was made that, where companies cannot resolve problems with partners, they might prefer to run their multinational activities in-house. This begs the question of how such operations are to be structured. Chapter 10 tries to provide an answer.

Case study 9.3

From Spain to your doorstep: Inditex goes global

Having grown within one generation from a small provincial company to one of the world's two largest clothing manufacturers, Inditex's internationalization trajectory deserves close analysis. After an early period where the company (http://www.inditex.com) merely made clothes, founder Amancio Ortega Gaona decided on a forward integration strategy in 1975 and opened up his first Zara brand store in La Coruna in north-west Spain. His new 'fast fashion' concept of ensuring that changing consumer tastes are quickly reflected in changing product lines was very successful and within a decade his commercial brand, Zara, had a chain of stores throughout Spain. The next step was to look abroad.

In 1988, Inditex opened its first foreign outlet in Portugal. This choice was very much in line with theories stating that most managers' first internationalization efforts are in a country that is physically and/or culturally close to their home market. Having gained confidence in its own ability to operate internationally, Inditex quickly expanded into the larger retail markets like Paris and New York that are capable of giving a brand the kind of high profile shop window that it needs to gain global visibility. This process accelerated through the 1990s, although a variety of approaches were used. On some occasions, Inditex's market entry would be based on organic growth, with the company using its own resources to undertake downstream FDI in markets defined by strong retail demand and the absence of significant barriers to entry (cost, regulation, consumer culture). On other occasions, Inditex's growth strategy revolved around the acquisition of existing outfits, such as Massimo Dutti or Stradivarius. In 2009, Inditex signed a joint venture with India's powerful Tata Group before opening stores in that country the following year, reasoning that the challenge of entering this dynamic but complicated emerging market required greater local input. MNEs may have a preference for one or the other kind of market entry mode but it is rare to find one that has not implemented a combination of different approaches.

By 2004, the Group had opened its 2000th store (in Hong Kong) and was a recognized high street presence in most major cities in the developed and, increasingly, the developing world. There had also been some attempts at product diversification over the years. For instance, 2003 saw the opening of the first Zara Homes outlet, which opened its own online store in 2007. 2010 saw Inditex extend online retailing to its basic Zara products, while also focusing on the development of a new 'Strategic Environmental Plan'. But in general, the group stayed focused on its initial competitive advantage, based on quick communications and concentrated production and distribution transiting through very few logistics centres.

While the business model for many other clothing companies had been based on outsourcing production to low-cost countries like China, Sri Lanka, Bangladesh, or Indonesia, Inditex sources more than half of its products in Spain and neighbouring Morocco and Portugal (Economist 2012). Its reasoning is that this shorter supply chain allows the company to react more quickly to changing customer preferences, allowing the group to compete on that basis as well as price.

Inditex still has a number of risks to manage in the future, starting with the fact that in 2011 it achieved 70 per cent of its €13.8 billion revenues in the European market. This concentration is dangerous, especially given concerns that as households spend more and more on energy and food, they will have less available income for more discretionary items like the kind of fast fashion clothing it offers. Hence the group's decision to accelerate Zara's move into Asia generally and China in particular, opening respectively 179 and 156 new stores there in 2011 alone. One problem is that unlike the situation in Europe, Zara clothes are not especially cheap in China, especially items that need to be shipped all the way from the group's main production centres in south-west Europe. To overcome this problem, the group might consider adapting its historical model and open up new production centres in China itself. It could also increase the proportion of designers it employs in Shanghai as opposed to the more than 250 working out of its La Coruna home base. The decision it finally takes in this respect will depend to some extent on its strategic philosophy, which might change when Mr Ortega retires and is replaced by a new CEO who is less focused on the commercial side of the business and more on its financial aspects. Like other areas of international business, decisions relating to the way in which MNEs approach certain markets depend on the attitudes of the individuals involved.

Case study questions

1. To what extent will the market entry decisions of MNEs like Inditex be planned and to what extent will they be reactions to sudden opportunities?
2. What are the advantages of Inditex's particular value chain organization?
3. Should Inditex change its organization because of the Chinese venture, and why?

Advanced logistics help Inditex to focus its production activities in fewer locations than most other MNEs

Source: INDITEX

Discussion questions

1. Is a 'global' mindset necessarily riskier than a 'domestic' one?

2. What determines the speed at which a company internationalizes?

3. Can SMEs ever be as comfortable with internationalization as large MNEs?

4. What effect will future environmental constraints have on the choice of greenfield vs. brownfield expansion?

5. When do the risks of international partnerships outweigh the advantages?

Online resource centre

Go online to test your understanding by trying multiple-choice questions, and assignment and examination questions.

Further research

Readers will note that this chapter contains more references than usual from academic reviews, starting with the *Journal of International Business Studies* (*JIBS*), published by the Academy of International Business (AIB), a leading association of scholars and specialists in this discipline. This was intentional. Not only has *JIBS* been a benchmark review since the 1970s, but the 'modes of internationalization' topic treated here is a key topic for international business authors.

Similar to *JIBS* is the *International Business Review* (*IBR*), a publication by the European International Business Academy (EIBA), which was founded in 1974 under the auspices of the European Foundation for Management Development. Both AIB and EIBA are active associations that, in addition to publishing reviews, organize regular events and themed conferences.

Barber, J. and Alegre, J. (eds.) (2010). *Reshaping the Boundaries of the Firm in an Era of Global Interdependence*. Bingley, UK: Emerald Group Publishing Limited

This compilation volume combines two basic themes in international business studies: continued global interconnectedness, despite the recent financial crisis; and the way in which companies continue to test new organizational arrangements as they seek optimal international configurations.

References

Abdul-Aziz, A. and Wong, S. (2011). 'Business networks and internationalisation of contractors from developing countries: An explorative study', *Engineering, Construction and Architectural Management*, 18/3, pp. 282–296

Anand, J. and Delios, A. (2002). 'Absolute and relative resources as determinants of international acquisitions', *Strategic Management Journal*, 23, pp. 119–34

Barba Navaretti, G. and Venables, A. J. (2004). *Multinational Firms in the World Economy*. Princeton: Princeton University Press

Barkema, H. and Drogendijk, R. (2007). 'Internationalizing in small, incremental or larger steps?', *Journal of International Business Studies*, 38/7 (December)

Bellman, E. and Rohwedder, C. (2007). 'Metro cultivates system to grow in India', *Wall Street Journal-Europe*, 28 November, p. 4

Bosshart, B., Luedi, T., and Wang, E. (2010). 'Past lessons for China's new joint ventures', December, available at http://www.mckinseyquarterly.com/, accessed 28 January 2012

Braithwaite, T. (2012). 'Wells Fargo eyes European bank assets to power expansion plans', *The Financial Times*, 27 February, p. 19

Cassman, B. and Golovko (2011). 'Innovation and internationalization through exports', *Journal of International Business Studies*, 42, pp. 56–75

Chetty, S. and Campbell-Hunt, C. (2003). 'Paths to internationalization among small to medium-sized firms', *European Journal of Marketing*, 37/5–6

Contractor, F., Kundu, S., and Hsu, C.-C. (2003). 'A three-stage theory of international expansion: The link between multinationality and performance in the service sector', *Journal of International Business Studies*, 34/1 (January)

Desislava, K. and van Witteloostuijn, A. (2007). 'Foreign direct investment mode choice: Entry and establishment modes in transition economies', *Journal of International Business Studies*, 38/6 (November)

Doukas, J. and Lang, L. (2003). 'Foreign direct investment, diversification and firm performance', *Journal of International Business Studies*, 34/2 (March)

Economist (2012). 'Inditex: Fashion forward', *The Economist*, 24 March, pp. 71–72

Fernandez, Z. and Nieto, M. (2006). 'Impact of ownership on the international involvement of SMEs', *Journal of International Business Studies*, 37/3 (May)

Gilpin, R. (2001). *Global Political Economy: Understanding the International Economic Order*. Princeton: Princeton University Press

Glader, P. and Whalen, J. (2008). 'GE in cancer clinic deal', *Wall Street Journal-Europe*, 13 November, p. 6.

Hooi, A. (2011). 'Tapping into technology', *China Daily—European Weekly*, 7–13 October, p. 6

Hutchinson, K., Quinn, B., and Alexander, N. (2006). 'SME retailer internationalization: Case Study evidence from British retailers', *International Marketing Review*, 23/1

Hutson, E., Sinkovics, R., and Berrill, J. (eds.) (2011). *Firm-Level Internationalization, Regionalism and Globalization*. Basingstoke: Palgrave Macmillan

Kontinen, T. and Ojala, A. (2010). 'Internationalization pathways of family SMEs: Psychic distance as a focal point', *Journal of Small Business and Enterprise Development*, 17/3, pp. 437–454

Lankhuizen, M., de Groot, H. L. F., and Linders, G-J. M. (2011). 'The trade-off between foreign direct investments and exports: The role of multiple dimensions of distance', *The World Economy*, 34/8, pp. 1395–1416 (1 August)

Li, J. and Rugman, A. (2007). 'Real options and the theory of foreign direct investment', *International Business Review*, 16/6 (December)

Lloyd-Reason, L. and Mughan, T. (2002). 'Strategies for internationalization within SMEs: The key role of the owner-manager', *Journal of Small Business and Enterprise Development*, 9/2

Lu, L-T. (2010). *International Joint Ventures: A Cultural Perspective*. Saarbrucken, Germany: Lap Lambert Academic Publishing

Macduffie, J. (2011). 'Inter-organizational trust and the dynamics of distrust', *Journal of International Business Studies*, 42, pp. 35–47

McKinsey (2011). 'The making of an emerging-market champion', August, available at http://www.mckinseyquarterly.com/, accessed 28 January 2012

Manzoni, J.-F. and Barsoux, J.-L. (2006). 'Untangling alliances and joint ventures', *Financial Times*, 19 October, http://www.ft.com, accessed 11 April 2008

Moody, A. (2011). 'Different ways of doing business', *China Daily—European Weekly*, 7–13 October, p. 21

Nadkarni, S. and Perez, P. (2007). 'Prior conditions and early international commitment: The mediating role of domestic mindset', *Journal of International Business Studies*, 38/1 (January)

Nadolska, A. and Barkema, H. (2007). 'Learning to internationalise: The pace and success of foreign acquisitions', *Journal of International Business Studies*, 38/7 (December)

Philippe, J. and Leo, P. (2011). 'Influence of entry modes and relationship modes on business services internationalisation', *The Service Industries Journal*, 31/4, pp. 643–656 (March)

Prashantham, S. (2011). 'Social capital and Indian micromultinationals', *British Journal of Management*, 22/1, pp. 4–20 (March)

Ripollés, M., Blesa, A., and Monferrer, D. (2011a). 'Role of international precocity in born global firms', *International Journal of Technology Transfer and Commercialisation*, 10/3–4, .pp. 247–267 (June)

Ripollés, M., Andreu, B., and Monferrer, D. (2011b). 'Factors enhancing the choice of higher resource commitment entry modes in international new ventures', *International Business Review*, 21/4 (August)

Ruzzier, M., Hisrich, R. D., and Antoncic, B. (2006). 'SME internationalization research: Past, present, and future', *Journal of Small Business and Enterprise Development*, 13/4

Sender, H. (2012). 'HSBC sets target of 800 branches in China', *Financial Times*, 15 February, p. 15

Sivertsen, C. (2012). 'A mixed year for M&A', January, available at http://www.mckinseyquarterly.com/, accessed 28 January 2012

Slangen, A. and Hennart, J.-F. (2008). 'Do multinationals really prefer to enter culturally distant countries through greenfields rather than through acquisitions?', *Journal of International Business Studies*, 39/3

Slovin, M., Sushka, M., and Mantecon, T. (2007). 'Analyzing joint ventures as corporate control activity', *Journal of Banking & Finance*, 31/8 (August)

Song, H. (2011). 'Chinese private direct investment and overseas Chinese network in Africa', *China and World Economy*, 19/4, pp. 109–126 (July)

Thomas, D. and Sakoui, A. (2012). 'Vodafone keeps its merger powder dry', *Financial Times*, 15 February, p. 19

Thompson, C. and Jones, A. (2012). 'InterContinental Hotels checks out growth in emerging markets', *Financial Times*, 15 February, p. 19

Tseng, C.-H., Tansuhaj, P., Hallagan, W., McCullough, J., and Tseng, C.-H. (2007). 'Effects of firm resources on growth in multinationality', *Journal of International Business Studies*, 38/6 (November)

Tuppura, A., Saarenketo, S., Puumalainen, K., Jantunen, J., and Kyläheiko, K. (2008). 'Linking knowledge, entry timing and internationalization strategy', *International Business Review*, 17/4 (August)

UNCTAD—United Nations Conference on Trade and Development (2012). *World Investment Report annex tables*, available at http://www.unctad.org, accessed 4 November 2012

Vahne, J., Ivarsson, I., and Johanson, J. (2011). 'The tortuous road to globalization for Volvo's heavy truck business: Extending the scope of the Uppsala model', *International Business Review*, 20/1, pp. 1–14 (February)

Zhang, Y., Haiyang, L., Hitt, M., and Cui, G. (2007). 'R&D intensity and international joint venture performance in an emerging market: Moderating effects of market focus and ownership structure', *Journal of International Business Studies*, 38/7 (December)

10 Organization of multinational enterprises

Learning objectives

After reading this chapter, you will be able to:

✦ track changes over time in MNEs' organizational paradigms

✦ assess how MNEs organize themselves in relation to their circumstances

✦ apply sociological principles to MNE structures

✦ link the location of power within an MNE to its strategic purpose

Case study 10.1

MNE restructuring: Unilever united

When a company has survived for as long as Unilever (http://www.unilever.com) it knows that new challenges often necessitate new strategies and structures. This grand old name in European consumer goods, the manufacturer of famous household brands like Lipton tea, Knorr soup, Lux soap, and Vaseline, has traditionally run a decentralized organization, partially reflecting its dual Dutch and British origins. Moreover, like most companies in the fast-moving consumer goods sector, it has long considered adaptation as its key factor of success, even before consumer markets began globalizing. This vision remains central to Unilever's self-image, with the company claiming a 'multi-local' focus even as it coordinates operations in nearly 100 countries worldwide. The problem in today's hyper-competitive environment is that multinationals running similar operations in several countries are not very cost-effective.

With Unilever achieving lower operating profits in the early 2000s than its great rival, Proctor and Gamble, CEO Patrick Cescau sensed the need to streamline the organization and launched an initiative called 'One Unilever'. The first step of this process involved thinning out Unilever's top ranks, with half of all 1200 executives worldwide losing their job by the end of 2005 (Ball and Patrick 2007). A new senior team was established, consisting of three Regional Presidents (for Europe, the Americas, and Asia/Africa), two Product Category Heads, one Chief Financial Officer, and one Chief Human Resources Officer. This compact but diverse committee, pooling competencies in functional, product, and geographic areas, set the tone for leaner management structures at lower, more operational levels. A case in point was the change made to the European Foods research and development (R&D) centre that,

having once employed 1160 people on 60 sites stretching across Europe, was now asked to run only 29 sites, leading to a loss of 240 jobs. In this simpler and tighter R&D structure, new product development would be run out of six European 'Centres of Excellence', sized to both ensure a concentration of technical capabilities across all categories and encompass all global, regional, and local innovations. A decision was also made to consolidate and amalgamate different country and factory teams, making each more diverse and adapted to local circumstances; a key factor in the implementation of food innovation.

By the completion of 'Unilever One' in 2009, the group had a very different look from its traditional model of autonomous national subsidiaries. Yet this initiative was just one step in an ongoing restructuring process. In mid-2011, Unilever announced on its website that it had decided that to 'drive speed-to-market behind further simplification and efficiency' and achieve 'scalable innovation', it needed to lodge responsibility for all of its 'go-to-market' activities in the hands of one individual, Chief Operating Officer Harish Manwani. This further step towards centralization meant that the Unilever of 2012 barely resembled its ancestor of just one decade before.

Case study questions

1. Why has Unilever traditionally had a decentralized multinational structure and why was this decentralization no longer considered appropriate by 2005?
2. How might Unilever's post-2005 restructuring organization be described?

236

Figure 10.1
Organizational
intentions, structures,
circumstances, and
performance are
interrelated.

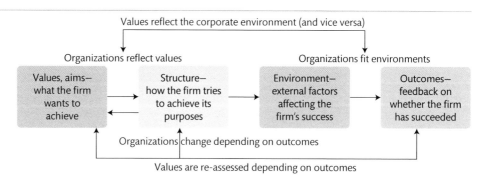

Values reflect the corporate environment (and vice versa)

Organizations reflect values

Organizations fit environments

| Values, aims— what the firm wants to achieve | Structure— how the firm tries to achieve its purposes | Environment— external factors affecting the firm's success | Outcomes— feedback on whether the firm has succeeded |

Organizations change depending on outcomes

Values are re-assessed depending on outcomes

Introduction

Where Chapter 9 highlighted market entry, this chapter considers how MNEs manage their existing operations. The two topics are not entirely unrelated, since many internationalization decisions are specifically taken because an MNE wants to assume a particular cross-border shape, referred to here as a 'configuration'. Above all, MNEs can face considerable difficulties when coordinating the activities and objectives of subsidiaries that can be geographically distant and culturally diverse.

There are several reasons why MNEs are so difficult to configure. As Figure 10.1 shows, organizations can evolve and are susceptible to internal and external influences. The structures that a group executive establishes to achieve certain goals are likely to affect employees' world views and future behaviour. What cannot be predicted with certainty is the feedback effect that these new attitudes and actions will have on the structures in which they take shape. In addition, as executives' organizational efforts are often focused on corporate objectives, there is a risk that MNE configurations will be poorly adapted to the diverse and sometimes contradictory environments in which they operate. Sociologists like Talcott Parsons (1964) have studied the ways in which the efforts of a system (such as an organization) to adapt to its circumstances can be at odds with its need to ensure internal coherency. In international business as in other social sciences, structures and mindsets influence one another. When examining the succession of structures and modes of control that MNEs have implemented over time, it is worth remembering that philosophies fall in and out of fashion.

Section I: Multinational theories and structures

Management theorists have developed a wide range of models to explain companies' international behaviour. For example, cross-cultural studies have highlighted issues such as national identities or else the interaction between worker and manager perspectives when companies acquire overseas subsidiaries (Moore 2011). Internationalization studies have advanced constructs like the Uppsala 'stages' model (see Chapter 9), which stresses the role that organizational learning plays in helping firms to enter new markets. Strategy studies have offered perspectives like George Yip's 'global transformations' thesis, with its emphasis on MNEs' strategic integration and adoption of unified structures serving to globalize their pricing, production standardization, and account management approaches (Yip 2007). All of these theories, and many others (**see ORC Extension material 10.1**), are relevant to the discussion of MNE structures and control.

> Go online

In terms of the specific way in which MNEs manage existing operations, however, the theories that stand out most are those that try to pinpoint the connections between companies' ambitions and the systems they create to achieve their goals. MNE organizational theories are generally based on different conceptions of the location of power within an international

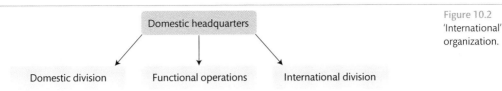

Figure 10.2
'International'
organization.

group. Broadly speaking, these range from simple 'multi-domestic' orientations (see Chapter 5) where each national subsidiary enjoys maximum autonomy, to globalized orientations characterized by all-powerful head offices. This spectrum typifies the core distinction that Chapter 1 makes between international business and globalization.

Historical MNE configurations

MNEs have long sought to develop configurations that will enable them to benefit from the international business opportunities they encounter. In 1960, a young economist named Stephen Hymer wrote a seminal text analysing how companies shape their international operations (Hymer 1976). One of the many outcomes of the FDI studies that Hymer carried out was to divide MNE organizational history into three distinct stages, each characterized by its own particular logic. This is a good starting point for tracking how MNE structures have evolved.

According to Hymer, most companies that became world leaders began life under the tight control of a few key managers working on a single product out of a single location. At this early stage of development, managers tend to view their first foreign operations as mere 'appendages to dominant domestic operation' (Bartlett and Ghoshal 2002: 5). Thus, a company's first foreign moves often involve separating overseas activities from the bulk of their business and grouping them into an international division comprised of specifically offshore activities such as trade documentation or international funding (see Figure 10.2). This type of structure might seem appropriate to firms that do most of their business domestically and consider their home market a priority. It also expresses the 'ethnocentric' attitude discussed in Chapter 7, where managers see the world exclusively from the perspective of their home country. But it is also deeply flawed, since it can create a mindset where the group executive underestimates national specificities. As a result, few MNEs opt for this structure today.

Hymer considered that one of the main drivers behind internationalization is companies' desire to exploit their 'monopoly advantages', or the unique capabilities that often materialize in the way they manage their value chains. As discussed in Chapter 5, many firms at the time that Hymer wrote (in the 1960s and 1970s) tried to internationalize along vertically integrated lines, largely because the general managerial paradigm at the time held that it was in companies' interest to control as much of their global value chains as possible. Usually this meant that the group executive would take direct responsibility for the cross-border implementation of strategy. In turn, this often resulted in a division-based structure known as the 'Unitary (U-form)', illustrated in Figure 10.3. For Hymer, this was the second organizational stage that most MNEs were destined to experience once their capabilities had reached a certain level.

+ International
division
Structure based on the idea that all foreign environments share certain characteristics that differ from a company's domestic market and should therefore be combined in a specific division.

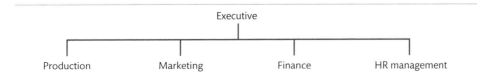

Figure 10.3
'Functional' organization. Departments are divided into the different value chain functions. All report directly to the group executive.

+ Functional
organization
Structure where power
is centralized, based on
the idea that internal
capabilities are key in
corporate organization.

One of the configurations typifying second-stage MNEs is the functional organization, a U-form in which each division is defined by a corporate function (such as manufacturing, marketing, or finance). Here, it is the 'centre' (head office) that controls the 'periphery' (the foreign subsidiaries), whose mission is to implement strategies and technologies that have been handed down from the top. For this reason, the tendency within such organizations is also to follow an ethnocentric approach to international challenges.

In a functional MNE the focus is on the different value chain operations being performed, irrespective of products or locations. This works best in companies like oil companies, with their relatively undifferentiated product portfolios, or ones that operate within a relatively new sector of activity still characterized by narrow product ranges. The first examples of functional organizations were in the early twentieth century when the configuration was applied by trailblazing MNEs like General Motors, Shell, Standard Oil, and above all Ford, whose early internationalization efforts generally involved transferring the same 'methods of organization and production as [those] developed in the parent company' (Bélis-Bergouignan et al. 2000). The MNE's main priority in structures of this kind is to ensure headquarters' operational control.

As the international business environment evolved throughout the twentieth century, Hymer detected the rise of a third organizational stage, one he called the 'multi-divisional (M-form)'. To respond to global consumers' increasingly differentiated demands, MNEs began to need structures that were more flexible than the U-form. For some, this meant adopting a product organization, with each division being set up as an independent profit centre (see Figure 10.4). Structures of this kind reflect situations where decisions made by one division have little or no effect on sister units, which should remain free to pursue their own product policies in line with local market conditions. This is especially important in conglomerates (such as Westinghouse and General Electric, and also some Japanese *keiretsus*—see Chapter 11) characterized by the absence of any real overlap between product lines. It is no use focusing an MNE's efforts on its internal functions when each of its product lines requires entirely different capabilities.

+ Product
organization
Structure based on
the idea that each
product division
should be run as an
autonomous business.

Another variant of the multi-divisional M-form structure, and one that became very popular among MNEs that view responsiveness to local specificities as their key priority, is the 'geographic' organization (see Figure 10.5). Where consumer attributes (or production conditions) vary widely from one country to another, structuring efforts along 'functional' or 'product' lines makes less sense than empowering front-line units, i.e. the national subsidiaries, because they have most knowledge about local circumstances. This structure places emphasis on international differentiation instead of global strategy, an approach that in corporate culture terms corresponds to the 'geocentric' approach detailed in Chapter 7. Thus, power in an MNE with this type of structure shifts from the centre to the periphery, with group headquarters performing little more than resource allocation, performance control, and strategic coordination missions. A leading example of an MNE promoting this kind of structure is Nestlé, which has traditionally given each of its national subsidiaries a great deal of autonomy to make key product portfolio decisions. In geographically organized MNEs, being a country manager is a very desirable position, often even more so than working out of headquarters.

Responsiveness
Ability and inclination
to react quickly to the
perceived needs of a
situation.

Figure 10.4
'Product' organization.

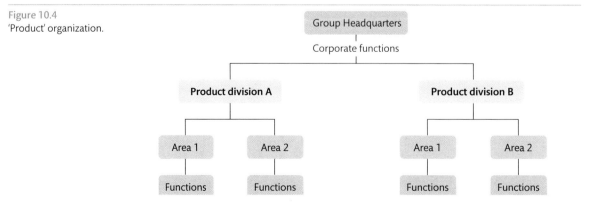

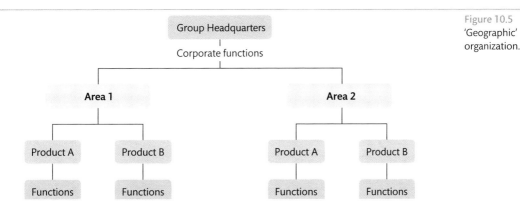

Figure 10.5
'Geographic'
organization.

By stressing local autonomy over central power, a geographic organization approaches the 'multi-domestic' logic where national subsidiaries are almost run as if they were standalone businesses with little coordination or crossover. To a certain degree, this is a conception where MNEs are viewed as little more than the sum of very different parts.

Power in multi-domestic firms is very fragmented. Greater responsiveness to local circumstances is a strength but also a weakness, since it can lead to a wasteful duplication of certain functions (such as R&D or manufacturing) across several countries. This increases overheads, making it harder to achieve group-wide economies of scale. It is one of the reasons why Unilever, as discussed in Case study 10.1, has started to re-centralize some of its group functions. The role of the head office can also be confusing in a multi-domestic firm, especially where it is asked to make both investment and operational decisions instead of focusing only on the former and leaving the latter to local managers (Rugman and D'Cruz 2000). Lastly, transferring knowledge from one subsidiary to another can be difficult in multi-domestic organizations because employees in this type of configuration often communicate solely within the confines of their immediate geographic unit. This is a crucial shortcoming in a world in which reduced barriers to trade have intensified global competition, forcing MNEs to seek any kind of advantage that they can find. One key source of competitiveness is a group's ability to ensure that the knowledge developed by one unit operating on one location can be shared with a sister unit operating elsewhere. This is particularly crucial when ground-breaking technological progress and generic innovations are involved. Conversely, anything causing poor intra-firm communications or coordination is counterproductive. This explains why many MNEs have abandoned pure multi-domestic geographic organizations over the past few decades.

+ Geographic organization
Structure based on the idea that the MNE's overriding organizational aim is to maximize adaptation to local circumstances.

Global vs. regional focus

Renowned observers like Theodore Levitt were already proclaiming the convergence of international markets as far back as the 1980s, particularly where branded consumer goods were involved. For MNEs in many sectors, this meant that what mattered was no longer differentiation along national lines (the main focus in a multi-domestic logic) but the ability to service global customers. Facing rivals who were increasingly sized to do battle on a global scale, companies would need to organize operations in a way that maximized their own economies of scale. The new goal of achieving a global reach and efficiency called for appropriate organizational configurations.

Rationale for global MNEs

The key objective for firms pursuing a global strategy is to achieve efficiency by coordinating the performances of subsidiaries in one part of the world with sister units elsewhere. By adopting this approach, units might have to subsidize one another from time to time (Hamel and Prahalad 1985). This will occur only if the group executive has sufficient authority over local managers to compel them to share surpluses with fellow subsidiaries. Thus, the rise of global structures in the late twentieth century was to a certain extent the reassertion of headquarters' power over subsidiaries. Emphasizing standardization, global MNEs tend to organize production around highly coordinated specialist factories scattered strategically across the globe (see Chapters 7 and 11). The difference with geographic organizations is that factories in this latter configuration tend to be less specialized. Globally run MNEs also try to sell similar products where possible to achieve downstream economies of scale, although in many sectors this has become increasingly difficult due to savvy consumers' demand for differentiated products. The end result in multinational corporate terms has been a 'polycentric' approach mixing elements of both ethnocentrism and geocentrism.

Above all, throughout the 1980s and 1990s, MNE reorganization was driven by the growing consensus that globalization was destined to dominate future organizational thinking. The publicity attached to a given paradigm is crucial to its acceptance. This is because managers risk their careers if their actions are at odds with what everyone else is thinking. After all, if the decisions they make correspond to received wisdom at a certain point in time and things then go wrong, they can always escape personal blame by pointing out that everyone else committed the same mistake. It is harder for them to defend themselves, on the other hand, if their original decision was unusual. In international business as in other disciplines, mavericks are always likely to stand out—for better or worse.

Shortcomings of the global approach

In recent years, a number of observers have started to take a negative view of the global approach. One criticism is that little room remains for independent thinking at the local level when subsidiary missions are decided by headquarters executives whose sole interest is a group's overall activity portfolio (Dicken 2007). A similar concern is that local units might suffer from de-skilling as headquarters shift competencies from one subsidiary to another in a game of global chess that ignores each unit's specific ambitions. In addition, subsidiary employees may feel resentment at having to follow the orders of foreign decision-makers working out of distant global headquarters. At a more psychological level, they can also be confused by a global organization's 'de-territorialized' nature (Held and McGrew 2002), one in which physical proximity has little to do with the location of power. After all, working next to one's boss usually enables better interactions than reporting to someone sitting thousands of miles away. Note also the risk in a global company that knowledge will be transmitted only vertically, from headquarters to subsidiary or vice versa, undermining the possibility of subsidiary–subsidiary information flows. Lastly, in more financial terms and as described in Chapter 9, when global organizations serve local markets from distant central manufacturing locations, they tend to suffer higher 'trade costs'.

Thus, after having been so popular in the late twentieth century, global configurations are now generally acknowledged to be imperfect. Like other international business solutions, they are applicable in some situations but not all. As Figure 10.6 shows, in some cases it makes sense to centralize particular functions, like supply chain management, because this helps an MNE to 'achieve worldwide optimisation, monitor supplier performance, check alternatives and monitor demand throughout all of the pipeline' (Christopher 2005). Conversely, it is often just as good an idea for operations like customer service to be run on a local basis, in part because this strengthens the interpersonal relations that are a key factor of success in downstream functions. One example of this is the way in which major international airliners like British Airways (BA) run representative offices in many of the countries they serve. BA could save money by fielding all of the phone calls that it receives worldwide out of just one site. However, this kind of centralization runs counter to the marketing approach that customers prefer. Broadly speaking, an MNE's decision about where to locate functions varies depending on whether the priority is internal cohesion or external

+ De-skilling
Where lesser competency is required of a business unit, often because it is asked to specialize in one or very few value chain operation(s).

	Function	Rationale	
Functions that are likely to be centralized, thus lodged in MNE headquarters	R&D	Confidentiality	Figure 10.6 Certain functions, by their nature, tend to be run out of an MNE's headquarters, and others from its subsidiaries.
	Manufacturing, logistics	Economies of scale, coordination	
	Finance, IT	Shared platforms	
Functions that are likely to be decentralized, thus lodged in MNE subsidiaries	Design	Market intelligence	
	Sales	Customization	
	Human resources	Personal culture	

adaptation. Indeed, MNEs must often simultaneously juggle global and multi-domestic orientations, the two opposite ends of the spectrum of possible organizational logics. Of course, having extremes also hints at the existence of intermediary solutions. One is the figure of the regional MNE.

Rise of regional MNEs

Some leading international business analysts have started to doubt how many truly global firms really exist today. Their contention is that most MNEs focus on their region of origin, which regularly accounts for at least 70 per cent of their global revenues (Rugman 2005). Most companies derive their main economies of scope and scale from services or products that they produce within their home region. Thus, there is little advantage or incentive for them to venture further abroad. As Chapter 9 explained, managers tend to feel more comfortable with a regulatory environment and general business culture that is more familiar to them. This latter factor is particularly important at the personal psychological level. 'Reading a contract is useful but you also need to be able to read people. Even as free trade and electronic communications bring the world closer together, kinship still counts' (Economist 2012).

+ Economies of scope
Production efficiencies that companies achieve because they can manage their product portfolio in a way that creates synergies. This occurs, for instance, when a marketing initiative sells more than one item at a time.

Moreover, running units on a global basis can often mean spreading managerial resources too thinly. In financial terms, this can be expressed by saying that global operations often incur higher transaction costs. Some reflect external factors, like economic, political, and social barriers to entry (i.e. import tariffs, discriminatory regulations, and xenophobic reactions, respectively). Other costs are internal and relate to the 'governance and organization of the activities within the MNE, [including] the costs of information acquisition and transmission, the costs of coordination, and the costs of aligning the interests of different stakeholders within the MNE' (Buckley and Strange 2011).

Despite this, many firms continue to apply an at least partially global logic to their activities, particularly towards the upstream side of their value chains and especially in sectors (like pharmaceuticals) where the cost of transporting goods is low in comparison with the cost of building production facilities. Observers have noted that much world production in sectors like automobiles or chemicals takes place in 'clusters' (see Chapter 11) organized to maximize the benefits of proximity between supply chain partners. Similarly, a number of MNEs situate their R&D activities close to the home country headquarters, because it is easier for them to register patents in the legal environment that they know best. As for downstream activities, with the exception of a few sectors like consumer electronics, it is questionable whether Levitt's prediction of a mass global convergence in consumer preferences has actually come true. Indeed, many MNEs expand regionally via horizontal integration (see Chapter 9) precisely because it is easier for them to cater to populations that share existing customers' social, economic, and cultural attributes. It is also more likely (especially in service sectors like banking or insurance, where a sense of proximity is key) that customers will have a great sense of familiarity with companies originating from another country from the same region. Furthermore, firms often find that market structures in neighbouring countries have a better chance of possessing at least some similarities with what they are accustomed to back home. This is particularly true in regional associations (see Chapter 4) like the European Union that have made great progress towards institutional integration. Lastly, the trend towards 'nearsourcing' supplies (see Chapter 11) to assure greater responsiveness to customer demands but also because of the rising logistics cost of long-range supply chains, also makes it more attractive for MNEs to work in their home region. Globalization clearly exists, but may not be as widespread as its supporters think. In many cases, headquarters' role usually involves little more than ensuring inter-regional transfers of assets and knowledge.

However, some analysts disagree with this idea that international business is dominated by MNEs' home regions, offering evidence that many operate regularly on a bi-regional and/or global basis (Osegowitsch and Sammartino 2008). Moreover, the growing number of MNEs that come from emerging economies like China and India but sell into the world's wealthier regions means that at least some companies are being drawn into configurations that can only be described as global in nature, at least in terms of the way that value chains are being organized. Over the next few years, it is worth monitoring the breakdown in MNEs' global and regional volumes, in part to assess the impact that this has on MNE configurations. One very good source of information is UNCTAD's World Investment Report, whose 'Transnationality Index' assesses the geographic distribution of sales and assets in the world's largest companies. Whereas the 2005 report had highlighted an ongoing home bias, it is noteworthy that one of the main trends discussed in the 2007 and especially the 2010 reports was Western MNEs' accelerated interest in Asia for both manufacturing and commercial purposes. The growing attraction of the Far East for MNEs worldwide could work against the regional thesis and strengthen the idea that global networks will dominate in the future as companies sell into this new growth region as well as their traditional markets. The 2010 report found that the degree of internationalization characterizing the world's largest companies had actually risen during the 2008 financial crisis, with the exception of MNEs from developing and transition countries, whose transnationality scores fell because of increased revenues in their fast-growing home countries. The question then becomes whether MNEs from dynamic emerging economies might end up adopting more regional configurations than MNEs from the older industrialized countries, forced to go global due to comparative stagnation in their home regions.

Glocalization: Juggling global and local perspectives

During the 1980s, recognition of different multi-domestic, regional, and global MNE models gave birth to the so-called 'parenting theory', which states that companies will adopt the specific organization that they think best suits their strategic purpose at a particular point in their internationalization trajectory (Goold and Campbell 1987). In this view, some managers, often working out of headquarters, will see long-term strategy as a key factor of success and therefore try to centralize all planning activities. Others, however, will consider it more effective for subsidiaries to take fuller responsibility for their own performance and favour decentralization, as it is almost impossible in today's widely flung corporate empires for headquarters to have complete understanding of everything that national subsidiaries are doing (Andersson and Holm 2010). The almost political negotiations between the two sides are reconciled (Balogun et al. 2011) in a structure that, although it can be expected to evolve, reflects the consensus view of what constitutes the best parent–subsidiary relationship at a given point in time.

On the other hand, if companies focus excessively on the appropriateness of their structures to the current strategy and exclude other considerations, they might imprison themselves in a rigid and bureaucratic mindset of their own making. Despite the unifying pressure of globalization, specific local contexts will always survive, forcing MNEs to engage in the difficult juggling act of managing subsidiaries' 'multiple embeddedness' both within the group framework and also within their host setting (Meyer et al. 2011). As noted by Jack Welch, CEO of General Electric (GE) during the 1980s and 1990s, managers will be discouraged from showing much-needed initiative if asked to strategize (and/or communicate) only within the narrow boundaries of whatever official role they have been allocated in a particular structure (Byrne 1998). In other words, MNEs should not be forced to choose between global integration and local adaptation, since both are key to success in today's international business environment. The key challenge is how to configure a multinational so that it can achieve these two apparently contradictory goals. This search gave birth to the figure of the transnational firm (Bartlett 1986).

+ Transnational firms
Companies whose aim, and therefore organization, simultaneously targets global efficiency, local flexibility, and shared learning.

Managers' mentality can be just as important as MNE structures

Transnational theorists argue that attitudes and relationships are just as crucial to an MNE's success as official reporting lines. They believe that companies must develop a 'multidimensional' mindset (Levy et al. 2007) nudging people into looking beyond their 'administrative heritage' and culture of origin and getting them to accept ideas that have originated elsewhere. In truth, it does not matter whether a useful innovation starts in a firm's headquarters or subsidiaries; all that counts is that it spreads throughout the group. In Bartlett's opinion, this is best achieved by encouraging two-way flows between headquarters and subsidiaries, as well as multilateral flows among subsidiaries. This insight has become a cornerstone of modern international business theory. It is imperfect because it hints that learning can only take place if the MNE puts in formal structures to promote this effect, an assumption that neglects the possibility of subsidiaries making conscious efforts to enhance knowledge levels (Saka-Helmhout 2011). Nevertheless, it is a very strong construct, in part because it acknowledges international managers' capacity for embracing multiple perspectives at once.

One of the aims of the transnational approach is to avoid the problems that often arise when a head office tries to force foreign subsidiaries to reproduce its strong home country culture. An example of this from the early 2000s was when Toyota executives brought Japanese working methods to the plant that they had opened in Valenciennes in northern

France. Many staff members were angry because of the pressures they were put under following the implementation of an ambitious new performance system. Today, it is rare that an MNE's centre can simply dictate to its periphery. According to the 'knowledge-based theory of the firm' (Kogut and Zander 1992), the main driver of corporate organization is knowledge but, because this is deeply embedded in a unit's local culture and practices, it is almost impossible to fully replicate it elsewhere. Hence the need for staff members to develop a wide range of capabilities that they can apply in varying circumstances. MNE structures must also be adapted so that innovation processes become more open and quicker, making it easier to apply in one location the good ideas being developed elsewhere (Löscher 2012).

In short, the transnational approach is meant to replace the one-way, top-down (or bottom-up) information flows that characterized, respectively, global and multi-domestic MNEs. One expression used to describe the new vision is 'glocalization'. Many companies apply this phrase nowadays, one of the best-known examples being the advertising campaign that the British banking giant HSBC has run over the past decade to publicize itself as an organization that is local everywhere (see Chapter 12). A similar construct (see Unilever example in Case study 10.1) involves 'multi-local' firms ready to manage challenges at the national, regional, and global levels simultaneously, depending on whether a given situation is driven by domestic or international factors (Ghislanzoni et al. 2008). This is facilitated by the fact that 'host country nationals' working within an MNE tend to differ from the rest of the local population, largely because they have adopted the corporate culture of the company for which they are working (Caprar 2011). Staff members that are capable of switching back and forth between different paradigms can be said to have reached an advanced level of organizational flexibility.

A transnational approach is a useful compromise, but it can also create a serious organizational dilemma. An example is the kind of transnational working arrangements where people are asked to assume a leadership role in certain situations but not in others. This mixing of assignments raises questions about the permanency of multinational structures and has spawned a body of management literature devoted to concepts such as 'management by projects' and 'flexible working teams' (**see ORC Extension material 10.2**). On other occasions, the dilemma is rooted in people's sense of self-interest. In a structure like an MNE, certain selfless actions are always necessary for the common good. Examples include the need to share an innovation or to prospect customers that a sister unit will subsequently serve and for which it will receive credit. Where subsidiary managers focus exclusively on their unit's competitiveness or are not rewarded sufficiently for contributions to other teams, they will be less motivated by the overall group interest (Ghoshal and Gratton 2002). Even worse, group and subsidiary interests sometimes conflict directly. The two levels may disagree, for instance, about a product's pricing or whether it should have simple or advanced technological attributes, possibly because it is at a different stage of its life cycle in the subsidiary's territory than in the other markets where the MNE is competing. Such conflicts of interest mean that hierarchical relations in MNEs run according to a transnational logic are often full of tension.

Other problems associated with the transnational approach are cultural in nature. As discussed, colleagues working in a company's headquarters and subsidiaries can be expected to interact more positively, and exchange more information, when they possess similar national, cultural, and/or linguistic backgrounds. Conversely, when people's backgrounds are very different, the information exchanges upon which a transnational company relies can be difficult to achieve. This obstacle can be overcome if employees learn to recognize the value of different cultural practices, however foreign they may seem. Thus, the Japanese business culture is just as foreign to US workers as it is to the French, yet employees at the Toyota plant in Huntsville (Alabama), unlike their Valenciennes counterparts, had relatively few problems adopting Japanese 'quality circle' practices where ideas are shared from the bottom up. In essence, this tolerance for foreign thought processes meant that the company's US workers were closer to a transnational mentality than their French counterparts. Flexible structures are difficult to implement in the absence of flexible mindsets.

+ Organizational dilemma
Where employees are confused by the contradictory interests that they are asked to represent at different levels within their organization.

> Go online

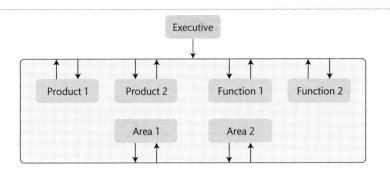

Figure 10.7
'Matrix' organization.
Everyone shares
knowledge, with
variable teams
comprised of people
from different
departments.

Creating the conditions for a transnational MNE

All in all, the transnational company seeks to maximize vertical (hierarchical) and horizontal (geographical) exchanges between all units—a principle embodied in a relatively recent structure called the 'matrix' organization (see Figure 10.7). Thus, irrespective of people's unit of origin, there are many occasions when they might be temporarily allocated to ad hoc structures specifically created to fulfil a particular task. The matrix logic became especially popular during the 1990s, when it was applied by several leading MNEs, most notably the Swedish–Swiss engineering company Asea Brown Boveri (ABB). The hope was that by encouraging multiple reporting lines and developing forums for information sharing, new synergies would arise, benefiting all product, function, and geographic divisions. The main goal was to ensure that the whole of a company would be in a position to use the knowledge held 'explicitly' (openly) or 'tacitly' by any one of its units (Davenport and Prusak 1998). Indeed, many large MNEs struggle to analyse data and knowledge stored in different departments and sites. Getting useful information to the right people at the right time is a major concern for international managers. Most MNEs have organized a range of systems and roles to achieve this (newsletters, multi-site videoconferencing, internal communications specialists, and/or peer visits). At a deeper level, however, the decision to share information via these or other methods depends on the amount of trust that an MNE's employees have in foreign colleagues sometimes working on the other side of the world. Trust, in external partners like suppliers but also in colleagues, is a major topic in international business studies.

+ **Matrix organization**
Structure based on the idea that multiple reporting lines broaden employees' vision of the business and can create synergies.

Because of its multiple reporting lines and potential for information overload, a matrix organization can confuse members and will often only really succeed if certain individuals within the organization are capable of (and willing to) act as traffic controllers. These key staff members will have the job of identifying and redirecting colleagues' competencies. That is no easy task, seeing as the knowledge that a company holds is often very compartmentalized. In many cases, this steering role will be played by national subsidiary (country) managers, who are once again starting to receive the kind of attention that they used to enjoy back in the days when multi-domestic structures were dominant. At the same time, because it is considered very complex to manage, the matrix organization is starting to lose some of its popularity.

MNEs as alliances of equals

Since national subsidiaries, on the one hand, and regional or global headquarters, on the other, are all capable of contributing to an MNE's collective welfare, there is also a strong argument to make that the only accurate way of representing a group's different constituencies is to view them all as equal members in a network (Birkinshaw 2000). The goal then becomes to encourage 'dispersed entrepreneurship' with proactive subsidiary managers communicating head office initiatives as well as their own across the whole of the group (Williams and Lee 2011). Figure 10.8 visualizes this concept. In some cases (for example, US construction and mining equipment manufacturer Caterpillar or Japanese electronics

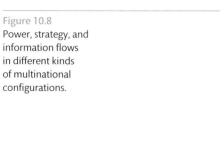

Figure 10.8
Power, strategy, and information flows in different kinds of multinational configurations.

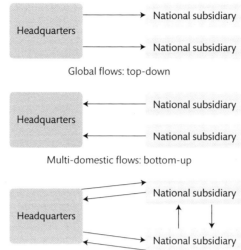

Global flows: top-down

Multi-domestic flows: bottom-up

Transnational flows: bilateral and multilateral

+ Heterarchy
Organizational principle that corporate units are allies and therefore equals in the management of their joint enterprise. In an MNE, this signifies that no one unit should take a global lead any more.

> Go online

+ Internal market
Idea that different corporate units deal with one another as buyers and sellers of resources. Related to 'intrapreneurship', or the notion that individuals behave as entrepreneurs within large organizations.

+ Federative organization
Structure whose sub-units are recognized both as autonomous entities with freedom to manoeuvre and as members of a unified group.

firm Matsushita), a strong headquarters culture means that group technology and strategies tend to be determined by the centre. In other cases, the periphery sets the pace—one example being the way that competencies developed by Fuji Xerox's Japanese marketing subsidiary in reaction to local standards helped it to become the group's lead R&D centre. Contrary to the general organizational principle of top-down authority, the key to international success today might be a more balanced relationship between head offices and subsidiaries, or what Hedlund (1986) has called the heterarchy of an organization that combines diverse and equal power bases. What head offices provide are an overview and the ability to coordinate. What subsidiaries offer are alertness to global opportunities and, depending on their size, a certain capacity for driving initiatives in domestic or international markets (not to mention across the firm itself). Because subsidiary managers are in constant touch with suppliers and customers, they are fertile sources of information, and thus useful drivers of change. They deserve as much credit as head office strategists do.

By hypothesizing that a company is just as likely to accumulate advantages abroad as at home, the transnational logic is at odds with 'transaction cost theory' (see Chapter 9), which assumes that most firm-specific advantages are generated in the firm's home country. It also contradicts resource-based theories (**see ORC Extension material 10.3**) rooted in the idea that capabilities develop at the level of the whole of the firm. What it emphasizes instead is that different units contribute in different ways to overall performance. This is an important advancement in general understanding of how MNEs function.

If power and knowledge are created at the subsidiary level, the real challenge becomes ensuring that they can be disseminated throughout an MNE's internal market system. In turn, this raises the issue of which mission should be assigned to which unit. Things can get complicated if subsidiaries are empowered to show too much initiative, since they might compete with one another for whatever 'good' jobs will increase their usefulness to the rest of the group. In this case, the centre's main authority over the periphery is to ensure fair competition among subsidiary managers competing to extend their missions. What remains after this is a model of modern MNEs as federative organizations in which headquarters and subsidiaries compete constantly over their respective competencies (Andersson et al. 2007).

Ultimately, the suitability of a multi-domestic, global, or transnational configuration depends on subsidiaries' assigned missions and degree of autonomy, which is itself a function of their size (Johnston and Bulent 2007). If a subsidiary's role is to respond to specific local market needs, then coordinating its marketing and/or production processes with fellow subsidiaries becomes somewhat less useful and a multi-domestic logic seems more feasible.

On the other hand, in some MNEs, subsidiaries exist only to contribute inputs to the rest of the regional or global value chain, or to provide customers worldwide with one standardized product. Under these circumstances, a global logic might make more sense. Lastly, in hybrid situations where subsidiaries serve both domestic and global purposes, and where managers live in a world of 'semi-globalization' (Ghemawat 2007), a more useful approach might be a transnational decision-making system, which does not obey a rigid organizational chart as much as it tries to let human initiative flourish at all levels.

> **Strategic business unit**
> Identifiable entity within a corporation, large enough to plan strategy and organize resources on its own.

Case study 10.2

MNE controls: Tata no longer in tatters

In its early days, the giant Indian conglomerate Tata Enterprises (http://www.tata.com) would export any product for which it could find an overseas market, ranging from rice, jewellery, and castor oil to cars, marine products, and pharmaceuticals. As with many firms, Tata's initial exploration of foreign markets through exports was followed by a series of foreign direct investments (FDI). The problem was that, with such a wide product range, there was little coherency between Tata's overseas subsidiaries. Coordinating this vast empire became very difficult for the group's Indian headquarters.

As the twenty-first century dawned, Chairman Ratan Tata felt a need for change. The decision he took was to abandon less strategic activities and leverage his company's internal strengths by regrouping remaining product lines into eight strategic business units (SBUs)—leather, steel, minerals, power projects, engineering (including automotive and chemical products), textiles, commodities, and information technology. The next step was to create an atmosphere in which knowledge, capital, expertise, products, and processes could flow easily between all units. It was decided that a good way to start this process would be to organize an International Synergy Meeting. This was held in Mumbai in December 2001.

The meeting, attended by senior and middle management executives from India and overseas, created a platform enabling Tata's overseas entities and SBUs to 'develop and evolve an aligned corporate strategy and to share a common vision'. Finding a common purpose was crucial at a time when Tata was looking to implement new structures. Henceforth, industry experts located in different countries would report not only, as previously, to local country heads but also to global SBU chiefs. These dual reporting lines were specifically set up in recognition of the dual local–global identity that has become a feature of many modern MNEs. For this organization to be accepted, however, it was crucial that transnational attitudes take root. This is where Ratan Tata's Synergy agenda came in.

Things evolved quickly and by 2008 the conglomerate had organized its 98 companies into 'promoter operations' groups (like Tata Financial Services or Tata Interactive Systems) alongside seven business sectors (engineering, materials, energy, chemicals, services, consumer products, and information systems and communications).

With its longstanding presence in a wide range of countries, Tata had always benefited from strong differentiation capabilities. Now, in the early twenty-first century, key employees were being asked to think along more integrated, cross-border lines. One way to achieve this involved reconfiguring Tata's organizational chart to 'combine the strengths of its various parts' (Economist 2011). The other involved reconfiguring employees' mindsets. Ratan Tata sought to achieve this by spreading the values of innovation, frugality but also social responsibility throughout the group. By the time he retired in November 2011, he could look back on his efforts with more than a little satisfaction.

Case study questions

1. Why did Tata's management decide to change its conglomerate organization?
2. How did Tata build up its corporate unity?

Diversified product ranges in conglomerates like Tata make organizational structure decisions more complex

Section II: Managing people across borders

Irrespective of whether an MNE has implemented a local, global, or transnational configuration, international managers will run it according to a set of sociological principles that are themselves worth studying in greater depth. A century ago, eminent sociologists like Max Weber (1921) had analysed the nature of bureaucratic procedures to monitor their effects on employee behaviour. Group dynamics constitutes a special branch of management studies. It is no coincidence that, in many languages, a 'firm' or 'enterprise' is often referred to by a word translating in English to 'company', or an activity undertaken by groups of persons working together and not alone. Business is a highly social profession. It is also an emotional one, as established in numerous studies revealing the significant role that intra-firm communications play in many situations, best exemplified by employees' often negative attitudes and behaviour in the wake of international merger and acquisition operations (Sinkovics et al. 2011). As expressed throughout this book, international management is best analysed as an art, not a science.

Principles of organization

When MNE executives reflect on the types of structures that will help them to achieve their objectives, they are generally guided by a set of overriding principles. Many derive from the field of organizational sociology. It is worth repeating that international business is a multidisciplinary field of study.

Centralization

This principle refers to the extent to which an MNE's head office (the centre) shares power with subsidiaries (the periphery). It is rare that headquarters possess all of the power within MNEs, since subsidiaries' greater access to local information gives them a 'micro-political bargaining' chip that they can use to negotiate some independence (Dörrenbächer and Gammelgaard 2011). The fact remains, however, that in most MNEs, the centre starts out with more power than the periphery.

Figure 10.6 offered business reasons why various corporate functions might be run out of different parts of an MNE, but in reality centralization is also a psychological phenomenon. Companies concentrating power in their centre must find a way to motivate subsidiary managers so that they feel valued. If subsidiary employees are asked to focus on their host country alone, it is important that they feel at home there. Otherwise, if they are not being asked to focus locally, they will need to have more of a regional and/or global outlook. This raises the issue of whether employees are satisfied with the particular role they have been assigned. This depends in turn on their psychological make-up, specifically their openness, attitude towards risk, and ability to compromise (Roth 1992). It is one thing drawing organizational charts but another finding people willing to fit into the slots.

Studies have detected connections between employee performance and the different ways that MNEs coordinate and control their businesses worldwide (Kim, Park, and Prescott 2003). It was no surprise, for example, when Apple announced in January 2012 that it was hiring a British national, John Browett, who had previously helped revive the fortunes of British electronics retailer Dixons, to lead its global retail expansion. Working out of its headquarters in the state of California, this relatively centralized American MNE was aware that its historic strength had been the vision of recently deceased founder Steve Jobs and the technological geniuses he employed at group headquarters. As impressive as these capabilities are, they differ from the more downstream talents required to spearhead the kind of foreign retail penetration that Apple considered key to its future as it transitioned from a product producer to a service provider. Turning to a manager who was British and could therefore empathize with the US business culture yet keep an emotional distance from it seemed a good solution. In addition to the need for appropriate structures, international business also means getting people with a balanced vision of the requirements of particular cross-border situations.

Hierarchy

This principle is rooted in the recognition of authority. In corporate environments, which are more or less undemocratic and have often been compared with military organizations, this would appear to be relatively straightforward. In reality, MNE reporting lines can be very confusing. Where employees in domestic companies usually work in proximity to their boss and are therefore clear about who determines their objectives and judges their performance, MNE employees often have two bosses: the local-country manager, and the person in charge of their product or functional area. Things can get complicated when the latter manager works out of a different time zone. Dual reporting lines have the advantage of ensuring greater coordination of local and global strategies, but if a person has two bosses pursuing two different business philosophies (with regards, for instance, to pricing, product adaptation, or customer segmentation), it can be hard to know whom to please. It is true that this kind of confusion is also quite empowering, since it can let employees play one boss against another. At the same time, it often causes a great deal of tension (see Case study 10.3).

Specialization

One solution to the confusion over people's multiple roles within an MNE is specialization. Implementing this can be difficult, however. In small and medium-sized enterprises (SMEs), for instance, defining narrow missions is not always possible given that, by definition, fewer people are employed, meaning that each has to fulfil several roles. There are many cases of SMEs where the person in charge of marketing must also assume legal responsibilities like international contracts. The advantage for large MNEs of having specialized staff members is that everyone gains greater expertise in a particular area of competency. This explains the growing tendency towards 'shared services' in companies seeking to achieve economies of scale across their administrative functions. One example is the way that Austrian-based plastics company Borealis Polymers has production facilities throughout Europe and in the

The Borealis Polymers plant in Stenungsund, Sweden. It often makes sense for an MNE to centralize certain global operations while dispersing others

USA and Brazil, yet runs 'treasury, payables and receivables, general ledger, cost and inventory accounting, reporting and business intelligence' for all of them out of a single service centre located in Belgium (Ernst & Young 2012).

Conversely, it is much harder in specialized MNEs to ensure that knowledge circulates adequately. Employees are generally supposed to avoid 'tunnel vision', which occurs when they cannot see how their personal mission fits in with what colleagues in other departments or locations are doing. Indeed, unless a company pursues an active policy of lifelong learning or career enrichment (see Chapter 14), specialists normally only get a chance to really broaden their competencies once they have been promoted. Generalists, on the other hand, may find it easier to develop a broader overview, but the cost will be shallower knowledge.

Coordination

The more specialized employees' missions are within an organization, the harder it is to coordinate them. A good way to visualize this is by imagining that each employee has a 'territory' to manage. This territory can be defined along functional lines (a stage in the firm's value chain) but also in terms of products or geographic area. The company needs to ensure that all these territories fit together in a cost-efficient manner and so that the way they are defined minimizes any duplication of efforts while maximizing speed of action. This can be achieved through organizational planning and design, and by getting different territories to adopt similar 'language systems', thereby enhancing knowledge-sharing (Luo and Shenkar 2006). This latter factor is one of the reasons why so many non-English-language MNEs (such as Switzerland's Credit Suisse or Germany's Deutsche Post World) use English as the corporate language at management meetings.

Problems can arise when boundaries change between employees' territories: because the company perceives a need for greater coordination; because one employee has the ambition of taking over another's territory; or due to external circumstances. However carefully an organization is designed, the human nature of business means that things do not always go as planned. Moreover, despite the efficiency benefits of coordination, studies of multinational laundry detergent manufacturers' product range choices in Western Europe have revealed that it also has a cost, since it discourages the kind of decentralized decision-making that can lead to optimized outcomes (Thomas 2011). It is important to recall that organizational principles should always be analysed in conjunction with one another.

Control

Companies spend considerable resources on control—or 'organizational performance' (**see ORC Extension materials 10.4**). In widely dispersed MNEs where executives are physically remote from the teams they monitor, getting feedback on whether performance matches expectations can be difficult. Multinational managers will want to visit their foreign teams, but in general this can only happen sporadically. MNEs all establish global (or at least regional) reporting systems to compensate for this deficiency. However, information transmitted over long distances does not always paint a full picture of what is happening in far off subsidiaries. First, country managers have a vested interest in protecting their local units from head office interference and therefore may not communicate all relevant facts. Secondly, head office executives suffering from information overload may not have the time to cope with anything more than a short and necessarily incomplete document. It is common, for example, for a manager seeking permission to enter a new market to be asked to describe the opportunity on a single sheet of paper. Indeed, this is what happened to one of the book's authors when he began prospecting in Sweden. He returned from Stockholm with a seven-page report on the local economy only to be told by his manager that this was too long. One constant in international business today is that people are incredibly busy. However, the ensuing need for abbreviated communications necessarily undermines managers' overall control.

> Go online

Practitioner insight

Philippe Pascual is Director of International Sales and Marketing at BPI Management Consultancy. The company offers three main services: collective and individual outplacement of recently dismissed staff members; recruitment and training of senior managers; and change management, often as part of a post-merger restructuring process. BPI's headquarters are in Paris but it operates globally, with particular focus on cross-border takeovers in Europe and North America.

'My role means that I travel a lot, which is no surprise given that our human resources focus requires us to be very localized. BPI has offices throughout Europe but that's the nature of our business. You can't just show up with a travelling team. Instead, BPI lets its local organization do a large part of the work, relating to things like work organization, recruitment, and how people are managed. At the same time, for financial reasons, we coordinate our different entities out of headquarters, using a huge information exchange system. In that sense, we are like our customers.

In terms of our actual consultancy services, one of the first things to say is that companies from non-Latin cultures must be very careful when making an acquisition in France. It's not really a problem at the beginning if the purchaser can reassure French workers about their jobs, activities, or personal development. After that, however, you get into the day-to-day management and that's where things depend on where the new manager comes from. It may not be much of a problem for an Italian or British boss coming into France but things might be unfamiliar for someone from China, or even America. Even so, I'm not sure that nationality is the only important factor in a new relationship.

In reality, the first thing that the purchaser looks to manage is finance and financial reporting. Aside from that, it depends on who the purchaser is and the target's state of health. If everything is fine, there will be no need to change the existing organization. If purchasers have the habit of purchasing several companies a year to integrate them into their groups, then clearly many things will have to change. But they'll need to be careful with the reorganization's social aspects. What people design on paper can be very different from what is feasible and will perform well.

Internally things will have to be explained, because people's connections will change and they'll need to know about their new role and often new contract. But this is probably a useful experience for the purchaser, who will have arrived with a strong idea about what they would like the new company to do in the market but might suddenly discover things that can be done to improve the sales or production organization. Actually, I think companies usually find it easier to change production since it is a more technical and less localized function.'

Learning

The difficulties that managers face in communicating complete information in a busy MNE environment explain why a new element has been added in recent years to the traditional list of key organizational principles—learning. There have been many studies on this and related phenomena, including 'knowledge management', covered in some detail by Chapter 11. The actual mechanics of learning varies, however, depending on whether the recipient of the knowledge being transferred is the parent company or another subsidiary (Miao et al. 2011). The particular mode that an MNE has used to enter a foreign market also matters at this level (Park 2011). Different companies have different traditions in terms of managers' willingness to trust one another with knowledge transfers. This is not necessarily something that will be determined by formal procedures alone.

At a practical level, MNEs often hire international corporate communications professionals to publish internal newsletters and run regularly scheduled (video) conferences. Others invest huge sums in information systems enabling a multi-site sharing of information, relating, for instance, to customer preferences. In emerging economies like India, there is even a recent tendency for companies to build in-house universities ensuring that raw talents receive the training that will enhance their ultimate usefulness (Bishop 2012). MNEs like Nestlé have also historically incurred huge travel bills flying managers to sister units worldwide to enhance their information exchanges. Getting colleagues from one time zone to service customers working out of another is a great source of commercial synergies for a company, since it extends the number of hours in a day during which a group-wide commercial relationship might be mined. Learning has become a very real source of profitability for most MNEs.

In addition, international managers also learn through their interactions with external partners. As discussed in Chapter 9, one key element in modern international business is the kind of relationship that companies entertain with suppliers. After all, it is only by accessing all of the relevant knowledge held by all of the partners within a value chain that an MNE can achieve real global reach and efficiency. This is the specific route followed, for instance, by Japanese *keiretsus* (see Chapter 11), whose historical approach has been to embed supply chain relationships in knowledge exchanges instead of emphasizing less strategic factors like pure pricing. It is a conception where knowledge flows are elevated to a priority principle in multinational organization.

Push vs. pull paradigms

The factor driving MNEs' efforts to consolidate their overseas presence is their organizational paradigm. Broadly speaking and as explained earlier, a key divide in international business is whether a company seeking to develop a new configuration pursues a headquarters-oriented vision or starts with a local subsidiary perspective. This fundamental choice plays out at the level of individual managers' cultural mindsets (see Chapter 7) but also, more widely, in regard to companies' strategic choices.

This dilemma, which some have called the 'integration–responsiveness' dilemma (Prahalad and Doz 1987), can also be referred to as 'push' vs. 'pull' choices. 'Push' multinationals consider that internationalization should be an extension, and sometimes even a direct reproduction, of the strategies, configurations, and mindsets that they first developed in their home markets. They tend to be more focused on their organization's internal strengths than on its fit with different national environments. Their preference will be to centralize power in headquarters and allocate to foreign subsidiaries the task of rolling out existing products and processes with as little adaptation as possible. Fully confident in their upstream capabilities and technological prowess, market studies may seem less crucial to them. In general, they will be animated by the idea that theirs is a new and better product or service that should be able to command a high price everywhere.

If they are right, 'push' MNEs can achieve fantastic first-mover advantages. The best success stories for such firms usually occur in innovative hi-tech sectors. Microsoft's success, for instance, clearly derives more from its invention and diffusion of top performance software than from its cultural adaptability. It remains that the potentially higher rewards of a 'push' approach are associated with much greater risks, mainly because firms enacting this kind of approach are never entirely certain of foreign demand for their brand new products. Nor can they ever be certain, when exporting new knowledge into a country, that local workers and suppliers will be able to take full advantage of the associated learning (Chung et al. 2003). A 'push' approach is always a shot in the dark.

'Pull' firms, on the other hand, specifically start by checking demand in foreign markets before working backwards and calculating how they might be able to satisfy it. They will often decentralize power to subsidiaries and empower them to accumulate local knowledge.

In turn, this helps to determine the product portfolio that the MNE will offer in each location. Using market signals as a starting point is safer, since it gives the company the certainty that the goods it produces are what customers actually want. At the same time, this lesser risk is associated with lower returns. First, to please an international clientele, 'pull' companies tend to have wider product ranges and will therefore standardize less and achieve lesser economies of scale than more specialized companies will. Secondly, the signals to which they respond will also be heard by their rivals, who might rush in to satisfy the very same demand. Since no one operating in a 'pull' market achieves first-mover advantage, there is no possibility of imposing premium pricing.

Despite these limitations, in sectors such as food or clothing that are deeply embedded in national cultural differences, success will usually require the adoption of a 'pull' approach. 'Pull' MNEs might try to gain competitive space by developing new niches, as French baker Brioche Dorée did in the USA with its croissant fast-food concept, taking an existing product and positioning it in a novel manner. Ultimately, however, firms operating in 'pull' markets are forced to adapt. They cannot ignore local specificities in the same way as 'push' organizations can in the new markets or segments that they have created. Of course, this also means that locals are less likely to resent 'pull' MNEs. The key to success, as so often in international business, lies in determining which approach balances an MNE's internal needs with its external environment.

Challenges and choices

→ International recruitment is a strategic challenge for MNEs. If they hire people who are deeply rooted in the culture of their host country, they will be able to benefit from the new employees' specific knowledge but must also ensure that they internalize group values.

Where MNEs hire cosmopolitan managers, there is a greater risk that the corporate strategy will, at some point, run afoul of host country interests. For many companies, the 'glocalization mindset' is more of an ideal than a reality.

Chapter summary

The chapter began with an analysis of three main business configurations that have historically guided international managers' efforts to shape their cross-border activities. Each of these approaches (multi-domestic, transnational, and global) varies in terms of subsidiary autonomy, production process fragmentation, and product standardization. At different points in history, and depending on whether the MNEs involved focused mainly on internal capabilities, local responsiveness, or information circulation, there has been a tendency to adopt varying international, functional, product, geographic, and matrix structures. Each has its strengths and weaknesses.

The chapter's second section showed that, however coherent an MNE's organization is, it can only succeed if employees agree with its goals. Collective enterprise is guided by a number of basic principles, including centralization, hierarchy, coordination, specialization, control, and learning. Work groups develop routines integrating these factors, and anything upsetting their habits, like a foreign takeover, creates severe change management problems to which companies must attend. International managers' approaches to these kinds of challenges tend to break down into 'push' vs. 'pull' orientations. These generally apply not only at the level of MNEs' organizational structure but also with respect to their value chain approaches.

Case study 10.3

MNE structures: When books and e-books don't mix

This case study describes a real situation, but names have been changed for reasons of confidentiality.

'Democracy' is a company that operates two separate but related product lines: academic texts manufactured and sold by the 'Books' department; and learning packages (comprised of interactive e-books and tablets that offer users access to a whole range of online resources in addition to the paper book) run out of the 'E-books' department. The headquarters and main office is in Toronto, but a substantial European operation is run out of Edinburgh. Both centres have a 'Books' team and an 'E-books' team. The global Head of Books is a Scottish national and, as the most senior manager in the UK subsidiary, she also serves as Country Head. The global Head of E-books works out of Toronto in an office next to the CEO, a fellow Greek with whom her family has a longstanding personal relationship.

The 'E-books' team is widely, and justifiably, seen as possessing greater technical competency than the 'Books' department. 'E-book' professionals are also better paid, since their high-margin, low-volume product potentially offers more value added than books, which is more of a commodity business. This difference in status has caused some resentment between the two departments. There are other sources of conflict as well.

Because the 'Books' department sells more of a standardized product, it has a wider range of customers than the 'E-book' department does. Many customers only purchase books, making it clear which of the two departments has responsibility for servicing the account. Others, however, buy both book and E-book packages, meaning that the two departments then have to fight over who should take credit for the business. Similar disputes have erupted regarding which department should be allowed to make initial contact with attractive prospects, many of whom are organized differently from Democracy. Clearly, because they want to build up their own department's bonus pools, 'Book' and 'E-book' specialists both want to take the lead role in developing potentially lucrative customers, without having to share any of the glory (or profits) that come from a new account. One solution would be to have salespersons from both departments make separate visits to the same customers, each marketing a different product. This is not very realistic, however, since it would waste customers' time and irritate them. Another solution would be to get a single salesperson working out of one or the other department to sell both products when visiting prospects. In reality, however, 'Books' employees are incapable of selling complicated 'E-book' packages, and 'E-book' employees are uninterested in selling books when their annual bonuses are determined by the profits recorded by their own department.

The battle over marketing territories has gone on for years. The tensions are particularly poignant for Edinburgh 'E-book' professionals doing early morning deals before their product boss gets to the office at 7 a.m. Toronto time (1 p.m. in Scotland). Above and beyond a certain deal size, all Democracy managers have to get executive approval before they can finalize a transaction. In the UK morning, this means asking the Head of Books, since she is also the local Country Head. The problem is that she will often take advantage of this situation to get 'E-book' professionals to do things that are in her interest but not theirs, forcing them to lower prices on hi-tech packages almost below cost, in an attempt to get customers to purchase more books, thereby enhancing the profits of her own department. The Head of Books justifies this stance with the argument that the entire company benefits from this increased turnover. But she is thinking along the lines of a low-margin business in which volume is everything. In a hi-tech business like 'E-book', each deal comes with specific after-sales service costs and is only worth it if margins are big enough. When UK E-books staff members protest because of the policies that the Head of Books is forcing on them in the UK morning before the Head of E-books gets to the Toronto office, they are accused of being selfish and thinking only of their own narrow interests rather than the company as a whole. They are also criticized for not agreeing to spend time accompanying 'Books' salespersons on courtesy calls to major book customers whose interest in educational packages is at best vague and therefore not worth their while.

Complaints from the UK team have filtered up to the Head of Education in Toronto, who is not entirely sure how to deal with them. On the one hand, if she goes to the CEO to argue her department's case, she will be suspected of misusing family connections to gain favourable treatment within the company. On the other hand, there is no doubt that the current structure is being abused by the Head of Books seeking to manipulate Edinburgh E-books personnel for her own purposes. After lengthy reflection, the Head of E-books has decided that her best option is to offer the CEO a review of alternative forms of organization.

Case study questions

1. What are the strengths and weaknesses of Democracy's current product organization?
2. List and justify the alternative organizations that Democracy's CEO might consider adopting.
3. How would Democracy's current managers and employees react to each of these alternatives?

Different markets' variable receptiveness to modern technology makes it harder for MNEs to coordinate product lines

Source: Tetra images

Discussion questions

1. Why is an MNE best advised to adopt a global strategy in certain sectors of activity and a local strategy in others?

2. What are the different ways in which MNEs coordinate subsidiaries' actions?

3. Is there anything significant about the location of an MNE's headquarters?

4. What mechanisms can MNEs use to optimize knowledge flows?

Online resource centre

Go online to test your understanding by trying multiple-choice questions, and assignment and examination questions.

Further research

Barber, J. and Alegre, J. (eds.) (2010). *Reshaping the Boundaries of the Firm in an Era of Global Interdependence*. Bingley, UK: Emerald Group Publishing Limited

This book is based on the idea that MNEs' boundaries have changed in recent years to the extent that it is no longer accurate to distinguish between what happens inside and outside of them. Instead the focus should be on 'new organizational forms, such as inter-firm networks, global strategic alliances, alliances with NGOs, cross-border mergers and acquisitions, franchising organizations, offshoring/outsourcing structures, international new ventures, international entrepreneurs and on-line communities.'

McCarthy, K., Fiolet, M., and Dolfsma, W. (eds.) (2011). *The Nature of the New Firm: Beyond the Boundaries of Organizations and Institutions*. Cheltenham: Edward Elgar Publishing Ltd

Technological advances, led by ICT, have flattened corporate hierarchies and narrowed the borders of the firm, facilitating outsourcing and other kinds of relationships with external contractors.

References

Andersson, U. and Holm, U. (2010). *Managing the Contemporary Multinational: The Role of Headquarters*. Cheltenham (UK), Northampton (USA): Edward Elgar Publishing Ltd

Andersson, U., Forsgren, M., and Holm, U. (2007). 'Balancing subsidiary influence in the federative MNC: A business network view', *Journal of International Business Studies*, 38/5 (September)

Ball, D. and Patrick, A. (2007). 'How a Unilever executive is thinning the ranks', 26 November, available at http://online.wsj.com, accessed 23 May 2008

Balogun, J., Jarzabkowski, P., and Vaara, E. (2011). 'Selling, resistance and reconciliation: A critical discursive approach to subsidiary role evolution in MNEs', *Journal of International Business Studies*, 42, pp. 765–786

Bartlett, C. A. (1986). 'Building and managing the transnational: The new organizational challenge', in M. Porter (ed.). *Competition in Global Industries*. Boston: Harvard Business School Press

Bartlett, C. and Ghoshal, S. (2002). *Managing Across Borders: The Transnational Solution*. Boston: Harvard Business School Press

Bélis-Bergouignan, M.-C., Bordenave, G., and Lung, Y. (2000). 'Global strategies in the automobile industry', *Regional Studies*, 34/1

Birkinshaw, J. (2000). *Entrepreneurship in the Global Firm*. London: Sage Publications

Bishop, M. (2012). 'It's war', *The Economist: The World in 2012*, p. 131

Buckley, P. and Strange, R. (2011). 'The governance of the multinational enterprise: Insights from internalization theory', *Journal of Management Studies*, 48/2, pp. 460–470 (March)

Byrne, J. (1998). 'How Jack Welch runs GE', available at http://www.businessweek.com, accessed 2 July 2008

Caprar, D. (2011). 'Foreign locals: A cautionary tale on the culture of MNC local employees', *Journal of International Business Studies*, 42, pp. 608–628

Christopher, M. (2005). *Logistics and Supply Chain Management: Creating Value-Added Networks*, 3rd edn. Harlow: Prentice-Hall

Chung, W., Mitchell, W., and Yeung, B. (2003). 'Foreign direct investment and host country productivity: The American automotive component industry in the 1980s', *Journal of International Business Studies*, 34/2 (March)

Davenport, T. and Prusak, L. (1998). *Working Knowledge: How Organizations Manage What They Know*. Boston: Harvard Business School

Dicken, P. (2007). *Global Shift: Mapping the Changing Contours of the World Economy*. London: Sage

Dörrenbächer, C. and Gammelgaard, J. (2011). 'Subsidiary power in multinational corporations: The subtle role of micro-political bargaining power', *Critical Perspectives on International Business*, 7/1, pp. 30–47

Economist (2011). 'Out of India', *The Economist*, 3 March, available at http://www.economist.com, accessed 5 February 2012

Economist (2012). 'Schumpeter: The power of tribes', *The Economist*, 28 January, p. 62

Ernst & Young (2012). 'Sharing the load', *The Economist: Performance insert*, p. 23

Ghemawat, P. (2007). 'The hard reality of semiglobalization and how to profit from it', 14 November, available at http://changethis.com, accessed 19 May 2008

Ghislanzoni, G., Penttinen, R., and Turnbull, D. (2008). 'The multilocal challenge: Managing cross-border functions', March, available at http://www.mckinseyquarterly.com, accessed 19 May 2008

Ghoshal, S. and Gratton, L. (2002). 'Integrating the enterprise', *MIT Sloan Management Review*, 44/1

Goold, M. and Campbell, A. (1987). *Strategies and Styles*. Oxford: Blackwell

Hamel, G. and Prahalad, C. (1985). 'Do you really have a global strategy?', *Harvard Business Review* (July–August)

Hedlund, G. (1986). 'The hypermodern MNC: A heterarchy?', *Human Resource Management*, 25/1

Held, D. and McGrew, A. (2002). *Globalization/Anti-Globalization*. Cambridge: Polity

Hymer, S. H. (1976). *The International Operations of National Firms: A Study of Direct Foreign Investment*. Cambridge, MA: MIT Press (originally a PhD thesis, 1960)

Johnston, S. and Bulent, M. (2007). 'Subsidiary size and the level of subsidiary autonomy in multinational corporations: A quadratic model investigation of Australian subsidiaries', *Journal of International Business Studies*, 38/5 (September)

Kim, K., Park, J.-H., and Prescott, J. (2003). 'The global integration of business functions: A study of multinational business units in global industries', *Journal of International Business Strategy*, 34/4 (July)

Kogut, B. and Zander, U. (1992). 'Knowledge of the firm, combinative capabilities, and the replication of technology', *Organization Science*, 3/3

Levy, O., Beechler, S., Taylor, S., and Boyacigiller, N. (2007). 'What we talk about when we talk about ' "Global Mindset" ': Managerial cognition in multinational corporations', *Journal of International Business Studies*, 38/2 (March)

Löscher, P. (2012). 'Less is more', *The Economist: The World in 2012*, p. 131

Luo, Y. and Shenkar, O. (2006). 'The multinational organization as a multilingual community: Language and organization in a global context', *Journal of International Business Studies*, 37/3 (May)

Meyer, K., Mudambi, R., and Narula, R. (2011). 'Multinational enterprises and local contexts: The opportunities and challenges of multiple embeddedness', *Journal of Management Studies*, 48/2, pp. 235–252 (March)

Miao, Y., Choe, S., and Song, J. (2011) 'Transferring subsidiary knowledge in the global learning context', *Journal of Knowledge Management*, 15/3, pp. 478–496

Moore, F. (2011). 'Holistic ethnography: Studying the impact of multiple national identities on post-acquisition organizations', *Journal of International Business Studies*, 42, pp. 654–671

Osegowitsch, T. and Sammartino, A. (2008). 'Reassessing (home-) regionalization', *Journal of International Business Studies*, 39/2 (March)

Park, B. (2011). 'What changes the rules of the game in wholly owned subsidiaries? Determinants of knowledge acquisition from parent firms', *International Business Review*, 21/4 (August)

Parsons, T. (1964). *The Social System*. New York: Free Press

Prahalad, C. and Doz, Y. (1987). *The Multinational Mission: Balancing Local Demand and Global Vision*. New York: Free Press

Roth, K. (1992). 'Implementing international strategy at the business unit level: The role of managerial decision-making characteristics', *Journal of Management*, 18/4

Rugman, A. (2005). *The Regional Multinationals: MNEs and 'Global' Strategic Management*. Cambridge: Cambridge University Press

Rugman, A. and D'Cruz, J. (2000). *Multinationals as Flagship Firms: Regional Business Networks*. New York: Oxford University Press

Saka-Helmhout, A. (2011). 'Learning from the periphery: Beyond the transnational model', *Critical Perspectives on International Business*, 7/1, pp. 48–65

Sinkovics, R., Zagelmeyer, S., and Kusstatscher, V. (2011). 'Between merger and syndrome: The intermediary role of emotions in four cross-border M&As', *International Business Review*, 20/1, pp. 27–47 (February)

Thomas, C. (2011). 'Too many products: Decentralized decision making in multinational firms', *American Economic Journal: Microeconomics*, 3/1, pp. 280–306 (February)

Weber, M. (1921). *Economy and Society*. Berkeley and Los Angeles: University of California Press

Williams, C. and Lee, S. (2011). 'Political heterarchy and dispersed entrepreneurship in the MNC', *Journal of Management Studies*, 48/6, pp. 1243–1268 (September)

Yip, G. (2007). *Managing Global Customers: An Integrated Approach*. Oxford: Oxford University Press

Portugal Telecom (PT) is a medium-sized global telecommunications operator that enjoys the reputation of being 'national leader everywhere it operates' (Portugal Telecom 2012). This starts with the group's home market (where 11,180 out of its total global staff of 72,347 are employed) but also includes ex-Portuguese colonies like Cape Verde, Mozambique, Timor, Angola, and above all Brazil, where PT's presence is manifested through its stakes in Oi, South America's largest telecommunications operator, and Contax, Brazil's leading contact centre services company (Portugal Telecom 2012). PT's consolidated group revenues hit €6.2 billion in 2011, up an exceptional 64 per cent from the previous year. This expansion was largely due to a series of initiatives it has taken in several locations worldwide developing traditional product areas as well as new sectors, including 'mobile voice and data services, multimedia and broadband internet access' (Portugal Telecom 2012). Its future performance will depend both on the mainly partnership-based strategies that it has followed in PT's different international markets, and on the ease with which the group can restructure its internal organization to maximize the integration of so many new activities.

The main opportunity, and challenge, is associated with PT's strategic investments in Brazil, where the company has secured 'significant governance rights and proportional consolidation' of 25.6 per cent in Oi and 44.4 per cent in CTX, Contax's controlling holding (see 'Investors Presentation', 26 January 2012, available at http://www.telecom.pt/). Henceforth, PT will have direct input into the appointment of Oi's CEO along with relevant subsidiary directors and committee chairs, covering such crucial policy areas as Engineering and Networks, Technology and Innovation, and Product Offering. This level of involvement comes at a steep price and reflects the decision taken by an increasing number of CEOs from firms starting in medium or smaller sized markets to create a 'second home market' (Meffert 2011) in the emerging world. The challenge then becomes integrating a new group that dwarfs the original company.

In an in-depth interview with McKinsey Quarterly (Meffert 2011), PT CEO Zeinal Bava, who took over in 2008, spoke of his ambition to increase the group's international activities by half before 2012, by which time he hoped that foreign revenues would account for 66 per cent of the consolidated total. To some extent, this goal is based on the calculation that given the high fixed costs in the telecommunications business, it would be impossible for PT to achieve the critical mass enabling it to compete with rivals if it continued to emphasize a homeland that has fewer than 11 million residents. On the other hand, the combined power of the PT-Oi group, supplied with fresh capital through new rights issues, should be enough to operate competitively not only in Brazil, where the market is not yet fully saturated, but also throughout the rest of South America, a growth region. Additionally, Bava accepted the general consensus that the developing world is finally emerging and should experience higher growth rates than the older industrialized countries, some of which are already at a mature and almost declining stage of development. The comparative attraction of the emerging world is particularly true given the spread of wealth in an increasing number of countries from a narrow population of wealthy consumers to a much bigger number of potential middle class customers, many of whom are leapfrogging directly to more advanced technological solutions, such as mobile telephones, instead of fixed lines. At times like this, CEOs can be excused for viewing accelerated internationalization more as an obligation than as a choice.

This is particularly true given that PT had just made the opportunistic decision to sell its stake in Brazil's leading mobile operator, Vivo, to PT's big Spanish rival Telefonica, which had been its partner in Brazil up until that point. To maintain a footing in its giant former colony, where Portuguese businesses enjoy a small advantage due to linguistic and cultural affinities, Bava had decided to reinvest nearly 50 per cent of the proceeds from the Vivo sale back into Brazil. This became the stake in Oi.

PT's decision to change its Brazilian partner from Vivo to Oi was based on Bava's perception of greater synergies with Oi, which, like PT, offers the full range of telecoms services. Bava considered this essential given the ongoing evolution towards a full scale integration of voice, video, and data services. The compatibility in PT and Oi's capabilities is cemented by the Portuguese arm sending specialists to Brazil to work in joint project teams, while also hosting Oi technicians back home. Such technical collaborations are crucial as the combined group embarks on important new ventures, such as the installation of fibre networks driving the new Pay TV business. They may also change the culture at PT, where managers have learnt to take a more international perspective when considering the resources they might mobilize when addressing technological and commercial challenges. PT had once enjoyed a monopoly status in its own market but that business culture is long gone, with a premium now being placed on innovativeness and the willingness to adopt new business models and products, most of which do not originate in Portugal.

The internal transformation is best epitomized by PT's 'Meo' programme, named after its new Pay TV offer. One of the main goals of the MEO programme is to get staff members to realize that PT is open all the time and does not shut down at the end of the Portuguese working day. This cultural shift has been crystallized in the launch of an 'innovation platform' called Open, available to all employees worldwide. The focus is not just on products but on processes, or as Bava says, 'instilling a mindset of continuous and planned improvements, where the innovation team works with colleagues in each customer segment to understand the market opportunities and customers' needs' (Meffert 2011). The attitude shift is implemented on a segment-by-segment basis and is shared with PT's partners, including Oi, to ensure its broad diffusion. The net effect is PT's transformation from a sleepy nationalized company managing a legacy

infrastructure in one relatively small European market to a dynamic global competitor with hunger for further expansion.

Case study questions

1. What are the arguments in favour or against Portugal Telecom increasing its equity stake in the Brazilian company Oi?
2. Should Portugal Telecom look to expand into other South American countries or does its cultural and linguistic proximity to Brazil mean that it should concentrate on this one country alone?
3. To what extent might Portugal Telecom's old business culture as a former state-run monopoly still affect managers' vision of international business?

References

Meffert, J. (2011). 'Remaking Portugal Telecom: An interview with CEO Zeinal Bava', April, available at http://www.mckinseyquarterly.com, accessed 6 April 2012

Portugal Telecom (2012) http://www.telecom.pt/, accessed April 2012

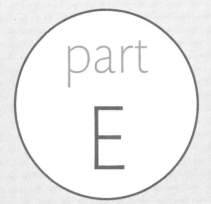

part

E

International functions

11 International production

Learning objectives

After reading this chapter, you will be able to:

- ✦ perceive the role that knowledge plays in international production
- ✦ understand the link between different stages in supply chain management
- ✦ apprehend the strategic aspects of supplier relationships
- ✦ compare manufacturing orientations
- ✦ analyse upstream operations within a broader value chain context

Case study 11.1

Nearsourcing: Homeward bound supply chains

Outsourcing is not a new idea in international business. MNEs whose first experiences in this area occurred many years ago have had time to reflect upon and, potentially, adjust their strategy. It is generally difficult to avoid the temptation to move production activities to the lowest cost locations, irrespective of the distance. Yet many companies have started to conclude that it makes even more sense to manufacture closer to home, even if this involves a higher cost location.

This strategy, known as 'nearsourcing', is particularly prevalent in certain sectors, like clothing. Influenced by the many images and cultural icons broadcast globally nowadays, consumers' clothing preferences can be volatile. In turn, this has sparked a move towards 'fast fashion', with many leading MNEs in this trillion dollar industry working to reduce the 'time-to-market' it takes to move goods from their place of manufacturing to their place of consumption. Thus, where the first outsourcing efforts for global clothing giants such as Gap or Nike involved Asian suppliers (China

but also Indonesia, Bangladesh, and Sri Lanka), by the mid-2000s, some major European names (such as Mango) started to source out of Tunisia and Turkey, specifically because goods could be shipped more quickly to EU markets. Calculations in this area are very complicated, however, as clothes manufacturing requires the coordination of many supply chains, including cloth made from processed raw materials, zippers made from mined metals, or stitching, itself a very labour-intensive activity. Achieving an optimal balance between two upstream activities (logistics and manufacturing) can be a challenge.

The robotization of modern production is also likely to reverse the trend towards long distance outsourcing (Economist 2012b). Manufacturing has been revolutionized by tools such as 'layer-by-layer 3D computers' that replicate most factory operations, marginalizing workers' importance. Given rising Chinese labour costs (around 20 per cent in 2012) and the difficulties of doing business in many emerging countries (see Chapter 15), this technological innovation reduces Western MNEs' incentive to outsource. The list of MNEs that began nearsourcing in 2011–2012 is impressive, ranging from big industrialists like Rolls Royce or Volkswagen and pharmaceuticals like Novartis, to SMEs like toy producer Trunki or Chesapeake Bay Candle. This has caused a major shift in general understanding of international production, supported by the discovery that out of the Apple iPad's total (2012) cost of $499, only $33 involved manufacturing labour costs. If this distribution of value added starts to generalize, determining where goods are produced will no longer be as important as the value generated in each production location.

Technological progress means that even SMEs like Trunki have started nearsourcing product inputs

Copyright of Trunki

Case study questions

1. At what point do the costs of international outsourcing outweigh the benefits?
2. What sectors of activity are particularly attracted to nearsourcing?

Introduction

One of the most crucial value chain decisions that international managers will ever make is how wide a product range their companies should offer. At one extreme, MNEs can emphasize the high-volume production of a narrow range of goods. At the other, they can focus on their ability to adapt and customize. Generally speaking, production specialists are interested in standardization, since this enables economies of scale and helps them to achieve their operational goal of manufacturing cost-effectively and efficiently. Their downstream colleagues, on the other hand, tend to support a wider product range, since this makes it easier for them to sell into different national markets. The tension caused by these contradictory outlooks forms a key part of the 'push' vs. 'pull' model that is discussed in Chapter 10.

Because upstream and downstream functions are so closely intertwined, it is useful to view the present chapter in conjunction with Chapter 12's presentation of international marketing. There is also a close connection to the corporate responsibility issues raised in Chapter 8, given that the main ethical problems associated with globalization today often materialize at the level of a firm's manufacturing function. Lastly, this chapter's outsourcing debate also links to Chapter 9's discussion on the 'boundaries of the firm'. Intersecting all these debates, international production is too important a topic to be overlooked, even by students not planning to work in manufacturing.

To visualize a value chain's different upstream stages, readers may wish to revisit Figure 1.2. Production is defined as all of the steps taken to create a product or service. Unprocessed inputs (raw materials) are transformed into components (or parts) that are combined into modules and subsequently assembled into the final goods sold in the market. The good increases in value at each of these stages, which is why the whole process is called a 'value chain'. It is crucial for readers' understanding of international production that they envisage the final outcome as the sum of all the intermediary transformations. A complex machine like a computer, for example, is made out of many different modules (microprocessor, motherboard, hard drive), themselves built from many components. An example from the service sector would be an insurance policy, built on the foundation of an administrative infrastructure (customer call centres, claim processors) on top of which advanced mathematical and financial models are applied. The skill of producing a good or service often means piecing together different constituents.

+ **Modules**
Components assembled into a unit that fulfils a particular function in a system. Such units can be plugged without alteration into the rest of the system. Groups of modules are known as 'sub-assemblies'.

Section I: International knowledge management

As Chapter 2 discussed, classical analyses of economic advantage by theorists like Adam Smith or David Ricardo have traditionally been formulated in terms of factor inputs such as capital, labour, or physical resources. Over time, however, it has become apparent that differences in economic performance reflect another factor as well—knowledge, or the sum total of people's experience, ability to handle complexity, judgement, intuition, values, and beliefs (Davenport and Prusak 1998). Much work has been done on how knowledge management (KM) increases 'organizational learning' (Nonaka and Takeuchi 1995). This analysis is relevant, for instance, to the Uppsala 'stages of internationalization' model discussed in Chapter 9. KM has become an increasingly important production factor since the 1980s due to advances in information technology, the rise of the knowledge economy, and the growing share of global wealth produced by knowledge-intensive service sectors such as biotechnology or computing.

KM is not only an upstream phenomenon. Marketing specialists will have their own knowledge to manage (customer lists and consumer preferences), as will financial professionals (currency regulations, capital controls, etc.). Nevertheless, many of the world's

+ **Knowledge management**
Systems that companies use to maximize the benefits of internal and external knowledge.

+ **Knowledge economy**
Sum total of the markets that help economic actors to access knowledge.

best-known MNEs have built their success on production advantages specifically derived from transforming knowledge into new products or services. Examples include Microsoft's operating systems and the Toyota Prius (a hybrid car running on both petrol and electricity). KM becomes a particularly important aspect of production when goods or services are conceived as 'bundles' not only of tangible materials but also of intangible inputs like technology and know-how (Ietto-Gillies 2012). Stated simply, some products are more knowledge-intensive than others.

Lastly, it is important to note that knowledge management extends beyond R&D activities to include the development and transfer of data, information, and management practices. It remains that most MNEs would view research as the cornerstone of their KM efforts and the spark triggering all of their upstream activities.

National research efforts

Corporate R&D environments vary greatly from one country to another, with analysis often placing these efforts within the broader context of the so-called 'national innovation system' (**see ORC Extension material 11.1**). Figure 11.1, for instance, offers statistics on leading companies' R&D efforts worldwide. These statistics are actually more helpful than data on 'national R&D intensity', a frequently used indicator that measures the percentage of GDP spent on R&D but does not acknowledge that MNEs whose headquarters or main operations are located in certain countries may use other countries for research activities. Similarly, countries also vary in terms of the knowledge spillover possibilities for the MNEs operating there. Most companies fund their own R&D but want to benefit as well from breakthroughs achieved by neighbouring researchers. MNEs often set up operations in places like Silicon Valley in California or Bangalore in India specifically because a hi-tech cluster already exists there. By working more closely with other firms, MNEs hope to achieve synergies in the knowledge accumulation process. Host governments tend to

> Go online

+ Knowledge spillover
When companies gain knowledge through proximity to external sources such as universities, research centres, or other companies.

The challenge for many countries is to get universities and industry to work more closely together

Source: Green Templeton College, Oxford

Figure 11.1
Geographic breakdown
in R&D by world's
top 1400 companies
(European Commission
2011).

Country	% of 2010 total of €455.9 billion
USA	35.1
Japan	21.7
Germany	10.1
France	5.3
Switzerland	4.5
UK	4.4
South Korea	3.0
Netherlands	2.1
China	1.7
Taiwan	1.6

actively welcome such moves because they facilitate the inward transfer of technology. This is often achieved by getting the foreign MNE to create a strategic alliance with a local interest (see Chapter 9) or by establishing helpful institutional and legal frameworks, such as the European Research Area or the World Intellectual Property Organization.

Research by MNEs

As revealed in Figure 11.2, R&D often involves huge sums. It is rarely certain that a product innovation will sell well enough globally to justify initial R&D outlays, which can be enormous. In the 2011 EU scorecard, for instance, research spending as a percentage of sales ('corporate R&D intensity') reached 15.3 per cent in the pharmaceutical/biotechnology sectors, the world's leading R&D investors, ahead of software and computer services (9.6 per cent). Together with 'automobiles and parts' (whose companies spend huge sums on R&D in absolute terms but slightly less as a percentage of sector revenues), these industries

Figure 11.2
MNEs ranked by global
R&D investment
(European Commission
2011).

Rank	Name (country of origin)	Sector	2010 R&D investment (in billions of euros)
1	Roche (Switzerland)	pharmaceuticals	7.18
2	Pfizer (USA)	pharmaceuticals	7.02
3	Microsoft (USA)	information technology	6.74
4	Toyota (Japan)	automotive	6.67
5	Merck (USA)	pharmaceuticals	6.40
6	Volkswagen (Germany)	automotive	6.26
7	Samsung (Korea)	information technology, telecommunications	6.18
8	Novartis (Switzerland)	pharmaceuticals	6.02
9	General Motors (USA)	automotive	5.19
10	Johnson & Johnson (USA)	pharmaceuticals	5.10
11	Nokia (Finland)	telecommunications	4.94
12	Daimler (Germany)	automotive	4.83

account for the lion's share of global corporate spending on research, with normal R&D/ revenue ratios in other sectors remaining in the 2–4 per cent range.

MNEs may spend so much on research that they cannot afford the commercial networks they need to distribute their innovations—even though global sales are the only hope of recouping heavy upfront R&D outlays. Thus, many international alliances between rival MNEs are rooted in each partner's sense that it lacks the resources to undertake R&D by itself (Branzei et al. 2011). For example, in 2011 US technological giant GE partnered with Australia's Commonwealth Scientific and Industrial Research Organisation (CSIRO) in areas ranging from green technology to health care. Similarly, Nokia (Finland) worked with Microsoft (USA) on products like the Windows smartphone or the Bing internet browser. R&D's cost factor is a particular constraint for SMEs, whose smaller size means that they are often unable to achieve sales volumes justifying the initial expenditure.

With knowledge being key to international competitiveness, confidentiality constitutes a major part of MNE strategy. Generally, this involves legal efforts to extend exclusive rights over intellectual properties—one famous example being pharmaceutical companies' attempt during the 1990s and 2000s to control the production of AIDS medicine (WHO 2006). Confidentiality can be difficult to preserve as a company internationalizes, however, especially given the recent trend towards MNEs establishing foreign R&D centres, increasingly in Asia because of this region's abundance of new science graduates. For this reason, companies often take great care to only transfer to subsidiaries certain strategic categories of knowledge relating, for instance, to management practices instead of product characteristics. This may change, however, if consumers in emerging markets like China start to require locally conceived products instead of ones that were first researched in places like Germany or the USA (Moody 2011).

Lastly, as summarized in Figure 11.3, the same 'pull' vs. 'push' concepts that Chapter 10 used to analyse MNE organizations are also key to international R&D.

'Push' R&D. In this orientation, the MNE imposes its new idea on the market instead of starting by reacting to signals. Push MNEs often concentrate R&D activities on a single site, usually global headquarters, to maximize confidentiality and cost control. This means, however, that researchers are not working in proximity to the different markets that their new product will affect. Less concerned with international variations in consumer preferences, they may be tempted to seek a single global standard. The example of Microsoft, with its powerful R&D unit in Redmond (Washington State, USA), springs to mind. Where a new standard (like Windows Operating System) is a superior innovation, 'push' R&D can be very successful and attain first-mover advantage. But problems also arise when researchers are so distant from markets that they focus on things that are irrelevant to customers. Hence the growing trend among some MNEs to transfer their R&D activities abroad to enjoy both greater proximity to dynamic emerging markets and access to a wider range of researchers (He and Zhao 2011).

'Pull' R&D'. Responsive MNEs see their business as starting with customer signals and will therefore often try to maximize researchers' exposure to the outside world. This can be done by offshoring R&D centres (Martínez-Noya and García-Canal 2011) or by using information technology to help designers stay abreast of market changes beyond their home environment. A famous example of this latter approach is the way that Inditex (brand name Zara) links cash registers from stores across Europe directly to its design centre at home in Spain.

Pro-centralization (push R&D)	Anti-centralization (pull R&D)
Assemble critical mass of scientists	Mobilize diverse teams of scientists
Better chance of protecting secrets	Possibility of alliances
Lower overhead costs	Greater customer focus
ICT used for scientific communications	More opportunities for knowledge spillovers

Figure 11.3
Arguments for and against centralizing MNE research.

Design

+ Design
Activities aimed at
defining a product's
final shape and
attributes.

A similar debate on the applicability of 'push' or 'pull' approaches is also found in international design, defined as the stage at which an idea is modelled into a physical shape. In the hope of achieving economies of scale, an MNE might try to 'push' a single design into all its foreign markets. A famous example from the 1990s was when Ford spent $6 billion designing a 'world car' (known in its first version as the Mondeo in Europe and the Contour in North America). Global sales were disappointing, however. Conversely, other MNEs' design efforts are driven by a 'pull' logic that aims to keep staff in touch with local preferences. In the late 1980s, for example, US toolmaker Black and Decker ran design centres in more than 20 countries. This seemed a good idea given that the company built appliances that were adapted and sold well. However, duplicating design centre overheads was so expensive that it became untenable, with Black and Decker changing course in the 1990s and running its design efforts out of a few sites only.

It is impossible to overstate the importance of knowledge management as an international production function. Decisions taken at the beginning of a value chain will have crucial knock-on effects as products or services evolve towards their final shape. For instance, Dell's original decision to offer IBM PCs instead of Apple Macs has clearly affected many other supply decisions relating to components that are compatible with one standard but not the other. Upstream decisions are almost never taken without managers considering their ripple effects.

Section II: International supply chain management

Supply chain management (SCM) refers to all the operations involved in sourcing, producing, transporting, assembling, and finalizing a product or service. Global SCM occurs when firms are in a position to purchase and take delivery of raw materials, components, and modules anywhere in the world. As discussed in Chapter 1, these are developments that can be analysed in both macro-level political, economic, social, and ecological terms, and from a more micro-level corporate and business perspective. It is this latter focus that the 'International outsourcing' section below will emphasize.

The first dividing line in global SCM is whether an MNE sources raw materials and components from a domestic source, from a foreign plant that it owns (called 'offshoring', this is part of the international vertical integration strategy discussed in Chapter 5), or from a foreign supplier. This last instance, called international outsourcing, has been a leading driver of international business in recent decades.

International outsourcing

There is a large body of academic work that tries to explain MNEs' growing tendency to focus on their own core competencies and outsource any other value chain functions to external partners. When a company outsources functions to its suppliers or subcontractors, it benefits from the other parties' competitive advantages, which can derive from a combination of lower costs and greater competency in particular products or services. Advantage seeking is particularly crucial in an international context, where performance differentials are even greater than if a company only considers domestic partners. In addition, as discussed in Chapter 5, many MNEs now prioritize financial performance indicators like return on equity (ROE) over traditional corporate objectives like market share. One way that companies can increase ROE is by 'shrinking the balance sheet'. If they run fewer functions in-house then they will have fewer assets to finance. Lastly, outsourcing increases a company's productive flexibility, a key factor of success in an era of global competition and rapidly changing consumer demand. After all, during periods of economic downturn,

Since the early 1990s, a host of new *maquiladora* factories have been built in North Mexico to supply US manufacturers with components

Source: iStock

it is easier and cheaper to renegotiate supplier contracts than to shut down factories. An example of this approach was the speed with which companies from the USA and Europe cut orders to Asian suppliers following the 2008–2009 crisis.

In turn, this highlights the way that outsourcing trends evolve over time. The main driver for outsourcing towards the end of the twentieth century, for instance, was the procurement of low-cost components or finished products manufactured in the world's poorer regions such as South East Asia, which tended to specialize in textiles and basic semiconductors, or Latin America, particularly after US car-makers began buying parts from North Mexican *maquiladora* factories. Protests against manufacturing job losses in the industrialized world were often met with the argument that LDCs were less capable of higher value-added production, which would therefore be dominated by OECD countries in a new international division of labour. However, with today's emerging market companies demonstrating their ability to engage in increasingly sophisticated work, Western MNEs are outsourcing all sorts of corporate functions today, not just manufacturing. It was always wrong to imagine that developing economies could not compete in the knowledge economy. Quite the contrary, service activities account for a growing proportion of all international outsourcing today.

+ Procurement
Act of purchasing resources or inputs.

Product outsourcing

Companies are no longer daunted by the coordination problems that can arise when outside partners are brought into their production process. Inter-firm communications have been greatly enhanced by the development of electronic data interchanges (EDI) and Internet-based applications such as vendor managed inventory, collaborative planning forecasting, and replenishment or efficient consumer response (Naim et al. 2004), all of which optimize inter-firm flows of goods. It is easier than ever for a company to work hand in hand with its overseas suppliers to monitor key parameters such as inventory levels, delivery times, and standards. This has had enormous consequences for MNEs' value chain strategies. Many of the world's best-known names (car-makers like Volkswagen but also computer-makers like Dell or TV-makers like Sony) manufacture only a small percentage of the final products they sell. Boeing's Dreamliner programme involves the direct delivery of parts from 1200 'tier-one' suppliers working in 5400 plants in 40 countries worldwide (Economist 2012a). Fed in turn by thousands of 'tier-two' suppliers, Boeing has had to set up a 'war room' to monitor its global supply of parts and raw materials, hiring hundreds of examiners to visit suppliers worldwide. Indeed, for some MNEs, outsourcing has become so important that 'hollow firms' like Nike run almost no physical production activities (and few if any retail outlets). Nike's main activity is branding and coordinating the different firms that make up its network.

For simpler goods, outsourcing often involves companies trying to take advantage of suppliers' cost advantages or economies of scale. Evidence suggests that companies acquiring new resources and foreign knowledge through outsourcing improve their competitive position and perform better in their own export markets (Bertrand 2011). For more complex goods, there is the added advantage of accessing, albeit indirectly, whatever technology the supplier uses to make an input. In both cases, by outsourcing non-essential functions, firms are freeing themselves to focus on those functions where they can be most productive.

Even as the strategic principles of MNE outsourcing remain constant, received wisdom about the best way to organize it varies. Companies just starting their international outsourcing activity may feel comfortable dealing with a single partner but over time some might see an advantage in getting suppliers to compete on price and innovation, and will break their outsourcing needs up into smaller contracts with different companies (called 'multi-sourcing'). This protects prime contractors against supply chain disruptions. Otherwise, MNEs might also try to improve their bargaining position by centralizing global procurement for all subsidiaries and demanding competitive bulk purchasing rates. However, this kind of coordinated procurement requires a top performance communications and logistics system.

Over the past decade, a number of MNEs have taken a nuanced view of the benefits of outsourcing to certain destinations simply because the cheapest suppliers are found there. As explained in Case study 11.1, the nearsourcing trend spreading through several sectors is driven by the calculation that the delays inherent to long-distance procurement no longer justify the advantages. More radically, some MNEs' level of disappointment with the whole concept of externalization has caused them to revert to 'in-sourcing', a strategy where an MNE brings back in-house functions that it used to allocate externally (see Figure 11.4). This makes most sense in hi-tech sectors where cost is less of a factor and where companies risk losing valuable knowledge and handing foreign suppliers a real advantage. This happened, for instance, with light-emitting diode (LED) technology, where Western MNEs outsourced production to China only to discover that suppliers there had soon innovated new forms of the product (Ernst & Young 2012). Companies from less hi-tech sectors, such as Master Lock or GE's appliances division, also announced a return to in-sourcing in 2011 for a range of reasons including quality control, delivery problems, rising fuel prices, and higher labour costs (and currency rates) in several key product outsourcing destinations, starting with China. The benefits of outsourcing, including productivity gains, must be weighed against its disadvantages. There is no guarantee that the conditions that made a strategy viable in the past will still apply in the future.

Services outsourcing

Recent years have seen a sharp rise in the outsourcing of services. One explanation relates to the division of MNEs' activities between their internal processes and their external

+ Bulk purchasing
When goods or services are bought in large quantities, there is a greater chance of negotiating a lower per-unit price since the seller will achieve economies of scale that it can pass on to the buyer.

+ Externalization
Where a firm gives an outside party responsibility for some of its business functions. The opposite of internalization.

Figure 11.4
Different ways of organizing international supply chains.

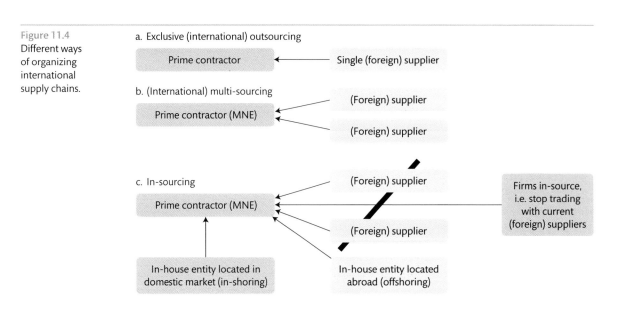

a. Exclusive (international) outsourcing

Prime contractor ← Single (foreign) supplier

b. (International) multi-sourcing

Prime contractor (MNE) ← (Foreign) supplier
← (Foreign) supplier

c. In-sourcing

Prime contractor (MNE) ← (Foreign) supplier
← (Foreign) supplier

Firms in-source, i.e. stop trading with current (foreign) suppliers

In-house entity located in domestic market (in-shoring)
In-house entity located abroad (offshoring)

interface with customers. To a large extent, most of the outsourcing wave that was such a key characteristic of international business in the late twentieth century and early 2000s involved MNEs sourcing from foreign suppliers products (or at the very least, product components) that they would then market. Over time, this first wave was accompanied by a growing interest in outsourcing the services associated with running a company's internal processes. In addition, there has been a general reappraisal of the kinds of activities that are capable of being run out of the low-cost, emerging economies that account for such a large proportion of international outsourcing today. As Chapter 15 explores in greater detail, whereas 20 years ago the received wisdom was that the older industrialized countries would specialize in higher value-added activities with the developing world focusing on low-cost, labour-intensive operations, it is clear nowadays that emerging economies possess the human capital to engage in all kinds of work. The lack of formal education characterizing many workers in the developing world is increasingly being addressed by employers organizing the professional training, certifications, and performance standards (Fernandez-Stark et al. 2011) that will allow them to compete effectively with the more expensive workforce operating out of Europe, North America, and Japan. The end result is that services have started to overtake products as the main focus of international outsourcing initiatives.

Studies show that more and more MNEs are in fact outsourcing services simply to reduce transaction costs, choosing locations based on factors such as the relative complexity of the service in question or the host country's institutional quality and cultural proximity (Liu et al. 2011). Thus, whereas China remains the world's leading destination for product outsourcing, the top of the list for services features, in order: India, with its strong computing skills; the Philippines, dominating the global market for medical transcriptions; and the ex-Soviet Union (Russia and Ukraine), accounting for a rising share of global software development. In general, the outsourcing of these kinds of in-house functions tends to be divided between technological services such as telecommunications infrastructure and computing networks; business processes, ranging from invoicing to payroll, human resource management, and customer contacts; and, most ambitiously, knowledge processes, starting with R&D and patents work (the kinds of efforts often undertaken as part of the strategic alliances discussed in Chapter 10).

Suppliers' key argument when bidding for service activities is not so much their lower cost resulting from economies of scale, a factor that is much more important for manufacturing operations, but the ability to automate and standardize the processes in question (Knowledge@wharton 2011). Since the use of a shared language facilitates information exchanges, there is some evidence of particular linkages between, for instance, English and UK MNEs with suppliers working out of India or South Africa; French MNEs with North African service suppliers; or Spanish MNEs working with counterparts in Latin America, a region whose general share of the global outsourcing market is predicted by many to rise in the not so distant future (IAOP 2011). It remains that the constraint of physical proximity is understandably not as important for the outsourcing of services as it is for products.

Limitations on international outsourcing

As Figure 11.5 shows, outsourcing also has a number of shortcomings. The company purchasing the inputs (the 'prime contractor') becomes dependent on suppliers, losing the ability to produce inputs and the specialist knowledge that comes from this. Dependency creates vulnerability at several levels: if adverse currency or raw-material price movements increase the component's price and the buyer cannot find a substitute; or if prices rise suddenly due to sudden wage hikes in those countries where the company has developed its main outsourcing relationships, as is the case in China where several provinces have suffered labour shortages as a result of rapid industrialization. Worst of all, if suppliers go bankrupt and shut down, the MNE might be forced to cease its own operations until it can organize alternative channels. This chain reaction was a real possibility in the wake of the

Advantages	Disadvantages
Lower costs	Will not develop knowledge/experience
Access to supplier technology	Dependent on supplier
Productive flexibility	Potential quality problems
Higher return on equity	Delivery risks

2008 and 2011 credit crunches when many suppliers suffered from the double shock of falling global demand and banks' increased unwillingness to lend funds. To prevent their outsourced supply chains from drying up, some prime contractors provide upstream partners with financial assistance. This is done as a matter of course by MNEs such as Benetton and IKEA but can also happen in response to ad hoc crises, such as the aid that Toyota provided to certain subcontractors in the wake of Japan's destructive 2011 earthquake. This kind of joint financial planning is a sign of how crucial supply chain collaboration has become in many sectors of activity.

There is also the strategic risk that suppliers might decide to pursue a forward integration strategy (see Chapter 5) and expand the scope of their activities down the value chain, ultimately becoming competitors to their own customers. One example is the Estonian rare earth processing company Silmet, which was taken over in April 2011 by a US mining company, Molycorp, that used to supply its facilities with raw materials but now wanted to develop the full range of competencies on the 'mines to magnets' value chain. In addition, the US small aircraft producer Cessna created a similar risk with its 2007 decision to outsource the production of complete models to China's Shenyang Aircraft Corporation. Where Boeing is only outsourcing the production of certain parts, Cessna's strategy has put it in danger of being crowded out of its own value chain if its supplier feels sufficiently empowered to expand downstream. Luckily for the company, Shenyang has shown no such ambition, at least for the first four years of the contract, meaning that through 2012 at least Cessna could continue to work in harmony with its supplier.

Another problem arises when suppliers, particularly ones operating in emerging countries marked by lax regulations, deliver poor-quality goods or services. This is why quality controls have become a key part of negotiations between order-givers and suppliers. An example of what can happen when quality goes wrong is the uproar that US toy-maker Mattel faced in 2007 after selling allegedly unsafe products it had bought from suppliers in China. This debacle raised doubts in many consumers' minds about the safety of any toys made in China, with leading German teddy bear maker Steiff terminating its Chinese outsourcing contracts in 2010 simply to avoid possible public recrimination. Similarly, a number of MNEs are now being held to account for problems relating to 'child labour, indigenous peoples' rights, forestry, intellectual property and conservation or biodiversity' in the countries where they outsource (Timlon 2011). Thus, if an MNE sources from suppliers who do not offer the kind of workforce protections considered acceptable in the final markets where the goods are being sold, it might be accused of contributing knowingly to human exploitation. Examples include the campaign led by the NGO Clean Clothes Campaign criticizing sporting goods specialist Adidas for outsourcing football production to Pakistan, a country where factories allegedly employ children to work long hours for little pay in difficult conditions. Similarly, in 2012 the UK Parliament Energy and Climate Change Committee determined that by moving production to countries with low pollution standards, international outsourcing can wreak havoc on the environment, as witnessed by the terrible air quality in many Chinese factory towns. Furthermore, additional fuel consumption and emissions caused by the long-distance transportation of components and finished products is a contributor to global warming. Recent analysis suggests that 'for consumer goods makers, hi-tech players, and other manufacturers, between 40 and 60 percent of a company's carbon footprint [see Chapter 16] resides upstream in its supply chain—from raw materials, transport, and packaging to the energy consumed in manufacturing processes. For retailers, the figure can be 80 percent' (Brickman and Ungerman 2008). All of these risk factors (product safety, labour standards, environmental damage) can cause indirect harm to an MNE's reputation. The damage can even become quite direct when, for instance, customers are unhappy with the service they receive from a department that the MNE has outsourced to an overseas provider. This can lead to the company moving the service in question back in-house, with examples including bank Santander UK's decision in 2011 to switch its call centres from India to Britain, or a similar decision taken that same year by British Telecom to open up a new call centre in the UK (Kavanagh 2011). Following a wave of similar repatriation decisions taken over the previous five years by banking, energy, and other MNEs concerned that their customers' cultural sensitivities were being upset, this trend shows how the business logic of international outsourcing can run afoul of some consumers' preference for a local service.

Lastly, outsourcing can contradict the lean production principles that many firms have adopted in recent years. One such principle highlights the need to reduce inventory costs by delivering components 'just in time' before they are required on the customer's assembly line. It can be risky for a company to source materials from the other side of the world, since the necessarily longer lead times increase the likelihood of late arrivals undermining production schedules. For instance, natural catastrophes can destroy critical infrastructure and have effects extending far beyond the country where they occur, because today's global supply chains are so fragmented and interdependent. In the case of the 2011 Tohoku earthquake and tsunami, for instance, the destruction of Japanese supply chains was also felt by American manufacturer Chevrolet, which relied on transmissions made in Japan for an electric car, the Volt, that it was manufacturing in the USA. In Europe, telecommunications MNEs Nokia and Ericsson also expressed concerns about their ability to continue sourcing components from their Japanese subcontractors. Indeed, to counter the risk of uncertain long-distance deliveries, some firms are starting to hold larger inventories—thereby defeating the very purpose of a just-in-time organization (Tabrizi and Tseng 2007).

Solutions exist for many of these distance-related problems, but they can be expensive. For example, a real-time tracking and inventory management software solution called radio frequency identification (RFID) technology allows contractors to monitor components' location. In turn, this helps them to forecast deliveries and manage inventories more accurately. On a more structural level, some component-makers have taken to building supplier parks immediately adjacent to contractors' overseas plants (for example, the 'Blue Macaw' project near Volkswagen's Gravatai factory in Brazil). Such initiatives strengthen the argument that it is better to analyse MNEs' actions as members of a supply chain network than to focus on what each does separately. Indeed, an increasing number of today's MNEs define themselves primarily by their facilitating and coordinating capabilities.

+ **Lean production**
Production philosophy that emphasizes saving resources through less waste, better inventory management, better quality, and shorter industrial cycles. Largely derived from the 'Toyota Production System'.

+ **Lead time**
Time it takes, once an order has been placed, to deliver a good to the order-giver's premises.

+ **Supplier park**
When industrial suppliers cluster together to provide components and modules to their prime contractor.

Case study 11.2

Dellism: A new model value chain?

When a customer buys a personal computer from a Dell salesperson (http://www.dell.com), the order is transmitted immediately to one of the company's 'manufacturing facilities' as soon as payment has been verified. The decision as to which facility should fill the order depends on geographic proximity and the particular product in question. For example, most laptop notebooks that Dell sells worldwide are made in Asia.

What Dell calls its 'manufacturing facilities' might also be described as 'assembly plants'. The company makes few if any of the components used in its computers. When

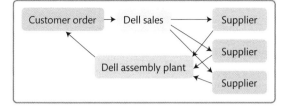

Figure 11.6
The Dell supply chain involves a full integration of communications, manufacturing, logistics, and assembly functions.

Dell's information technology capabilities are at the heart of its own production processes
Source: Dell

notification of a laptop notebook purchased in the USA reaches Dell's Malaysian plant, for instance, the parts will be immediately ordered from a 'supplier logistics centre' comprised of the many supply chain partners running operations immediately adjacent to every Dell plant worldwide. Each supplier is in constant communication with the company, determining future delivery quantities and tracking current parts. As illustrated in Figure 11.6, communications lie at the very heart of the Dell system.

Dell's supplier system is what allows the company to meet its three commitments. The first is to provide a customized product. This is feasible because of Dell's ability to vary the sub-systems that it orders from suppliers. The second is to make a quick delivery, something enabled by the company's ultra-rapid communications and efficient supplier parks. Lastly, Dell promises low prices thanks to the volume discounts it negotiates with suppliers but also because its just-in-time delivery system cuts inventory costs.

The arrangement shifts certain manufacturing responsibilities to suppliers, who must also respond to Dell's policy of multi-sourcing certain products to ensure that plant deliveries are done in a timely fashion. The reason they work with such a demanding customer is the sheer volume of orders that Dell gives them. Having one

of the world's biggest computer retailers as a customer enables companies to achieve economies of scale that they would otherwise struggle to attain. Largely specialized in upstream functions, many of Dell's rivals lack its commercial competencies, infrastructure, and brand recognition.

Dell's own industrial competencies involve relatively straightforward assembly operations, to the extent that one risk the company faces is the possibility of its suppliers trying to bypass it and deal directly with its customers. It is unlikely that they would succeed, however, given the difficulty in replicating Dell's exceptional prowess in using modern communications and logistics to link the different threads that make up its international production process. Excellence in international production nowadays is not only what a company does itself but how it links up with suppliers and customers worldwide.

Case study questions

1. What is Dell's international manufacturing system?
2. What risks are associated with Dellism?

Supply relationships

Depending on their strategy and corporate culture, prime contractors can establish different kinds of relationships with suppliers (Harland et al. 2004). Examples include the 'integrated hierarchy' of single product firms that depend heavily on specific suppliers or else the 'semi-hierarchy' of multidivisional firms characterized by less dependency. Other supplier relationships include the 'coordinated revenues links' typifying licensing/franchising arrangements or 'medium-term trading commitments' by companies that prefer to work with supplier shortlists. These relationships often evolve if the balance of power shifts between a contractor and its suppliers, as witnessed, for instance, in the Dutch cut flower agroindustry when growers formed cooperatives to gain more power (Patel-Campillo 2011).

Things can also change simply because the two parties learn to trust one another, with some studies speaking of a general tendency for relationships to evolve over time from competition to cooperation (Loppacher et al. 2011).

A simpler way to categorize supplier relationships is to differentiate between the short-term, so-called American model, the longer-term Asian model, and the compromise 'flagship' model.

Short-term supply relationships

In this model, subcontractors are asked to bid anew every time that a contractor wants to replenish its supplies. This means that they will only be as good as their latest bid and are at a constant risk of losing the business if they slip on quality and/or price. There is little room for loyalty or joint planning in this kind of relationship, but it does force suppliers to remain competitive. An interesting case is the Covisint online auction platform that Ford and General Motors developed to force potential suppliers worldwide to compete for contracts. Covisint has grown over the years to cover different kinds of inputs, including IT services. It is a way for prime contractors to pass on to their upstream partners the competitive pressures that they face themselves.

Long-term supply relationships

The focus in longer term supply models is on collaboration up and down the supply chain. Encapsulated in Japanese vertical or horizontal *keiretsus* but also in Korean *chaebols* and Chinese *guanxi* networks with their roots in close, long-term relationships (see Chapter 6), these supply systems are prime examples of business being embedded in a cultural context. They reflect the Asian emphasis on social harmony as opposed to individual success. In a *keiretsu*, for instance, a prime contractor will lend its name (for example, Mitsubishi, Mitsui, Sumitomo) to a network of companies that work together to cover all the upstream operations needed to bring a good to market. Firms typically take an equity stake in one another and plan investments, research, and product design together. This is a comfortable arrangement based on extremely stable contracts that are usually renewed without non-*keiretsu* members having any opportunity to compete. Even in cases of 'follow sourcing' where subcontractors build factories abroad to service their prime contractor's overseas operations, Japanese *keiretsu* suppliers can still count on winning most contracts, whether or not an explicit *keiretsu* agreement exists (Solis 2003). Predictability of this kind is priceless, since it helps suppliers' industrial planners to decide between small capacities that cost less but cannot accommodate peaks in demand, and large capacities that can cope with bigger orders but cost more. Being able to size plant capacities correctly is an advantage resulting in lower costs that the supplier can then share with the contractor.

Asian supply networks are not without their faults. For instance, the difficult recession that Japan experienced during the 1990s has often been blamed on *keiretsu* members' tolerance for partners' poor investment decisions. Over-dependence on external partners can also be dangerous, as Toyota discovered when the 2011 earthquake flattened many of its suppliers' facilities, causing enormous disruption to its 'just in time' system. At the same time, there is no doubt that Asia's rise as a centre of international manufacturing is partially rooted in the success of its supply chain organization. This has drawn the attention of many Western MNEs. In manufacturing, as in other international business functions, success breeds imitation.

Compromise 'flagship model'

A number of Western MNEs have moved over the years to establish similarly collaborative supply chains, possibly to imitate the success of Japanese *keiretsus*. This approach, described as the 'flagship' concept (Rugman and D'Cruz 2000), is often pursued by prime contractors

+ **Vertical *keiretsu***
Japanese corporate network based on very long-term cooperation between companies specializing in different production activities. A vertical network will include a bank for funding purposes.

+ **Horizontal *keiretsu***
Japanese corporate network where similar firms ally with trading companies to ensure the widest possible market coverage.

+ **Chaebol**
South Korean equivalent of Japanese *keiretsu* but with the founding family generally maintaining a majority holding.

who compete in markets under their own names, acting as figureheads for networks of dedicated suppliers that tend to be organized into clusters. The benefits for the network's flagship firm are that it can count on reliable sourcing and faces less of a risk that suppliers will raise prices when supplies are low. Flagship leaders can also internationalize more quickly because they do not have to build their own manufacturing facilities. One example cited by Rugman and D'Cruz is IKEA, the Swedish furniture retailer. Confident that centralized control over subcontractors' product design and quality operations guarantees adequate sourcing and protects its brand name, IKEA has been free to focus resources on opening stores in Europe and elsewhere. The extra management costs that it has incurred because of the need to supervise suppliers have been more than offset by the savings achieved by sticking to its core competencies. In a sense, the flagship arrangement is a microcosm of the division of labour concept.

As for the flagship suppliers, they will benefit from the prime contractor's expertise in production and materials planning, quality control, and technical assistance. On occasion, suppliers can piggyback the leader's ability to buy raw materials in bulk, hence cheaply. Above all, flagship suppliers benefit from greater stability, with guaranteed sales volumes allowing them to size their production capacities more accurately. This is the kind of umbrella that Italian clothing-maker Benetton, for example, offers the different companies that produce the wool it processes.

However, flagship suppliers will also incur extra costs. New members of the network are often forced to build expensive, capital-intensive facilities to manufacture the components they are expected to provide. Indeed, one analysis of the flagship arrangement is that it involves prime contractors passing on to their suppliers some of the performance pressures that they themselves face. This is particularly true in sectors characterized by very demanding customers, such as mass retail and fast food, although it also applied in the Dell example.

Not all pressures are cost-based, however. For many suppliers, it is just as important to offer technological competencies, such as the ability to share supply chain information. Many flagship leaders are interested in 'concurrent engineering', or the possibility for partners to design in parallel the different value chain stages for which each is responsible (Nassimbeni 2004). Today, industrial collaboration often starts as early as a product's pre-production phase, with suppliers and contractor cooperating openly ('tacitly') on basic component designs to ensure that they fit seamlessly into the modules being built (Kotabe et al. 2007). The priority in this 'fractal production' approach is ensuring coherency between different sub-systems that, when combined, comprise the final product. To the extent that such operations reflect group efforts, it is clear that international production is shaped by the way a company draws the boundaries between its own operations and its partners'. Like most aspects of international business, manufacturing must be analysed in conjunction with managers' strategic intent.

Section III: International manufacturing

The only way that an MNE can satisfy consumer demand for a timely delivery of different goods to different locations worldwide is to have an efficient manufacturing and logistics network. Dominant thinking about the most efficient way of building such networks varies. The principle of this book, as set out in Chapter 1, is that no one best way of doing international business exists. This means that there is value in analysing the full range of industrial models that MNEs have pursued over the years.

Industrial models

On a broad level, the concept of industrial models not only refers to the different ways that companies organize production activities but also how this helps to structure the allocation of power and wealth within society as a whole (**see ORC Extension materials 11.2**). In a purely business context, a good place to start applying the concept is the mass production system that Henry Ford first implemented in the early twentieth century. This model offered the advantage of standardization and efficiency, featuring specialized workers stationed along an assembly line and completing a succession of tasks and outputs to be assembled in a final product. By enabling economies of scale, Ford's system cut costs, leading to lower retail prices and, in turn, expanded sales. One of the first applications of this logic was the Ford Model T car, a trailblazer among mass-manufactured and mass-consumed products. For much of the twentieth century, this industrial model was the starting point for many managers' economic vision.

+ **Industrial models** Manufacturing systems determining the sequencing of operations within factories. Also refers to flow of goods before and after industrial transformation, and to the distribution of the income generated.

> Go online

Critiques of Fordism

As powerful as Henry Ford's approach was, it had several flaws, starting with its emphasis on uniformity. This may have been acceptable in the early stages of a new product, but as markets mature, consumers tend to require greater diversity. This was problematic for Fordist manufacturers. Offering a broad product range is expensive, both because it takes time to switch factory equipment from one production line to another, and because shortening a production run reduces economies of scale.

To solve this problem while continuing to reap the benefits of mass production, Ford's great rival at General Motors during the 1920s, Alfred Sloan, devised a strategy that has been described as a 'volume and diversity' approach (Boyer and Freyssenet 2002). Sloan's idea was that manufacturers can achieve economies of scale by making invisible sub-assemblies that use the same components even as they give consumers a sense of customization by differentiating the visible parts bolted onto the product at the end of the manufacturing process (see Figure 11.7). Car buyers can see, for example, whether a particular vehicle comes with a sunroof, but the brand name of its carburettor (for example, Holley or Edelbrock) will be less apparent. The practice of standardizing for as long as possible before differentiating as late as possible has been referred to as deferred differentiation, 'platform strategy', or 'postponement' (Kumar and Wilson 2007). The advantage of this approach is that it allows manufacturers to combine scale with diversity. Moreover, it is easier for companies to manage stocks if their production system involves a deferred differentiation logic where they store cheaper generic modules instead of expensive sub-assemblies that are specific to one model only (Christopher 2005). Indeed, the only real problem with this approach is the difficulty of balancing factory workloads when product differentiation occurs at different times on different lines (Ko and Hu 2008). The production engineers who overcome such mathematical challenges are the quiet heroes of international production.

Sloan's ideas drove many of the consolidations that have marked international business since the 1920s. His platform strategy would become particularly widespread in the

+ **Deferred differentiation** Manufacturing strategy that combines economies of scale with product diversity by standardizing inputs for as long as possible and introducing adaptation as late as possible.

Figure 11.7
Deferred
differentiation in a
Chinese restaurant
kitchen. Customers get
different dishes but
the restaurant owner
also achieves some
economies of scale.

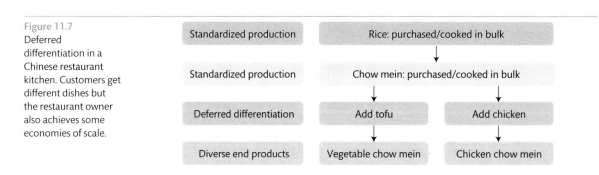

automotive industry, where famous takeovers such as Volkswagen's purchase of Spain's SEAT Motor Company in the 1970s or Renault's more recent acquisition of Nissan were designed to save money by rationalizing factories that had previously manufactured different chassis (platforms). On the surface, VW and SEAT cars, like Renault and Nissan cars, continued to look different, satisfying consumers' desire for choice. Most shared the same platform underneath, however, enabling manufacturers to achieve economies of scale.

The Fordist mass production model also had problems because of its assembly line organization. Disruptions to operations anywhere along the line (for example, if a workstation ran out of parts) would shut down the whole process. To offset this risk, Fordist manufacturers tended to carry large inventories of parts, an expensive undertaking. Secondly, the Fordist factory's lack of flexibility meant that it was not particularly suited to a world where MNEs were increasingly expected to serve diverse customer bases. It was largely in reaction to these challenges that a new industrial model, called 'Toyotaism', became the dominant international manufacturing paradigm from the 1970s onwards.

A Japanese manufacturing model

The Toyota Production System was built on the idea that, contrary to received wisdom, volume manufacturing can coincide with product flexibility, as long as uncertainty about the level and timing of factory flows ('throughput') is minimized. The goal is for assembly lines to 'handle different models and specifications without missing a beat' (Caulkin 2007). This is achieved by getting staff members to adopt what the Japanese call a *kaizen* (continuous improvement) attitude, seeking a 'permanent reduction in costs' (Boyer and Freyssenet 2002). The Toyotaist approach is bottom-up, because the people responsible for production are in the best position to increase efficiency. Employees meet regularly in 'quality circles' to discuss process improvements. In a world featuring increasingly knowledgeable consumers, quality has become a factor in all industrial models, but none more so than in Toyotaism, dominated by a Total Quality Management (TQM) philosophy targeting zero output defects.

TQM is an ambitious goal that firms usually achieve only through a combination of approaches. Contractors need to audit themselves and/or their suppliers. One of the leading systems in this area is 'Six Sigmas'. First developed by Motorola in the 1980s, it involves asking managers to improve business processes by establishing thresholds for quantitative defects and keeping statistics about performance. Corporate controls of this kind can be relatively difficult to implement, however. Moreover, for cultural reasons, not all workers cooperate with quality controls as readily as Japanese employees traditionally do. Lastly, inspectors may not always be welcomed in some workplaces, since it might not be in employees' interest to share information about how their roles are designed. Inspections are also expensive to run, and in some cases (i.e. where a TQM approach is supposed to be implemented) it is unclear whether the contractor or the supplier is supposed to bear the cost.

One solution has been the creation of autonomous quality assessment organizations. The leader in this area is the Geneva-based International Organization for Standardization

> Go online

(http://www.iso.org), often referred to as the ISO (**see ORC Extension materials 11.3**). This body has determined more than 16,500 standards covering all aspects of quality, relating notably to management systems (ISO 9001) and environmental performance (ISO 14001). Most MNEs are prepared to enact the changes they need to receive ISO certification because they want to demonstrate their commitment to quality. ISO's success is a sign of how quality attitudes have spread since the 1970s, when leading Japanese MNEs first began marketing quality as a key attribute.

Aside from quality and in addition to the 'just in time' and 'lean' principles discussed above, another noteworthy aspect of the Toyota Production System is its revolutionary inventory management process. Instead of ordering supplies based on predictions of future demand, a Toyotaist prime contractor asks subcontractors to replenish stocks at a rate defined by real customer demand. In this *kanban* (automatic signalling) logic, supplies to each level of the value chain are 'pulled' by the next level downstream, and ultimately by orders from end users. This is opposed to a system where replenishment is 'pushed' by factory schedules, which are poor predictors of flows in firms serving volatile global markets. *Kanban* prevents the distortions ('bullwhip effects') that Fordist supply chains cause when factory production volumes are misjudged. By stopping surplus production from piling up, *kanban* keeps inventory costs down. Conversely, when supplies run short, *kanban* reduces bottlenecks and delays. Much of Japanese companies' international success has been attributed to their ability to run 'lean' supply chains.

Despite Toyotaism's success since the 1980s, it would be wrong to assume that this is the only successful industrial model possible. Depending on a company's objectives, other models can succeed in other circumstances. The Dell case study shows a firm that has been extremely successful in replacing a traditional manufacturing function with an assembly/logistics focus. Also noteworthy is the industrial model developed by the Swedish car-maker Volvo, which specialized in top-of-the-range products and stressed worker knowledge more than output volumes or product diversity. Against the backdrop of Sweden's commitment to lifelong adult learning, the company created a hybrid production system called 'Volvoism'. This combined a standard 'platform strategy', in which Volvo vehicles largely shared the same chassis as their Ford group counterparts, with an enrichment of tasks. Workers would be encouraged to raise their general skill levels by doing different jobs over the course of the year—a polyvalent approach that was the exact opposite of Fordist (and, to a lesser extent, Toyotaist) specialization. As long as they are accompanied by efficient sourcing and logistics strategies, different industrial models can be implemented in response to today's international manufacturing challenges.

+ Polyvalent
Ability to perform many different functions, i.e. the opposite of specialization.

Physical operations

Clearly, a vertically integrated company making its own components faces different pressures from one that outsources everything and whose only real physical activity involves assembling inputs or branding finished products built by other companies. For many MNEs, the reality lies between these two extremes, since they run some strategic operations in-house and outsource the rest. The ability to link the whole physical process via logistics is therefore crucial.

Logistics

All levels of the supply chain are affected by logistics, from initial inputs to the recycling of used products and packaging ('reverse logistics'). Global competition means that deliveries of raw materials, components, and finished products must be quicker and more flexible than ever. This puts enormous pressure on logistics professionals. Sometimes the demands are commercial in nature, coming from retailers who require suppliers to replenish outlets scattered worldwide, or from knowledgeable online shoppers who force companies to compete on delivery. On other occasions, logistics must address production problems. This can involve the replenishment of globally dispersed assembly operations, the vulnerability of many supply chains to political risk or natural catastrophes, and the accumulation of finished products, which is the most expensive form of inventory (Christopher 2005). It is only through top logistics performance that international manufacturers meet these challenges.

However, most MNEs do not possess the competency for this. Logistics requires not only physical capabilities but also much specific knowledge, about geography and infrastructure, as well as documentary and regulatory requirements, customs administration, and banking practices. For instance, sometimes an importer receives goods on a cost, insurance, and freight (CIF) basis, meaning that it lets the exporter organize the transportation and pays a higher price for the delivery. On other occasions, the importer organizes the transportation itself and pays the exporter the lower free on board (FOB) price. The distinction between CIF and FOB is important not only because it reflects a firm's confidence in its ability to organize logistics but because each of these formats implies different legal rights and obligations. Documents like 'bills of lading' have evolved to convey information about the nature of goods in transit, carriage details, and transfer of ownership procedures. Specialist customs house brokers and freight forwarders 'clear' goods through border controls on MNEs' account, paying duties where required and organizing further transportation from the port of arrival to final destination. Bank 'trade finance' departments offer an array of financial instruments, led by 'letters of credit' where sellers are reassured that they will be paid once buyers or their agents receive the ownership documents for the goods in question. Logistics in the broadest sense of the term refers to a very wide range of 'trade operations' (**see ORC Extension material 11.4**) that are just as important as the physical movement of goods. Their significance explains, for instance, the attention paid at the 2009 London G20 summit to reviving trade finance in the wake of the 2008 credit crunch. At a very basic level, international business would be impossible without the vast number of trade intermediaries exercising their profession worldwide.

Indeed, it is precisely because logistics are so complicated that MNEs increasingly outsource their needs in this area to specialist 'third party logistics providers'. The largest of these '3PLs' (German firms DHL Logistics and Schenker, and Japan's Nippon Express) offer a full range of logistics services (see Case study 11.3). With their ability to consolidate different parties' shipments, they can transport larger volumes, thereby achieving economies of scale that an MNE working alone could not match. Moreover, patchy transportation infrastructure in some of the regions currently experiencing the fastest growth in trade (Western China and Eastern Europe) requires specialist knowledge that few companies possess (Rushton and Walker 2007).

> Go online

Factory locations

Logistics affect MNEs' upstream organization in different ways. One is by enabling 'centralized inventories'. Many companies have taken to storing their global stocks of semi-finished and finished products in just a few key regional distribution centres. Examples include German chemicals firm BASF operating a central staging platform for all of Asia in Singapore, or US office equipment-maker Katun's running a centre for all of its South American operations out of the Uruguayan free trade zone. The approach has the advantage of saving on overheads, but it also increases the distance between the MNE's storage facilities and consumer markets, potentially slowing delivery times. To compensate, many companies have organized the same kinds of joint information systems with their customers as the ones they operate with suppliers. This too is a logistics solution.

An associated development is the rise of 'focused factories', where companies specialize each of their plants worldwide in a specific production. One example is the climate control plant that automotive supplier Visteon has built at Dubnica in Slovakia, the only unit in its group to make this kind of sub-assembly. As Chapter 9 explained, the advantage of this approach is much higher economies of scale at the factory level. On the other hand, it also

+ **Free trade zone**
Tariff-free 'export processing zones' that many countries have set up to attract industrial activity. Little or no tax is paid as long as the items being assembled or temporarily stored there are re-exported.

causes longer lead times and complicates packaging and communications. This can be particularly difficult for an MNE when the customer requires delivery to different global locations of the different products that the MNE is producing in each of its focused factories (see Figure 11.8). In this case, the rationale for the MNE's plant location decisions must be juggled against the logistics problems linked to their location and the fit with customer locations. One attempt to address this problem is the new 'dual shore' manufacturing model that Indian automotive firms Amtek Auto and Bharat Forge have developed, characterized by a division of labour where focused factories in India specialize in labour-intensive activities due to the country's lower wage level, with more sophisticated production activities being carried out in plants situated in the older industrialized countries. In this instance, factory location is determined by different locations' variable endowments in factor inputs like, respectively, labour and capital (see Chapter 2).

Practitioner insight

Maite Irizar is Air Operations Manager at Ceva Logistics, an international supply chain logistics provider resulting from a 2007 merger between an Australian and an American company. The group employs more than 50,000 people worldwide in a multitude of offices and is largely structured into two business units: Contract Logistics and Freight Management. Maite works out of the Madrid Airport office in Freight Management.

'We offer every type of international logistics service, including customs house brokerage, multimodal transport and tax-free bonded import/export warehousing. My position consists of coordinating five departments to ensure they provide the best possible service. Our work starts when an international deal takes place. At that point, we will be contacted by the seller or buyer (either here in Spain or abroad through our office network) and asked to find a cargo relocation solution.

One of our strengths is that we provide a full range of logistics solutions. Depending on what stage of the international supply chain is involved and how responsibilities have been specified in the contract, a customer working by themselves might have to get in touch with many different specialists (air, maritime, road, etc.). This can be very complicated and instead of having their own logistics team manage the process, more and more companies find it easier to deal with us. By outsourcing this activity, they get us to assume much of the financial risk while taking advantage of our legal and, above all, technical know-how.

Ultimately, this means much lower costs for them, especially since we can negotiate much better deals with airliners or maritime carriers. In addition, you can't underestimate the value of our customs house brokerage, which takes care of all sorts of sensitive duty and tax payments.

Our business is so broad that the very word 'logistics' seems vague to me. It implies too many different things. Basically we're a service company and the fact that our business doesn't necessarily require a large capital investment means that a lot of new players have joined the sector in recent years. But many are transport companies and don't offer a complete supply chain service.

That doesn't mean that the big players like DHL, K+N, Schenker, or CEVA control the whole market because smaller local companies still get a piece of the pie. But the big question now in logistics isn't size but technology, particularly relating to tracking services, GPS, and communications systems. I expect that some of the processes that people currently handle (like documentation) will eventually be fully computerized. Still, the future is bright, since there will be growing demand for our services as companies continue to internationalize their operations to save money. I mean, why warehouse your goods in Europe when you can do this infinitely more cheaply in Asia? These kinds of calculations imply increasing volumes of cargo requiring relocation across the world. That will be good for us.'

Figure 11.8
Complicated
logistics in modern
manufacturing.

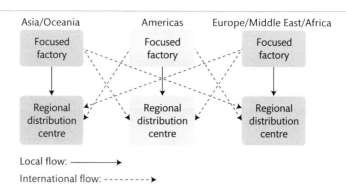

Business research tends to discuss MNE factory location in terms of considerations like cost and proximity to resources, along with the strategic thinking that Vernon outlined in his product life cycle theory (see Chapter 2). It is increasingly clear, however, that corporate decisions in this area are also based on a whole range of other criteria, including knowledge spillover possibilities, host government attitudes, and most importantly the size and importance of the market(s) that a plant is being asked to service. To a certain extent, the mission that an MNE attributes to a particular production unit will depend on where its output is being sold. Some plants serve only the countries or regions where they are located. Others send their output globally, either to sister MNE units or directly to customers (Dicken 2007). A key distinction must also be made between plants that merely assemble modules produced elsewhere, and others that manufacture their own generic goods. The former are cheaper and less capital-intensive, and can therefore be dispersed more easily. This differs from big manufacturing plants, which cost more and are therefore less likely to be spread worldwide. The terms 'manufacturing' or 'production' are often applied wrongly insofar as they refer to different things. Precise use of terminology is a crucial skill for international managers.

Challenges and choices

→ One major challenge for international business managers is determining to what extent they should skew their international value chain to suit upstream or downstream interests. The two strategies have a completely opposite focus (standardization vs. adaptation) and in most MNEs the group executive must spend an enormous amount of time juggling this conflict. It is impossible to overstate the amount of tension that exists in most companies between production and marketing.

Chapter summary

The chapter divided the international value chain's upstream portion into three sections. In recent years, academic analysis has determined that knowledge management is an increasingly crucial factor in international success, justifying analysis of the different factors influencing MNEs' innovation efforts. The second section focused on supply chain management, specifically on the trend towards international outsourcing that has played such a key role in the expansion of international business over the past few decades. The chapter concluded with an exploration of international manufacturing, starting with industrial models, each of which emphasizes different principles (like specialization for Fordism or quality for Toyotaism). A connection was also noted between companies' logistics possibilities and plant location decisions.

Case study 11.3

International transportation

The physical handling and/or delivery of raw materials, semi-processed components, or finished goods is a key aspect of international business. In part, this is because the transportation market has always been seen as a leading barometer of the international economy's health. Many forecasters base their predictions on vessel charter rates quoted on the London Baltic Exchange, the market where global bulk freight contracts are priced. Trade operations have always been a key international business function.

The explosion in international transportation over the past 30 years, caused by the trend toward market liberalization, fragmented supply chains, and focused factories, has had two main effects. First, a great deal of strain has been placed on global transportation infrastructure owing to the explosion in long-distance deliveries. The ever-larger vessels that shippers require to carry cargo have saturated the handling capacities of many ports worldwide. Governments invest heavily to renew ageing transportation infrastructure and avoid the delays regularly witnessed, for instance, at some Chinese ports or US–Mexico border crossings. Transportation companies engage in similar infrastructure productivity and capacity investments by purchasing bigger and better cranes to roll containers on and off ocean freighters as quickly as possible.

Rising international trade volumes also impact on the vehicles that companies use to carry freight. One key challenge involves matching transportation capacity to the demand for such services, measured in the shipping business, for instance, by the relative activity of ship-building vs. ship-breaking yards. Above all, there is the problem of rising fuel prices. Logistics companies meet this challenge in different ways, many of which involve environmental transportation initiatives. In terms of road freight (trucking), for instance, American carrier UPS is working to develop a 'green fleet' of delivery vans, some of which are expected to run on hydrogen fuel cell technology or hybrid electricity systems. One noteworthy advance in ocean freight is Danish shipping group Maersk's installation of waste heat recovery systems on its ships to save engine power. Rail companies worldwide have been investing in energy-saving devices such as regenerative braking systems, not to mention GE's Trip Optimizer technology, which calculates the most fuel-efficient speed for a train on any particular journey. For air cargo, however, the outlook is less rosy, despite the work to develop lighter aircraft and more efficient engines. Even the International Air Transport Association (IATA) accepts that this transport mode is destined to grow more slowly than ocean freight, its main rival for long-distance voyages. Airliners will try to save costs by easing the heavy administrative burdens associated with their business but this is a marginal improvement. For routine port-to-port carriage, ships and trains have a much brighter future than planes.

The outlook is more mixed for road haulage, the one mode of transportation that is flexible enough to move freight from a port to a factory or warehouse. On the one hand, carrying goods by road is expensive on a per kilogram basis and destined to suffer further cost disadvantages as fuel prices and taxes increase. Yet trucks' flexibility means that they are the only way of satisfying the growing demand from leading transportation customers (international manufacturers and large retailers) for integrated, end-to-end solutions. As such, they often figure in the product portfolio of dedicated third party logistics specialists, who are increasingly expected to provide a number of trade services above and beyond the full range of transportation modes. These added services include warehousing, customs house brokerage, freight forwarding, order tracking, and consolidation/deconsolidation facilities. Only the largest companies can afford to be present in all of these sectors. This explains the succession of synergy-seeking mergers and acquisitions that has characterized international transportation over the past decade, exemplified by Deutsche Bahn's 2010 acquisition of British rail and bus provider Arriva or the mid-2011 move by Korean industrialists Samsung Electronics and Posco to take a stake in the country's leading logistics firm, Korea Express Co. At the same time, transportation remains highly fragmented, not only for historical reasons (states' traditionally strong presence in this field) but because competencies vary widely worldwide.

It bears repeating that much growth in international trade occurs in emerging or transition economies, where the transportation infrastructure can be of variable

Adjusting port handling capacities to variations in international trade volumes can be difficult

Source: iStock

quality. In China, for instance, initial industrial expansion in eastern coastal cities offering easy access to modern ports has been followed by growth in western regions inland that are much harder to reach. Accessing remoter destinations requires adapted modes (like river barges) and good relations with government officials. In this most globalized of industries, local knowledge remains crucial (Rushton and Walker 2007).

Case study questions

1. How might rising fuel costs and climate change issues affect the future of international transportation?
2. How does the prospect of economic boom and bust cycles affect MNEs' management of their transportation needs?
3. How much further consolidation can be expected from third party logistics specialists?

Discussion questions

1. What can governments do to encourage national research and development?
2. What forms can international outsourcing be expected to adopt in the future?
3. Can Japanese *keiretsu* networks be replicated in other business cultures?

4. How have the 2008 and 2011 crises affected international manufacturing?
5. What are the strategic dangers facing a company like Dell whose entire production system relies on logistics performance?

Online resource centre

Go online to test your understanding by trying multiple-choice questions, and assignment and examination questions.

Further research

McKinsey Quarterly online review, 'Operations' section

McKinsey is a leading consultancy firm that operates an Internet journal featuring articles of great value to readers interested in issues such as international outsourcing, manufacturing performance, product development, purchasing, supply chain, and logistics. Readers should consult McKinsey about registration possibilities.

Kollar, M. (2012). *Production Structure in the Context of International Trade: Towards a General Theory of International Production*. Lap Lambert Academic Publishing

The author uses as his starting point the trade of similar goods between similar countries to develop a theory of production that links specific manufacturing phenomena with international business debates such as an industry's degree of vertical integration or fragmentation.

References

Bertrand, O. (2011). 'What goes around, comes around: Effects of offshore outsourcing on the export performance of firms', *Journal of International Business Studies*, 42, pp. 334–344

Boyer, R. and Freyssenet, M. (2002). *Productive Models: The Conditions of Profitability*. Basingstoke: Palgrave Macmillan

Branzei, O., Nakamura, M., and Vertinsky, I. (2011). 'Learning in collaborative R&D: When multinationality matters', *Asian Business & Management*, 10/1, pp. 9–36 (February)

Brickman, C. and Ungerman, D. (2008). 'Climate change and supply chain management', July, available at http://www.mckinseyquarterly.com, accessed 28 November 2008

Caulkin, S. (2007). 'Toyota's never-to-be-repeated all-star production', *The Guardian*, 2 December, available at http://www.guardian.co.uk, accessed 20 June 2008

Christopher, M. (2005). *Logistics and Supply Chain Management: Creating Value-Added Networks*, 3rd edn. Harlow: Prentice-Hall

Davenport, T. and Prusak, L. (1998). *Working Knowledge: How Organizations Manage What They Know*. Boston: Harvard Business School

Dicken, P. (2007). *Global Shift: Mapping the Changing Contours of the World*, 5th edn. London: Sage Publications

Economist (2012a). 'Faster, faster, faster', *The Economist*, 28 January, p. 59

Economist (2012b). 'A third industrial revolution', *The Economist*, 21 April, special insert

Ernst & Young (2012). 'Why manufacturing matters', *Performance Preview 3*, January, p. 10

European Commission (2011). 'Monitoring industrial research: The 2011 EU Industrial R&D Investment Scorecard', available at http://iri.jrc.ec.europa.eu/research/docs/2011/SB2011_draft_October.pdf, accessed August 2012

Fernandez-Stark, K., Bamber, P., and Gereffi, G. (2011). 'The offshore services value chain: Upgrading trajectories in developing countries', *International Journal of Technological Learning, Innovation and Development*, 4/1–2, pp. 206–234

Harland, C., Knight, L., and Cousins, P. (2004). 'Supply chain relationships', in S. New and R. Westbrook (eds.). *Understanding Supply Chains: Concepts, Critiques and Futures*. London: Oxford University Press

He, Q. and Zhao, J. (2011). 'R&D transfer of MNCs: The perspective of China', *International Journal of Learning and Intellectual Capital*, 8/2, pp. 155–166 (April)

IAOP International Association of Outsourcing Professionals (2011). 'Will 2011 be the year people start talking differently about outsourcing?', available at http://www.iaop.org, accessed 10 December 2012

Ietto-Gillies, G. (2012). *Transnational Corporations and International Production: Concepts, Theories and Effects*, 2nd edn. Cheltenham: Edward Elgar

Kavanagh, M. (2011). 'Santander India call centre: Back to UK', 8 July, available at http://blogs.ft.com/beyond-brics, accessed 10 December 2011

Knowledge@wharton (2011). *Outsourcing: New Pressures to Stay Home, Old Reasons to Go Abroad*, 11 January, available at knowledge.wharton.upenn.edu, accessed 10 December 2011

Ko, J. and Hu, S. (2008). 'Balancing of manufacturing systems with complex configurations for delayed product differentiation', *International Journal of Production Research*, 46/15 (August)

Kotabe, M., Parente, R., and Murray, J. (2007). 'Antecedents and outcomes of modular production in the Brazilian automobile industry: A grounded theory approach', *Journal of International Business Studies*, 38/1 (January)

Kumar, S. and Wilson, J. (2007). 'A manufacturing decision framework for minimizing inventory costs of a configurable off-shored product using postponement', *International Journal of Production Research*, 45/17 (September)

Liu, R., Feils, D., and Scholnick, B. (2011). 'Why are different services outsourced to different countries?', *Journal of International Business Studies*, 42, pp. 558–571

Loppacher, J., Cagliano, R., and Spina, G. (2011). 'Key drivers of buyer-supplier relationships in global sourcing strategies', *International Journal of Procurement Management*, 4/2, pp. 156–180 (March)

Martínez-Noya, A. and García-Canal, E. (2011). 'Technological capabilities and the decision to outsource/outsource offshore R&D services', *International Business Review*, 20/3, pp. 264–277 (June)

Moody, A. (2011). 'The China strategist', *China Daily—European Weekly*, 7–13 October, p. 32

Naim, M., Disney, S., and Towill, D. (2004). 'Supply chain dynamics', in S. New and R. Westbrook (eds.). *Understanding Supply Chains: Concepts, Critiques and Futures*. London: Oxford University Press

Nassimbeni, G. (2004). 'Supply chains: A network perspective', in S. New and R. Westbrook (eds.). *Understanding Supply Chains: Concepts, Critiques and Futures*. London: Oxford University Press

Nonaka, I. and Takeuchi, H. (1995). *The Knowledge Creating Company*. New York: Oxford University Press

Patel-Campillo, A. (2011). 'Transforming global commodity chains: Actor strategies, regulation, and competitive relations in the Dutch cut flower sector', *Economic Geography*, 87/1, pp. 79–99 (January)

Rugman, A. and D'Cruz, J. (2000). *Multinationals as Flagship Firms: Regional Business Networks*. London: Oxford University Press

Rushton, A. and Walker, S. (2007). *International Logistics and Supply Chain Outsourcing: From Local to Global*. London: Kogan Page

Solis, M. (2003). 'On the myth of the Keiretsu network: Japanese electronics in North America', *Business and Politics*, 5/3

Tabrizi, B. and Tseng, M. (2007). *Transformation through Global Value Chains: Taking Advantage of Business Synergies in the United States and China*. Stanford, CA: Stanford University Press

Timlon, J. (2011) 'Building legitimacy within a Scandinavian MNC: An analysis of the factors that influence sustainable strategic sourcing decisions', *Strategic Direction*, 27/8, pp. 22–24

WHO—World Health Organization (2006). 'Access to AIDS medicine stumbles on trade rules', *Bulletin of the World Health Organization*, 84/5 (May)

12 International marketing

Learning objectives

After reading this chapter, you will be able to:

- ✦ appreciate a range of key issues related to international marketing
- ✦ recognize the strategies and phases for marketing overseas by MNEs
- ✦ assess standardization and adaptation in international marketing
- ✦ recognize and analyse the impact of culture on international marketing and advertising
- ✦ evaluate key developments in international marketing, including Internet marketing

Case study 12.1

Hero Bikes and advertising in India

One of the most interesting phenomena of the early part of the twenty-first century has been the 'reverse imperialism/ colonialism' of companies in the emerging economies taking over companies from the more developed and industrialized world. An example of this was the ending of the Indian joint venture between Honda of Japan and Hero Motocorp of India in August 2011. The joint venture had been in place from 1985 and had proved to be an exceptionally successful combined activity. From 2011–2012 onwards, the challenge for the Hero Motocorp and its owners, the Munjal brothers, is whether they can continue both the high sales and market share of the joint venture and the innovative approach to advertising that had characterized Honda's involvement in the venture.

Hero Honda advertisement. The clever marketing campaign for Hero Honda scooters resulted in strong sales (reproduced with the kind permission of Honda).

For an MNE such as Honda, its international marketing strategy enabled it to target a range of markets and segments through the massive purchasing power that it wielded globally. In addition, the attraction of the joint venture for Honda had been the local knowledge, expertise, and production capacity of the Munjal brothers. For Hero Bikes, the attraction of Honda was not only its name and its engineering strengths but also its innovative approach to advertising, such as its use of television with its keynote slogan of 'The Power of Dreams' and the 2006 advertisements for the Honda Civic: the 'Choir' that associated this relaxing mode of cultural expression with the sounds made by an automobile. With the joint venture in India, Honda took a different approach to the selling of very colourful motor scooters, the Hero Honda, into the Indian market. Among the range of about six different scooters one was branded as 'Hero Honda Pleasure', aimed directly at young female customers. The advert emphasized weddings, children playing in a park, and the independence of women and hooked into the slogan: 'Why should boys have all the fun?'

There is no doubting the success of this range of motor scooters: in 2010–2011 Hero Honda had about 50 per cent market share in India, with sales of over 5.2 million per year. These successful sales figures are partly accounted for by the advertising campaigns that demonstrated such a clever approach to a particular segment of the Indian market. It will be interesting to see whether Hero Motocorp will be able to maintain this level of sales and market share without the support of Honda.

Case study questions

1. Why did Honda decide to abandon its international marketing strategy for scooters and motorbikes in India?
2. What are the key challenges facing Hero Motocorp over the next few years as it stands on its own in the competitive Indian two-wheeled vehicle market?

Introduction

For many companies, the new markets for their goods are international so their corporate marketing strategies have to consider the implications of moving from their original domestic markets to developments beyond their own borders. International marketing is as vital for smaller companies as for massive MNEs. For all of them, their international expansion strategies are driven by pull or push marketing.

The concepts of 'pull' and 'push' marketing are extensions of views introduced in Chapter 10, where companies' structures and operations are seen as being developed from different approaches to internationalization. The pull or push orientation reflects the attitude of the company as the consumer demand for products and services has expanded on a global scale. International marketing is designed to ensure that global consumers' needs and desires are met and satisfied.

Part of the international expansion of the marketing function of companies is related to the development of and fascination with brands. Brands are global assets used by marketers to differentiate their products, services, and images from those of their competitors. In the scramble for international market share, companies seek to maximize their advantages from the economies of standardization and the specificities of adaptation, especially in relation to branding, and the use of the many facets of the Internet.

+ Brand
Collection of images and ideas representing a company or other organization or economic producer; it can refer to specific symbols such as a name, logo, slogan, and design scheme.

Section I: International marketing choices

When managers market internationally, they face a spectrum of strategic choices. They take decisions within the context of the key forces that shape the international corporate environment: the expansion of world trade, the growth and enlargement of trading blocs, and the staggeringly rapid development of new communications networks (including the Internet and IT communications). The way these choices are made helps to identify different kinds of international marketing effort.

Pull vs. push marketing

+ Pull marketing
Form of marketing reflecting the way in which a company is 'pulled' into the market by reacting to demand from the market.

The overriding approach taken in this chapter is to consider the marketing of goods and services from the perspective of where each international company locates itself on the spectrum of pull marketing or push marketing, as shown in Figure 12.1. These concepts relate in part to the pull and push corporate structures discussed in Chapter 10.

Pull marketing is when a company reacts to signals from the market. Companies that undertake pull marketing are generally more accurate in the methods they use to carry out market research, may face more competition, tend to offer lower prices, and are unlikely to benefit from any first-mover advantage. By contrast, push marketing is generally more risky internationally. It occurs when a company sells goods that are relatively unheard of and usually undertakes less accurate market research. If the new product is right for the market,

+ Push marketing
Form of marketing characterized by the way a company 'pushes' itself into the market by providing and selling goods that are new and relatively unknown.

Figure 12.1
Pull vs. push marketing.

Market expresses needs   Company reacts

Pull marketing effort

Company proposes idea   Market reacts

Push marketing effort

it can be launched at a premium price and, hopefully, has the potential to gain very large market share.

In the 1950s and 1960s, the Japanese were considered to be the key producers of 'copy-cat' products. Their companies developed and grew beneath the shadows of US industry and were known as imitators of whatever was produced in the Western world: this was the era of pull marketing for Japanese companies, which produced copies of already established items, including motorbikes and cars, electrical equipment, and plastic products. Later in the twentieth century, Japanese companies moved towards push marketing as they became greater innovators, particularly in the area of electronics, with products such as the most successful format for video recorders (VCRs)—JVC's VHS system—and the Sony Walkman.

An example of push marketing is the highly innovative approach taken by Apple in developing cutting-edge products in the i-range, for example iPods, iTunes, iPhones, and iPads. Although Apple was not necessarily the absolute first into these developments or products, its approach to the customer was such that it was thought to be a key innovator. Pushed by its late founder and CEO, Steve Jobs (1955–2011), and guided by Sir Jonathan Ive (Senior Vice President of Industrial Design), Apple always emphasized style and innovation, and this often paid dividends in its niche sales. With the launch of different versions of the iPad, Apple managed to reach very high worldwide sales, predicted to be as much as 66 million by the end of 2012 (Perez 2012). However, as is often the case with highly competitive products and markets, there grew up a whole series of rivals: other tablet computers, increasingly more sophisticated smartphones (Apple's iPhone achieved only about 10 per cent of worldwide sales of smartphones), and e-readers such as Amazon's Kindle (Arthur 2012). Indeed, the new market (from 2007 onwards) for e-readers has had a major impact not only on printed books and bookshops but on that aspect of the attraction of the iPad; the main competitors in 2011–2012, as well as the Kindle, were the products of Barnes & Noble (Nook), Kobo, Sony, Hanvon, Jinke, iRex Technologies, and Onyx International (Falcone 2011). For Apple in the decade from 2010–2020, there will be the usual high risk of international push marketing; the company has made major initial investments and commitments but the likely outcomes are deeply uncertain.

Standardization vs. adaptation

Few companies operate entirely at one end of the spectrum of standardization (most closely related to the push imperative) or adaptation (most closely related to pull marketing). Part of what differentiates each choice is the extent to which a company seeks to sell the same product or service worldwide or adapts them to the local market (Vrontis et al. 2009).

+ Adaptation
Extent to which a company's products and services are adapted for each market, meeting the particular needs of the customers.

Within the marketing function, the standardization of products refers to the extent to which a company can sell the same product in its domestic and international markets, whatever their location and size. Among the prime advocates of such an approach has been Microsoft, which has endeavoured to capitalize on economies of scale and to ensure that only one system is used on personal computers (PCs). Although Microsoft has faced a number of challenges to its top position in the world as far as PCs and operating systems are concerned, its intention to dominate the computing world has been clear since the late 1980s (Coyle 1998).

MNEs that are focused on standardization apply the principle of deferred differentiation (see Chapter 11) so that they postpone as long as possible any change from a globalized standard product (or service) to the various local adaptations that may be recommended at the regional or local level. The countervailing trend to standardization is adaptation (or customization). This approach requires that products and services are adapted for each market, meeting the particular needs of customers. Chapter 11 referred to deferred differentiation as the way in which MNEs' production function attempts to address the scale/scope dilemma; 'glocalization' is the downstream version of this international management approach—the idea of 'think global, act local'.

Figure 12.2
The BCG portfolio
matrix from the
product portfolio
matrix.

© Boston Consulting
Group 1970.

In the early years of the twenty-first century, glocalization became the claim of a world-wide bank, HSBC. Using the tag line 'the world's local bank', HSBC stressed its global reach simultaneously with its understanding of local and national norms, and cultural behaviour. Its advertising played on the dangers of bank representatives who did not fully understand local cultures and were liable to offend local businesspeople. Obviously, the HSBC banking representatives were seen as being sensitive to national cultures and possessing local knowledge (Jacobs 2010). Similarly, Danone, the French food products MNE, stressed its 'world-wide presence' and its culture of 'pragmatism, adaptability and local decisions' (Danone 2012). For many years, the company has been prepared to have its products marketed as national rather than French brands, even to the extent of Americanizing its name in the USA to Dannon. The MNE stresses that its international marketing strategy is driven not by the French headquarters but by the needs of local markets and the inventiveness of subsidiaries in a range of economies around the world (Danone 2012).

Another model in international marketing that helps to determine a company's approach to the standardization–adaptation issue is the Boston Consulting Group's (BCG's) growth share matrix explaining why companies market products differently in different countries, depending on their stage of development. Whereas Vernon's 'product life cycle' theory (see Chapter 2) noted that an MNE will move its main focus of production from more developed to less developed countries as the product itself moves from being a new to an older product, this chapter looks at the role of the product depending on the state of the market. The BCG matrix—see Figure 12.2—is applied to international marketing as the MNE's products reach different life cycle stages in national markets around the world.

A modern example of the use of the growth share matrix is in the communications revolution led by mobile phone developments. For a company such as Apple, its 'standard products'—computers, laptops, music players, smartphones, and iPads—are located in the 'cash cows' box, generating major proportions of revenue from the established OECD markets; such products are classified as 'stars' in the growing Asian markets and as 'question marks' in the more slowly developing markets of Africa. For Apple, the 'dogs' category will be achieved in the OECD markets when its older products are being run down or possibly abandoned completely. The growth share matrix provides a way of understanding that well-established MNEs will permit certain products, and sometimes entire product divisions, to be sold off once they have moved from the 'cash cow' box towards the 'dogs' category. An MNE can also find that its misunderstanding of the market for a particular product can undermine its international marketing strategy.

+ Ethnocentric
Company's replication in the international market of the way in which it markets its products and services in its domestic market—'this approach has worked well at home so it does not need to be changed'.

Marketing errors and failures

The successes and failures of international marketing strategies are likely to be more expensive than domestic ones. There are a number of ways in which MNEs can make poor decisions when addressing their international marketing dilemmas. There can be errors such as misinterpretation of signals (cultural, social, or economic), MNE managers' projection of their own tastes, and an ethnocentric view of consumers' product preferences.

Practitioner insight

Robert Dennis, Advisory Board Member, Zafesoft .

'Zafesoft, a small hi-tech company operating in the field of digital information security, faces particular challenges in the international marketing of its security solutions. As a niche vertical player, it needs to make decisions on how it generates leads and how it delivers solutions to customers in different sectors with different needs and of different sizes. Zafesoft has to be smart in its approach in order to be competitive with its larger rivals.

Zafesoft is a software start-up company focused on the security and control of digital information. It targets government agencies, companies that deal with electronic health information, financial information, other proprietary and commercially valuable information, where the loss or compromise of this information can result in a breach of national security, loss of privacy and/or illegal financial transactions (credit cards and so on) or loss of competitive advantage. Companies that outsource their operations to countries that have less strict or lax information property rights, for example, to Asia, Eastern Europe, or countries in the Middle East, are especially vulnerable to these risks. Zafesoft markets its software solution through a series of partnerships with specialist security re-sellers, personal contacts, by directly approaching and getting face time with chief security officers, chief technology officers, or chief administrative officers, and through other vendor partnerships.

The company has dedicated teams that cover a particular region or set of accounts and, while there are clear divisions between sales and account management in terms of the job function, the overall goal is the same. Marketing efforts are global and vertical, the goal being to generate warm leads that can be funnelled to the appropriate sales channel. Each team is separately responsible for prospecting for business; once a new account has been won and a solution implemented, it is the responsibility of a designated account manager to maintain the relationship and keep the customer happy. Any problems raised by the customer are resolved by Zafesoft as a whole.

Staff work very closely together to ensure that the functionality within the solution meets the needs of the customer base. In a dynamic company of this size the corporate structure is relatively flat, and as a result there is no real division between employees working in business development, product management, or sales, other than their natural expertise. The company adapts to its different markets in a variety of ways. For example, the approach to foreign markets requires Zafesoft to have local re-sellers acting on its behalf to help build relationships and navigate local bureaucracy; as a result there is usually a much longer sales cycle. In some cases, there is resistance to the approaches of new and foreign companies such as Zafesoft, particularly if there are similar home-grown solutions and services.

The size and demands of its customers often dictate the Zafesoft development roadmap. In addition, market research coupled with continuous customer feedback mean that Zafesoft will often adapt its offering to the growth areas in the market and the needs of its largest customers. Currently, the company is not large enough to offer multiple solutions, so this allows it to focus on specific products and services, and as a result makes Zafesoft very agile and able to respond very quickly to its customers' demands within days and weeks rather than months, as in the case of larger organizations.

The Internet has really opened up the world for companies such as Zafesoft, allowing organizations to find such a company, and similarly the company gains access to the wider market, and to a wealth of information through industry technical and business sources.'

Upstream focus Ethnocentric	Geocentric	Downstream focus Polycentric
Standardized product		Locally adapted product
Advantages of scale		Benefits of scope
Market is identical		Market is dissimilar
Customers are the same		Customers are different
High specialization		Maximum variety

Figure 12.3
Competing logics of upstream ethnocentrism vs. downstream polycentrism.

In the attempts to explain MNEs' successes and failures in international marketing, it is helpful to consider the three basic approaches that they follow as they face the issue of standardizing or adapting their products or services internationally: ethnocentric, geocentric, and polycentric. The two contrasting management approaches (ethnocentrism and polycentricism), as well as the mid-point of geocentrism, have been mentioned in Chapter 7 and are discussed below in further detail from the perspective of international marketing (see Figure 12.3). These approaches are fundamentally derived from business arrogance (ethnocentric) or corporate accommodation to the specific nature of individual local markets (polycentric).

Some of the world's largest retailers have found that foreign markets can be very difficult and some of the classic cases are set out below. The giant US retailer Walmart has failed to do well in a number of markets, including Japan, Brazil, South Korea, and Germany. The problems for Walmart included an inability to understand the consumer and retail environment (Japan), too much emphasis on low prices (South Korea), and attempting to replicate the same store format (Brazil) (Gandolfi and Strach 2009; ICMR 2009). The classic case of Walmart failing to export its American systems to other countries occurred in Germany where it acquired the wrong chain of stores in the wrong locations, was unable to adapt culturally to the different needs of German employees by treating them in the same way as American workers, and ignored the desires and needs of German customers by arranging the store layout in a way that was favourable in the USA but not suited to the German market (Knorr and Arndt 2003). This demonstrates the crucial importance of understanding the particular nature of any market where a foreign company intends to operate (Pioch et al. 2009).

Similarly, like many other British companies, Marks & Spencer discovered that the American market is very different from the UK and, after nearly 20 years of activities in the USA, the company admitted that its acquisitions and attempts to operate across the Atlantic had failed. Although such large retailers engage in a considerable amount of preliminary survey work and undertake detailed plans for entry into the US market, they appear to be misled by the apparent similarities of language, culture, and style. Marks & Spencer's purchase (and subsequent sale) of Brooks Brothers was shorter lived and less successful than its operation of King's supermarkets, but even the latter were finally sold off in 2006 (Cope 2001; Finch 2006). One of the latest British ventures into the US retailing market was that of Sir Philip Green's Topshop in 2009–2010; thus far, this appears to have succeeded but it has not expanded beyond three key stores located in New York, Chicago, and Las Vegas (Grazia 2011).

Even for Starbucks, a few markets have proved resistant to the normally worldwide marketing success of the North American coffee company. Notably, in Israel in 2003, Starbucks decided that it had failed to understand the existing coffee culture of the country, including its need for security, and pulled out of its six coffee houses in Tel Aviv (Barnea 2011; Starbucks Newsroom 2012). Starbucks had erred on a number of counts relating to the choice of partner (the Delek Group) and the type of market entry mode, and to misunderstandings about the competition in the market for coffee drinking.

+ **Polycentric**
Company adapts its marketing and sales strategy as closely as possible to the target country—that is, the market that it is entering is so particular that the marketing strategy and the products themselves must be adapted to the local conditions.

In the media sector, there is the interesting case of the launch of the Russian edition of the Condé Nast magazine *Vogue* in 1998 (BBC Education 1999). Apart from the major financial and economic impact of the crash of the rouble in August 1998, there was cultural ignorance in the company's approach to a Russian version of the magazine. This was compounded by the misguided assumption that there was no need to research a new market in any great depth. Ironically, it was the son of the publisher/owner, Jonathan Newhouse, Jr, who assumed that his own Russian-origin background (his grandfather was born Solomon Neuhaus in Russia) and the expert Americans he had assigned to the Moscow office could put together a version of the magazine that would meet the needs of the Russian market. This was a failure and, after the first few issues, *Vogue* was restyled with more Russian themes and covers, Russian (or Russian-looking) models and Russian editors—the latest being Viktoria Davydova who was appointed in July 2010 (Conde Nast Russia 2010).

Kodak also failed to adapt when it showed over-confidence in its own brand name on first entering the Japanese market in the 1980s, although its difficulties have also been attributed to technological challenges from Fuji and its own mismanagement (Hopkins 1990; Finnerty 2000). Kodak assumed it could trade on its well-established name in the USA and Europe without fully realizing the power of existing rivals in the Japanese market, especially Fuji, which had an established position and a better name for the Japanese consumer. It took Kodak a few years to adapt its original strategy to a more positive position within Japan. On a broader scale, the parent company of Eastman Kodak filed for bankruptcy in the USA in January 2012 and, in its attempt to cut worldwide costs, the inventor of the digital camera ironically decided to cease operating in that sector of business (*New York Times* 2012).

International marketing strategy and marketing mix

The international marketing department of an MNE needs to devise and carry out a full and proper international strategy, classically based on its marketing mix decisions, referred to as the 4 Ps or the extended version of 7 Ps. The corporate strategy is designed to optimize the marketing of the MNE's products or services.

+ **Marketing mix**
Different phases of a corporate marketing strategy—product, price, promotion, and place.

Phases and 4 Ps

The basic elements of an international marketing mix are reflected in the phases of the marketing strategy, whether international or domestic: *product, price, promotion,* and *place*; the extended version adds *process, physical evidence,* and *people*. The first steps in devising such a strategy relate to establishing the nature of the product and its price. This process takes the product from its creation, research, and design through to final production and sale. Increasingly, international marketers need to consider the growing focus on products suited to consumers' lifestyles and modern ways of living. Marketing research can uncover knowledge about consumer preferences so as to enhance product development and satisfy the preferences that are based on expectations about both the functional and experiential benefits of a new product (**see ORC Extension material 12.1 on consumer behaviour**).

> Go online

International product

These phases of strategy definition and implementation are at the heart of success or failure in bringing goods to market. A central debate within international marketing is whether increasingly global markets are ready for truly global goods, thus requiring little or no adaptation of the product (or service) itself. Were this to be the case, the global good would have the same characteristics wherever it was sold; the only variations would be in relation to pricing, methods of promotion, and location or place of sale/purchase. In certain cases—such as, for example, perfumes and drinks—this appears to be the way the product is sold worldwide, with the promotion and even the place being the same. The same strategy has also been tried in the automobile/car business with the launch of so-called global cars, such as the Ford Ka with a single model produced in 1996–1997 but since created in different versions, including after its re-launch in 2008.

The reasons for product adaptation range from the cultural to the technological. In some circumstances, companies have to adapt their products because the countries in which they are being marketed and sold have specific laws and requirements.

In India, Australia, New Zealand, Kenya, Ireland, and the UK, for example, all road vehicles drive on the left and thus most are designed as right-hand drive. However, the majority (about two-thirds) of the world's drivers are in left-hand drive markets. This means that car manufacturers seeking to sell worldwide have to be prepared to adapt their designs and production for both left-hand and right-hand drive markets. This requires certain marketing decisions that have an impact on the technological make-up of their production systems.

Another cultural product adaptation based on legal reasons is the German purity law (the *Reinheitsgebot* of 1516) related to the production and sale of beer. German breweries adhere to these regulations (amended in 1993 as the *Biergesetz*) and use their compliance as a valuable marketing tool, so that German consumers continue to give enormous credence and loyalty to beers that are 'pure'. The Germans have followed EU requirements and allowed the importation of foreign beer brewed with added ingredients such as rice, corn, and other un-Germanic additives. Since the EU ruling and the introduction of foreign beers to the market, however, such beers have not made dramatic inroads into the German market. In a sense, therefore, foreign brewing companies trading their own beers into the German beer market are inclined to follow the lead set by German breweries.

The German purity law is one of the best worldwide examples of marketing seeking to exploit its identification with positive attributes of a so-called leading country. It may be assumed, for example, that the best pasta comes from Italy, that Japan sets the standard for electronic goods, that the best steak is from Argentina, and that the highest-quality vodka is from Russia.

Companies follow different competitive strategies in different markets to maximize their impact, whether in terms of price or product. Rather like the increasing adoption of air conditioning in cars as standard, this kind of marketing strategy changes over time. Whereas Northern European car purchasers of the 1970s would have regarded air conditioning as an unnecessary luxury, the clientele of the 2010s think of it as essential for their lifestyle. Within each national market, as well as in the world as a whole, different messages have different resonances at different times. To some extent, this is a reflection of changes in advertising literacy; as products become more complex, advertising becomes more subtle and consumers more sophisticated.

Within the standardization and adaptation spectrum, most companies operating internationally endeavour to optimize their ability to target as many segments as possible with

The Lord of the Rings has been a global success

Source: NEW LINE/SAUL ZAENTZ / WING NUT / THE KOBAL COLLECTION / VINET, PIERRE

a single product or service; more specialized companies tend to target only a selection of segments. The success of global products such as Levi's, Coca-Cola, Pepsi-Cola, and McDonald's demonstrates that broad market segments can be reached internationally. Even on a more restricted basis, there are other products, including film series such as *Harry Potter*, which grossed $7.7 billion in global ticket sales (Box Office Mojo 2012), and *The Lord of the Rings* that have been successfully marketed into a wide range of sectors, thus bypassing 'the filter of national cultures' (Usunier and Lee 2009).

International pricing

As with domestic pricing decisions, the key choices made by international managers depend on the overall corporate strategy for the market, product, or service. Companies may decide to stick with the cost basis for pricing by ensuring that the price fixed is in line with the costs of producing the good; this may also be a decision to adhere to a price floor—the minimum price that can be afforded—or to a price ceiling—the maximum price that the market can tolerate. MNEs also base pricing decisions on the international distribution costs.

An MNE can opt for standard or adaptive pricing. Standard pricing means that the product is offered at the same basic price throughout the world, whereas adaptive pricing gives greater decision-making power to managers in subsidiaries, so that they can adapt the price to the local market (Hollensen and Opresnik 2010). In any MNE, there are pricing specialists located in different divisions, and their separate inputs need to be coordinated in such a way as to produce a coherent pricing strategy. For initial entry into a new market, an MNE decides whether or not it will adapt its normal strategy and opt for an artificially low price (penetration pricing), as was used by Sky TV in establishing large market share in competition with terrestrial television channels in many OECD countries. The marketing of luxury products usually requires the opposite strategy of maintaining the brand image with a high price (premium pricing); this choice usually applies to five-star hotel chains, first-class airline tickets, and high-quality pens, watches, and jewellery. In some cases, the MNE that is first into the market can raise its prices to benefit from its temporary competitive advantage (skimming strategy). Many electronic goods when first sold in new international markets are priced in this way until such time as the competitive advantage is lost.

In general, international costs will almost always be significantly higher than domestic ones. The additional factors that impact on the international marketing of products are the need for labelling and packaging that may be country specific; the tariffs, taxes, customs duties, or other charges related to importing and exporting; possible administration fees; and the extra costs of logistics and transportation (Hollensen and Opresnik 2010). Sometimes a simple change in the exchange rate between the producing country and the importing country can overturn the careful working-out of costing and pricing so that very quickly the price in one currency is no longer feasible in another.

International promotion

The challenges of international promotion are that MNEs are unsure whether the methods of communicating the message of their products or services in the domestic market can be replicated in the international arena. The use of marketing budget, media, and sales forces may be entirely different and advertising via television, billboards, magazines, websites, or social media is subject to different rules and regulations, as well as to different consumer reaction.

Some of the problems of international promotion, including advertising, are covered in Section II. Key factors for the international marketing division of a company is the accessibility of media in which the products and services are promoted, and the level of 'advertising literacy' in different countries. Advertising needs to be pitched appropriately and, as Goodyear (1991) suggested, five different levels can be identified. At the most basic level, advertising is focused on repetitive, factual messages about the product. The next two levels reflect a shift from the product's attributes towards the brand and the benefits that consumers will obtain from purchase and use of the product. At the fourth level, the advertiser is engaged in very little selling of the product, as the emphasis is on reinforcing the consumer's identification with the brand. The fifth and most sophisticated level is where the emphasis is virtually on the advertising itself; the advertisement makes little or no direct reference to the product (or even the brand) but simply provides stimulation and entertainment to the consumer. In the international market, these levels mean that, in general, the most advanced and complex consumer societies of the OECD countries will accept promotion and advertising towards the more sophisticated end of the spectrum. In the same countries, however, there are some restrictions on other forms of promotion. For example, in Germany there are considerable restrictions on promotions such as cold calling, mail shots, prizes, and promotional draws (Yeshin 2006).

There are other differences, too, in the use of print media within OECD countries. Loose inserts in newspapers and other printed materials are more common in the UK and Germany than in France and Spain. Perhaps as a result of the use of this form of promotion, inserts are commonly ignored by Germans and Britons, whereas the French and Spanish public pay more attention to them (Elms 2001).

The international communications revolution has brought the promotion of global products to the world through the use of satellite and cable television, evident by the worldwide reach of magazines such as *Vogue* and *Cosmopolitan*, and the Internet. The growth of the web has brought globalized messages to consumers and is sophisticated enough to permit the transmission of localized messages with the international promotion strategy of an MNE. The medium of company websites has increasingly become the main method of promotion for MNEs in the developed world, but it needs to be remembered that only 33 per cent of the world's population has access to the Internet (Internet World Stats 2012), so much international marketing must still be conducted in more traditional ways. For the more sophisticated markets within the developed world and among younger consumers, interconnectedness is achieved through various forms of digital marketing and particularly social media networks, such as Facebook (see Case study 12.3), LinkedIn, and Twitter (Tuten and Solomon 2012). Whether the promotion of products and services is to more or less developed markets, it is constrained by the budgets of MNEs or their international marketing departments; the pricing issue is, therefore, crucial. The tension between the marketers and the accountants can have a major impact on international marketing strategies.

International place

MNEs pay particular attention to place within their marketing strategy. This involves channel management—that is, the control of the systems by which the product is brought to market: logistics, transportation, distribution, delivery, and the locations for sales of the products. For most companies, their products are sold through a variety of outlets: hypermarkets, supermarkets, shopping malls, discount stores, open-air markets, boutiques, department stores, and so on. Some new methods of distribution rely primarily or solely on the Internet.

Large MNE retailers, such as Carrefour, Walmart, and Tesco, have established such a predominant position in the marketplace that they have great influence with their producers, suppliers, and distributors. Their dominance of the supply chain reinforces their ability to establish ever larger super- and hypermarkets, as shown by the massive growth of hypermarkets in the Shanghai area of China. Their presence in online sales is also impressive; in the UK by 2012, Tesco had approached 50 per cent of the online grocery market, far ahead of their domestic competitors such as Sainsbury's, Asda, Waitrose, and Ocado (Thompson 2012). Even by 2016, however, it is anticipated that the Internet will only account for 6 per cent of total expenditure in the grocery sector (Thompson 2012).

The purpose of the international marketing mix and the strategy adopted by companies is to demonstrate how the MNE is meeting the needs and desires of consumers throughout the world. To succeed in this, the company must ensure that it prepares and plans its marketing operations in the most thorough manner.

Market research, marketing information, and market position

The main reasons for success and failure in international market entry and marketing are related to the collection of marketing data, research into market segmentation, targeting of customers, methods for getting close to consumers, and ways in which companies can ensure customer loyalty to goods and services. Far-sighted MNEs with sufficient financial power are able to spend a significant proportion of time and money on attracting and retaining customers.

A key example of apparently good market research was demonstrated in 2007–2008 by the large UK-based supermarket Tesco with the launch in parts of south-west USA of its Fresh & Easy stores. These outlets were designed as stores for healthy foods at good value—neither at the top end of the market nor attempting to match Walmart's 'rock-bottom prices'. In its domestic market (the UK) and others, Tesco had established a loyalty card (the Tesco Clubcard) to give it an exceptionally rich source of customer data.

Before creating the new stores in California and other states, Tesco undertook an extensive process of research that included a number of Tesco executives and anthropologists living with 60 families in an attempt to understand their eating, drinking, and buying habits and the use of a mocked-up store to track the movement of customers. Despite this thorough work, Tesco's expansion plans have slowed—though it had reached over 180 stores by early 2012, some stores have been closed and it has realized that it may have misjudged the habits of American consumers (Li 2012). It was reported that some 'cultural norms imported from Britain [had] proved mystifying to US shoppers'. These included pricing own-label products higher than 'their brand-name counterparts' and having some 'fresh produce tightly wrapped in cellophane for freshness' (Li 2012).

Despite this temporary blip in the USA with Fresh & Easy stores, Tesco continues to show a commitment to this kind of investigation and understanding of its markets and customers. As Townsend (2007) commented, 'Tesco has long relied on in-depth research to inform its international growth; cash-and-carry aisles were introduced to its Thai stores, for example, as a direct response to local competition'. According to an industry analysis, 'Tesco's international business has a depth of management which is sector-leading among its peer group . . . Each country is run as a stand-alone business, with predominantly local management coupled with ex-pat specialists' (Townsend 2007).

It is not only large MNEs that can undertake successful international marketing into unexpected markets; the possibility also applies to small and medium-sized enterprises (SMEs). An interesting case of international expansion by a medium-sized firm is PAUL bakery, established in 1889 in Lille, France. Domestically, the expansion of PAUL began in the 1950s and 1960s, to the point where the company had nearly 500 outlets in 25 countries in 2012. It expanded extensively into new markets within the EU (Spain, the UK, Holland, and the Czech Republic) and outside (Bahrain, Florida (USA), Japan, Qatar, and Turkey). In the UK in 2012, there were nearly 40 shops/restaurants, mostly in and around London, but also at Edinburgh airport, with planned expansion to about 50. The supposed unique selling proposition (USP) of PAUL is the quality and exclusiveness of its bread and other products (http://www.PAUL-uk.com). It markets itself as being uniquely French ('L'amour du pain' —or a passion for bread) and has made this a successful proposition in the UK, where there can sometimes be resistance to products that originate in France (Mattinson 2010).

The case of PAUL illustrates the peculiar position and the specificities of international marketing for SMEs: they tend to be too small to run a volume product, so they are either condemned to work as a niche seller or are able to relish this position as long as their international order books are full or their international expansion continues at a measured and manageable pace. Regardless of the company's own view of its position, any SME operating internationally can be a target of vertical integration for a larger company. This would occur, for example, if a large restaurant chain decided that it should acquire PAUL as part of its extensive provision of a range of restaurant experiences. It would also suit a food and drink MNE that did not have this kind of product/service offering within its range or wanted to purchase a larger share of this market.

+ **Market segmentation**
Identification of customers with similar characteristics so that a commercially viable marketing strategy can be devised and implemented.

+ **Targeting**
Designing and aiming of a message at specific types of customers within markets that have been selected as the focus for a company's offering.

PAUL is an example of international expansion and successful marketing (reproduced with the kind permission of PAUL)

Case study 12.2

What is it about Coca-Cola and water? Dasani, VitaminWater, and Glaceau in the UK

In 2004, the launch of Coca-Cola's bottled water product, Dasani, became a classic case of failing to understand the market and of nearly wrecking the image and product range of a major MNE through the marketing failure of one product (Anderson and Kumar 2004). The growing British market for bottled water (about 10 per cent per year) was dominated by foreign brands such as Perrier, Vittel, and Evian, with strong competition from many UK private-label waters and supermarket brands. Bottled water sales in the UK were dominated by Danone (about 35 per cent of the market) and Nestlé (about 15 per cent of the market). Coca-Cola viewed the market as ripe for entry and exploitation. Its strategy was to use the UK as the springboard for entry and expansion of its non-carbonated beverages within Europe.

Certain market issues might have prevented Coca-Cola's launch of Dasani: a sophisticated market with strong existing consumer identification and loyalty; and increased market competition, which was squeezing industry profit margins. This might have put off a less powerful MNE, but Coca-Cola persisted in its determination to enter the UK and European markets. Dasani is 'manufactured' rather than taken directly from springs or other natural water sources: it is effectively tap water that undergoes what Coca-Cola calls a highly sophisticated purification system. Most American consumers regarded this as a valid hi-tech way of producing good-quality bottled water. Once this method was known in the UK, British consumers clearly did not regard it as acceptable. Of course, the customers who bought and drank it did not fully understand that it was not natural until a health scare led to the recall of Dasani.

In March 2004, it was discovered that the levels of bromate in Dasani were higher than legal levels and were caused by its manufacturing process. Quite correctly, the company consulted the Food Standards Agency and, although there was no direct threat to public health, it agreed to recall the entire stock of 500,000 bottles in the UK within about 24 hours. Media coverage of the recall led to a public realization of the manufactured rather than the natural quality of Dasani and to scathing comments about it being 'just tap water'. The public, therefore, felt that they were paying a great deal of money simply to have filtered water that had come out of the normal piped water system.

Dasani is not the only Coca-Cola water product to have been criticized in the UK. In 2011, campaigners objected to the claims of Glaceau (an 'enhanced water') that it used 'spring water with fruit juice', and to VitaminWater that it was 'nutritious'. In the latter case, the UK's Advertising Standards Authority banned the advertising on the grounds that the drink contained too high a level of sugar (nearly a quarter of a consumer's guideline daily amount) to be called nutritious. In the case of Glaceau, campaigners objected to the fact that only three of the eight flavours contained any form of fruit (O'Brien 2011). In spite of these problems, Coca-Cola has continued to witness significant increases in the sales of many of its water products as a result of the MNE's massive production and marketing strength.

Case study questions

1. Why did Dasani's launch in the UK fail?
2. What steps should an MNE take to ensure that its entry into a new market is successful?

Seven types of cultural adaptation

The combination of an MNE's location on the push–pull marketing axis and the ethnocentric–polycentric spectrum can be used as a measure of its international marketing strategy and, to some extent, the likelihood of its international success. To consider some of these issues more fully, this section outlines the main cultural factors to be taken into account in international marketing (see Figure 12.4). Obviously, the separation of these factors is not always as clear-cut as Figure 12.4 might suggest; some factors are related to the product or the form of the advertising itself.

(a) *National and country-specific* factors often incorporate some of the other listed factors, but some general approaches to life, living, and lifestyles can be identified; these factors are sometimes a reflection of real or perceived national stereotypes. The British attitude towards humour, for example, means that products can often be advertised and sold with a touch of fun and comedy. For both print and visual advertising of international brand motor cars, such as Audi or BMW, the stereotypical approach to be taken for the British is far more humorous than it is for other countries such as Italy or France (more inclined to an emphasis on style, luxury, and sex), or Germany (more susceptible to a technical sales message). In a market such as Japan, it is very important to have celebrity endorsements (about 60 per cent of all advertisements), whereas the German market tends to be unimpressed by this (about 6 per cent of all advertisements) (Usunier and Lee 2009).

(b) The *religious factor* within international marketing is most evident when comparing countries where Islam, Hinduism, or Christianity are most prominent. Global brands and MNEs realize that they need to tailor their products and messages to fit the dominant religion. For McDonald's, the essential constituent of a burger worldwide is beef but, in India, where

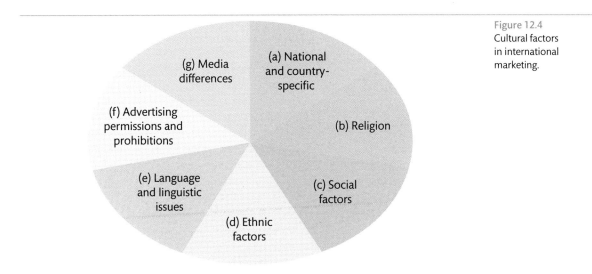

Figure 12.4
Cultural factors in international marketing.

Hindus revere cows, this is replaced by chicken or lamb. Similarly, beverage companies operating in Muslim societies need to focus on non-alcoholic products within their portfolio.

(c) Marketers operating across borders have to take into account a vast array of *social factors* as they seek to research, analyse, and segment these international markets. These include the demographic pattern of each country—for example, the age distribution of the population, the degree of urbanization, the structure of families, the extent of education, and the proportion of men to women. Each of these factors, and many others, can have a significant impact on the marketing of certain products and services. For example, where women have equal status to men in a society, they will tend to represent an equally import-ant market for many goods. In Western and industrialized countries since the 1990s, a new market has been revealed with the purchasing power of retired people, the so-called grey market: they have well-developed tastes for products such as travel, pensions, or recreational facilities and they wield enormous spending power.

(d) *Ethnic factors* have a role to play both within countries and between them. Within some countries, there are often groups that have different needs, tastes, and purchasing patterns. In the USA, Americans of Hispanic origin demand food and drink products that remind them of their ethnic/national origins in the Latin American countries from which they come, or with which they identify (Usunier and Lee 2009). Similarly, the high pro-portion of workers from India (and other parts of the Indian subcontinent) who reside in the United Arab Emirates (about 50 per cent of the population) greatly affects the marketing and sale of products there.

There are cases, too, where a famous MNE misreads the ethnic messages that it intends to attach to a product and its accompanying advertising. In spring 2009, Burger King launched in the UK and Spain its 'Nuevo Texican Whopper': 'the taste of Texas with a little spicy Mexican'. The TV adverts showed a tall Texan cowboy and a short Mexican wrestler wear-ing the Mexican flag as a cape. It should not have surprised Burger King that this attracted serious criticism from people such as the Mexican ambassador to Spain, whose complaint was that Burger King 'improperly use the stereotyped image of a Mexican'. The criticism resulted in the adverts being pulled from TV and not being released into the US market with its large Hispanic population, many originally from Mexico (Feldman 2009).

(e) Many countries are not only socially and ethnically diverse but also have *different languages and linguistic* traditions. What appeals to the French speakers of Belgium may not appeal to the Flemish speakers; the same applies, obviously, to other bilingual countries such as Canada and Wales, as well as to the many multilingual societies. In addition to the political and economic consequences of these linguistic splits, MNEs and other firms need to prepare marketing and selling strategies to take account of these differences. For Belgium, advertising agencies usually create advertisements simultaneously in Flemish and French, whereas, for example, in South Africa (which has 11 official languages, though the most used are English and Afrikaans), the agencies usually conceptualize an advertisement in English and then translate it. The translated adverts often fail to take into account the cultural factors that are crucial to selling into that sector of the market. Aside from the inevitability of having marketing campaigns and packaging in different languages, in a coun-try such as India, with 15 official languages, including English, there are different shopping patterns to consider. Clearly, these are not solely linguistically determined but are a reflec-tion of the socio-cultural aspects of the different groups (Hollensen and Opresnik 2010).

(f) Each country, especially in the industrialized world, has specific laws and regulations in relation to what is *permitted and prohibited in advertising*. For all countries, the regulatory framework for advertising covers a range of areas, such as no use of pornographic or overtly sexual images, regulations banning violent messages, and prohibitions on the exploitation of children. In particular, since the 1990s, there has been concern about the obesity of chil-dren and the consequent need to restrict (or ban) the advertising of unhealthy products, such as fast food, high-sugar drinks, sweets, and chocolates, to children.

In the Western world, the tobacco industry has found that the advertising and marketing of products have been increasingly restricted. This has primarily been a consequence of the evidence of health risks associated with the consumption of tobacco. Progressively, cigarette advertising has been removed from all media in many OECD countries, so that tobacco MNEs have had to move their message to sports sponsorship and LDCs. In the EU, the Directive of 2003 related to the approximation of the laws, regulations, and administrative provisions of the EU members states in connection with the 'advertising and sponsorship of tobacco products'. It classified tobacco products and their associated promotion as being cross-border issues that needed to be regulated within the EU as well as by national legislation and restrictions. For example, the UK's law (Tobacco Advertising and Promotion Act of 2002) was then supplemented by 2004 regulations on point of sale and brand-sharing (see Department of Health 2009). The international marketing consequence of the Western prohibitions on smoking has increased attention by the tobacco companies to markets in Asia and other parts of the less-developed world.

(g) Within the category of *media* (which includes newspapers, magazines, billboards, and online), there are differences such as patterns of television broadcasting, coverage, and viewing (Usunier and Lee 2009). A country like the UK, which has high viewing figures (in 2012, the average viewing time per week was about 28 hours), will respond more to high levels of advertising on television and to products that are particularly susceptible to such advertising (BARB 2012). For example, TV advertising in the UK includes massive campaigns tied into children's programmes. These products include the obvious ones such as toys, as well as a whole range of food and drink items. Many are thought to have contributed to the problem of obesity among young people and, as indicated above, have been restricted by law.

This wide range of culture, or culture-related, factors shows how complex the task is for international managers as they seek to make decisions about what products to market, where, and how. The challenges they face require them to take the right decisions and, perhaps above all, to avoid choosing strategies that could lead to embarrassment, failure, or scandal.

Section II: Issues in international marketing

There are three issues of current and growing significance to be highlighted in international marketing: business-to-business (B2B) marketing, international branding, and Internet marketing. Obviously other issues that could be stressed as being of similar importance to these include the complexities of international market segmentation and targeting, ethical or green marketing, international market research, and the role of marketing in the strategic decisions of MNEs considering market entry and the mode(s) of such entry. All these have been mentioned in this chapter—or elsewhere in the book—but here the focus is on three selected issues.

Business-to-business (B2B) marketing

While most of this chapter has been concerned with marketing to final customers or consumers—that is, members of the general public who buy goods and services for their personal consumption, or business-to-consumer (B2C) marketing—it is important to acknowledge the significance of B2B marketing, as this accounts for a considerable proportion of international marketing activities.

For companies marketing and selling in the B2C sector, their emphasis is usually on seeking a large target market, being product driven, and maximizing the value of the transaction. Being product-driven they emphasize merchandizing and point of sale, and try to create a single-step purchasing process (a short sales cycle), and stress emotional buying decisions (based on price, desire, or status) in the customer. The original distinction between

+ **Business-to-business (B2B) marketing**
Marketing of products and services to businesses—i.e. the marketing and sales relationship between one company and those other companies to which it supplies, or from which it receives, products and services.

+ **Business-to-consumer (B2C) marketing**
Marketing of products and services to the end consumers or customers—i.e. members of the general public who consume the products or services directly for themselves.

B2C and B2B arose from an attempt to differentiate between those buying 'online' (B2B) and those buying in more traditional ways. The development of Internet availability and access has made this distinction less valid, and the difference is now acknowledged to be between commercial/industrial (B2B) and personal (B2C) purchasers. It should be noted that there are also other categories such as B2G (business to government), G2B (government to business), and C2C (consumer to consumer).

The size of the B2B market is difficult to determine with any accuracy, but it has been estimated at more than $500 billion, or about 10 per cent of the total amount spent annually on international marketing activities and global sales transactions (QFinance 2012). What is not in doubt is the different nature of the B2B market, where, as Minett (2001) has suggested, the nature of the product development is 'linear' (rather than 'cyclical' as in B2C marketing), the driver is 'technology' (not 'fashion'), the customer motivation is 'organizational need' (not 'individual wants or desires'), and the focus is on 'sales and application' (not 'consumer characteristics').

The dimensions of B2B marketing can be exemplified by an MNE such as IKEA, which requires regular supplies of items that will eventually be sold to the consuming public. For IKEA, this means competition between suppliers of the different types of furniture (and other products). Each supplier will promote its products to the buyers at IKEA, compete on design, quality, manufacturing schedules, and price, and endeavour to secure as large a contract as possible with IKEA. The successful supplier(s) will have achieved substantial sales of its products to a mainstream MNE in the home-furnishings business. IKEA has about 1800 suppliers in more than 50 countries (Kotler et al. 2008). However, none of the final consumers (the public) will ever know the suppliers' names; the products that are bought will all be under the IKEA brand.

Another instance of the B2B market is the supply to airlines of all the customized components for its aircraft, the provision of catering, the supply of fuels, and so on. Apart from the names of such suppliers as Rolls Royce or Pratt and Whitney for engines, and BP or Esso for fuels, it is unlikely that any flying passengers will know who provided the seats, seat belts, air-conditioning system, or flooring. For several airlines, including JetBlue, American Airlines, and Lufthansa, seats are supplied by Recaro, a German company, which provided 85,500 seats to airliners in 2011 (Recaro 2012). The main difference involved in such B2B

Recaro supplies seats to several airlines including JetBlue, American Airlines, and Lufthansa

Source: Recaro

Rank	Brand	Brand value ($ m)
1	Apple	153,285
2	Google	111,498
3	IBM	100,849
4	McDonald's	81,016
5	Microsoft	78,243
6	Coca-Cola	73,752
7	AT&T	69,916
8	Marlboro	67,522
9	China Mobile	57,326
10	GE	50,318

Figure 12.5
The world's top 10 most powerful brands, 2011 (Millward Brown Optimor 2011).

(Note that Interbrand (http://www.interbrand.com) produces a similar list in which, for example, Coca-Cola is ranked 1st, Apple 8th, and Intel, Disney, and HP replace AT&T, Marlboro, and China Mobile—see Interbrand 2011.)

marketing is the scale of the activity: very large budgets but usually involving fewer suppliers and buyers; and more targeted promotional activities, including the building of personal relationships between the professional buyers and sellers in the market.

International branding

Over the years, marketers have stressed that it is not so much the product or the service itself that is important in influencing consumers but the branding. The idea of a brand is that the name, image, and symbols of the product or service are equally important. International branding has, therefore, become a key aspect of the marketing of products and services, especially where the brand is perceived to be able to cross borders.

The right branding can be critical for the success of any company's domestic or international business. For MNEs, a well-planned and executed international branding campaign is crucial for expanding into new markets, as well as securing and strengthening existing markets. International branding has the added complication of trying to ensure that the brand message remains intact regardless of the cultural differences. The branding of services, as can be seen from Figure 12.5, has been focused on the Internet and computing (Google, Microsoft, IBM, and Apple) and on mobile phones (Apple, AT&T, and China Mobile). Note the pre-eminence of Apple's brand since the iPhone (and later iPad) was added to the computing products of the company. This reflects the centrality of Apple design and products, as the iPhone drives 'the real-time communications revolution'. The iPhone is 'the critical engine of the new media economy . . . [as it] has swept away the traditional barriers between a mobile telephone, a web browser, a computer, a portable entertainment system and even an e-book reader' (Keen 2009).

Other areas in which successful international branding has occurred involves products such as drinks (alcoholic and non-alcoholic), perfumes and other toiletry products, cars, and luxury products, such as top-range watches (Hublot, Breitling, Raymond Weil, Patek Philippe, and Bulgari). For many successful brands, part of their appeal has been the close relationship between the design of the product and its function or its image. Design management and design within marketing are critical to the impact of the brand and, in some cases, to the enduring longevity and appeal of the product (**see ORC Extension material 12.2**).

Many criticisms of international branding have been broadcast by the popularity of the nologo website (http://www.naomiklein.org/nologo) and the writings of Naomi Klein. Her book, entitled *No Logo*, was originally published in North America and the UK in 2000 and

> Go online

is now available in over 25 languages. Klein's principal idea is that big brands (such as McDonald's and its character symbol Ronald McDonald) target young children worldwide in a kind of mass psychological experiment that turns consumers into robots. The more robotic the consumer can be, the smaller the need for product or service differentiation. This means that companies can sell the same thing everywhere, thus saving themselves adaptation costs. This raises the issue of whether international consumers are thought to be converging or diverging. Where they converge, they are more accepting of 'global' brands; where they diverge, they tend to resent the attempted homogenization of their lifestyles.

Concerns about the impact of brands can be seen in the mixed responses to international brands that are believed to illustrate the American lifestyle. Resistance to Americanization has been led in France, for example, by José Bové, a farmer and political activist, who has campaigned against the spread of fast-food restaurants, especially McDonald's, against the introduction of genetically modified (GM) foods, and for the international peasant movement, now called 'La Via Campesina' (http://viacampesina.org).

The more that the world moves towards sourcing products locally, the less likely it is to encourage global brands—unless they are made close to the customer. Therefore, the trend in the first half of the twenty-first century may be towards the encouragement of less FDI and greater closeness of producer and customer.

Internet marketing

One extraordinary development within the world of marketing, selling, and purchasing has been the rise since 1995 of the World Wide Web, the Internet. The best estimates suggest that about 2 billion people (of a world population of 7 billion) have access to the Internet; this is a growth in Internet access from less than 10 per cent of the world to about 33 per cent since 2005–2006 (CIA 2012). A key issue is whether the Internet represents a dramatic change in the conduct of international business or whether it is simply a different medium and means of getting products to consumers. The potential of the Internet is still being tapped and it is making great strides towards not only being a source of social interaction and information gathering but also as a dramatic new phase in business.

The question of how much Internet services, and the Internet itself, are standardized rather than adapted is one that is still to be resolved, as are the issues about how successful these networks will become as international advertising and marketing vehicles. Indeed, the development of social networking has reinforced the view that viral marketing is a key trend for the future of increasing marketing reach and sales in the next few decades.

There is an infinite amount of 'shelf space' on the Internet, even though, as is evident from companies such as Amazon, it still requires vast amounts of warehousing in order to satisfy consumer demand. Anybody who has seen the vast storage depots that supply Amazon customers with their books, DVDs, and CDs realizes that some of what the Internet does is little different from what is provided through the distribution of catalogues and mail-order sales. The key difference between old warehousing and the Amazon system is the ruthless application of technology to the Amazon structures. The Amazon warehouses in the USA were expensive to build (about $50 million each) and expensive to operate. They have become, however, models of efficiency because of the high degree of computerization, the interactivity between people and computers (signals to workers, collection of items, weighing and dispatch), and the generation of large amounts of data on factors such as line speed, robot-picking, productivity, conveyor belt blockages, and bottleneck problems. The warehouses have become so efficient that Amazon turns over its inventory about 20 times per year, whereas other retailers are fortunate to achieve a rate of 15 times.

The successful growth of the Internet in its many forms may be a result of the theory of the Long Tail (**see ORC Extension material 12.3**), which claims that the world's culture and economy are increasingly shifting away from a focus on a relatively small number of 'hits' (mainstream products and markets) and towards a huge number of niches ('the tail'). As the

> Go online

costs of international production and distribution fall, especially online, narrowly targeted goods and services can be as economically attractive as mainstream items.

Of course, the question can be asked as to whether the success of Amazon (over 56,000 employees worldwide and profits continuing to rise on revenue of about $48 billion in 2011) is a result of it offering goods on the Internet rather than through older media or a result of the efficiency of its warehousing systems—and the drive and skills of its CEO, Jeff Bezos (Kirby and Stewart 2007). This is likely to remain a debatable point until later in the twenty-first century, when there will be some historical perspective on the international marketing of goods via new Internet businesses.

Challenges and choices

→ A key challenge for international marketing over the next few years is the extent to which the use of the Internet and social networking sites becomes the industry norm, and the impact this will have on other methods of marketing.

→ This involves difficult decisions about the information management systems to be purchased, maintained, and extended; the staffing levels required in this new marketing world; and the likely development of affordable, single-platform home-entertainment systems that combine the current features of TV, DVD, computer, telephone, gaming, and the purchase of goods and services. A key choice for the industry is the extension of online marketing to children. As long ago as 2008, there were about 100 youth-focused virtual worlds, some aimed at children as young as 5 years old; by 2012 this had grown to nearly 500. For the industry, the key challenge is to provide 'legitimate reassurance to parents that the sites their children use adhere to strict codes and standards' (Richard Deverell, Controller of BBC Children, cited in Carter 2008).

Chapter summary

The coverage of international marketing in this chapter has addressed a range of key issues including strategies for marketing overseas, questions of standardization and adaptation, push and pull marketing, the impact of cultural aspects on marketing and advertising, the key role of branding, the importance of good research and closeness to customers, and the emergence and future of Internet marketing.

There are many problems attached to the possible expansion outside a company's domestic market, even for major MNEs. Success in international expansion is often related to good market research, intelligent understanding of different cultures, sensible advertising and marketing approaches, and a quality product or service being delivered to the right market segment at the right time and in the right way. Although the most significant roles in international marketing are played by large MNEs, it should be clear that SMEs can also take the strategic option of successful international sales, marketing, and distribution.

The great marketing phenomenon of the early part of the twenty-first century was the development of advertising and sales through social networking. The main social networks included Facebook, Twitter, MySpace, Bebo, LinkedIn, and Flickr. The market leader was Facebook, which made a rapid fortune for its young founder, Mark Zuckerberg. Born in 1984, he was estimated to be worth $15 billion at the age of 23 in 2007 and in 2012, in an action that he may live to regret, he floated the company on the stock market with an initial public offering (IPO) in which each share was priced at $38 and at an initial total value of about $104 billion. However, the share price fell within hours and within a few weeks had lost over 15 per cent of its value (Demos et al. 2012) and by November 2012, Facebook stock had lost 44 per cent of its value since its offer price of $38.

In a very short time, all these social networks expanded from their original base (usually the USA) into an international phenomenon. As with most developments on the Internet, the American impetus has remained strong but, as the networks have expanded, they have become genuinely global—within the communities that are web-connected.

Facebook started in February 2004 and was initially a social networking site restricted to students of Harvard College. It rapidly extended to other Boston colleges and universities, then to all international academic and educational institutions, and finally to anybody anywhere in the world. Facebook's growth rates were astounding, rising from the 60th to the 7th most-visited website between September 2006 and September 2007. By September 2007, the website had achieved the largest number of registered users with over 42 million internationally active members; by February 2012, it had nearly 845 million users worldwide, a rocketing growth rate, an annual revenue of $3.7 billion, and a profit margin of 27 per cent (Harris 2012).

Many other companies involved in the Internet and computing, such as Google and Microsoft, competed to buy into Facebook. Microsoft paid $240 million for a minority stake (1.6 per cent) in the company, thus buying the exclusive rights to sell advertising on Facebook. The value of this small stake was estimated to be $1.6 billion in 2012.

Facebook and the other social networks are inevitable developments from the user-generated content feature of the Internet. Whereas earlier developments within the commercial exploitation of the Internet tended to mirror normal sales and marketing patterns, the rise of the social networks threatened to break new ground. The early users of the Internet tended to create cyberspace catalogues—the goods were easily viewed, ordered, and paid for through their websites, but there was still a crucial delivery of a physical product, such as CDs, books, foodstuffs, computer hardware, and other goods. The later users (that is, social networkers) looked at the Internet in an entirely different way. Not only were they looking at the features of cyberspace in the way that Manuel Castells (2001) had foreseen, but they were also able to attract large volumes of advertising onto their websites.

For Facebook, registered members join for no charge, since the idea is for Facebook to make money out of domestic and international advertising. The real battle in the market is for the competing firms, such as Microsoft and Google (with Google+), to contend for shares of online advertising. The value of Facebook is its extensive and international membership: 'a goldmine waiting to be tapped' (Ashworth and Heath 2007). What has not yet been fully developed, even with its potentially ill-fated 2012 IPO, is how advertisers will connect with users. An investor in Facebook is assuming that each of the 845 million international users is worth about $100 each, and thus likely to generate that sum in advertising and commercial value. Such spending power—or anything approaching it—represents a gigantic international market over a long period of time.

The potential of Facebook was seen in the possibilities of international crossover marketing. Facebook's progress by 2020/2025 will demonstrate how well social networks have become an integral part of product and service marketing for all generations, not just young people who have grown up with it in the early part of the twenty-first century. Above all, it can be contended that 'the capacity for interactivity is greater on the web than with any other mass media' (Yeshin 2006). This means that customers

The growth of social networking sites such as Facebook has provided new opportunities for product and service marketing

Source: Getty

have far greater control over the way in which they interact with the advertising message, with the marketing of goods and services, and with the manipulation of the content of the medium. The customer has the real possibility of choosing and responding to particular marketing messages that they like—they have become more active consumers than ever before. The interactivity of the World Wide Web as an international marketing medium is reaching its zenith with the rise and success of social networks such as Facebook.

Case study questions

1. For international consumers and MNEs, what are the marketing benefits of social networks and other Internet sites?
2. Why has Facebook spread so quickly across the world?
3. Why are Facebook and other Internet sites such a threat to established industries and authority structures around the world?

Discussion questions

1. What are likely to be the most internationally successful Internet marketing websites by 2020? Why?

2. What are the key benefits for an international retailer of 'loyalty cards'?

3. Why are popular, internationally sold bottled waters (such as Perrier, Evian, Dasani, etc.) now thought to be a less ethical purchase than ten years ago?

4. What are the most common reasons for successes and failures in the international marketing of products and services?

5. Why do MNEs so often make cultural mistakes in their product launches and/or advertising?

Online resource centre

Go online to test your understanding by trying multiple-choice questions, and assignment and examination questions.

Further research

Ruzo, E., Losada, F., Navarro, A., and Díez, J. A. (2011). 'Resources and international marketing strategy in export firms: Implications for export performance', *Management Research Review*, 34/5.

Using a sample of Spanish companies, the purpose of this article is to use the resource-based view (RBV) to analyse the relationship between the resources available for export activity—the company's size, structure, and experience—and the international marketing strategy adopted. The overall conclusion of the article is that, although the international expansion strategy does not generally affect export performance, the decisions taken about whether to standardize or adapt the marketing-mix elements do have a considerable impact. The authors seek to allocate corporate resources in identifying the optimal fit for firms' export strategies.

References

Anderson, J. and Kumar, N. (2004). 'Dasani UK: Brand under attack', *European Case Clearing House*, ECCH 504-022-1

Arthur, C. (2012). 'Kindle fire may have singed iPad sales . . .', *The Guardian*, 4 January

Ashworth, J. and Heath, A. (2007). 'Because he's worth it: Facebook hits the jackpot', *Business*, 29 September

BARB—Broadcasters' Audience Research Board (2012). 'Weekly total viewing summary, 1992–2009', available at http://www.barb.co.uk, accessed 18 February 2012

Barnea, A. (2011). 'Lack of peripheral vision: How Starbucks failed in Israel', *African Journal of Marketing Management*, 3/4, April

BBC Education (1999). 'To Russia with Vogue', *Trouble at the Top*, Episode 2, Series 3

Box Office Mojo (2012). 'Franchises—Harry Potter', available at http://boxofficemojo.com/franchises/chart, accessed 14 June

Carter, M. (2008). 'Is this harmless child's play—or virtual insanity?' *Independent*, 2 June

Castells, M. (2001). *The Internet Galaxy: Reflections on the Internet, Business and Society*. Oxford: Oxford University Press

CIA—Central Intelligence Agency (2012). 'Internet users', *The World Factbook*, available at http://www.cia.gov, accessed 19 February

Conde Nast Russia (2010). 'Viktoria Davydova named editor-in-chief of Vogue Russia,' 28 July, available at http://condenast.ru/en/news, accessed 9 June 2012

Cope, N. (2001). 'Marks & Spencer disposes of Brooks Brothers for a knock-down $225m', *Independent*, 24 November

Coyle, D. (1998). 'The simple idea that lies behind Microsoft's aim to rule the world', *Independent*, 19 February

Danone (2012). '2010 growth first – interview with Franck Riboud, CEO of Danone', available at http://www.danone.com/en/company/strategy.html, accessed 9 June 2012

Demos, T., McCrum, D., and Alloway, T. (2012). 'Investors sue Facebook and banks on IPO', *Financial Times*, 23 May, available at http://www.ft.com, accessed 14 June 2012

Department of Health (2009). 'Tobacco publications', available at http://www.dh.gov.uk, accessed 19 April 2009

Elms, S. (2001). 'Multi-country communication planning', *Admap*, January

Falcone, J. (2011). 'Kindle vs Nook vs iPad', *CNet News*, 23 November

Feldman, C. (2009). 'Burger King's whopper of an ad', *Houston Chronicle*, 16 April

Finch, J. (2006). 'M&S quits America with sale of supermarkets', *The Guardian*, 1 April

Finnerty, T. C. (2000). 'Kodak vs Fuji: The battle for global market share', Lubin School of Business, Pace University (paper written under the supervision of Dr Warren J. Keegan)

Gandolfi, F. and Strach, P. (2009). 'Retail internationalization: Gaining insights from the Wal-Mart experience in South Korea', *Review of International Comparative Management*, 10/1, March

Goodyear, M. (1991). 'Global advertising: The five stages of advertising literacy', *Admap*, March

Grazia (2011). 'Topshop's parent company will close up to 250 shops due to the recession', 24 November, available at http://www.graziadaily.co.uk/fashion/archive/2011, accessed 9 February 2012

Harris, P. (2012). 'The risks and rewards that lie in wait for Facebook', *The Observer*, 5 February

Hollensen, S. and Opresnik, M. O. (2010). *Marketing: A Relationship Perspective*. Munich: Verlag Vahlen

Hopkins, H. D. (1990). 'Kodak vs Fuji: A case of Japanese–American strategic intervention', paper, Temple University

ICMR—IBS Center for Management Research (2009). 'Wal-Mart's Foray in Brazil', BSTR332, available at http://icmrindia.org/casestudies, accessed 9 June 2012

Interbrand (2011). 'Best global brands 2011,' 4 October, available at http://www.interbrand.com, accessed 18 February 2012

Internet World Stats (2012). 'Internet usage statistics: The Internet big picture', available at http://www.internetworldstats.com, accessed 18 February 2012

Jacobs, E. (2010). 'Navigating cultural differences', *Financial Times*, 19 July

Keen, A. (2009). 'Why Apple isn't feeling the bite even as other tech Titans tumble', *Independent*, 27 April

Kirby, J. and Stewart, T.A. (2007). 'The institutional yes: An interview with Jeff Bezos', *Harvard Business Review*, available at http://hbr.org/2007/10/the-institutional-yes/ar/1, accessed 19 February 2012

Klein, N. (2000). *No Logo*. London: Flamingo

Knorr, A. and Arndt, A. (2003). 'Why did Wal-Mart fail in Germany?' *Materialien des Wissenschsftsscherpunktes 'Globalisierung der Welwirtschaft'*, Instituts für Weltwirtschaft und Internationales Management (IWIM), Universitat Bremen, 24 June

Kotler, P., Armstrong, G., Wong, V., and Saunders, J. (2008). *Principles of Marketing*, 5th European edn. Harlow: Pearson Education

Li, S. (2012). 'Fresh & Easy to close 7 stores in California', *Los Angeles Times*, 11 January

Mattinson, A. (2010). 'Frank PR takes on Paul bakery and café consumer brief following pitch', *PR Week*, 5 August

Millward Brown Optimor (2011). 'BrandZ top 100 most valuable global brands 2011', available at http://www.millwardbrown.com, accessed 18 February 2012

Minett, S. (2001). *B2B Marketing: Different Audience, Different Strategies, It's a Different World*. Harlow: Pearson Education/FT Prentice Hall

New York Times (2012). 'Kodak says it will stop making digital cameras,' 10 February, available at http://www.nytimes.com, accessed 18 February 2012

O'Brien, L. (2011). 'The real thing? Coca-Cola water rebuked for its health claims', *Independent*, 31 December

Perez, S. (2012). 'iPad sales may reach 66 million in 2012', *Tech Crunch*, 20 March, available at http://techcrunch.com/2012, accessed 8 June 2012

Pioch, E., Gerhard, U., Fernie, J., and Arnold, S. J. (2009). 'Consumer acceptance and market success: Wal-Mart in the UK and Germany', *International Journal of Retail & Distribution Management*, 37/3

Q-Finance (2012). 'E-Commerce industry', available at http://www.qfinance.com, accessed 18 February 2012

Recaro (2012). www.recaro.com, accessed 18 February 2012

Starbucks Newsroom (2012). 'Facts about Starbucks in the Middle East', available at http://news.starbucks.com/article, accessed 9 June 2012

Thompson, J. (2012). 'Tesco bids for a virtual supermarket sweep', *Independent*, 24 February

Townsend, A. (2007). 'Coming to America', *Business*, 6 October

Tuten, T. and Solomon, M. R. (2012). *Social Media Marketing*. Upper Saddle River, NJ: Prentice Hall

Usunier, J.-C. and Lee, J. A. (2009). *Marketing Across Cultures*, 5th edn. Harlow: Pearson Education/FT Prentice Hall

Vrontis, D., Thrassou, A., and Lamprianou, I. (2009). 'International marketing adaptation versus standardisation of multinational companies', *International Marketing Review*, 26/4–5

Yeshin, T. (2006). *Advertising*. London: Thomson Learning

Other sources of information

Brassington, F. and Pettitt, S. (2007). *Essentials of Marketing*, 2nd edn. Harlow: Pearson Education

Carr, D. (2008). 'You want it, you click it (waiting is not an option)', *Observer*, 13 April, *New York Times* insert

Carroll, E. (2007). 'The rise of the social network phenomenon', *Independent*, 26 September

Chaffey, D., Ellis-Chadwick, F., Johnston, K., and Mayer, R. (2006). *Internet Marketing: Strategy, Implementation and Practice*, 3rd edn. Harlow: Pearson Education/FT Prentice Hall

Chong, W.K., Shafaghi, M., Woollaston, C., and Lui, V. (2010). 'B2B e-marketplace: An e-marketing framework for B2B commerce', *Marketing Intelligence & Planning*, 28/3

Clark, A. (2007). 'Microsoft stake in Facebook values site at $15bn', *The Guardian*, 25 October

Cohen, N. (2007). 'Stand up for Tila, an unlikely web warrior', *Observer*, 30 September

Fill, C. and Fill, E. (2005). *Business-to-business Marketing: Relationships, Systems and Communications*, 4th edn. Harlow: Pearson Education/FT Prentice Hall

Hillebrand, M. (2000). 'Forecasters fuel feeding frenzy on B2B projections', *E-Commerce Times*, 27 January

Hindustan Times (2011). 'Hero Honda: Hero Motocorp' available at http://blogs.hindustantimes.com/car-nama/2011/08/18/hero-honda-//-hero-motocorp, accessed 3 February 2012

Hopkins, H. D. (2003). 'The response strategies of dominant US firms to Japanese challengers', *Journal of Management*, 29/1, pp. 5–25

Immelt, J. R., Govindarajan, V., and Trimble, C. (2009). 'How GE is disrupting itself', *Harvard Business Review*, October

Independent (2009). 'Tesco admits it misjudged US shopper', 23 February

Moen, O., Madsen, T. K., and Aspelund, A. (2008). 'The importance of the internet in international business-to-business markets', *International Marketing Review*, 25/5

Pettey, C. and Stevens, H. (2011). 'Gartner says sales of mobile devices grew . . .', *Gartner Newsroom*, 15 November, available at www.gartner.com/it, accessed 3 February 2012

Sanchez-Hernandez, M. I. and Miranda, F. J. (2011). 'Linking internal market orientation and new service performance', *European Journal of Innovation Management*, 14/2

Schiffman, L. G. and Kanuk, L. L. (2007). *Consumer Behavior*, 9th edn. Upper Saddle River, NJ: Pearson Prentice Hall

(13) International finance

Learning objectives

After reading this chapter, you will be able to:

- ✦ identify the different corporate activities that create foreign exchange risk
- ✦ apply financial risk management strategies
- ✦ evaluate different sources of MNE funding
- ✦ trace movements of funds within MNEs
- ✦ analyse tax issues that MNEs face

Case study 13.1

Currency risk is small beer for Heineken

With its network of 140 breweries and countless distributors in more than 71 countries worldwide, Heineken face foreign exchange (FX) risk on a daily basis (Heineken 2012). In general, the company seeks protection against the risks associated with the changing value of the currencies that its business units use in their daily transactions. Its general policy is to eliminate up to 90 per cent of the routine exposures that it forecasts, generally comprised of the gap between revenues that it accumulates in US dollars and production costs that it incurs in local currencies. At year-end 2011, for instance, Heineken estimated that a 10 per cent fall in the value of the dollar would have reduced its equity position by approximately €14 million (down from €38 million the year before). Its currency management policy had succeeded in keepng this risk under control, especially in light of the group's €1 billion in consolidated 2011 profits.

Retrospectively, however, it is difficult to say whether Heineken's prudent policy of always protecting itself against a weaker dollar was a good thing. In fiscal year 2008, for instance, the company averaged selling the US currency at around $1.26 per euro. Compared with 2009's lower average exchange rate of $1.43, this might seem to have been a good move. But then in 2010, the company sold the dollar at an average 1.35, meaning that Heineken would have benefited greatly had it not already sold off its 2009 dollar revenues and just held on to them until 2010. Of course, regrets can be a double-edged sword. Had Heineken decided to change its risk management policy to take advantage of future dollar strength, it would have suffered in 2011 when the currency fell to close to 1.50 against the euro—before turning around to hit a new high of around 1.20 in 2012.

Heineken's currency management programme smoothes out any risks
Source: Heineken

This kind of volatility means that without a crystal ball, the corporate treasurers in charge of Heineken's currency exposure can never be sure what the dollar exchange rate will be in one day's time, much less in one year. That makes it very risky not to cover the company against its worst case scenario. The problem is that protective strategies of this kind also prevent it from making unexpected, so-called 'windfall', profits in case the dollar strengthens. In this sense, Heineken's decision to cover its FX risks creates a new risk.

Case study questions

1. Why does Heineken cover some potential FX risks but not others?
2. With hindsight, has Heineken been successful in recent years in covering its currency risks?

Introduction

Exposure
Where assets do not match liabilities for a financial asset, such as a currency, whose price might fluctuate.

The two main topics in multinational finance are FX management and funding. To avoid adverse currency moves wiping out profit margins, MNEs need to monitor their market risks at all times. It can be hard tracking the many different positions that a group's headquarters and different subsidiaries accumulate, explaining why most MNEs spend large amounts of money on information systems centralizing data about their currency exposures (Bergendahl and Sjögre 2011). As for funding, the key issue here is MNEs' ability to access capital for both short- and long-term purposes. Being able to raise to funds when times are tough can be crucial to a company's survival. Capital also allows MNEs to acquire strategic assets when opportunities arise. Like labour and materials, it is a key factor input in business enterprise.

Section I: Foreign exchange

The first task when identifying FX exposure is to clarify why firms operating in multi-currency environments are at risk when prices move. Following this, analysis will explore the main foreign operations that generate FX risk.

The concept of exposure

There are many occasions when MNEs handle currencies other than the one traded in their home country. The US dollar, for example, is the standard currency of transaction in commodity markets such as oil or rubber but also for many complex goods like aeroplanes. For non-dollar-based companies, trading in these sectors entails FX exposure. Conversely, firms whose entire value chain involves the use of one single currency can trade with foreign counterparts without exposing themselves to direct FX risk (although they will still face an indirect 'economic risk' because of the way that currency movements can affect rival firms' competitiveness).

+ Denominate
Specifying the currency in which a transaction takes place.

+ Home currency
Currency that a firm uses to calculate its consolidated global accounts.

+ Long position
Owning more of a commodity in the form of assets than the amounts owed in the form of liabilities.

+ Short position
Owing more of a commodity in the form of liabilities than the amounts owned in the form of assets.

Managing FX exposure is a costly and difficult process that most MNEs like to avoid if at all possible. For this reason, a key aspect of international contract negotiations is the currency of transaction. The party that is in the stronger position (usually the one that is larger in size or technologically more advanced) will tend to demand that the deal be denominated in its own currency, forcing its counterpart to cope with the FX exposure.

An MNE is exposed to FX risk if the three following conditions are met:

1. It manages several currencies on both the asset and liability sides (respectively, sums owned and owed).

2. Its assets in any one currency do not match its liabilities in that same currency (creating an 'asset–liability gap'). For instance, the British discount airline EasyJet tends to sell to UK and European customers, accumulating assets in pounds and euros, while many of its liabilities are in dollars.

3. The price of the currency in question varies against the price of its home currency.

FX management is based on two fundamental risks. Where an MNE has a long position and more assets than liabilities in a given currency, the risk is that the value of this currency will fall before the assets can be sold. Where an MNE has a short position and more liabilities than assets in a given currency, the risk is that the value of this currency will rise before the liabilities can be acquired, increasing their cost. Thus, regardless of the MNE's currency of origin, it will be exposed to FX price variations as long as its different currency positions are not equal to zero at all times.

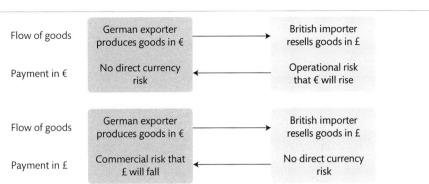

Figure 13.1
FX risk of a German
export to the UK
depends on currency
of transaction.

Once the existence of an FX exposure has been established, the next step is to identify what caused this risk, and what impact it might have. The answer will depend on factors such as: the nature of the company's international operations (trade or foreign direct investment); the volumes in question (different for small and medium-sized enterprises (SMEs) and large MNEs); and the company's configuration, i.e. the locations where it produces and sells.

Sources of FX exposure

The main sources of FX risk are 'transactional' exposures that MNEs incur as a result of daily value chain activities. These risks occur constantly in companies such as global retailers that deal in foreign currency all the time, or they can be more irregular in companies for whom overseas transactions are more sporadic (including, for instance, the construction sector).

Transactional FX risks

The first category is *commercial risk*, which occurs when a company sells goods or services to a customer and receives foreign currency in payment. Sales of this kind increase the exporter's 'long' exposure, and thus the risk that the foreign currencies it receives will fall in value before it can resell them. As Figure 13.1 demonstrates, one example would be a euro-based German SME that exports solar panels to the UK. If the foreign currency in which the exporter denominates its sales (pounds sterling) differs from the domestic currency in which it incurs costs (euro), it is exposed to the risk that the pound falls in value before it can be sold for the euro. The British importer, on the other hand, would be buying foreign goods in its home currency and therefore has no exposure.

Operational risk arises when a company buys goods or services from a supplier and pays in foreign currency. These purchases increase the importer's 'short' exposure, and hence the risk that the foreign currencies in which it pays its liabilities will become more expensive before it gets a chance to acquire them. In the example of the Germany–UK solar technology trade, if the UK importer were to pay its German supplier in euros, the deal would expose it to the risk that this currency might rise in value against the British pound, the currency in which the importer manages its accounts. In this case, the German exporter's foreign transactions would be in its own home currency, meaning that it would have no direct FX exposure. Thus, it is the currency of transaction that determines whether the exporter will face a commercial risk or the importer an operational risk.

The above example presents a simple situation where one firm faces a single exposure generated by one cross-border deal. Things are very different for most MNEs, since they operate in a multi-currency environment on a daily basis, incur costs in many currencies worldwide, and accumulate revenues in many countries as well. It is commonplace for an MNE subsidiary in one country (i.e. in Switzerland) to accumulate assets and liabilities denominated in euro, USD, yen, and other currencies, while a sister unit (i.e. in Japan) has its own exposure to these currencies and to others as well. This is why almost all MNEs calculate their operational exposures on a net basis, not only within each unit but among

+ Net basis
Exposure remaining
after a firm's short
positions in a given
financial category have
been subtracted from
its long positions in the
same category.

	Position subsidiary A	Position subsidiary B	Net group exposure	Risk
in USD ($)	+10	−5	Long $: +5	$ will sink
in yen (¥)	−20	+10	Short ¥: −10	¥ will rise
in euros (€)	+5	−20	Short €: −15	€ will rise
in sterling (£)	0	+5	Long £: +5	£ will sink

all units worldwide. Thus, as Figure 13.2 shows, a group will not calculate its exposure to each of the four currencies based on the position of subsidiary A or B separately, but only after combining the two.

Non-transactional FX risks

A third category of FX exposure is *translational risk*, which occurs when FX variations affect a company's efforts to convert foreign assets or liabilities back into its home currency. This includes profits that an MNE's foreign subsidiaries send back to headquarters in the form of dividends, foreign currency loans that an MNE makes or receives, and, above all, the value of foreign assets. Take a Japanese MNE that owns a plant in the USA. Figure 13.3 shows how currency variations could affect its year-end results without the company having completed any new deals. In this example, the value of its overseas assets does not alter in host country terms but changes when translated back into the home currency.

Analysts have long questioned whether it is desirable for companies to protect themselves against translational risk (Hyman 2006). The issue arises because some companies intentionally configure their international operations in such a way as to diversify exposures so that risks faced in one currency zone are offset by risks elsewhere. In this case, hedging any component of the group's FX risk would disturb the overall balance and create new exposures.

A fourth source of FX exposure is *speculative risk*. MNEs are free to decide what percentage of their currency risk they want to offset. A company might reason that its treasury specialists are as competent at currency trading as the bank with which they currently offload their exposures, and authorize them to trade in the markets on the company's behalf. The most successful example of this approach is Porsche, famously said to have made more money from 'active' FX management in 2007 than it did from selling cars (Shipman 2007). This kind of trading can just as easily go badly, however, as exemplified by the sums that some famous emerging MNEs (including Hong Kong's CITIC Pacific and Mexico's Grupo Alfa) lost 'playing roulette' with the currency markets in the wake of the 2008 credit crunch (Holstrom 2010). The explanation for these companies' sudden appetite for risk might lie in their newly internationalized circumstances, which freed their managers from the kinds of currency controls that most had faced in their Global South country of origin. Strong academic research indicates that a company's tendency to speculate in the financial markets reflects the value systems of its senior managers (Beber and Fabbri 2011). Whether a firm should (or can) cover all of its risks is a central debate in currency management.

+ Hedging
Where a party offsets a risk through a new deal exposing it to the exact opposite risk. The original exposure is called the 'underlying' risk. The new exposure is called the 'hedge'.

	Year 1	Year 2
Value of US plant in dollars	$100 million	$100 million (unchanged)
Dollar/yen exchange rate	$1 = ¥110	$1 = ¥100
Value of US plant in yen	¥11 billion (100 million × 110)	¥10 billion (100 million × 100)
Book loss between Year 1 and Year 2	¥1 billion	

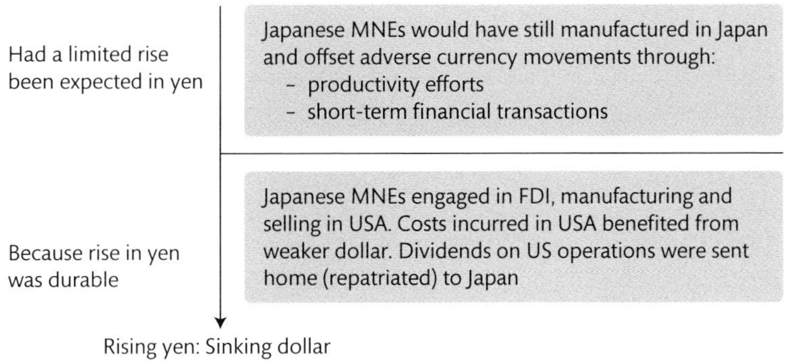

Figure 13.4
Historic Japanese
responses to dollar
weakness.

Lastly, it is worth noting that the FX exposures discussed above all involve risks that can be identified, hence managed immediately. This differs from *economic risk*, which involves the long-term fortunes of the currencies of the countries where an MNE has interests. An interesting example of economic risk is the decades-long rise in the Japanese currency's value from a 1949 rate of 360 yen per dollar to a June 2012 rate of around 78. In the 1950s and 1960s, Japanese companies, incurring manufacturing costs in their home currency, the yen, began exporting products (like automobiles) in US dollars. The dollar's long-term downtrend against the yen therefore had the effect of squeezing their profit margins. Japanese exporters could have decided to raise retail prices in dollars to restore earnings but this would have made them less competitive in the USA at a time when they were trying to increase market share. Hence their initial decision to keep their prices stable in USA and offset the falling margins by improving productivity at home. This is one rationale behind the Toyota Production System (see Chapter 11).

At a certain point, however, the yen had risen so high, and the dollar had fallen so low, that it was no longer possible for Japan-based manufacturers to compete profitably. As shown by Figure 13.4, Japanese MNEs would have understood that the yen's strength was a long-term trend and reacted accordingly. The currency squeeze, in conjunction with the quotas that the US authorities decided to levy on Japanese car imports, was one of the factors behind Toyota's decision to engage in FDI in the USA from the 1970s onwards. Once the company had diversified its production locations, the negative effect of further dollar weaknesses on its US revenues were largely offset by their positive effects on its new US liabilities (production costs). Of course, FDI is a major, structural action that should be undertaken only if a firm believes it is facing a lasting problem. As noted in Chapter 5, currency shifts are only one of many factors at stake in FDI.

Indirect economic risk can occur when a competitor has production facilities located in a country characterized by a weak currency, and seeks competitive advantage by exporting goods from this cheap location. One example is the way that many EU car-makers such as Volkswagen rushed to build plants in East European transition economies that are relatively inexpensive, not only because of lower wages or taxes but also because their currencies are fragile and not yet part of the Eurozone. MNE strategies for managing currency risk range from short-term tactics to long-term strategy. In international business, foreign exchange is much more than a mere treasury function.

Managing foreign exchange risk

As exemplified by Japanese exporters' historic responses to the long-term rise in the yen, whenever a company fears that an adverse currency movement is destined to have lasting effects, reconfiguring its entire global value chain may become a viable option. Immediate exposures, on the other hand, tend to be dealt with through simpler mechanisms, above all short-term financial hedging.

Long-term 'natural' hedging

An MNE is subject to a foreign exchange 'squeeze' if its configuration means that it tends over the long term to accumulate assets in a weak currency and/or liabilities in a strong one. The only possible responses in this case are to change the currencies in which it denominates its operations or accounts and/or ensure that its long and short exposures are more evenly matched.

In terms of increasing liabilities (i.e. developing a cost base) in a currency whose long-term trend has been downwards, there are two ways to achieve this. The quickest and easiest is to source more components from suppliers who invoice in the currency. This is one explanation for the explosion in outsourcing since the 1980s. More recently, this has also been witnessed in the decision taken in 2011 by several Swiss pharmaceutical MNEs (along with engineering giant ABB) to increase the percentage of components bought outside Switzerland, whose currency had risen sharply in recent years.

A costlier and less flexible but more structural way to develop an overseas cost base is through FDI. In the case of offshoring (see Chapter 5), this usually involves setting up a plant in a country specifically because its currency is traditionally weak. Where the aim is to reduce overall FX exposure, an MNE can establish industrial operations in the markets where it realizes a significant proportion of its global revenues. With this approach, if the currency in question weakens in the future, the company's sales will fall but so will its costs. In this way, FDI helps MNEs to offset their long-term 'long' exposures.

Still, it is not always clear how expectation of future FX rates affects managers' FDI decisions. One view is that companies will be reluctant to invest in a country whose currency is subject to future volatility, if only because the assets it owns there will be devalued if they are consolidated back into the MNE's global accounts at a lower exchange rate in the future (Morrissey and Udomkerdmongkol 2008). The opposing view predicts that outwards FDI from a country such as China will increase if (as is widely predicted) its currency were to strengthen, since this would lower the cost of overseas acquisitions (Sauvant and Davies 2010). Given the sizable sums usually at stake, it is unsurprising to discover that there are a variety of perspectives on the role of FX in FDI decisions.

Examples of FX-driven FDI include actions undertaken by Australian and Swiss manufacturers in 2011 to cope with strong rises in their domestic currencies: because the Australian dollar tends to track commodity prices, which are on a long-term uptrend (see Chapter 16); and because the Swiss franc is often seen as a safe haven in times of crisis. One case involving Australia was when drinks maker Coca-Cola Amatil warned that it might have to shut down food processing plants in Victoria province and move operations to Indonesia, arguing that consumers would have to choose between inexpensive foreign imports or subsidizing the domestic farming industry (Korporaal 2011). The same year, Swiss electric parts manufacturer Huber + Suhner announced on its website that it was moving approximately 80 jobs to Poland and Tunisia, primarily for currency-related reasons. In both of these cases, FX was the key factor in the company's internationalization decision.

Similarly, to offset long-term 'short' (buy-side) exposures, MNEs can try to increase revenues denominated in the strong currencies in which they pay their suppliers, or in the currencies of the countries where they already incur manufacturing costs. A case in point is the situation facing many Western MNEs that source products in China. Given China's massive export surpluses, its currency (the yuan) is likely to appreciate should the national government ever allow this to happen. Until now, most MNEs have used China solely as a manufacturing base, but the prospect of a higher yuan, combined with Chinese consumers' rising purchasing power, means that many are now looking to develop their retail network there, in the hope that the expected increase in yuan-denominated production costs will be offset by higher revenues in this currency. There are many examples of companies with operations in China currently seeking to expand their sales networks here. One is US car-maker Chrysler, which announced in 2011 that it wanted to expand its Chinese dealer network by 39 per cent within two years. Another is giant German conglomerate Bayer, which also announced in 2011 that within less than five years it expected to more than

+ **Safe haven**
Assets that investors tend to purchase to store value in times of crisis. Often includes gold, US$, and Swiss francs.

Most MNEs operate in multicurrency environments, complicating their risk management operations

double its sales of diabetes and hypertension medicine in China. Of course, it is rarely clear whether a company's motive for increasing sales in one country stems from a desire to offset currency risk or to take advantage of market growth, since the two often go hand in hand (countries with rising incomes should theoretically have stronger currencies). What is clear is that FX considerations influence many MNE decisions.

Short-term financial hedging

Where companies have no more than a short-term vision of a given FX risk—that is, where they have no view on the currency's long-term strength—they will often offset any exposure they face by hedging it through the foreign exchange market. By creating new exposures that are the polar opposite of the risks associated with their normal transactions, MNEs' hedges will protect them against potentially adverse price changes. To achieve their aims, they can use a variety of currency instruments (**see ORC Extension material 13.1**), including forwards, which is when counterparts set the price today for a specified future delivery price (that will differ from the current 'spot' price by an amount reflecting the interest rate differential between the two currencies). Fundamentally, however, the long/short approach described above will always apply.

Unlike long-term structural reconfigurations in a company's value chain, short-term hedges do not prevent the initial exposure from reappearing once the cover runs out, and there is always the possibility that the next hedge will be transacted at a worse rate. Moreover, recurring short-term hedges increase transaction costs (Hughes 2006), largely because the market-maker who the company calls to make a deal will buy at a lower price and sell at a higher price, with the spread between the two prices working to the price-taker's disadvantage (**see ORC Extension material 13.2**). Of course, it is always possible that when one hedge matures, the next might be done at a better rate. Lastly, it is worth recalling that short-term financial hedges are quicker and cheaper to organize than huge structural reconfigurations. Aside from exceptional circumstances, such as the 2008 credit crunch or 2011–2012 European sovereign debt crisis, it is fairly easy for an MNE to find a counterpart, usually a bank, on which it can offload its exposures.

Managing short-term exposures

A useful example of the kinds of short-term hedging choices that MNEs typically have to make came between May 2010 and July 2011 when the Brazilian real rose from almost 1.87 against the US dollar to around 1.56: a jump of almost 23 per cent. This was very

+ Foreign exchange (FX) market
Virtual marketplace(s) where currency prices are set through market supply and demand.

> Go online

+ Market-maker
Trader who is always prepared to quote other market participants a price to buy ('bid') and sell ('offer') a given commodity.

+ Spread
Difference between the market-maker's 'bid' and 'offer' prices. In the FX markets, this is usually calculated in 'basis point' terms (four digits after the zero, i.e. .0001).

> Go online

Figure 13.5 Offsetting a long exposure with a short hedge.		Step 1. Samsung notes long exposure, i.e. risk that $ will fall vs. won	Step 2. It therefore shorts (sells) $ against won to hedge this risk	Net effect
	Scenario (a). If the $ subsequently falls …	the underlying position loses money as feared (−)	the hedge makes money (+)	Zero: the profit on the hedge offsets the underlying loss
	Scenario (b). If the $ subsequently rises …	the underlying position makes an unexpected 'windfall' profit (+)	the hedge loses money (−)	Zero: the loss on the hedge offsets the underlying profit

painful for Brazilian exporters since it made them less competitive in the world markets. Part of the problem was the uncertainty about how long the real's strength would last. A number of Brazilian companies ended up taking the view that they had to protect themselves against a further fall in the value of the dollar against the real and sold forward their expected revenues in the US currency at what they hoped might be a higher rate than what they would get in the future. With hindsight, they were wrong to panic, since by mid-2012 the dollar was back up above 2.00 to the real, having climbed by about 30 per cent over the previous 12 months. The exporters who had already sold their dollar assets at the lower price could not benefit from this.

Another instructive example from 2011 was provided by Korean conglomerate Samsung Heavy Industries, whose ship-building division incurred most of the company's manufacturing costs in its home currency (the Korean won) but accumulated revenues in dollars (see Figure 13.5). Samsung's risk was that the dollar would weaken before the revenues it received could be sold back into Korean won. The company therefore implemented a short hedge against this long risk, selling 100 per cent of its currency exposure. When the dollar weakened by about 5 per cent against the Korean won between May and June 2011, Samsung lost money on any dollar-denominated assets that it sold during this period but made money on earlier hedges where it had sold the dollar at a higher rate. When the dollar subsequently strengthened by about 8 per cent over the following two months, the opposite happened, with Samsung making money on any dollar-denominated assets that it sold during this period but losing money on earlier hedges where it had sold the dollar at a lower rate.

This same principle works the other way around for importers whose risk is that the currency in which they pay their suppliers will rise before the bills are paid. Like retailers importing consumer goods for resale in their domestic markets, industrialists importing raw materials for use in their production processes face this short risk on two levels, since they are exposed to a rise in both the currency and the commodity. From late February 2012 onwards for one month, for instance, Turkey's leading petroleum importer, state-owned BOTAS, saw Brent crude oil prices rise from about $118 to $125 a barrel while the Turkish lira fell from 1.75 to 1.82 against the US dollar. It is one thing hedging against a single risk (see Figure 13.6) but it is very difficult when this is compounded by an adverse price rise in the underlying good. However, where this commodity is as widely traded as oil is, MNEs can

Figure 13.6 Offsetting a short exposure with a long hedge.		Step 1. BOTAS notes short exposure i.e. risk that $ will rise vs. Turkish lira	Step 2. It therefore goes long (buys) $ to hedge this risk	Net effect
	Scenario (a). If the $ subsequently rises …	the underlying position loses money as feared (−)	the hedge makes money (+)	Zero: the profit on the hedge offsets the underlying loss
	Scenario (b). If the $ subsequently falls …	the underlying position makes an unexpected 'windfall' profit (+)	the hedge loses money (−)	Zero: the loss on the hedge offsets the underlying profit

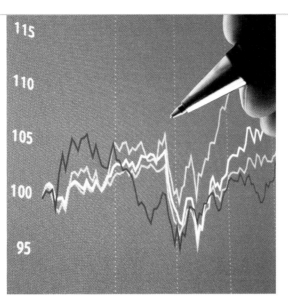

Energy companies must plot whether currency and commodity price movements are correlated

Source: iStock

apply the same hedging approaches as they do for FX risks. In this case, BOTAS would have covered its exposure by buying oil on a forward basis (i.e. fixing prices today for future delivery) in the same way as it hedged its USD exposure. The mechanism for hedging via an immediate, so-called 'spot' or else longer term 'forward' instrument is the same, however.

As these examples demonstrate, hedging reduces volatility but also affects potential returns. Some stakeholders prefer the prospect of less uncertainty. This includes executives who think that a company should stick to its original mission and not speculate on currencies, or creditors reassured because borrowers' earnings will be more stable. Others are less enthusiastic about hedging, however. Even if it turns out that the hedge was unnecessary because the worst-case scenario never materialized, hedging always costs money, especially in situations where market prices swing back and forth, and emit unclear signals (Mattioli and Schoenberger 2011). Furthermore, companies that lock in prices through hedging exclude the possibility of windfall profits, unlike their unprotected rivals. Lastly, there is also the notion in modern portfolio theory that investors may hold a stake in an MNE specifically because its currency risk offsets the other exposures in the shareholder's asset portfolio. In short, it is just as possible to criticize MNE treasurers for over-hedging as for under-hedging their exposures.

Hedging as an expression of attitude towards risk

Decisions about the extent to which an MNE should hedge FX risk depend on several factors: the size of the firm (SMEs might find it harder to manage hedging programmes); whether the treasury department is viewed as a profit or cost centre; the size of the currency risk compared with the company's total activity; and shareholders' or managers' cultural attitudes towards earnings volatility. The broader question is whether the company is viewed as a mere tool for profit maximization or, instead, is expected to behave prudently to ensure long-term survival. As Figure 13.7 shows, the profits of companies that refuse to speculate and hedge as a matter of course are less volatile, since they experience no unexpected FX profits or losses on top of their regular activities. Yet because of hedging transaction costs, their profits will be slightly lower. This is normal, since hedging reduces risk, an advantage for which the company should have to pay.

Few MNEs hedge all or none of their exposures, with most deciding upon a percentage of coverage. For instance, Swedish outdoor power products producer Husqvarna stated on its website in June 2012 that it hedges between 75 and 100 per cent of its invoiced and forecast

Figure 13.7
Hedging changes a
company's earnings
patterns.

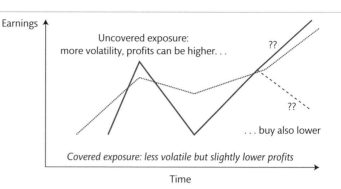

Earnings

Uncovered exposure:
more volatility, profits can be higher. . .

??

??

. . . buy also lower

Covered exposure: less volatile but slightly lower profits

Time

flows up to six months, but only 50 to 75 per cent of longer term flows. Aside from the implied assumption that short-term price swings even out in the long run, this policy means that the group does not fully protect itself against possible rises in the currency (Swedish kroner) in which it incurs most of its manufacturing costs. Conversely, it benefits from falls in the kroner, which is what happened in summer 2011 when the currency dropped 5.4 per cent from 8.90 to 9.38 to the euro. Of course, by summer 2012, the kroner had gone back up to 9.00. As always, the question is at what level Husqvarna should have decided to transact its hedge.

Ultimately, the problem for MNEs is their inability to predict whether a currency will strengthen or weaken in the future. Different models exist to help forecasts, humorously exemplified by the annual 'Big Mac Index' calculating different currencies' purchasing power parity in terms of this particular dish. No one has a crystal ball, however, meaning that managers' FX management decisions will always be at least partially subjective.

+ Purchasing
power parity
Theory that future
currency rates will
adjust upwards or
downwards to ensure
that each reaches a
level where it allows
users to purchase the
same basket of goods.

+ Working capital
Excess of circulating
assets over short-term
liabilities. Indicates
level of long-term
funding available
to companies to
help finance their
operational cycle.

Section II: Multinational funding

One of corporate treasurers' most crucial missions is securing the capital that is vital to companies' survival: working capital for operational purposes; useful assets on an opportunistic basis; or simply to give the company a margin of safety when times get tough. Aside from an exceptionally cash-rich company like Apple, it is hard to imagine an MNE generating enough cash to cover all of its needs. This means that MNE financial officers usually entertain some relationship with external fund providers.

Case study 13.2

MNEs following the money

One of the main consequences of the 2007–2008 subprime crisis (also known as the 'credit crunch') was a steep drop in the kind of cross-border debt or equity financial flows upon which MNEs rely. These fell from $10.9 trillion in 2007 to $1.6 trillion two years later (Roxburgh et al. 2011). Volumes recovered to $4.6 trillion in 2010, but the markets remained fragile, with confidence being dented again by the subsequent European

sovereign debt crisis, sending cross-border volumes to new lows. MNEs could no longer count on external fund providers under these conditions. Instead, they had to rely on internal resources that are necessarily more limited.

The funding channel that suffered most in both 2008 and 2011–2012 was lending by banks, both to one another and to corporate borrowers. The supply of capital was

particularly tight in the USA following the 2008 crisis, and in Western Europe when the sovereign debt crisis erupted in 2011. In Asia, however, bank lending rose sharply throughout 2011, with two leading British banks, Standard Chartered and HSBC, expanding their loan books by anywhere between 20 and 40 per cent year-on-year in the continent's different sub-regions, reaching as high as 50 per cent in Indonesia (Goff 2011). Asia's growing importance can also be witnessed in the steep rise in stock market activity in the continent's emerging economies in 2010, when the sector exceeded $400 billion, accounting for almost 40 per cent of the world's total new share issues (ADB 2011). This percentage continued to rise throughout 2011, with volumes falling in Asia less quickly than elsewhere. To some extent, this reflected the growth in total savings in Asia and in intra-regional financial flows.

The third funding channel, the bond markets, witnessed strong growth globally after the first financial crisis, with non-financial corporations issuing a total of $1.3 trillion in bonds in 2010 vs. $800 billion two years before. This expansion can be explained by the difficulty that many companies had in accessing bank funding, forcing them to seek other sources of capital. Events affecting one MNE funding channel will often have a spillover effect

In recent years, Standard Chartered's loan book has expanded much more quickly in Asia than anywhere else

Source: Standard Chartered Bank

on others. This makes it essential that financial officers take a global view.

Case study questions

1. What factors help to explain funding channels' different performances over 2008–2012?
2. To what extent can Asia's share of the global capital markets be expected to increase further?

External sources of funding

Where the capital that the MNE raises through its internal operations does not suffice for its needs, it must turn to outside sources. Generally, these are divided into two categories: debt (borrowings) and equity (shares).

Debt finance

MNE debt tends to be divided between borrowings from banks or from financial markets.

Bank lending

The banking industry has developed a range of practices tailored to the many different situations that MNEs face when conducting international business (**see ORC Extension materials 13.3**). Very few banks offer a full spectrum of debt instruments, if only because of the difficulties that non-resident banks have in tightly controlled financial systems like China where local institutions possess certain advantages. For this reason, MNEs tend to work with shortlists of global banks, alongside a few local ones offering specific national services and information.

> Go online

The traditional 'transformation' model of corporate lending involved savers depositing short-term funds with banks who would then lend them to borrowers, often for a longer period. In this model, the bank acts as a screen between providers and users of capital. Its gross margin is the difference between the interest it pays on deposits and receives on its loans.

This model revealed weaknesses during the 1980s when several large debtor nations, such as Peru and Brazil, defaulted on their repayments, raising fears about the solvency of some of the world's largest banks. To reinforce the global financial system, the Bank for International Settlements (BIS) sponsored a capital adequacy agreement in 1988 called Basel I (extended over the years by Basel II and III) specifying that banks should have equity capital equal to at least 8 per cent of their assets. To meet this so-called Cooke ratio, many banks cut direct lending and focused on acting as intermediaries between investors and borrowers. The new emphasis became the issuance of securities in capital markets, with banks receiving commissions for this service. Such 'securitization' processes explain the explosion in international financial volumes since the 1980s.

Greater securitization does not mean that banks no longer lend directly to corporations. Indeed, for SMEs too small to issue securities, banks remain crucial partners. All that has happened is that bank lending is now one funding source among several.

Market funding

In terms of the stocks and bonds that an MNE issues (acting through the intermediary of its 'lead manager' bank), two crucial factors are whether investors are attracted by the general interest rates that companies are paying on their debt, and how a specific borrower's creditworthiness is perceived. Lenders confident of recovering a loan demand less interest than those worried about whether they will be reimbursed. The standard way of representing confidence is the 'risk premium' (or 'credit spread'). Expressed in basis points, this is the difference between the yields that creditors require from one class of debt vs. what a zero-risk borrower (usually the government) might pay. Clearly, the more people worry about an MNE's ability to repay its debts, the greater the risk premium that it will be asked to pay.

The same applies to the duration of the borrowing. Because the distant future is more uncertain than the near term, generally there will be a lower credit spread on short-term 'money market' loans, which tend to be priced in line with recognized benchmarks such as the London Interbank Offered Rate (LIBOR). MNE treasurers seeking to fund their companies at the lowest possible cost pay close attention to the difference between short- and long-term interest rates (called the 'yield curve').

The problem is that credit spreads can shift rapidly if investors reassess borrowers' situations. The 2011–2012 European sovereign debt crisis, for instance, saw money pouring out of bank securities (or debt issued by countries like Greece, Spain, or Italy) into bonds issued by reputedly safer governments such as the USA or Germany. Effectively, this raised the cost of capital for the borrowers whose bonds were being sold off. Perceptions of creditworthiness are influenced by scores awarded by 'ratings' agencies like Standard & Poor's or Moody's. A highly rated (i.e. 'Triple A') borrower pays much lower interest charges than one

+ Issuance of securities
Act of creating tradable capital market instruments like stocks and bonds that firms sell to investors to raise capital.

+ Capital markets
Sum total of all medium- and long-term debt and equity transactions.

+ Basis points
One hundredth of 1 per cent. A common unit in international finance.

The British economy may have lost ground in the international league tables but London remains one of the world's leading financial centres

Source: Photodisc

with a lower rating (i.e. 'Triple B'). This explains why being upgraded or downgraded is such a big event in an MNE's life. The downgrading of famous household names (such as Citigroup or Bank of America) in late 2011, followed by a number of European banks in spring 2012, caused creditors to withdraw funds at the very moment when they were most needed.

A second factor in MNE's market funding efforts is whether they want to sell their securities to domestic or offshore investors. This is largely a question of who has the greatest appetite for a particular company. There are also a number of technical considerations. Offshore markets often feature lower transaction costs and tax advantages. Domestic exchanges offer greater transparency and investor protection. Some providers of capital, like fund managers, are required by statute only to purchase domestically traded securities. Others do this by choice. Despite much press coverage about the globalization of savings, most people invest primarily in their home markets.

Given the uneven global distribution of capital (partially a reflection of variations in national savings rates), the world's different financial markets are all keen to attract foreign companies ready to list their securities. One key element in this competition between financial centres is the degree of regulation characterizing a particular market. First, different markets require different amounts of disclosure about a company's accounts. Providing in-depth information on group activities is an expense that some MNEs might try to minimize (although it might also be analysed as an ethical obligation; see Chapter 8). Indeed, variations in national accounting and governance rules are a prime focus for MNE financial officers. Aside from obvious differences in banking systems and tax policies, financial environments also vary in more subtle ways. For instance, some countries (like Germany) offer relatively greater protection to creditors, whereas others (like Australia) tend to support shareholders (Anderson et al. 2012). Factors such as these affect how MNEs structure their funding efforts to ensure maximum access to capital. The end result is that multinational funding networks often resemble a patchwork of different channels.

> **+ Disclosure**
> Provision of information, often in a specified form to comply with legal requirements.

One other way that credit considerations affect corporate borrowings involves guarantees. MNEs often record debt in the name of a small subsidiary, sometimes an offshore vehicle specifically established for this purpose. This practice, known as 'ring-fencing', ensures that, if times are tough and loan reimbursements become problematic (as exemplified by the problems Disneyland Paris faced in the 1990s), creditors can only make claims against assets held by this one subsidiary. From the lenders' perspective, of course, it is safer to have loans secured against the assets of the whole group. One surprising aspect of an international business career is the time spent negotiating which entity is responsible for a particular liability.

Equity finance

The second external source of funding is equity capital. Here, investors purchase shares in the hope that their price will rise in the future. Share price changes not only reflect general economic conditions but also expectations of a company's future profitability, which is influenced by many different factors.

One factor that is specifically under the control of an MNE's financial officers is the extent to which it tries to increase its return on equity (ROE) ratio by increasing debts and reducing equity funding. This 'leverage' strategy, also called 'gearing', has a high risk/reward profile. As shown in Figure 13.8, if things go well, the company can achieve a higher return on equity by using borrowed funds. However, if things go poorly, the company must still reimburse its debt, increasing the risk of bankruptcy. Generally, leverage is more typical of American MNEs, which have historically had higher debt-to-equity ratios than their European and Japanese counterparts. This means that US companies often achieve higher returns, possibly in response to domestic investors' greater preference for shares instead of bonds. At the same time, the indebtedness of some US financial institutions was a major factor in the 2007–2008 financial crisis.

Company A
If equity = 100, debt = 100 and profits = 20
(or a profit rate of 10 per cent of the sum of equity + debt)

Then: Debt to equity ratio 100/100 = 100 per cent, and
return on equity = 20/100 = 20 per cent

Company B
If equity = 100, debt = 150 and profits = 25
(or a profit rate of 10 per cent of the sum of equity + debt)

Then: Debt to equity ratio 150/100 = 150 per cent, and
return on equity = 25/100 = 25 per cent

A second distinction in equity financing exists between 'passive' or 'active' approaches. A passive approach involves situations where the investor is not seeking to take an active role in the management of the company whose shares are being bought. An active approach represents situations where the investor does intend to intervene directly in the management of the target company. One trend since the 1980s has been the rise of active international shareholders seeking to maximize short-term financial returns and ready to pressurize CEOs into adopting strategies to serve this purpose (Froud et al. 2006). Active foreign shareholders are unwelcome in some cultures, where they might be accused of preventing executives from pursuing policies (such as job security, health and safety) that could benefit local stakeholders. This is particularly true in societies with a strong sense of 'economic patriotism' (see Chapter 3).

MNEs often organize worldwide 'road shows' to convince current or potential investors of the attractiveness of keeping or buying their shares. The question then becomes where such investors might be found. At this point, it is worth recalling the problems that many SMEs face in trying to source equity finance. Because most of the larger stock exchanges have minimum size thresholds that exclude SMEs from this particular funding source, many countries try to create an incentive for entrepreneurship by developing stock exchanges that are specifically meant to host smaller firms, often operating in hi-tech sectors. Examples include Nasdaq in the USA, Japan's Nippon New Market Hercules, and the UK's Alternative Investment Market.

Another dynamic source of equity funding for hi-tech SMEs is 'venture capital'. This is 'private equity' finance provided by small groups of professional investors who want to take a direct stake in a growing firm. It was the main funding vehicle used to launch the companies that drove the information technology revolution that swept out of California's Silicon Valley in the 1980s, with many former start-ups like Intel, Google, and Cisco having since turned into the world's largest MNEs. This category of equity finance is imitated in many countries seeking to achieve similar success.

Alongside this, there has been a trend over the years towards the concentration of global equity capital in the hands of relatively few big 'institutional investors'. These can range from huge pension funds such as CALPERS (representing California state employees) to speculative 'hedge funds', investment funds like unit trusts (called mutual funds in the USA), and, increasingly, sovereign wealth funds, a sector that according to http://www.swfinstitute.org already totalled nearly $5 trillion of assets under management by the year 2012 (see Figure 3.6).

One effect of this evolution is the rise of a class of professional fund managers trained to look globally to maximize portfolio returns. In turn, this has led to a rise in cross-border share ownership, to the extent that in countries like France today, for example, non-resident investors hold more than 40 per cent of domestic companies' total stock market capitalization (Bayart 2010). This trend has come under increasing criticism, owing to fears that because foreign shareholders are potentially less attached sentimentally to the

+ Sovereign
wealth funds
Large pools of capital
run by government-
appointment
managers. Usually
originating from
countries with large oil
surpluses and/or where
the state centralizes
control of savings.

+ Stock market
capitalization
Total number of shares
issued multiplied by
the share prices for all
companies listed on a
particular exchange.

companies they own, they might demand higher returns than domestic owners and show less concern for local stakeholders' welfare (see Chapter 3). A second concern is that foreign shareholders might make equity decisions based solely on their global portfolio's overall risk/return profile (Markowitz 1991) rather than on a company's own strategic needs. Offshore shareholding is a key element in the 'financialization' logic (Froud et al. 2006) that characterizes modern international business and has come under great scrutiny in the wake of the 2008 'subprime' financial crisis.

Practitioner insight

Matthew Bowyer works as Global Equity Portfolio Manager at Allianz Global Investors in London. Prior to joining RCM in 2004, he was consultant to the Chief Investment Officer of BNP Paribas Asset Management. From 1985 until 2002, Matthew was at Citigroup Asset Management where he was responsible for managing over $4 billion. He was educated as an economist in the USA and UK.

'Multinationals' three main sources of external funding (banks, and the debt and equity markets) have each gone through changes in recent years, sometimes suddenly, like when French banks abruptly withdrew from commodities trading finance in 2011. European banks generally retreated after the 2008 financial crisis, even from growth regions like Asia. They needed to de-leverage their balance sheets, as did many American banks, to meet capital ratio targets imposed by banking regulators. Other players will step in, however, often established global operators like Standard Chartered, HSBC, Citigroup, and the Australians. Some sectors will see new players, like the sovereign wealth funds that have shown an interest in collateralized aircraft leasing and project finance. As for banks from emerging economies, such as China or Brazil, they have sufficient lending opportunities domestically to maintain rapid growth.

Actually, many companies aren't seeking bank funding at present. Cash holdings are historically high, perhaps as a precaution against a repeat of the credit crunch associated with the 2008 financial crisis. This makes the recent jump in bond issuance surprising, until you realize how attractive today's low interest rates are to borrowers. For investors, bonds from corporations like McDonald's, Tesco, or Pfizer are attractive; their ratings are as good as or better than some sovereign nations but they still pay an extra credit spread.

Regarding equity funding, for companies in advanced economies, share issues tend to fund acquisitions, whereas emerging market companies look to fund investment projects. A prime example was when Brazil's Petrobras raised $70 billion in 2010 to fund its offshore exploration and production. Otherwise, new issues (initial placement offerings) tend to come in waves. Investor interest is attracted by high growth prospects in emerging markets, sustained rises in resource markets, but above all by market momentum. Generally it has become easier to invest in shares issued by emerging market companies, either in their home markets, where transparency has improved, or in places like New York or Hong Kong, where companies can list American Deposit Receipts or A shares, respectively, to access new investors and diversify their shareholder base.

Lastly, it's worth commenting on attitudes towards the way that multinationals manage foreign exchange risk. The question here is whether a company has a transparent and well-defined hedging policy, so that investors can analyse and estimate currency movements' impact on profits. Investors tend to prefer companies that hedge operational exposure, reducing volatility of earnings. Conversely, profits made in foreign exchange speculation are not rewarded by the equity market. It's risky and rarely sustainable.'

Internal sources of funding

An MNE treasury department has many responsibilities. Some (like FX and funding) are externally oriented and depend on the company's long-term strategy. Others are more internally oriented and involve the implementation of short-term tactics. Examples include investment planning, simulation, budgeting, management control, accounting, reporting, cash management, insurance, and tax management. The sum total of these responsibilities gives treasurers an overview of all corporate processes. Arguably, finance is the most strategic of an MNE's value chain functions.

MNE treasurers not only manage relationships with external fund providers but also supervise the distribution of cash among all group units. This is crucial for several reasons. Due to the specialist role assigned to many MNE subsidiaries nowadays, internal funds tend to be distributed unevenly between units that are 'long' cash (i.e. have more than they need) and others that are 'short' (i.e. have less than they need). Such imbalances require close monitoring. In addition, as MNEs transact more and more of their business in LDCs characterized by comparatively underdeveloped financial markets, they may find it harder to fund subsidiaries operating in these locations and will therefore need to rely more on capital sourced from elsewhere within their group (Islam and Mozumdar 2007). In this vision, MNE treasurers must often act as bankers to their own group.

Netting

As they do in the FX markets, banks will usually quote debt market prices with a bid–offer spread or, more rarely, charge fees for this service. Thus, every time a company gets funding from a bank, it incurs a cost: lending at below the market rate; or borrowing above the market rate. It is, therefore, in companies' interest to do as few operations as possible. Towards this end, many MNEs create a 'netting' department that recycles some subsidiaries' surplus cash to fund other units' deficits. By internalizing this clearing process, MNEs can reduce their transactions with the outside world.

+ **Clearing**
Process of calculating and paying net differences between the amounts due to/owed by market participants.

To perform this function, MNE treasurers must take a snapshot of the different cash positions that each group subsidiary accumulates in each of its currencies. This is a challenge for firms running global operations, one requiring a high performance information system, the backbone of all global finance. Indeed, with their Reuters screens, spreadsheets, cash-flow simulation models, and economic research papers, MNE treasury departments often resemble bank trading rooms.

As discussed in Chapter 10, finance is one of the corporate functions that is most likely to be centralized. MNE subsidiaries may have their own accounting and cash teams but to get a full view of group needs and save on overhead, most companies lodge strategic financial operations in a Regional Treasury Centre (Barlow 2011). Such offices are often in tax jurisdictions that treat MNEs' internal flows favourably. One example is Belgium, explaining why MNEs like Monsanto, Proctor & Gamble, and IKEA all run major treasury operations and/or netting services near Brussels.

To demonstrate the principle of netting (see Figure 13.9), take an MNE whose Berlin office has a cash surplus of €10 million to deposit for a period of six months to earn interest. At the same time, its sister unit in Paris needs to borrow €20 million, also for six months. If at that moment a bank quoted six-month euro deposits at an annual rate of 1.50–1.75 per cent (a typical bid-offer spread in June 2008 before the credit crunch erupted), and if the two units operated separately, the Berlin office would lend its €10 million for six months at the bank's 1.50 per cent borrowing rate—receiving €75,000 in interest—whereas the Paris office would borrow €20 million from the bank at its six-month, 1.75 per cent lending rate—paying €175,000 in interest. In total, the group would pay the difference between these two sums, or €100,000. If, on the other hand, a netting procedure were in place, Berlin could deposit its €10 million surplus with a central netting office, located, for instance, in Brussels,

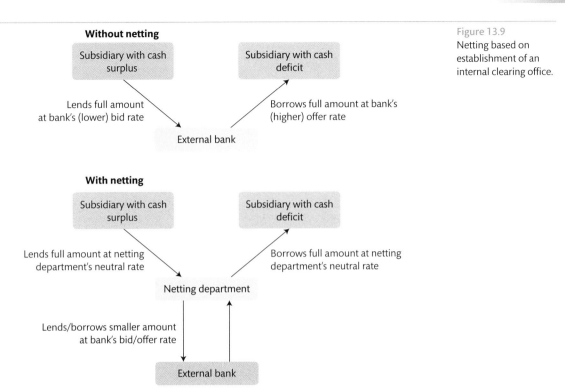

Figure 13.9
Netting based on
establishment of an
internal clearing office.

which would then shift the funds to Paris, whose only external transaction would involve borrowing the remaining €10 million it requires at the bank's 1.75 per cent lending rate, for a total six-month cost of €87,500. By having subsidiaries grant one another internal loans at a neutral interest rate—and in the absence of any tax considerations—the group would save €12,500 just by netting.

As is the case with all intra-MNE capital movements, the price that one unit pays its sister unit will have an effect on the geographic location where the group declares its profits or losses at the end of the accounting period. Unsurprisingly, this mechanism is of deep interest to MNEs.

Transfer pricing and tax implications

MNE subsidiaries and headquarters trade a wide range of assets with one another: tangible items such as raw materials, parts, and finished goods; but also capital or intangible items like loans, fees, royalties, trademarks, and dividends. MNEs are obliged to put a price on all such deals because they involve an exchange of value between entities that are supposedly independent of one another (if only because each might file a tax statement to a different national authority). Given the large percentage of contemporary international business that is comprised of such 'intra-firm' trade (see Chapter 5), such transfer prices have become a topic of great importance.

Although international standards vary in this area, most authorities (including the US Internal Revenue Service and the OECD) favour transfer prices being calculated according to the 'arm's length' principle, where an MNE's different business units price any and all deals as if each entity were unrelated to the other, and traded goods and services were in a state of perfect competition. The concept is relatively vague, however, leaving MNEs much freedom to establish their own transfer prices, especially if no comparable market exists for the item in question, as is often the case when intangible assets such as trademarks are being exchanged. The main categories of transfer prices include:

- 'cost pricing': where the item is transferred without any mark-up
- 'cost plus pricing': where a defined margin is added to the return price of the item, often a finished product
- 'profit split' pricing: where the ultimate operating profit realized on an item after it has been sold is split between the manufacturing and sales subsidiaries, after an objective measurement of the contribution made by each.

Because such dealings occur between related units, it is tempting to manipulate the pricing for two reasons: to influence each unit's assessed performance; and, above all, to minimize the group's overall tax exposure. In terms of the first reason, any decision to transfer capital or goods at a high price will leave more money in the hands of the unit making the transfer, whereas a transfer made at a lower price will favour the receiver. Thus, the unit benefiting from intra-firm pricing policies will declare higher profits at year-end and feel justified in demanding higher bonuses. The fact that a sister unit is the source of their profits makes no difference.

Much time is spent in multi-site MNEs negotiating transfer prices with other units. Understandably, an international manager might feel the greatest loyalty to the particular unit employing them rather than to the MNE as a whole, since, as often as not, this is the level where remuneration and career prospects are determined. Some firms actually engage in double accounting practices, quantifying employees' contribution to sister units to motivate them to see beyond their own unit. Interdepartmental competition, often occurring up and down the value chain, is ferocious in many MNEs.

In terms of transfer pricing's second aspect (tax minimization), the starting point here is shareholders' interest in seeing losses declared in higher tax regimes and profits declared in countries where taxes are low. It is important to remember that transfer prices are only one aspect of MNEs' tax management. There is a great deal of international variation at this level, whether in terms of customs duties, foreign tax credits, value-added taxes, double taxation measures, and, above all, corporation tax rates. For most MNE tax directors, however, especially in industries such as pharmaceuticals characterized by complex value chains and large transferable profits, transfer prices are the most crucial element in their tax-reduction strategies (Ernst & Young 2008). In part, this is because of the wide variation in transfer price rulings worldwide.

Figure 13.10 demonstrates how MNEs might use transfer price manipulations to give tax authorities an inaccurate picture of their economic activity (Sikka and Wilmott 2010). Note that the practices outlined here are highly dishonest and therefore completely unacceptable. The authors of this book entreat all students to pursue the highest standards of conduct throughout their careers. However, for analytical purposes, it is useful to visualize the mechanism by means of which a hypothetical MNE might lower its overall tax bill.

Where an MNE's accounting principles comply with national legislations, actions taken to minimize its taxable income are called tax avoidance. If not, the talk is of tax evasion, an illegal and often criminal offence. Even if tax avoidance is legal, some consider it unethical. Indeed, MNEs' tax behaviour is a key aspect of their corporate governance, a broad concept that has attracted growing attention in recent years. In general, there have been concerns about accounting quality and transparency, in part due to problems harmonizing US Generally Accepted Accounting Principles (see http://www.fasb.org) with the International Financial Reporting Standards (http://www.ifrs.org) that dominate elsewhere. Without convergence in accounting, it becomes difficult to analyse MNE financial statements and correctly analyse items such as foreign sales, employments, or assets. As Figure 13.10 shows, a further complication is the possibility that an MNE's internal pricing mechanisms differ from real accounting. More broadly, corporate governance asks political and economic questions about whose interests a company represents (**see ORC Extension material 13.4**).

One element in this debate is the huge differential between many older industrialized countries' corporation tax rates of 25–35 per cent and levels as low as 10 per cent found elsewhere. Even more striking are the fiscal policies practised in some of the world's tax havens,

+ Tax avoidance
Use of legal means to avoid paying taxes.

+ Tax evasion
Use of illegal means to avoid paying taxes.

> Go online

+ Tax haven
Country with particularly low tax rates and regulations.

	Country A (place of production): Normal tax regime (30% tax rate)	Country B: Tax haven (5% tax rate)	Country C (place of sale): Normal tax regime (30% tax rate)
A. Real transaction			
Real operation	Return cost €800,000	n.a.	Revenues €900,000
Gross profit	€100,000 (€50,000 declared in Country A, €50,000 in Country C)		
Tax calculation	€50,000 × 30% = €15,000	n.a.	€50,000 × 30% = €15,000
Total tax	€15,000 + €15,000 = €30,000		
Net profit	€100,000 (gross profit) − €30,000 (total tax) = €70,000		
B. Tax evasion transaction			
Fictionalized operations	*Declares export to B at €700,000*	Declares export to C at €1 million	Declares payment of €1 million
Profit calculation	*Reminder: Real return cost = €800,000*	Declares payment of €700,000	*Reminder: real sale = €900,000*
Stated profit	(−€100,000)	+€300,000	(−€100,000)
Tax calculation	(−€100,000) × 0% = €0 (+ tax credit?)	€300,000 × 5% = €15,000	(−€100,000) × 0% = €0 (+ tax credit?)
Total tax	€0 + €15,000 + €0 = €15,000		
Net profit	€100,000 (gross profit) − €15,000 (total tax) = €85,000 (+ tax credits)		

Figure 13.10
Using transfer pricing to locate profits in tax havens and locate losses in countries with higher tax levels.

like Bermuda, which levies no income tax on foreign earnings, or the British Virgin Islands, which levies no corporation or capital gains tax at all. Booking transactions in these locations can be very tempting for MNE financial officers focusing on their fiduciary responsibility of maximizing shareholder returns.

There have been many examples of household-name MNEs taking advantage of transfer pricing mechanisms, accounting loopholes, and/or tax havens to pay little or nothing in tax. In the USA, for example, where corporation tax is around 35 per cent, American giant General Electric paid the American government no tax at all in fiscal year 2010 despite profits of around $5.1 billion in the country that year (Kocieniewski 2011). In the UK, where large corporations should normally pay around 28 per cent, Barclays Bank paid £113 million in tax on 2009 global annual profits of £4.6 billion, or just 2.4 per cent (BBC 2011). Large and vocal NGOs such as the Tax Justice Network or UK Uncut have sprung up in recent years specifically to denounce such practices. They are not the only critics of MNEs' fiscal behaviour. Less tax paid means less revenue for government (Christensen 2006). MNE taxation is a social issue as well as a business one and in many countries it has risen to the top of the political agenda, particularly at a time of deep budget deficits.

In turn, it has become increasingly difficult for MNEs to file questionable tax returns without a reaction from national tax authorities. Moreover, such disputes can be very expensive. In 2011, for instance, it cost Anglo-Swedish pharmaceuticals company AstraZeneca $1.1 billion to settle a long-running transfer price dispute with the US tax authorities (Jack 2011). Of course, MNEs can also be at odds with tax authorities for reasons other than transfer pricing. In 2008, for instance, Vodafone went to court to challenge the Indian government's decision to tax a stake that it had acquired in a company that was listed outside India but possessed substantial assets in the country. That same year, ExxonMobil and Shell received a $2 billion tax bill from the Nigerian government for old offshore oilfield contracts. The desire to avoid maximum penalties explains why more and more deals are being struck between governments and MNEs, where the latter agree to bring home ('repatriate') funds currently lodged offshore in exchange for minimal taxation

(Gravelle 2010). Such actions may satisfy tax authorities but it is doubtful that they reduce reputational damage (see Chapter 8). It is dangerous analysing multinational finance in isolation from the rest of an MNE's behaviour.

Challenges and choices

→ MNEs require centralized real-time information on their current and prospective currency and funding positions to understand potential risks accurately. In turn, this suggests a centralization of the power to determine whether the company should cover financial risks systematically or sporadically. The problem is that managers working out of MNE headquarters may be too distant from the frontlines where knowledge can best be accumulated about different currencies and securities. Similarly, the incentive schemes set up to motivate financial officers can distract them from their company's prime purpose and encourage undesirable speculation. The jury is still out on whether finance should be a technical or strategic function for MNEs.

Chapter summary

+ Liquidity
Volume of funds in a market. Markets are liquid if there are sufficient funds so that an asset can be bought or sold without any noticeable impact on price.

The chapter began with an analysis of foreign exchange exposures before defining different sources of risk: transaction (commercial and operational), translational, speculative, and economic. A distinction was made between risks that can be identified and managed immediately, and those that materialize over the longer term and need more structural adjustment. The second section started with a brief comparison of debt vs. equity as sources of external finance, with the former largely dependent on borrowers' perceived creditworthiness and the latter focusing more on MNEs' access to different investor pools. Lastly, the final section reviewed internal sources of finance, primarily MNEs' efforts to shift surplus cash from one site to another to achieve wider group objectives and avoid the costs associated with external funding.

Case study 13.3

MNE treasury operations: Nokia knocking on Asia's door

Finance is one of the functions that MNEs tend to centralize to achieve economies of scale. Not only is it cheaper to run a single global team than many local units but some services benefit from large, streamlined operations. These include cash management services provided by corporate 'payment factories' and the netting operations that many MNEs run out of central units serving as in-house banks (Polak 2010).

Yet it can be hard staffing one location on a 24/7 basis. Not only does this require personnel working through the night but it is also questionable whether people working out of a central location have the in-depth knowledge required to master each of the three time zones (Asia, Europe–Middle East–Africa, and the Americas). Hence the decision taken by many MNEs to spread finance specialists across the world, organizing them into two or three regional centres coordinating units in their time zone and providing them with the help they need relating to funding, risk management, tax, and liquidity. One example of this approach is Nokia, the Finnish telecommunications giant, which used to manage all its global treasury needs out of Geneva. Since the mid-1990s, the group's 80-member-strong global treasury department has been working along more or less regional lines, with functional groups broken down into FX risk management (identification and validation), insurance and risk finance (hazard risk management), customer finance (sales support and credit risk management), corporate finance, and cash management solutions (gtnews 2008). Each group features a mixture of local and expatriate hires. The goal is to develop capabilities that are both global and local in nature.

Nokia's Singapore centre runs treasury operations on behalf of the group's operating companies in Asia, serving as their in-house bank and helping them to manage their banking and funding relationships. A treasury team accumulates an enormous amount of knowledge that may not be widespread in an MNE whose main focus is on other core competencies. It is therefore crucial that this financial knowledge be shared, although this is easier said than done. Some MNE treasurers unaccustomed to the Asian environment might struggle with the region's long tradition of state interventionism producing a patchwork of national regulations, fiscal constraints, and payment systems that can be difficult for non-specialists to master. Nokia subsidiaries here and elsewhere benefit from the proximity of knowledgeable colleagues possessing an overview of all regional flows of goods and capital. This is especially useful during financial crises, like the one that hit Asia during the late 1990s. The effects of this crisis were minimized at Nokia because of its expert treasurers' effective utilization of up-to-date simulation techniques such as Value at Risk (VAR), a process that models potential future losses on a probabilistic basis (Curry 2000; Wood 2006). Nokia has so much confidence in its treasury specialists that it has classified their activity as a profit centre. Indeed, working under strict controls, Nokia's treasury staff are encouraged to engage in speculative trading from time to time. The aim is to enhance their understanding of how local financial markets work, in the hope that this will improve the advice that they offer regional operating companies. This attitude is very different from many other MNEs, which view finance solely as an administrative function.

To pool this know-how, the IT platforms used by Nokia's different units must be more or less compatible. This relates, for instance, to daily intra-unit data transfers, a key task for all MNEs. Such exchanges involve communication between operating companies and their treasury centre(s), or between different treasury units. Harmonization helps to make things run smoothly, especially when operatives are trained, as they are at Nokia, to emphasize teamwork. Nokia may have

For MNEs like Nokia, Singapore remains the gateway for Asian finance
Source: Photodisc

decentralized power to its regions but its treasury centres reign supreme within each zone.

At the same time, some functions are still exercised at a lower, national level. Where a country's financial system or market is complex and/or favours resident firms, MNEs often empower the national treasury team to oversee certain operations. Thus, Nokia Singapore runs a branch in Beijing specifically because this gives the group direct access to China's growing onshore yuan–dollar forward market. It is also an opportunity to improve relations with Chinese banks, a great advantage in this economically attractive but complex country. Another decentralization example is the requirement formulated by Nokia's NSN entity in Vietnam that any letters of credit issued by local banks in that country be confirmed by an international bank in Singapore to mitigate counterparty and sovereign risk (Macknight 2011). This is one way of getting large functional banking networks to back relatively unknown local financial systems.

All in all, Nokia's Singapore treasury centre is destined to retain a key role in the group's global configuration, if only because its work enhances Nokia's general standing across Asia. In this area of MNE activity, as in so many others, the region offers an optimal compromise between local and global levels of organization.

Case study questions

1. What are the different tasks that an MNE treasury department performs?
2. What factors dictate where an MNE should locate its treasury operation(s)?
3. To what extent is an MNE treasury team a strategic or an administrative function?

Discussion questions

1. What kinds of companies are more likely to be exposed to what kinds of FX risk? Why?

2. When does a short-term transactional risk turn into a long-term economic one?

3. To what extent should a company hedge all, some, or none of its FX (or interest rate) exposures?

4. When should MNEs fund themselves through debt or equity?

5. What factors determine the credit spread that an MNE has to pay at a given point in time?

Online resource centre

Go online to test your understanding by trying multiple-choice questions, and assignment and examination questions.

Further research

Bragg, S. (2010). *Treasury Management: The Practitioner's Guide.* Hoboken: John Wiley & Sons

Includes chapters covering cash transfer methods, cash forecasting, cash concentration, working capital management, debt management, equity management, investment management, foreign exchange risk management, interest risk management, clearing and settlement systems, and treasury systems.

Sinn, H. (2010). *Casino Capitalism: How the Financial Crisis Came About and What Needs to be Done Now.* Oxford: Oxford University Press

Examines the causes of the banking crisis and presents a master plan for the reform of financial markets. The judgement here is that the only way to induce more prudent behaviour in the long term is to require governments to help the banks, but not their shareholders, by both becoming a temporary co-owner and restricting riskier activities.

References

ADB—Asian Development Bank (2011). *Asia Capital Markets Monitor,* August, available at http://asianbondsonline.adb.org, accessed 24 November 2011.

Anderson, H., Welsh, M., Ramsay, I., and Gahan, P. (2012). 'The evolution of shareholder and creditor protection in Australia: An international comparison', *International and Comparative Law Quarterly,* 61, pp. 171–207 (January)

Barlow, J. (2011). 'The rise of regional treasury centres', 30 August, available at http://www.financeasia.com, accessed 23 November 2011

Bayart, B. (2010). 'Les étrangers investissent le CAC 40', 8 August, available at http://www.lefigaro.fr, accessed 23 November 2011

BBC (2011). 'Barclays UK corporation tax bill for 2009 was £113m', 18 February, available at http://www.bbc.co.uk, accessed 23 November 2011

Beber, A. and Fabbri, D. (2011). 'Who times the foreign exchange market? Corporate speculation and CEO characteristics', available at http://www1.fee.uva.nl, accessed 19 November 2011

Bergendahl, G. and Sjögre, S. (2011). *The Effects of Changed Policies and Regimes within European Financial Markets on MNCs' Foreign Exchange Exposure Management,* available at http://snee.org/filer/papers/619.pdf, accessed 19 November 2011

Christensen (2006). 'Follow the money: How tax havens facilitate dirty money flows and distort global markets', available at http://www.taxjustice.net/, accessed 6 March 2008

Curry, C. (2000). 'A star is born', available at http://www.cfoasia.com, accessed 7 March 2008

Ernst & Young (2008). 'Precision under pressure: Global transfer pricing survey 2007–2008', available at http://www.ey.com/, accessed 10 May 2008

Froud, J., Johal, S., Leaver, A., and Williams, K. (2006). *Financialization and Strategy: Narrative and Numbers.* Abingdon: Routledge

Goff, S. (2011). 'Lenders expand Asian loan books', *Financial Times,* 7 August, available at http://www.ft.com, accessed 25 November 2011

Gravelle, J. (2010). *Tax Havens: International Tax Avoidance and Evasion*, 3 September, Congressional Research Service

gtnews (2008). 'Finding best practice for corporate treasury in the deepening credit crisis', 7 October, available at http://www.gtnews.com, accessed 23 November 2011

Heineken (2012). *2011 Annual Report*, available at http://www.annualreport.heineken.com, accessed 3 June 2012

Holstrom, L. (2010). 'Meet the new multi-dynationals', 1 October, available at www.eurofinance.com, accessed 19 November 2011

Hughes, J. (2006). 'Companies too shortsighted when hedging', *Financial Times*, 26 January, available at http://www.ft.com, accessed 15 June 2007

Hyman, M. (2006). *New Ways for Managing Global Financial Risk: The Next Generation*. Chichester: John Wiley and Sons

Islam, S. and Mozumdar, A. (2007). 'Financial market development and the importance of internal cash: Evidence from international data', *Journal of Bank and Finance*, 31/3 (March)

Jack, A. (2011). 'AstraZeneca pays $1bn in US tax settlement', *Financial Times*, 29 March, available at http://www.ft.com, accessed 23 November 2011

Katz, D. (2011). 'You make me feel like a natural hedge', 5 July, available at http://www.cfo.com, accessed 21 November 2011

Kocieniewski, D. (2011). 'G.E.'s strategies let it avoid taxes altogether', *New York Times*, 24 March, available at http://www.nytimes.com, accessed 23 November 2011

Korporaal, G. (2011). 'Exporters feel pain of soaring Aussie dollar', 7 May, available at http://www.theaustralian.com.au, accessed 19 November 2011

Macknight, J. (2011). '2011 global corporate treasury awards', 23 August, available at http://www.gtnews.com, accessed 23 November 2011

Markowitz, H. (1991). *Portfolio Selection: Efficient Diversification of Investments*, 2nd edn. Malden, MA (USA), Oxford (UK): Wiley

Mattioli, D. and Schoenberger, C. (2011). 'For some, currency hedging is no gain', 19 February, available at http://online.wsj.com, accessed 22 November 2011

Morrissey, O. and Udomkerdmongkol, M. (2008). *Foreign Direct Investment and Exchange Rates: A Case Study of US FDI in Emerging Market Countries*, available at http://www.bot.or.th, accessed 21 November 2011

Polak, P. (2010). 'The centre holds', 22 June, available at http://www.gtnews.com, accessed 23 November 2011

Roxburgh, C., Lund, S., and Piotrowski, J. (2011). 'Mapping global capital markets 2011', August, available at http://www.mckinsey.com, accessed 24 November 2011

Sauvant, K. and Davies, K. (2010). 'What will an appreciation of China's currency do to inward and outward FDI?', *Columbia FDI Perspectives*, October, No. 30. Reprinted with permission from the Vale ColumbiaCenter on Sustainable International Investment (http://www.vcc.columbia.edu)

Shipman, A. (2007). 'Active currency management', *FinanceWeek*, 3 December, available at http://www.financeweek.co.uk/, accessed 13 February 2008

Sikka, P. and Willmott, H. (2010). 'The dark side of transfer pricing: Its role in tax avoidance and wealth retentiveness', *Critical Perspectives on Accounting*, 21, pp. 342–356

Wood, J. (2006). *Remote Control Treasury?* available at http://www.cfoasia.com/, accessed 7 March 2008

14 International human resource management

Learning objectives

After reading this chapter, you will be able to:

✦ appreciate and analyse issues related to international human resource management (IHRM)

✦ identify and analyse the key strategic problems of international assignments, including changes to twenty-first century jobs

✦ assess the advantages and disadvantages of expatriation

✦ evaluate the main issues related to the role of women in international business, to diversity in workforces, and to issues of executive pay

✦ identify the key tasks that managers face when managing international workforces

Case study 14.1

Ericsson and human resource management in India

Ericsson, the large Swedish telecommunications company, is the world leader in this field and has operated in India since it supplied manual switchboards to India in 1903. By 2012, Ericsson was operating half the country's telecommunications networks, had about 11,500 employees across 24 offices, and a wireless market share of about 34 per cent. The company offers a full range of telecom services from 'basic telephony, intelligent networks, datacom and the most advanced telecom integration and services to mobile office applications and multimedia applications' (Maki and Soudakova 2008). In 2011, Ericsson was awarded India's first 4G/TD-LTE (4th Generation/Time Division-Long Term Evolution) contract, including end-to-end TD-LTE solutions, managed services, and network operations, and renewed its managed services agreement with Bharti Airtel for 2G and 3G services within the multi-vendor network (http://www.ericsson.com).

Given the size of its Indian operation, Ericsson decided to establish a full Human Resource (HR) Department at its headquarters at Gurgaon in the state of Haryana, just south of New Delhi. Recognizing the irreplaceable importance of staff, Ericsson set up People and Culture (P&C) within the Indian operation. P&C was designed to bring together and nurture competent employees, combining global HR philosophy and practices with local flavour and content; the significant features were the policies on staffing, appraisal, compensation packages, and training.

Ericsson's approach to staffing in India is to encourage both internal (Indian) and external (Swedish and global) recruitment. The company prides itself on its culture and values: perseverance, respect, and professionalism. It encourages staff to understand, appreciate, and practise these as 'ways of working' when dealing with internal and external customers. Ericsson's positive attitude towards its Swedish employees working in India stresses the need for them to be open-minded and culturally aware. Employees selected for international assignments are managed in a uniform and professional manner by Global International Assignments (GIA), acting as a competency centre within the global HR function. When work appraisals are conducted, individual performance is assessed the same way in India as elsewhere. As far as compensation packages are concerned, the policy is to give a small amount of additional benefit (supplementary payments for a car, living costs, and additional salary) to employees working abroad—for example, Swedes in India.

The most interesting aspect of Ericsson's human resource management (HRM) operations in India is cross-cultural training, which is seen as preparation for employees working outside their home country. Ericsson focuses on three provisions: meetings with the HRM department on the practical aspects of working in India; meetings for new employees with members of staff who have served there; and a guide or mentor to assist new employees working in India. Ericsson's approach to the induction of all employees into their new working environments treats them the same and appears to be very successful. The company sees no reason to adopt a 'third culture' between the Indian and the Swedish: both sets of managers need to adapt to one another on an equal basis.

Introduction

Firms that operate on an international level face major people challenges in all aspects of their activities. MNEs' key tasks are whether they can (a) facilitate effective integration across their many locations and operations and (b) take advantage of local differences in culture. The analysis of international human resource management (IHRM) explores general principles, with a focus on three basic orientations: *ethnocentric*, *polycentric*, and *geocentric*, and a consideration of expatriation. Many MNEs have developed such complex international structures, linkages, and reporting systems that the effective running of the business is often conducted as much through informal methods and linkages as through formal reporting and formal organizational charts. The main issues for IHRM departments relate to their role in the strategic direction of the MNE, the development of new international assignments, the nature of cross-cultural training, performance management, and equality of opportunity. A key factor for firms operating internationally is the need, therefore, to apply integrative management development skills or what Paul Evans (1992) called 'glue technology'. At the start of the twenty-first century, 'multi-domestic operations, joint ventures and strategic alliances were increasingly common forms of business structures across regions or across the world' (Grainger and Nankervis 2001: 83). To ensure maximum effectiveness in very complex organizations, the crucial areas that need to be faced and resolved are the roles of people within these organizations and the management of all levels of people—from assembly line workers to top corporate executives.

+ Expatriation
Process of international transfer of managers, often used as a strategic tool to achieve specific organizational goals.

+ Performance management
The approach within a business to ensuring its increasing effectiveness by improving the performance of its employees and by developing the capabilities of teams and individuals.

Section I: Strategic development of IHRM

International human resource management (IHRM) has increasingly been incorporated within the strategic direction of the vast majority of MNEs, so that it is recognized as having equal importance with other main functions like production, operations, finance, and marketing. Corporations have realized that the management of their human resources is as crucial for success as the management of capital and sales. In addition to the need to recruit, retain, train, and develop the best managers, firms acknowledge that they must adopt an overall—or holistic—approach to people within the firm: they must participate fully at all stages, such as creating the vision, devising and implementing the strategy, and organizing managerial and working structures. This is not just a matter of managing people once they have been hired but of ensuring their full contribution to the direction of the company. Certain firms, such as W. L. Gore, the makers of Gore-Tex (a waterproof material), have not only created excellent products but have maintained a reputation for excellence in their standards and practices of good employee relations. W. L. Gore (http://www.gore.com) employs more than 9500 associates in about 30 countries and, in 2012, it continued to be named as one of the top employers by *Fortune* magazine (http://www.fortune.com); ever since the rankings began in the 1980s, W. L. Gore has been ranked among the top 100 US companies. Only four other companies have maintained this record of ranking in the *Fortune* listing.

The essential purpose of an IHRM within an MNE department is to ensure that the company is competitive throughout the world: operating efficiently; being flexible, adaptable, and locally responsive; and being capable of transferring knowledge and learning throughout its globally organized business units (Schuler et al. 2002). In order to carry out these functions, the IHRM department can be structured in three different ways: decentralized (small), transition (medium-sized), and centralized (large) (Scullion and Starkey 2000). The model of small, decentralized departments in all companies within the group may lead to limited resources for training and preparation of staff for international assignments, possible shortages of well-qualified international managers, and the downsizing of central operations in the HRM area. With the medium-sized transition departments, each business unit or company within the MNE's group has a moderately resourced and staffed operation. Frequently, the problem with this size of department is that it does not carry sufficient influence to ensure that the best people are released from their existing duties to undertake international assignments. Divisional managers hold onto their best staff, and the battle between the IHRM department and the division is usually resolved in favour of the latter. As the MNE grows, it often attempts to resolve the problems that have been noted above by creating a large centralized IHRM department. The key roles of this department are to carry out comprehensive and sophisticated planning across the group, engage in strategic staffing under centralized control, and establish and maintain control over all high-grade international jobs, usually with an emphasis on jobs being given to managers from the MNE's home country. This centralized department will be well resourced, highly regarded within the MNE, and able to implement its overall IHRM strategies (Scullion and Starkey 2000). This search for global talent, i.e. highly qualified people at all levels of the business, and their effective deployment within the MNE has become an essential task of the IHRM function around the world (Scullion and Collings 2011).

Ethnocentric, polycentric, and geocentric orientations

As discussed in earlier chapters and in Chapter 12 in relation to international marketing, one of the key approaches to the behaviour of MNEs derives from Perlmutter's classic study in 1969 on the three different international orientations within IHRM of ethnocentric, polycentric, and geocentric, as noted in Figure 14.1. These orientations play out at the human-resource level as well as from structural, cultural, production, and marketing perspectives. Perlmutter (1969) made a distinction between the different ways in which companies organize themselves, such that the ethnocentric orientation emphasizes the primacy of the home country, i.e. the original headquarters' values prevail; the polycentric orientation stresses the importance of local decision-making, i.e. the main power is held by the subsidiary; and the geocentric orientation emphasizes a global integrated business strategy towards staff and talent management.

Within these three overall views, there is also a range of international models for different firms' engagement in IHRM. The place of IHRM within business organizations can be considered at the strategic, managerial, and workforce levels, all of which are considered below.

Once the importance of IHRM has been established at the strategic level, it is essential that the crucial nature of its role be transmitted throughout the organization to all managers and members of the workforce. The advantages spelt out at the top—in the boardroom, and among directors and senior managers—can filter down to the rest of the firm's employees at all managerial levels and throughout the workforce. While this cascading operation is normal in all good firms, it is even more crucial in firms with major international activities. The management of other members of staff—both white collar and blue collar—becomes more complex when such people come from different countries, are located overseas, work in cross-cultural teams, and/or are globally mobile. The next sections deal with the issues of expatriation and managing workers in foreign locations.

Headquarters Orientation		
Ethnocentric	**Polycentric**	**Geocentric**
Recruit and develop people of *home country*	Develop people of *local nationality*	Develop *the best people* everywhere in the world

Figure 14.1
Ethnocentric, polycentric, and geocentric orientations (adapted from Harzing 2004; Morris 2004).

Expatriation

Increasingly less importance is attached to some of the classic issues concerned with the expatriate role in international workforces, the balance between staff members of different national origins, and the treatment of managerial staff in international jobs. Historically, MNEs and other organizations operating internationally were always concerned with ensuring that they could establish, maintain, and retain international workforces and, in particular, accommodate overseas or expatriate staff carrying out specialized functions or roles in senior management. IHRM literature is full of concern about staffing policies relating to parent country nationals (PCNs), host country nationals (HCNs), and third country nationals (TCNs). To some extent, this concern is still relevant and applied within IHRM policies, but it is increasingly common in the twenty-first century for workforces at managerial and specialized levels to become truly international. For example, the staffing of major banks, industrial companies, and computing software firms around the world are increasingly very similar in composition, regardless of where they are located.

To illustrate the current situation and recent changes in IHRM staffing strategies, it is essential to consider studies from the start of the twenty-first century (e.g. Harzing 2004; Morris 2004) that have identified MNE trends. Harzing's survey of 2689 subsidiaries of nearly 250 MNEs indicated that about 40 per cent of the subsidiaries had a parent country national in the position of managing director. Within this survey, Japanese and Italian companies were the most likely to have parent country nationals in top positions, and Danish companies the least likely; this suggests a greater concern among the former that their senior people were of the same background and culture as the company itself, whereas other companies from Scandinavia (including Denmark) and elsewhere were more comfortable with executives of other national origins. There are clearly advantages and disadvantages to the employment of nationals of different origins in senior and middle positions, as set out in Figure 14.2.

Varied approaches to the employment of nationals of different origins will probably continue to expand during the twenty-first century. If the globalization of business continues, it is likely that the patterns of employment established since the mid-nineteenth century may change quite dramatically. However, there may still be some established rationales for corporate motives in organizing and arranging international postings and transfers. Based on the pioneering work of Edstrom and Galbraith (1977), and developed by a succession of other writers (mentioned below), the three main rationales for international transfers are thought to be:

* position filling (transfer of technical and managerial knowledge)
* management development (enhance the manager's international experience)
* coordination and control (to further the development of the organization).

	Advantages	Disadvantages
Figure 14.2 Possible advantages and disadvantages of employing host country nationals (adapted from Harzing 2004; Morris 2004).	Familiarity with socio-economic, political, and legal environment and business practices	Communication difficulties with home-office (headquarters) staff
	Lower cost of hiring people	Difficulties in exercising control of fellow local nationals
	Effective response to demands for localization	Perceived problems of authority and seniority in dealing with headquarters
	Familiarity with MNEs' subsidiary operations	Need for fluency in language of parent country
	Fluency in language and customs of host country	

Practitioner insight

Elisa Nardi is the Chief People and Services Officer, Virgin Media.

Virgin Media is a media, entertainment, and telecommunications company with a primary listing on the US Nasdaq but all its operations in the UK. The company sells a 'quad' solution made up of broadband, TV, fixed-line telephone, and mobile products. Virgin Media's fibre optic cable passes almost 13 million homes in the UK and the company serves over 5 million customers.

'I am responsible for all people or HR-related activity in Virgin Media—whether this is strategic or operational. This includes employee attraction, recruitment, engagement and development, reward, performance management, and training.

The nature of the workplace is changing and expectations around jobs are also changing as more of the millennial generations enter the workplace. We see the changing expectations of different generations: demands for more flexible working, adoption of social media technologies, and different innovative and collaborative working practices.

When making appointments in Virgin Media, the nationality of the person is less important. However, where unique geographies require local knowledge, complete language fluency, and an understanding of specific customs and cultures, nationality plays an important part and is one of the recruitment criteria.

As far as "expatriation" is concerned, it has changed somewhat in recent decades. In the last 20 years it has become easier to move geographically and more career opportunities are available. However, the governance and personal liability implications of doing this have also become more complex.

It's difficult to establish and maintain the right work–life balance but it has to be about two things. First, the company you work for needs to provide you with the opportunity for flexible working (working at home, from different offices, remotely, flexible hours, job shares, and so on) and, secondly, the individual has to decide what's important and what needs to be managed in what way.

Work-related stress is a relative thing: one person's stress is another person's energy. On the whole, people "feel more under pressure" because the work environment feels more 24/7. We are now so connected all of the time through technology that it's more difficult to switch off.

For women in business, there are still many challenges. For some women, career progression at work will feel like a glass box not a glass ceiling. Depending on your choices it's still difficult for some women to have exactly the same kind of career experiences as men—particularly if they choose to bring up a family. Women need good role models in senior roles and flexible working arrangements to ensure that the best possible options exist. For some women it's also about realizing that working differently is fine, if it's affordable. Organizations have to accept that they need to think differently to keep getting the best talent out of this group of people.

Corporate social responsibility has grown massively in the last few years and is a key driver of Virgin Media's strategy and business. Virgin Media's real passion is in helping the UK become an amazing digital economy. We want to help grow digital confidence in Britain—particularly investing in and supporting young disadvantaged Britons who have loads of entrepreneurial ideas but fewer ways to channel them and make them a reality.'

+ **Glass ceiling**
Artificial barriers based on bias that prevent qualified individuals from advancing upward in their organization into management-level positions.

It is worth commenting on some of the main variations in the rationales of large firms of different national origins. Harzing (2004) has suggested that position filling is more important in British and American MNEs than in other firms. By contrast, and perhaps because they are historically more established and developed MNEs, it appears that British and American companies tend to use international transfers much less frequently as a matter for coordination and control. For Swiss, Dutch, and German MNEs, there is a 'higher than average use of international management training (as a control mechanism)' (Harzing 2004: 263).

The main trend apparent within IHRM at the beginning of the twenty-first century is that MNEs will witness a continued diminution of the traditional role of the expatriate. Not only is the prevalence of expatriates in the management of MNEs likely to decline, but the rise of the truly global CEO, manager, working team, and project group will rewrite the traditional concerns about staff members' national, ethnic, or perceived allegiance. The possible march towards globalization, especially within international business, has ensured that the management of MNEs is increasingly in the hands of the best talent, regardless of origin (Ryan and Tippins 2009). As Grainger and Nankervis (2001: 90) pointed out at the start of the century: 'Traditional approaches to expatriation and IHRM are increasingly out of step with contemporary global business realities. Essentially, a new approach to IHRM should recognize that for many companies, international operations are increasingly "normal", reflecting the reality that globalization is making international assignments more common, more frequent and shorter term in duration, and will be based on the understanding that into the future, those who work for international corporations will be increasingly recruited offshore from a wide variety of labour markets.' The systems for global selection within MNEs have developed in line with the rapid changes in the world of work in recent decades (Ryan and Tippins 2009).

+ Recruitment process outsourcing (RPO)
A form of process outsourcing by businesses in which part or all of its staff recruitment is contracted to an outside provider.

Case study 14.2
Kenexa and recruitment process outsourcing (RPO)

One of the key developments within IHRM has been the outsourcing of many HRM processes, including that of recruitment and selection. Many large IHRM specialists are engaged in this kind of business and one of the increasingly successful niche players is Kenexa, a global provider of business solutions for human resources. Based in Wayne, Pennsylvania, USA, Kenexa is headed by its Chairman and CEO, Nooruddin (Rudy) Karsan who co-founded the original company in 1987 and has been Chairman of the Board since 1997. Kenexa operates in over 20 locations around the world, employs over 2500 people, and has an impressive list of partner companies and clients, including Deutsche Bank, KPMG, Google, HSBC, Adidas, LinkedIn, BDO Seidman, BullseyeEvaluation, and Deloitte (http://www.kenexa.com). Kenexa provides a range of 'solutions' for many

companies that decide not to carry out all or some of their HRM functions but prefer to outsource them to Kenexa, or similar specialist providers.

Kenexa offers many different services: assessment guidance, talent acquisition, employment branding (including cultural research, career site development, cultural fit surveys, recruitment marketing, and retention strategy), compensation solutions, recruitment technology, learning management, strategic 'onboarding', and recruitment process outsourcing (RPO). The definition of RPO—as approved in 2009 by a group of the Human Resources Outsourcing Association—is that it is 'a form of business process outsourcing where an employer transfers all or part of its recruitment processes to an external service provider'. Kenexa's RPO services are organized around a

team of 'solutions architects' with a senior Kenexa manager as the leading architect. The team will pitch and bid for the service and once it has been secured, Kenexa manages the entire recruitment/hiring process from job profiling to 'onboarding' of the newly hired members of staff, and the operation of the appropriate technology, methods, and reporting. The proper functioning of a Kenexa RPO is designed to increase a client company's time to hire people, increase the quality of the candidate pool, provide verifiable metrics, reduce costs, and improve the company's compliance with regulatory requirements.

In August 2011, Kenexa acquired the Ashbourne Group within the UK, thus further expanding

Kenexa's operations into the public sector. The Ashbourne Group holds contracts with the Central Government Procurement Service for the design and delivery of assessment, recruitment, learning, organizational development, and leadership interventions. The combination of Kenexa and Ashbourne enables them to assist the UK public sector at a time when the austerity cuts and reductions in expenditure have made efficient recruitment operations a vital matter. The founder of Ashbourne, Trevor Pons, commented: 'We're confident that our customers will benefit from the combined synergies of our companies' (http://www.kenexa.com).

International assignments

As MNEs use fewer expatriates there are new types of international assignment, as set out in Figure 14.3. The advantages of the more 'distant' assignments, especially in the 'frequent-flyer' and 'virtual' categories, are that they provide flexibility, reduce costs, and avoid staff resistance to moving. Modern assignments are not only common at the highest levels—where CEOs and chairmen have always employed the latest means of communication and can combine flights around the world with teleconferencing—but have increasingly been established at lower managerial levels. Marketing and finance managers, for example, have taken to this newer kind of assignment. The advent of modern communications systems like smartphones (such as Blackberry and iPhone), worldwide visual telephony (such as Skype), and Internet access has meant that many lower level employees can mimic the working patterns of their superiors.

Global staff postings used to distinguish between normal and hardship postings. The latter clearly identified with less-developed countries and consequently attracted additional allowances, extra holiday, special arrangements, and more pay. Increasingly, this has changed, as it is now difficult to argue, for example, that a posting to Sao Paulo, Singapore, Shanghai, or other modern metropolises can be regarded as hardship. Clearly there remains a distinction between being posted to office jobs in major cities or to production facilities or mining areas in 'up-country' regions.

+ **Hardship posting**
Traditional overseas assignment (or posting) that was thought to be undertaken in worse conditions than assignments at home and was thus rewarded with additional allowances, special arrangements, and increased remuneration.

Modern communication systems like smartphones have allowed lower level employees to imitate their superiors' working patterns

Copyright © 2012 Research In Motion Limited

Figure 14.3
New international
assignments (based on
categories adapted
from research by M.
Fenwick, cited in
Harzing and Van
Ruysseveldt 2004).

Type of assignment	Characteristics of assignment
Long-term or expatriate	Over one year Family accompany staff Residential accommodation
Short-term	Specific duration (months) Family may accompany staff
International commuter	Weekly or bi-weekly trips Occasional temporary relocation Family stays at home
Frequent-flyer	Regular international trips No relocation
Virtual	Senior managerial responsibility at home and abroad 'Frequent-flyer' combined with email, video conferencing, telephoning

Even though the trend in IHRM may be away from expatriates or PCNs towards the truly global or TCN, there is still a relatively strong impetus within large MNEs for some of their key staffing abroad to consist of expatriates (Ghafoor et al. 2011). In order to operate this sort of staffing policy, the MNE needs to be able to reward or compensate the member of staff who will be working outside his or her home country. The compensation package is at the heart of international staffing, whether it is a Swede working in India, a Japanese employee in the UK, or a Chinese manager in Argentina. The essential linkage within the compensation arrangements is between performance on the international assignment and the pay and benefits that are associated with it. There is also a cultural aspect to pay related to the different ways in which people choose to be paid. Depending on the national culture, there will be a greater or a lesser tendency to prefer the security of a higher fixed salary (even if this means a lower bonus). Other people prefer to accept a lower fixed salary in the hope of possibly earning a large bonus. The latter system is preferred by a risk-taking person who is likely to be more receptive to innovative but unproven ideas or products. In cultures that are less bonus-oriented, the greater preference for stability may create greater receptivity to well-established ideas and products.

The 2008–2012 financial and economic crisis led to many employees being made redundant and to higher levels of uncertainty in employment, particularly in the financial and banking sectors. In this sector, the payment traditions, especially in North American and British institutions, were that a high proportion of staff were paid large bonuses, either as a reward for very good performance or as a guaranteed amount paid at the end of the year. This bonus culture encouraged risk-taking and a degree of irresponsibility in personal expenditure. By contrast, people from countries cited in Chapter 6 as being less comfortable with uncertainty are more likely to want a higher proportion of their pay to be guaranteed in a fixed salary. This direct link between corporate culture in particular business sectors, the culture of a host country, and pay structures may also impact on the staffing decisions taken by MNEs, including when the company is looking at overseas pay packages.

There are commonly three types of package: home-based, headquarters, and host-based. In the home-based method, the expatriate receives similar pay (and other benefits) as would be given for the equivalent position in his or her home country—that is, a Swede working for an Italian company in India receives a similar package to his or her Swedish counterparts working at home in Sweden. This method tends to be the most common among large international firms, with about 60 per cent of them using this method for long-term assignments and about 75 per cent for short-term jobs. The headquarters method means that the expatriate receives the same package as for a comparable job in the city or country where the MNE has its headquarters, so that the Swedish manager would get the same as equivalent managers in Italy. Effectively, this method means that the Italian salary package is the standard throughout the world for managers in jobs of similar rank. The third method is where the expatriate receives the local or host country salary; this is sometimes called localization or destination pricing. Depending on various factors, such as the manager's home country, negotiations with the IHRM department, and the status of the post, the expatriate may also receive additional benefits (extra allowances, taxation compensation, international assignment premiums, and so on) to adjust the package upwards. In the end, the IHRM department has to ensure that its expatriates are not being penalized for taking on international assignments but also that employees in equivalent posts around the world are not being awarded very different compensation packages.

For many overseas postings, there may still be financial, linguistic, and cultural difficulties associated with certain locations for some potential expatriates. However, it has become an integral responsibility of IHRM professionals to ensure that 'internationally assigned employees are chosen, and appropriately supported, in ways which reflect not only their managerial and technical abilities, but also their capacity and willingness to undertake such positions' (Grainger and Nankervis 2001: 81).

In this context, there are important IHRM functions that are activated so that staff are properly prepared and supported, such functions include: language and cultural training, advice on legal matters, performance management, personal and family assistance, and help with relocation. Many of these factors are considered in Section II.

The increasingly strategic role and operations of IHRM departments within MNEs was emphasized in the aftermath of the 2008–2009 credit and financial crisis when thousands of relatively well-paid and highly trained employees lost their jobs. The speed and depth of the crisis meant that IHRM managers were over-burdened with the consequences of such a massive number of redundancies, with an estimated 100,000–200,000 financial jobs lost (Wilson and White 2011). Ironically, some analysts blamed the previous practices of the IHRM departments for inflating salaries and benefits for employees in the financial and other sectors. For many IHRM departments, too, the consequence of the financial crisis was that, at the same time as they were having to handle job cuts and redundancies, they were no longer in a position to continue with normal levels of recruitment. For most companies in the financial sector, it is unlikely that there will be a return to pre-2008 staffing levels, nor any upturn in new recruitment until beyond 2013.

A further consequence of the financial crisis was that certain elements of the IHRM departments' own budgets were being reduced. One report, focused on central and East European employers, noted that the key cuts within firms were changes in benefits (34 per cent of firms surveyed), freezing of recruitment (28 per cent), layoffs (28 per cent), reduced travelling costs (15 per cent), and, specifically for the HR departments, a reduction in their own costs (13 per cent) (Anderson Willinger 2009).

The financial crisis has had a tremendous impact on IHRM managers

Source: iStock

The changing face of IHRM rides on the impacts of the 2008–2012 economic and financial crises, and on the general international trends within work practices. The perceived reduction in the use of expatriates and the increasing variety of international assignments indicate that the role of IHRM will remain central to the strategic operation of MNEs in the twenty-first century.

Section II: Managing international workforces

In modern international business, international workforces are made up of a variety of employees from a range of countries. Whatever the mixture of PCNs, HCNs, and TCNs, and at whatever level of management, it is essential that the workforce is properly managed. A key component of the management of international workforces is the preparation, training, and development of staff (Sylvain 2012), followed by a system of thorough performance management. The majority of MNEs operating globally, as well as smaller firms, undertake programmes of cross-cultural training (CCT). Increasingly, such programmes have come to be delivered at distance or electronically and are known as e-CCT programmes.

The rationale for these programmes is that well-prepared individuals will be able to work more effectively with the employees they meet on their overseas assignments. They will learn about the language, local customs, and different cultural expectations of the host country, thus enabling them to integrate more smoothly with the HCNs who make up the bulk of the firm that they are joining.

Cross-cultural training

The key elements within CCT (or e-CCT) programmes are:

- identifying the types of global assignments for which CCT is required
- determining any specific CCT needs
- establishing the goals and measures for determining the effectiveness of CCT
- developing and delivering CCT
- evaluating the effectiveness of the programme.

The design and implementation of an effective CCT programme must usually match the degree of participant involvement with the rigour of the training. There are various elements for these two parameters, as can be seen in Figure 14.4.

There are broadly considered to be four types of global assignment (a typology devised by Caliguri and Lazarova, as set out in Harzing 2004), each requiring a different amount of CCT work. The first global assignment is *technical*, which is considered to be similar in content to the domestic activities already carried out by the member of staff. These assignments include staff in the oil and gas business involved in drilling and refining, technicians such as quantity surveyors in construction projects, systems engineers, and analysts interfacing

Figure 14.4
Parameters for effective CCT (adapted from Black et al. 1999, reproduced with kind permission).

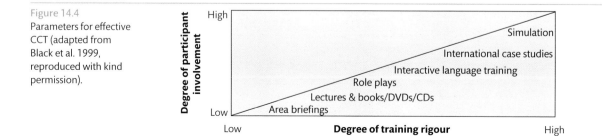

with computer systems. The member of staff is being employed primarily for his or her technical skills; it is these that will largely determine the outcome of the assignment and, therefore, a minimal amount of CCT is required. The second—and most common—global assignment is described as *functional/tactical*. In this, the essential requirement is a high level of interaction between the member of staff being assigned and the locally employed nationals: a good CCT programme is vital. For some MNEs, the third type of assignment is part of a broader IHRM strategy in which the main purpose is *developmental/high potential*. One of the primary goals is the individual development of the manager being deployed; this may, of course, be the designation of a younger HCN to take on a task in his or her own country, as well as assigning a rising executive to work abroad. Finally, there are global assignments that are very high profile and at the level of general managers, vice presidents, managing directors, and so on. These *strategic/executive* assignments are often at the core of the competitive development of the MNEs' strategies around the world. The tasks of these top people will include masterminding entry into new markets, turning around failing companies or subsidiaries, establishing a new joint venture, and developing a market base in certain countries.

Clearly the extent and content of the CCT programme will depend on the type of assignment, the personal characteristics and existing skills of the manager(s), and the short- and long-term goals of the assignment. There will be an emphasis in most CCT programmes on pre-departure training, a selection of language and culture-specific elements (Sylvain 2012), and a balance between one-off or continuous training. Whether the training is delivered within an e-CCT system or by a more traditional method, it needs to be evaluated in terms of a number of key factors, which include the following:

- How effectively was the assignment carried out?
- How far did the CCT contribute to the success of the assignment?
- How well were new cultural values explained, learnt, absorbed, and applied?
- What form of assessment (and self-assessment) was provided for the member of staff and his or her family?
- How well did the member of staff respond to the challenges of the global assignment?

The international skills required include a broad knowledge of HRM environments and practices in different countries, including not only knowledge of HRM and industrial relations systems, but also of the effects of national culture and values on work ethics and customary workplace behaviour. Other elements of a CCT programme may include the use of structured mentoring for all kinds of international employees, and corporate initiatives to seek appropriate work for spouses and partners in host countries. Issues related to the adaptation of the spouse as well as the employee may become even more urgent if, as some authors have suggested, 25 per cent of these 'trailing partners' will be male in the near future (Grainger and Nankervis 2001).

One of the aspects of CCT that is sometimes neglected is the training or counselling that is required when a manager's international assignment finishes. It might be assumed that, for anybody going 'home', there is no need for any help; after all, the manager and his or her family are going back to an environment with which they are entirely familiar: their own house, town, and country. However, there are a number of key problems that can be associated with repatriation or reverse culture shock (**see ORC Extension material 14.1**). These are often very dependent on the length of time that the employee and family have been abroad. The main changes are readjustments to the corporate structure and life at the MNE's headquarters, changes (usually a reduction) in the employee's financial package, changes in the home country that have not been fully understood after years of service abroad, and readjustment to life at home where the family may be living in a smaller house, children are having to settle into another school, and all of them are having to relearn some of what they took for granted. The process of repatriation requires as much careful planning and preparation as CCT for employees embarking on international assignments.

> Go online

The relationship between effective CCT and business success is taken for granted, but there are still cases in which large companies fail to understand this. The failure of the American retailer Walmart to understand and accept national employment practices and labour conditions, including a reluctance to appoint German managers for its 1998 takeover of the Wertkauf and Interspar stores in Germany, has—quite rightly—been held out as a classic example of this. More of these cases were explored in earlier chapters on the importance of culture in international business.

Performance management

An interesting aspect of IHRM relates to the management of international performance throughout an organization. There are extensive systems of performance management that are explored in traditional HRM textbooks and manuals; they comprise the key steps of recruitment, retention of staff, including appraisal and rewards, and training and staff development. The best companies are usually praised for their successes in nurturing and retaining good staff, and for their ability to combine good HR relations with the maximization of profit and value.

Within Virgin Media (see 'Practitioner insight'), Elisa Nardi has noted that performance management is more an art than a science, with the challenge of management confidence and competence—managers being able to make discerning judgements about the 'what' and the 'how' of performance management—and the challenge of individuals taking personal ownership of performance rather than seeing it as something the company 'does to you'. There is the great challenge of connecting performance and reward—and then the need to ensure that all reward mechanisms are transparent, well-governed, fair, affordable, and equitable. Performance management is fully embedded in Virgin Media so that their process drives and is connected to reward (annual bonus, long-term incentive, etc.). The objective-setting process is closely connected to role grading and job specifications. The company uses performance management to determine objectives, set development plans, discuss career ambitions, and think about its values (Nardi 2012).

A very visible aspect of IHRM relates to the payment and overall remuneration packages of the highest paid and most prominent executives, particularly the worldwide CEOs (Thomas and Hill 2012). Even though much has changed in international business since the 1980s, it is still true that the dominance of US-origin MNEs within the world of international business is reflected in the continuing pay gap between American CEOs and other CEOs. As Randall S. Thomas noted in his ground-breaking study, most pay gaps exist because of market forces (Thomas 2003). In 2010–2011, the average overall compensation package (pay plus other benefits and shares) for CEOs in the top 350 US-based companies was $9.3 million, with the largest package being $84 million paid to the boss of Viacom, Philippe Dauman (Lublin 2011; Wall Street Journal 2011; Singer 2012).

+ Pay gap
Different levels of payment between the top CEOs (or other employees) and those at other levels, or between male and female employees.

Historically, it has been argued that top managers of non-American firms had not enjoyed the same increase in bargaining power in relation to pay. The structures of their firms, the shareholdings, and the management meant that 'foreign' (non-American) CEOs were not in a position to benefit from large takeovers in the earlier years of MNE growth, and perhaps until the 1990s this imbalance remained a significant factor. By contrast, American CEOs (or CEOs of US origin or US-based firms) were able to 'capture' their boards of directors and/or their passive and widely dispersed shareholders so as to overpay themselves excessively.

Randall Thomas put forward four arguments related to market-driven forces that may have accounted for this traditional pay difference. Thomas's first argument rested on 'the marginal revenue product of executive labour'. He noted that American CEOs should be paid more, on average, than foreign CEOs, because American CEOs contributed more to their firms' value. American firms had greater growth opportunities and had greater resources to be deployed because they were bigger. American CEOs played a much larger role in the decision-making process at their firms than CEOs at foreign firms. They also received more of their pay in the form of stock options, and might hold more of their wealth in company stock than foreign CEOs, and therefore their pay would reflect a risk premium (Thomas 2003).

His second argument on the international pay gap came from an examination of the workings of corporations' internal labour markets and the competition to become CEO. In this view, American firms were different because their CEOs had so much more power than foreign counterparts. After all, in the USA, the CEO was (and is) normally also the Chairman of the Board, whereas in other countries this was rarely the case. For example, in the early part of the twenty-first century, there were significant difficulties for Sir Stuart Rose, then CEO at Marks & Spencer, and for Lakshmi Mittal, CEO at Arcelor Mittal, when they tried to persuade their boards and shareholders to permit them to combine the two top jobs. American CEOs' power was further enhanced compared with those of their biggest foreign rivals, such as Japan and Germany, because boards of directors were smaller in the USA than in Japan, and had only one tier, instead of the two-tier structure in Germany.

Thomas's third point was to note the differences in the opportunity costs for American and foreign CEOs. The opening-up of financial markets between the early 1980s and the start of the 2008–2009 financial crisis gave US CEOs better access to capital markets for financing their own start-up businesses, raising the value of their alternative opportunities. This occurred first through the use of leveraged buyout (LBO) or management buyout (MBO) as a method of financing a new firm, then with the tremendous growth in venture capital financing, and later on (at least for a period of years) when the technology boom made available massive amounts of capital to finance start-ups. Established American businesses that wished to compete for managerial talent were thereby forced to offer executives larger pay packages.

By comparison, non-US CEOs did not have nearly the same access to financial markets to launch their own businesses. For them, the expansion of executive job opportunities only came with the deregulation of some capital markets and increased managerial migration. These changes increased pressure on foreign companies to pay their executives more, but in general they have yet to catch up.

Thomas's final point related to the differential bargaining power that American CEOs had compared with that of foreign CEOs. This different level of power derived from two important forces at work in the USA: first, the shift in the 1980s in the relative bargaining strength of American CEOs in vetoing takeovers of their corporations; and secondly, the concurrent acceptance of the idea of pay-for-performance by domestic institutional investors. These changes gave American CEOs tremendous power to stop a hostile takeover unless the sale of the firm was perceived as being in that executive's personal best interests.

Since the 1990s, there has been a more significant change to the dominance of 'American' CEOs. This has come from two contrasting developments: the rise of global corporations and their CEOs, and the scandals associated with certain US MNEs, related to failures in corporate governance, accounting abuses, and/or straightforward corporate and CEO greed. This affected CEOs and senior executives such as Bernie Ebbers at WorldCom; Gary Winnick of Global Crossing; Dennis Koslowski of Tyco; Andy Fastow, Jeff Skilling, and Kenneth Lay at Enron; Richard Fuld, Jr. at Lehman Brothers; and Stan O'Neal of Merrill Lynch (Harvard Law School 2000; Treanor 2010).

Perhaps more significantly, there has been the rise of global/international corporations from all over the world, so that their CEOs are neither European nor American. Key examples were the top Indian businesspeople: Vijay Mallya, CEO of the Indian United Breweries group (originally founded by a Scotsman); Lakshmi Mittal, CEO of the global steel giant Arcelor Mittal (half of which is based in Europe); Sunil Bharti Mittal (no relation), CEO of the telecommunications Bharti Group; and Sanjay K. Jha of Motorola.

Beyond these examples, there are CEOs/senior executives whose worldwide experience has been regarded as more important than their original nationality in their rise to the top jobs. Examples of this type of CEO were Indra Nooyi, the Indian-born CEO of PepsiCo; Carlo

Carlos Ghosn, CEO of Renault–Nissan (reproduced with the kind permission of Nissan)

Radicati, an Italian in charge of Russian Standard vodka; Willie Walsh, an Irishman as CEO at BA, following on from Rod Eddington, an Australian who was CEO from 2000 to 2005; Andrea Jung, a Canadian of Chinese origin as CEO of Avon Products (due to stand down in 2012); Andre Navarri, a Frenchman in charge of the Canadian transportation company Bombardier; and Carlos Ghosn, a Brazilian-born Lebanese who is now a French citizen and runs Renault–Nissan Alliance as Chairman and CEO. These developments within corporate promotion and achievement demonstrate that there has been a greater smoothing-out of US and non-US pay for CEOs and other leading corporate executives.

Women in international business

A related issue in the world of leadership in international business has been the move towards a greater role for women as CEOs and senior managers in MNEs. This involves reducing the gaps between men and women in the posts they hold, as well as in their pay. It is evident that women have begun to achieve top positions in MNEs, most notably Indra Nooyi and Andrea Jung. There are also women in charge of other large corporations: Meg Whitman (HP), Virginia Rometty (IBM), Ellen Kullman (Dupont), Marjorie Scardino (Pearsons), Anne Mulcahy (Xerox), Oprah Winfrey (Harpo Inc.), and Irene Rosenfeld (Kraft Foods).

It might be expected that MNEs and other business organizations in the developed world, including Europe, would be more advanced in establishing equality of treatment, pay, and seniority for women. While the picture is reasonably positive in certain areas (see Figure 14.5), it is also evident that progress has not been as great as anticipated. In 2007, 'far from powering through the glass ceiling, women take up just 8.5 per cent of seats in corporate boardrooms in Europe's biggest 300 companies' (Attwood 2007). By 2012, there had been some progress in certain countries so that it could be claimed in the UK that 'getting more women in the boardroom is now a mainstream agenda' (Urwin 2012). As can be seen from Figure 14.5, there is a wide difference across the world, with the most advanced and favourable companies (within the European countries cited) being in Norway and Sweden, then Germany, France, and Britain, and the least favourable being from Spain.

In 2011–2012, it has been proposed within Europe and elsewhere that a key remedy to the relative lack of women entering the highest levels of business is to introduce quotas by means of national legislation, or EU-led proposals. Within Europe, the Norwegian government aimed to get company boards to be 40 per cent women by 2008–2009; this has largely been achieved but there were questions as to the extent of this being 'window-dressing' (Economist 2011). Viviane Reding, the EU Commissioner for Justice, proposed in March

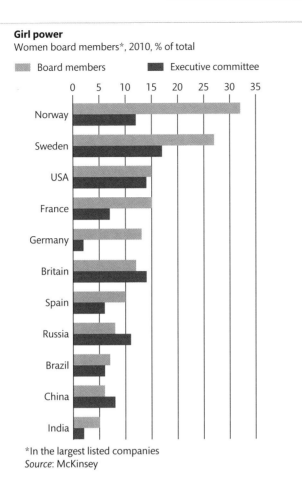

Girl power
Women board members*, 2010, % of total

*In the largest listed companies
Source: McKinsey

Figure 14.5
Girl power (McKinsey, cited in *The Economist* 2011).

2011 that companies should promise that women 'will make up 30% of their boards by 2015 and 40% by 2020' (Economist 2011).

A consequence of women's lack of success in getting senior jobs in international business has been the growth in the number of businesses set up and led by women. This is true both in LDCs, with the growth of micro-finance, and in the more developed OECD countries. In the UK, for example, it is 'estimated that between 34 and 42 per cent of the UK small business stock is owned or co-owned by women' (Attwood 2007). Part of the reason for this expansion in the creation of women-led businesses is that, in all sizes of company, there is a perceived and real degree of inflexibility in the working regime imposed on members of staff. This often means that these companies perform poorly in allowing staff to achieve a proper work–life balance.

Much of the excellent work on the role of gender in the IHRM aspect of businesses has been carried out by female researchers, academics, and practitioners, especially Professor Nancy Adler (Adler and Izraeli 1988; Adler and Gundersen 2008). For many women in international business, the key factor that has been described as most limiting to their careers is the glass ceiling; this was true even in 2012 in a country such as the UK (Urwin 2012). The term implies that the actual level to which women can rise in business is lower than that of men, even though it is not stated explicitly—that is, the real ceiling for women is invisible or transparent, like glass (Glass Ceiling Commission 1991–1996).

In 1995, the Glass Ceiling Commission said that the barrier was continuing 'to deny untold numbers of qualified people the opportunity to compete for and hold executive level positions in the private sector'. It found that women had 45.7 per cent of America's jobs and more than half of master's degrees being awarded. Yet 95 per cent of senior managers were men, and female managers' earnings were on average a mere 68 per cent of those of their male counterparts (Glass Ceiling Commission 1991–1996).

There are certain factors that indicate continuing discrimination against women in international business, as established by the Professional Women's Network (PWN) of Europe in 2006–2007. These factors include the following:

* Women lack visibility: women's public profiles are significantly lower than men's; 28 per cent of the top 100 businesswomen cannot be 'googled'.

* Only 8 per cent of women are heads of committees, against 27 per cent of men; for example, audit committees are almost exclusively headed by men.

* In non-executive board positions, men had 84 per cent of line management positions against women's positions, which are reported as only 57 per cent.

* Only 9.5 per cent of women hold PhDs against 33 per cent of men; most PhDs received by businessmen are honorary, whereas women have generally studied in order to achieve their status. PWN's researchers wonder whether this indicates that men 'work smart and women work hard'.

In their research, PWN have also established certain other key differences between women and men. For example, women executives have significantly more social science degrees; women dominate as employee representatives (28 per cent vs. less than 1 per cent for men); men tend to retire, whereas it is usual that women serve until they reach the end of their tenure; female executive board members have fewer expatriate assignments than their male counterparts (in general 0.8 vs. 2.4 over the course of their career); and, in the accumulation of other posts, executive board women hold more corporate board positions than men, but male non-executives hold more corporate and not-for-profit board positions than women.

According to PWN, there are also a number of key similarities between men and women on international boards. All executive board members tend to hold a low proportion of MBA degrees (only 12 per cent of women and 15 per cent of men) and a similar number of not-for-profit board positions (that is, 2.5 positions per person).

The European PWN's advice to women in international business, based clearly on the elements set out above, is extensive and mirrors in many respects the view of other professionals and academics concerned about the gaps between men and women. Because women often lack visibility, PWN advises companies that they can make women aware of the importance and difficulties of these issues and proposes that each woman needs to design a strategic plan for self-promotion. Similarly, women need to be aware of the importance of networking to gain access to and flourish in the topmost levels of MNEs. As women lag behind in expatriate assignments, which often are still a requirement for getting to the top, companies tend proactively to include women in their expatriate planning. Since significant differences in profiles at non-executive level (age, staff/line, expatriate assignments, accumulation of posts) may place women in a disadvantageous position, this requires a strong and inclusive chairperson of the board to take counterbalancing action. Companies that experience an under-representation of women executives but an over-representation of women in staff positions should develop strategic action plans to maximize the promotion of female talent to a higher level.

Above all, consideration of the position of women within international business requires a focus not only on the 'glass ceiling', but on other factors that inhibit the mobility and career development of women. Various other factors are described by terminology such as 'off- and on-ramps', 'glass walls vs. class accelerator', the 'labyrinth', the 'glass shoe', and the 'glass cliff'. Of these many other terms that can be applied to the difficulties facing all sorts of employees, but most associated with those facing women, the most significant is perhaps the concept of the glass cliff. This suggests that, once a woman has overcome the difficulties of the glass ceiling, she may then be given an exceptionally risky and complicated assignment in which she is likely to fail, and thus to fall over the cliff edge.

In contrast with the study and practice of women in international management, there has been less work on the role of different ethnic backgrounds within MNEs. There are a number of international organizations trying to rectify this situation, such as the International Society for Diversity Management, established in Germany, and TCO—International Diversity Management, based in Italy and the UK. Part of the relative neglect of this area derived from the fact that people have tended to focus on the PCN, HCN, and TCN issues (see above) and partly because non-white men appear to have succeeded in achieving top positions within MNEs in a way that has not yet been possible for women. There are genuine benefits to diversity, as it helps to ensure that companies mirror the market, encourage innovation, improve decision-making, enforce ethics, attract talent, and raise the bottom line. It seems that international business is heading towards the position where all managers can share equally in the ups and downs of corporate life.

Stress in international jobs

One of the most serious impacts of international management at all levels is work-related stress. It is clear that modern corporate thinking considers stress to be a potential hindrance to the smooth functioning of international operations. There is far greater concern with assisting employees to achieve a better work life balance than has been the case in the past (Lightfoot 2008). Some sectors of MNE activity, including work in the financial and market-trading operations, may still favour and reward punishing work schedules, long anti-social hours, and a 'macho' working atmosphere. In some cases this environment is made even worse by the way in which such tensions reflect a considerable degree of political manoeuvring within the workplace—the impact of office politics (**see ORC Extension material 14.2**). However, in general, there is a greater understanding of, and proactive attempts to overcome, stress in the workplace. With modern developments such as the smartphone and Skype, many globally operating employees are always 'at work' or 'on platform'. Managers who travel the world are expected to be in touch with the office at all times and to be on call 24/7 (a modern phrase denoting round-the-clock working for the whole week). For such international employees, the lines between work time and social life, or 'down time', have become increasingly blurred.

> Go online

There is a strong view among the IHRM professionals that stress at work can be a massively negative factor in the productivity of a company. Excessive stress can be extremely expensive for employers, leading to greater absenteeism, lower performance, and a higher rate of employee turnover. The impact of this on business productivity can be significant and is starting to be taken more seriously by MNEs. The evidence for this is demonstrated by the increase in activities such as mentoring and coaching, stress-relieving workshops, and a general call for a more holistic approach to the needs of all corporate workers.

A number of MNEs have established programmes designed to assist employees with stress, including GlaxoSmithKline (GSK) and PriceWaterhouseCoopers (PwC). The giant British–American MNE GSK combines health assessments, discussion groups, and follow-up evaluations in a programme called 'Team Resilience' that is intended to deal with workplace stress. Various groups within GSK have undergone this process, completing questionnaires about workplace stress and then participating in workshop discussions within their functional areas. The programme has produced proposals for improving conditions within the workplace, including desire for more flexibility in how work is organized (GSK 2006–2008; Holland 2008). In a similar fashion, PwC has addressed the issue of stress through annual surveys, the provision of more coaching, and greater opportunities to connect with experienced colleagues throughout the firm's worldwide operations. The creation of 'market teams' has led to higher satisfaction levels and lower employee turnover within PwC. The managing director for People Strategy at PwC, Michael J. Fenlon, was reported as noting the successful achievement of creating 'an environment where there's openness and a sense of mutual support' (Holland 2008).

Changes in employment and the workplace

There are three key factors that are beginning to have a large impact on IHRM for the twenty-first century. These are: (1) the changing roles, varying from country to country, of trade unions and workers' associations in the operations of businesses around the world; (2) changes in employment legislation in different parts of the world, with particular emphasis on laws relating to a range of forms of discrimination in the workplace; and (3) greater emphasis on flexible working and improving the work–life balance.

> Go online

Traditionally, battle lines within domestic and international business are drawn up between employer (the company) and employees, often gathered together and represented by a workers' association or a trade union (**see ORC Extension material 14.3**). The hard-line employer was, and still is, keen to get as much work out of its employees as it can while at the same time paying as little as possible and providing the minimum in the way of good working conditions. This may well still be true for many employers, whether in the developed or the developing world. On the other side, there have always been more enlightened employers who have been convinced that the best way of getting the maximum effort from their workforce is to ensure that employees have good pay and good working conditions. A classic example of this is the German concept and practice of co-determination (*Mitbestimmung*), which provides two levels of employee participation in work decisions. Co-determination is established through representation of workers on two 'boards': a works council and the company's supervisory board. This principle is now in the process of being extended to the formation of the 'European Company', which will be a form of co-determination derived from German, Dutch, or French variants of this principle.

One of the key impacts on international business is the MNE's relations with the workforce and its representatives. Much of the data on these relations is collected and analysed by the International Labour Organization (ILO). In addition to the official facts, figures, and interpretations, it is evident from the authors' experience and that of their business contacts that some national governments and MNEs are more hostile to fair employee status than others. Certain governments, such as Saudi Arabia and Indonesia, are perceived as being particularly hostile to good relations with trade unions and, on occasion, even to their existence. Trade unions are perceived by many regimes as 'socialist' or 'communist' and condemned by the political elites as subversive, and opposed to the safety and ongoing operations of the state. The use of repressive legislation permits such regimes, often with the connivance of the national business class, local companies, and MNEs, to deny workers some of the most basic human rights. In such situations, workers may have to work for longer hours than normally permitted, carry out successive work shifts, be denied the appropriate number of breaks for drinks or meals, be forced to work in excessive temperatures, and even not be paid or compensated properly for their work.

It is essential for future international business managers that they analyse and understand the labour relations of any country in which they operate. They will be involved in the position that their company adopts regarding the nexus of business–labour relations, employment laws, the legal position of trade unions, and the social and legal framework for workers and working conditions.

At a further stage of FDI strategy, or any other form of involvement abroad (see Chapter 7), the MNE will make a detailed assessment of the relative attractiveness of target countries in terms of factors such as employment laws and customs. For many MNEs, this is an assessment of the business environment and range of risks connected with the associated legislation, including laws relating to contracts, pay and conditions, and job discrimination.

In the countries of the EU, the development of employment legislation has produced major changes in legislation. Some of the key developments have been in the area of employment discrimination, relating in particular to gender and sexual identity, racial and ethnic origin, and varying types of disability. In the most advanced applications of this legislation, the new framework is founded on the principles and interpretations of European Human Rights. In a country such as the UK, for example, employee rights were enhanced by the British acceptance of European rights as from October 2000. The new legislation in the UK includes laws on equal pay, ageism, civil partnerships, racial equality, and disability discrimination.

The increasing burden on employers, whether domestic companies or MNEs operating in the UK, is aggravated by the fact that there is greater responsibility placed on the employer to show that positive action has been taken in relation to these varying laws. Some critics complain that such legislation harms business and typifies 'discredited 1970s feminist ideology' (Ruth Lea, former Head of Policy at the Institute of Directors, quoted in Lightfoot 2008). The new laws impose, for example, a burden of proof on both sides in any disputes, but the employer increasingly has to show that it has a full set of policies and procedures and all employees have been informed of these, full records are kept on all matters related to employment, and decision-making is transparent. For MNEs it is essential that both the legal department and the HR specialists understand all the legal requirements of employment, the frequent changes that occur, the impact of EU directives and regulations, the rulings of the European Court of Justice, and the implications of forthcoming legislation.

The final aspect for IHR managers to deal with in some of the more advanced workplaces in the twenty-first century is the extension of modes of flexible working (see Case study 14.3) and the emphasis placed on establishing a work–life balance. The importance of flexible working is that it helps companies to address and solve skills shortages, open up new markets of talent, and retain workers who would otherwise leave the organization.

One of the outcomes of the legislative changes mentioned above has been the increased legal right to request flexible working arrangements. Whereas employers in the UK, for example, are not bound to grant the employee's request, they are required to consider it. In 2010–2011 the giant telecommunications MNE BT (formerly British Telecom) had about 12 per cent of its 100,000 employees in the UK working full-time from home, using broadband connections to log into BT's system. The encouragement of flexible working enabled the company to balance the firm's needs and interests with those of its employees. Within most OECD countries, there has been a general trend towards more of these flexible arrangements, thus encouraging companies to adopt this form of employment as 'many of them start to choose the flexible working . . . policy to optimize their human resources and save cost' (Antal International 2009).

A further feature of flexible working is the creation of job-sharing, where usually two employees fulfil the functions of one job. This tends to occur more frequently among women employees than men. Although job-sharing is most common at lower levels of work within MNEs, it has also happened at relatively senior management levels. For example, in 2007–2008, two very senior female managers at Credit Suisse successfully shared their working week and two women departmental and branch managers at NatWest (since 2008 part of the RBS Group) operated successfully in a similar fashion (Lightfoot 2008).

The developments in flexible working have frequently been expected to affect international managers more rapidly and thoroughly, but it is apparent that people at all levels of work still value the traditions of personal and face-to-face contact. Managers still do not view communicating by email and video conferencing in the same light as knowing exactly with whom they are doing business across the world.

The many changes in international workforces' management have posed key challenges for IHRM departments within MNEs. The adoption of cross-cultural training, extension of diversity within the international workforce, and greater emphasis on the work–life balance are hallmarks of the most enlightened IHRM professionals. Within the context of technological and economic uncertainty, these are real challenges to the managers of the twenty-first century.

Challenges and choices

→ Managers engaged in international human resource management (IHRM) in the twenty-first century face choices that are strategic level in nature. What sort of national staffing composition best suits the company? What sorts of performance management systems are best for the highest paid executives? How different are these for other levels of managers and workers? How far are certain employees held back by workplace discrimination or different legal structures? The range of issues is immense and central to international business development. The greatest challenge will possibly be the need to develop more sophisticated and permanent forms of flexible working for a higher proportion of the workforce. Even in 2012, it is still only a small percentage of people worldwide who can work flexibly: mainly professionals, hi-tech workers, and job-sharers. In an increasingly international world of work, it is ironic that most workers have little choice about how they work and are still restricted to nine to five office jobs and, even worse, to production shifts in factories, sometimes in sweatshop conditions.

Chapter summary

This chapter has set out a number of key issues of international human resource management (IHRM) and focused on some of the major developments of the twenty-first century in relation to the world of work. The principal arguments have shown a move away from 'foreign' domination of international work to increasing participation and management by host country nationals (HCNs) in the affairs of MNEs. This reflects the relative decline in the role and influence of expatriates, although cross-cultural training of employees on international assignments remains important.

On completing the chapter, students should appreciate and understand the importance of the development of IHRM at the strategic level within MNEs. Modern IHRM attempts to establish greater diversity and equality in the international workforce, better work–life balance, and the reduction of stress among managers. Organizations that take care of their people are more likely to be successful, both in the short term and in the long run.

Case study 14.3

Cisco: Remote workers and greater security

Cisco (http://www.cisco.com) is a worldwide leader in networking that transforms how people connect, communicate, and collaborate. Cisco's 2008 global study and its range of further studies (*Cisco Connected World Technology Reports* 2010 and 2011) offered some key findings on remote workers' security awareness and online behaviour. The study indicated how they could inadvertently heighten risks for themselves and their companies. The study's findings prompted Cisco security executives to offer recommendations to information technology (IT) professionals on how to protect their companies against threats and maximize the business benefits of distributed and mobile workforces. The conclusions of the study also highlighted the way in which IHR departments and managers could bring themselves and their companies into closer contact with their more distant employees. The 2011 *Connected World Technology Report* noted that young workers regarded 'mobile networking, device flexibility, and the blending of personal and work lifestyles' as key components in their preferred work environment and culture (Cisco 2011).

The significance and importance of the 2008 global study were emphasized by the growing number of employees worldwide who were working outside their office

Remote employees are becoming less disciplined in their online behaviour

Source: iStock

locations. In the early part of the twenty-first century, 'the worldwide corporate teleworking population of individuals that spend at least one day a month teleworking from home is expected to show a compound annual growth rate (CAGR) of 4.3 per cent between 2007 and 2011 . . . In the same period, the worldwide corporate teleworking population of individuals that spend at least one day a week teleworking from home is expected to show a CAGR of 4.4 per cent. This population will likely reach 46.6 million by the end of 2011' (Jones 2007).

The 2008 study involved surveys of more than 2000 remote workers and IT professionals from various industries and company sizes in ten countries: the USA, the UK, France, Germany, Italy, Japan, China, India, Australia, and Brazil. The ten countries were chosen because they represent a diverse set of social and business cultures, stable and emerging network-dependent economies, and varied lengths of Internet adoption.

One of the more important findings is that remote workers feel less urgency to be vigilant in their online behaviour. While most believe that they are more vulnerable outside the office than inside, their perceptions of security threats are softening. In just one year, the number of remote workers who believe the Internet is safer increased by 8 per cent, from just under half (48 per cent) to more than half (56 per cent). This trend is especially prevalent in Brazil (71 per cent), India (68 per cent), and China (64 per cent), three of the world's fastest growing economies whose workforces are depending more and more on the Internet and corporate networks.

According to the study, IT respondents believe that remote employees are becoming less disciplined in their online behaviour. More than half of the companies (55 per cent) believe that their remote workers are becoming less diligent towards security awareness, an 11 percentage point increase from the year before. Some of the key findings in terms of risky behaviour include:

- *Opening emails and attachments from unknown or suspicious sources.* China (62 per cent) is the worst offender. It is arguably more disturbing that this is a growing trend in entrenched Internet-adopter countries like the UK (48 per cent), Japan (42 per cent), Australia (34 per cent), and the USA (27 per cent).

- *Using work computers and devices for personal use.* A 3 percentage point increase year-on-year shows that more remote workers use corporate devices for personal use, such as shopping, downloading music, and visiting social networking sites. This trend occurs in eight of the ten countries, with the highest year-to-year increase occurring in France (27–50 per cent). In Brazil, this trend rose 16 per cent despite an increasing number of respondents agreeing that this was unacceptable behaviour (37 per cent to 52 per cent year-on-year). Reasons offered: 'My company doesn't mind me doing so', 'I'm alone and have spare time', 'My boss isn't around', 'My IT department will support me if something goes wrong'.

- *Accessing work files with personal, non-IT-protected devices.* Accessing corporate networks and files with devices that are not protected by an employee's IT team presents security risks to the company, its information, and its employees. As the number of remote workers grows, the study reveals an annual rise (45 per cent in 2006 to 49 per cent in 2007) in this behaviour. It is widespread in many countries, especially China (76 per cent), the USA (55 per cent), Brazil (52 per cent), and France (48 per cent).

The 2008 Cisco study contained a number of strategic recommendations for protecting this increasingly dispersed workforce. It is imperative for any company's IT department (including Cisco's) to reassess how it is perceived by employees and how it can proactively influence corporate security. As part of an overall company IHRM strategy, the IT department can spearhead a consultative engagement with employees.

In the 2008 study, Cisco's John Stewart stressed: 'How you communicate and educate employees about essential security practices and policies will be different in Japan than in the United States. It will be different in China than in France. Security awareness and education requires an understanding of your audience's culture. You have to relate to them and earn their trust. Through trust comes respect and cooperation.'

Case study questions

1. For employees who work in an MNE like Cisco, what are the greatest temptations of the IT systems?
2. What security measures can be taken to protect both employees and companies in an increasingly 'porous' global information age?
3. What needs to be done to ensure that IT systems continue to develop in line with changes in the international workplace?

Discussion questions

1. What performance management systems would be most suitable for the highest paid executives or expatriate middle-level managers in MNEs?

2. How far are women held back by workplace discrimination or by legal structures in different countries?

3. Why are expatriates less in demand at the highest levels of international management in the twenty-first century?

4. What common characteristics are held by CEOs of international companies?

5. What causes stress for international businesspeople? How can IHRM processes assist staff in getting the correct work–life balance?

Online resource centre

Go online to test your understanding by trying multiple-choice questions, and assignment and examination questions.

Further research

Wai, I. L., Siloran Udani, Z. A., and Arches, A. A. (2011). 'Social adjustment of expatriates in Macau: Evidence from the gaming industry', *EuroAsia Journal of Management*, 21/1–2, December

This article focuses on the expatriates or non-resident workers in Macau, with particular emphasis on the gaming industry. There are over 75,000 non-resident workers in Macau, with the main groups being (by place of origin) from Mainland China (55.2 per cent), the Philippines (15.1 per cent), Vietnam (10 per cent), and Hong Kong (6.3 per cent). The study focuses on ten interviews, with eight men and two women engaged in the gaming industry. In line with the theoretical issues set out within the study, the authors recommend the need for continuing acculturation and language training programmes for expatriates. They note that the four key factors for the social adjustment of expatriates are: (a) language ability, (b) spouse-family adjustment, (c) co-worker support, and (d) logistical support.

References

Adler, N. J., and Izraeli, D. N. (1988). *Women in Management Worldwide*. Armonk, NY: M. E. Sharpe

Adler, N. J., with Gundersen, A. (2008). *International Dimensions of Organizational Behavior*. 5th edn. Mason, OH: Thomson South-Western

Anderson Willinger (2009). 'What employers think about effects of the financial crisis on their companies', 13 January, available at http://www.andersonwillinger.com, accessed 21 April 2009

Antal International (2009). 'Global survey finds out companies chose flexible working hours for cost saving', available at http://www.antal.com.cn, accessed 1 May 2009

Attwood, K. (2007). 'Business misses the female touch', *Independent*, 7 December

Black, J. S., Gregersen, H. B., Mendenhall, M., and Stroh, L. K. (1999). *Globalizing People through International Assignments*. Harlow: Addison-Wesley

Cisco (2008). http://www.cisco.com, accessed 23 August 2012

Cisco (2010). *Connected World Technology Report*, available at http://www.cisco.com/go/connected report, accessed 23 June 2012

Cisco (2011). *Connected World Technology Report*, available at http://www.cisco.com/go/connected report, accessed 23 June 2012

Economist (2011). 'Still lonely at the top', *The Economist*, 21 July

Edstrom, A. and Galbraith, J. R. (1977). 'Transfer of managers as a co-ordination and control strategy in multinational organizations', *Administrative Science Quarterly*, 22 (June), pp. 248–63, cited in Harzing and Van Ruysseveldt (2004)

Evans, P. (1992). 'Management development as glue technology', *Human Resource Planning*, 15/1, pp. 85–106

Ghafoor, S., Khan, U. F., Idrees, F., Javed, B., and Ahmed, F. (2011). 'Evaluation of expatriates' performance and their training on international assignments,' *Interdisciplinary Journal of Contemporary Research in Business*, 3/5 (September)

Glass Ceiling Commission (1991–1996). US Department of Labor, various reports available at http://www.dol.gov

Grainger, R. J. and Nankervis, A. R. (2001). 'Expatriation practices in the global business environment', *Research and Practice in Human Resource Management*, 9/2, pp. 77–92

GSK (2006–2008). GlaxoSmithKline, interviews with employees

Harvard Law School (2000). The Harvard Law School Forum on Corporate Governance and Financial Regulation, available at http://blogs.law.harvard.edu/corpgov

Harzing, A.-W. (2004). 'Composing an international staff', in Harzing and Van Ruysseveldt. *International Human Resource Management*, 2nd edn. London: Sage

Harzing, A.-W. and Van Ruysseveldt (2004). *International Human Resource Management*, 2nd edn. London: Sage

Holland, K. (2008). 'The tension builds', *New York Times*, 23 March

Jones, C. (2007). 'Teleworking, the quiet revolution', dataquest insight: update 14 May, Gartner, Inc., available at http://www.gartner.com, accessed 21 April 2009

Lightfoot, L. (2008). 'How to improve work–life balance', *Independent*, 10 April

Lublin, J. S. (2011). 'CEO pay in 2010 jumped 11%', *Wall Street Journal*, 9 May

Maki, D. and Soudakova, V. (2008). 'MNCs' management of human resources in India: Case studies of two Swedish companies', unpublished Master's thesis, Lulea University of Technology

Morris, K. (2004). 'Expatriate training in the corporate and non-corporate sector', unpublished MSc dissertation, Sheffield Hallam University

Nardi, E. (2012). Information from Virgin Media

Perlmutter, H. V. (1969). 'The tortuous evolution of the multinational company', *Columbia Journal of World Business*, Jan/Feb, pp. 9–18

Ryan, A. M. and Tippins, N. T. (2009). *Designing and Implementing Global Selection Systems*. Bognor Regis, Sussex, UK: Wiley

Schuler, R., Budhwar, P. and Florkowski, G. (2002). 'International human resource management: Review and critique', *International Journal of Management Reviews*, 4/1 (March), pp. 41–71

Scullion, H. and Collings, D. (eds.) (2011). *Global Talent Management*. Abingdon: Routledge

Scullion, H. and Starkey, K. (2000). 'In search of the changing role of the corporate human resource function in the international firm', *International Journal of Human Resource Management*, 11/6 (December), pp. 1061–1081

Singer, N. (2012). 'Boardroom bonanza', *New York Times* in *The Observer*, 15 April

Sylvain, N-M. (2012). 'How to make cross-cultural training effective,' *International HR Forum* (February), available at http://www.internationalhrforum.com, accessed 22 June 2012

Thomas, R. S. (2003). 'Explaining the international CEO pay gap: Board capture or market driven?', *Vanderbilt Law Review*, at SSRN: available at http://ssrn.com/abstract=407600 or DOI: 10.2139/ssrn.407600

Thomas, R. S. and Hill, J. G. (2012). *Research Handbook on Executive Pay*. Abingdon: Edward Elgar

Treanor, J. (2010). 'Solving the Lehman insolvency', *The Guardian*, 15 September

Urwin, R. (2012). 'The broad room', *Evening Standard*, 16 March

Wall Street Journal (2011). 'The Wall Street Journal/Hay Group Survey of CEO Compensation', *Wall Street Journal*, 8 May

Wilson, H. and White, A. (2011). 'Thousands more City banking jobs could go', *Daily Telegraph*, 17 November

Other sources of information

Bhatti, A. P. (2009). 'Cross-cultural issues in HRM,' unpublished MBA project, Simon Fraser University

Bolino, M. C. (2007). 'Expatriate assignments and intra-organizational career success: Implications for individuals and organizations', *Journal of International Business Studies*, 38/5 (September)

Bonache, J. and Zarraga-Oberty, C. (2008). 'Determinants of the success of international assignees as knowledge transferors', *International Journal of Human Resource Management*, 19/1

Briscoe, D. R., Schuler, R. S., and Claus, L. (2008). *International Human Resource Management: Policy and Practice for the Global Enterprise*, 3rd edn. Abingdon: Routledge

Davies, M. [Lord Davies of Abersoch] (2011). *Women on Boards*, UK BIS Dept., February

Hutchings, K., Dawn Metcalfe, B., and Cooper, B. (2010). 'Exploring Arab Middle Eastern women's perceptions of barriers to, and facilitators of, international management opportunities,' *International Journal of Human Resource Management*, 21/1

Kamenou, N. (2008). 'Reconsidering work–life balance debates: Challenging limited understandings of the "life" component in the context of ethnic minority women's experiences', Special Issue on Gender in Management: New Theoretical Perspectives, *British Journal of Management*, March

Lauring, J. (2007). 'Language and ethnicity in international management', *Corporate Communications: An International Journal*, 12/3, pp. 255–66

Mendenhall, M. E., Oddou, G. R., and Stahl, G. K. (2007). *Readings and Cases in International Human Resource Management*, 4th edn. Abingdon: Routledge

Nieto, M. L. (2006). *An Introduction to Human Resource Management*. Basingstoke: Palgrave Macmillan

Pitroda, S. (2012). 'Building a better India', *Ericsson Business Review*, 1

Schneider, S. C. and Barsoux, J.-L. (2003). *Managing across Cultures*, 2nd edn. Harlow: Pearson/FT Prentice Hall

Scroggins, W. and Benson, P. (2010). 'International human resource management: Diversity, issues and challenges', *Personnel Review*, 39/4

Shen, J. (2011). 'Developing the concept of socially responsible international human resource management', *International Journal of Human Resource Management*, 22/6 (April)

Tobin, L. (2012). 'Putting women on the board,' *The Independent*, 23 February

Visser, M. and Gigante, A. (2007). *Women on Boards: Moving Mountains*. European Professional Women's Network (PWN)

Part case study

Duelling expats: The conflict between headquarters and subsidiary mentalities

Financial intermediaries such as stock brokers are in a complicated position and must work conscientiously to avoid conflicts of interest. On the one hand, they can earn money by receiving commissions on deals transacted on behalf of customers (many of whose own trading decisions are at least partially based on their broker's advice). On the other hand, brokerage houses can also earn money through their own trades. Given this dual mission, there is always a possibility that brokers might be tempted to talk customers into bad trades and keep the good ones for themselves. To avoid such temptations, most countries have 'Chinese wall' legislation keeping trading and sales staff working for a given bank or brokerage from communicating certain details to one another. At a more subjective level, however, many people in this sector will feel relatively more loyalty to upstream production (trading) rather than downstream sales, or vice versa. This will then have an effect on the business decisions they make.

Employed in the early 1980s by a medium-sized California stock brokerage as a young systems designer, Jeff had had a brilliant early career developing a computerized trading system that soon became the industry standard. Within a decade, Jeff had been promoted to a senior position managing a team of brokers whose advice and transactional capabilities were largely based on the effectiveness of his product, which the company both used to manage its own positions and also sold to other brokerages (both in the USA and abroad) to generate extra revenue. These system sales often involved repeat business where wholesale customers would order customized or updated versions of the system. This ensured Jeff's ongoing reputation at his company more than anything he achieved with the teams of stock brokers for whom he became responsible as he was promoted.

Around the year 2000, however, competitors came out with newer and better software. Jeff's system continued to sell but it was no longer a cash cow for the company. Jeff's personal position was further undermined by the fact that, over-confident in the success of his now ageing system, he began to neglect most of his responsibilities aside from trading stocks for the company's own account.

This created a dilemma for the group executive. On one hand, they were grateful to Jeff for all he had done in the past. On the other, he was no longer nearly as valuable as

he once had been. When the director at the big branch office in Frankfurt resigned, the company decided to send Jeff over to replace him, arguing that internationalization might offer his career an exciting new direction. Jeff was not very excited about the prospect of going abroad. He was left little choice, however.

The Frankfurt office was 90 per cent staffed by German nationals, who as is normal in their culture paid no special attention to the new boss and simply got on with their work. This irritated Jeff greatly, as he considered Germany's customarily more egalitarian approach to be disrespectful. He missed the American culture, which tends to celebrate stardom. Jeff's hostility was also exacerbated by what he saw as local brokers' cosy relationships with customers. He felt that even though 'his' software was no longer state-of-the-art in the USA, European customers should be happy to pay the company a premium commission because he considered Europe a step behind the USA. When local sales personnel disagreed, he saw this as another sign of their excessive 'pride', telling them at an open meeting that if they were 'any good', they should be able to get customers to pay the higher commissions he was now demanding.

Jeff decided to show who was boss and, in particular, make an example of Susan, an American sales officer who was a local hire in Frankfurt. Susan had left the USA many years before. She had fallen in love with Europe, finished her university studies on the Continent, and learnt several languages. Married to a Dutchman, she was raising a young family in Frankfurt. Her sales relationships were based on her personal understanding of local customers' needs, and her sense of what the company's competition was offering them. Her target market was comprised of second-tier European trading companies, a segment that the local branch had been happy to service up until now. However, Jeff scorned them because they were less prestigious names than the ones he had been used to dealing with back home when his trading system was new and had attracted attention from the big investors, whose transaction size gives them a great deal of power in many financial markets.

Up until that point, Susan had almost always met or exceeded her sales volume targets. However, she had also developed a tendency to disagree with her production-side colleagues back in the USA about what the Frankfurt office should pay for the back-up services it was receiving from headquarters. Susan argued that she needed her internal return price to remain competitive because further down the value chain she could not be expected to knock any higher costs on to her European customers. With so many other US companies willing to equalize commissions between the two regions, charging more in Europe would have made the company uncompetitive in this part of the world.

Jeff had no complaints about Susan's performance but was irritated by her ongoing policy disagreements with headquarters, which he still considered home. Despite having only just arrived in Frankfurt, Jeff decided to side with his old US colleagues against Susan, and ordered her to charge local customers higher commissions. Susan tried to arrange meetings for Jeff with her biggest customers so he could get a feeling of how sophisticated the European market really is but this irritated him further. The conflict intensified, with Jeff loudly accusing Susan of 'going native' and ordering her to return to HQ to sit in the office for a month and re-acclimatize herself. Susan decided to consider other options.

(Real-life case study; names and other elements changed for reasons of confidentiality)

Case study questions

1. To what extent was Jeff justified in worrying that his European salespeople were getting too close to their customers?
2. How will Susan's life experience have influenced her international business decisions?
3. What is the best way of resolving the conflict between Jeff and Susan?

Future

part

F

15 The changing geography of international business

Learning objectives

After reading this chapter, you will be able to:

✦ trace developing countries' breakthrough in the world of international business

✦ analyse particularities of operating in emerging economies

✦ evaluate the particularities of selling into emerging economies

✦ forecast growth prospects for MNEs originating in the developing world

Case study 15.1

Macro adjustments in micro-finance

Despite progress in most developing countries, many people worldwide still live in poverty. One contributing factor is the general absence of adequate support systems in LDCs, one example being many entrepreneurs' difficulty in accessing the finance they need to grow their businesses. LDCs have historically lacked effective funding channels that are often found in wealthier nations. Moreover, the huge loans that big international banks typically offer small LDC borrowers are often unsuitable to their needs. In many LDCs, entrepreneurs must deal with loan sharks who charge extortionate interest. This creates a debt trap that undermines development. Enabling the poor to escape this vicious circle may be the last great frontier in international business (Bruton et al. 2011).

Responding to the deprivations afflicting his Bangladeshi community following the famines of the early 1970s, Muhammad Yunus founded the Grameen Bank in the hope that it might offer competitively priced loans to the small entrepreneurs that many LDC villages rely upon for their economic vitality. Yunus's vision gave birth to a whole new sector, micro-finance, which has contributed greatly to the world's development dynamic in recent decades. The effect has been so positive that, in 2006, Yunus was awarded the Nobel Prize for his efforts.

The micro-finance approach has been copied worldwide, with upwards of 5000 institutions adhering to its principles. Arguably, the movement has become a victim of its own success. The basic principle that loan costs be fully disclosed (something lacking in many LDCs previously) is not being obeyed by some institutions (Sitkin and Bowen 2010). Others originally created for non-profit purposes now have a for-profit status. Without adequate regulation, micro-finance could lose its identity and purpose.

This explains recent attempts to establish sector standards, most notably a transparency initiative developed by Chuck Waterfield, an independent consultant and a friend of Yunus. Waterfield has built a 'self-monitoring organization' (http://www.mftransparency.org/) that compiles and diffuses data, creating truth-in-lending standards that empower customers and prevent exploitation. This evolution is interesting because it mirrors the quality agenda that many of the world's older industrialized economies have pursued since the Toyota Production System was first rolled out in the 1970s (see Chapter 11). It is one of the many different ways that the Global South is leapfrogging the emergence phases that the Global North experienced during its own development (Ho 2008). It also indicates that micro-finance has reached a level of maturity.

Case study questions

1. Why do large international banks struggle to satisfy some LDC borrowers' needs?
2. How has the micro-finance sector performed so far? (see http://www.microfinancegateway.org)

Introduction

Despite the financial crises of 2008 and 2011–2012, many analysts continue to predict further integration of the global economy, largely driven by FDI flows (Sachs 2011). This is especially likely given the way in which many so-called less developed countries (LDCs) flourished even as the older industrialized nations entered a period of economic turmoil. The net effect is that 'for the first time ever, the number of poor people is declining everywhere' (Economist 2012b). This positive trend cannot help but have a major impact on international business.

It is important to state from the outset that 'LDCs' is a vague term referring to countries with very different prospects, ranging from highly indebted poor countries (HIPCs) struggling to survive without foreign aid to 'higher lower income' or 'lower middle income' countries whose recent performance has turned them from marginal players on the international business scene into key drivers of future growth. This latter category includes country-continents (the famous BRICs: Brazil, Russia, India, and China) and a group called CIVETS (comprised of Colombia, Indonesia, Vietnam, Egypt, Turkey, and South Africa), as well as other emerging powers like Malaysia, Mexico, Nigeria, and Taiwan. Terms such as the Global South, newly industrialized countries, and above all 'emerging' economies apply to both groups and are used throughout this chapter and book.

There are different ways to categorize emerging economies. In addition to performance indicators such as GDP rates or per capita income, the countries vary in terms of population size, natural resources, and proximity to trade routes or other growth markets. Their institutional backgrounds can also differ depending on colonization history or political traditions. For instance, so-called 'transition' countries like the Czech Republic in once communist Eastern Europe have clearly followed a different path from other emerging economies with less of an industrial tradition. Similarly, China has used cheap labour to build its manufacturing sectors whereas India focuses more on service activities. Another distinction is between Chile, with its preference for free-market 'neo-liberal' policies (see Chapter 3) and Malaysia, which tends to take a more critical view of deregulated markets. MNE managers must have a differentiated vision of each emerging market in which they operate. Their approach must also vary depending on whether the country in question is viewed as a manufacturing platform, consumer market, birthplace of new rivals, or a combination. The sequencing of these stages (manufacturing, sales, corporate development) typifies much of the Global South's emergence and provides a logical way of structuring this chapter.

Section I: Emerging operational locations

Despite industrialized countries' ongoing dominance of global trade and investment, the data provided in Chapter 1 shows a strong rise in the proportion of international business transacted in the emerging world. One prime example at this level is China, a country that experienced starvation as recently as the 1960s yet now possesses foreign exchange reserves of nearly $3 trillion, making it the most cash-rich nation in the world. The change has been monumental and is exemplified by the way that EU leaders turned to China in the autumn of 2011, hoping that this vast country-continent would help fund the bailout package being organized in the wake of the Greek and EU sovereign debt crisis. Previously this role might have been played by the USA but it is also deeply in debt to China, which holds about one-third of its total reserves in US Treasury bonds. This same power is felt at an international business level, with Chinese interests leading global investment in sectors ranging from natural resources and simple components to sophisticated technology and all kinds of global finance. In January 2011 alone, German companies including Volkswagen and Mercedes signed $8.7 billion in car, machinery, and energy deals with Chinese interests. Transactions of this size are eye-watering, especially at a time of recession. The emerging world has truly emerged.

The rise of the Global South

In 2006, Goldman Sachs economist Jim O'Neill estimated that more than 25 per cent of world growth over the previous five years had come from BRIC countries. He also predicted, accurately, that this percentage would rise. Whereas average annual GDP growth during most of the 2000s was between 1 and 4 per cent in the older industrialized countries, the original BRICs regularly experienced annual growth rates of 5–6 per cent (and often well above, in the case of China).

In 2011, O'Neill updated his vision with a 'Next 11' concept that identified a set of fast-growing countries capable of emerging at a BRIC-like speed. This new list of emerging powerhouses (Bangladesh, Egypt, Indonesia, Iran, Mexico, Nigeria, Pakistan, Philippines, South Korea, Turkey, and Vietnam) contained several surprises, if only because of the still high poverty levels in these countries. Yet it is a view that has come to be shared by many international business analysts. One example is the study that HSBC Bank published in 2011 predicting major shifts in countries' relative rankings between now and the year 2050 (see Figure 15.1).

One interesting aspect of this increasingly widespread vision of the future is the way in which many LDCs have continued to emerge at a time when their older and supposedly more advanced rivals were performing less well (see Figure 15.2). This underlines the importance of determining the particular development dynamics dictating emerging countries' performance.

Country	Predicted size of economy in 2050
1. China	24,617
2. USA	22,270
3. India	8165
4. Japan	6429
5. Germany	3714
6. UK	3576
7. Brazil	2960
8. Mexico	2810
9. France	2750
10. Canada	2287
11. Italy	2194
12. Turkey	2149
13. S. Korea	2056
14. Spain	1954
15. Russia	1878

Figure 15.1
The world's top 15 economies in the year 2050, ranked by predicted GDP (amounts in billions of constant 2000 US$) (Ward 2011).

Figure 15.2		Older industrialized economies	BRICs	Next 11 countries
2011 GDP growth rates for different categories of countries (CIA 2012).	**Americas**			
	USA	2.8		
	Brazil		7.5	
	Mexico			3.8
	Europe/Middle East/Africa			
	Germany	2.7		
	UK	1.1		
	Russia		4.3	
	Nigeria			6.9
	Turkey			4.6
	Asia			
	Japan	–0.7		
	China		9.2	
	India		7.8	
	Indonesia			6.4
	Vietnam			5.8

Stages of emergence

Many observers have scrutinized these growth trajectories to determine if they have any shared characteristics. One discovery is that rapid wealth accumulation over the past 20 years (and even more recently for the 'Next 11' countries) started for most with exogenous drivers, meaning increased exports to foreign markets and/or greater manufacturing on behalf of foreign MNEs. To some extent, this is a continuation of the explosion in outsourcing that has typified international business in recent years, with many upstream operations that used to be staged in the Global North being run out of the developing world today (see Chapter 11). It is impossible to overstate the scale of this shift in the geography of international manufacturing.

The ensuing growth in GDP has been accompanied by rising household income and increased government tax revenues. In turn, this has paved the way for a future of endogenous growth, driven by consumption and infrastructure investment, which are internal factors. The power of this two-step development model for so many countries (manufacturing-for-export, followed by newly solvent consumers) makes it worth studying in greater detail.

Stages of emergence

Several factors explain emerging countries' rise as international manufacturing powerhouses, marking the first stage of their recent development process. First, the depletion of natural resources (see Chapter 16) has sparked global investment in the primary sector. The Global South has benefited from this since some of the world's leading reservoirs of untapped fossil fuels and minerals are located here (mainly in Russia, the southern ex-Soviet republics, Mongolia, sub-Saharan Africa, and parts of South America). Secondly, the much

+ Exogenous
Outwardly oriented. In economics, this term is often used in reference to export-driven growth.

+ Endogenous
Inwardly oriented. In economics, often used in reference to consumption and internal investment-driven growth.

Country	Minimum monthly wage in purchasing power parity US$ (most recent year)
Americas	
USA	1257
Brazil (BRIC)	286
Mexico (Next 11)	170
Europe, Middle East, Africa	
France	1443
UK	1507
Russia (BRIC)	223
Nigeria (Next 11)	83
Turkey (Next 11)	609
Asia	
Japan	944
China (BRIC)	173
India (BRIC)	121
Indonesia (Next 11)	148
Vietnam (Next 11)	85

Figure 15.3
Global Wage Report
2010–2011 (ILO 2011).

lower wage levels characterizing emerging economies gives them an enormous cost advantage over the Global North (see Figure 15.3). This is especially important given that their productivity levels have improved so much in recent years.

This latter development is particularly significant in light of many economists' predictions that the older industrialized world would continue to monopolize high value-added activities while outsourcing less advanced operations to emerging economies (see Chapter 11). A rich school of analysis called 'global value chains' has taken form in recent years to discuss the breakdown of value added between countries like China, where an increasing proportion of international manufacturing occurs, and the Global North, which continues to dominate many higher end design and engineering activities. Taking the example of products like the Apple iPad, much research in this area has suggested that labour and capital in the Global South continues to be poorly rewarded, with questions being raised about whether workers in the countries involved are being 'upgraded' as much as producers are (Appelbaum and Gereffi 1994)—and whether the main effect of the current geography of international business is simply to increase the part of the total value added being appropriated by shareholders located in the older industrialized countries, to the detriment of other stakeholders worldwide (Chakrabortty 2012).

Other studies question such assumptions (Inklaar and Timmer 2012). First, the great success of some emerging MNEs, whose trajectory started with responsibility for simple outsourced production tasks, has given them the means to invest in higher value-added activities. One example is Taiwanese Hon Hai Precision Industry, which made so much money assembling Apple products that it was able, by March 2012, to take a large equity stake in Japanese consumer electronics company Sharp's liquid crystal display panel operations. Secondly, huge numbers of young engineers and scientists are being trained in Chinese, Russian, and Indian universities—not to mention the huge international scholarship programme that Brazil's government announced in March 2012, sending students

Advanced R&D at
Novo Nordisk's R&D
Centre China in Beijing,
China

Source: Novo Nordisk

worldwide to sharpen their skills in different fields of science and engineering. The end result will be to make technological capability, always a key driver of international business, much more widespread. At present, the Global North's advanced telecommunications infrastructure distinguishes it from (and gives it an advantage over) the Global South, especially in knowledge-related industries. This gap is being closed, however, as emerging economies play catch up in terms of general broadband access. As discussed in Chapter 11, there are countless cases today of innovative activities in fields such as pharmaceutical research or software development being conducted out of emerging economies. One example is the giant Danish pharmaceutical company Novo Nordisk's plans to give its Chinese subsidiary direct responsibility for applied bacterial research (Pogrebnyakov and Kristensen 2011). The current mission of this unit is to simply implement existing knowledge, but in the future it will be expected to develop its own innovation capabilities, providing the whole of the group with so-called immune technology. This evolution is only possible because so many highly qualified researchers are joining the labour market in China.

Other factors explaining the Global South's increasingly knowledge-intensive capabilities include the development of fibre optics infrastructure directly linking LDCs while avoiding communications hubs located in the developed world, or the rise of new clusters of hi-tech industries working in close proximity to one another and creating new opportunities for knowledge spillover (see Chapter 11). Recent studies have identified the existence in many emerging societies of technical cooperation processes linking national industries, universities, and research and development institutions, all engaged in the pursuit of a knowledge-based economy (Kuchiki and Tsuji 2009). Many emerging countries are consciously trying to improve their terms of trade (see Chapter 1) by getting value chain partners to cooperate and leverage knowledge-sharing into higher value-added precision work. One example is the automobile industry cluster in Malaysia, where domestic brands such as Proton and Perodua have, within a few short years, developed to the extent that today they rival longer established global rivals.

The shift upscale is not just a choice—it is also a necessity. High demand for workers is causing above-inflation wage settlements in industrial centres like China's Guangdong province. Local producers are reacting in two ways: by automating production, as exemplified by electronics giant Foxconn Technology's recent acquisition of 1 million manufacturing robots (Hooi 2011); and by shifting towards less cost-sensitive, higher value-added activities.

Changing political environments

Changes in many emerging countries' political and institutional frameworks have also made it much easier for MNEs to operate in the Global South. In general, the dominant trend of the past 30 years has been towards a greater integration of global markets. This contrasts with the more or less isolationist policies being pursued by most developing and/or transition Eastern European countries prior to this. The change is particularly noteworthy in those countries that had once identified themselves as communist regimes (**see ORC Extension material 15.1**). For many other LDCs, the experience of decolonization meant that the political priority in the 1950s and 1960s was to achieve independence on an economic level as well as a political one. In left-wing regimes such as Tito's Yugoslavia or Nyerere's Tanzania, this materialized in the form of 'self-management' policies where the countries consciously tried to engage in as little cross-border business as possible. Elsewhere, the same orientation translated into widespread 'import substitution' policies where governments' main priority was to invest in sectors where they once relied on foreign imports, specifically in an attempt to reduce dependence (see Chapter 2, Case study 2.1).

By the end of the century, however, this kind of economic isolation was being actively rejected by most regimes worldwide, with a new consensus being built around the idea that trading with MNEs can be a positive growth driver. This shift in outlook is exemplified in the decision made by almost all emerging regimes to join the World Trade Organization and accept its policy prescriptions, first and foremost being to reduce barriers to trade (see Chapter 4). It can also be witnessed in the recurring news that a BRICs or Next 11 country is liberalizing a sector of activity (e.g. in 2011, the electricity markets in Turkey or the telecommunications industry in Indonesia) or that a large global MNE has signed yet another strategic alliance in the Global South.

This is not to say that market liberalization has taken the same form across the emerging world. Brazil, for instance, features relatively few nationalized companies any more and has implemented a laissez-faire financial system authorizing more or less free capital flows. There has been a similar loosening of financial controls in India, but FDI in certain sectors (e.g. retailing) in this country is subject to tight restrictions due to fears that large foreign MNEs such as Walmart (USA) or Metro (Germany) might enter the market and displace local shopkeepers. India's emphasis on protecting small entrepreneurs contrasts with Russia, where much power is concentrated in the hands of a few oligarchs, although the state continues to exercise significant control, particularly in the resource sector. As for China, the regime's communist allegiance means ongoing state interference in so-called strategic sectors such as banking—unlike Next 11 countries such as Pakistan or Nigeria, where competition between rival political constituencies makes it impossible to concentrate this kind of power. Despite such differences, however, there is no doubt that all these emerging countries have one feature in common, namely the radical difference in the market orientation of their policies today and 20 years ago.

Difficult operating conditions

It would be wrong to portray the emergence dynamic of recent years as having completely reversed the balance of power in international business. The fact remains that the vast majority of Fortune 500 top global MNEs continue to originate from (and operate in) the Global North, where circumstances are generally very different from those found in the developing world. Generalizing about operational conditions anywhere is impossible but it should be remembered that many newly industrialized economies were characterized until recently by poverty. Many still are. This has had a number of consequences.

Chapter 8 stated that after the category of heavily indebted poor countries (HIPC), it is the emerging world that performs worst in terms of corruption. For instance, out of the 178 countries featured in the Transparency International rankings, China was 78, India 87, Indonesia 110, and Russia 154. Types of corruption can vary (state bureaucracy, private sector transactions) but the general effect is to complicate negotiations and decision-making. There is no doubt that success in the emerging world requires a specific managerial understanding that may not always be widely available throughout an MNE.

+ **Isolationist**
Refers in international trade to a policy of interacting as little as possible with foreign interests. Stands in contradiction with principle of international division of labour.

+ **Transition**
In evolution. Often used in economics to refer to ex-communist countries shifting towards more market-based economies.

> Go online

+ **Oligarch**
Dominant business figure, often used in Russia to refer to an entrepreneur who gained control of formerly state-owned assets in the immediate aftermath of the communist regime.

Another major problem affecting operations in emerging environments is price instability, historically caused by central bank mismanagement but nowadays reflecting volatile growth instead. This uncertainty plays out at an operational level when MNEs consider purchasing physical assets in countries whose rapid development has made them prone to property bubbles, a concern that was widely expressed in 2010–2011 in relation to several markets across Asia. Moreover, the stop-start nature of volatile 'hot capital' flows (see Chapter 3) means that LDCs that rely on FDI run a risk of sudden outflows at times of crisis (**see ORC Extension material 15.2**). This can weaken the national currency and undermine asset values in the country (see Chapter 13). MNEs may try to offset such risks through local currency funding, as Coca-Cola sought to do in 2011 when it started negotiating with Chinese authorities about whether it might list shares on the Shanghai stock exchange. It remains that many currencies in the Global South are not convertible and cannot be purchased without administrative permission, diminishing the liquidity of MNE holdings in this part of the world.

Price instability also has social effects. Where the benefits of globalization are poorly distributed, the higher standard of living enjoyed by citizens engaging in international business can cause inflation as their purchasing power rises. This makes things harder for poorer fellow citizens excluded from the growth dynamic, especially given the strong rises in 2007 and again in 2010 for many foods that serve as staples in the developing world (rice, wheat, maize). There can be widespread anger where MNEs allegedly undermine the national interest, one example being when Argentinian tax inspectors raided the premises of grain traders Dreyfus, Cargill, and Bunge (Lawrence 2011), accusing them of evading taxes on profits from their local operations. Indeed, throughout the developing world (and particularly in South America in recent years), MNEs face many regulatory risks that are less frequent in the Global North, including unequal treatment by courts or governments; unilateral denunciations of investment treaties; expropriation (Alvarez 2010); and at certain points in time (like in Nigeria in early 2012), concern for managers' physical safety. Otherwise, patents suffer in some LDCs from insufficient intellectual property protections, meaning that MNEs cannot be sure of their ability to protect trade secrets from local partners with whom they might collaborate through a joint venture. In sum, the regulatory environment in many emerging societies does not always facilitate corporate operations (see Figure 15.4).

Relations with MNEs

Many emerging countries have started to address these legal and regulatory vacuums. One example is the new patent protections enacted in both India and China to convince pharmaceutical sector MNEs to collaborate with local partners in the hope that this will upgrade national manufacturing capabilities (Rakhi 2011). It is significant that such steps remain necessary even now, long after both countries have integrated the global economy. To some extent, they confirm Dunning's 'OLI' theory that the need for confidentiality lies at the heart of many companies' internationalization strategies (see Chapter 2).

Clearly, many LDCs are still debating to what extent globalization serves their national interests. MNEs can provide some reassurance in this respect by demonstrating a willingness to negotiate deals stressing loyal long-term collaboration with local partners (i.e. through the transfer of technologies or training and promotion of local executives). Similarly, the common LDC requirement that MNEs agree joint ventures with local firms does not have to be viewed as an obstacle but instead as an opportunity to create mutual trust and even solidarity. Finding a local sponsor might also help to protect the MNE against legal discrimination. More subjectively, it may address the resentment still felt in many formerly colonized countries towards Global North interests.

This is not to say that MNEs are greeted with hostility throughout the emerging world. Quite the contrary; there is growing recognition that MNEs can also produce 'significant

> Go online

+ Upgrade
Where a company (or country) improves its terms of trade by intensifying the value-added content of its output.

Country	Ranking out of 183 countries
Americas	
USA	4
Brazil (BRIC)	126
Mexico (Next 11)	53
Europe, Middle East, Africa	
Germany	19
UK	7
Russia (BRIC)	120
Nigeria (Next 11)	133
Turkey (Next 11)	71
Asia	
Japan	20
China (BRIC)	91
India (BRIC)	132
Indonesia (Next 11)	129
Vietnam (Next 11)	98

Figure 15.4
'Ease of doing business'
rankings (World Bank
2011).

positive welfare impacts through employment creation and labour market participation' (Maertens et al. 2011) and often pay higher wages than local firms. Similarly, the level of scrutiny that increasingly holds MNEs to account for their behaviour worldwide (see Chapter 8) means that an increasing number bring their best governance practices to societies unaccustomed to such approaches. A case in point is corporate pollution. Younger and relatively less wealthy companies originating in the Global South often cannot afford to comply with environmental management legislation. Indeed, in the absence of pressure from global NGOs, they may not even feel any need to do so (Boudier and Bensebaa 2011). This contrasts, for instance, with energy giant Shell's recent conduct in Nigeria's Ogoni region, where the MNE now applies modern de-pollution techniques to mitigate the negative environmental side-effects of its local operations, having been loudly criticized in the past by Greenpeace and other NGOs for less constructive practices (Sitkin and Bowen 2010). When relations improve to this extent, it becomes reasonable to argue that MNEs' positive engagement with local civil society and government in an emerging country can have a beneficial effect on its overall development dynamics (Rugman and Doh 2008).

Thus, the difficulties affecting operations in the Global South need not be viewed in negative terms only. Indeed, some analysts (Khanna and Palepu 2010) see them as an opportunity for practitioners capable of addressing the 'institutional voids' that characterize many emerging markets. Where it used to be possible to conduct international business careers in the older industrialized world alone, this is no longer the case in many sectors. Instead, students and young managers should see their ability to work in countries characterized by very different levels of socio-economic emergence as a distinct career advantage. From that perspective, operational difficulties should be embraced as a challenge to overcome.

Case study 15.2

Brazil emerges with a beat

Once synonymous with economic instability, for many years Brazil suffered from triple-digit inflation and crippling debts that it was not always in a position to repay. Things got so bad that the old national currency had to be scrapped in 1994. Bringing in a new currency was beneficial, however, mainly because accompanying measures calmed the inflationary expectations that had caused so many of Brazil's earlier problems. One such measure was the Cardoso administration's budget-balancing policy. Although economically necessary, this meant fewer social programmes attacking poverty, which is one root cause of Brazil's high crime rate. The 2002 election of ex-union leader Lula helped here. The new president steered an even course between encouraging entrepreneurship and sensitivity to poverty. The rich got richer in Brazil but the poor became much less poor, due to private sector jobs but also because of generous monthly Bolsa Familia benefits paid to disadvantaged families. The resulting social harmony means that Brazil can focus on economic emergence today. It does this to great effect.

Despite lagging behind its fellow BRICs in GDP growth, Brazil performed excellently through the mid-2000s,

Brazil's emergence has made it one of the world's new economic powerhouses

Source: Photodisc

creating an average of 1.4 million jobs annually, keeping annual inflation to 4.7 per cent and accumulating $100 billion in foreign exchange reserves. Unsurprisingly, international investors flocked to its equity markets. Like everywhere else, Brazil was hit by the 2008 credit crunch. By 2010, however, its annual growth rate returned to 7.5 per cent, before falling sharply in 2011–2012 (albeit continuing to grow at a somewhat faster rate than most of the older industrialized countries).

Brazil's economic diversity bolsters business confidence. The energy sector features a well-developed ethanol industry and energy giant Petrobras, which after discovering major offshore oil fields generated a record $70 billion in receipts when it was partially privatized in late 2010. Otherwise, in an era of rising commodity prices, Brazil's traditional agribusiness and mining surpluses have gone from strength to strength, to the extent that China, which has become the leading foreign investor in Brazil (as in other South American countries) has recently built the world's largest industrial super-port at Acu near Rio de Janeiro, a so-called 'Highway to China' that will be used to ship millions of tonnes of raw materials abroad. Construction and banking have also benefited from the growth dynamic, as has Brazil's aerospace sector. It would be wrong to forget Brazil's ongoing problems: poor living conditions for favela ghetto inhabitants; or the environmentally and socially damaging destruction of the Amazon. Nevertheless, for the first time in decades, Brazilians have reasons besides football and samba to dance.

Case study questions

1. What is the link between Brazil's social and economic progress?
2. How much confidence should MNEs have in Brazil's ongoing emergence?

Section II: Emerging consumer markets

The greater solvency of emerging country households worldwide is one of the most promising trends in international business today. It has also changed people's consumption behaviour. As income rises, people tend to spend in certain areas (consumer durables, transportation, and leisure) that were once beyond their means. This is a great opportunity for the companies operating in the sectors concerned.

Similarly, a distinction can be made between markets in a 'first equipment' phase vs. markets that are in their 'product renewal' stages. The former involves products being bought for the first time and logically implies much higher volumes than the latter, where consumers simply purchase items to replace those that have become obsolete. Recent examples of products sold in the emerging world on a first equipment basis include cars and refrigerators. Where such products have been tried and tested elsewhere and do not require any major adaptation, they can be particularly attractive to MNEs since the business model (manufacturing location, product adaptation, and funding) is straightforward. This is one reason why the world's leading companies are so interested in accelerating sales into the emerging world. Conversely, where new consumers' requirements differ greatly from the more established markets, there is a significant opportunity for new MNEs originating in the Global South, especially since they can transform any initial successes into a platform for future expansion in their older Global North rivals' home markets. The rest of this chapter will analyse these two stages.

Greater solvency for billions of households

Early studies on the emerging world's new middle class consumers, defined as households with a per capita annual income of $3,000 or more (expressed in constant 2003 dollars), have largely focused on the four BRICs. Many MNEs, especially ones whose existing markets are saturated, monitor studies in this area in the hope of being able to identify new consumer demand for their goods and services. It is worth recalling Goldman Sachs economist Jim O'Neill's expectation that the BRICs will, for the foreseeable future, remain poorer than their Western counterparts on a per capita basis, if not in terms of national GDP. Nevertheless, if O'Neill is right that these countries are likely to experience a fourfold increase to 1 billion middle-class consumers by the year 2015 (before doubling to 2 billion by 2025), the outlook for growth remains excellent in the BRICs. It becomes phenomenal once O'Neill's Next 11 group is added to the equation (see Figure 15.5). As noted in a 2011 HSBC Bank study (Ward 2011), whereas per capita income is expected to grow over the next generation by a factor of between 1.5 and 2.1 in most of the world's older industrialized countries, the corresponding number is much higher in the emerging economies.

There is, of course, some uncertainty about the speed of this trend. A certain tension exists, for instance, between MNEs that want to see developing country wages rise because this ensures the solvency of future customers, and others who worry that higher wage costs mean LDCs become less competitive as production locations (Lewis 2008). The general direction of travel is clear, however, and rather than questioning future increases in wealth in the Global South, a more interesting question is whether Global North incomes must fall in exchange (**see ORC Extension material 15.3**).

> Go online

Sectors where emerging markets already set the tone

Emerging market demand is already a determinant in a number of international sectors. The first is energy, due in large part to the Global South's rise as a low-cost manufacturing centre. Similarly, the rapid urbanization of many emerging societies is associated with increased energy use, not only because cities require more energy (for buildings, transportation systems, even lifestyles) but because the new urban districts being built have a significant environmental footprint (see Chapter 16). Another factor is the high population growth characterizing much of the developing world (one notable exception being Russia). A classic example is the rapid urbanization of China, where 350 million more people are due to move to cities by the year 2025 (Branigan 2011). To visualize the effect of this huge internal migration, the number of new skyscrapers being built over the next decade or so in

	Income per capita, 2050	Income per capita, 2010	2050–2010 per capita growth factor
China	17,372	2396	7.25
Russia	16,174	2394	6.76
India	5060	790	6.41
Malaysia	29,247	5224	5.60
Indonesia	5215	1178	4.43
Turkey	22,063	5088	4.34
Iran	7547	2138	3.53
Mexico	21,793	6217	3.51
Brazil	13,457	4711	2.86
S. Korea	46,657	16,463	2.83
Germany	52,683	25,083	2.10
UK	49,412	27,646	1.79
France	40,643	23,881	1.70
Japan	63,244	39,435	1.60
USA	55,134	36,354	1.52

Figure 15.5
Predicted rise in per capita income between 2010 and 2050 in BRICs and selected Next 11 and older industrialized countries (in constant US$) (Ward 2011).

this country is the equivalent of another ten New Yorks being added to the planet. Aside from the potential negative environmental consequences, this unprecedented shift will put enormous pressure on global commodity prices as construction firms seek the natural resources they need for their projects. More generally, emergence is wreaking havoc on many developing countries' ecosystems. For example, in Mexico, recent industrialization trends have caused a widespread contamination of water tables as well as the pollution and erosion of the country's best agricultural land and forests. This creates an urgent need for de-pollution investment—another international business sector that is likely to centre in the developing world within a few decades.

The rapid urbanization of China is unprecedented in human history and is creating a huge demand for scarce natural resources

Source: iStock

Information and communications technology is another sector increasingly dominated by the developing world. Paradoxically, here it is the emerging economies' lack of infrastructure that gives them an advantage since they are free to purchase more up-to-date technology instead of being required to lay modern systems on top of older ones. An example of this is the way that Asia has started to dominate the global market for smartphones, with China featuring 785 million mobile subscribers in 2010 and India another 635 million, even before the two countries fully implement 3G or even 4G technologies (OECD Communications Outlook 2011). The end result has been a mini-boom, not only for established MNEs but also, and increasingly, for emerging market firms capable of addressing the demand for new hi-tech consumer goods (see Section III).

Alongside this, emerging market demand has also become central to a number of medium-tech sectors. At the upper end of this range, nouveau riche customers from Cairo to Karachi to Shanghai have reinvigorated several luxury segments. Much more significantly, the Global South is already providing a much needed boost for car-makers and components suppliers worldwide. Goldman Sachs economist Jim O'Neill had originally predicted, for instance, that with 200 million car-owners projected by the year 2025, the Chinese automobile market

Practitioner insight

Parvez Shahid worked for the Abu Dhabi Group in various capacities, ranging from acquisitions principal to advisor on different investments, primarily in Pakistan. His main area of responsibility in this country was Bank Alfalah, which rose from being one of Pakistan's smallest banks when it was privatized in 1997 to the sixth largest bank, with over 400 domestic branches and operations in Bangladesh, Bahrain, and Afghanistan.

'The potential return on capital investments in emerging markets is far better than in developed markets like Europe or the USA. This is because developed country leaders are unwilling to take certain hard decisions. The end result is that their economies are bleeding with sovereign and private debt, whereas in emerging countries like China, India, and Pakistan, private and public sector leveraging is fully backed by the amount of gold and other tangible assets that ordinary citizens own.

About 200 hundred years ago, China, the Indian subcontinent, and South Asia accounted for 50 per cent of world GDP. This could happen again within 40 to 50 years unless developed countries take the unpopular decisions of running their social support systems on a more reasonable and practical basis.

A similar problem is debt-driven consumerism, which undermines the very foundations of countries that try to resolve fundamental problems by adopting this short-term strategy.

Another issue receiving insufficient attention is negative or zero population growth in the developed world. Countries like India and Pakistan are teaming with a large base of young persons who will provide huge potential for future growth.

Little is known about emerging economies' real size or the amount of assets that residents hold outside these countries. There is evidence that Pakistanis living in Pakistan hold about $300 billion in undeclared foreign assets. For Indians living in India, the equivalent number is about $1 trillion. Once confidence returns, these funds will be repatriated, providing impetus for even further growth.

Then there are those who left these countries in recent decades to seek better opportunities available in the USA or Western Europe. They hold good degrees from prominent foreign institutions and can be expected, when the time is right, to return home, bringing their knowledge and experiences of the first world.'

was in the process of becoming the largest in the world (O'Neill 2011). This explains why many MNEs have invested so heavily in this country, as exemplified by the corporate campus that General Motors built near Shanghai to house R&D activities developing environmentally friendly technologies that target the local market. The southern Indian city of Chennai has also started to host new car plants built by leading global automakers including Nissan, Toyota, BMW, and Ford, all enthusiastic to enter what is expected to become yet another growth market. With the emerging economies' vast expanses, large populations, and comparatively low levels of car ownership, it is no surprise that they are becoming a top focus for much of the global automotive sector. The question then becomes to what extent this will require MNEs to change their productive and commercial organizations.

Consumers with different requirements

Products that dominate in older industrialized markets are not necessarily the ones that are most likely to appeal in the developing world. The $3,000 threshold commonly used to define entry into the middle class remains very low, and although this level of income represents much greater purchasing power in some countries than in others, there is no doubt that the Global North still features a far greater number of comfortably affluent households than the developing world does. The relative lack of physical and social infrastructure in many poorer societies adds to this picture, as does the fact that many future members of the Global South's middle classes have yet to develop the purchasing power that they need to join the consumer society. Thus, even as MNEs can rejoice at the prospect of so many potential new customers, they must pursue a different strategy when approaching this segment.

There is a growing literature on how companies might market profitably to these 'bottom-of-the-pyramid' customers (Prahalad 2009). Factors such as 'local monopolies, inadequate access, poor distribution and strong traditional intermediaries' prevent huge numbers of poor consumers (up to 40 per cent of the urban population in many developing countries) from accessing consumer markets. Conversely, this means that MNEs stand to benefit greatly if they can overcome these obstacles by establishing their own 'large presence' distribution channels—after all, the urban poor in most LDCs tend to frequent small local retailers. Such approaches can create strong brand loyalty, because bottom-of-the-pyramid consumers are often enthused when offered aspirational products associated with personal betterment, and because their densely populated living environment means that they already network intensively, often via modern wireless communications devices for which they already constitute an enormous market.

Frugality as a way of doing business

+ **Frugal**
Characterized by an economical or thrifty use of inputs.

One adaptation that MNEs must make to cultivate this new market successfully involves the development of frugal innovations, 'good-enough' affordable products that enhance currently insolvent customers' ability to consume (Zeschky et al. 2011). Like the micro-finance loans discussed in Case study 15.1, a whole range of sectors have seen products downsized and simplified to appeal to emerging bottom-of-the-pyramid segments. An example from the early 2000s was when European conglomerate Unilever entered Africa and decided that the only way to satisfy the demand of the continent's poor households was to sell smaller detergent packages at much lower prices. Unilever realized that this meant tiny per unit profit margins and was probably justifiable only if it helped the company gain durable brand loyalty. It is the same calculation as Proctor & Gamble has made with the single-serve shampoo sachets that it sells in India, or Danone with the tiny vitamin-enhanced yogurt pots that it retails at 11 cents per unit in Bangladesh. In a different product sector, Dutch MNE Philips has also started selling low-cost, solar power lighting products to Africans lacking connections to an electric grid. All these actions break even at best, but they do teach the companies in question a great deal about accessing bottom-of-the-pyramid markets.

Famously low China prices set competitive standards that many Western companies struggle to match

Source: iStock

The problem for many Global North MNEs, however, is that the particular production and marketing techniques associated with these frugal approaches differ greatly from their traditional business models based on more hi-tech innovations targeting top-of-the-pyramid customers in the world's wealthier countries. Conversely, many companies originating in the Global South have developed a great deal of experience in being frugal. Examples include the Tablet PCs that Indian company Aakash is selling in its home market at $35; the functional but inexpensive Nano car models that Tata is selling for $2,500; the battery-powered refrigerator that Godrej & Boyce is selling for a mere $70; and more generally, the countless companies in Eastern Asia whose products sell at the famously competitive so-called China price (see Figure 15.6).

LDC retail prices are being driven up as the countries involved finally emerge. They are affected by external factors like strong demand for exports and higher raw material prices, but also because domestic workers expect to share in the fruits of their companies' success and be paid higher wages. In addition, as emerging consumers become accustomed to quality goods (and as local companies accumulate their own intellectual property to protect), the tolerance for cheap counterfeits diminishes. For instance, whereas 31 per cent of Chinese respondents to a study in 2008 said that they were willing to buy fake jewellery, by 2011 that figure had fallen to 12 per cent (Economist 2012a). Yet despite these trends, the differential between prices practised in the Global North and South remains enormous, giving the latter a huge competitive advantage.

+ China price
Reference to the comparatively very low retail price of goods and services originating in China.

Driver	Relative contribution to overall effect (in percent)
Low wages for high quality work	39.41
Export subsidies	16.71
Industrial network clustering	16.02
A chronically undervalued currency	11.44
Piracy and counterfeiting	8.63
The catalytic role of FDI	3.09
Minimal worker health and safety regulations	2.44
Lax environmental regulations and enforcement	2.26

Figure 15.6
Factors contributing to the 'China price' (Navarro 2006).

There has been much discussion in many large MNEs about how they might integrate emerging markets' new frugal focus into their portfolio of activities. One idea is to ask subsidiaries located in these zones to specialize in this kind of approach. More ambitious is the decision taken by some Global North companies to introduce frugal approaches in their home markets. Examples include GE developing in China a $1000 portable scanner that can rival the only slightly more complicated $10,000 version the company was already selling in the world's wealthier markets. At first glance, this was a bad idea, since GE would be competing with its own product line. On the other hand, the company reasoned that given the financial difficulties facing many once rich economies, it was a good idea to learn to adopt to a new age of austerity. Besides, whether or not GE sold new frugal products in the West, it was highly likely that its new LDC rivals would (Economist 2012c).

Section III: New competitors in international business

Many emerging societies are characterized by an attraction to foreign products associated with a lifestyle and standard of living that few consumers could access until recently. Long queues celebrating the opening of new McDonald's restaurants from Russia to Indonesia, at a time when the company suffers from a saturation effect in some of its more established markets, confirm this fascination. Yet Global South consumers can be just as ethnocentric as their counterparts from the older industrialized world, as witnessed by the demonstrable preference in many emerging markets for products bearing a local label (Ehmke et al. 2008) while offering value for money (St-Maurice et al. 2008). Many emerging MNEs seem aware of this effect, with studies revealing that they tend to distinguish between LDC markets, where they publicize their own brand names (Fetscherin and Marc 2008), and Global North markets, where they tend to pay to acquire established brand names (Hope et al. 2011). As discussed throughout this book, international business is permeated by economic patriotism issues, especially during times of crisis. There is no evidence that such attitudes are any less prevalent in the developing world than elsewhere. This will be another advantage for emerging market companies as national income levels rise.

Emerging markets as launchpads for future MNE leaders

With observers commonly predicting that the combined GDP of the Global South countries will far exceed their Global North counterparts within a few short decades, companies originating in the Global South are likely to enjoy a significant advantage. Not only are they physically closer to (and better known in) the world's most dynamic growth markets, but they are also more accustomed to the kinds of 'non-market' problems that companies face when operating in the developing world (Cuervo-Cazurra and Erdem 2011). Above all, as aforementioned, increasing numbers of emerging market MNEs have expanded their technological and design capabilities, used this advancement to break out of the low-end segments where they operated previously, and now compete with their more established rivals in higher value-added markets (Loren and Thun 2011). Indeed, there are more and more examples of successful products starting in the developing world before being sold globally. Chinese appliances manufacturer Haier, a white goods company with little brand recognition in the West despite being a global leader in its sector, has innovated the world's first completely wireless TV. Brazil's avionics giant Embraer has moved to the top of the global market for regional jets, in part because of its invention of a 'double bubble' fuselage offering passengers much greater headroom. South African energy company Sasol is global leader in coal-to-liquid technology. Mexico's Modelo Group has become one of the world's

	Primary sector (energy, mining, agriculture)	Secondary sector (consumer durables, capital equipment)
Africa	– Sasol, South Africa (energy) – Sonatrach, Algeria (gas)	– Orascam, Egypt (telecoms, construction)
Asia (misc.)	– Bumi, Indonesia (coal) – PTT Thailand (oil/gas)	– Hon Hai; HTC, Taiwan (electronics) – Indorama, Thailand (plastics)
Brazil	– CVRD Vale (mining/metals) – Petrobras (energy/oil)	– Gerdau (steel) – Embraer (aviation) – Votorantim (metallurgy)
China	– China National Petroleum (oil) – Sinochem (chemicals) – Baosteel Group (metals)	– Chery; Donfeng; Sinotruk (automotive) – Haier (appliances, telecoms) – Huawei (telecoms) – TCL (electrical equipment)
E. Europe (misc.)	– MOL, Hungary (oil/gas) – PKN Orlen, Poland (refinery)	– Tungsram, Hungary (lighting)
India	– Reliance (oil/gas)	– ArcelorMittal (steel) – Bharti (telecoms) – Tata (automotive, mechanical) – Videocon (electronics)
Mexico	– PEMEX (oil/gas) – CEMEX (concrete)	– Modelo (beverages) – America Movil; Carso (telecoms) – Alfa (intermediary goods)
Russia	– Lukoil; Gazprom (oil/gas) – Severstal; Rusal (metals/mining)	– Avtovaz (automotive) – RSCC (satellites)
S. America (misc.)	– Arcor, Argentina (food products) – PDVSA Venezuela (oil/gas)	– Technint Argentina (energy industry equipment)
Turkey	– BOTAS (energy)	– Kalik; Dogus; Koc; Sabanci (conglomerates)

Figure 15.7

Emerging primary and secondary sector MNEs from selected BRICs and Next 11 countries, characterized by strong growth in foreign assets, strong foreign sales (Sauvant et al. 2011), and/or strengthening brand image.

leading beer exporters, launching brands considered trendsetters everywhere. Chinese telecoms giant Huawei is a global leader in patent registrations across a whole range of hi-tech sectors (starting with ICT software and hardware) and took the decision in 2012, after years of producing components anonymously on behalf of famous Western companies, to start selling consumer goods in its own brand name. In short, where emerging market firms once tried to catch up with Global North MNEs by developing customized products and/or acquiring existing technologies, the 'new strategy to succeed is innovation-based differenti-ation, developing core technologies and advanced product offerings that are delivered at a low cost and with excellent customer service' (Gao 2011). Moreover, many emerging manufacturers' strategic position is improved by the fact that they operate in close physical proximity to primary sector (agriculture, mining) producers who can provide the new factories with the raw materials they need (see Figure 15.7).

At the same time, the Global South is also showing leadership in a number of service activities (see Figure 15.8). Bumrungrad International Hospital in Bangkok (Thailand) has successfully implemented the world's first paperless patient record system, a procedural innovation destined to be imitated in medical institutions worldwide. A Bolivian financial services company called Prodem FFP has devised multilingual smart ATMs that recognize fingerprints and use voice recognition software. Combining technologies this way will facilitate cash point access for populations that were previously excluded from this service, while also setting convenience standards that may take over in the world's more established markets. Emergence means that many of the companies leading global product and service innovation are less known today than they will be tomorrow.

Figure 15.8
Emerging service
sector MNEs from
selected BRICs and
Next 11 countries
(Sauvant et al. 2011).

	Tertiary sector (banks, IT, pharmaceuticals)
Asia (misc.)	– ACER, Taiwan (IT)
Brazil	– Banco do Brasil, Banco Itau (finance) – TV Globo (media)
China	– Bank of China (finance) – CITIC (financial services) – Lenovo (computers)
E. Europe (misc.)	– Mercator, Slovenia (retail)
India	– Ranbaxy; Dr. Reddy's (pharmaceuticals) – HCL; Infosys; WIPRO (IT) – State Bank of India, ICICI (finance)
Mexico	– Televisa (media)
Russia	– Sberbank, Vneshtorgbank (finance)
South Africa	– Standard Bank Group (finance)

Different managerial philosophies

It is not only at the output level that the new MNEs are using their home markets as launch-pads. The managerial philosophies characterizing many of these companies also differ from paradigms originating in the Global North. Although generalizations are impossible, international business theory must be updated to encompass the new realities of the Global South. It is not at all certain that tomorrow's leading companies, an increasing number of whom will have originated in an LDC, will pursue the same international trajectory that their predecessors did.

A good example is the growing body of literature on the 'Indian way of doing business'. Some authors writing in this area emphasize how the difficulties of operating in a country like India, which still suffers from a number of 'institutional deficiencies', prepares executives to drive their companies' future expansion by teaching them to 'manoeuvre and mould key agents in the external environment' (Nayak 2011). Another school of thought looks at the possibility that companies originating in India focus less on shareholder value and profitability than their Western counterparts, because they are more in tune with national interests and broader societal issues (Cappelli et al. 2010). This can be witnessed at the level of companies' philanthropic activities (see Chapter 8) but also in terms of the way that Indian managers engage with employees, who are encouraged to be intuitive and imaginative, show respect for seniority, and share a general sense of national purpose. By taking this longer view, Indian executives hope to free frontline operatives to consider 'creative advantage where no one is looking' with a view towards developing innovations that will help their companies move up the value chain.

Some Indian MNEs try to 'springboard' into markets by acquiring going concerns to compensate for their latecomer status (Luo and Tung 2007). One successful example in the UK is Tata's 2008 takeover of Jaguar, using the Indian formula of good labour relations and management creativity to sharply increase the group's return on equity (Economist 2012b). However, several similar efforts have struggled in terms of producing satisfactory returns or operating profits, including Tata's 2007 takeover of British-Dutch steelmaker Corus, Bharti Airtel's 2010 purchase of Zain Africa's mobile telecoms network, or Hindalco's acquisition of North American aluminium firm Novelis. Although the Indian MNEs involved benefited in terms of acquiring new skills, in sheer financial terms the results were disappointing, in part because they hesitate to seek equity capital (see Chapter 13), meaning that these operations were funded by debt, increasing financial charges. The lesson here is that habits adopted in certain national business cultures may be problematic in other international business situations.

On other occasions, however, Indian MNEs' internationalization efforts have been very successful in pursuing the frugal engineering and bottom-of-the-pyramid focus that they first developed back home. Many Global North rivals neglect this segment, one with which Indian companies have a great deal of experience. The end effect is that in certain sectors, Indian MNEs seem to be establishing a new business model that could give them a serious global advantage, much in the same way as other developing country MNEs trained in 'China price' constraints have increased market share everywhere.

The rise of South–South and South–North flows

The internationalization of Global South MNEs has become a major new research topic. The sheer scale of this phenomenon—with outbound FDI from emerging markets (as detailed in Chapter 1) expanding faster in recent years than FDI from developed countries (Sauvant et al. 2011)—has attracted much interest. In terms of destinations, many Global South companies' first outward investments are in the developing world, although this should change as they gain confidence in their internationalization capabilities. Of course FDI motives vary widely. Some emerging MNEs internationalize to acquire the raw materials they need to sustain their expanded manufacturing operations back home. This generally involves South–South flows. Others are seeking technology or expanding to diversify their asset portfolio. This increasingly involves South–North flows. It is this phenomenon that is so new in international business.

Categories of FDI coming out of the Global South

Resource-seeking

The hunt for energy and other resources has dominated FDI headlines in recent years. In 2011, for instance, Chinese company Citic Pacific signed a 25-year contract to mine at least two billion tons of iron ore in north-west Australia, with cargo being shipped to China on purpose-built container ships. This was a significant operation since it varied from previous trade arrangements where Chinese interests would buy commodities from BHP Billiton and other Australian mining interests. China's focus now is on vertical integration to maximize control over its supply of strategic inputs. Similarly, Chinese oil companies such as CNOOC (along with the Brazilian Petrobras) have been making a concerted move to tap the oil and gas fields of Eastern Africa. This has raised concerns over whether South-South flows are any better at promoting an equitable distribution of benefits (technology transfers) than North-South flows have been.

There is much debate today about the extent to which developing host countries benefit from FDI in so-called 'extractive sectors' like mining or oil. Evidence exists that many countries that enjoy large endowments of natural resources but lack control over FDI in these sectors do not perform as well as their poorer neighbours, with the royalties and taxes they receive from MNEs leading to lower growth rates, greater corruption, and even 'devastating civil wars' (Humphreys et al. 2007). In the absence of good planning mechanisms and strong institutions, some LDCs have failed to use the proceeds of their natural resource sales to move into higher value-added activities. This resource curse affects their development dynamic in comparison with fellow LDCs that have developed more equal relations with MNEs, as well as a greater level of public accountability.

+ Resource curse
Temptation for a country possessing significant natural resources to market its commodities without seeking to develop a value-adding industry.

Technology-seeking

Recent examples of South-North technology-seeking FDI include the product development centres being built worldwide by Nemak, an automotive components subsidiary of Mexican conglomerate Grupo Alfa (BCG 2011); or the hi-tech assets being acquired by budding Indian giants Reliance (developing its telecommunications infrastructure capabilities in the USA) and Tata (which bought digital media company Mosaic from BT). In terms of South–North asset-seeking FDI, examples might include the purchase by Mexico's CEMEX of British firm RMC, a global leader in ready-mix concrete; or Thai plastics giant Indorama's September 2011 purchase of Wellman International's European recycled PET business. Of course, there are also many examples of South–South asset-seeking FDI, reflecting emerging market managers' comparatively greater adeptness at operating in fellow LDCs.

The human factor has also attracted analysts' attention, partially because some emerging MNEs follow other models than those predicted by most internationalization theories (see Chapter 9). Emerging market MNEs seem to go abroad when they are smaller than their Global North predecessors had been at a similar stage, take greater risks, and implement less formalized policies (Alvarez 2010). Within this generalized view, however, it is also clear that 'each emerging country has its own particular reasons and agenda for investing outside its national boundaries' (Ramamurti and Singh 2010). This can best be expressed using a regional classification.

Regional categorization of emerging MNEs

+ **Paternalistic**
Sense of managing a company with a view towards ensuring the well-being of employees and other stakeholders rather than for pure profit maximization motives.

Studies of the internationalization behaviour of Latin American MNEs have highlighted the paternalistic attitudes of companies that often began either as state-owned concerns or that have a long experience of close dealings with their home country governments and are therefore well equipped for the public–private interface that is an integral part of international business (Cassanova 2009). The region had suffered recurring crises until recently and many senior managers have become skilled at remaining focused on long-term objectives even as they deal with immediate concerns. Foreign assets are often viewed as hedges against the problems that these 'puma' MNEs first faced at home, with some of the leading Latin American names (the Mexican Cemex or the Brazilian Vale) having famously embarked in the late 2000s on billions of dollars of acquisitions all across the Global North. A similar diversity can be witnessed in the kinds of overseas strategies being pursued by other puma MNEs, with some (like Mexican telecoms company America Movil) rolling out new business models in different markets and others (such as Brazil's Natura Cosmeticos) doing the opposite and simply taking their local brands global. In general, Latin American MNEs are very sensitive to cost competition from China and often try to protect themselves by starting their internationalization drives in other Spanish- or Portuguese-speaking countries, where managers may feel more at ease. An example here is rising Chilean wine company Vina Concha y Toro, whose slow growth overseas reflects the owners' more conservative internationalization strategies.

This slower approach contrasts with the recent FDI behaviour of Russian MNEs (Kalotay 2010), the only companies from transition Eastern Europe to invest abroad to any notable extent. Over the 2000s, the leading names in Russia's resource-focused economy, led by Gazprom, Lukoil, Norilsk Nickel, and Severstal, have undertaken a series of acquisitions across the Global North. The deals were either horizontal in nature, involving other energy and mining interests, or vertical, with the Russians purchasing downstream distribution channels for the commodities they produce. What is particularly noteworthy here is the sheer magnitude of these investments at such an early stage in these companies' existence, as well as the complicated relations that these MNEs, like their Latin American counterparts, have historically entertained with home country politicians.

The same observations also apply to the final category of emerging MNEs, the so-called 'yang' multinationals from Asia. The internationalization pattern here generally started with the export of commoditized components or generic products under outsourcing arrangements, followed by upgraded high-tech joint ventures with foreign partners, and culminating in outwards FDI (Larçon 2009). Certainly this was the pattern followed by two of China's leading MNEs, TCL and Haier, which only varied insofar as the former pursued an

Uppsala model (see Chapter 9) and started with FDI in Vietnam and the Philippines (China's neighbours), whereas the latter went straight to the USA and Europe. As noted in Chapter 3, there is also Asian states' historical tendency to intervene, either because they actively coordinate national companies' foreign and domestic activities ('developmental economics') or else, as is the case in China, because many leading companies are still state-owned (**see ORC Extension Material 15.4**). This overriding sense of strategic national interest has necessarily affected the behaviour of emerging MNEs originating from this zone. One example is the way that the Chinese government's March 1986 '863 program' led to enormous subsidies being paid over the years to help local telecoms companies such as Huawei and ZTE catch up with their Western rivals' capabilities.

> Go online

Emerging MNEs' sense of mission

Lastly, emerging MNEs' greater sense of national political interest (and often closer relationship with government officials) might have a secondary effect on their international business activities. As discussed in Chapter 4, for reasons of democratic legitimacy but also to reflect their growing financial power, it is likely that developing countries' voice will receive greater airing at bodies such as the WTO or the IMF where decisions are made about global trading and investment systems. Similarly, the general expectation is that BRICs and Next 11 country currencies will strengthen over time, with companies from these zones accounting for an increasing share of global stock market capitalization. Indeed, China has already become the global creditor upon whom all debtor nations, led by the USA, rely for funding. It is impossible to imagine that all this economic power can do anything but translate into major political power.

This is important because there are differences in attitudes towards state power in the developed and developing world. Whereas many countries in the developed world have witnessed a 'retreat of the state' (see Chapter 3) over the past 30 years, political elites in almost all of the Global South retain as much if not more power than business leaders. This may be expected in a communist state such as China, where the leading consumer group, Bright Food, is managed by a municipal administration (Shanghai), something that would be unheard of in the Global North. Yet government officials retain just as much power over corporate decision-making in emerging countries such as Russia or Malaysia that operate under an entirely different kind of regime. The clear contrast between European and US banks' extensive involvement in the 2008 subprime crisis and the more prudent approach adopted in more interventionist developing nations such as India hints at the kinds of changes that might be expected once the Global South becomes a fully fledged participant in the different initiatives that shape the international business framework. International managers specializing in emerging markets will need to learn how to incorporate non-market-related considerations into their strategic vision.

Challenges and choices

→ The emergence of the BRICs and Next 11 countries may be an opportunity for MNEs originating in the Global North but it also challenges their longstanding domination. For political and cultural reasons, they often feel uncomfortable about entering emerging markets without a local partner. Yet where an MNE chooses to develop an alliance, there is always the risk that it is arming a future rival. It is hard to determine when the benefits of penetrating an emerging market justify the extra costs and risks.

Chapter summary

The chapter started by identifying a group of emerging economies (the BRICs and Next 11 countries) whose positive outlook means that they are destined to become a key focus of international business. The countries' development dynamics often started with political reform encouraging inwards investment by MNEs, albeit in an operating environment quite different from the Global North. LDCs' improved manufacturing capabilities caused national household income levels to rise, leading in turn to the arrival of a newly solvent middle class characterized by its own particular consumption patterns. The final section discussed how this population has become a target for MNEs but also a launchpad for local companies, which can leverage their experience to develop a new international profile. Given the growing capabilities of companies originating from the Global South, in time they can be expected to compete with their older established rivals. In turn, this is likely to impact upon international governance decisions.

Case study 15.3

BYD looking for a recharge

Founded in 1995, BYD (http:// www.byd.com) is a Chinese company that started out as a rechargeable battery specialist, developing technological competencies (and achieving International Organization for Standardization certification) that won it the trust of leading telecommunications MNEs including Nokia, Motorola, and Samsung. The company's original IT business (information technology and electronic parts) was very successful, with its nickel and lithium ion batteries becoming global benchmarks and BYD achieving a significant share of the world market for mobile phone batteries. The real strategic innovation, however, was when the company decided to apply its competencies to electric cars.

The idea behind this strategic move reflected more than an attempt to expand downstream into a more complex product. The growing concentration of international manufacturing in the Global South increased the amount of pollution being generated in the newly industrialized countries, which often lack the necessary de-pollution equipment. This problem is particularly acute in China, which has recently become the world's largest source of climate change-inducing greenhouse gases and where smog caused by factory and automobile emissions has created a real health hazard. This has raised awareness in the country that something needs to be done to tackle pollution. At the same time, the scale of the problem makes it a real business opportunity. In turn, this has

caused Chinese companies to intensify their industrialization efforts in the field of environmental technologies and products in the hope that this will place the country at the forefront of a new industrial revolution, allowing it to leapfrog the development stages that Global North countries experienced on their own road to sustainability (Ho 2008).

BYD's diversification strategy began in the early 2000s with a number of acquisitions and capital investments. After about five years of preparation during which it leveraged existing competencies in ferrous oxide batteries, the company rolled out a revolutionary electric vehicle called the F3e. Publicized as creating 'zero pollution, zero emission and zero noise', the car had a driving range of 350 km per charge, much more than earlier battery prototypes. The hope was that this greater range would reduce concerns about the lack of a supporting industry for electric cars, much in the same way as the availability of petrol stations reassures drivers of traditional cars. Prices were also lower than rival electric vehicles being sold outside China, in part because BYD hoped that breaking through in its domestic market would help it to achieve economies of scale and lower overall costs, making it in turn more competitive in the international marketplace.

Within a few years, however, terrible sales showed that Chinese consumers were not ready for an innovation of this kind. Out of the 13.8 million cars and trucks sold in the country in 2010, only a handful were electric or hybrid, with the global leader in this segment, Toyota, selling just a single Prius in China that year (Watts 2011). Despite efforts to update its model (now called the E6), BYD ultimately felt that it had no choice but to postpone the domestic production of 100 per cent electric vehicles. For the moment at least, the diversification drive had to be considered a failure.

Enjoying a solid financial position because of its battery business (and helped by US investor Warren Buffett's $230 million equity stake in 2009), BYD did not abandon all hopes for the electric car, however. Indeed, its next move was to set up a divisional headquarters in Los Angeles to spearhead entry into the US market. Whether BYD will succeed in the Global North remains to be seen. When emerging MNEs sell low-tech products in the older consumer markets, their cost advantages make a huge difference. The effect is less meaningful with innovative products where technology and credibility are the key success factors. This explains why new Chinese automobile purchasers seem to be congregating towards some of the better known Western brand names. It is in recognition of this that BYD decided to create a joint venture with Germany's Daimler Chrysler, culminating in the new brand being introduced at the April 2012 Beijing auto show. Over time, as MNEs from the Global South compete for Global North markets and vice versa, success will be determined less by country of origin and merely reflect the suitability of the international business strategy. The day when emerging market companies face the same expectations as MNEs from the older industrialized world is the day that they will have fully emerged.

Rapid growth in Chinese automobile ownership is creating major environmental problems
Source: iStock

Case study questions

1. What are the prospects for China becoming a global leader in new hi-tech sectors involving the production of environmentally friendly products?
2. Is it still accurate to characterize Chinese industry as low-tech?
3. How likely is it that MNEs from emerging markets will dominate the global automotive sector one day?

Discussion questions

1. What other development models exist asides from the manufacturing-for-export path followed by most of today's emerging economies?
2. Which countries might be added or subtracted from economist Jim O'Neill's list of Next 11 emerging markets?
3. How quickly might MNEs be expected to adapt their product ranges to meet the specific demands of emerging market consumers?

4. Is 'frugal innovation' destined to become a major global marketing trend in the future?
5. What implications does Asia's rise as a centre of international business have for the political paradigm that shapes the international business framework?

Online resource centre

Go online to test your understanding by trying multiple-choice questions, and assignment and examination questions.

Further research

Gipouloux, F. (2011). *The Asian Mediterranean*. Cheltenham: Edward Elgar Publishing

Uses a cross-disciplinary approach to analyse the new 'East Asian economic corridor' intertwining all of the economies between Vladivostok and Singapore.

Radjou, N., Prabhu, J., and Ahuja, S. (2012). *Jugaard Innovation: Think Frugal, Be Flexible, Generate Breakthrough Growth*. San Francisco: Jossey-Bass

Makes the argument that the West would benefit by looking to the East and copying its frugal and flexible innovation processes.

References

Alvarez, J. (2010). 'The rise of emerging market multinationals', in K. Sauvant, G. McAllister, and W. Maschek (eds.). *Foreign Direct Investments from Emerging Markets: The Challenges Ahead*. New York: Palgrave Macmillan

Appelbaum, R. and Gereffi, G. (1994). 'Power and profits in the apparel commodity chain', in E. Bonacich et al. (eds.). *Global Production: The Apparel Industry in the Pacific Rim*. Philadelphia, PA: Temple University Press

BCG—Boston Consulting Group (2011). *Companies on the Move: Rising Stars from Rapidly Developing Economies are Reshaping Global Industries*, available at http://www.bcg.com/documents/file70055.pdf, accessed 17 November 2011

Boudier, F. and Bensebaa, F. (2011). 'Hazardous waste management and corporate social responsibility: Illegal trade of electrical and electronic waste', *Business and Society Review*, 116/1, pp. 29–53 (spring)

Branigan, T. (2011). 'Special report', *The Guardian*, 3–4 October

Bruton, G., Khavul, S., and Chavez, H. (2011). 'Microlending in emerging economies: Building a new line of inquiry from the ground up', *Journal of International Business Studies*, 42, pp. 718–739

Cappelli, P., Singh, H., Singh, J., and Useem, M. (2010). *India Way: How India's Top Business Leaders Are Revolutionizing Management*. Cambridge, MA: Harvard Business School Press

Cassanova, L. (2009) *Global Latinas: Latin America's Emerging Multinationals: The New Latin American Jaguars*. Chippenham and Eastbourne: Palgrave Macmillan

Chakrabortty, A. (2012). 'Apple: Why doesn't it employ more US workers?', *The Guardian*, 23 April, available at http://www.guardian.co.uk, accessed 3 June 2012

CIA—Central Intelligence Agency (2012). *The World Factbook*, available at https://www.cia.gov/library/publications/the-world-factbook/rankorder/2003rank.html, accessed 3 April 2012

Cuervo-Cazurra, A. and Erdem, M. (2011). 'Obligating, pressuring, and supporting dimensions of the environment and the non-market advantages of developing-country multinational companies', *Journal of Management Studies*, 48/2, pp. 441–455 (March)

Economist (2012a). 'Brands in China: Pro logo', *The Economist*, 14 January, p. 64

Economist (2012b). 'Running with the bulls', *The Economist*, 3 March, p. 69

Economist (2012c). 'Asian innovation', *The Economist*, 24 March, p. 76

Ehmke, M. D., Lusk, J. L., and Tyner, W. (2008). 'Measuring the relative importance of preferences for country of origin in China, France, Niger, and the United States', *Agricultural Economics*, 38/3 (May), pp. 277–285

Fetscherin, M. and Marc, S. (2008). 'Chinese brands: The build or buy considerations', *International Journal of Chinese Culture and Management*, 1/4 (August)

Gao, X. (2011). 'Effective strategies to catch up in the era of globalization: Experiences of local Chinese telecom equipment firms', *Research-Technology Management*, 54/1, pp. 42–49 (January/February)

Ho, P. (2008). *Leapfrogging Development in Emerging Asia: Caught Between Greening and Pollution*. New York: Nova Science Publishers Inc.

Hooi, A. (2011). 'Auto mode', *China Daily – European Weekly*, 7–13 October, p. 1

Hope, O., Thomas, W., and Vyas, D. (2011). 'The cost of pride: Why do firms from developing countries bid higher?', *Journal of International Business Studies*, 42, pp. 128–151

Humphreys, M., Sachs, J., and Stiglitz, J. (2007). *Escaping the Resource Curse*. New York: Columbia University Press

ILO—International Labour Organization (2011). *Global Wage Report*, available at http://www.ilo.org/, accessed 16 December 2011

Inklaar, R. and Timmer, M. (2012). *The Relative Price of Services*, February, available at http://www.ggdc.net, accessed 2 April 2012

Kalotay, K. (2010). 'Takeoff and turbulence in the foreign expansion of Russian multinational enterprises', in K. Sauvant, G. McAllister, and W. Maschek (eds.). *Foreign Direct Investments from Emerging Markets: The Challenges Ahead*. New York: Palgrave Macmillan

Khanna, T. and Palepu, K. (2010). *Winning in Emerging Markets: A Road Map for Strategy and Execution.* Cambridge, MA: Harvard Business School Press

Kuchiki, A. and Tsuji, M. (2009). *From Agglomeration to Innovation: Upgrading Industrial Clusters in Emerging Economies.* Basingstoke: Palgrave Macmillan

Larçon, J. (ed.) (2009). *Chinese Multinationals.* New Jersey: World Scientific

Lawrence, F. (2011). 'Argentina accuses the world's largest grain traders of huge tax evasion', *The Guardian*, 1 June

Lewis, C-P. (2008). *How the East Was Won: The Impact of Multinational Companies on Eastern Europe and the Former Soviet Union 1989–2004.* London: Coptic

Loren, B. and Thun, E. (2011). 'Going mobile in China: shifting value chains and upgrading in the mobile telecom sector', *International Journal of Technological Learning, Innovation and Development*, 4/1–2, pp. 148–180 (August)

Luo, Y. and Tung, R. (2007). 'International expansion of emerging market enterprises: A springboard perspective', *Journal of International Business Studies*, 38, pp. 481–498

Maertens, M., Colen, L., and Swinnen, J. (2011). 'Globalisation and poverty in Senegal: A worst case scenario?', *European Review of Agricultural Economics*, 38/1, pp. 31–54

Navarro, P. (2006). *The Economics of the 'China Price'*, available at http://chinaperspectives.revues.org/3063, accessed 16 November 2011

Nayak, A. (2011). *Indian Multinationals: The Dynamics of Explosive Growth in a Developing Country Context.* Basingstoke: Palgrave Macmillan

OECD (2011). 'OECD Communications Outlook', available at http://dwmw.files.wordpress.com/2011/06/oecd-commoutlook-2011.pdf, accessed 20 August 2012

O'Neill, J. (2011). *The Growth Map: Economic Opportunity in the BRICs and Beyond.* New York: Viking Press

Pogrebnyakov, N. and Kristensen, J. (2011). 'Building innovation subsidiaries in emerging markets: The experience of Novo Nordirsk', *Research-Technology Management*, 54/4, pp. 30–37 (July/August)

Prahalad, C. (2009). *The Fortune at the Bottom of the Pyramid: Eradicating Poverty Through Profits.* Upper Saddle River, NJ: Prentice Hall

Rakhi, R. (2011). 'India and China as partner of choice for the Western multinational companies in the era of globalisation', *International Journal of Learning and Intellectual Capital*, 8/2, pp. 128–154 (April)

Ramamurti, R. and Singh, J. (2010). *Emerging Multinationals in Emerging Markets.* Cambridge: Cambridge University Press

Rugman, A. and Doh, J. (2008). *Multinationals and Development.* New Haven, CT: Yale University Press

Sachs, J. (2011). 'The context: Foreign investment and the changing global economic reality', in J. E. Alvarez and K. P. Sauvant with K. G. Ahmed and G. P. Vizcaino (eds.). *The Evolving International Investment Regime: Expectations, Realities, Options.* Oxford: Oxford University Press

Sauvant, K., Govitrikar, V., and Davies, K. (2011). 'MNEs from emerging markets: New players in the world FDI market', January, available at http://www.vcc.columbia.edu, accessed 28 October 2011

Sitkin, A. and Bowen, N. (2010). *International Business: Challenges and Choices*, 1st edn. Oxford: Oxford University Press

St-Maurice, I., Süssmuth-Dyckerhoff, C., and Tsai, H. (2008). 'What's new with the Chinese consumer', September, available at www.mckinseyquarterly.com, accessed 26 September 2008

Ward, K. (2011). 'The world in 2050: Quantifying the shift in the global economy', 4 January, available at http://www.research.hsbc.com, accessed 2 April 2012

Watts, J. (2011). 'SUV good, Prius bad . . .', *The Guardian*, 24 August, p. 25

World Bank (2011). *Ease of Doing Business Rankings*, available at http://www.doingbusiness.org/rankings, accessed 16 December 2011

Zeschky, M., Widenmayer, B., and Gassmann, O. (2011). 'Frugal innovation in emerging markets: The case of Mettler Toledo', *Research-Technology Management*, 54/4, pp. 38–45 (July/August)

16 International business and the environmental challenge

Learning objectives

After reading this chapter, you will be able to:

+ identify the environmental problems that MNEs face
+ compare different ways that MNEs might deal with these issues
+ address the difficulties in greening multinational value chains
+ analyse the prospects for greener international business in the future

Case study 16.1

Steeling South Africa against pollution

Having originated in a developing country (India) to become global leader in its sector of activity, Mittal exemplifies globalization in its most modern form. With its volume strategy based on maximizing geographic coverage, Mittal tends to internationalize via brownfield FDI (see Chapter 9), acquiring rivals and integrating them into its network. Economies of scale and capacity utilization are crucial to a resource like steel, which is very sensitive to variations in global demand. In short, Mittal needs its factories to be running at all times.

In 2002, Mittal bought a 5683 acre plant at Vanderbijlpark in South Africa. For as long as local residents could remember, the plant's chimneys had produced heavy smoke and poisonous black dust (SAPA-AP 2009). The hope was that the new owners would have the means and desire to cut emissions.

Developing countries may wish to attract manufacturing units but the pollution from factories can be devastating

Source: Corbis

Years later, the question is whether Mittal has done enough. The company has rehabilitated Vanderbijlpark's waste disposal sites and plans to cover over its slagheaps of spent materials. However, residents still suffer from pollution-related health disorders, livestock are often born deformed, and metal surfaces rust uncontrollably (SAPA-AP 2009).

The issue came to a head in January 2010 when Mittal South Africa was shortlisted for the Public Eye Global Award awarded by the Davos World Economic Forum to firms accused of lacking corporate responsibility. Vanderbijlpark was nominated for dumping toxic waste, failing to clean up contamination, opposing air quality controls, and lacking transparency. A local environmental activist denounced Mittal for using political connections to 'protect [its] polluting industry', asserting that it is guilty of similar behaviour at facilities in Kazakhstan and Ohio (USA) and has an 'appalling safety record' (GAAM 2010).

Mittal's website (http://www.arcelormittal.com/) has an environmental responsibility section that portrays sustainability as a core value, exemplified in its active recycling programme. Mittal's website recognizes that steel making is carbon-intensive but goes on to state that 'real progress will mean substantial expenditure on new technologies, and we will be looking to governments and regulators for support'. The question is whether such investments will actually happen if no state funding is on offer.

Case study questions

1. How much of a priority is de-pollution for MNEs?
2. How quickly should MNEs be expected to remedy environmental problems inherited from the past?

Introduction

MNEs have a tremendous impact on the natural environment. Given the ecological problems facing planet Earth, companies are increasingly coming under internal and external pressure to adapt their products and processes in a way that diminishes their overall footprint. This affects MNEs' international configurations as well as their upstream operations and marketing approaches.

Historically, some members of the international business community have displayed apathy and even hostility towards environmentalists, dismissing the issue as irrelevant and/or utopian (Monbiot 2007). Indeed, early green business thinkers like Jeremy Rifkin blamed modern capitalism itself for today's ecological crisis. Nowadays, however, there are strong signs of growing cooperation between these two worlds (Anshelm and Hansson 2011), exemplified by the World Business Council for Sustainable Development (http://www.wbcsd.org). If this continues, there is every chance that tomorrow's MNEs will view environmentalism as an essential corporate activity alongside traditional functions such as production or marketing (Bresciani and Oliveira 2007). At the same time, the many other challenges that MNEs face today limit how much they can focus on environmental issues alone—explaining why some managers continue to view this as part of the broader ethical trade-off referred to in Chapter 8 rather than focusing on the environment for its own sake.

Section I: MNEs and the environmental challenge

International business practitioners are just as likely today to view ecological problems as opportunities instead of obstacles. To some extent, this reflects the value systems of modern managers raised at a time when ecological knowledge is widespread (Jackson 2011). Indeed, given rising raw material prices and a deteriorating ecosphere, MNE inaction could cost more than their adopting a proactive attitude in this area.

+ Ecosphere
Sum total of living flora or fauna whose interactions with one another and other inanimate elements enable life on Earth.

A finite planet

Industrial activity has traditionally involved the transformation of raw materials into products but also the generation of unwanted waste. In economic terms, this scheme relies on two conditions: that inputs are available at an affordable price; and that outputs are acceptable. These constraints embody the ecological challenge as most managers experience it.

Depletion of natural resources

A World Wildlife Fund report (2012) announced that in 2008 planetary resources are being consumed about 30 per cent faster than they are replenished. At this rate, two Earths would be needed by the mid-2030s to sustain modern civilization. The word 'sustainability' has various meanings in different contexts, but at a basic level it is clear that this rate of resource consumption is unsustainable.

Energy

There is a strong argument that the main interface between economy and ecology is the energy that businesses use to run operations. The problem for MNEs is that almost all of the raw materials they use are finite and will run out one day (see Figure 16.1). Certainly this is the premise of the theory of 'Peak Oil', developed to explain the declining production from many of the world's largest oil fields (**see ORC Extension material 16.1**). Much hope has been placed in recent years in new solutions such as deep sea drilling, tar sands, or shale

> Go online

Energy source	Total 2011 consumption	Percentage of total primary energy consumption	Years of proven reserves vs. current global production
Oil	4059	33.1	54.2
Coal	3724	30.3	112 (vs. 210 in 2010)
Natural gas	5906	23.7	63.6
Hydroelectricity	792	6.5	N/A
Nuclear	599	4.9	80 (see http://www.world-nuclear.org)
Renewable	195	1.6	N/A
Total	**12,275**		

Figure 16.1
2011 primary energy consumption statistics in million tonnes oil equivalent (BP Statistical Review of World Energy 2012, BP plc).

gas, but each creates its own problems in terms of engineering issues and produces large quantities of carbon dioxide (CO_2). Calculations that the world will need four times Saudi Arabia's daily output of oil by 2030 just to maintain current supply levels offer another way of describing the scale of the energy supply challenge (Chazan 2008).

On the demand side, projected global energy consumption is expected to rise through 2020 by at least 10.2 per cent, or even 27.3 per cent if the main corporate consumers fail to implement eco-efficiency technologies or adapt their modes of organization (MGI 2009). Indeed, despite poor trading conditions in 2011, global energy consumption rose by 2.5 per cent, driven by higher demand in the Global South (BP 2012). Without radical change in behaviour or technology, an energy crunch is imminent.

One surprise in these trends is that they contradict classical economists' prediction that demand falls as prices rise. Higher primary energy prices seem to have little effect on demand. Some managers' inability or unwillingness to process available data on resource depletion may contribute to this. Studies show that some business thinking on energy supplies is driven by psychological or institutional influences (Steininger 2009) instead of rationality. The first step towards addressing a crisis is to recognize its existence.

The slow transition towards alternative energies is also surprising. Normally, where a company suffers from higher input costs and struggles to pass them on to customers, it will try to innovate, increase input productivity (Barbiroli 2009), and find substitutes. However, many companies have tremendous sunk investments in energy-specific infrastructure (internal combustion engines, gas-fired power plants, etc.) whose re-engineering seems prohibitively expensive. The International Energy Agency has predicted that up to $26 trillion dollars of new investment are needed just to meet projected growth in energy demand by 2030, with a further $10.5 trillion to combat climate change. Some managers place their faith in future scientific solutions. Others view the capabilities required to overcome these challenges as opportunities to develop different kinds of firm-specific advantages (Kolk and Pinkse 2008).

Initial responses to the ecological challenge

MNEs and governments have responded to the impending energy crunch by investing in energy infrastructure, conservation, and alternative sources. For instance, work has been done to reduce the estimated 30 per cent of all primary energy lost during transportation (via tanker, pipeline, liquefaction, or electric lines) from the place where it is produced to where it is consumed. The result has been the rise of 'smart grid' technology, a new sector of activity intersecting between electric equipment and information technology. Leading MNEs such as IBM and Siemens are investing heavily in this growth sector. Another example is the £500 million BritNed high voltage undersea cable linking the UK to Holland in 2011, opening the door to an efficient transmission of renewable electricity across a 'European super-grid'. Technology in this area creates space where many contemporary international business students can hope to build a career. Similarly, in 2012, the UK was exploring the possibility of 'connectors' running along the bottom of the North Atlantic and allowing the country to tap into geothermal energy produced by the volcanoes in Iceland. Other initiatives are more localized: many of the world's largest consultancies now offer eco-efficiency advice; several clean technology sectors (i.e. compact fluorescent lighting, electric vehicles) are expanding; not to forget solar or wind power. The problem here is not whether demand exists for the new professions but whether the timing is right. It may seem uneconomic to invest in new systems as long as prices for today's energy sources remain acceptable. But if managers wait until prices skyrocket before starting the new business, the transition may be too costly.

A further complication relates to energy consumption factors, which can vary across the world. For instance, many of the older industrialized countries have experienced a 'Jevons Paradox', with energy-efficient technology actually causing people to consume more energy because they feel less urgency to save. Conversely, total consumer demand in the developing world has risen due to rapid population growth, energy-intensive urbanization, and increased concentration of manufacturing operations here (see Chapter 15). This latter aspect is key because factories in the Global South tend to be more energy-intensive, especially where they involve low-margin firms lacking funds to buy energy-saving technology (King and Slesser 2009). Lastly, there is the cumulative effect of MNE supply chains' internationalization, with growing volumes of materials, components, and modules being manufactured in distant specialist locations before shipment to final assembly or sales sites (see Chapter 11). MNE configurations of this kind rely greatly on logistics, hence on fuel. The first victim of the energy crunch might be globalization.

+ Energy-intensive
Description of activities requiring a higher than average injection of energy resources.

Other natural resources

Modern industry also consumes large volumes of minerals. Many of these resources have a lifespan of centuries, partially because they are recyclable. Some minerals like gold and copper keep their characteristics after first use, whereas others like chromium lose strength and require chemical additives before they can be used again. These factors, and the cost of organizing a recycling channel, influence the decision to recycle materials.

Minerals

There is some concern that global mineral stocks will deplete if developing countries consume them as intensively as older industrialized nations have done. Certainly, sharp price rises in recent years indicate that markets fear shortages. One problem given the often significant distance between where minerals are mined and consumed is the difficulty in adjusting output to inventory or demand levels. Note that an MNE's access to mineral resources often reflects its position in a supply chain, with many industrialists (increasingly from China) seeking to secure inputs by acquiring mining companies in Africa and Brazil (see Chapter 15). It is also interesting to track new markets for 'rare earths' such as dysprosium, terbium, and neodymium, used in wind turbine generators and hybrid automobile engine parts; or lanthanum, used to enhance battery performance. These minerals, key to many hi-tech products, are mainly located in one country (China), which can therefore dictate their global supply. Indeed, there was much concern following Beijing's decision to cut export quotas by 72 per cent in 2010. Hence the importance of determining which resources will become the technological standards of the future. In the battery market, for instance, there is still a question over whether future products will run on Chinese lanthanum or on lithium-ion, which is mainly mined in Bolivia and Chile. The answer will help shape future international business flows.

Biological resources

Another depletion concern relates to biological resources, which can be exhausted as a result of pollution or because they are being used more quickly than they regenerate. The leading biological resource is water, which companies use to cool machinery, evacuate and dilute waste, etc. Water is increasingly scarce, with large-scale purification projects becoming a significant growth area for many engineering MNEs. The UN has called for a doubling of water infrastructure investment from current annual levels of $80 billion. This means huge construction projects that will create international jobs for years to come (Jowit 2008).

Wood is another resource worth studying; because timber is a valuable commodity but also because forests are key to many ecospheres. Forests embody biodiversity principles by providing a habitat and nutrients for other living beings that, in turn, help trees to sustain their own regeneration cycles. Removing any one participant from these systems undermines the natural equilibrium. Yet biological resources such as the tropical forests (Indonesia and the Amazon) that serve as 'green lungs' for the planet continue to experience accelerated deforestation. This too makes forest management an international business issue.

A final area of biological distress is food, either for direct human consumption or within other species' food chains. One example here is fishing, with ocean and river stocks collapsing worldwide following long years of over-exploitation and the pollution of aquatic habitats. Another is soil quality, which has deteriorated worldwide due to over-farming. The net effect has been a reduction in the supply of the commodities affected by these problems.

+ Biodiversity
Extent to which living organisms vary within a given ecosystem.

Pollution

Industrial activities often generate unwanted chemical waste (see Figure 16.2). Foundries that make steel produce smog and pollutant heavy metals. Paper mills that make stationery emit chemicals that infiltrate water tables. Farmers who raise crops may spray them with noxious pesticides. Service industries that use electricity will source it from power stations that generate radioactive waste (nuclear plants) or carbon dioxide (coal-powered plants). All these unwanted emissions circulate in a way that depends on natural factors (winds,

Type	Sources include
Gaseous pollutants	
– Solid particles (inc. asbestos)	Mineral extraction, cement / steel / glass works.
– SO_2 Sulphur dioxide	Power stations, refineries, large combustion plants
– Nox Nitrogen oxides	International combustion engines, forest fires
– CO Carbon monoxide	Motor vehicle exhaust fumes
– CO_2 Carbon dioxide	Fossil energy
– CH_4 Methane	Coal mine, landfill sites, livestock
Heavy metals	
– As Arsenic	Glass-making, metalworking
– Cd Cadmium	Burning solid mineral fuels, heavy fuel oil
– Cr Chromium	Production of glass, cement, ferrous metals
– Hg Mercury	Chlorine production, waste incineration
– Pb Lead	Fusion of lead, manufacture of batteries
– Se Selenium	Glass production, use of heavy fuel oil
Other pollutants	
– NH_3 Ammonia	Agricultural activities
– PCDD-F Dioxins	Incineration, fuel combusion

Figure 16.2
Examples of industrial pollutants (http://www.citepa.org/pollution/sources.htm).

Pollution doesn't respect national boundaries

ocean currents, geological formations) and ignores national borders. By definition, pollution is an international problem.

It is hard to say whether companies or consumers have greater responsibility for pollution. Passenger cars emit smog, household heating aggravates global warming, and the inadequate disposal of trillions of plastic shopping bags has created a several hundred square kilometre island of rubbish in the middle of the Pacific Ocean. Some argue that business is not accountable for waste generated by households. The opposing argument is just as strong, since consumers can use only goods that companies make. Households seeking to reduce their environmental footprint increasingly ask companies to provide products and services to help them to live more sustainably. It is consumer demand for low-emission, fuel-efficient cars that has caused car-makers such as Toyota, Honda, and General Motors to invest in hybrid automotive technology. It is also consumers' desire to buy from ethical firms (see Chapter 8) that has sparked many sustainable practices, exemplified by supermarket efforts to phase out plastic bags.

Still, it can be argued that companies, starting with large MNEs, bear special responsibility for addressing this problem. It has been calculated (Trucost 2010) that the costs associated with cleaning up the pollution produced by the world's 3000 largest companies would amount to nearly 7 per cent of their combined revenues. The logic here is that having benefited from the activities that generated this pollution, it is reasonable that they assume the costs (see Figure 16.3). Secondly, in many industrial economies, final consumer products account for only 6 per cent of total output, with the remaining 94 per cent comprised of pollutant 'non-products' such as perfluorocarbons, dioxins, or PCBs generated during the industrial process (Friend 2009). Much of this hidden pollution is only visible to (and can only be solved by) the upstream suppliers who created it. Lastly, the sheer scale of international business means that MNEs alone have the power to help.

+ Mitigation
Corporate efforts to lessen the effects of pollution they have already generated.

+ Abatement
The act of not generating any pollution in the first place.

Different de-pollution approaches

A major obstacle to MNEs' pollution efforts is that they rarely have incentives to mitigate the effects of their pollution, much less implement costly zero-waste abatement processes. To some extent, MNEs' motivation to de-pollute depends on what penalties they must pay, and

Source	External costs in 2008 (US$ bn)	in % GDP 2008	External costs in 2050 (US$ bn)	in % GDP 2050
Greenhouse gases	4,530	7.54%	20,809	12.93%
Water abstraction	1,226	2.04%	4,702	2.92%
Pollution (SOx, NOx, PM, VOCs, mercury)	546	0.91%	1,926	1.20%
General waste	197	0.33%	635	0.39%
Natural resources (Fish, Timber)	96	0.16%	543	0.34%
Other ecosystem services, waste . . .	NA	NA	NA	NA
Total	6,596	10.97%	28,615	17.78%

Figure 16.3
Annual environmental costs for the global economy (http://www.unpri.org/).

whether costs can be passed on to consumers. Moreover, MNEs are often unaware of their footprint. Few companies inventory toxic releases systematically: national regulations mean they are not obliged to and many will not want to draw attention to this area (Hitchcock and Willard 2009). On the other hand, growing numbers of MNEs proactively develop and publicize pollution remedies for a variety of motives: brand reputation (viewing this as part of their corporate social responsibility agenda); health concerns; corporate value systems; or legal liabilities (e.g. the bill awaiting BP as a result of the 2010 Gulf of Mexico Deepwater Horizon oil disaster).

Certain pollution topics draw more attention than others, with global warming topping the list in recent years. More broadly, national governments create frameworks placing greater and lesser emphasis on dealing with the negative externalities of pollution. This can involve anti-pollution regulations or, increasingly, the development of carbon emission trading systems (**see ORC Extension material 16.2**). Many of these have been formulated as market-based solutions adopted under the aegis of the United Nations Framework Convention on Climate Change, which was enacted at Kyoto (Japan) in 1997 and has led since then to a string of further conferences, including May 2012 in Bonn (Germany). The idea here is that companies will be motivated to reduce their CO_2 emissions since by so doing they will be able to sell their unused allocation rights off for a profit.

> Go online

Other business responses have included a number of construction-related initiatives (smart meters, insulation, lighting, etc.) focused on reducing energy and CO_2 emissions. This mirrors the kind of adaptive behaviour that has been witnessed in response to other air-quality concerns in the past. For example, since the 1970s worries about smog have led to legislation being enacted in many countries. Manufacturers have responded too, fitting platinum-based catalytic converters on automobiles and creating a new sector ('green driving') manifested today in zero-emission vehicles. Similarly, steel-making has also cleaned up its operations in much of the Global North, as exemplified by stringent US Environmental Protection Agency requirements that have forced companies since the 1990s to allocate up to 30 per cent of new plants' capital costs to de-pollution technology (Sitkin 2011) Generally, companies operating in the world's older industrialized countries today cannot expect to engage in manufacturing without filing detailed environmental impact statements. Pollution has become a mainstream topic.

The same does not necessarily apply to emerging economies, however. This is because countries in a pre- or early industrial stage have neither the resources nor the inclination to over-spend on eco-efficiency, which only becomes a priority once a certain comfort level is achieved (see Figure 16.4). There are countless examples of environmental stress in the

Figure 16.4
The Kuznets curve links
de-pollution efforts to
a society's level of
wealth.

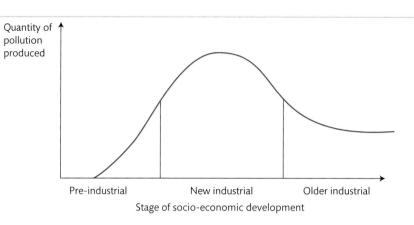

Global South: killer smog in Beijing; dysentery in South Asia; or huge smoke clouds over South East Asia caused by forest fires set intentionally to create farmland. As always, some entrepreneurs view such problems as opportunities, one example being the invention of 'biolite' stoves that reduce black carbon emissions by 90 per cent (Siegle 2010). There are even some efforts afoot to develop technologies making it possible to extract from the atmosphere the harmful excess CO_2 resulting from centuries of industrialization. To some extent, green business makes a virtue out of necessity.

One pollution risk that the whole world faces is global warming. Two leading effects that may be attributed to global warming include frequent droughts (causing starvation and higher food prices) and rising sea levels. The latter is dangerous for coastal populations everywhere, flooding farmland in countries such as Bangladesh and endangering drinking water systems in many great metropolises (ranging from Shanghai, Mumbai, and Buenos Aires to New York, Amsterdam, and Tokyo). Some companies will benefit from climate change (i.e. construction firms building flood barriers or water purification plants) but others, such as insurance, are devastated by natural catastrophes like Hurricane Katrina, which battered New Orleans in 2005. This aggravates managers' sense of uncertainty in a dangerous world.

Managerial awareness of environmental problems

Managers vary in terms of the particular environmental concern capturing their attention. Recent studies (Carbone and Moatti 2008) have found that one factor is an MNE's region of origin. For instance, North American MNEs focus more on water problems, which is unsurprising given frequent droughts in their homeland, whereas Europeans are more concerned by packaging and general resource availability. The implication here is that green outlooks develop under specific circumstances (see ORC Extension materials 16.3).

> Go online

External drivers of environmental responsibility

Given considerable international variations in environmental policy, it is impossible for any MNE to possess all the knowledge it needs. This explains why environmental law has become one of the fastest growing service sectors in recent years. Some factors relevant to trade discussions also apply to environmentalism, like debates between interventionists who want to see ecological awareness permeate all decision-making vs. neo-liberals opposed to governments forcing environmentalism on companies (see Chapter 3). Other factors are specific to national cultures. For instance, the pressure to go green differs for MNEs in Germany or in a poor country desperate for FDI. As discussed in Chapter 5, MNEs are usually aware of a host government's bargaining position. This may make it tempting to threaten to take their FDI elsewhere whenever environmental regulations are stringent. In response, some governments feel forced to relax their standards, allowing their country to degenerate into a pollution haven. The concepts of 'regime arbitrage' forcing a 'race to the bottom' apply as much to environmental as to social or economic policy.

> + Pollution haven
> Country that does not make stringent environmental demands on local producers.

We must then consider whether environmental policy is only effective if enacted on a global scale. Unlike trade, which is governed by the World Trade Organization (WTO), environmental global governance is almost non-existent (see Chapter 4). This is particularly problematic because some WTO decisions actually undermine the greening of international business. For instance, WTO reciprocity principles can stop governments from subsidizing infant industries. Yet without such funding, nurturing certain green sectors is almost impossible. Indeed, there is a whole array of green international business practices that the WTO finds discriminatory: de-taxing domestic green products to make them more competitive; stipulating that labels on imported products contain green information that is not readily available abroad; requiring that imports of energy-efficiency devices be accompanied by technology transfers; or allocating a product's carbon footprint to its foreign production site instead of to the finished product itself (Cottier et al. 2009). In some quarters, there is deep concern that the trade and environmental agendas contradict one another.

The only international body capable of governing both areas is the United Nations, which has regularly organized the negotiation of environmental treaties by national governments. However, the UN has no policing authority, so these agreements generally only have power if they are ratified by signatory countries' domestic legislatures. Thus, almost all environmental policy is determined and policed at the national level, shaped by the pressures that stakeholders put on national politicians. These vary greatly, with activist NGOs such as Greenpeace or Friends of the Earth having views diametrically opposed to those of, for example, Irish airline Ryanair's CEO Michael O'Leary with his attack on 'eco-nuts' and 'environmental headbangers' (Harrison 2006).

Auditing frameworks

Sometimes the MNE is free to choose its level of environmental commitment. On other occasions, this is determined in national law. In France, for instance, the *Nouvelles Régulations Economiques* legislation specifies that companies operating locally engage in triple bottom line accounting. If managers have to publish their economic (and social) performance, this is an incentive to behave more sustainably. More and more MNEs are trying to receive environmental ratings (see Chapter 8), being audited by bodies such as the GRI (http://www.globalreporting.org/) or the ISO (http://www.iso.org/), or simply developing environmental management systems to monitor internal performance and drive an improvement dynamic. The effectiveness of such systems will vary depending on whether the MNE runs its environmental standards and reporting activities out of global headquarters or its different national subsidiaries. Such green business decisions are not unlike many of the others that MNE managers are accustomed to taking.

> + Environmental management systems
> 'Framework through which [a company's] environmental performance can be monitored, improved and controlled' (see http://www.envirowise.gov.uk/).

Internal drivers of environmental responsibility

MNE managers vary in terms of recognizing the need for greater environmental action and being willing to pay for this. Those who view eco-efficiency as a competitive advantage tend to welcome stringent green regulations since this forces them to toughen up (Jain and Kedia 2011). Others imitate competitors and want to avoid criticism for lagging behind new standards. Hopeful of avoiding a negative reputation, their approach is less proactive.

Where staff members come from different cultures, each with its own attitude towards environmentalism, senior management alone is in a position to unify the MNE's greening efforts, especially in centralized companies (see Chapter 10). Yet, because of the pressure to maximize shareholder profits, some senior executives find it hard to commit to costly and difficult green transformations. This makes it all the more noteworthy when the opposite happens and a CEO almost singlehandedly drives a company to reduce its environmental footprint.

Middle managers' frontline knowledge may help them to drive corporate greening processes but at times they can also be a source of resistance to progress in this area, because of poor communications, managerial complacency, departmental isolation, or staff apathy (Werbach 2009). Uncertainty can also exist around how an MNE should behave in all of the countries where it operates. Spending a maximum everywhere could also put the company at a competitive disadvantage. This realization may spark a reluctance to change things. In response, companies worldwide are introducing programmes (and cross-departmental task forces) that motivate, train, and reward personnel contributing to the overall sustainability effort. Examples include the 'Personal Sustainability Projects' that Walmart has run since 2007 to encourage employees to set environmental and health-related objectives and disseminate knowledge in this field, at work and at home. The incentives can also be negative, like Dow Chemical's 'internal waste tax', where each of its business units pays a notional pollution fine to a central body (Epstein 2008).

Practitioner insight

David Cotton started in research with Shell before assuming a more commercial role with group headquarters in London. This was followed by a 30-year career with consultants Metra Martech, where he worked with scientific and technical products in different sectors, including alternative fuels. David was also involved in economic and industrial planning in Nigeria and the Middle East, gaining experience in statistical analysis that would subsequently lead to his publishing a book, *Climate Change: What You Need to Know*.

'I have become increasingly concerned about vast differences in wealth, thus in resource consumption, and believe we should strive for a more equal distribution both internationally and within countries. I am also very concerned about our obsession with growth. If Chinese GDP continues to grow as at present, by 8 per cent annually, it will be double that of the USA in only 30 years. If the whole world reaches current US consumption levels, then global GDP will rise by a factor of six over the next century and we won't have enough resources to cope. Nor do I agree with blind faith in technological solutions. People who talk about them are seldom very specific. I figure that if a solution hasn't been found yet, it will take a very long time to find a viable one. Fuel cells have been around for 50 years but they are still not commercially viable.

Having said that, in practice there are considerable opportunities for increasing the efficiency with which we use energy and other resources. The problem is that most business-people look at the short term but are not interested in what happens over the next 50 years. I remember from my own earlier career when we used to do cashflow calculations using discount rates of 5 or 6 per cent. Anything that would happen after, say, eight years would be immaterial to the decision. But I have grandchildren and what happens in the longer term is very important to me.

By and large, multinationals are self-centred and are only really interested in how decisions will affect their own business rather than their impact on the rest of the world. This mindset can be put to good use, however, if energy-efficiency investments are discussed in terms of saving money rather than saving the planet. The problem is that many renewable energy sources need subsidies to be competitive in the short term. That should change soon, however, both because prices for conventional fuels will jump, and also because large scale production will lower the cost of solar panels or wind turbines, etc. A lot of people complain about taxes on fuels but I think they're actually good—they make us use energy more carefully. And it is important that we change quickly, given the speed of problems like climate change. We haven't yet hit a so-called tipping point but we soon could do if we do not move quickly.'

Section II: The future of green international business

To some extent, eco-efficiency is an extension of the 'quality revolution' principle that has dominated international business since the Toyota Production System first spread in the 1970s (see Chapter 11). This approach affects internal factory operations but also MNEs' productive configurations. In a world of prohibitively expensive logistics costs (fuel, packaging), future MNEs might want to shorten their supply chains. Instead of fragmented global production organizations, they might return to multi-domestic strategies focused on autonomous local subsidiaries. Physical deliveries might also become less important than knowledge sharing. Managers' lifestyles would also change, with interactions based on video-conferencing and long-term overseas assignments instead of repeated short-term travel, as is currently the case. Tomorrow's greener international business is likely to look very different from today's version.

Operational greening

Ever since the Industrial Revolution, manufacturing stands accused of 'commoditizing nature', forcing harsh synthetic processes on the ecosphere instead of working within its boundaries (Braungart and McDonough 2009). Operational greening means replacing this approach with an 'industrial ecology' method that restructures value chains to minimize resource utilization and waste. A frequent analogy at this level involves self-sufficient forests that require almost no new inputs (aside from renewable fuels such as sunlight and water) because they reconvert any waste generated into nutrients. One example is an industrial cluster near Middlesbrough in England where waste from a local chemicals plant heats greenhouses whose vegetable outputs feed back into the original plant. This kind of 'closed loop' system relies on companies not only greening their own operations but also working closely with partners.

Supply chain management

Green design takes natural principles and uses them to maximize eco-efficiency. Some 'biomimicry' (according to Janine Benyus) and 'biomorphism' approaches create products that replicate the 'intelligent patterns' found in the natural world. Examples include curtains that react spontaneously to sunlight or airplane wings mirroring bird flight. Others focus on internal corporate processes, most famously designer William McDonough's 'cradle-to-cradle' concept (see Figure 16.5), where goods are designed from the outset in a way that reduces their footprint. To achieve this, a company's manufacturing processes should differentiate between 'biological nutrients' returned to the natural environment at the end of a product's working life, and 'technical nutrients' comprised of substances like synthetic chemical compounds or materials and minerals whose disposal is toxic. The basic idea is that companies should inventory everything going in and out of their production processes.

McDonough's vision constitutes an ideal that few companies can implement fully without abandoning their existing product ranges or manufacturing facilities. As a result, green design often focuses on more achievable objectives that can be attained either individually or in combination: lightweighting materials; extending products' useful life via upgradeability; and enhancing end-of-life disassembly (Blackburn 2008). Most companies cannot afford to green every single aspect of their production processes and must make choices. There is evidence (Carbone and Moatti 2008) that logistics is the function that MNEs are most successful at greening. One example is the way that the home delivery vans operated by British supermarket Sainsbury's feature an electric fleet, thereby reducing the group's carbon

+ **Lightweighting**
Engineering initiatives aimed at reducing the mass of materials comprising a manufactured item.

+ **Upgradeability**
Ease with which an object can accommodate modernization.

+ **Disassembly**
Act of breaking an item down into its component parts, usually at the end of its working life.

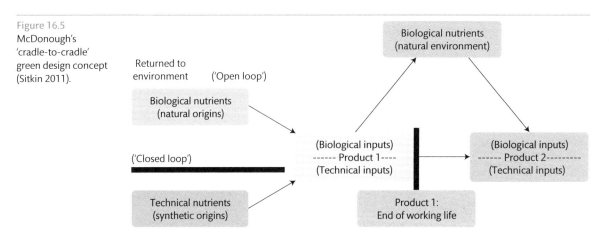

Figure 16.5
McDonough's 'cradle-to-cradle' green design concept (Sitkin 2011).

footprint. The same study also indicates that many companies tend to focus on product design, components, and packaging (the last of these being another area where Sainsbury's has taken a lead through its efforts to reduce the use of plastic bags). Different MNEs stress different areas of operational greening.

Monitoring suppliers' footprints

Because MNEs are increasingly accountable for products' total footprint, it is important that they monitor suppliers' environmental behaviour. The goal can be to reduce legal liability, one 2007 example being when Mattel imported toys from China containing toxic substances. Supplier monitoring can also be useful to protect a company's reputation, so it can avoid being criticized for the environmental quality of the inputs it purchases. Similarly, the high non-product ratio characterizing certain goods (e.g. computers, household appliances) means that some companies inherit up to 60 per cent of their carbon footprint from suppliers (Brickman and Ungerman 2008). To achieve change, MNEs have started offering suppliers environmental incentives and/or dictating Environmentally Preferable Purchasing

+ Non-product ratio
Percentage of inputs that are transformed into waste over the course of a production process.

Logistics are a key part of many companies' environmental improvement efforts

Reproduced by kind permission of Sainsbury's Supermarkets Ltd.

(EPP) specifications. Thus, Walmart gives its suppliers worldwide specific directives about carbon emissions, preferred chemicals, energy-efficiency, and packaging (with changes in the final area saving the company, according to its 2010 Global Sustainability Report, upwards of $20 million). Similarly, office products chain Staples is sourcing more of its paper or wood stocks from certified sustainable timber sources, and textiles giant Levi Strauss pressures suppliers to consume less water. Many MNEs also target incoming and outgoing packaging waste. Efforts here include 'rightsizing' smaller containers; making them sturdier or reusable; introducing recycled, biodegradable, or bio-based materials; and developing 'reverse logistics' schemes to accelerate recycling or remanufacturing. These activities are fast turning into a major new international business sector in their own right, as exemplified by US equipment manufacturer Caterpillar's December 2009 announcement that it had agreed to a global service joint venture with a Chinese partner named Yuchai. The work involves remanufacturing Yuchai diesel engines and components alongside Caterpillar diesel engines and components. The output will add to the more than 100 million pounds of end-of-life iron that Caterpillar already recycles annually. To facilitate such 'end-of-life' activities, MNEs are increasingly basing product design on identifiable, inter-changeable modules that can be replaced easily to extend product usefulness. For instance, 60 per cent of all equipment parts used by photocopier specialist Xerox are retrieved from earlier models. Combined with an active product take-back scheme, this approach is said to save the MNE several hundred million dollars a year (Blackburn 2008). Recycling nowadays is about profits as much as social responsibility.

A final area of operational greening is transportation, which can become particularly problematic in MNEs that are characterized by globally dispersed value chains and outsource logistics to third-party providers. Aside from the strategic benefits of nearsourcing (see Chapter 11), problems at this level include recurrent oil spills caused when transporters charter sub-standard, accident-prone tankers. The question then becomes how much control the MNE has over its service providers' environmental behaviour.

Green marketing

Corporate social responsibility (CSR) (see Chapter 8) is one framework that can be used to analyse modern consumers' green sensitivities. It is important to remember that CSR is comprised of many sub-categories, with recent studies indicating that even as environmental responsibility has become the dominant reference for companies looking to prove their CSR credentials, it is the category that is least important to consumers' estimation of a company's CSR image (Anselmsson and Johansson 2007). For many consumers facing a purchasing decision, the environment is not the prime consideration. At a deeper level, green (and more broadly, ethical) marketing may satisfy customer desires but it also asks potential customers to behave in a selfless way that might not correspond to what they perceive as their immediate material interest. At a psychological level, there is a conflict between self-interest and group-interest (Sitkin 2011). This is particularly difficult when the economy is weak and there is evidence that in times of recession, demand falls for environmental products (such as the kinds of cleaning products that American MNE Clorox produces under its Green Works brand). Environmental issues can also seem distant in time (depletion of fish stocks by 2050, fear of global warming by 2100) and place (i.e. the melting of the polar ice caps). There is much debate over whether green marketing can really take off without a revolutionary shift in global cultural values.

A further complication is that green consumers do not represent a unified whole but constitute an accumulation of segments characterized by contrasting needs and perceptions (Finisterra do Paço 2009). For instance, studies have found that in Hong Kong women tend to buy more eco-products than men (Lee 2009) whereas in Egypt men are more positive towards green purchases than women (Mostafa 2007). Like other sectors, green marketing makes most sense when broken down into sub-categories.

Case study 16.2

Lenovo and its Greenpeace rankings

China's industrial boom has raised living standards for tens of millions of citizens. This outcome is very welcome but the environmental effects are much less so. Not only do China's rising CO_2 emissions contribute to climate change, but the country faces many other problems, including, according to the World Resources Institute (http://www.wri.org), groundwater pollution and lethal air pollution ('killer smog').

Hence the general delight in March 2007 when Chinese computer-maker Lenovo came top of Greenpeace's list of the world's most environmentally friendly electronics company, largely reflecting its work to eliminate hazardous substances and organize take-back/recycling programmes. This was a great achievement, given the huge volumes that Lenovo had been trading since acquiring IBM's Personal Computing Department in 2005. Lenovo had been conscientiously developing a green strategy for a number of years and continued in this vein after heading the Greenpeace table, setting up a division called Lenovo Asset Recovery Services (ARS) to help customers 'manage their end-of-life technology equipment by providing computer take-back, data destruction, refurbishment and recycling' (http://www.lenovo.com). The company's green reputation seemed secure despite criticism of its manufacturing processes' use of toxic substances. Lenovo's subsequent announcement that it would work to eliminate PVCs and brominated flame retardants (BFRs) within a few short years was meant to consolidate its Greenpeace ranking.

By January 2010, Lenovo was down to fourteenth in the table, having received penalty points for allegedly backtracking on its commitment to eliminate PVCs and BFRs. Its recycling activities were also penalized for

E-waste from old electronic appliances is rapidly becoming a major international problem

Source: iStock

unclear data. Above all, Lenovo scored poorly in terms of two new criteria that Greenpeace had added: carbon footprint and energy consumption. Having created expectations that it could become one of the global electronics sector's greenest representatives, Lenovo was discovering that brand image is a double-edged sword. A year later in November 2011, Lenovo had edged back up to eighth place, as a reward for its sustainable operations and reduced greenhouse gas emissions (http://www.greenpeace.org/international/en/campaigns/toxics/electronics/). Other competitors were also raising their game, however. Like most areas of international business, green marketing is an ongoing battle.

Case study questions

1. What triggered Lenovo's interest in sustainability?
2. How important are the Greenpeace rankings to Lenovo's brand image?

The green marketing mix

For MNEs operating in market segments that are relatively ignorant of (or apathetic towards) the environment, the first step is to educate potential consumers about the benefits of green consumption (see Figure 16.6). This can be quite difficult at a psychological level. Lacking previous knowledge on how innovative green products work, potential buyers' initial reaction is often one of incredulity. The degree of resistance that companies encounter at this level depends on whether consumers are being asked to accept a green product that has objective qualities or a green brand, which is a more subjective choice.

	Green product marketing	Green brand marketing
Consumers already sensitized to environmental problems: responsive approach	competition argument, i.e. value for money	emotional argument to create 'halo effect'
Consumers not yet sensitized to environmental problems: proactive approach	long-term argument focused on benefits such as 'lifecycle' costs	educational argument to increase comfort level with green purchases

Figure 16.6
Proactive vs. responsive green marketing matrix (Sitkin 2011).

1. Green products

There are different ways of categorizing green products. One is to distinguish between items that generate no direct environmental benefits themselves but are manufactured using environmental principles. A second is to highlight the green benefits that end users realize upon consumption.

Professional goods

One leading example of an industrial MNE with a green product line is General Electric (GE) (http://www.ge.com), whose 'Ecomagination' programme sells industrial systems enhancing industrial customers' operational and environmental performance. GE's main areas of focus have been renewable energy, transportation, and water use and purification. To sustain this activity, the MNE has invested substantial sums and its website contains a pledge that it will allocate $10 billion to green R&D by the year 2015. Today, it is well placed for the large domestic infrastructure contracts that the US government is expected to put out to tender over the next few years. It can also bid on contracts for similar green construction projects overseas. The main rivals with whom GE will be vying in its sector are ABB from Switzerland, Siemens from Germany, and Mitsui from Japan.

Consumer goods

An early example of a green consumer product derives from a decision taken at the 1987 UN conference in Montreal to reduce the global production of ozone-depleting CFC chemicals. Following this directive, companies worldwide, led by the giant American conglomerate Westinghouse and European white goods specialist Electrolux, designed a new range of refrigerators featuring coolant systems that use a less hazardous chemical compound called HCFC. Within a few short years, HCFC refrigerators became the sector standard. Another example from the same period involves children's nappies. In response to public concerns about the amount of non-biodegradable used nappies being sent to landfill, manufacturers such as Proctor & Gamble in the USA or Unilever in Europe began experimenting with 'super-absorbent' polymers producing the same functionalities but requiring fewer material inputs. Otherwise, many recent green consumer products focus on energy efficiency. Examples include solar-powered mobile phone chargers such as those produced by China Solar, as well as low power computers and household appliances. Lastly, for some other green products, the main sales argument is their durability or non-toxicity (e.g. SJ Johnson's 'Greenlist' cleaning products). This latter category appeals simultaneously to consumers' emotions (they are fashionable) and rationality (they are characterized by lower life cycle costs). Clearly, this dual argument enhances their chances of success.

+ Life cycle costs
Total cost of an item taking all impacts into account, including running costs, environmental impact, and end-of-life disposal.

2. Green pricing

Green products' generally higher point-of-sale pricing has several causes. Companies may take advantage of goods' novelty value to charge more. Also, few green products have achieved significant production scale. Return costs are further increased by the care taken during their manufacturing phase to use higher quality inputs, minimize waste, and organize end-of-life recycling. Unlike non-green rivals, green products are supposed to incorporate all ecological costs not only for the company but for society as a whole. This puts them at

Green pricing incorporates a product's 'life cycle costing', including disposal

a price disadvantage and condemns them to a niche positioning unless consumers have other arguments to overcome this barrier. Different factors come into play at this level: consumers' cultural values and demographic characteristics; prevailing economic conditions; or the extent to which consumers are educated in life cycle cost valuation. Some of these factors have their roots in national cultural variations (see Chapter 6).

3. Green places

Green marketing originally involved specific distribution channels, often based on small local stores or cooperatives staffed by environmental devotees trying to escape the corporate lifestyle. Even today, specialist outlets continue to account for a large percentage of all green product sales, although less than before, with most of the world's leading retail chains now offering green product ranges. Whether these goods are mixed with non-green goods in store sections defined by product category, or sold separately in dedicated organic produce sections, depends on whether management's priority is to normalize customers' transition to green consumption or sharpen the store's reputation as a green provider.

4. Green promotions

+ Halo effect
Where consumers feel positively about a company because it has a track record of virtuous behaviour.

+ Green redemption
Where a company restores its tarnished environmental reputation through positive actions.

Green promotion sends out concrete signals that a particular company is not only aware of stakeholders' ecological concerns but is also proactive about protecting the environment. This approach is intended to produce a halo effect, something that is particularly important to MNEs that have been accused of environmental mismanagement in the past. One example of this kind of green redemption is McDonald's (Juniper 2008). Criticized in 2006 by the environmentalist NGO Greenpeace for meat procurement policies that allegedly contributed to the destruction of the Amazon rainforest, the MNE is now praised by the Rainforest Alliance (http://www.rainforest-alliance.org) for selling certified sustainable coffee. Similarly, MNEs such as BP, Shell, or Exxon Mobil, all of whom have been criticized for their association with oil spills in the relatively recent past, now produce advertisements highlighting their investments in renewable energy. Green promotion appeals to potential consumers' social conscience, helping them to view the purchasing act as something virtuous. On other occasions, the appeal may be to consumers' self-interest, with the green product being depicted as healthier or more natural. In both instances, the purpose is to provide arguments helping purchasers to overcome green products' double handicap of being new and expensive. Lastly, it is important to note that some products can be promoted differently across the world. One example is the way that Shell highlighted its Pura zero-sulphur diesel liquid's cleaner aspects in Thailand, where cities can be very smoggy, but stressed engine performance in the Netherlands, where air pollution is a lesser problem (Esty and Winston 2006).

Unfortunately, the explosion in green promotions over the past 20 years has led to some exaggerated and sometimes even false green claims—one example being the oil company Chevron claiming credit for using 'solar energy to power pumps at one of the oldest and dirtiest oilfields on the planet' (Pearce 2010). There is rising concern about some MNEs' 'greenwashing' tendency to overstate the environmental benefits of their products or processes. This can undermine green promotions' credibility and strengthen consumer resistance. To counter this, an international eco-labelling system has been developed to certify product authenticity (**see ORC Extension material 16.4**). The problem is the lack of international standardization in labelling standards. Green international business will only be able to take off if markets believe in its basic proposition.

> Go online

Looking to the future

Many commentators predict that resource productivity will become the main driver of global economic growth within a few short years. The sectors that are most likely to be affected include 'the built environment, transport and industry, material productivity including steel, concrete and timber, chemistry, engineering, water efficiency and sustainable agriculture' (Weizsäcker et al. 2009). The United Nations itself has predicted a global explosion in the number of green jobs, reaching as many as 20 million by the year 2030. It is clear that some of these jobs will be filled by today's international business students.

Growth sectors

Future rises in natural resource prices should trigger a range of new international business activities. The most dramatic changes are likely to relate to the direct production of energy. In addition, it is also worth remembering other sectors driven by the effects of the environmental problems discussed in this chapter.

Food

Food will always be in demand. Yet largely due to technological progress, food prices fell relative to other sectors all throughout the twentieth century. Since the turn of the twenty-first century, however, this trend has reversed (see Figure 16.7). On the supply side, ecological problems (such as sustained drought in Australia) have disrupted harvests, newly

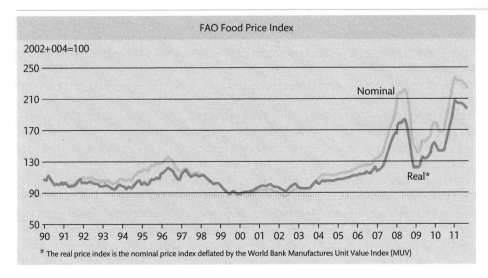

Figure 16.7
Global food prices have jumped over the past decade (http://www.fao.org/ worldfoodsituation/ wfs-home/ foodpricesindex/en/).

urbanized spaces pave over what used to be fertile farmland (a big problem in China), and energy inflation has increased farmers' costs (fertilizers, transporting goods to market). On the demand side, the world's population now exceeds the seven billion mark and is still rising; biofuels add to demand for crops; emerging consumers now buy less energy-efficient dairy and meat products; and an estimated 30 per cent of all food continues to go to waste in the older industrialized societies. The result has been rapidly rising prices for staples such as rice, causing food riots from Haiti to Bangladesh.

The outlook for future supply is good: technology and crop diversification should help agricultural productivity to improve in Africa and South Russia; planners worldwide are increasingly creating urban space for city farming; and genetically modified (GM) strains offer greater resilience to blight (although NGOs such as Greenpeace are concerned by GM's biodiversity risks and the fact that Global North MNEs such as Monsanto and Novartis monopolize GM seed supplies). Even so, food demand is projected to rise even faster than supply, meaning that price pressures are set to continue.

A second aspect of international agribusiness is the distance between where food is produced and where it is consumed. Most food markets are dominated by a few big MNEs that organize global supply chains to keep supermarkets stocked with produce all year long, even when it is out of season. Once this distribution system has been set up, there is a vested interest in keeping it running. The end result, however, is an accumulation of 'food miles' that will become unsustainable if fuel prices soar. A shift towards greater localism in this sector is now widely expected, especially given national concerns about food self-sufficiency. The problem is that farming in the Global North costs more.

Water

According to current estimates (McKinsey-WRG 2009) and all else remaining equal, global water requirements are expected to rise from 4.5 to 6.9 trillion m^3 by the year 2030, largely due to population growth. This is a full 40 per cent above current reliable supplies. Investing in water infrastructure has therefore become a growth sector for MNEs. The activity ranges from building huge dams and other infrastructure to repairing leaky pipes, protecting reservoirs from pollution, and generalizing rainwater harvesting systems. Water is especially important in emerging countries whose development is often undermined by households' lack of access to drinkable sources (http://www.wateraid.org/). It is also crucial to agriculture.

Buildings

Given the urbanization and industrialization of many emerging countries, plus the stimulus packages implemented by many industrialized countries following the 2008–2011 crises, the outlook is promising for the global construction industry. This is a great opportunity for big construction MNEs, such as world leader Vinci from France, CCCC from China, or US giant Bechtel. In addition, there should also be work for SME suppliers with technical competency in different green building activities, ranging from eco-equipment manufacturers to post-construction performance monitors. The actual work can vary depending on whether a building's construction or operational phase is involved, or even the surrounding infrastructure (i.e. combined heat and power systems). Designing eco-efficient natural features into buildings is relatively straightforward nowadays and generally equates to a surcharge of between 2 and 10 per cent (Blackburn 2008), money easily recaptured through lower life cycle operating costs. Retrofitting older units is harder and therefore more expensive. In this sector as in others, it is easier to implement green solutions when they are part of the design from the very outset.

In addition, the building industry is increasingly subject to green construction standards. One benchmark is the United States Green Building Council standard (http://www.usgbc.org/), widely referred to as LEED or Leadership in Energy and Environmental Design. A signature example of a top category LEED project is the Shanghai Engine Centre facility built by Pratt & Whitney's joint venture with China Eastern Airlines. At least one-eighth of this structure's total energy needs come from renewable sources; it has energy-efficient and reflective windows and roofs; and water use has been cut by around 40 per cent (Greenbiz 2010). Design features of this kind are particularly important in rapidly emerging markets such as China, which adds about 2 billion m^2 of new buildings every year.

Variability in international standards means that this level of performance is not always achieved, however. For instance, current UK codes accept that a building in this country leaks three times as much energy as its German equivalent would (Monbiot 2007). Many European developers and architects work to BRE Environmental Assessment Method specifications (http://www.breeam.org/), although Italy's Green Building Council has recently decided to adopt LEED. These holistic codes are often complemented by targeted efficiency standards, such as Energy Star.

Transportation

Greening this sector will involve engineering a wholesale shift from energy-inefficient modes of transportation such as airplanes and internal combustion engine automobiles to cleaner and more sustainable alternatives. Examples include the development of an electric train system in Lima (Peru) to facilitate congestion and reduce smog (Economist 2012a) or the fast-train corridors being built between major Russian cities in the run-up to the 2018 World Cup. This sector is dominated globally by industrialists from countries where integrated systems of this kind have already been established. The leaders are Alstom for the French TGV, Hitachi for the Japanese 'Bullet Train', and Siemens for the German ICE. The Canadian Bombardier is also a big name in this sector.

Mega-projects of this kind feature significant upfront costs, however, meaning that their payback period can be very long. Governments may therefore find it difficult to make such commitments at times of severe budgetary constraints, such as the 2011–2012 European sovereign debt crisis. As is often the case in greening calculations, high short-term costs often overshadow benefits (i.e. the lower life cycle cost) that accrue over a longer term.

The same applies to the green car sector. Given worsening congestion and pollution worldwide, the sector was expected to expand rapidly but its take-off has been slower than predicted, with the stock of 20 million vehicles expected by 2020 accounting for a mere 2 per cent of global light-duty vehicle stocks by that time (IEA 2011). This disappointing result is partially caused by conflicting technological standards, with the market divided between Toyota or Honda's petrol-electric hybrid vehicles and Renault or GM's 100 per cent electric cars—a confusion that feeds fears about performance. Above all there is a price barrier, with green premiums reaching 25 per cent in the sector. This will last until oil prices reach a point where today's internal combustion engines become comparatively more expensive, green car production achieves economies of scale, and/or battery technology improves. Supporting industries must also take off, with one contender here being an Israeli SME called Better Place that is installing battery recharging points worldwide to overcome concerns about new vehicles' driving range.

+ Green premium
Surcharge paid for a green product over the equivalent non-green product.

Clean ventures

Clean technology's main promise is that it helps produce outputs with minimal environmental footprints. Within this category, there is a clear emphasis on renewable energies. Given resource depletion and global warming, and with nearly one-third of 2010 international mergers and acquisitions involving energy activities against just 14 per cent a decade ago (http://www.ft.com), many students today can expect their future careers to revolve around this line of business.

Like almost all infant industries (see Chapter 2), renewables have experienced a bumpy take-off. Entrepreneurs worldwide have long been aware of the need to find substitutes for fossil fuels, with 2011 renewables investments having risen to $257 billion, 17 per cent more than the year before and up sixfold since 2004 (UNEP/Bloomberg 2012). What this mainly reflects, however, is the industry's low starting point. Given the possibility that the global economy must rely almost entirely on renewable energy within a few decades, the real question is why growth is so slow. Explanations include the new technology's expensiveness compared with fossil fuels, plus governments' inability (or unwillingness) to offer subsidies overcoming this disadvantage at a time of severe budget deficits (IEA 2011). Renewable energy is as much a financial challenge as a technological one.

The first distinction to make is between experienced MNEs diversifying into new activities and dedicated start-up SMEs. Examples of the former include Boeing, which is a world leader in concentrated photovoltaic solar power technology; ABB, which builds photo-voltaic solar plants; and Johnson Controls, which makes batteries for electric and hybrid vehicles (Sitkin 2011). Larger companies' deeper pockets might mean that they are in a better position to fund an infant industry, but because institutional shareholders demand short-term returns, their renewables departments are under pressure to produce quick profits. This has led to major energy names exiting the market quickly, as BP did in 2009.

Funding green ventures

Most funding for start-ups is external, starting with government investments and incentives in the form of grants, subsidies, production tax credits, guarantees, co-investment arrange-ments, or cheap loans. Public funding became particularly important in the wake of the 2008 credit crunch, when the G20 group of leading global economies allocated around $184 billion in green stimulus funds (including $67 billion in the USA and $47 billion in China), mainly for disbursement within three years (Pew 2010b). MNEs also bid for these funds, but given the strategic nature of the business, national governments tend to favour local interests (see Chapter 3). There is also significant international variation in the availab-ility of government or private sector funding for clean technology ventures. In the USA, for instance, most funding for green ventures involves bank loans, largely dominated by 'asset financing', which is when a borrower secures a loan by pledging assets (Pew 2010a). Far behind comes private equity (a particularly American funding mechanism) and investment funds, including 'socially responsible' interests. A distinction exists between purely financial investments in clean energy, which fell by 14.6 per cent in 2010 (UNEP/Bloomberg 2011), and industrial investments, which rose by 32 per cent the same year. In part, this reflects varying perceptions about the future of green international business in different parts of the world. With the exception of small-scale rooftop solar arrays in Germany that benefit from government-subsidized feed-in tariffs, the older industrialized countries have generally suf-fered from over-capacity in the large-scale renewable sector and reduced state aid. China, on the other hand, has enjoyed strong growth in new financial investment in utility-scale renewable energy projects and provision of equity capital for renewable energy companies (Pew 2012; see Figure 16.8). For the first time ever in 2010, clean energy investments in the Global South surpassed the North ($72 billion vs. $70 billion), although strong growth in American renewables the following year meant that by year-end 2011, the USA had returned to the top of the global table. One key aspect of this discussion is to what extent the geographic shifts observed in many industrial sectors (see Chapter 15) apply to green business as well. In part, this will depend on whether emerging economies are able to leapfrog the stages of development that the older industrialized countries went through (Ho 2008).

Highlighting solar and wind ventures

Alongside offshore experiments in the UK and elsewhere with electricity from tides or waves, solar and wind power are the two main categories of renewable energy and have several characteristics in common. Both are 'intermittent', meaning that supplies are incon-sistent, i.e. the sun does not always shine or the wind blow. Moreover, large-scale solar and wind arrays tend to be most efficient in deserts or stormy zones that seldom host large populations. This means that any energy produced has to be stored, sparking major efforts

Rank	Nation	Investment in 2011 ($bn)	Investment in 2010 ($bn)
1	USA	48.0	33.7
2	China	45.5	45.0
3	Germany	30.6	32.1
4	Italy	28.0	20.2
5	Rest of EU-27	11.1	15.2
6	India	10.2	6.6
7	UK	9.4	7.0
8	Japan	8.6	7.0
9	Spain	8.6	6.9
10	Brazil	8.0	6.9

Figure 16.8
Renewable energy investment in different countries (Pew 2012).

in recent years in battery technology or 'pump-stored hydropower', based on the 'combination of water and gravity to capture off-peak power and release it at times of high demand' (Economist 2012b). Conversely, solar or wind arrays situated in urban areas where most power is consumed tend to be smaller, hence less efficient. Solar and wind are also far from 'grid parity', or the cost enabling them to compete with traditional fuels. Hence their need for government support, involving development frameworks often expressed as 'renewables obligations' where countries agree that solar and wind should account for a particular percentage of final energy consumption (in the EU, this is 20 per cent by the year 2020). Lastly, both solar and wind are divided between upstream equipment manufacturing, which is a relatively international activity, and downstream systems installation, a business run by local companies that may or may not be vertically integrated with manufacturers.

Examples abound of MNEs using renewables projects to grow internationally. Numerous information sources publicize such activities. One is http://www.cleantechnology-business-review.com/, whose April 2012 highlights included French energy giant Areva's contract to build a 250 megawatt concentrated solar power installation in India; Swiss conglomerate Landis + Gyr's installation of a smart grid demonstration project in New York state; and the turbines that the Spanish group Acciona's wind power subsidiary is supplying in Brazil. All of these cases involve the same kinds of internationalization decisions as the ones that this book has addressed in other chapters, relating respectively to vertical integration, outsourcing, FDI, and joint ventures. Increasingly, green international business looks like a sector of activity like any other.

Challenges and choices

→ There is broad international consensus that the environmental challenge is one of the greatest problems ever faced. What is less certain is what role MNEs will play in addressing this problem. Companies that invest heavily in the environment should be able to improve their operational efficiency and brand image. It remains that the process of adaptation is expensive and may not be justified at current price levels. The real question is to what extent international managers prefer to manage the future proactively or simply maintain the status quo. Like many other decisions, change is a matter of temperament.

Chapter summary

The chapter started with a review of the main environmental problems facing MNEs: the depletion of natural resources (leading to higher future input costs), and pollution. It then reviewed possible responses in terms of corporate strategy (reflecting awareness of this problem, something that depends in part on whether a Global North or South culture is involved), operational greening (design measures, and adapted international supply chains and production processes), and green marketing. The chapter concluded with a section on the environmental challenge's effects on different key sectors, before analysing the rising power of new green ventures, particularly in sectors such as energy generation. The key message throughout the chapter is that students with capabilities in this field are likely to have a competitive advantage as they build their careers.

Case study 16.3

Powering the renewal of international business

Given current technology, wind power is closer than solar power to achieving grid parity, or the level of performance that makes it competitive with traditional fuel sources. This should mean better short-term growth prospects for wind as countries try to stabilize energy supplies and fulfil their climate change-related renewables obligations (Ren21 2011). Growth in different wind sub-sectors (offshore and onshore, community projects, etc.) has accelerated in recent years to account presently for almost half of all renewable capacity vs. 32.5 per cent for hydro and 12.9 per cent for solar (Kinver 2012). Along with improved turbine and blade technology, the main drivers have been projects in western China, underpinning the international expansion of Chinese MNEs such as Goldwind and Sinovel, whose rise has turned their country into the world's largest wind market, accounting for half of total global capacity. Conversely, difficult trading conditions in the US and Europe, explained by the credit squeeze and falling electricity demand, mean that champion MNEs in these regions (including, respectively, GE and Vestas or Vattenfalls) have fared less well. Renewables, like other business sectors, are subject to international product life cycle variations.

Even as wind power carves out a space for itself in the energy mix of the future, solar continues to fascinate many entrepreneurs' imaginations. The problem is accessing this power source in an economically viable way. Much exploitable sunlight falls on desert regions (the Sahara in Africa, the Gobi in Asia, the Arabian Peninsula, or the Mojave/Sonora in California/Mexico) that are almost uninhabitable. At that point, exploiting solar power requires enormous investments in long-term distribution networks that consume much of the primary energy captured in the first place. The loss of power can be diminished by using long-distance direct current transmission cables, like German giant RWE is considering for a concentrated solar thermal array it wants to build in the Sahara to supply Europe with electricity—a mega-project that is likely to raise Africa's profile as an international centre of energy production. A second obstacle is that the technology used in thin-film solar cells has yet to achieve a level of performance ensuring its economic efficiency. Much progress is expected at a sub-molecular level, involving nanotechnology capabilities similar to the ones that many computer companies develop when imprinting memory on computer hard drives (Pernick and Wilder 2007). The synergy between these areas may explain Silicon Valley computer firms' growing presence in the solar sector (alongside leading Asian chip makers such as Taiwan Semiconductor Manufacturing). The hope is that a combination of supply-side improvements and greater demand will enable output to reach the critical threshold beyond which economies of scale occur, helping solar to join wind in achieving grid parity.

What remains to be seen is the breakdown in this sector between mega-projects, the reserve of big MNEs capable of coordinating consortiums and delivering turnkey projects, and local solutions, which are more geared towards groups that can integrate upstream production with downstream installation capabilities. An example of a consortial mega-project was the 2010 agreement between California company eSolar (http://www.esolar.com) and China's Penglai Electric to build solar thermal plants in the Mongolian desert capable of generating 2 gigawatts of electricity. An example of a more local project was a €50 million arrangement in 2008 where General Motors leased 2 million square feet at its Zaragoza automobile plant in Spain to a Franco-American consortium (Veolia Environnement and Clairvoyant Energy) that bought 85,000 lightweight photovoltaic panels from US manufacturer Energy Conversion Devices to produce 12 megawatts of electricity. Multi-partner transactions of this sort are imaginative and hold a great deal of promise for the future.

The main hurdle facing such arrangements is capital expenditure. To overcome this, some suppliers (such as Sunedison) are devising schemes where they pay for initial installation work as long as customers sign a 20-year supply contract. Otherwise, in countries where governments remain committed to solar, incentives and subsidies exist to support demand. Relying on such subsidies is risky, as evidenced in 2010 by the dramatic demise of Puertollano, Spain's solar panel production centre, after state subsidies were slashed by one-third. Similarly, the decision taken by the British government to reduce feed-in tariffs by March 2012 dampened sectorial dynamics in that country at the same time as the German government was deciding to stop all nuclear energy and accelerate the move into renewables. Confidence in the sector's future should not blind practitioners to the different speeds at which this plays out worldwide.

There is a global market for renewable energy equipment but installers tend to work on a local basis
Source: iStock

Nevertheless, with total renewable capacity having risen by 15 per cent over 2011 despite a weak global economy, to total 565 gigawatts of generation capacity or about 47 per cent more than nuclear (Kinver 2012), the general pattern is clear. Renewable energy is bound to make the international business headlines for years to come.

Case study questions

1. How would you assess SMEs' prospects in the international renewables sector?
2. To what extent will this sector be driven by domestic or international companies?
3. How do different national government policies affect MNEs' decisions in this sector?

Discussion questions

1. How will the depletion of natural resources affect MNE configurations?
2. How should cost factor into MNEs' anti-pollution efforts?
3. What are the different ways of adapting green marketing to local circumstances?
4. How might international variations in culture affect MNEs' willingness to go green?
5. At what point will green sectors take off in different countries worldwide?

Online resource centre

Go online to test your understanding by trying multiple-choice questions, and assignment and examination questions.

Further research

Sitkin, A. (2011). *Principles of Ecology and Management: International Challenges for Future Practitioners*. Oxford: Goodfellow Publishers Ltd

Uniquely highlights the factors impeding the transition towards greater corporate environmentalism.

Dietz, S., Michie, J., and Oughton, C. (2011). *Political Economy of the Environment*. Abingdon: Routledge

Compilation text seeking to understand how alternative thinking from different social sciences, starting with economics, might enhance mainstream approaches to environmental and natural-resource problems.

References

Anselmsson, J. and Johansson, U. (2007). 'Corporate social responsibility and the positioning of grocery brands: An exploratory study of retailer and manufacturer brands at point of purchase', *International Journal of Retail & Distribution Management*, 35/10

Anshelm, J. and Hansson, A. (2011). 'Climate change and the convergence between ENGOs and business: On the loss of Utopian energies', *Environmental Value*, 20/1, pp. 75–94 (February)

Barbiroli, G. (2009). 'The limitedness of natural and environmental resources as an opportunity for sustainable yet competitive solutions', *International Journal of Business Environment*, 2/3 (March)

Blackburn, W. (2008). *The Sustainability Handbook: The Complete Management Guide to Achieving Social, Economic and Environmental Responsibility*. London: Earthscan

BP (2012). 'Statistical review of world energy', available at http://www.bp.com, accessed 9 November 2012

Braungart, M. and McDonough, W. (2009). *Cradle to Cradle: Re-Making The Way We Make Things*. London: Vintage Books

Bresciani, S. and Oliveira, N. (2007). 'Corporate environmental strategy: A must in the new millennium', *International Journal of Business Environment*, 1/4

Brickman, C. and Ungerman, D. (2008). 'Climate change and supply chain management', July, available at http://www.mckinseyquarterly.com, accessed 5 March 2010

Carbone, V. and Moatti, V. (2008). *Greening the Supply Chain: Preliminary Results of a Global Survey*. Paris: ESCP-EAP

Chazan, G. (2008). 'Oil-field production drops are accelerating', *The Wall Street Journal-Europe*, 13 November, p. 10

Cottier, T., Nartova, O., and Bigdeli, S. (eds.) (2009). *International Trade and the Mitigation of Climate Change*. Cambridge: Cambridge University Press

Economist (2012a). 'The train leaves platform one at last', *The Economist*, 14 January, p. 46

Economist (2012b). 'Packing some power', *The Economist Technology Quarterly*, 3 March, p. 13

Epstein, M. (2008). *Making Sustainability Work: Best Practices in Managing and Measuring Corporate Social, Environmental and Economic Impacts*. Sheffield: Greenleaf Publishing

Esty, D. and Winston, A. (2006). *Green to Gold: How Smart Companies Use Environmental Strategy to Innovate, Create Value and Build Competitive Advantage*. London: Yale University Press

Finisterra do Paço, A., Barata Raposo, M. L., and Filho, W. L. (2009). 'Identifying the green consumer: A segmentation study', *Journal of Targeting, Measurement and Analysis for Marketing*, 17/1 (March)

Friend, G. (2009). *The Truth About Green Business*. New Jersey: Natural Logic

GAAM (2010). 'ArcelorMittal's polluting South African plant shortlisted for Public Eye Global Award', 19 January, available at http://www.globalaction-arcelormittal.org/, accessed 2 February 2010

Greenbiz (2010). 'Pratt & Whitney earns first LEED-Platinum rating in China', 8 April, available at http://www.greenbiz.com/, accessed 25 May 2010

Harrison, M. (2006). 'Ryanair boss labels flight critics "econuts, idiots and headbangers"', *Independent*, 7 November, available at http://www.independent.co.uk, accessed 26 December 2009

Hitchcock, D. and Willard, M. (2009). *The Business Guide to Sustainability: Practical Strategies and Tools for Organizations*, 2nd edn. London: Earthscan

Ho, P. (2008). *Leapfrogging Development in Emerging Asia: Caught Between Greening and Pollution*. New York: Nova Science Publishers

IEA—International Energy Agency (2011). *Clean Energy Progress Report*, available at http://www.iea.org, accessed 21 October 2011

Jackson, T. (2011). *Prosperity without Growth: Economics for a Finite Planet*. London: Earthscan

Jain, S. and Kedia, B. (2011). *Enhancing Global Competitiveness Through Sustainable Environmental Stewardship*. Cheltenham (UK), Northampton, MA (USA): Edward Elgar Publishing Ltd

Jowit, J. (2008). 'Environment: Huge increase in spending on water urged to avert global catastrophe', *The Guardian*, 11 September, available at http://www.guardian.co.uk, accessed 22 October 2011

Juniper, T. (2008). 'How McDonald's finally got green', *The Guardian*, 30 November, available at http://www.guardian.co.uk/, accessed 2 May 2009

King, J. and Slesser, M. (2009). 'Can the world make the transition to a sustainable economy driven by solar energy?', *International Journal of Environment and Pollution*, 5/1 (September)

Kinver, M. (2012). 'US tops global clean energy investment rankings', 12 April, available at http://www.bbc.co.uk/, accessed 13 April 2012

Kolk, A. and Pinkse, J. (2008). 'A perspective on multinational enterprises and climate change: Learning from "an inconvenient truth"?', *Journal of International Business Studies*, 39, pp. 1359–1378

Lee, K. (2009). 'Gender differences in Hong Kong adolescent consumers' green purchasing behavior', *Journal of Consumer Marketing*, 26/2

McKinsey-WRG (Water Resources Group) (2009). 'Charting our water future', available at http://www.mckinsey.com/, accessed 4 June 2010

MGI—McKinsey Global Institute (2009). 'Exploring global energy demand', June, available at http://www.mckinseyquarterly.com, accessed 15 January 2009

Monbiot, G. (2007). *Heat: How We Can Stop the Planet Burning*. London: Penguin

Mostafa, M. (2007). 'Gender differences in Egyptian consumers' green purchase behaviour: The effects of environmental knowledge, concern and attitude', *International Journal of Consumer Studies*, 31/3

Pearce, F. (2010). 'Chevron's solar panels won't clean up its filthy oilfield', *The Guardian*, 8 April, available at http://www.guardian.co.uk, accessed 1 April 2012

Pernick, R. and Wilder, C. (2007). *The Clean Tech Revolution*. New York: HarperBusiness

Pew Charitable Trusts (2010a). 'Who's winning the clean energy race? Growth, competition and opportunities in the world's largest economies', available at http://www.pewtrusts.org/, accessed 26 April 2010

Pew Charitable Trusts (2010b). 'Global clean power: A $2.3 trillion opportunity', available at http://www.pewtrusts.org, accessed 21 October 2011

Pew Charitable Trusts (2012). 'Who's winning the clean energy race? G-20 investment powering forward', available at http://www.pewtrusts.org/, accessed 23 April 2012

REN21 (2011). 'Global status report', available at http://www.ren21.net/, accessed 26 October 2011

SAPA-AP (2009). 'Arcelor Mittal South Africa dismisses pollution claims', 25 September, available at www.corpwatch.org, accessed 2 February 2010

Siegle, L. (2010). 'Ethical living', *The Observer Magazine*, 12 September

Sitkin, A. (2011). *Principles of Ecology and Management: International Challenges for Future Practitioners*. Oxford: Goodfellow Publications

Steininger, K. (2009). 'Environmental illusion in the depletion of common property resources', *International Journal of Environment and Pollution*, 4/3–4 (September)

Trucost (2010). *Universal Ownership: Why Environmental Externalities Matter to Institutional Investors*, UNEP Finance Initiative—PRI

UNEP/Bloomberg (2011). *Global Trends in Renewable Energy Investment*, available http://fs-unep-centre.org/, accessed 21 October 2011

UNEP/Bloomberg (2012). *Global Renewable Energy Investment Powers to Record $257 Billion*, available at http://www.unep.org, accessed 9 November 2012

Weizsäcker, E., Hargroves, K., Smith, M., Desha, C., and Stasinopoulos, P. (2009). *Factor Five: Transforming the Global Economy through 80% Improvements in Resource Productivity*. London: Earthscan

Werbach, A. (2009). *Strategy for Sustainability: A Business Manifesto*. Boston: Harvard Business Press

WWF (2012). 'Living Planet Report 2012: Biodiversity, biocapacity and better choices', available at http://awsassets.panda.org/downloads/1_lpr_2012_online_full_size_single_pages_final_120516.pdf, accessed 20 August 2012

Part case study

Global treasure hunt: China's insatiable hunger for resources

Historically, one of the main manifestations of one country having a dominant position in global manufacturing has been the proliferation of supply chains bringing raw materials to its factories from regions that are less industrialized but resource-rich. When the 'first golden age of globalization' began in the late nineteenth century, this kind of transformative activity could be seen in the large share of world trade involving the sale (and often colonial expropriation) of commodities such as cotton from India or minerals from Africa, destined, respectively, to become inputs in British textiles or steel-making plants. US dominance during the late twentieth century was characterized by arrangements organizing huge imports of crude oil from the Middle East, South America, or anywhere that had fuel to sell to thirsty American factories and cars.

China's rise as a global manufacturing power in the early twenty-first century has been no different. In fact, the hunt for resources to nourish factories back in its homeland has been particularly intense for two reasons. First, China lacks a significant supply of natural resources, aside from coal and rare earths (see Chapter 16). Above all, many of the main oil fields that international energy companies have exploited over the past 50 years are starting to deplete. Hence the need to discover new locations capable of supplying China's growing industrial base. The country's industrial planners are well aware of this challenge and are taking a number of steps to address it. It is worth analysing the different forms that the search has taken worldwide.

Business news has been dominated for several years now by stories of Chinese companies securing natural resources in Africa, a region whose oil resources, for instance, have been less fully exploited than the Arabian peninsula for a number of years. That is about to change with the discovery of large new fields in eastern Africa, which finally looks like it will catch up with the proven reserves that have already been identified in the west of the continent , previously estimated to be ten times greater (Economist 2012b). This is particularly important due to the fact that Nigeria and Gabon, western Africa's two largest oil-producing nations, have long awarded extensive drilling concessions to companies linked to their former colonial powers, respectively BP and Shell from the UK or Total (ex-Elf) from France. Things are somewhat different in the east, however, where longstanding political instability in countries like Somalia or Sudan has daunted the Europeans to some extent, creating a vacuum that budding Chinese giants such as CNOOC can fill. Similarly, the recent gas find in Ethiopia's Ogaden desert has attracted the attention of a Chinese company, PetroTrans, which is looking to invest $4 billion there. Other Chinese MNEs have also spent significant sums to improve shipping ports up and down this coast so that any resources extracted locally can be shipped home. Such investments require confidence that the proposed ventures can overcome the frequent wars and acts of piracy from which this region has suffered for so long. Chinese companies may feel more confidence in this respect due to the greater support they receive from their national government.

Another area where the Chinese have increasingly been looking for resources in recent years is Latin America. China has become Brazil's most important economic partner, with trade between the two countries rising by a factor of 17 in the decade since 2002 (Economist 2012a). What is particularly interesting is the breakdown of this business—Brazil is a net importer of manufactured goods from China but more than compensates for this with massive exports of commodities such as iron ore, soy beans, and crude oil. This might be explained by the competitive advantage that many Chinese MNEs have developed compared with their Latin American rivals, based in part on Beijing government support for market-seeking investments (Fornes and Butt-Philip 2011). It remains that a number of Brazilian policy-makers are angered by their country's competitive disadvantage in higher value industrial products and have started advocating protectionist measures such as increased taxes on Chinese car imports. This may run counter to the rule of the WTO, of which both countries are members, but it also indicates that some governments are more at ease with China's global resource hunt than others.

One example of this ambivalent attitude is the intention announced in February 2008 by different Australian government officials to exercise tighter control over Chinese FDI when the MNE in question is a state-owned enteprise (Wilson 2011). Australia has become the number one destination for Chinese FDI, most of it directed to the mining sector (Drysdale 2011). Historically, the Australian political tradition has been to tolerate inwards investment, an open attitude that, along with the country's significant endowment in natural resources, partially explains why it has survived recent crises in relatively good condition. Thus, any move towards 'resource nationalism' raises fears that additional scrutiny will undermine foreigners' willingness to invest in Australia. This is not a likely prospect, however—sellers are in such a dominant position in the global markets for raw materials that demand for Australian resources is bound to stay strong even if the state intervenes to a greater extent in their extraction. A better analysis of what is happening in Australia is that it has a growing sense of the need to get the national government involved in the energy business, given that companies driving this activity on the Chinese side are state-owned.

There are many sectors of activity where a wide international consensus exists that things can be managed satisfactorily without excessive state intervention. The situation is different with natural resources, however, if only because an absence of basic commodities makes it impossible for many other sectors to operate. When facing a problem as fundamental as the entire ecology of international business, and indeed of the planet, it is no surprise that governments want to be involved alongside MNEs.

Case study question

1. What (if any) areas of international business activity might a country hope to dominate if it has little access to energy resources?
2. How would you differentiate between China's energy supply policies in various parts of the world?
3. What is the outlook for the global energy business as natural resources continue to deplete?

References

Drysdale, P. (2011). 'A new look at Chinese FDI in Australia', *China & World Economy*, 19/4, pp. 54–73

Economist (2012a). 'Brazil's trade policy: Seeking protection', *The Economist*, 14 January, available at http://www.economist.com, accessed 6 April 2012

Economist (2012b). 'African energy: Eastern El Dorado?', *The Economist*, 7 April, p. 51

Fornes, G. and Butt-Philip, A. (2011). 'Chinese MNEs and Latin America: A review', *International Journal of Emerging Markets*, 6/2, pp. 98–117

Wilson, J. (2011). 'Resource nationalism or resource liberalism? Explaining Australia's approach to Chinese investment in its minerals sector', *Australian Journal of International Affairs*, 65/3, pp. 283–304

Glossary

Abatement Act of not generating any pollution in the first place.

Absolute advantage Where one country, providing the same input of a good as another, achieves greater output and can therefore be said to produce it more cheaply.

Accountability Idea that actors must take responsibility for their actions.

Adaptation Extent to which a company's products and services are adapted for each market, meeting the particular needs of the customers.

Advocacy Speaking out on behalf of a certain constituency in order to influence policy-makers to adopt a friendly stance.

Autarky Where an entity operates self-sufficiently and in isolation.

Autocratic management Management style that is domineering and dictatorial, sometimes with the exercise of unrestricted authority.

Barriers to entry Regulatory, competitive, financial, and other obstacles that make it difficult for a firm to enter a particular market.

Basis points One hundredth of 1 per cent. A common unit in international finance.

'Beggar thy neighbour' policies Where one country manipulates its competitive position (i.e. via currency devaluations) to its trading partners' detriment.

Biodiversity Extent to which living organisms vary within a given ecosystem.

Black market Economic activities occurring outside an official framework.

Boundaries of the firm Range of value chain operations that a company does by itself without turning to outside partners.

Brand Collection of images and ideas representing a company or other organization or economic producer; it can refer to specific symbols such as a name, logo, slogan, and design scheme.

BRICs Term first developed by US investment bank Goldman Sachs, referring to Brazil, Russia, India, and China as a bloc to highlight the emergence of these continent-sized countries.

Brownfield investment Where a firm enters a new market by buying existing facilities.

Bulk purchasing When goods or services are bought in large quantities, there is a greater chance of negotiating a lower per-unit price, since the seller will achieve economies of scale that it can pass on to the buyer.

Business cycle Period during which the economy alternates between boom and bust.

Business-to-business (B2B) marketing Marketing of products and services to businesses—i.e. the marketing and sales relationship between one company and those other companies to which it supplies, or from which it receives, products and services.

Business-to-consumer (B2C) marketing Marketing of products and services to the end consumers or customers—i.e. members of the general public who consume the products or services directly for themselves.

Capital flight When investors or savers take large sums of money out of a country because of concerns about local risks or disagreements with policy.

Capital markets Sum total of all medium- and long-term debt and equity transactions.

Cartel Groups of producers that collaborate with one another on supply quantity and pricing decisions instead of competing.

Chaebol South Korean equivalent of Japanese *keiretsu* but with the founding family generally maintaining a majority holding.

China price Reference to the comparatively very low retail price of goods and services originating in China.

Clearing Process of calculating and paying net differences between the amounts due to/owed by market participants.

Cluster Where firms in a similar line of business operate in close physical proximity to one another and build close ties. This can reflect historical factors or strategic intent.

Code of conduct List of rules detailing accepted behaviour within an organization.

Commitment to internationalization Depth of a company's engagement of human, physical, and financial resources abroad. Ranges from simple import/export to running large, wholly owned foreign subsidiaries.

Comparative advantage Where one country makes all goods more efficiently than another but agrees not to make (and hence to import) those goods whose production makes the least efficient use of its resources.

Competitive intelligence Firm's compilation and analysis of information on the outside world. Generally used as a guide for future action.

Configuration How a company locates its different corporate functions like research, production, marketing, and finance.

Consolidation Where producers within a sector join forces via takeovers or mergers in an attempt to reduce over-capacities.

Conspicuous consumption Extravagant purchase and use of expensive goods and services, usually by a leisure class, in order to demonstrate status and wealth.

Corporate culture Common values shared by employees at all levels of a business. This can sometimes form an implicit or explicit control mechanism within the company.

Corporate governance Laws and processes regulating corporate management, including composition of the Board of Directors, protection of minority interests, executive control, and accounting practices.

Corporate responsibility Idea that a company should ensure that all its actions are both legal and ethical.

Coupling Where countries' economic fortunes are linked due to the inseparability of their economic and financial interests.

Critical mass Minimum threshold beyond which positive, size-related benefits arise.

Cultural context (high and low) Definition of the situational framework by which it is possible to distinguish the degree to which a special code is needed to understand the signals and communications of a culture.

Culture Broad term that covers many patterns of human activity that exemplify the ways of life of a certain population.

Currency/capital controls Where a government places administrative restrictions on people's ability to buy/sell or lend/borrow assets denominated in the national currency.

Current account Country's 'balance of trade' (exports minus imports) plus or minus its financial flows from abroad (interest or dividend payments, cash transfers).

Debt relief Idea that poorest borrowers should not be asked to reimburse debt: because the original borrowings had been misused or embezzled; or because the borrower is too poor to pay.

Default Where a debtor does not fulfil a contractual obligation to repay a debt.

Deferred differentiation Manufacturing strategy that combines economies of scale with product diversity by standardizing inputs for as long as possible and introducing adaptation as late as possible.

Demography Statistical study of all populations and the specific features of such populations related to their size, structure, and distribution.

Denominate Specifying the currency in which a transaction takes place.

Design Activities aimed at defining a product's final shape and attributes.

De-skilling Where lesser competency is required of a business unit, often because it is asked to specialize in one or very few value chain operation(s).

Disassembly Act of breaking an item down into its component parts, usually at the end of its working life.

Disclosure Provision of information, often in a specified form to comply with legal requirements.

Downstream Late value chain activities undertaken when selling or distributing a product or service.

Dumping Where exporters sell goods at a loss or below the normal price to gain market share and put rivals out of business.

Economic patriotism Idea that a society might show preference for domestic firms by purchasing their products and/or preventing foreign ownership.

Economies of scale When a company increases output using the same equipment, its per-unit production costs fall.

Economies of scope Production efficiencies that companies achieve because they can manage their product portfolio in a way that creates synergies. This occurs, for instance, when a marketing initiative sells more than one item at a time.

Ecosphere Sum total of living flora or fauna whose interactions with one another and other inanimate elements enable life on Earth.

Emissions Outflow following an industrial transformation process. Include air-borne gases and water-borne sewage, also known as 'effluents'.

Endogenous Inwardly oriented. In economics, often used in reference to consumption and internal investment-driven growth.

Energy-intensive Description of activities requiring a higher than average injection of energy resources.

Environmental footprint Ecological impact of a human activity.

Environmentalism Attitude that ecological sustainability should be a priority factor in personal and organizational decision-making.

Environmental management systems 'Framework through which [a company's] environmental performance can be monitored, improved, and controlled' (see http://www.envirowise.gov.uk/).

Ergonomics Analysis breaking physical human activities down scientifically into a series of micro-tasks. Also called time and motion studies.

Ethical premium Surcharge that consumers are prepared to pay for a good certified as being associated with ethical business practices.

Ethical report group Associations of companies and other organizations promising to respect certain ethical standards.

Ethics Study of moral values. For the purposes of this book, behaviour is considered ethical when it is characterized by an intention not to cause harm.

Ethnocentric A company's replication in the international market of the way in which it markets its products and services in its domestic market—'this approach has worked well at home so it does not need to be changed'.

Exogenous Outwardly oriented. In economics, this term is often used in reference to export-driven growth.

Expatriates Employees working outside their home country.

Expatriation Process of international transfer of managers, often used as a strategic tool to achieve specific organizational goals.

Exposure Where assets do not match liabilities for a financial asset, such as a currency, whose price might fluctuate.

Expropriation Where private property is seized by a government, often without compensation.

Externalities When the effect of an economic action falls upon parties not directly involved in it. This effect can be positive or negative.

Externalization Where a firm gives an outside party responsibility for some of its business functions. The opposite of internalization.

Factor endowments The human, financial, and physical capital that an economic entity (often a country) can use in its production process.

Factor mobility Propensity of factor inputs (capital, resources, labour, etc.) to move in time and/or place.

Fair trade Business defined by the equitable distribution of profits up and down the value chain to ensure that upstream producers receive a decent 'living' wage.

Federative organization Structures whose sub-units are recognized both as autonomous entities with freedom to manoeuvre and as members of a unified group.

Financial globalization Deregulation of global capital markets leading to an acceleration in cross-border capital transfers.

Financialization View that a firm's mission is to maximize financial returns and shareholder value.

First-mover advantage Benefit of being the first party to move into a market segment in a certain location.

Foreign direct investment (FDI) Where companies fund a permanent or semi-permanent unit overseas. The OECD defines FDI as a situation where a foreign owner has an equity stake of at least 10 per cent in a company's ordinary shares and aims to establish a 'lasting interest' in the host country.

Foreign exchange (FX) market Virtual marketplace(s) where currency prices are set through market supply and demand.

Franchising Contract where a franchiser grants permission to a franchisee to run a business bearing its name, often using supplies that it provides. In return, the franchiser will receive income, often based on the franchise's performance.

Free ride Where a party derives benefits from an economic activity without contributing to its costs.

Free trade Belief that goods and services should be negotiated in private domestic and foreign markets without government interference.

Free trade zone Tariff-free 'export processing zones' that many countries have set up to attract industrial activity. Little or no tax is paid as long as the items being assembled or temporarily stored there are re-exported.

Frugal Characterized by an economic or thrifty use of inputs.

Functional organization Structure where power is centralized, based on the idea that internal capabilities are key in corporate organization.

Generic Reference to goods that are not meant for a specific use but serve a variety of applications.

Geocentric Company adopts the most suitable marketing strategy, taking into account the values of the company and those of the target market.

Geographic organization Structure based on the idea that the MNE's overriding organizational aim is to maximize adaptation to local circumstances.

Glass ceiling Artificial barriers based on bias that prevent qualified individuals from advancing upward in their organization into management-level positions.

Global corporate ethos Essential set of characteristics that define the ways in which the MNE is organized and has its staff operate and behave.

Global firm Company designed to serve a single world market instead of different national markets.

Global governance Regulatory and supervisory functions fulfilled by authorities whose responsibilities exceed national borders.

Globalization Process whereby the world becomes increasingly interconnected at an economic, political, and social level.

Goodwill Difference between the price at which a company can be purchased and the break-up value of its assets.

Greenfield investment Where a firm enters a new market by building new facilities.

Green premium Surcharge paid for a green product over the equivalent non-green product.

Green redemption Where a company restores its tarnished environmental reputation through positive actions.

Gross domestic product (GDP) National income, defined by national consumption plus/minus investment plus/minus government spending plus/minus balance of trade.

Guanxi Chinese concept in which personal relations and the establishment of mutual trust and obligations are seen as essential for the conduct of business.

Halo effect Where consumers feel positively about a company because it has a track record of virtuous behaviour.

Hardship posting Traditional overseas assignment (or posting) that was thought to be undertaken in worse conditions than assignments at home and was thus rewarded with additional allowances, special arrangements, and increased remuneration.

Hedging Where a party offsets a risk through a new deal exposing it to the exact opposite risk. The original exposure is called the 'underlying' risk. The new exposure is called the 'hedge'.

Heterarchy Organizational principle that corporate units are allies and therefore equals in the management of their joint enterprise. In an MNE, this signifies that no one unit should take a global lead any more.

Hierarchy of needs Maslow's concept sets out a pyramid of layers of human need, from basic needs such as food, water, and shelter to the realization of personal potential and self-fulfilment.

Home bias Preference for domestic counterparts rather than foreign ones.

Home/host countries People and companies originate from a 'home country'. When they operate abroad, they are working in a 'host country'.

Home currency Currency that a firm uses to calculate its consolidated global accounts.

Horizontal integration Where a firm establishes a presence in a new market by running activities similar to the ones operating in its home market.

Horizontal *keiretsu* Japanese corporate network where similar firms ally with trading companies to ensure the widest possible market coverage.

Import substitution Trade policy of supporting the domestic production of goods that would otherwise be imported.

Industrialization policies Concerted efforts by states to increase the role of value-added manufacturing in their national economy or to support industrial sectors they consider strategic.

Industrial models Manufacturing systems determining the sequencing of operations within factories. Also refers to flow of goods before and after industrial transformation, and to the distribution of the income generated.

Infant industry Sector of activity that has only recently developed in a particular country and whose prospects for survival are uncertain because it lacks the capital and experience to compete with existing (foreign) producers.

Infographics Graphic visual representations of information, data, or knowledge.

Insiderization Where a person or company has become so integrated into a particular host society that locals forget its foreign origins.

Integration Where different units' activities are coordinated to the extent that their missions are defined in light of one another.

Intellectual property rights Exclusive enjoyment of the benefits derived from intangible assets like trademarks, patents, and copyrights.

Internalization When a company decides to run a particular function itself (using its own employees) instead of delegating it to an external party.

Internal market Idea that different corporate units deal with one another as buyers and sellers of resources. Related to 'intrapreneurship', or the notion that individuals behave as entrepreneurs within large organizations.

International division Structure based on the idea that all foreign environments share certain characteristics that differ from a company's domestic market and should therefore be combined in a specific division.

Internationalize Decision to enter foreign markets; involves upstream and/or downstream activities.

International tax competition Where countries try to attract offshore funds by offering investors lower tax rates than they can find in competitor nations.

Interventionism Belief that the state has a role to play in ensuring that market mechanisms are both efficient and lead to a fair and viable distribution of income.

Intra-firm Activities occurring within the confines of one and the same firm.

Isolationist Refers in international trade to a policy of interacting as little as possible with foreign interests. Stands in contradiction with the principle of international division of labour.

Issuance of securities Act of creating tradable capital market instruments like stocks and bonds that firms sell to investors to raise capital.

Joint venture Business unit specifically created by different companies to achieve a particular mission. Usually involves pooling resources like equity capital, knowledge, processes, and/or personnel.

Knowledge economy Sum total of the markets that help economic actors to access knowledge.

Knowledge management Systems that companies use to maximize the benefits of internal and external knowledge.

Knowledge spillover When companies gain knowledge through proximity to external sources such as universities, research centres, or other companies.

Lead time Time it takes, once an order has been placed, to deliver a good to the order-giver's premises.

Lean production Production philosophy that emphasizes saving resources through less waste, better inventory management, better quality, and shorter industrial cycles. Largely derived from the 'Toyota Production System'.

Learning effects Added production efficiency and lower costs that companies gain from accumulating experience in a particular activity.

Less developed countries (LDCs) Countries whose industrial base and general level of human welfare does not enable most citizens to achieve a decent living standard. This is an umbrella term covering a vast range of economic, social, and demographic situations, ranging from 'emerging' or 'newly industrialized' countries that are on a clear industrialization path to 'heavily indebted poor countries' (HIPC) with very poor growth prospects.

Licensing Contract where a licensor grants permission to a licensee to use one of its assets, usually intellectual property. In return, the licensor will receive royalties.

Life cycle costs Total cost of an item taking all impacts into account, including running costs, environmental impact, and end-of-life disposal.

Lightweighting Engineering initiatives aimed at reducing the mass of materials comprising a manufactured item.

Liquidity Volume of funds in a market. Markets are liquid if there are sufficient funds so that an asset can be bought or sold without any noticeable impact on price.

Lobbying Attempts to influence policy-makers, often elected officials.

Long position Owning more of a commodity in the form of assets than the amounts owed in the form of liabilities.

Luddism Term used to characterize any resistance to change and innovation in technology. It is derived from the actions of the Luddites, who campaigned against the introduction of textile machinery in the early nineteenth century.

Market failure Where markets perform inefficiently by not allocating resources optimally.

Marketing mix Different phases of a corporate marketing strategy—product, price, promotion, and place.

Market-maker Trader who is always prepared to quote other market participants a price to buy ('bid') and sell ('offer') a given commodity.

Market segmentation Identification of customers with similar characteristics so that a commercially viable marketing strategy can be devised and implemented.

Matrix organization Structure based on the idea that multiple reporting lines broaden employees' vision of the business and can create synergies.

Mergers and acquisitions Mergers are when two companies agree to combine their operations into a new company and both have more or less equal powers. Acquisitions indicate that one company has become the main shareholder of another.

Meritocracy Form of social organization in which the leaders have achieved their status by their own efforts—on merit.

Mission statement Defines in a few words or sentences the reason for existence of any entity or organization. It embodies its philosophies, goals, ambitions, and values.

Mitigation Corporate efforts to lessen the effects of pollution they have already generated.

Modules Components assembled into a unit that fulfils a particular function in a system. Such units can be plugged without alteration into the rest of the system. Groups of modules are known as 'sub-assemblies'.

Multi-domestic Management approach emphasizing autonomy of differentiated national markets as opposed to the coordination of unified global or regional markets.

Multinational enterprises (MNEs) Companies whose regular activities cause them to engage with and/or operate in more than one country at a time.

Nearshoring Where operations are outsourced to a low-cost location relatively close to the company's country of origin.

Neo-liberalism Belief in minimal interference from government in the economy.

Net basis Exposure remaining after a firm's short positions in a given financial category have been subtracted from its long positions in the same category.

Non-governmental organizations (NGOs) Associations created by members of the general public to address specific problems or promote an overall ethos or policy.

Non-product ratio Percentage of inputs that are transformed into waste over the course of a production process.

Nouveau riche French expression referring to a population that has recently come into wealth and whose consumption behaviour is changing.

Offshore Transactions or actors over which national regulators have no authority.

Offshoring Where a firm moves an activity that it once ran domestically into a subsidiary that it owns abroad, usually to cut costs.

Oligarch Dominant business figure, often used in Russia to refer to an entrepreneur who gained control of formerly state-owned assets in the immediate aftermath of the communist regime.

Oligopoly Market dominated by few sellers, who might therefore have a disproportionate power to collude outside the market framework and fix prices in a non-competitive manner.

Opportunity cost Cost of doing something in a certain way, thus not receiving the benefits of doing it another way.

Organic growth Where a company expands by growing its internal capabilities instead of through external acquisitions.

Organizational dilemma Where employees are confused by the contradictory interests that they are asked to represent at different levels within their organization.

Outsourcing Where a company delegates to another company certain tasks (like the production of components) that it might otherwise undertake itself.

Paradigm World view or vision of how things are and/or should be organized.

Paternalistic Sense of managing a company with a view towards ensuring the well-being of employees and other stakeholders rather than for pure profit maximization motives.

Pay gap Different levels of payment between the top CEOs (or other employees) and those at other levels, or between male and female employees.

Performance management The approach within a business to ensuring its increasing effectiveness by improving the performance of its employees and by developing the capabilities of teams and individuals.

Philanthropy　Long-term charitable donations to worthy causes.

Pioneering costs　Costs associated with the mistakes that companies make when entering an unfamiliar market.

Pollution haven　Country that does not make stringent environmental demands on local producers.

Polycentric　Company adapts its marketing and sales strategy as closely as possible to the target country—that is, the market that it is entering is so particular that the marketing strategy and the products themselves must be adapted to the local conditions.

Polyvalent　Ability to perform many different functions, i.e. the opposite of specialization.

Post-industrial society　Defines the development of a late capitalist society with such features as the growth of free markets, greater mass consumption, and, ultimately, more leisure time.

Prime contractor　Company at the heart of a corporate network, whose orders trigger partners' production plans.

Procurement　Act of purchasing resources or inputs.

Product organization　Structure based on the idea that each product division should be run as an autonomous business.

Protectionist　General attitude that a national government should adopt policies restricting foreign interests' ability to access its domestic market.

Psychic distance　People's sense of the degree to which a foreign business culture differs from their own, adding to the sense of 'foreignness'.

Public good　Good that is 'non-exclusive' (i.e. available to everyone) and whose use by some does not decrease its availability for others.

Pull marketing　Form of marketing reflecting the way in which a company is 'pulled' into the market by reacting to demand from the market.

Purchasing power parity　Theory that future currency rates will adjust upwards or downwards to ensure that each reaches a level where it allows users to purchase the same basket of goods.

Push marketing　Form of marketing characterized by the way a company 'pushes' itself into the market by providing and selling goods that are new and relatively unknown.

Race to the bottom　Where competition among disadvantaged producers forces them to accept lower remuneration for their services.

Real interest rate　Nominal interest rate minus inflation rate.

Reciprocity　Notion that all parties to a transaction should grant and receive benefits of equivalent value.

Recruitment process outsourcing (RPO)　A form of process outsourcing by businesses in which part or all of its staff recruitment is contracted to an outside provider.

Regime　General system organizing interactions between different groups. Often refers to a system of regulations and the institutions that formulate and enforce them.

Regime shopping/arbitrage　Decision to locate an MNE's activities based on the relative laxness of a host country's requirements (taxes, regulations, etc.).

Regional association (RA)　Cooperation between neighbouring countries in building an institutional platform where issues of mutual interest can be discussed and decided.

Relative pricing　Price of a given category of goods or services expressed in relation to the price of a different category.

Reserve currency　Currency that, by consensus, is viewed as the safest vehicle for storing value.

Resource curse　Temptation for a country possessing significant natural resources to market its commodities without seeking to develop a value-adding industry.

Responsiveness　Ability and inclination to react quickly to the perceived needs of a situation.

Safe haven　Assets that investors tend to purchase to store value in times of crisis. Often includes gold, US$, and Swiss francs.

Salaryman　White-collar worker (based on a Japanese model) who works in the large bureaucracy of a business (or government office). The salaryman has long working hours, low prestige in the corporate hierarchy, and an absence of significant sources of income other than salary; the term is almost always used only for male employees.

Segmentation　Identification of customers with similar characteristics so that a commercially viable marketing strategy can be devised and implemented.

Shareholder value　Idea that the purpose of a company is to maximize returns to shareholders.

Short position　Owing more of a commodity in the form of liabilities than the amounts owned in the form of assets.

Sister units Separate corporate entities sharing the same parent company.

Small and medium-sized enterprises (SMEs) 'Enterprises which employ fewer than 250 persons and which have an annual turnover not exceeding 50 million euros, and/or an annual balance sheet total not exceeding 43 million euros' (Extract of Article 2 of the Annex of Recommendation 2003/361/EC).

Social contract Idea that people will hand some of their rights over to an authority that offers them order in return.

Social network A social structure consisting of a set of individuals and/or organizations and the dyadic (or bilateral) links between them.

Solvent Having sufficient funds to pay for goods or services.

Sovereign wealth funds Large pools of capital run by government-appointment managers. Usually originating from countries with large oil surpluses and/or where the state centralizes control of savings.

Spread Difference between the market-maker's 'bid' and 'offer' prices. In the FX markets, this is usually calculated in 'basis point' terms (four digits after the zero, i.e. .0001).

Stakeholder Anyone affected by an organization's actions. Often understood to include employees, local governments, suppliers, consumers, and host communities.

Standardization Extent to which a company sells exactly the same product in its domestic and international markets.

Stereotype Simplified and/or standardized conception or image with specific meaning, often held in common by people about another group.

Stock market capitalization Total number of shares issued multiplied by the share prices for all companies listed on a particular exchange.

Strategic business unit Identifiable entity within a corporation, large enough to plan strategy and organize resources on its own.

Strategic change Radical reorganization and restructuring of the direction and operation of a company.

Strategic trade policy Trade policy of strengthening local firms' export competitiveness in specific sectors.

Subsidiaries (Foreign) Unit belonging to a company's head office.

Supplier park When industrial suppliers cluster together to provide components and modules to their prime contractor.

Supply chain management Ways of directing the transformation of a physical good. Includes: purchasing supplies and stocks; coordinating and training of suppliers and sub-suppliers; and overseeing the logistical flow of goods and information.

Sustainability Approach where activities are organized in a way that will ensure their long-term economic, social, and ecological viability.

Synergy Idea that the value of a newly combined company will be greater than the separate value of its constituents.

Targeting Designing and aiming of a message at specific types of customers within markets that have been selected as the focus for a company's offering.

Tariffs Taxes that governments levy on goods (usually imports) when they cross national borders.

Tax avoidance Use of legal means to avoid paying taxes.

Tax evasion Use of illegal means to avoid paying taxes.

Tax haven Country with particularly low tax rates and regulations.

Technology transfer Where technology belonging to one country or company is shared with another under a formal partnership arrangement.

Terms of trade Relationship between the value added inherent to the goods/services that a country imports or exports.

Time to market Lag between a product's design and/or value-chain transformation and its being made available to end users.

Trade balance Relationship between the value of a country's exports and imports. When exports exceed imports, the country has a trade surplus. When imports exceed exports, the country has a trade deficit.

Trade diversion When imports come from less efficient producers located within an RA instead of from more efficient outside producers.

Transition In evolution. Often used in economics to refer to ex-communist countries shifting towards more market-based economies.

Transnational firm Companies whose aim, and therefore organization, simultaneously targets global efficiency, local flexibility, and shared learning.

Triad/OECD countries World's older industrialized nations. Triad refers to the three regions of Western Europe, North America, and Japan/Oceania. The Organization for Economic Cooperation and Development (OECD) is a Paris-based association whose membership is comprised of the world's advanced economies.

Trickle-down economics Idea that policy should reward the economically successful because their gains ultimately benefit the rest of society. Often used to justify low tax regimes.

Triple bottom line Idea that firms should report not only financial but also social and environmental outcomes.

Turnkey project Large projects where a group of companies, called a consortium, bids to win the right to build an asset (plant, infrastructure).

Upgrade Where a company (or country) improves its terms of trade by intensifying the value-added content of its output.

Upgradeability Ease with which an object can accommodate modernization.

Upstream Early value chain activities undertaken when processing or transforming a product or service.

Value chain Succession of acts that successfully add value to an item as it is transformed from a raw material or input stage to a finished product or service.

Venture capital Funds provided by a small group of investors to support the expansion of a new firm, often in a hi-tech sector.

Vertical integration Where a firm controls, and/or moves towards controlling, both the upstream and the downstream sides of its value chain.

Vertical *keiretsu* Japanese corporate network based on very long-term cooperation between companies specializing in different production activities. A vertical network will include a bank for funding purposes.

Viral marketing Strategy that encourages individuals to pass on marketing messages to others, creating a multiplier effect spreading the message's exposure and influence.

Welfare systems Provisions made alongside the productive economy to support vulnerable members of society. Usually government-sponsored.

Working capital Excess of circulating assets over short-term liabilities. Indicates level of long-term funding available to companies to help finance their operational cycle.

Work–life balance Life choices that many people make in order to balance the demands of work with other important areas of their lives, such as family, friends, and hobbies.

World culture Growing concept of a universal culture that rises above national cultures and emphasizes global events and world organizations.

Xenophobia Fear of things that are foreign.

Index